INDUSTRIAL RELATIONS RESEARCH
ASSOCIATION SERIES

COLLECTIVE BARGAINING:
CONTEMPORARY AMERICAN EXPERIENCE

GERALD G. SOMERS, editor

AUTHORS

JACK BARBASH

ROBERT E. DOHERTY

MARK L. KAHN

KAREN S. KOZIARA

JAMES KUHN

HAROLD M. LEVINSON

J. JOSEPH LOEWENBERG

WILLIAM H. MIERNYK

RICHARD U. MILLER

D. QUINN MILLS

JACK STIEBER

i

COLLECTIVE BARGAINING: CONTEMPORARY AMERICAN EXPERIENCE.

Preparation of this volume was supported by funds granted to the Industrial Relations Research Association under Contract No. J-9-P-6-0074 from the Labor-Management Services Administration, U.S. Department of Labor. Since contractors conducting research under government sponsorship are encouraged to express their own judgments freely, this report does not necessarily represent the official opinion or policy of the Department of Labor. Moreover, the contractor is solely responsible for the factual accuracy of all material developed in the research reported in this volume.

First edition

Library of Congress Catalog Card Number 79-90030

Price $20.00

INDUSTRIAL RELATIONS RESEARCH ASSOCIATION SERIES

PROCEEDINGS OF THE ANNUAL MEETING (Spring publication)

PROCEEDINGS OF THE SPRING MEETING (Fall publication)

Annual Research Volume (Fall publication)

(MEMBERSHIP DIRECTORY every sixth year in lieu of research volume)

IRRA NEWSLETTER (published quarterly)

Industrial Relations Research Association
7226 Social Science Building, University of Wisconsin
Madison, WI 53706 U.S.A. Telephone 608/262-2762

Pantagraph Printing, 217 W. Jefferson, Bloomington, IL 61701

CONTENTS

DEDICATION

Jerry Somers was an exceptional person. His scholarship in the areas of employment and training and industrial relations are well documented. The breadth of his activities was amazing. His influence was widespread. Yet, despite the scope of his activities as educator, researcher, and valued consultant, he found time to advance his profession through the Industrial Relations Research Association. He was editor of the *Proceedings* from 1958 through 1974 and president in 1975. Beginning in 1976, he directed the activities which culminated in this volume for the IRRA, and then unexpectedly, he passed on while attending the IRRA's Annual Meeting in December 1977. It is most fitting, therefore, that we dedicate this volume to Gerald G. Somers with all the respect and affection that he gave to the profession and the IRRA during his distinguished and productive life.

RAY MARSHALL
Secretary of Labor

INTRODUCTION

The literature of collective bargaining, both scholarly and practical, is immense. Nevertheless, there has been lacking for the contemporary period a work which collects in one place authoritative, industry-by-industry accounts of key collective bargaining relationships. This is what we have tried to do here.

Collective Bargaining: Contemporary American Experience is a joint effort of eleven authors. The conception, administration, and execution of the volume represents an undertaking by the Industrial Relations Research Association in consultation with the Labor-Management Services Administration of the U.S. Department of Labor. The project director was Professor Gerald G. Somers of the University of Wisconsin-Madison in his capacity as IRRA president, and the coordination of the undertaking was largely his doing. In the ordinary course of events Somers would have also written this introduction (which is adapted from the original project proposal) and the concluding commentary, but his tragic passing intervened. Accordingly, Jack Barbash, Professor of Economics and Industrial Relations at the University of Wisconsin-Madison and president-elect of IRRA, was asked to write the introduction and commentary. Richard U. Miller, Professor of Business, University of Wisconsin-Madison, secretary-treasurer of IRRA at the time, took over Professor Somers's administrative responsibilities. Barbara D. Dennis has continued to act as editor throughout this period.

This study provides a detailed description and analysis of contemporary collective bargaining in ten major industries. In addition, a commentary draws upon the industry reports to summarize and interpret current trends, practices and results of collective bargaining, and their implications for public policy.

In one sense the study updates the classic *How Collective Bargaining Works*, edited by Harry A. Millis and published by the Twentieth Century Fund in 1940. Much has happened in the intervening generation to justify a new overview of collective bargaining in the United States from the standpoint of the 1970s, and this is precisely what the objective of this volume is.

The authors bring to their respective investigations proven records of research and scholarship in the industries that they are reporting on here. Each study uses a common time perspective and follows a consistent format of detailed description and analysis of bargaining structure, procedure, and outcomes, all examined against the background of economic and institutional forces.

The common framework, it is hoped, will facilitate a comparative analysis of collective bargaining in leading industries and the policy implications thereof. In some measure this is what the commentary is about.

We hope we have produced a volume that scholars and practitioners alike will find authoritative, useful, and stimulating. In any case, we have tried.

JACK BARBASH

Madison, Wisconsin

vi

CHAPTER 1

Coal*

WILLIAM H. MIERNYK
West Virginia University

The Product and the Industry

Coal has been mined commercially in the United States since well before the Civil War. Thus, it is one of the nation's older forms of non-agricultural economic activity. The coal sector grew rapidly between 1890 and the 1920s, as the national rail network expanded and industrialization proceeded at a rapid pace.

Throughout most of its history, coal was sold in aggressively competitive markets, and the industry was characterized by the kind of instability such competition engenders. In the early days of pick-and-shovel mining there were few skilled workers in the industry, and it was a natural target for unionization on an industrial rather than a craft basis. But effective unionization came only after decades of organizing effort. Paradoxically, stable labor-management relations came at a time when the industry was going through a period of difficult adjustment to declining demand. As this is written, in the late 1970s, the industry is expanding again, but the future of its largest union, and of collective bargaining in coal, is once again clouded by uncertainty.

There are four broad classes of coal: bituminous, subbituminous, lignite, and anthracite. The most recent distribution of demonstrated reserves in 1975—expressed both in physical and heat units—is given in Table 1.

Coals vary in terms of moisture, ash content (following combustion), gases or vapors driven off when the coal is heated, and fixed carbons. Lignite contains the highest amount of moisture, has a relatively low content of volatile matter, and contains the lowest quantity of fixed carbon. Anthracite, at the other extreme, averages 92 percent fixed carbon, 5 percent volatile matter, and 3 percent moisture. Bituminous and subbituminous coals range between these extremes. As Table 1 shows,

* The author wishes to acknowledge helpful comments on an earlier draft, and research or secretarial assistance, provided by Gus Cantfil, James Cassell, Jean Gallaher, Leon Lunden, James Maddy, Jeanne Miernyk, Robert Munn, Carla Uphold, Melissa Wolford, and the editor of this volume. The author, of course, is solely responsible for any errors or shortcomings that remain.

TABLE 1
Distribution of Demonstrated Reserves[a]

Type of Coal	Tons (billions)		Btu (quadrillions)	
	Number	% of Total	Number	% of Total
Bituminous	233	53	6,100	64
Subbituminous	169	39	2,800	29
Lignite	28	6	400	4
Anthracite	7	2	200	2
Total	437	100	9,500	100

Source: *Bituminous Coal and Lignite*, U.S. Department of the Interior, Bureau of Mines, Preprint from Bulletin 667, a chapter from *Mineral Facts and Problems*, 1975 Edition, pp. 3–4.

[a] Demonstrated reserves are located at depths less than 3,000 feet below the surface, and are those which the Bureau of Mines considers to be "amenable to present mining and economic conditions." The U.S. Geological Survey estimates *total* reserves at this depth to be 1,700 billion tons. On the basis of "broad geological knowledge and theory," the Survey "surmises" that there might be "additional reserves of 2,200 billion tons" within the nation's confines.

bituminous coal accounts for more than three-fourths of demonstrated reserves in terms of heat content.[1]

Coal is produced by both underground and surface methods. Major technological advances in heavy earth-moving equipment were required before surface mining could be practiced on a large scale. In 1963, for example, 66 percent of all U.S. coal was mined underground. By 1975, more than half the nation's coal was produced by surface methods, and the most rapid expansion was taking place in western coal fields where thick seams lying close to the surface lend themselves to large-scale, area strip mining.

These changes have had an effect on the relative strength of the United Mine Workers of America (UMWA), since the union has had less success in organizing western surface miners than those who work in the older underground and surface mines of the East. This is partly due to technological differences between surface and deep mining; the skills of strip miners resemble those of engineering construction workers more than they do those of deep miners. Some western surface miners have been organized by the International Union of Operating Engineers (IUOE), but many workers in the capital-intensive and highly productive surface mines of the West have chosen to remain nonunion,[2] since most of them earn more than their UMWA counterparts.

[1] Btus are usually expressed in quadrillions, generally abbreviated as "quads," or simply "Qs" in the jargon of energy specialists.

[2] See "The UMW Is Learning How to Lose the West," *Business Week*, April 18, 1977, pp. 128–30; George Crago, "Western Miners Earn $100 Daily, UMW Leaders Face New Pressures," *Dominion-Post* (Morgantown, W.Va.), June 19, 1977; and A. H. Raskin, "Coal Is Booming But the Miners' Union Is Not," *New York Times*, June 19, 1977.

Underground coal, which contains less moisture and more heat per pound than surface coal, has a higher average value, f.o.b. the mine mouth, than surface coal. Moreover, the spread widened from $1.50 per ton in 1965 to $8.00 per ton in 1975,[3] thus maintaining the attractiveness of investment in eastern deep mines. It also has allowed the UMWA to negotiate substantial wage and fringe settlements in recent years, in spite of the fact that coal produced in UMWA mines has been a declining share of total coal production.[4] This somewhat unusual circumstance is a result of the structure of coal markets. Because of the high cost of transportation, most of it is sold in regional rather than national markets.

The distribution of reserves is given in Map 1; and major coal uses are summarized in Figure 1. The West has far more surface reserves than the East. Western coal contains less sulfur than eastern coal, but also less heat per pound. The differences are not as large in the case of underground coal as they are for surface coals, but still are large

MAP 1

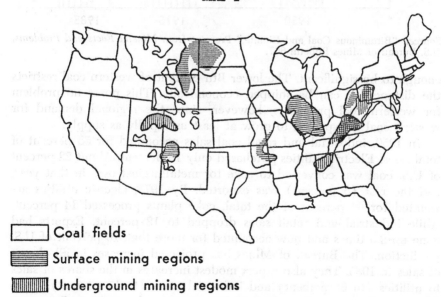

☐ Coal fields

▤ Surface mining regions

▥ Underground mining regions

Source: Energy: Use Conservation and Supply, ed. P. H. Abelson (Washington: American Association for the Advancement of Science, 1974), p. 74.

---

[3] "Bituminous Coal and Lignite," p. 13. [The complete citations of all footnote references are listed at the end of the chapter.]
[4] Business Week, April 18, 1977, p. 128.

FIGURE 1

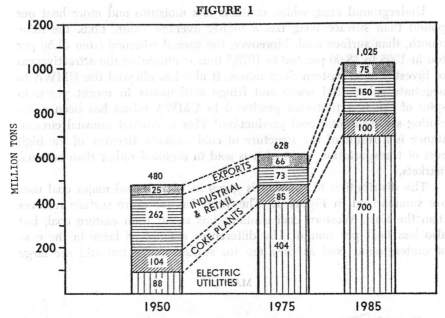

Source: "Bituminous Coal and Lignite," Preprint from *Mineral Facts and Problems*, U.S. Bureau of Mines Bulletin 667.

enough to be significant. The lower Btu content of western coal restricts the distances it can be shipped economically. This poses no problem for western coal producers, however, since the regional demand for western coal is expected to grow at least as rapidly as supply.

In 1950, industrial and retail coal sales accounted for 55 percent of total sales. Electric utilities purchased only 18 percent. About 22 percent of U.S. coal was converted to coke for metallurgical uses in that year, and the rest (5 percent) was exported. By 1975, electric utilities accounted for 64 percent of the total, coke plants processed 14 percent, while industrial and retail sales dropped to 12 percent. Exports had gone up 2.6 times and now accounted for more than 10 percent of U.S. production. The Bureau of Mines has projected increases in all classes of sales to 1985. They also expect modest increases in the shares of sales to utilities (to 68 percent) and industrial users (to 15 percent). Coke processing is expected to drop to 10 percent and exports to 7 percent of the total.[5]

Coal reserves are located in 34 of the 50 states, and in 1976 coal was mined in 29 states. In some states, however, the amounts mined are miniscule compared with the leading producers. In the early 1970s, al-

---

[5] "Bituminous Coal and Lignite," p. 12.

most 90 percent of all coal produced in the nation came from eight states, and 43 percent came from Kentucky and West Virginia. The industry is still highly localized, compared to many other kinds of economic activity, although with rapid increases in western production it is becoming more dispersed.

Historically, the coal industry has been highly unstable, with pronounced production and employment cycles. From the turn of the century to the end of World War I there was sustained growth; the production of bituminous coal increased 2.7 times, and employment just about doubled (see Chart 1). The number of jobs reached an all-time peak in 1923 when nearly 705,000 workers were employed in 9,331 mines.[6] But this level of capacity could not be sustained.

During the roaring twenties, while the nation's industrial sector prospered—and speculators were busily undermining financial markets—coal mining joined agriculture in a long period of secular decline. By 1932, bituminous production had dropped to 310 million tons—down 47 percent from the wartime peak; employment had been cut to 406,000, a drop of 42 percent; and the number of mines had shrunk to 5,555—40 percent fewer than the 1922 peak.[7] The price of soft coal, which had climbed from $1.04 per ton in 1900 to $3.75 in 1920, had dropped back to $1.31 by 1932.

The situation in anthracite coal was much the same. An important industrial fuel in the past, anthracite was used primarily for home heating in recent decades. But even this market could not withstand competition from residual fuel oil and natural gas. In 1928, for example, 160,000 anthracite miners produced 75 million tons of hard coal. By 1973, production had dropped to 7 million tons and employment to 15,000 (see Chart 2). The anthracite sector, which is located entirely in northeastern Pennsylvania, was no longer a significant part of the coal industry by the 1970s.[8] In the remainder of this chapter—unless specific mention is made to the contrary—all references to "coal" and the "coal industry" will mean bituminous coal.

Coal production climbed erratically around a rising trend from 1932 until the nation began to gear up for World War II. Production hit a new peak of 631 million tons in 1947, then dropped sharply to 437 million tons in 1949. A slow decline continued from 1949 until 1961, but there was a precipitous drop in employment which lasted until the mid-1960s. The job contraction continued after the revival in output started

[6] Baratz, p. 40.
[7] Ibid.
[8] See Bob Harwood, "Anthracite Industry Barely Survives in U.S.; Costs Up, Demand Off," Wall Street Journal, June 2, 1972.

CHART 1

BITUMINOUS COAL TRENDS, 1900-1976

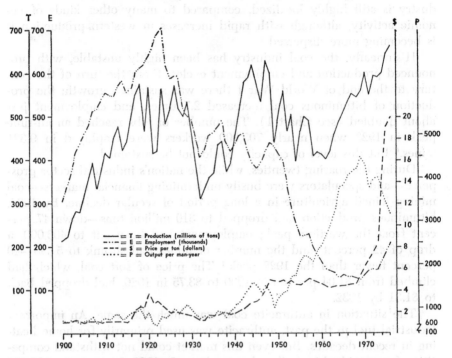

Sources: Morton S. Boratz, *The Union and the Coal Industry* (New Haven, Conn.: Yale University Press, 1955), pp. 40–41; *Minerals Yearbook* (Washington: U.S. Bureau of Mines, various years); *Coal Week*, February 14, 1977, p. 4.

in 1963, and it was not reversed until 1969. These divergent trends will be discussed later in this chapter.

The bituminous coal industry entered a new era in 1969, one which is likely to have a substantial impact on collective bargaining in the industry. That year marks the end of "cheap" coal in the United States. Between 1948 and 1968, average coal prices fluctuated within the narrow band of $4.39 to $5.08 per ton. By 1976, however, the average price had increased to $20.00, and industry experts were projecting further price increases on the basis of anticipated increases in the demand for steam coal.[9]

Another significant event in 1969 was passage of the Federal Coal Mine Health and Safety Act, which established "the strongest single

---

[9] For a discussion of the factors affecting coal production and prices after 1969, see Miernyk et al., especially ch. 1.

CHART 2
ANTHRACITE COAL TRENDS, 1928–1974

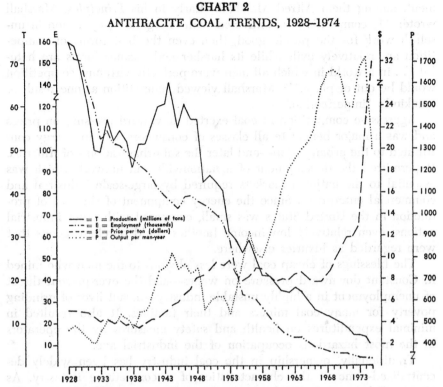

——— = T = Production (millions of tons)
–·–·– = E = Employment (thousands)
– – – = $ = Price per ton (dollars)
········ = P = Output per man-year

Source: 1928–74, *Minerals Yearbook* for given year; 1975 production figures: *Keystone News Bulletin,* January 1976, p. 23; 1975 employment and production figures: *Keystone Coal Manual* (1977), p. 947.

Note: Figures for 1951–present not strictly comparable with earlier years. See Production and Employment sections, Pennsylvania Anthracite chapter, *Minerals Yearbook* (1951). After 1951, data from independent operators were included in this chart.

code of health and safety that the country had known."[10] One consequence of this legislation was a marked decline in coal mine productivity. Less widely publicized, however, was the accompanying decline in fatal accidents—particularly in UMWA mines.

Market Structure

From Adam Smith to Milton Friedman, economists have extolled the virtues of competition. "Competition," said Smith, "can never hurt either the consumer, or the producer." It was, he said, "the only cause of good management."[11] There have been dissenters from this judg-

[10] Conaway, p. 95.
[11] Smith, p. 147.

ment, among them Alfred Marshall. Early in his *Principles*, Marshall wrote: "If competition is contrasted with energetic co-operation in unselfish work for the public good, then even the best forms of competition are relatively evil; while its harsher and meaner forms are hateful . . . in a world in which all men were perfectly virtuous, competition would be out of place."[12] Marshall viewed competition as one result of mankind's "imperfection."

Aggressive competition in coal exerted downward pressure on prices and was a major benefit to all classes of consumers. Cheap energy contributed to the urbanization—and later the suburbanization—of America. It permitted the development of a nationwide rail network which was essential to the national markets required by large-scale industrial and commercial enterprises. Since the energy component of the cost of production in the United States was small, compared with other industrial nations, even relatively low-income families could purchase goods that were regarded as luxuries elsewhere.

The blessings of cheap coal were less obvious to the men who mined it. Constant downward pressure on wages—and the ever-present threat of unemployment in a highly unstable industry—meant lives of grinding poverty for many coal miners and their families. It also resulted in minimal expenditures on health and safety measures by the operators in the most hazardous occupation of the industrial age.

Traditionally, ownership in the coal industry has been widely decentralized—one of the characteristics of a competitive industry. As Waldo Fisher put it, "[E]xcept perhaps during . . . World War [I], and under the Bituminous Coal Act of 1937, competition has been ruthless."[13] In 1929, Fisher reported, "4,612 companies operated 6,057 mines." About 20 percent of total output was from 221 mines operated by the 17 largest companies (0.37 percent of the total). The next 23 percent was produced by 416 mines owned by 70 other companies (1.52 percent of the total). The remaining 57 percent was produced by 5,420 mines operated by 4,525 companies (98.11 percent of the total).[14]

The structure of the industry has continued to change slowly in the direction of a greater degree of concentration. A few large companies account for a substantial percentage of total output. At the other extreme, a large number of small companies produce the remainder. In 1941, 15 percent of the companies produced more than 88 percent of total tonnage, while 98 companies (1.8 percent of the total) accounted for more than 39 percent of total tonnage. The situation had not changed

---

[12] Marshall, pp. 9–10.
[13] Fisher, "Bituminous Coal," p. 229.
[14] *Ibid.*

much by 1975 when 15 percent of the companies produced more than 88 percent of total tonnage, and 2.8 percent of the companies accounted for nearly 60 percent of all the coal produced.[15] The Lorenz curves in Figure 2 show the inequality of size distributions of coal companies in 1941 and 1975. While the degree of inequality increased during the 34-year period, it changed at a slow rate.[16]

FIGURE 2
LORENZ CURVES OF DISTRIBUTION OF COAL PRODUCTION BY COMPANY, 1941 AND 1975

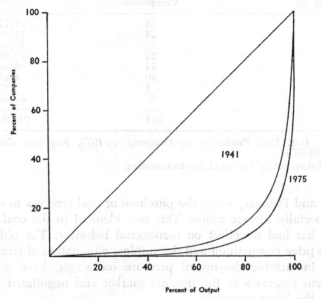

Source: U.S. Coal Production by Company, Keystone Coal Industry Manual (1941 and 1975).

There has been another change in the industrial structure of the coal industry more subtle than that revealed by a simple examination of changes in the degree of concentration. In 1941, the large coal com-

[15] The large corporations have a disproportionate influence on collective bargaining, however, since they largely determine the strategy to be followed by the industry's collective bargaining arm, the Bituminous Coal Operators Association (BCOA). They are also the dominant influence in the National Coal Association which handles much of the industry's national public relations and lobbying activities.

[16] This can be demonstrated by comparing Gini coefficients for the two years. In 1941, the Gini coefficient was .8036. By 1975, it had increased to .8520. These coefficients were calculated by a modification of the formula given by Kafoglis and Neeoy in *The Bell Journal of Economics* (Spring 1975), pp. 377–87.

panies were just that; they produced and marketed coal. By 1975, however, several of the large companies operating coal mines were energy
conglomerates (see Table 2). A number of oil companies had entered
the coal industry, either by merging with existing coal companies (such

TABLE 2

Ownership of Coal Companies Producing One Million Tons or More

Affiliation of Parent Company	Number of Companies	% of[a] Total
Coal	53	24.77
Oil	24	11.21
Utilities	22	10.28
Steel	22	10.28
Metal	14	6.54
Chemical	10	4.67
Railroad	1	.47
Others	67	31.31
Total	214	100.00

Source: U.S. Coal Production by Company . . . 1975, Keystone Coal Manual
(1976), pp. 36–37.
[a] Detail does not add to total due to rounding.

as Consol and Pittston) or by the purchase of coal reserves to open new
mines, especially surface mines. This new element in the coal industry
no doubt has had an effect on managerial behavior. The old days of
aggressive price competition and the ruthless elimination of rivals, which
produced ineluctable downward pressure on wages, have given way
to long-term contracts in the product market and negotiated wage increases in the labor market.[17]

The tables have been turned. Consumers now pay high prices for
energy derived from coal, and the straight-time average hourly earnings

[17] Those who believe that the "capitalist world" is ruled by a conspiratorial elite
take an ominous view of the trend toward increasing concentration—and even more
so, the "takeover" of the three largest coal companies by corporate giants, two of
which are oil companies. For an excellent review of this attitude, see "How International Energy Elite Rules." For a somewhat less emotional, but still decidedly
concerned, treatment of the energy conglomerates, see Ridgeway.
  A detailed statistical presentation is given by Mulholland and Webbink, especially
"The Coal Industry," pp. 67–80. Despite the procompetition flavor of most FTC
reports, Mulholland and Webbink's conclusions are decidedly not alarmist. They feel
that concentration in coal is fairly low, although they point out that it has been
rising. They also feel that "[b]ecause there are some economies of scale in coal
production, it seems likely that concentration in this industry may continue to rise
in the future" (p. 85). They do not, however, foresee any dire consequences stemming from this trend.

of coal miners are among the highest earned by industrial workers in the nation—and quite possibly in the world (see Chart 3). Weekly earnings also have remained above the average for manufacturing workers since the industry has started to grow again.[18]

For the first 40 years of this century, there was virtually no improvement in productivity in the mining of bituminous coal (see Chart 1). Technical change was a stranger to the coal industry. Long-term swings in output were followed closely by similar swings in employment.[19]

There was a moderate increase in productivity in both anthracite and bituminous coal during World War II, which was almost entirely the result of increased labor effort (despite widely publicized wartime strikes) and the steady demand for coal. But the wartime gains were virtually eliminated by 1950, a year that marks a turning point in the history of collective bargaining in coal. Employment declined sharply after 1951, while output per man-year showed a correspondingly steep increase. A major cause of these changes in trend was the 1950 agreement negotiated by John L. Lewis and the coal operators, which will be discussed in detail later in this chapter. Few labor-management agreements have had more sweeping consequences for a union and an industry than this one.

The United Mine Workers of America

The UMWA is the third largest independent union in the United States, ranking behind the Teamsters and the Auto Workers. It ranks 27th among all unions in the United States. The 1977 reported membership was 277,000, but the union had a much smaller "working" membership of 180,000. The latter represented a gain of 30,000 members, or 17 percent, over the figure reported for 1975. The UMWA may be unique in having such a large proportion of nonworking members active in union affairs. Retired members have no vote on contract matters and cannot hold national office, but they do vote in national union elections and thus may play an important role in the determination of union

---

[18] Because of fairly frequent interruptions in production, either due to strikes or short time resulting from temporary declines in orders, a comparison on an annual basis would not be as favorable as that shown by Chart 3. But after adjustment for time worked, annual earnings plus fringe benefits in coal mining would probably still compare favorably with other industries.

[19] To a lesser extent this was also true of anthracite coal between 1928 and 1948 (see Chart 2).

CHART 3
EARNINGS IN BITUMINOUS COAL MINING, MANUFACTURING AND TOTAL PRIVATE NONAGRICULTURE, 1923–1976

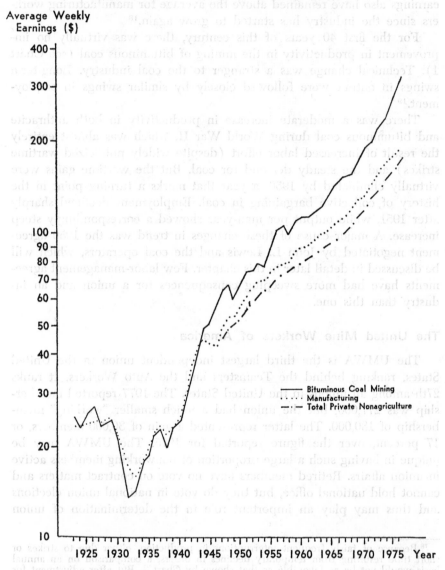

Source: *Employment and Earnings, United States, 1909–75*, pp. 3, 15, 39; *Employment and Earnings*, March 1977, Vol. 24.

policies which impinge upon their health care and economic status.[20]

The UMWA is a relatively simple organization. Locals are organized into 21 districts.[21] An elected representative of each district serves on the International Executive Board. This board, which also includes the elected international officers, governs the union between conventions. The principal elected officers are the international president, vice-president, and secretary-treasurer.

The international headquarters is organized into nine departments or divisions. A brief statement about the function of each, where this is not obvious from the title, follows:

1. The *Coal Miners Political Action Committee* (COMPAC) handles political and legislative matters. Each active member of the union is assessed $7 annually to support COMPAC's activities.

2. The *Publications and Press Department* handles public relations, but its primary responsibility is publication of the *United Mine Workers Journal*, the official voice of the UMWA which was first launched in 1889. The *Journal* is published semimonthly.

3. The *Contract Administration Department* is responsible for day-to-day administration of the various agreements negotiated by the union.

4. The *Compensation Department* is responsible for handling black-lung and worker's compensation matters.

5. The *Research Department* is responsible for the collection and analysis of data.

6. The *Legal Department* handles all legal matters.

7. The *Occupational Health Division* is concerned with occupational health legislation and maintains liaison with federal and state occupational health agencies. It also administers the EMT program under which emergency medical technicians are trained and assigned to working areas.[22]

---

[20] Before the 1969 election, for example, Tony Boyle, then president of the UMWA as well as chairman of the trustees of the union's retirement fund, pushed through a 30 percent increase in pensions. Although Boyle received only a slight majority of the votes of working miners, 87 percent of the pensioners voted for him. See Thomas O'Hanlon, "Anarchy Threatens the Kingdom of Coal," *Fortune* (January 1971), p. 80.

[21] District boundaries appear to be largely determined by the density of membership in a given area. Pennsylvania, for example, has four districts. There are three complete districts in West Virginia, and a fourth which covers part of Ohio. Kentucky has three districts, and the following states have one each: Indiana, Illinois, Virginia, Alabama, Arkansas, and Utah. Two districts cover the remaining western states (Arizona, Colorado, Kansas, Missouri, Montana, and the Dakotas). The other two districts are in Canada.

[22] COMPAC also has been involved in this effort. The Political Action Committee lobbied for more than a year, for example, to obtain passage of a law in Pennsylvania which requires that EMTs be assigned to each shift of every underground mine and to each surface mine that employs 20 or more miners. See *UMW Journal*, July 15–31, 1976, pp. 11–13.

8. The *Safety Division* is responsible for the regular inspection of mines to insure that negotiated safety provisions are being enforced. This division has its headquarters at Bridgeport, West Virginia, and has a substantial field operation covering all districts.

9. The *Organizing Division* is responsible for all efforts to organize nonunion workers.

An ancillary operation in which the union is deeply involved, but which is a separate legal entity, is the trust that administers the UMWA Welfare and Retirement Funds first established in 1946. Over the years the trust has evolved into a complex organization which has been altered in successive negotiations as the fortunes of the industry have waxed and waned, and as the legal requirements of union-related retirement programs have changed. There are now four separate funds administered by three trustees. More will be said about the history, structure, and functions of these funds in a later section.

Rivals to the UMWA

The UMWA is widely regarded as *the* coal miners' union, although it has had to face the problem of rival or "dual" unionism. Until recently, the most serious threat came from the Progressive Mine Workers of America, founded by UMWA dissidents in Illinois in 1932. Before the break, District 12, covering Illinois, had been one of the strongest in the union, enjoying "a closed shop in the shipping mines of the district."[23]

In 1924, John L. Lewis had negotiated a $7.50 daily wage rate for District 12, the highest achieved up to that time in the industry. But Kentucky and West Virginia were "open shop" areas, and output in these states went up 50 percent over the next four years while it declined substantially in Illinois. Lewis countered by accepting a wage cut, but the members of District 12 resisted and broke away to form the Progressive Miners of America in September 1932. Later, the PMA affiliated with the American Federation of Labor to become the Progressive Mine Workers of America.

Paid membership in the PMWA reached a peak of 19,576 in 1934, but in spite of aid and comfort from the AFL, it was unable to sustain this membership. Districts established in Kansas, Kentucky, and West Virginia did not survive, and by 1942 paid membership had dropped to 10,000.[24] The most recent estimate places PMWA membership at

[23] Hudson, p. 10.
[24] *Ibid.*, p. 152.

COAL   15

about 5,000.[25] Since 1932, District 12 of the UMWA and the Progres-
sives have lived a competitive coexistence in Illinois, but except for a
few years during the depressed 1930s, the PMWA has not constituted
a serious threat to the older UMWA.[26]

A more recent, and potentially more serious, threat to the UMWA
has come from the International Union of Operating Engineers (IUOE),
which has undertaken an aggressive organizing campaign in the West.
Many of the heavy machine operators in the West are relatively young
and apparently prefer higher wages now to generous pensions later.
Some western operators have also voiced a preference for the IUOE over
the UMWA, stating that they believe the latter to be "too militant and
strike-prone."[27] The UMWA responded to the IUOE presence by negotiating a separate western surface mine agreement in 1975. Rival unionism in the western coal fields remained a clear and present danger to
the survival of the UMWA in the West in the late 1970s.

To complete the record, another organization—the Southern Labor
Union—should be mentioned. This organization, founded in 1959, has
been called a "company-oriented alternative" by UMWA spokesmen. It
has made little headway, and its estimated 2,500 members in 1975 were
located entirely in Kentucky. The union's general counsel and highest
paid official that year was Ted Q. Wilson who, in addition to being the
chief executive of the union, was also a coal operator. Although the
UMWA does not appear to be seriously threatened by this "dual" union,
union leaders would be happy if they could win the allegiance of its
members.[28]

The Bituminous Coal Operators Association

Before 1950, the UMWA negotiated agreements with three major
groups of operators. The Northern Coal Operators Association represented companies in Pennsylvania, northern West Virginia, Ohio, Illinois,
and western Kentucky in these negotiations. A separate agreement was
negotiated with the Southern Coal Producers Association, which represented operators in southern West Virginia, Virginia, eastern Kentucky,

[25] I am indebted for this estimate to Dr. Keith Dix of the Institute of Labor
Studies, West Virginia University.

[26] For a detailed history of the PMWA, see Hudson. "When John L. Lewis took
his United Mine Workers back into the AFL fold in January, 1946 . . . the obstinate
little Progressive union thumbed its nose at the dignity of the AFL and the power
of the UMW by withdrawing and declaring itself independent. The same house
could not hold John L. Lewis and the Progressive Mine Workers of America." Young,
p. 330.

[27] *Business Week*, April 18, 1977; Crago, *Dominion-Post*, June 19, 1977; and
Raskin, *New York Times*, June 19, 1977.

[28] For further details, see *UMW Journal*, February 1–15, 1975, pp. 4–11.

Tennessee, and Alabama. The third agreement was negotiated with the owners of captive mines.

In 1950, however, the northern operators and the owners of captive mines agreed to negotiate jointly, the result of this merger of interests being the creation of the Bituminous Coal Operators Association (BCOA). Initially, BCOA members accounted for about half of total coal production in the United States. By 1954, the Southern Coal Producers Association had joined the BCOA which by then spoke for most of the large bituminous coal operators who had recognized the UMWA. Although many small operators do not belong to the BCOA, those who recognize the UMWA sign agreements that are identical to the one negotiated by the union and the association.

The BCOA is a small organization established exclusively for collective bargaining purposes. It is concerned, of course, both with the negotiation and administration of agreements. Its principal officers are the president and the general counsel, who are backed up by a legal and research staff.

Other UMWA Agreements

The key contract in bituminous coal, which determines the wage contour and pattern of fringe benefits throughout the industry, is that between the UMWA and the BCOA,[29] but this is not the only contract the union negotiates. It has a separate agreement with the Association of Bituminous Contractors, Inc., which "covers all work related to the development, expansion, or alteration of coal mines, including the erection of tipples and preparation plants and other facilities placed in, on, or around the coal mines" operated by the BCOA.[30] As noted above, the UMWA has also negotiated a separate subbituminous and lignite agreement with six western surface mine operators.[31]

There also is a separate contract between the UMWA and the Anthracite Coal Miners of northeastern Pennsylvania. The anthracite branch of the coal industry was moribund throughout most of the 1950s and 1960s, but during the 1970s the revived demand for fossil fuels led to a modest amount of anthracite production. In 1975, there were about

---

[29] For discussion of the concept of "wage contour," see Dunlop, pp. 131–34.

[30] *United Mine Workers of America and Association of Bituminous Contractors National Coal Mine Construction Agreement*, December 23, 1974, p. 1.

[31] *Western Surface Coal Wage Agreement of 1975.*

2,200 anthracite working miners, and about 15,000 anthracite pensioners belonged to the UMWA.

A new anthracite agreement was reached in May 1975 following a 21-day strike. Because anthracite production had come to a virtual standstill, wages and fringe benefits in this segment of the industry lagged far behind those of the more prosperous bituminous branch, as did the pensions received by retired anthracite miners. The 1975 agreement called for an immediate increase in anthracite wages of $1.50 per hour, with further scheduled increases up to $2.10 per hour. This would raise the average daily wage in anthracite mining from $28 to $42.70, a figure which still lags far behind prevailing wages in the bituminous sector. The new anthracite agreement also called for an increase in health and welfare royalties from 50 cents per ton to $1.40 per ton at the end of the third year. As a result of this increase, the pensions of retired anthracite miners were scheduled to be raised, although they were not expected to reach the levels of those received by retired bituminous miners.[32]

The Historical Development of Collective Bargaining in Coal[33]

FORERUNNERS OF THE UMWA

The first recorded union of coal miners in the United States—the American Miner's Association—was formed at Belleville, Illinois, in 1861. A work stoppage in 16 St. Clair County mines spread to Missouri, Ohio, and Pennsylvania, and miners from these states joined to form the association. Membership grew for a while, but the union could not survive the deflation that followed the Civil War. Following a series of unsuccessful strikes in 1867–68, the union gradually dissolved as local after local disappeared.[34]

The operators had not accepted the idea of unionism with equanimity. Following a successful strike in the Belleville district in 1863, a number of operators met in Chicago to plan a defensive strategy. Their decision was, quite simply, not to deal with members of the Miner's Association. Instead, each employee would be hired on the basis of an individual contract which would forbid him to be a member of any

---

[32] For further details, see *UMW Journal*, May 1–15, 1975, p. 5.

[33] Only the highlights of the early days of coal unionism will be given here. For more complete treatments, see Baratz, Fisher.

[34] Fisher, "Bituminous Coal," pp. 230–31. See also Finley, p. 18.

"association of miners." This is one of the first recorded instances of the use of yellow-dog contracts.[35]

While the first bituminous coal union was gradually withering away, miners in the anthracite fields of northern Pennsylvania were making significant organizational progress. In 1867, local unions in the Lehigh and Schuylkill fields organized the Workingmen's Benevolent Association. In 1868, while the bituminous locals in Missouri and Illinois were falling apart, the WBA negotiated a 10 percent wage increase in the anthracite fields.[36] The WBA did not survive the economic turbulence of the last quarter of the 19th century, but for a time it appeared to be in a relatively strong bargaining position.

Encouraged by the successes of the anthracite miners, workers in the bituminous coal fields had begun to organize again. Between 1868 and 1872, locals were established in Illinois, Indiana, Pennsylvania, Maryland, Michigan, Kentucky, and West Virginia. In 1872, delegates from Illinois, Indiana, and Missouri established the Miner's Benevolent and Protective Association. The following year, joined by representatives of local unions in Ohio, Pennsylvania, and West Virginia, they formed the Miners' National Association of the United States. Despite employer resistance and prosecution for violation of the conspiracy law, the new union grew for the next three or four years. By 1875 it had more than 30,000 members in 347 local unions covering 12 states and the Indian Territory.[37]

The brief period of success was followed by disaster. Overproduction, a recurring problem in the coal industry until fairly recent times, caught up with the union in 1876. Operators responded by cutting prices and slashing wages. Local unions responded by going on strike, despite pleas from national officers not to do so. Most of the strikes were lost, and the locals disbanded. Soon the national treasury was drained, and the national offices were closed. "After more than a decade of determined effort the miners lacked the solidarity, self-discipline, and experience to force union recognition of interstate or industry-wide collective bargaining."[38]

The last quarter of the 19th century was a period of short-term instability around a rising growth trend. Coal was mined by a large number of small producers, and price competition was severe. Efforts by the industry to stabilize prices were not successful. Low wages and long stretches of unemployment led miners to organize local unions once

[35] Finley, p. 19.
[36] Fisher, "Anthracite," pp. 281–82.
[37] Fisher, "Bituminous Coal," p. 231.
[38] Ibid., p. 232.

again. The Knights of Labor achieved the greatest success in organizing miners during this period of economic turbulence. As late as 1888, most organized miners belonged to the Knights, having joined during the brief but meteoric rise of membership following 1885.[39]

Some local union leaders, however, remained outside the Knights of Labor. They were convinced that earlier efforts to establish an interstate agreement had failed because of the lack of a united front. Miners from Illinois, Indiana, Ohio, Pennsylvania, West Virginia, Iowa, and Kansas had met in 1885 to form the National Federation of Miners and Mine Laborers, and they invited the operators to meet with them to work out an agreement which not only would prevent strikes and walkouts, but also would stabilize production, prices, wages, and profits. A limited number of operators participated, and in 1886 the first interstate stabilization agreement was reached. Employers continued to complain about high wages. Again the competing unions were unable to present a united front and the agreement collapsed.

Following the end of the interstate agreement, a loose federation was formed between the National Federation of Miners and National Trades Assembly No. 135 of the Knights of Labor. From this relationship the United Mine Workers of America was born on January 25, 1890.[40] At first, the UMWA tried to preserve the essential features of both organizations, but membership in the Knights declined as suddenly as it had increased and by 1898 the Knights of Labor was no longer an effective spokesman for the coal miners of America. From that day to the present, the UMWA has been the dominant voice of organized labor in both the bituminous and anthracite fields.

Membership in the UMWA rose from 17,000 to 60,000 during its first year, but the panic of 1893 cut into the ranks of the new union and, by 1896, membership had dropped to 10,000. It appeared that the national union was again in jeopardy. Economic conditions improved in 1897, however, and UMWA membership more than tripled during the first year of recovery. The union also managed a successful three-month strike in 1897.[41]

Two important events affected the UMWA in 1898. First, the Knights of Labor component was dissolved, and the UMWA was reorganized as a national industrial union, a structure it has retained to the present day. The second event was a joint conference of miners and operators. At this conference collective bargaining was accepted, in principle, in the coal fields of Illinois, Indiana, Ohio, and western Pennsylvania.

---

[39] Millis and Montgomery, pp. 65–72.
[40] Baratz, p. 52.
[41] *Ibid.*

THE UMWA

During its early days, the UMWA's fortunes were determined to a large extent by exogenous forces. When market conditions improved, membership rose and the union achieved gains, but the union lost ground during recessions when prices and wages were cut. The union sought to break the cycle by establishing the "principle of competitive equality" which would, in essence, "take wages out of competition."[42] Its goal was not uniform piece rates, since these varied with thickness of seam and other conditions in the mines, but equality of earnings.

A major influence on the success of the UMWA during its early days was the quality of its leadership. The international president, John Mitchell, was an astute and knowledgeable labor leader. His statement on the impossibility of individual bargaining, and the need for collective action by organized workers to improve their conditions, has become a classic pronouncement of organized labor's position.[43] Mitchell also recognized the need for mechanization, but argued that it should proceed gradually so as to minimize dislocation and to allow for orderly adjustment to change.[44]

Mitchell's career as president was a stormy one. Throughout his tenure he had to cope with attacks from within as well as opposition from the operators.[45] But one thing worked in Mitchell's favor; mine employment rose steadily while he was president, passing the half million mark in 1907 when production amounted to almost 400 million tons.[46]

An outstanding accomplishment of the UMWA during its first 20 years was negotiation of the Central Competitive Field Agreement which covered Illinois, Indiana, Ohio, and western Pennsylvania. First negotiated in 1898, it established "the basic eight-hour day, a uniform wage scale for daymen, and tonnage rates at basing points in each area for the men who actually mined the coal."[47] Thereafter, new agreements were negotiated annually until 1904, biennially between 1904 and 1916, and then for periods ranging from seven months to three years until it collapsed in 1927.

---

[42] Ibid.
[43] See Mitchell, pp. 2–4. Cf. Millis and Montgomery, pp. 357–58.
[44] Mitchell, pp. 249–50. See also Baratz, pp. 53–55. Another early UMWA leader who should be mentioned, at least in passing, is John McBride. At the 1893 convention of the AFL he was narrowly defeated by Samuel Gompers for the presidency of the federation. The following year McBride, a Socialist, succeeded in unseating Gompers and served as president of the AFL for the subsequent year. Gompers again won the presidency in 1895 and held the post until his death in 1925. See Millis and Montgomery, p. 112.
[45] Gluck, p. 27.
[46] Although Mitchell served as president from 1899 until 1908, he retired at the comparatively early age of 38. Later he was to become chairman of the Trade Agreement Department of the National Civic Federation. Gluck, p. 219.
[47] Fisher, "Bituminous Coal," p. 238.

John L. Lewis and the Rise of the UMWA

John L. Lewis became president of the UMWA at a difficult time in its history.[48] The trend in production during the 1920s was nearly horizontal, although there were wide fluctuations around that trend. Coal production did not drop until after the crash of 1929, but coal employment had been decreasing since 1923. At the bottom of this decline it was only slightly above the 1903 level. There were 493,000 organized coal miners in 1923, accounting for 57 percent of wage earners in the industry. By 1930, membership had dropped to 205,000 and included slightly less than 32 percent of all employed miners.[49]

Despite stagnation in the national economy, coal production expanded throughout most of the 1930s, and coal employment rose steadily between 1931 and 1937. Union membership recovered. According to Wolman's estimate, unions accounted for almost 91 percent of all employees in coal mining in 1934.[50] Production declined again in 1939, but it rose throughout World War II. After a brief drop at the end of the war, it reached a new record peak of 630 million tons in 1947. In spite of wartime price controls, there were modest increases in coal prices. Prices did not level off until 1948 when another protracted decrease in production set in and continued until 1963.

It is difficult to manage a contracting organization, and the UMWA was in a state of decline after 1950. That year it reported a membership of 416,000; nine years later this figure had dropped to 180,000. Lewis was more than a passive observer of this decline; he contributed to it. But he did so in what he believed to be the best interests of the men he led. The greatest need for the industry, in Lewis's view, was stability of production and employment, and this could be achieved, he felt, only if major increases in productivity could be realized. The two goals that Lewis sought were mechanization of the mines and a pension system to take care of displaced miners too old to shift to other occupations. These goals could be achieved only with the full support of UMWA officials.

Article III, Section 2, of the UMWA Constitution states: "Charters of Districts, sub-Districts, and Local Unions may be revoked by the International President . . . ." Lewis used this provision of the constitution liberally. In 1948, the union was organized into 31 districts. Over

[48] John P. White was succeeded as president by Frank Hays in 1918, and Hays appointed Lewis as vice-president. Hays resigned in 1919, and Lewis took over the presidency. Lewis ran for election for the first time in 1920 and won by a small margin. He remained president until 1960 when he was succeeded by Tom Kennedy.

[49] Wolman, p. 229.

[50] Ibid. This figure includes membership in both the UMWA and the Progressive Miners of America.

the years, Lewis had suspended the elected officers of 21 of these districts and had replaced them with men known to be loyal to his views. He had the vote of a majority of executive board members in his hippocket. In spite of what most observers have regarded as shocking abuses of power, Lewis retained the support of most rank-and-file miners.[51]

The UMWA Health and Retirement Fund

The initial agreement establishing the Health and Retirement Fund in 1946 was not negotiated with the coal operators, but by the UMWA and the U.S. government. Lewis led the miners in an industrywide walkout that year. The government, however, used its wartime powers to seize the mines, as it had during the war years. Following the seizure, a new agreement was negotiated by Lewis and Julius Krug, who served as Secretary of the Interior under President Truman. A wage increase was granted. Far more important, however, was the "Krug-Lewis agreement" establishing the UMWA Welfare and Retirement Fund.[52]

The Krug-Lewis agreement specified that the fund would be financed by a royalty payment of 5 cents per ton of coal produced for use or sale. It also provided for a survey of medical and sanitary facilities to be made by the Coal Mines Administrator. The only part of the agreement that proceeded without a hitch was the survey conducted under the direction of Rear Admiral Joel T. Boone. The first four years of the fund's life were marked by disagreement over procedures and objectives, and several changes were made before the activities of the fund were stabilized following the landmark National Bituminous Coal Wage Agreement of 1950.

The original Krug-Lewis agreement called for three trustees to administer the fund. Lewis represented the UMWA, and Captain Collison, the Coal Mines Administrator, represented the government. The two could not agree on the third impartial trustee, however, and while collections were started, disbursements were frozen until the issue of the neutral trustee could be resolved. On April 8, 1947, the government agreed to the selection of T. E. Murray as the impartial trustee, and the first payments from the fund went to dependents of the Centralia, Illinois, mine disaster of March 25, 1947, in which 111 men were killed. The

---

[51] Lewis's role in the formation of the Congress of Industrial Organizations and his widely publicized political activities are not discussed here since they have no direct bearing on collective bargaining in coal. They did, however, help keep him in the public eye and added to his status as a legend in his own time. For a detailed account of these activities, see Dubofsky and Van Tine.

[52] Only the highlights of the four years following the Krug-Lewis agreement are given here. For further details, see *UMWA Welfare and Retirement Fund: Four Year Summary and Review for the Year Ending June 30, 1951*, pp. 23-45.

seized mines were returned to private operation on June 30, 1947, when the War Labor Disputes Act expired.[53] On July 1, a new National Bituminous Coal Contract went into effect which increased royalty payments to 10 cents per ton. Ezra Van Horn, representing the operators, replaced Captain Collison on the board of trustees.

The Drive Toward Industrywide Bargaining

There have been few periods in the UMWA's long and turbulent history to compare with the tumultuous years extending from January 1947 through March 1950.

Several strikes or slowdowns were called during this 26-month period. The Taft-Hartley Act was invoked against the UMWA three different times.[54] The union and President Lewis were fined $1,420,000 for criminal contempt of court, and Van Horn, the operators' trustee, filed four separate lawsuits to prevent activation of the Health and Retirement Fund. It also was the beginning of a long period of declining demand for coal which ultimately was to have an impact on employment and union membership.

The trouble started on December 17, 1947, when, during contract negotiations, Lewis asked for a pension of $100 per month for all miners reaching age 60 after 20 years of service. A month later, T. E. Murray, the neutral trustee for the Health and Retirement Fund, resigned over the pension issue. In March 1948, miners began leaving the pits to protest the operators' "dilatory tactics" during negotiations and, on March 23, the government secured a federal court injunction against the strike under the national emergency disputes provision of the Taft-Hartley Act.

Senator Styles Bridges of New Hampshire, who became the new neutral fund trustee in April, proposed a compromise on the pension issue: retirement at age 62 for those who had completed 20 years of service after the Krug-Lewis agreement. Lewis accepted this compromise, and a resolution was adopted putting it into effect.

Earlier in April, the Department of Justice had argued before District Court Judge T. Alan Goldsborough that Lewis and the UMWA should be adjudged guilty of contempt. Judge Goldsborough agreed that the union and Lewis had not purged themselves of contempt, although the miners were once again at work. On April 20, 1948, he levied fines of $20,000 against Lewis and $1,400,000 against the UMWA.

Although the pension issue had been settled—at least for the time

---

[53] *Ibid.*

[54] See *National Emergency Disputes Under the Labor Management (Taft-Hartley) Act, 1947–61*, Bureau of Labor Statistics Report No. 169, U.S. Department of Labor (Washington: U.S. Government Printing Office [revised July 1962]).

being—Lewis had not been able to negotiate new contracts with the operators. He was asking for both increased wages and higher contributions to the welfare fund. Unrest continued in the coal fields, and the Taft-Hartley national emergency disputes provision was invoked for the second time on June 19. The agreement reached later that month called for an increase of 10 cents per ton in royalty payments to the fund and a wage increase of $1.00 a day. But Harry Moses, representing the captive mines, had walked out of the bargaining sessions and, when the new contract went into effect in July, the captive mines remained closed. On July 13, however, Lewis and Moses signed a new pact, and labor peace returned to the coal fields.

A year later, when the industry was facing its chronic problem of overproduction, Lewis called for a one-week "stabilizing" work stoppage beginning June 13, 1949.

> This period of inaction will emphasize a lack of general stability in the industry and the dangers which will accrue therefrom if current harmful practices are not remedied. It will contribute constructively to the abatement of current economic demoralization; it will not adversely affect the public interest; it will help preserve property values in the industry; and it will help preserve the living standards of the mine workers, their dependents and the communities which depend upon mine workers' income.[55]

At the same time, George Love, president of Consolidation Coal Company, was asking for unified action to end "chaos in the industry." He recommended an organization of all operators not "to limit production or create an industrial monopoly to match the labor monopoly; the purpose is simply to bring order and dignity into labor relations. . . ."[56]

When the 1948 agreement expired on June 30, 1949, and a new agreement had not been reached, Lewis ordered miners in the eastern coal fields to limit themselves to a three-day work week starting July 5. Negotiations continued, but starting in September there were sporadic work stoppages with more and more miners staying out. By early October, 305,000 bituminous miners were on strike. By the time Lewis ordered the miners back to work, under terms of the old contract, on November 9, 1949, they had been out for 51 days.

In December, the first pattern-setting agreements were reached with several Kentucky and West Virginia companies, effective January 1, 1950. But not all producers had signed, and a number of them had filed unfair labor practice charges against the UMWA. Once again, the miners

---

[55] UMWA *Welfare and Retirement Fund*, p. 32.
[56] *Ibid.*

struck those companies that had not followed the Kentucky and West Virginia agreements. In February, there was a massive walkout when 370,000 miners failed to report for work. For the third time, President Truman invoked the Taft-Hartley Act against the UMWA, but the miners defied the injunction and remained off the job. On March 3, 1950, the President requested congressional authority to seize and operate the coal mines. Several hours later, representatives of the two associations and the captive coal operators reached an agreement with Lewis on "fundamental principles" for a new contract, and on March 5 the National Bituminous Coal Wage Agreement of 1950 was signed to run until June 30, 1952.

Basic wages were increased from $14.05 to $14.75 a day, and the Welfare and Retirement Fund royalty was increased to 30 cents a ton. Charles Owen became the new operators' trustee, and Josephine Roche, director of the fund, became the new neutral trustee. Although production continued to oscillate around a declining trend, prices were stable during the 1950s and the trust fund continued to grow and to provide expanded medical services. By 1960, for example, as a result of the Boone survey, it had built 10 memorial hospitals in eastern Kentucky, southern West Virginia, and western Virginia.

John L. Lewis and the 1950 Agreement

More than anything else, Lewis had proclaimed the need for order in an industry long noted for its instability. For more than three decades he had dealt with a large number of relatively small producers. As noted earlier, the UMWA negotiated separate agreements with two major associations and the captive mines. The 1950 agreement marked the beginning of a new era in collective bargaining in coal. With the formation of the Bituminous Coal Operators Association, the UMWA had for the first time successfully negotiated an industrywide contract.[57] The agreement, James Ridgeway wrote, "brought an end to chaos in the coal business, and allowed for a decade of orderly growth and reorganization . . . it marked the beginning of a curious partnership between George Love, the chief industry spokesman, and John L. Lewis, the leader of the mine workers."[58] However, this assertion, with its suggestion of a conspiratorial arrangement, is not quite a correct interpretation of the facts. What the 1950 agreement allowed for was a decade of more or less orderly decline in coal production, at the cost of

[57] The term "industrywide" is somewhat misleading since the coal industry has never been fully unionized. What it means is that the major operators and captive mines had signed a master agreement which also was accepted by many small operators outside the association.

[58] Ridgeway, pp. 17–18.

a substantial drop in coal employment. This, of course, had an adverse impact on "active" UMWA membership.

Lewis viewed displaced coal miners quite realistically as the victims of technological progress. He reasoned, however, that the industry had no alternative to mechanization.[59] Dieselization of the railroad and massive increases in imports of low-priced Middle Eastern oil—coupled with the backward state of the art of coal mining—made it abundantly clear that nothing short of major increases in productivity could save the jobs of those who remained in the industry.[60]

Sumner Slichter pointed out that despite opposition to mechanization by some locals, the 1934 convention adopted a resolution to accept the introduction of machinery. At that convention, Lewis had stated:

> There is no other modern solution to the machine problem of our present day and age than to increase the wages, shorten the working hours and shorten the working week to any degree necessary to let the machine do the work for mankind, but at the same time give to the workers and industry a wage produced by the machine that will maintain them and their families in comfort and with a provision for old age.[61]

And the report of the convention went on to state that:

> Rather than object to mechanization of industry, we should devote our efforts toward a shorter work day and work week, toward a greater participation in the blessings of invention, of science, of progress, with a fundamental objective of making mankind the masters of their destiny and subjecting machines, science, and modern developments of industry to humankind.[62]

The lofty language of the 1934 convention suggests a degree of optimism about the ease with which adjustments to mechanization could be made. Such oratory was less noticeable when the 1950 agreement was signed, but perhaps in part this was because in the meantime Lewis had been successful in his battle to establish the UMWA Health and

---

[59] For a detailed account of Lewis's views on the need for and benefits of mechanization, see the extended interview with him entitled "More Machines, Fewer Men—A Union That's Happy About It," *U.S. News and World Report*, November 9, 1959, pp. 60–64.

[60] This was not a new stance for the United Mine Workers. Writing shortly after the turn of the century—at a time when the coal industry was in a period of robust growth—John Mitchell had recognized the need for mechanization. He had argued, however, that employers had a duty to "make alterations gradually, so as to extend the effect of the change over a series of years, and thus permit the workmen to accommodate themselves to new conditions." Mitchell, pp. 249–50.

[61] United Mine Workers of America, *Proceedings of the Thirty-Third Constitutional Convention*, 1 (1934), p. 204. Cited by Slichter, p. 272.

[62] *UMWA Proceedings*, p. 188.

Retirement Fund of 1946.[63] He no doubt believed that older workers displaced from the mines by mechanization could maintain a decent standard of living on the pensions provided by the fund.

The 1950 agreement did not contain a specific mechanization clause. "The most important aspect of the 1950 contract . . . was its spirit, rather than its content."[64] The statement by George H. Love following signing of the agreement is indicative:

> . . . This two-and-one-half year Contract gives the industry its first real opportunity for stability in the last decade. . . . The Operators definitely established the right to control their production and their mining facilities. . . . We need stability and the Contract provides it. . . .[65]

Lewis added his support by stating that

> . . . the industry can apply itself—both management and labor —to the constructive problem of producing coal in quantity . . . *at the lowest possible cost permitted by modern techniques.* The Mine Workers stand for the investors in the industry and for a return on their capital. They stand for the public to have coal at the lowest possible price consistent with the Mine Workers having a decent life. . . .[66]

Lewis also realized that few if any of the small coal companies in an industry characterized by aggressive price competition would engage in market research. Another Lewis innovation was to establish a marketing division in the research department of the UMWA which would forecast demand and conduct other marketing studies. The results were made available to operators to help them plan future investment and production policies.

Finally, in 1959, Lewis took the initiative in organizing the National Coal Policy Conference, Inc., a venture sponsored jointly by the UMWA and other coal-related interests. The conference served a useful purpose. It published a number of informative and objective brochures dealing with a variety of fuel and energy issues. The nature and objectives of the conference were described in its publications as:

> An organization composed of coal producing companies, the United Mine Workers of America, coal-carrying railroads, electric utility companies, and the manufacturers of mining ma-

---

[63] For a discussion of the UMWA fund as an example of "vertical control" by the union, see Warren-Boulten, pp. 318–21.

[64] Dubofsky and Van Tine, p. 489.

[65] United Mine Workers of America, *Proceedings of the Forty-First Consecutive Constitutional Convention, October 7–15, 1952,* 1 (Cincinnati, Ohio), p. 125.

[66] *Ibid.,* p. 126.

chines and equipment and dedicated to creating a new awareness of coal as a vital source in the nation's energy fuels
complex and the need for a self sufficiency in energy fuels as
the key to the prosperous and secure future for the United
States.

The NCPC was dissolved on March 1, 1971, because, according to a
press release issued in February of that year, "the original objectives for
which NCPC was organized in 1959 had been achieved and . . . a new
approach to meet entirely new problems in the decades ahead will be
needed." It is not at all clear that these objectives had been achieved
at the time the conference was dissolved.[67]

Industrywide Bargaining

A new era in labor-management relations started in the American
coal industry in 1950. The UMWA had achieved one of the goals sought
since the days of John Mitchell—a *national* agreement. Now Harry
Moses, who was named head of the BCOA in September 1950, and John
L. Lewis could hammer out agreements that would be mutually satisfactory to the operators and the union.[68] Did the new agreement bring
the stability which both union leaders and operators appeared to yearn
for? It did indeed achieve stability in labor-management relations, but
conditions in the industry were anything but stable.

The industry faced problems created by shifts in demand and technological change. The large railroad market had been lost, and henceforth the major customers of coal would be electric utilities and steel
mills. But in many parts of the country the demand for steam coal declined as utilities shifted from coal to low-cost imported oil. Mine employment dropped steadily from 1948 until 1953; it leveled off then for
a few years at about 225,000 workers. The decline resumed in 1959,
however, and continued steadily for the next ten years. In 1969, only
125,000 workers remained in the mines. But the industry had been transformed, thanks in large part to the 1950 agreement. It was now more
capital intensive, it had experienced large increases in productivity, and
it had enjoyed two decades of relatively peaceful labor relations.

Collective bargaining was quite placid during the 1950s, at least by
comparison with the past. So John L. Lewis turned his talents in other
directions; he became involved in the world of finance. The UMWA

---

[67] When Lewis retired as NCPC chairman in 1963, Joseph P. Routh, then chairman of the Pittston Company, "ranked Lewis's two greatest achievements" as promoting modernization and initiating the National Coal Policy Conference. "It was
only because of this great man," he said, "that the industry survives today." Dubofsky and Van Tine, p. 521.

[68] It was not until the 1960s, however, that the UMWA was able to enforce uniform national wages in all the mines with which it had contracts.

purchased the National Bank of Washington.[69] Lewis also forged an alliance with Cyrus Eaton, the Ohio financier. Eaton served as a financial adviser to the UMWA, but he also participated more directly in its affairs. The union had tried for some time without success to organize the Western Kentucky Coal Company. Eaton began to buy shares in Western Kentucky, as did other companies over which he had control. The UMWA also invested heavily in Western Kentucky stock. By 1952, this combination controlled the board of directors, and in 1953 Western Kentucky signed the National Bituminous Coal Wage Agreement. Western Kentucky then took over another nonunion company. This strategy for extending organization appeared to be working. Unfortunately, Western Kentucky was one of the companies caught in the squeeze of declining coal demand. It began to suffer heavy losses and the price of its stock dropped. Ten years after it had signed its first agreement with the company, the UMWA liquidated its Western Kentucky stock. Finley reports that the union took an $8 million loss on this transaction.

John L. Lewis retired in 1960 and was succeeded by vice-president Tom Kennedy. William Anthony "Tony" Boyle was Lewis's hand-picked choice for vice-president. Lewis was a man who evoked strong feelings. He was frequently denounced by editorial writers for his alleged arrogance. It was also said that he placed the interest of his union above the national interest. But to the rank-and-file miners he was a great man. This assessment of Lewis was shared by many neutral observers, including some who disagreed with the tactics he employed.[70]

The End of an Era

Whatever else might have been said about John L. Lewis, he was never charged with being personally corrupt.[71] Nor was Tom Kennedy, who died in 1963. Tony Boyle then became the leader of the UMWA. Under Boyle's leadership, however, the UMWA was labeled by one observer as "The Corrupt Kingdom."[72]

Boyle took over at a time when coal production was rising steadily, although employment continued to decline as a result of further mechanization. The years from 1958 to 1969 covered a period of steadily increasing productivity, with output per worker increasing from about 2,100 tons per year to almost 4,500 tons per year. But while the eco-

[69] The exact date of the purchase and circumstances of the transaction were never widely discussed. Finley, p. 159.

[70] Cf. Dubofsky and Van Tine, *passim*.

[71] Lewis lived in a style that could not have been supported by his salary as union president. But he was an astute businessman and investor who did quite well in the stock market, as well as in business ventures which he organized. Dubofsky and Van Tine, *passim*.

[72] *Ibid*.

nomic health of the industry was improving, that of the union began to deteriorate.

Early in his administration, Boyle gave important positions to friends and members of his family, but this might have been among the least of his transgressions as a union president. He was a weak union official who could scarcely be characterized as a true labor "leader," and he soon lost control of a large part of his membership.[73] One indicator of his ineptness was his comment following the worst mine disaster of recent times. Speaking to the bereaved relatives of 78 miners killed in an explosion near Farmington, West Virginia, on November 20, 1968, he said: "As long as we mine coal there is always this inherent danger." And he went on to say that Consolidation Coal, which had operated the mine, was "one of the best companies to work with as far as cooperation and safety are concerned."[74]

Soon after he took office, Boyle was being criticized from within and without the UMWA. A reform movement known as Miners for Democracy started to grow. The man who emerged as the leader of the opposition to Boyle was Joseph "Jock" Yablonski, a UMWA officer who had been appointed director of Labor's Non-Partisan League. On May 29, 1969, Yablonski announced his candidacy for the office of president of the UMWA. Boyle immediately fired him, but Yablonski continued his campaign.

John L. Lewis died on June 11, 1969, and Boyle succeeded him as chairman of the Board of Trustees of the Health and Retirement Fund. In a move to win the support of pensioners in the upcoming election, he proposed an increase in pensions from $115 to $150 monthly, and he told the operators' trustee, George L. Judy, that Josephine Roche supported the move. In fact, it later came to light, the matter had not been discussed with her. Apparently, however, the pension increase had a major impact on the outcome of the election, which Boyle won.

Yablonski and his followers contested the election, charging that the UMW Journal had been used for campaign purposes, that staff salaries had been increased, that union funds had been improperly used, and that there had been numerous other campaign irregularities. The Department of Labor investigated the charges and obtained a court order for a new election.

One reason John L. Lewis had been able to maintain tight control over the UMWA, as noted earlier, was that its constitution permitted him to replace elected district presidents with his own appointees. Boyle, of course, had the same power and used it to maintain control of a

[73] Cf. O'Hanlon, p. 78.
[74] Dubofsky and Van Tine, p. 527.

majority of members of the international executive board. Lewis did not have to contend with the Labor-Management Reporting and Disclosure Act of 1959 (LMRDA), however, since it was enacted the year before he retired.[75] Boyle did, and he soon ran afoul of this law, which was one of the forces contributing to his downfall.

Miners for Democracy candidates challenged elections held in District 5 (Pittsburgh) and District 6 (Columbus, Ohio) in 1970, under terms of the LMRDA. A circuit court ordered new elections to be held under Labor-Management Services Administration (LMSA) supervision, both of which were won by Miners for Democracy candidates.[76]

On December 30, 1969, Yablonski, together with his wife and daughter, were murdered. Boyle remained in office, but the reform movement led by Yablonski refused to die. In December 1972 Boyle was successfully opposed in the court-ordered election by Arnold Miller, a retired rank-and-file miner and a leader in the black-lung movement. Yablonski's murderers were apprehended, tried, and convicted. Boyle was charged with being a participant in the conspiracy to kill Yablonski, and he, too, was convicted and imprisoned.[77]

Miller, in turn, attempted to eliminate Boyle appointees and supporters from key positions in the UMWA. In this he was only partly successful, and in the process he dismissed some able staff members who had not been involved at all in Boyle's schemes.

At the 1973 convention, the first which Miller chaired, a number of constitutional changes were made as part of the process of "democratization" of the union that Miller and the Miners for Democracy had promised. These changes were designed to guarantee the election of district officials, and to provide for ratification of new labor-management agreements. Miller's leadership in the move toward democratization was widely hailed, both within and outside the union, as were some of his austerity moves. The latter included a reduction in his own salary, elimination of some staff perquisites, and a cut in Boyle's pension. But the honeymoon between Miller and the rank and file was relatively short-lived. Four years later a veteran labor reporter could write that "the organization's internal affairs remain a shambles and conditions of near anarchy prevail in the mine fields."[78]

Miller conducted negotiations on the National Bituminous Coal Wage

---

[75] For discussion of the seven titles of the LMRDA, often called the Landrum-Griffin Act, see Miernyk, pp. 344–48.

[76] For further details, see Schubert, pp. 5–6.

[77] Later, in 1977, charges of irregularity in Boyle's trial were made. It was claimed that a lie-detector test, favorable to Boyle, was not admitted as evidence. A new trial was ordered, but had not been held as late as September 1977.

[78] Raskin, New York Times, June 19, 1977.

Agreement of 1974, and the subsidiary agreements covering construction
workers and western surface mine operations. The coal industry was in
excellent financial health in 1974. Annual production had again passed
the 600 million ton mark. More important, the average price per ton of
coal had reached a record high of $15.75, and it was still climbing. Under
these circumstances it was not difficult to negotiate a favorable agreement, in spite of the cumbersome new review and ratification procedures
that had been adopted at the 1974 convention.[79]

The UMWA had walked out on November 12, 1974, when the old
contract expired. The new settlement was reached on December 5, so
the strike was of relatively short duration.[80] It was also notably lacking
in rancor, particularly when compared with the strikes called by Lewis
in the late 1940s. An immediate wage increase of 10 percent was negotiated, with scheduled increases of 4 and 3 percent for the next two
years. More important, however, was the cost-of-living escalator clause
which had added about 75 cents per hour to the average miner's wage
by 1977.

A major consequence of the 1974 agreement, which itself was partly
a consequence of the Employee Retirement Income Security Act (ERISA)
of 1974, was a thoroughgoing change in the UMWA-BCOA health and
retirement program, now referred to as the UMWA Health and Retirement Funds. The 1974 agreement provided for four separate funds:
(a) the 1950 pension fund—essentially, for miners already on pensions,
(b) the 1974 pension fund—for miners scheduled to retire in 1976 and
thereafter, (c) a 1950 benefit or health fund, and (d) a 1974 benefit or
health fund. The administration of the funds, by three trustees, remained
unchanged.[81]

The 1974 agreement provided pensions of $250 per month to those
coming under the 1950 agreement, deducting $25 per month for miners
receiving federal black-lung payments. Retirees under the 1974 agreement were to receive graduated pensions ranging from $84.50 to $645,
depending on age and length of service at time of retirement. The financing of both pension and health funds was also altered. Before 1974,
employers had contributed 80 cents per ton. The new contribution was
based on both tons produced and hours worked, and was equivalent to
$1.55 per ton.

[79] The initial package negotiated by the bargaining team was turned down by the
bargaining council by a vote of 37 to 1. A revised package was accepted by a vote
of 22 to 15, but only after Miller had threatened to bypass the council if there were
further delays and to present the terms directly to the membership. For details of
this session and a summary of the settlement, see Monthly Labor Review (January
1975), pp. 82–83.

[80] The construction settlement was not reached until December 9.

[81] Miller, incidentally, broke the Lewis-Boyle pattern and did not serve as trustee.
The UMWA's trustee, and chairman of the funds in 1977, was Harry Huge.

The new agreement also called for more extensive job training; it provided that all new employees spend their first 90 days on "nonhazardous" jobs. It also gave safety committees the right to inspect all areas and provided that an individual miner could withdraw from an area he considered unsafe.[82]

Health and Safety Issues

Coal mining has always been the most hazardous of industrial occupations, but despite major disasters, such as the explosion at Monongah, West Virginia, in 1907, which killed 361 miners, safety legislation was slow in coming. The first Federal Coal Mine Safety Act was not passed until 1941. This act, and subsequent legislation passed in 1946, 1947, 1952, and 1966 did nothing to "disturb the general responsibility of the states for accident prevention despite a record indicating either an inability or unwillingness to discharge their responsibility."[83] But on November 20, 1968, there was another major mine explosion that killed 78 men in Farmington, West Virginia, a community not far from Monongah. Qualified observers believe this disaster was primarily responsible for the Federal Coal Mine Health and Safety Act of 1969, which established for the first time "a national code of health and safety standards which are more stringent than those contained in any previous federal law or those of any of the states."[84] Within two years, the "appropriation for the Bureau of Mines more than doubled . . . with the increase being entirely due to increased support for health and safety programs. . . ."[85]

Since 1969, the Bureau of Mines has been charged with two main functions: increasing mineral production, and improving mine health and safety. To separate these functions, the Mining Enforcement and Safety Administration (MESA) was established on May 7, 1973, by Order 2953 of the Secretary of the Interior. MESA is responsible for administering both the Coal Mine Health and Safety Act of 1969, and the earlier Metal and Nonmetallic Safety Act of 1966.[86]

The UMWA also has its own safety program. Safety committees set up in 1969 to study the dust problem in various districts were the predecessors of the Mine Safety Division established in 1973. Since 1974,

---

[82] *Monthly Labor Review* (January 1975), p. 83. A detailed account of the structure and functions of the funds was issued as a press release by the director. See *Dominion-Post* (Morgantown, W.Va.), January 10, 1977.

[83] Conaway, p. 96.

[84] *Ibid.*

[85] *Ibid.*, p. 98.

[86] The Bureau of Mines estimated that it would require an additional 750 inspectors and 250 new supervisors and technical specialists to enforce these acts. To provide for the training of inspectors and safety specialists, the National Mine Health and Safety Academy was established at Beckley, West Virginia.

union inspectors have been permitted to enter mines covered by the UMWA-BCOA agreement.[87]

One consequence of the 1969 Coal Safety Act, and the UMWA's increased attention to health and safety, has been a marked decrease in productivity. Average annual output per worker dropped from 4,488 tons in 1969 to 3,167 tons in 1976. On a daily basis, productivity declined from 16 tons per man-day to 9 tons per man-day. A recent study by the Office of Technology Assessment concluded: "Underground mining is now so thoroughly mechanized with existing technology that there seems to be no hope of reversing current productivity trends unless a new generation of equipment is deployed."[88]

Frequently overlooked in discussions of recent trends in productivity in the U.S. coal industry, however, has been the trend in fatalities and injuries. O. B. Conaway, writing in 1972, estimated that the 1969 Coal Safety Act has "increased the cost of producing coal by about a billion dollars annually."[89] But the frequency rate for all disabling injuries declined from 42.6 per million man-hours in 1969 to 36.4 in 1976. There was an even more dramatic drop, from .85 to .34, in the fatality rate per million man-hours over the same period.[90] In spite of this improvement, however, the occupational injury rate in coal mining remains high. In 1974, for example, it was 35.4 compared with an all-industry average of 10.2.[91] Union officials and staff members also point out that in spite of the decline in both productivity and injury rates, productivity remains higher in the U.S. than in other coal-producing countries, while the U.S. injury rate is also higher than that of other nations.[92]

Union officials are aware of the effects of the 1969 law, and of their own safety program, on productivity and production costs. Their position, however, is that higher productivity and lower production costs in the past exacted a price which the union is no longer willing to pay—the death or crippling of large numbers of miners. Before 1950, when the union was plagued by chronic overproduction, highly decentralized bargaining, and the threat of competition from nonunion mines, the basic UMWA slogan was: "No Contract, No Work!" In the late 1970s, with

[87] By 1976, the union employed 52 inspectors and, according to Nick DeVince, then Director of the Mine Safety Division, an increase in this number was planned.

[88] U.S. Congress, Office of Technology Assessment, *Analysis of the Proposed National Energy Plan* (Washington: U.S. Government Printing Office, August 1977), p. 49.

[89] Conaway, p. 102.

[90] Unpublished data provided by Francis E. O'Gorman, Public Information Specialist, Mine Enforcement and Safety Administration, U.S. Department of the Interior, July 19, 1977.

[91] United Mine Workers of America, *1976 Officers Report*, p. 41.

[92] Interview with Nick DeVince, late director of the UMWA Safety Division, and with Steve Weber and Bob Jennings, staff members, February 1, 1976.

the demand for coal rising steadily and prices rising at a faster rate than production, the slogan had become: "Coal Will Be Mined Safely or Not At All."

The UMWA is not opposed to productivity-increasing measures, provided they do not reduce mine health or safety. In an earlier day the objective of union policy was stabilization of the industry. The goal was to "take wages out of competition." Today, with relatively high wages, generous fringe benefits, and employment growth seemingly assured by an apparently insatiable demand for basic energy, union leaders have developed a new concept of the optimal level of output per man. This is the level that would maximize output while minimizing the risks of fatalities, serious injury, and the dreaded, debilitating pneumoconiosis— the medical term for "black lung."

Despite the preoccupation with health and safety issues in recent years, union leaders are aware that the well-being of members—and of the union itself—depends upon increases in productivity. John L. Lewis's influence lingers in this regard. The union's position on bargaining over safety vis-à-vis productivity can be expressed as a simple game-theoretic problem. The solution is the one given in the text—that combination of safety provisions and production arrangements which will minimize health and safety hazards while maximizing productivity.[93]

The Collective Bargaining Process

CONTRACT NEGOTIATIONS

Between 1950 and 1973, negotiations of new agreements between the UMWA and the BCOA was a matter that involved the officers of the two organizations. But the three-year agreement signed in 1974 was reached under a new set of procedures that involved the districts and the rank and file of the UMWA in the negotiations.

Before 1974, the only link between the negotiators and the membership was a 120-member National Scale and Policy Committee which ratified the agreements reached by union officers and the operators. During the tenures of Lewis and Boyle, this committee was not likely to include a substantial number of members whose views differed from their own. The actual negotiations are still conducted by the UMWA's principal officers—the president, vice-president, and secretary-treasurer, backed by a bargaining committee that includes staff specialists. But the major changes made in 1974 were establishment of a bargaining council, to serve as the nexus between the international headquarters and the membership, and provision for ratification.

[93] For a brief description of a game-theoretic model and an application to bargaining theory, see Miernyk, pp. 401–403.

For the 1974 negotiations, the bargaining council consisted of the international board members and the presidents of the 18 districts directly involved with the BCOA. This 36-member council had to approve the proposed agreement before it was submitted to the membership for ratification. The proposed agreement did not become effective until it had been ratified. This was accomplished after the terms of the proposed agreement had been explained to members in a series of regional meetings conducted by an estimated 800 miners from all the locals.[94]

CONTRACT ADMINISTRATION

Administration of the National Bituminous Coal Wage Agreement is quite conventional. A major change was made in the grievance procedure by the 1974 agreement, however, when it established the Arbitration Review Board (ARB). This board consists of one representative of the UMWA, a representative of the operators, and a chief umpire selected jointly by the two parties. The presidents of the UMWA and the BCOA also select panels of impartial arbitrators for each UMWA district.

Disputes which arise during the life of an agreement go through a five-stage grievance procedure. In the first stage the aggrieved employee contacts his immediate foreman who has authority to settle. The foreman must return a decision within 24 hours. If the decision is not satisfactory, the grievance goes to the mine committee and mine management within seven working days. At this stage a standard grievance form is filled out. If agreement is still not reached within seven additional working days, the grievance is referred to a designated district representative and a representative of the operator. The district and operator's representatives have seven working days to review the facts and relevant contract provisions. If the grievance is not settled at this stage, the two representatives prepare a joint statement setting forth the views and positions of both parties, and the grievance is referred to an appropriate panel arbitrator.[95]

If both parties agree, written testimony can be taken at stage three. If this has not been done, the arbitrator is required to hold a hearing within 15 days to accept such testimony, receive evidence, and consider arguments. If testimony was taken during stage three, the arbitrator is free to request a supplementary hearing. But if the step-three joint statement indicates that there is no disagreement about facts, the arbitrator may decide the case without a transcript on the basis of the joint statement and any supplementary statements and briefs he may request.

In many labor-management agreements, arbitration is the final step

---

[94] *Monthly Labor Review* (January 1975), p. 83.
[95] Cases are assigned to panel arbitrators in rotation.

of the grievance procedure. But the 1974 UMWA-BCOA agreement provided a fifth step; either party to the grievance may appeal the decision of the panel arbitrator to the Arbitration Review Board. An appeal can be made if the panel arbitrator's decision conflicts with earlier decisions by other panel arbitrators on the same issue of contract interpretation, or it may be appealed if the decision involves a question of contract interpretation not previously decided by the ARB, provided the board considers the matter to be a "substantial contractual issue."[96]

The Arbitration Review Board first decides whether there are grounds for appeal of the panel arbitrator's decision. If the board feels such grounds do not exist, it informs the parties; if it feels the appeal is justified, it reviews the decision of the panel arbitrator and makes whatever changes are necessary to resolve contractual questions and to ensure consistency with prior decisions of the board. The board's final decision must be issued within 15 days.

There has been disenchantment with the Arbitration Review Board, however. At the 1976 convention some delegates proposed a "right to strike" provision in the next agreement as a substitute for the ARB. Although the board had been operating for two years at the time of the 1976 convention, it had decided only 34 cases. The press reported a "huge backlog" of cases at that time.[97] Harry Patrick, then secretary-treasurer of the union, said: "It will continue until the current contract expires, but there will be no negotiating for it next year."[98] Patrick's comment followed presentation of a committee recommendation to continue the ARB. This recommendation was rejected by a vote of 1,336 to 946.

OTHER CONTRACT PROVISIONS

Article X of the 1974 agreement describes the first cost-of-living adjustment negotiated by the UMWA. It is geared to the BLS Consumer Price Index and calls for an adjustment of one cent per hour for each .4 point change in the CPI.

UMWA miners now receive payment for any disabling sickness. Coverage ranges from six weeks, for workers with more than six months but less than one year of employment, to 52 weeks for those employed 15 years or more. The agreement provides for 10 paid holidays and for a two-week "regular" paid vacation in late June and early July. Workers are entitled, in addition, to paid "graduated" vacation time based on

---

[96] The decision may also be appealed if it is considered "arbitrary and capricious, or fraudulent."

[97] *Dominion-Post* (Morgantown, W.Va.), October 4, 1976.

[98] *Ibid.*, October 2, 1976. The decisions through September 1976 were distributed as follows: 16 union wins, 17 company wins, and one draw.

length of continuous employment, ranging from one day for workers with seven years but less than eight years of employment to 13 days for those with 19 years or more of continuous employment.

Seniority is based on length of service and "the ability to step into and perform the job at the time the job is awarded."[99] The ability provision applies both to promotions and to possible reductions in workforce. Before a workforce reduction, management must submit to the mine committee a list of names of workers to be laid off or reassigned. Each worker destined for layoff then completes a standardized form which is a brief résumé of his work experience. Workers are called back to the job as the need arises, again on the basis of length of service and ability to perform the job that is open. Since larger companies may operate more than one mine in a single district, workers laid off at one mine may request that their names be placed on the panels of other mines operated by the same company. There they enter the eligibility list on the basis of length of service and ability to perform the job.

Job transfer, reassignment, and similar provisions are important in any resource-based activity. Some coal mines are always being worked out and new ones are started up. Thus, over the years the UMWA and BCOA have developed a rather elaborate procedure for permitting workers laid off at one mine to bid on job openings at another under the same management. There are no provisions for "bumping," however, so that younger workers in an expanding mine are not threatened by permanent reductions in workforce in other nearby mines.

Strikes, and the Cost of Strikes, in Bituminous Coal

Coal mining is unlike any other occupation, and coal miners develop a special set of behavioral characteristics. One that has been commented on by numerous observers is their propensity to strike. Operators also complain about excessive absenteeism. Miners themselves do not deny this. While there is perhaps no simple explanation, the comment of one veteran coal miner is revealing: "Any day I don't work in that mine is one more day it isn't going to kill me." The belief appears to be wide-

---

[99] Seniority is likely to be a major cause of worker discontent in a declining industry, and from 1948 until 1969 employment in the bituminous coal industry declined steadily. In his study of grievance settlements in coal mining, Somers found that claims to work, including seniority, ranked first among the causes of grievances in 1955, and second only to discipline and discharge cases for the period 1933–55. Somers, pp. 13, 16. Comparable data are not available for the 1970s when coal employment climbed steadily. But a survey of a large file of newspaper clippings dealing with recent "wildcat strikes" in Appalachia suggests that it may no longer be the dominant issue it was during the years of contracting employment and production. Miners appear to be willing to strike over a broader range of issues than they did in the past, including gasoline shortages and the kinds of textbooks used in local public schools.

spread that strikes and absenteeism have an adverse effect on the annual output of the coal industry.

In his study of the economic costs of labor disputes in coal mining, C. L. Christenson found that "there was no month during the 18 years without some time lost from disputes."[100] Much of this lost time is the result of unauthorized or "wildcat" strikes. There also are strikes in the coal industry during contract negotiations, but in recent years these have not resulted in as much time lost as they did in the past.[101] But Christenson's findings for the period 1933–50 undoubtedly still apply. The reason, of course, is the frequent occurrence of wildcat strikes.[102]

Christenson developed his "theory of the offset factor" after studying the relationship between coal production and dispute time losses. This, he says, is "merely a label for those forces which mitigate the impact of dispute time losses upon production."[103] There are two types of offset factors, both of which reduce (if not eliminate) the effects of labor disputes on coal production. Christenson called these the "current transfer offset factor" (CTOF) and the "time-shift offset factor" (TSOF).[104] The first refers to increased production at mines where there are no labor disputes to offset lost production at mines where output has been stopped by a walkout. The CTOF operates during contract as well as wildcat labor disputes since production at nonunion mines can be increased to offset in part losses in production at union mines. This type of offset has been particularly effective since the advent of large-scale surface mining.[105]

The time-shift offset factor (TSOF) has some influence on offsetting losses of production from wildcat strikes. It probably has its major impact, however, in maintaining annual production levels when there are

---

[100] Christenson, "The Theory of the Offset Factor," pp. 517–18.

[101] In 1946, for example, there were 19.5 million man-days idle in bituminous coal mining; the corresponding figure for 1949 was 16.7 million. Between 1950 and 1973, however, there were only two years (1952 and 1958) during which time lost due to coal disputes was more than a million man-days. The number of strikes reached an annual low of 120 in 1960. Since then the trend has been upward. There were, for example, 1039 strikes in 1973, but the number of man-days idle that year came to only 560,000. All data are from Dix et al., p. 5.

[102] At times individual operators have gone to court in an effort to reduce the incidence of wildcat strikes. In March 1976, for example, Consolidation Coal Company filed a $725,000 damage suit in U.S. District Court against District 29 and UMWA Local 6913 "for 25 allegedly illegal strikes in three years in a McDowell County mine." During the same month Judge Dennis Knapp issued temporary restraining orders against a similar walkout at a captive U.S. Steel mine in Mingo County by Local 8840, and another order to prevent a similar walkout at the Hazy Creek mine in Raleigh County. An injunction was also sought by Consolidation Coal "to prohibit future illegal strikes" in Jenkinjones. *Dominion-Post* (Morgantown, W.Va.), February 3, 1977, p. 3-A. These efforts have not been notably successful.

[103] Christenson, "The Theory of the Offset Factor," pp. 519–20.

[104] *Ibid.*, p. 523.

[105] Cf. Christenson, "The Theory of the Offset Factor," p. 544.

work stoppages due to the failure of contract negotiations. Several months before the termination of an agreement, large coal customers will increase their stockpiles in anticipation of a labor dispute. During the dispute these stockpiles may be drawn below those normally maintained. Following settlement, however, production levels tend to rise above the long-term trend line until inventory levels are back to "normal."

The industries directly affected by coal disputes are, of course, steel and electric utilities. The steel industry has somewhat less flexibility than utilities since metallurgical coal has more narrowly defined physical properties than does steam coal. Although boilers are designed to handle coal with specific physical qualities—particularly moisture content—steam coal can be obtained from a variety of fields at any given time. Throughout the period covered by his study—which included major coal-labor disputes in 1946, 1948, and 1949–50—Christenson found that "analysis of the monthly records for the entire period indicates no disturbance in consumption patterns for market-access consumers chargeable to coal mine labor disputes."[106]

During the coal walkouts of the late 1940s, the Taft-Hartley Act was invoked on three occasions—to "protect the national interest." At the time it may have appeared that the Taft-Hartley injunctions were necessary. On the basis of Christenson's studies, however, it appears that much less than a threat to the national interest, there was not even a threat of national inconvenience. The available evidence suggests that the two types of offset factors described by Christenson have served to protect consumers from losses due to coal disputes. This is not to say that no one loses from coal strikes. Since the UMWA funds are financed by employer contributions based on production, these contributions will decrease whenever the number of tons of coal produced by UMWA mines declines.

Wildcat strikes have become the leading cause of friction between the UMWA and the operators. At the 1976 convention of the American Mining Congress, Joseph P. Brennan, president of the BCOA, pointed out: "During 1975, the coal industry lost approximately 1.6 million mandays due to unauthorized work stoppages. This is the highest in our history and reflects an increasing degree of instability at the mine face."[107] The production loss might be made up elsewhere or at another time, but wildcat strikes affect the output of specific mines and exacerbate tensions between organized miners and the operators.

---

[106] Christenson, "The Impact of Labor Disputes," p. 111.

[107] Joseph P. Brennan, "Labor Relations and the Coal Industry," presented at American Mining Congress 1976 Coal Convention, Detroit, May 10–13, 1976, p. 8.

Most wildcat strikes are over conditions covered by the agreement, and machinery exists to settle such grievances without strikes. In a 1977 suit against the UMWA, Consolidation Coal charged that the issues over which its miners walked out could have been settled through this machinery.

Some wildcat strikes, however, are the result of issues which are not specifically covered by the 1974 agreement. In 1974, for example, there were numerous wildcat strikes in the central Appalachian coal fields because miners were unable to obtain gasoline for their journeys to and from work. In 1976, there were wildcat strikes over the issues of "the right to strike," one of which involved 120,000 workers.[108]

A wave of walkouts started in June 1977, following the announcement that after July 1 beneficiaries would be required to pay the first $250 of hospitalization cost and some additional costs to an annual maximum of $500. The strikes spread throughout southern Appalachia, and at one time the BCOA estimated that one-third of the nation's 180,000 active members were on strike. Arnold Miller announced that the 1977 wildcat strikes had cost the funds $40 million.[109] The *Wall Street Journal* had reported, on June 22, 1977, that up to then unauthorized work stoppages and the severe winter weather of 1977 had cost the funds an estimated $80 million in employer contributions. Harry Huge, the UMWA's trustee, was also quoted in the same story to the effect that the new wave of strikes could engender further cutbacks. The strikes continued to spread, however, since the miners appeared to be unaware that their actions could have a self-defeating feedback effect.

The union's response to the cutbacks was to request a reallocation of funds from the two pension trusts to the benefit trust. This had been done twice in the past, with the approval of the BCOA. But in 1977, the association refused to go along with the UMWA's request. There would be no need for this, the BCOA asserted, if the union would get its miners back to work.[110]

The 1977 strikes tapered off in early September, and before the end of that month the latest concerted wave of wildcat strikes had ended. From an actuarial point of view the benefit funds appear to be balanced on a very narrow edge. There is no large contingency account that can

[108] Almost half of the 2787 wildcat strikes in 1976 occurred in West Virginia according to the BCOA. About 39 percent of the West Virginia walkouts were sympathy strikes. Only 242 of 1252 strikes in West Virginia that year were over wages, hours, working conditions, or health and safety measures. *Dominion-Post* (Morgantown, W.Va.), May 31, 1977.

[109] Associated Press release, August 30, 1977.

[110] The BCOA claimed that wildcat strikes during the first five months of 1977—before the major wave of strikes started—had cost the benefit funds $17.9 million in lost employer contributions compared with $8.8 million for the same period in 1976. *Wall Street Journal*, June 20, 1977.

be drawn on if employer contributions decline when production drops in union mines. It is, essentially, a pay-as-you-go plan. The fund's problems have been exacerbated, moreover, by recent *increases* in union membership which boosted the number of health cardholders by 31 percent in 1975–76.[111]

The problem of wildcat strikes is not a new one,[112] but it is one of the most important problems facing UMWA leaders because of the damaging effects such strikes have on the benefit funds. The 1977 wildcat strikes tend to corroborate Christenson's theory of the offset factor. Although as many as one-third of all UMWA miners were out at the peak, weekly estimates of production issued by the Bureau of Mines showed a production drop of only 19 percent from the prestrike level. Following the strikes, weekly production exceeded 15 million tons, a figure well above the long-term trend line.[113]

UMWA Leadership—A House Divided

John L. Lewis's rule of the UMWA was completely autocratic. When opposition appeared, he replaced dissidents with loyalists. But he had the support of the rank and file. When he ordered them out on strike, they followed; when he ordered them back to work, they returned. Furthermore, Lewis enjoyed the respect of the operators—at one time an effort had been made to get him to switch sides.[114] For more than a decade Tony Boyle was able to coast on the achievements of his predecessor. But he had none of Lewis's leadership qualities and was unable to maintain his position of power.

When Arnold Miller succeeded Boyle as president of the UMWA, he was given a favorable reception, at least by the press. He had been a reform candidate, and the essence of his candidacy had been democratization of the union. He is also a man of modest demeanor, a veteran of the underground mines forced into retirement by the dreaded black-lung disease, and a man who came into office free of political debts. He

---

[111] At the same time the number of pensioners increased by only 4 percent, which explains why the benefit funds were in trouble in 1977 while the pension funds were not. For a detailed account, see Fund's news release. *Dominion-Post* (Morgantown, W.Va.), January 10, 1977.

[112] At the 1902 convention of the UMWA, John Mitchell argued that "if we expect the operators to carry out those provisions that are advantageous to us, we, in turn, must carry out just as explicitly those provisions which are unfavorable to us." And at the 1914 convention, President John P. White "strongly condemned the local unauthorized strikes—called sometimes in spite of the efforts of district officials to prevent them." Fisher, "Bituminous Coal," p. 251.

[113] U.S. Department of the Interior, Bureau of Mines, *Weekly Coal Report*, 3118 (June 17, 1977) through 3133 (September 30, 1977).

[114] In 1924, Joseph Pursglove, a Cleveland operator, asked Lewis if he would serve as chief executive of a new producers' association he was trying to establish. See Dubofsky and Van Tine, p. 109.

also took over the union at a time when conditions in the product market were better than they had been for decades; production and employment were rising and, partly as a result of the worldwide impact of OPEC on all energy prices, coal prices reached levels that could not have been imagined a decade earlier (see Chart 1).[115]

At the 1973 (Pittsburgh) convention, Miller's position seemed fairly secure, but he had been in office only a year. By the Cincinnati convention of 1976, however, it was clear that Miller was under attack. Even before this convention, Miller had been having trouble with the international executive board on which a number of Boyle supporters continued to serve.[116] When Miller fired an organizer in the western districts as well as his own executive assistant, the IEB voted to reinstate them.[117] This was only one of many causes of a continuing exacerbation of tensions between Miller and the IEB.

Miller's troubles with the IEB might have been anticipated because of the number of pro-Boyle members who had been elected to their posts. But his problems did not stop with the board. There was a falling-out between Miller and the other two principal officers of the UMWA: Mike Trbovich, vice-president, and Harry Patrick, the union's secretary-treasurer. The causes of this breakdown at the top are not entirely clear, but by early 1976 Trbovich had swung over to the opposition on the IEB.[118] By the time of the Cincinnati convention, *Business Week* reported: "For more than a year, the United Mine Workers' leadership has been all but immobilized by a split in its top ranks."[119] At that time Lee Roy Patterson, IEB member from western Kentucky's District 23— and a former member of Boyle's staff—had announced his candidacy for the office of union president. Although Harry Patrick had not yet announced his candidacy, there was speculation at the convention that he would do so, and Patrick did not discourage the rumors. To eliminate uncertainty about who would be in charge of scheduled contract negotiations in late 1977, the convention voted to advance the election from November to June, a move that was considered to be a blow to Miller and his chances for reelection.

Although the London *Economist* referred to the UMWA campaign as "bland and tired," and Ben A. Franklin, a veteran reporter on coal matters for the *New York Times*, claimed that voters were apathetic

[115] For further details, see Miernyk et al., especially chs. 2 and 4.

[116] Miller had been permitted to appoint new district directors and IEB members on an interim basis, but only until supervised elections could be held. Several such elections were held in 1973, and some were won by former Boyle supporters. See Schubert, p. 10.

[117] *Dominion-Post* (Morgantown, W.Va.), December 19, 1976.

[118] See "Feuding Stifles UMW Reform," *Business Week*, February 16, 1976.

[119] *Business Week*, October 11, 1976, p. 97.

two days before the election, the turnout was remarkably heavy in the districts where the UMWA remains a potent bargaining force.[120] When the final tally was reported by UPI on July 3, 1977, it showed that almost 139,000 miners had voted.[121] Miller won with 40 percent of the total, Patterson was a close second with slightly more than 35 percent, and Patrick ran a poor third, receiving only 25 percent of the votes. Patterson challenged the results, charging election bribery. But after what was described as a "stormy all-day session," the IEB sustained Miller's election by a vote of 84 to 55.[122] Patterson also appealed the election to the Department of Labor, but in October 1977 the department ruled that it had found no evidence of impropriety, and the results would stand.

Miller's election to a second five-year term as president of the UMWA could scarcely be called overwhelming. He had received less than a majority of the votes, and he displayed no new leadership characteristics after the 1977 election. During the wildcat strikes in the summer of 1977 he repeatedly asked for a return to work, but his pleas were ignored. Indeed, as a result of the health-fund cutbacks which triggered the strikes, there was a short-lived movement in southern West Virginia to recall Miller.[123]

Unrest and dissatisfaction with Miller's performance as chief executive of the union was not limited to the IEB and his fellow principal officers. Many of the union's staff members had also become disaffected. A number of young "liberal activists" were attracted to Miller and the Miners for Democracy, and several joined the staff after his election. It was fortunate that he was able to employ such talent since Miller himself had no experience in either contract negotiations or day-to-day administration of union affairs. As the union's internal affairs became more and more chaotic, relations between Miller and the staff became increasingly strained. He fired some staff members summarily.[124] Others,

---

[120] See *Dominion-Post* (Morgantown, W.Va.), July 10, 1977, for the *Economist* article, and *New York Times*, June 12, 1977.

[121] This amounts to 77 percent of the reported 180,000 active miners, or 50 percent of the estimated 277,000 UMWA members including retirees.

[122] Votes were weighted by size of district; the vote to accept the certified tellers' results was 11 to 8 before weighting. There was also a suggestion that Miller had picked up some strength on the board which voted 13 to 9 "to seat board member Martin Conners of Pennsylvania whose certification was challenged by the Patterson forces." *Dominion-Post* (Morgantown, W.Va.), July 22, 1977.

[123] There is no constitutional provision for the recall of elected officers in the UMWA, but this did not appear to dampen the enthusiasm of those who were circulating petitions for Miller's recall in District 17—his home district in the UMWA. See *Dominion-Post* (Morgantown, W.V.), September 7, 12, 15, 1977.

[124] His executive assistant was replaced by Sam Church, described by Miller critics as an "old crony." Church ran on the Miller slate in 1977 and was elected vice-president.

including some who were primarily responsible for the staff work behind the successful 1974 negotiations, resigned.[125] Miller's behavior also alienated a number of liberal supporters outside the UMWA, including Washington attorney Joseph Rauh, who supported Patrick in the 1977 election. With the departure of a number of able staff members, Miller had to turn elsewhere for technical support as he prepared to negotiate with the BCOA. A Washington consulting firm, Stanley Ruttenberg Company, was hired to provide this support.

By the fall of 1977, the reform movement that had toppled Boyle—and which had introduced such innovations in the UMWA as the bargaining council and the rank-and-file contract referendum—was in almost complete disarray. The men who had fought with Miller to wrest control from Boyle had abandoned him. Does this mean that the attempt to introduce democracy into the UMWA had failed after more than a half century of autocratic rule? There are many who feel that it had, including George Meany, president of the AFL-CIO. "I don't think they're any better off than they were three years ago," he said.[126] Even Miller has been forced to concede that there are serious internal problems, but he has referred to them as "the growing pains of democracy." Officials elected in 1972, he pointed out, "were rank and file miners with no previous exposure to the responsibility."[127] They had not had an opportunity to learn, he went on to say, and were thus forced to learn the hard way.

Some coal operators, such as Charles T. Jones, vice-president of Amherst Coal Company, also appear to feel that union democracy cannot succeed.[128] There is, unfortunately, no objective answer to the question. It is impossible to separate the experiment in union reform from the men who led the union when the reforms were introduced. Supporters of union democracy can only hope that Miller is right—that with increased experience the leaders of the UMWA will learn to administer the union both democratically and efficiently.

Current and Continuing Issues in Collective Bargaining in Coal

All of the major concerns in labor-management relations in the coal

---

[125] One of those who departed was Tom Bethell, described as "the union's key man in 1974 bargaining, the only aide in the reform administration of President Arnold Miller with a detailed grasp of industrial labor pacts." Other key staff members were departing. "The trend has accelerated recently as Mr. Miller has accused the staff of disloyalty. Researcher Bethell predicts the drain will mean 'complete chaos' in 1977 bargaining." *Wall Street Journal*, January 18, 1977.

[126] "Meany's implication was that the coming of democracy has not changed the union. UMWA officers considered this a gratuitous insult and asked Meany for an explanation. He has not replied." *Business Week*, February 16, 1976, p. 102.

[127] *Gazette-Mail* (Charleston, W.Va.), September 11, 1977.

[128] *Ibid.*

industry have been touched on in this chapter. They will be only summarized in this concluding section. The major concern of management,
expressed both publicly and privately, is that of unauthorized work
stoppages. The UMWA has a long tradition of honoring picket lines,
and a single worker can tie up an operation. But wildcat strikes cannot
be separated from the day-to-day administration of the contract. Management spokesmen claim that the machinery already exists to settle
grievances peacefully, but union spokesmen at the dictrict and local
levels claim that it is management that is guilty of bypassing the grievance machinery by going directly to the courts when a labor dispute
develops.

The Cincinnati convention endorsed the right to strike at the local
level after a secret-ballot majority vote. This procedure was proposed,
among other things, as the solution to wildcat strikes. The BCOA has
been obdurate in its opposition to this proposal.[129] Coal operators fear
it won't work because of low attendance at union meetings; they assert
that only those in favor of the strike would show up for the vote. Their
counterproposal is that the union discipline workers who strike without
authorization. But the BCOA proposal is scarcely compatible with the
union's attitude toward greater worker participation in labor-management decisions. Former Miller aide Tom Bethell maintains that no one
on either side of the bargaining table knows whether "the right to strike"
will work or not.[130]

If the union were in a stronger bargaining position, it might be able
to force acceptance of the right-to-strike proposal, at least on a trial
basis. But coal produced in UMWA mines has been a declining proportion of total production for more than a decade. Throughout the 1950s
and early 1960s, UMWA membership accounted for an average of 83
percent of total employment in bituminous coal.[131] By 1970 this percentage had dropped to 66, and there have been estimates that by 1977
non-UMWA mines produced almost half of the nation's coal.[132] A long
strike might do nothing more than reduce further the share of the
market served by UMWA mines. But of course this is also likely to
happen if something is not done to reduce the occurrence of wildcat
strikes. The union, it is clear, is on the horns of a serious dilemma.

Another major union problem has little to do with collective bargaining per se; it is a problem engendered by the recent history of

[129] It was one of the major proposals submitted by the UMWA in its initial meeting with the BCOA to discuss 1977 negotiations, however.
[130] "Wildcats—Are They Killing UMW?" *Wall Street Journal*, June 22, 1977.
[131] See John P. David, "Earnings, Health, Safety, and Welfare of Bituminous Coal
Miners Since the Encouragement of Mechanization by the UMWA" (Ph.D. dissertation, West Virginia University, 1972), p. 189.
[132] "Wildcats—Are They Killing UMW?" *Wall Street Journal*, June 22, 1977.

internal strife. Many rank-and-file miners have lost respect for union leaders.[133] They have never trusted the operators, however, so their attitude has become one of a "pox on both your houses!" They will continue to be responsive to local leaders, and their loyalty to *the union* remains as strong as ever. But until the national leaders regain the respect of working miners, it might be impossible for them to control wildcat strikes. If there is widespread distrust of national officers, locals are likely to take matters into their own hands, with or without a right-to-strike agreement. But another round of unauthorized strikes will have only two certain consequences: (1) a further reduction of employer contributions to the UMWA funds, and (2) an increase in the output of non-UMWA mines.

The UMWA is losing rather than gaining ground in the rapidly expanding western coal fields. Some observers consider this as another result of recent internal strife in the UMWA. But even with more effective leadership and more aggressive organizing efforts, the UMWA might have lost most of the surface mines of the West. The technology of western surface mining might have as much to do with the workers' choice of the Operating Engineers as their attitudes toward the UMWA.

Although a revitalized UMWA might reverse recent trends in the West, the pattern of collective bargaining that was established by John L. Lewis in 1950 might still break down. The UMWA now has a separate agreement with the handful of western companies it has been able to organize, and there could be further departures from the "national" bargain between the BCOA and the UMWA that was the industry standard for a decade and a half. Spokesmen for the BCOA have expressed concern about the declining share of coal produced by the union with which they have a master agreement, and the possibility of the proliferation of many separate agreements. This concern was expressed by E. B. Leisenring, Jr., president of Westmorland Coal Company and chairman of the BCOA: "If a way cannot be found to turn the tide," he said, "the percentage of United Mine Workers coal will dwindle to a pathetic fraction of its former share, and most of the bargaining clout of that once-great union will be gone."[134]

---

[133] See, for example, "New Breed of Miners Takes Over," *Sunday Dominion-Post* (Morgantown, W.Va.), September 4, 1977: "West Virginia Woman Accepted as the First to Head Mine Local," *New York Times*, October 9, 1977.

[134] *Wall Street Journal*, October 6, 1977.

List of References

Maratz, Morton S. *The Union and the Coal Industry.* New Haven: Yale University Press, 1955.

"Bituminous Coal and Lignite." *Preprint from Mineral Facts and Problems.* 1975 edition, U.S. Bureau of Mines Bulletin 667. Washington: U.S. Government Printing Office.

Christenson, C. L. "The Impact of Labor Disputes Upon Coal Consumption." *American Economic Review* 45 (March 1955).

————. "The Theory of the Offset Factor: The Impact of Labor Disputes Upon Coal Production." *American Economic Review* 43 (September 1953).

Conaway, O. B., Jr. "Coal Mining: New Efforts in an Old Field." *Annals of the American Academy of Political and Social Science* 400 (1972).

Dix, Keith, et al. *Work Stoppages and the Grievance Procedure in the Appalachian Coal Industry.* Institute for Labor Studies, Division of Manpower and Labor Studies, Appalachian Center. Morgantown: West Virginia University, 1974.

Dubofsky, Melvyn, and Warren Van Tine. *John L. Lewis, A Biography.* New York: Quadrangle/The New York Times Book Company, Inc., 1977.

Dunlop, John T. "The Task of Contemporary Wage Theory." In *New Concepts in Wage Determination,* eds. George W. Taylor and Frank C. Pierson. New York: McGraw-Hill Book Co., 1957.

Finley, Joseph E. *The Corrupt Kingdom.* New York: Simon & Schuster, 1972.

Fisher, Waldo E. "Anthracite." In *How Collective Bargaining Works,* ed. Harry A. Millis. New York: Twentieth Century Fund, 1942.

————. "Bituminous Coal." In *How Collective Bargaining Works,* ed. Harry A. Millis. New York: Twentieth Century Fund, 1942.

Gluck, Elsie. *John Mitchell.* New York: AMS Press, Inc., 1971.

"How International Energy Elite Rules." *Peoples' Appalachia* (April-May 1970).

Hudson, Harriet D. *The Progressive Mine Workers of America: A Study in Rival Unionism.* Bureau of Economic and Business Research Bulletin 73. Urbana: University of Illinois, 1952.

Marshall, Alfred. *Principles.* 8th ed. New York: Macmillan Company, 1948.

Miernyk, William H. *The Economics of Labor and Collective Bargaining.* 2d ed. Lexington, Mass.: D. C. Heath and Company, 1973.

Miernyk, William H., et al. *Regional Impacts of Rising Energy Prices.* Cambridge, Mass.: Ballinger Publishing Company, 1977.

Millis, Harry A., and Royal E. Montgomery. *Organized Labor.* New York: McGraw-Hill Book Company, 1935.

Mitchell, John. *Organized Labor.* Philadelphia: American Book & Bible House, 1903.

Mulholland, Joseph P., and Douglas W. Webbink. *Concentration Levels and Trends in the Energy Sector of the U.S. Economy.* Staff Report of the Federal Trade Commission. Washington: U.S. Government Printing Office, March 1974.

Ridgeway, James. *The Last Play: The Struggle to Monopolize the World's Energy Resources.* New York: E. P. Dutton & Co., Inc., 1973.

Schubert, Richard F. "Mine Workers Election Draws Lessons for Other Unions." In *Compliance, Enforcement and Reporting Under the Labor-Management Reporting and Disclosure Act,* USDL, LMSA. Washington: U.S. Government Printing Office, August 6, 1973.

Slichter, Sumner H. *Union Policies and Industrial Management.* Washington: Brookings Institution, 1941.

Smith, Adam. *Wealth of Nations.* New York: Random House Modern Library, 1937.

Somers, Gerald G. *Grievance Settlement in Coal Mining.* West Virginia University Business and Economic Studies, Vol. 4. Morgantown: West Virginia University, June 1956.

U.S. Congress, Office of Technology Assessment. *Analysis of the Proposed National Energy Plan.* Washington: U.S. Government Printing Office, August 1977.

Warren-Boulten, F. R. "Vertical Control by Labor Unions." *American Economic Review* 67 (June 1977).

Wolman, Leo. *Ebb and Flow in Trade Unionism.* New York: National Bureau of Economic Research, 1936.

Young, Dallas M. "Origin of the Progressive Mine Workers of America." *Journal of the Illinois State Historical Society* 40 (September 1947).

CHAPTER 2

Construction

D. QUINN MILLS
Harvard University

Introduction

Construction merits close study by persons interested in American industrial relations. The size and strategic role of construction in the economy give its labor relations significant interest in their own right, but construction also exerts considerable influence on labor relations in other sectors of the American economy.

Two aspects of the construction industry in particular are the source of its influence on other sectors. The first is the geographic dispersion of the industry. Unlike many industries that are concentrated in one or a few geographic areas, virtually every community in the nation has firms and labor organizations active in construction. The second aspect is the employment in construction of workers whose skills are widely used in other industries. Building and construction tradesmen are employed in large numbers on new construction work by nonconstruction firms and government agencies. There are substantial flows of workers between construction and other industries, reflecting changing wages and working conditions and fluctuations in the availability of jobs. Workers employed in construction and maintenance generally are aware of wages and conditions paid to persons of similar skills in other industries. Through the processes of mobility and comparison of wages and conditions, industrial relations in construction and other sectors interact continually with each other.

Construction is also of particular interest now because its industrial relations and manpower arrangements, worked out in a period of more than a century, are undergoing considerable change. Labor relations in construction now operate in three forms that are competing for dominance in the future: (1) the system under collective bargaining agreements; (2) open-shop (i.e., nonunion) arrangements under national or local policies of contractor associations (the "merit" or open-shop); and (3) the sector of individual enterprises pursuing policies apart from either collective bargaining or a formal organization of contractors, the

49

truly "unorganized" sector. In a sense, the "merit shop" associations (as they call themselves) have adopted many of the substantive industrial relations policies and procedures of collective bargaining (such as apprenticeship programs, health and welfare plans, and even, in some few instances, the hiring hall). But decision-making is under the control of a local or national employers' association without union involvement or participation. The direction of evolution in the sector's labor relations, and the form that will emerge dominant in the future, is by no means settled at this time.

Structure in the Construction Sector

Construction may be defined as a group of interrelated production activities involving the erection, maintenance, and repair of physical structures, including buildings, highways, earthworks, and so on. The value of materials, labor, and other inputs to the construction process (including both new construction and maintenance and repair) in recent years has constituted 11 to 14 percent of the total Gross National Product.[1] New construction averaged 11 percent of GNP in the early 1960s, but reached a low point of 8.5 percent of GNP in 1976, in the aftermath of the 1974–75 recession. Some 40 percent of total construction activity is maintenance and repair construction, and the sector employs some 5 percent of the nation's labor force. A large proportion of these workers are skilled, so that craftsmen employed in construction constitute 12 to 15 percent of the nation's skilled blue-collar workers.

Most construction is undertaken by private parties, but new construction expenditures by public authorities are roughly one-third of total construction volume, most of which is spent for projects owned by state and local governments (though much of the work is given financial assistance by the federal government). Residential construction expenditures constitute about one-third of total new construction, with nonresidential building and nonbuilding construction the remainder.

Construction contractors provided approximately 3.6 million year-long jobs in 1976 and, because of turnover, employed more than 6 million persons at one time or another during the year. During any given month, construction (including the self-employed) employs roughly 4 to 7 percent of the labor force in the United States, with seasonal shifts in the demand for labor largely accounting for the variance.

There are a great many firms in construction. Normally they are specialized by branch of the industry (for example, highway construction) or by trade (for example, carpentry). The most recent census of

---

[1] See current issues of *Construction Review* (U.S. Department of Commerce, monthly).

construction (1972) showed that 437,941 establishments with a payroll (that is, with any employees) were operating as contractors or as operative builders. "Operative" builders are firms that do construction not by contract but for sale or lease to others; most of them are homebuilders. Other data indicate that there are also almost 500,000 self-employed persons in the industry. The Standard Industrial Classification lists contractors by branch of the industry and by trade in a rough intermingling of the two systems of classification. Most establishments in the industry are special trade contractors (for example, electrical and plumbing contractors). However, no individual sector of the special trades includes as many firms as does the general contracting sector.

Contractual and subcontractual relationships in construction are very complex. Typically an owner hires a general contractor to erect a building according to a set of specifications. The general contractor then subcontracts the elements of the job he does not wish or is unable to perform himself. But there are wide variations from this practice. In some cases an owner signs independent (prime) contracts with a different firm for each phase of a job. Under legislation in some states covering public work, several prime contracts are awarded on a single job, and the general contractor is simply one of three or four firms holding contracts directly with the state or other government agency. Furthermore, subcontractors may subcontract elements of a job themselves. In all, the 1972 census reported that 25 percent of gross construction by value was subcontracted, with general contractors subcontracting 46 percent of value and specialty contractors 7 percent of value.

The contractual relationships among contractors and subcontractors, especially between generals and their subcontractors, are a constant source of divisiveness among employers in construction.[2] The precise nature of the obligations assumed by the different firms in their contractual relationships often determine the profitability of jobs for the firms. There is a constant struggle between employers in the courts, in the legislatures, and even on the job sites as to the nature of contractual responsibilities and their fulfillment. Since these disputes often involve large sums of money, the associations of general and specialty contractors (and in some cases the unions) often become engaged in the struggle. Especially important to labor relations behavior in construction is the assembling of contractors and subcontractors with various specializations to build a particular project with the resulting specialization

---

[2] Disputes among contractors are a not infrequent cause of jurisdictional disputes. See Dunlop, "Jurisdictional Disputes," p. 165. [The complete citations of all footnote references are listed at the end of the chapter.]

of the workforce and intermingling of the employees of different employers at the project site.[3]

The Labor Force

CHARACTERISTICS OF EMPLOYMENT IN CONSTRUCTION

The building construction labor force is composed of more than 20 crafts and many more specialties. Many contractors hire directly only one or two of these crafts, the numbers of persons and crafts hired depending on the type of work and geographic area in which the contractor operates. Different branches of the sector require a different combination of crafts in the production process. Nonresidential building construction (including office, commercial, and religious buildings, but excluding industrial facilities) employs perhaps the widest range of trades. Subcontracting is also most intensely developed in this branch of the industry, reflecting the high degree of specialization of firms. The general building contractor normally hires the basic trades (carpenters, operating engineers, laborers, cement masons, teamsters, and bricklayers), with subcontractors hiring the journeymen in their specialties. There is, of course, considerable variation in this pattern, depending on the nature of the project, its size and location, the practices of different geographic areas, and the methods of operation of different firms. Heavy and highway construction requires primarily five trades (carpenters, laborers, operating engineers, cement masons, and teamsters), usually hired by the general contractor. Residential building construction requires fewer trades than nonresidential, although more than heavy and highway work, but it also involves specialties not found in nonresidential building. The work is often nonunion, and jurisdictional lines among the trades are correspondingly less pronounced. Other branches of the sector require a relatively large proportion of men in specific trades. For example, laborers, operating engineers, teamsters, and pipefitters are needed in pipeline construction. Construction of industrial and power plants may require many pipefitters, often with special qualifications to do the complex piping work involved. Since each branch of the sector has its own labor requirements, the trades are confronted with different combinations of employment opportunities in the different branches. On the one hand, the sector is characterized by specialization of the labor force among its various branches; on the other, it is an incomplete specialization that creates a substantial pattern of interdependence as well.

---

[3] For a discussion of the management problems involved in contracting and subcontracting, see Grimes.

The fluctuating volume of construction has important consequences for the labor force. Sometimes large projects are built in an area that has seen very little major construction for years before and will see very little for years after. Other areas, especially large metropolitan areas, ordinarily experience a large and continuous volume of work, but sometimes have major downturns as well. And even then, some types of work may be declining in importance while others are increasing. In an unstable economic environment, employers greatly value flexibility of operations—the ability to hire and lay off men as job conditions demand. Equally important is the ability to hire men at a predetermined wage scale, so that the profit on a job is not eaten up by wage changes negotiated after the bid price has been established. The flexibility that the contractor requires for profitable operation, however, is sometimes translated into insecurity for the workingman. Labor organizations attempt to limit the effects on the employee of the changing conditions in which he and the contractor must operate.[4]

There are several aspects of construction employment that, taken as a whole, cause the sector to have a unique place in the American economy. The major characteristics of employment in construction are:

- Considerable shifting of employees among work sites.
- Considerable shifting of employees among employers.
- Identification by the employee with craft or occupation, not with employer.
- A relatively large portion of skilled workers, many of whom are trained by formal apprenticeship.
- Much self-supervision.
- Very unstable employment opportunity.
- Dangerous and often difficult work conditions.
- Intermixture of employees of different employers at a single project site.

UNEMPLOYMENT

In virtually every year, construction's unemployment rate has exceeded that of every other major industry group and has regularly been twice as high as the economywide average. Although the industry accounts for only about 5 percent of the total labor force, over the years it has represented between 9 and 12 percent of all unemployed workers.

The disproportionately high levels of unemployment in construction are attributable to a number of factors. In the first place, the industry is especially sensitive to cyclical changes in the general level of economic activity. Thus, between 1973 and 1975, while the all-industry

[4] See Bourdon.

unemployment rate was rising by almost four percentage points, the rate for construction rose by about 10 percentage points.

The industry also suffers an unusual degree of frictional unemployment. Since work is often intermittent, many workers experience spells of idleness between jobs. Finally, seasonal slowdowns in construction activity account for a substantial proportion of the industry's unemployment. In order to maximize employment opportunities, and thereby reduce unemployment, there are certain labor force flows among construction and other industries. Perhaps the most significant of these is the influx of temporary workers, such as college students, during the peak summer months. During the subsequent downswing, many of these workers return to school or other pursuits, dropping out of the construction labor force, and are hence not counted in the unemployment statistics. Some regular construction workers, moreover, customarily find employment in other industries during the off-season, or they may hire themselves out for small repair and maintenance jobs until contractors are hiring again.

OCCUPATIONAL COMPOSITION [5]

Recent decades have seen some noteworthy changes in the composition of construction employment. The proportion of the workforce engaged directly in production activity (i.e., construction work as opposed to clerical or engineering work) has declined, with a parallel increase in various nonproduction activities (as defined by the Bureau of Labor Statistics, U.S. Department of Labor). Thus, in 1947, 88.7 percent of construction's 2.0 million employees was classified as production workers; by 1974, that proportion had declined to 81.7 percent of 4.0 million employees.

There have also been important changes in the composition of the blue-collar workforce since 1950. Generally, skilled workers (craft and kindred workers) have continued to account for over half the total number of blue-collar employees. On the other hand, the proportion of unskilled workers has declined, while that of semiskilled workers (operatives and kindred workers) has risen.[6]

---

[5] Much of the information in this section is taken from Chapter 3 of the *Employment and Training Report of the President, 1976.*

[6] Data on construction employment are obtained from two separate sources, the nonagricultural survey of payrolls and the Current Population Survey (household survey). Data from the former relate to contract construction activities and cover only wage and salary workers on payroll records. The latter series covers all persons engaged in construction activities, including government and other force-account construction workers, those involved in speculative construction, and self-employed, without regard to pay status. Greater, but not complete, comparability between the two series can be achieved through the use of private wage and salary employment figures for the industry.

Finally, changes in construction technology, along with shifts in the composition of construction activity itself, have occasioned changes in the relative representation of various craft groups. The increasing size and complexity of much construction work have resulted in relative growth in the numbers of such craft workers as equipment operators, electricians, pipefitters, and supervisors. The major relative declines have taken place among such trades as carpenters, bricklayers, plasterers, and painters (see Table 1).

TABLE 1
Percent Distribution of Craft Workers in Construction
by Detailed Occupation, 1950–1970

Occupation	1950	1960	1970
Total: Number	1,934,400	2,052,193	2,559,697
Percent	100.0	100.0	100.0
Brickmasons, stonemasons, tile setters	7.5	7.9	5.5
Carpenters	38.1	31.6	24.7
Cement and concrete finishers	1.4	2.0	2.4
Crane, derrick, and hoist workers	.7	.8	1.1
Electricians	5.1	6.4	8.0
Excavating, grading, and road machinery operators	3.8	7.4	6.9
Mechanics and repairers	3.1	4.8	4.7
Painters	15.4	13.1	8.2
Plasterers	2.9	2.1	1.0
Plumbers and pipefitters	9.0	9.3	9.1
Roofers	2.1	2.2	2.2
Structural metalworkers	1.5	1.6	1.9
Supervisors, n.e.c.	3.0	4.7	5.9
Tinsmiths, coppersmiths, and sheet metalworkers	1.6	1.7	2.3
Crafts (allocated)			8.3
Other craft workers	4.8	4.5	7.9

Sources: U.S. Department of Commerce, Bureau of the Census, Census Subject Reports, *Occupation by Industry*, 1950, 1960, and 1970.
Note: Detail may not add to totals because of rounding.

RACIAL MINORITY REPRESENTATION IN CONSTRUCTION

The degree of minority employment in construction as a whole and in each occupational category has been a substantial public issue that has affected labor relations for more than a decade. Construction unions, in particular, have been accused of discriminating against minorities, and unions and employers have been the subject of legal and regulatory actions intended to increase minority representation in construction. The employers and unions have also developed programs of outreach and training for minority workers.

Racial minorities have a slightly larger proportion of jobs in construction in the United States than their proportion of the workforce as a whole (approximately 11 percent). To a disproportionate degree, however, minorities are represented in the laborers' classification. Certain skilled trades have a proportion of minorities higher than their proportion in the labor force as a whole, including especially roofers, cement masons, and bricklayers. Other skilled trades do not. The mechanical trades (including plumbers and pipefitters, electricians, boilermakers, and sheet metal workers) have relatively low minority representation, although to a limited degree this varies by geographic area.

In recent years legal proceedings under Title VII of the Civil Rights Act of 1964 have resulted in court orders establishing hiring and job-referral preferences for minorities in several local unions. Also, the federal government, many state governments, and some municipalities have established regulations requiring the employment of certain percentages of minorities in the workforce on construction projects financed in whole or in part with public funds. The overall effectiveness of these legal efforts is open to some controversy. Unfortunately, space does not permit a thorough review of these matters in this chapter.

UNION ORGANIZATION IN CONSTRUCTION

The degree of union organization in construction is subject to considerable statistical confusion.[7] Until recently there have been no continuous data reporting degree of organization for the industry as a whole or for its branches. Now, however, there are surveys of construction that offer some insight into organization. Perhaps most useful is the survey of union membership of full-time wage and salary workers, taken in recent years for the month of May as part of the Current Population Survey; union membership or nonmembership is based on occupation of current job. In May 1976, some 36.5 percent of private wage and salary workers in construction were reported to be union members. An earlier, somewhat different, survey made for 1970 showed that 54.7 percent of construction craftsmen and 29.9 percent of construction laborers were union members.[8]

The segment of construction not governed by collective bargaining agreements has usually been pictured as a fringe around the unionized segment. However, the segment outside of collective bargaining has apparently been growing rapidly relative to the whole sector.[9] Furthermore, significant parts of this segment are becoming structured and its

---

[7] See Mills, "Manpower in Construction," p. 270.

[8] U.S. Bureau of Labor Statistics, *Selected Earnings and Demographic Characteristics of Union Members*, 1970, Report No. 417 (Washington: U.S. Government Printing Office, 1972).

[9] See Northrop and Foster.

industrial relations formalized—not under labor agreements, but under policies adopted by nonunion employer associations.

Evaluating the degree of union organization in construction is complicated by the fact that employment is both seasonal and casual. The international unions report that their membership in construction (they have varying magnitudes of nonconstruction membership) varies less through the seasons than does employment in the industry generally. Depending, therefore, on the distribution of unemployment among union and nonunion workers, a higher percentage of the workforce may be union members in the winter than in the summer. Also, many persons who are not union members work under union contracts for brief periods at the peak of the construction season. Any estimates of the degree of organization in construction must therefore be treated carefully.

Some branches of the industry are more fully organized than others. Residential construction, accounting for perhaps a third of total construction employment (though this figure varies both seasonally and annually and must be estimated from expenditure data for lack of direct surveys), is probably the least organized. Nonresidential building is probably the most fully organized branch, with heavy and highway work following. Geographically, union organization is greatest in major cities, least in suburban and rural areas and the South. Finally, what little evidence is available suggests that union organization in construction had lessened substantially by the mid-1970s from what it was in 1936, when a Bureau of Labor Statistics study indicated that 68 percent of construction workers employed by general contractors or their subcontractors were union members.[10]

Organization for Collective Bargaining

The peculiar economic conditions and characteristics of employment in construction dictate that employers and unions are placed in a much more intimate relationship than they are in many other industries. Construction projects are normally of short duration, and the employment relationship itself is weak. Collective bargaining agreements, however, are areawide and provide a continuing relationship between the unions and the employers; they cover the contractor whenever and wherever he works in the area. Because employers are generally small and employment intermittent, training is normally done on an areawide, multiemployer basis. Contractors and unions therefore negotiate not only wages and working conditions, but also training and hiring practices. In an unstable industry, the development and retention of a skilled labor

[10] Sanford, pp. 281–300.

force require that employers and unions agree to practices that preserve the job opportunities of craftsmen. The problem is to adopt policies that are effective in protecting employment opportunities without either unduly restricting needed expansion of the labor force or promoting uneconomic practices.

The Building and Construction Trades

National Unions. Construction workers are largely organized into 19 international unions, 18 of which are affiliated with the Building and Construction Trades Department of the AFL-CIO. Table 2 includes a list of the AFL-CIO affiliates (the Teamsters are former affiliates), 1972 membership of the international union, and the proportion of the membership estimated to be in contract construction. Several other unions, including the United Steelworkers of America and the Allied Industrial Workers, also have construction membership. These unions have relatively small representation in the industry, largely confined to certain limited geographic regions, and they are self-proclaimed industrial unions rather than craft or craft-industrial unions.

The building and construction trades unions are organized, for the most part, on a craft-industrial basis. Craft unions (for example, the carpenters and bricklayers) are the result of the association in the union of persons doing a particular type of work, often involving a particular material (such as wood or masonry). With the historical growth of the union, related specialties were often absorbed into the international, in some cases through mergers or absorption of other national unions. Furthermore, as new materials replaced the traditional materials used by the craft (such as metal for wood or cinder block for brick), the jurisdiction of the union was extended to cover work with the new materials.[11] Craft-industrial unions are organized as much around an industry as an occupation and generally include several work specialties. For example, the electricians and the pipe trades have work jurisdictions that apply to the electrical contracting industry and to the plumbing and pipefitting industry, respectively. In the case of the pipe trades, the industry orientation of the union is especially clear, for steamfitters and plumbers were organized into separate international unions until 1911–13, when the United Association absorbed the steamfitters and was granted a charter by the American Federation of Labor as the only international union in the plumbing and pipefitting industry.[12]

Local Unions. The international unions are associations of American and Canadian local unions. Some 80 to 100 years ago, groups of locals

---

[11] For a description of this process in the carpenters' trade, see Christie.
[12] See Segal.

TABLE 2

Affiliates of the Building and Construction Trades Department,
AFL-CIO, 1975

Affiliated Organizations	Total Membership	% in Contract Construction
Asbestos Workers; International Association of Heat & Frost Insulators and	18,255	100
Boilermakers, Iron Shipbuilders, Blacksmiths, Forgers & Helpers; International Brotherhood of	138,000	22
Bricklayers and Allied Trades; International Union of	147,715	100
Carpenters and Joiners of America; United Brotherhood of	820,000	75
Electrical Workers; International Brotherhood of	991,228	19
Elevator Constructors; International Union of	18,902	100
Granite Cutters' International Association of America. The	3,200	n.a.
Iron Workers; International Association of Bridge, Structural & Ornamental	181,647	75
Laborers' International Union of North America	650,000	78
Lathers International Union; The Wood, Wire and Metal	14,428	n.a.
Marble, Slate and Stone Polishers, Rubbers and Sawyers, *Tile* and Marble *Setters'* Helpers and Marble Mosaic and Terrazzo Workers' Helpers; International Association of	8,000	90
Operating Engineers; International Union of	415,395	80
Painters and Allied Trades; International Brotherhood of	211,373	n.a.
Plasterers' and Cement Masons' International Association of the United States and Canada; Operative	65,000	99
Plumbing and Pipe Fitting Industry of the United States and Canada; *United Association* of Journeymen and Apprentices of the	228,000	90
Roofers, Damp and Waterproof Workers Association; United Slate, Tile and Composition	28,000	100
Sheet Metal Workers' International Association	160,860	65

Source: Bureau of Labor Statistics, U.S. Department of Labor, *Directory of National Unions and Employee Associations,* 1975 (Washington: U.S. Government Printing Office, 1977).

Note: *Italics* denotes short-reference to the particular organization. n.a. = not available.

in various trades participated in the founding of internationals in order to prevent the standards of the organized sectors of the trade from being undercut by the unorganized sectors. The local unions that participated in the founding gave the internationals the power to issue and remove charters and to organize and combine locals. The early period was marked by bitter struggles, which in some cases have continued to this date, between international union officers and large locals over their respective roles.[13]

---

[13] See Ulman.

Each local union owes its existence to a charter from the international union, despite the fact that many of them antedate the international's formation. The charter defines both a geographic and a work jurisdiction for the local. In some of the larger cities, for example, a single international union will have chartered several locals with distinctive work jurisdictions.

In the building trades, local unions have for the most part preserved a considerable degree of autonomy in the conduct of their affairs. The negotiation of collective bargaining agreements, their provisions, and their enforcement are largely matters of local authority, subject only to general supervision from the international unions. There are, of course, exceptions to this rule, some of which will be discussed later.

Locals in the building trades vary in size from very large organizations composed of thousands of members and with extensive geographic jurisdictions to groupings of only a few members and a geographic jurisdiction of a few square miles. Locals tend to be larger in the trades in which the geographic mobility of contractors and workers is greatest. In some crafts, small local unions in the same geographic area have been organized into district councils for collective bargaining and other purposes.

The Employer Associations

Contractors are organized into trade associations by sector of the industry, although not all contractors are members of an association. The associations normally have local, regional, and national bodies, with the national organization chartering local chapters. Often, however, national staffs are small and financing is limited, so that the associations are most active and vital at the local level. Major associations include the Associated General Contractors of America (AGC),[14] the National Constructors Association, the Mason Contractors Association, the National Electrical Contractors Association, the Mechanical Contractors Association, the Painting and Decorating Contractors Association, the Sheet Metal and Air Conditioning Contractors Association, the Roofing Contractors Association, the National (Steel) Erectors Association, the International Association of Wall and Ceiling Constructors, the Lathing Contractors Association, and the National Association of Home Builders. AGC chapters are often either heavy and highway or building chapters. They include both union and nonunion contractors. There is also an association of nonunion contractors, the Associated Builders and Contractors (ABC), which includes both general and specialty contractors.

The local associations perform a wide variety of functions for their

---

[14] For a description of the Associated General Contractors, see Mooney.

members, including public relations, lobbying, legal advice, labor relations activities, and members' benefits (such as group life insurance for contractors or types of liability insurance), and they deal with architects, owners, suppliers, and others. The national office of the association also conducts lobbying and public relations and provides legal and industrial relations advice. It often publishes periodicals carrying trade news, innovations, legislative reports, and analyses of the national scene as it affects members' concerns. Each national association normally holds a national convention and may sponsor trade shows as well.

The contractors' associations at the local level conduct labor negotiations and sign and administer collective bargaining agreements. A committee of contractors usually determines the industrial relations policies of the association, and they are approved by the membership. Negotiations are conducted by a team involving, variously, contractors, legal counsel, and association staff (if any). The national office of the association normally provides the local chapter with no more than information and advice on industrial relations.

The staffing of contractors' associations is generally sparse. Larger local associations may employ an executive director, and sometimes assistants for him, who may draw full- or part-time salaries. At the national level there is usually a full-time executive director, normally with only a small supporting staff. The Associated General Contractors, the National Association of Home Builders, and the National Electrical Contractors Association are unusual in having fairly extensive national staffs. Most of the activities of the associations at the local and national level are conducted by committees composed of and chaired by contractor members who are not compensated for their time, so that the operations of most associations depend on the voluntary efforts of individual business persons.

The disadvantages that result from the annual selection of a new chief executive officer in the employer associations are a continual source of problems in construction. Employer associations at the national level often experience frequent and abrupt changes in policy or, conversely, seem to have no capacity to adhere to any particular policy at all. National trade union leadership changes only infrequently. Employer association leadership changes constantly. Consequently, political turmoil and the direction of much of the energy of an organization to its own internal politics are perhaps more common in the national employer associations than in the unions. Each association employs an executive vice-president who attempts to provide continuity of policy and action, but the rotation of presidents often undermines this objective. In only one of the national associations may it now be said that the organizational structure which combines a rotating presidency with a continuing executive vice-president is such as to permit the association a certain stability and forcefulness in policy. Proposals are periodically made within the associations to remedy this administrative difficulty. One recent proposal made by the New England chapters of a national association was for the selection of a full-time national president who would serve a three-year term and be eligible to succeed himself. Proponents of the proposal argue that it would give the president sufficient time to incorporate programs and provide continuity of office.[15]

The size of an association's staff and the degree of professionalism in its administration are largely a function of financing. Both local and national chapter staff must be paid from the funds of the association. Funds are raised from contractor members as dues, although the methods of obtaining funds vary widely. The availability of funds to support a sizable national staff contributes strongly to the influence of certain associations on the actions of the industry as a whole.

Recent years have seen a discussion among the employer associations of the need to coordinate policy among themselves. In the phrase made popular by a former national president of the Associated General Contractors, construction has needed "a single voice," and a number of organizations competing for the opportunity to be that single voice in the area of labor relations have emerged. By mid-1977 there existed a greater proliferation of employer associations than when the unity movement began. In 1968 the Council of Construction Employers (CCE) was established as an informal grouping of national associations and was formalized as an association in 1972. CCE was intended to be counterpart to the Building and Construction Trades Department of the AFL-CIO, the coordinating body of the national unions. In 1971 another association, composed of major contractors, not associations, was formed: The Contractors Mutual Association (CMA). Apparently some of the impetus to the formation of CMA was provided by the Construction Users Anti-Inflationary Roundtable. The Roundtable was an organization of major industrial companies founded to encourage policies in construction which would be to the benefit of construction purchasers. In subsequent years, the Associated General Contractors and the National Constructors Association were affiliated first with CCE, then with CMA. By mid-1977 merger discussions were under way between the two organizations, conducted with the assistance of the Roundtable (now merged into the Business Roundtable, a group with broadened interests and membership).

Bargaining in construction often appears to be heavily weighted in

---

[15] *Contractor*, May 15, 1977, p. 1.

favor of the unions,[16] but the contractor's side of the bargaining table has had its own long record of success in negotiations with the building trades. In 1977, the executive vice-president of the Mechanical Contractors Association of America described his association's arrangements with the United Association as follows:

> Our method of construction with Building Trades Department workmen is still the most efficient in the Western world. The problem is that no one is recognizing this fact or talking about it.
>
> It is not only efficient, it is flexible in regard to the utilization of this labor, and this is the unique aspect of our arrangements with labor.
>
> We have flexibility unknown anywhere else in the Western world. When we need another 10, 20 or 100 pipefitters, we call the union hall, and within a reasonably short period we have these men working. Conversely, when our volume drops, these men are sent back to their labor depository to be called to work by some other contractor. We carry this flexibility through to the use of foremen and general foremen. Why should a contractor hold onto good supervision and run up his expense when this supervision could be put to work just as well by another contractor who has need for it?
>
> So a union contractor has this ready pool of trained men and this readily available degree of flexibility. A union employing contractor's only limitation on his volume of work is his ambition, financial capability and executive talent. A non-union contractor has these limitations plus the number of skilled men he has available, and this governs the volume of work he can perform.[17]

Probably a major reason why bargaining appears so one-sided in construction is that normally the unions restrict the scope of the issues that they raise within understood limits. For example, demands for job security (or seniority, for that matter) are rarely raised with the individual firm (a potentially disastrous issue for contractors). Were the unions more apt to challenge basic features of the industrial relations system in construction, there would certainly be a more visible reaction from employers. In 1971–72, the Sheet Metal Workers International Association decided to seek from their employers a package of benefits and obligations which was given the designation Stabilization Agree-

---

[16] See O'Hanlon, "The Stranglehold of the Building Trades," *Fortune* 78 (December 1968), pp. 102 ff., and "The Case Against the Unions," *Fortune* 77 (January 1968), pp. 170 ff.

[17] Walter M. Kardy, speech before the 17th Annual Construction Conference of the Builders Exchange of Columbus, Ohio, February 17, 1977, mimeo.

ment of the Sheet Metal Industry (SASMI). A major part of the package was a form of a supplemental unemployment benefit fund, a concept new to construction. Employers, fearing the precedent of paying unemployment benefits to persons who are not on the job in an industry with considerable intermittency of employment, have bitterly opposed the plan. As of this writing, SASMI has been incorporated in perhaps half the local collective bargaining agreements in the sheet metal construction industry, but has not progressed at all into other branches of construction.

Current Structure of Collective Bargaining

The structure of collective bargaining in construction is extraordinarily complex, and there is considerable variation by branch of the industry, geographic location, and craft. In consequence, only a very general description can be given. There are some 6,000 collective bargaining agreements in the industry, most negotiated between local unions and employer associations. The agreements run for from one to five years in length, and average about 18 months' duration. Each year, therefore, two to three thousand agreements are negotiated.

Table 3 summarizes bargaining structure in various branches of the industry. The only branch in which all the trades are involved in negotiations is building construction, and this branch is described in

TABLE 3

Bargaining Structure in Construction Generally

Branch of Construction	Geographic Scope of Agreements	Major National Employer Assoc.	Major Trade Unions Involved
Pipeline construction	National agreements	Pipeline Contractors National Association	Pipefitters Operating Engineers Teamsters Laborers
Highway construction	Local or statewide agreements	Associated General Contractors of America American Roadbuilders Association	Carpenters Cement Masons Operating Engineers Teamsters Laborers
Industrial and power plant construction	National and local agreements	National Constructors Association	Pipefitters Electricians Ironworkers Boilermakers Carpenters & Millwrights Laborers
Building construction (see Table 4)	Various	13 in number	18 in number

detail in Table 4. Table 3 also indicates the geographic scope of agreements. In the pipeline industry, each of the four trades listed negotiates a national agreement with the Pipeline Contractors Association, and the four unions and the association maintain a policy committee to resolve disputes. In the industrial construction industry, the individual companies and an association (the National Constructors Association) negotiate with the unions listed for national agreements, but also apply, in most instances, terms of the local building agreements where a project is located.

Table 4 lists the major national employer associations, the principal

TABLE 4

Bargaining Structure in Building Construction:
Major Employer Associations and Unions

Employer Association	Principal Unions	Geographic Coverage of Agreement
Associated General Contractors (AGC)	Carpenters Laborers Operating Engineers Teamsters Ironworkers (rod-men)	Local or state
National Association of Homebuilders (NAHB)	Carpenters Laborers Bricklayers	Local or state
Mason Contractors Association of America (MCAA)	Bricklayers	Local
National Electrical Contractors Association (NECA)	Electricians (IBEW)	Local
Elevator Constructors Employers Association	Elevator Constructors	National (except NYC)
Mechanical Constructors of America (MCA)	Pipefitters	Local
Sheet Metal and Air Conditioning Contractors National Association (SMACNA)	Sheet Metal Workers	Local
National Erectors Association	Ironworkers (structural)	Local
International Association of Wall & Ceiling Contractors (IAWCC)	Plasterers	Local
National Insulation Contractors Association (NICA)	Asbestos Workers	Local
Painting and Decorating Contractors Association (PDCA)	Painters	Local
National Roofing Contractors Association (NRCA)	Roofers	Local
Plumbing, Heating, and Cooling Contractors National Association (PHCCNA)	Plumbers	Local

unions with which they deal, and the geographic coverage of agreements in the building industry. The five or six trades with whom the Associated General Contractors negotiate are called the "basic trades." The electricians, pipefitters, structural ironworkers, boilermakers, and sheet metal workers are called the "mechanical trades." Bricklayers, plasterers, and cement masons are referred to as trowel or "wet" trades.

LOCAL AND REGIONAL BARGAINING

Collective bargaining agreements in construction are characteristically negotiated between a local union (or district council) in a single craft and the employers of that craft as represented by an association.[18] The agreements apply within the geographic jurisdiction of the local union (or district council) and apply to its work jurisdiction. Local negotiations are prevalent in building construction, but there are many exceptions. In some, regional agreements embracing many states have been established (for example, those covering boilermakers, operating engineers on dredging work, and electricians on transmission lines). In some states, local unions are so large that entire states are covered by a single contract with a single local. The structure of bargaining also varies greatly in the different regions of the country. In the West, bargaining on a regional or metropolitan area basis has become the standard for most crafts. In the rest of the country, local bargaining is still the rule. In some cases, special geographic areas have been established for coverage of pension plans, medical care, and work jurisdiction.

Contractor associations with collective bargaining responsibilities vary widely in composition and structure. In some areas of the Northeast, negotiations are conducted by a building trades employers' association in a metropolitan area, or by a builders' exchange. Negotiations with each craft are carried out by a committee including contractors or representatives of the trade association (for example, if negotiations are with the painters, the local association of the painting and decorating contractors will be included) and representatives of the building trades employers' association (BTEA) or the builders' exchange. The BTEA plays a central coordinating role when several negotiations are in progress at once or follow one another closely. In the remainder of the country, negotiations usually are limited to the individual trades and their employers, but the general contractors' associations (especially the AGC on the local level) will often attempt to provide some central leadership and negotiate their own contracts with the trades they employ.

Coordination of negotiations involving several trades in an area may

---

[18] Dunlop, "The Industrial Relations System in Construction," pp. 255–78.

take place formally at the bargaining table (through representatives of all the trades and employers' associations), informally through separate negotiations, or not at all, although there is always considerable interest in what each trade is doing or is going to do. In some cities, the building trades council and the BTEA traditionally hold formal negotiations for many trades at the same time. In others, unusual economic or other circumstances have led the unions to coordinate the negotiations themselves. Employers' associations sometimes do the same. Coordination of the bargaining among trades, when it succeeds, often avoids the succession of work stoppages that may occur as one trade after another negotiates a contract. However, the attempt by one side to impose formal coordinated bargaining where the other objects may lead to strikes or lockouts.

Another form of coordination of negotiations occurs when contract dates for several trades expire simultaneously, or nearly so. In this situation, the local building trades council and employers associations often try to settle any disputes that may arise without disruptive effects on the industry. Common expiration dates are not an unusual feature of the bargaining structure in some cities, and in many instances they appear to have contributed to industrial relations stability.

In recent years some leadership of the employers and unions has promoted wide-area or regional bargaining as a solution to the problems in bargaining created by a multiplicity of local negotiations. Both the CMA and CCE have assisted in the formation of regional bargaining groups among employers in various areas of the country. Generally, regional bargaining has involved multitrade negotiations with the basic trades, but in some instances with mechanical trades as well. The electricians remain outside such arrangements in virtually all instances. Both organizations have solicited direct affiliation of regional employer groups with the national association involved (CCE or CMA). Each publishes periodically lists and maps showing expansion in the number of regional bargaining groups. The degree to which the wider area bargaining groups have contributed to greater stability in construction bargaining cannot now be determined. Only after bargaining is conducted again in the context of a major construction boom, as it was in the late 1960s, will it be possible to ascertain whether or not regional bargaining has contributed to a lessening of inflationary pressures in those areas where it exists, as its proponents have hoped.

National Agreements

The structure of bargaining is complicated by the existence of the national agreement. Most international unions have either negotiated or adopted a standardized agreement for the traveling contractor. Normally these agreements are short documents providing that the contractor will do union work, subcontract all work union, and meet the local wages, fringes, and other working conditions. In return, the contractor is given assistance from the international union in manning his job and settling any disputes that arise in the course of it. Agreements of this type are to be distinguished from those establishing conditions in branches of the industry, such as pipeline construction, in which there is no local bargaining. The national agreement is much more important in some branches of the industry than in others. In the construction of industrial plants, the National Constructors Association (NCA) and the United Association of Plumbers and Pipefitters (UA) have an agreement that establishes terms and conditions of work on a national basis, but wages and fringe benefits are negotiated locally. Where no locally negotiated wage scales are applicable, the contractor and the international union negotiate the rates to be paid on the project.

The international union may use the national agreement in several different types of situations, often as a method of organizing the large contractor whose area of operation covers much of the country. The problems of the large contractor existed at the origin of the national contract some 50 years ago, and meeting them remains the national agreement's major function. Another use of the agreement is to organize contractors and their employees who perform specialties (which often involve new and unusual processes) within the work jurisdiction of a union.

There have been three major sources of dissatisfaction with the national agreement. While its most outspoken critics have been local contractors' associations, local unions have been hardly less bitter in some cases. The dissatisfaction of local contractors' associations is caused by the fact that the national agreement normally binds the national contractor to the conditions of the local agreement but not to the local contractors' association or bargaining unit. In consequence, contractors with national agreements often work through local strikes or lockouts and may appear in other ways to undermine the position of local contractors' associations. In recent years, in response to this criticism, the national unions and the NCA have inserted in some national agreements a clause permitting either the contractors or the national union, after due notice, to shut projects (i.e., lockout or strike) during a strike in the local geographic area. In 1976 the NCA contractors working in the state of Washington on large nuclear and fossil fuel power projects locked out members of a striking UA local for some five months in support of the bargaining position of a local association of mechanical contractors. At the height of the strike, some 300 UA members were idled by virtue of their strike against local contractors, while another 600 or so were locked out by NCA contractors. The strike ended with the employers' de facto acceptance of most of the union's demands, and the resignation of the executive vice-president of the local contractors' association. This unpleasant outcome, which cost the national contractors and construction purchasers many millions of dollars due to the lengthy lockout (the federal government was the major construction purchaser involved), has cast some doubt over the effectiveness, and the future, of the participation of contractors under national agreements in local bargaining disputes.

Ironically, large local unions often feel that the national contract, by binding the large contractor to the local agreement, deprives the local of the chance to extract concessions from him that it could not obtain from local builders. It is not uncommon to have resolutions from strong locals introduced at national conventions challenging the authority of the general president to negotiate national agreements or seeking to modify this authority.

In summary, the national agreement may tend to undercut local contractors during a strike, but it also prevents the local unions from exacting concessions from visiting contractors that local contractors would refuse to grant (a situation to which the local contractors are likely to be willing witnesses). By protecting the visiting contractor from local resistance, the national agreement tends to preserve competition in the industry. Finally, it helps local and national unions to organize contractors who might otherwise be nonunion.

PROJECT AGREEMENTS

For large projects involving a considerable volume of construction at a single site (or an interrelated group of sites) over a period of years, a special agreement will sometimes be negotiated. It may involve the owner of the project as well as his contractors, or it may be sought by the contractor at the owner's insistence. These agreements normally attempt to guarantee the progress of the work without interruption by strikes and to establish special mechanisms for dispute settlement. Sometimes they provide means for determining wages and conditions at the projects. While project agreements may be negotiated independently at the national level, at other times they are negotiated with the full cooperation of local parties.

In the 1970s, the Building and Construction Trades Department began to participate actively in the negotiation of project agreements to cover power plants, industrial facilities, and other large projects (such as the Disneyworld amusement park in Florida). By mid-1977 some 160 such project agreements were in effect. The owners of large construction projects have recently taken an increasing role in the negotiations of such agreements.

The TransAlaska Pipeline System Project Agreement is probably the most extensive, and perhaps the most successful, use yet made of the project agreement. The TAPS Project Agreement was negotiated between Alyeska Pipeline Service Co., a consortium of six major oil companies that built the pipeline, and some 18 international unions. The TAPS Agreement established certain standardized procedures among all trades, both for the handling of grievances and for many working conditions. It adopted wages and fringe benefits as established in the local collective bargaining agreements for each trade in Alaska; it incorporated a no-strike, no-lockout clause for the duration of the project, some four to five years; and it established a special mechanism for the resolution of jurisdictional disputes on the project. During 1975–77, Alyeska employed several hundred construction contractors and, at peak, some 15,000 construction workers to build the 800-mile pipeline across Alaska from the oil fields at Prudhoe Bay, within the Arctic Circle, to the ice-free port at Valdez. The port was also constructed under the TAPS Project Agreement. An attorney for Alyeska who was instrumental in the negotiation of the TAPS Project Agreement and in its application has described owner-negotiated project agreements as "the most significant improvement in the construction work site arrangements."[19]

The variety of provisions in project agreements, especially with respect to working conditions, has begun to cause certain problems. Contractors have objected to the inclusion of more favorable clauses in some project agreements than in others. Local employer associations also object to the no-strike provision of project agreements which, they maintain, undermines the bargaining position of local associations with the unions. In 1976, for example, the national office of the Associated General Contractors sent a letter to the Secretary of Transportation of the United States, objecting to plans of the agency to seek project agreements for the construction of urban mass transit systems. The letter charged that the unions sought no-strike project agreements as a means of obtaining employment for their members in the event of a strike against local contractors, and as a means of organizing nonunion contractors which might have subcontracts on an urban mass transit project.

[19] William J. Curtin, "Construction Labor Costs—Comment," *Public Utilities Fortnightly* 98 (October 7, 1976), p. 51.

"A no-strike agreement would have an extremely prejudicial effect on collective bargaining," the employers' letter concluded.[20] In this letter are set forth two major strains of national AGC policy: opposition to the unions' use of the selective strike (i.e., the strike against some employers but not others), and the attempt to protect, simultaneously, the interests of both unionized and nonunionized contractors.

There is also some opposition to the project agreement from local unions and union members. Local unions sometimes feel that project agreements, as contrasted to local collective bargaining agreements, include too many concessions to the employer. Also, local union members in some instances have filed suit against the national unions, alleging that the nationals have illegally permitted contractors to pay lower wages or to provide lesser working conditions under project agreements than under the existing local collective bargaining agreements.

These problems, which have developed as the number of project agreements has increased, now threaten the continued proliferation of such agreements. In 1977, negotiations between the Building and Construction Trades Department and various national contractors and contractor associations (in particular, the National Constructors Association) have been under way regarding consolidated national agreements for both power plant construction and the construction of large industrial facilities. These two agreements would probably replace many project agreements now in existence and would certainly obviate the need to negotiate any more.

The Process of Collective Bargaining

PECULIARITIES OF EMPLOYER ASSOCIATION BARGAINING

Most collective bargaining in construction is conducted by employer associations at the local level. Association bargaining has its own special problems of preparation for negotiations which differ from those encountered by the single company. The most characteristic problem arises from the potential for conflict among members of the association. The need to gain strength vis-à-vis the union causes the separate firms to join together in an association for bargaining, but many other circumstances tend to divide the companies and prevent their taking a common stand. In the first place, the firms are ordinarily competitors. They often mistrust one another and do not wish negotiations with the unions to end in a contract that benefits any other firm more than it benefits their own. In the second place, because the firms have different characteristics and difficult problems, sometimes their goals in bargaining conflict.

---

[20] Letter of J. M. Sprouse, executive vice-president of the Associated General Contractors of America, to William T. Coleman, Secretary of Transportation, June 30, 1976.

Some firms are large; some are small. Some firms may be very profitable; some are almost insolvent. Some firms utilize the newest technology; some the oldest. Some firms have a history of cordial relations with the unions; some a history of bitter disputes. Some firms have the loyalty of their employees; some do not. The union, which is usually aware of these differences among the firms, may exploit them for its own purposes.

At the outset of preparations for negotiations, the association must attempt to resolve internal disputes, reach a common position to present to the union, and agree on a joint course of action should a strike occur. However, the union has access to the individual companies that make up the association. It is very common for disputes between the association and the union to be resolved by the union splitting individual companies from the association (either in return for favorable treatment from the union, or simply in pursuit of the companies' own special interests) until the association collapses. To meet this threat, employer associations often adopt bylaws that legally bind each company to the association's position in bargaining and that provide a method by which the association decides on its bargaining stand. A company that fails to support the association as required by the bylaws may subject itself to a financial penalty.

Multiemployer bargaining has a peculiar status under the National Labor Relations Act. The National Labor Relations Board (NLRB) does not ordinarily certify a multiemployer bargaining unit, nor will it sanction the creation of a multiparty unit over the objection of either party, union or employer.[21] Therefore, labor and management create such units completely voluntarily and without NLRB involvement. The basic ingredient supporting the unit's appropriateness is the mutual consent of the parties, and the relationship is founded upon the unequivocal manifestation by the employer and union members of the group that all intend to be bound by the results of the prospective negotiations.

Under present law, once the group is formed and bargaining commences, neither the union nor the employer members are permitted to withdraw without the consent of all parties, except under unusual circumstances. Thus, while the decision to bargain jointly in a multiparty fashion is purely voluntary, and in fact must be based on the uncoerced agreement of all parties to enter this bargaining relationship, once the decision has been made and bargaining has commenced, neither the unions nor the employers or any part of those groups can withdraw without the consent of all the others or under specific "unusual circumstances."[22]

---

[21] See *Kroger, Inc.*, 148 NLRB No. 69 (1964).
[22] See *NLRB* v. *Hi-Way Billboards, Inc.*, 500 F.2d 181 (5th Cir. 1974).

The only escape under the "unusual conditions" exemption concerns those situations where the employer or the union is faced with dire economic circumstances, i.e., circumstances in which the existence of an employer as a viable business entity has ceased or is about to cease. In this respect, the NLRB has held that an employer may withdraw from a multiemployer association after negotiations with the union have begun where the employer is subject to extreme economic difficulties which result in an arrangement under the bankruptcy laws,[23] or where there is an imminent adverse economic condition which will require the employer to close its plant.[24]

Recently, a federal court of appeals has held that an employer may withdraw on its own initiative from association bargaining, even without union acquiescence, at the time that an impasse in bargaining occurs.[25]

SINGLE-TRADE NEGOTIATIONS

The most common form of collective bargaining in construction is negotiation between a local union in a single trade and an employer association.[26] Such negotiations always take place in the context of other negotiations, however. Each trade negotiates with the knowledge of the provisions of the existing agreements of other trades in the area as well as some knowledge about recent settlements in other trades. Also, the terms of employment and compensation in other local unions of the same trade in the geographic area are important factors in the negotiations environment.

Negotiations between a single trade and an employer association have certain advantages. They permit the persons most directly involved in the workplace to determine the conditions of work. Single-trade negotiations are as close to the individual employee and employer as is practical in construction. Negotiations between a local union and a single employer would not, in fact, be closer to the individual employee, since the employee probably works for more than one employer in the course of a year. A construction worker's attachment is ordinarily to a trade and a geographic locality rather than to a particular employer.

Also, single-trade negotiations permit employers, usually small firms, the maximum involvement in determining the conditions of work and compensation for the persons the firm hires. Flexibility in adjusting contract terms to conditions in the local construction market appear thereby to be maximized. Presumably, each trade and its employers are

---

[23] *U.S. Lingerie Corp.*, 170 NLRB 750 (1968).

[24] William J. Curtin, "Legal Aspects of Multi-Employer Bargaining," address to the Associated General Contractors of America, Chicago, January 16, 1975, mimeo.

[25] *NLRB v. Beck Engraving Co.*, 522 F.2d 475 (3d Cir. 1975).

[26] See Stokes.

able to adjust contractual provisions to the circumstances of their own peculiar situation, independently of the circumstances affecting others. This apparent flexibility in meeting local conditions is probably a key factor in explaining the persistence of decentralized collective bargaining in construction.

But the autonomy of single-trade negotiations is more apparent than real. Each trade's negotiations are largely determined by the context in which they occur. Ordinarily, for example, wage-setting in construction consists of only two major elements: first, the decision as to whether to follow the pattern of increases established by other trades in the same locality, or by the same trade in adjoining localities; and second, whether to follow the pattern in percentage terms or in cents-per-hour terms. Deviations from the patterns by a trade in negotiations occur only for unusual reasons.

Pattern-bargaining is pervasive in construction, but the patterns are more complex than usually encountered in other sectors of the economy. It is possible to identify certain leaders in establishing patterns, but there are frequent variations in leadership[27] as economic conditions change. Since some two to three thousand collective bargaining agreements are negotiated each year in construction, the opportunity for subtle alterations in pattern-bargaining are apparent.

The result of this bargaining structure is that each local union and contractor association perceives itself to have great independence of action, while in fact its opportunities are usually narrowly constrained by a process so decentralized that it lacks any coherent direction or policy. There is constant jockeying for position in the sequence of negotiations between various trades. Those negotiating early have the potential advantage of setting the pattern, while those who follow have the potential advantage of getting a somewhat higher settlement. This process of leap-frogging of settlements creates an inflationary bias in bargaining in construction during periods of rapid economic expansion. Attempts by employer associations to control the process often result in a sequence of strikes, by one trade after another, that can be very damaging to construction in a particular area.

Multitrade Negotiations

Several areas in the United States have experimented with multi-trade negotiations as a method of controlling leap-frogging and suc-

---

[27] See Shulenburger; see also Perloff, and Ross. These studies were made possible by the collection and maintenance of data on wages and fringe benefits in construction, 1961 to date, collected by the Construction Industry Stabilization Committee (1971–74) and maintained since 1974 by the Construction Services Division of the U.S. Department of Labor.

cessive strikes. In some instances multitrade negotiations are conducted formally; in others, by informal coordination.

In a few instances multitrade negotiations have successfully avoided the problems of single-trade negotiations over a period of years, but multitrade negotiations do involve certain difficulties which have limited their effectiveness. Foremost among these difficulties is that multitrade arrangements are, of necessity, purely cooperative in nature and are, therefore, subject to dissolution due to personal or political conflicts within either the union or employer side. Each trade is ultimately free to pursue its own objectives when it desires, because each local trade union is ultimately responsible not to a local building trades council, but to an autonomous national union. Ordinarily, national unions do not insist that local unions be involved in multitrade negotiations. Quite the contrary. Certain major national unions insist that their locals refrain from any such involvement, seeing it as one method by which a national union may protect the independence of the association of contractors with which it deals from the influence of other contractors' associations. This is a matter of special importance to certain associations of sub-contractors, which may fear domination by general contractors in a local association assembled for multitrade negotiations.

TACTICS IN BARGAINING

Employers and unions in construction utilize the full range of tactics characteristic of collective bargaining in the United States (there is not sufficient space to discuss them here), but construction bargaining also involves certain unusual tactics.

Employers ordinarily exert considerable effort to see that a strike, if called by a local union, is effective against all employers; their method is to try to get nonstruck employers to lock out members of the striking local. No weapon is more effective for the unions than the selective strike, because construction firms are usually small and poorly capitalized and lack the ability to sustain a strike unless their competitors are in a similar situation. Owners are apt to cancel a contract with a struck firm and transfer it to a nonstruck firm, if possible. Thus, not only can a strike cause a firm losses on its projects, it can cause the firm to lose its business entirely. Finally, if a union can strike some firms while its members are employed by other firms, it can usually continue the strike until the struck firms give in.

These circumstances result in certain rather bizarre, but common, occurrences in construction—for example, the "strike" during which the union's members are all at work. In one extreme case, when the carpenters "struck" contractors in a New Jersey city in a wage dispute, all members of the striking local were employed either by other contractors inside the city or by the "struck" contractors outside the city. The latter simply were employing members of the striking local union on their projects elsewhere.

Another common occurrence in construction is that the size of a settlement is larger after a strike, other factors similar, than if the strike had not occurred. In the parlance of collective bargaining, the fact that the employers took a strike raised the "settlement price." So effective is the selective strike in construction that unions often insist that their members be compensated for the inconvenience of a strike by raising the settlement price.[28]

The chief and most predictable union tactic in a strike is thus to divide the employers and to conduct a strike against some but not others. At the extreme, local unions will sometimes so pick apart an employer association that it disappears as an association, and the resulting collective bargaining agreements are between the union and individual contractors, or with a newly formed association which replaced the previous one.

PRINCIPAL ISSUES IN BARGAINING

Compensation is always an important issue in construction bargaining, and on occasion it is a difficult one. Often the pattern of compensation settlements in an area is so well established that there is little or no dispute as to the size of the settlement. At other times, the amount of an increase may occasion a bitter and lengthy struggle.

Construction settlements ordinarily are package settlements, and it is usually the package that constitutes the pattern. The division of the package between wages and fringe benefits is often left to the sole discretion of the union, and there have been instances when local unions have voted during the term of an agreement to reallocate part of the package from wages to fringe benefits, or vice versa. Such a reallocation is possible because both wages and fringes are defined in terms of an employer's contribution per hour worked.

Premium pay for overtime, for certain types of work, and for the use of certain materials and tools is often an issue in construction negotiations. In some agreements, premiums rather than base rates tend to constitute the real wage rates, because work involving the premiums is common. An example is an agreement in the painting industry that provides premium pay for the use of spray-painting equipment. Sometimes premiums are pyramided as, for example, when premiums are paid for spray painting, for high work, and for work on bridges; thus bridge-

[28] See Mills, "Explaining Pay Increases," pp. 196–201.

painting involves all three premiums. Employers and unions frequently dispute the form and amount of premium pay.

In some trades, manning is the subject of considerable controversy in negotiations—for example, the requirements for electricians and/or pipefitters on temporary lighting and heating in a building under construction. Similarly, requirements for operating engineers to man certain small equipment, including pumps and compressors, also occasion disputes. Provisions that limit the amount of work done by a journeyman, while often referred to in journalistic discussions of construction, are, in fact, very common. The often cited "rule" of bricklayers that allegedly limits the number of bricks a journeyman may lay in a day is virtually nonexistent. Other rules upon which the union sometimes insists—for example, those restricting the use of corner poles by masonry contractors —may, however, be the source of conflict between bricklayers' locals and mason contractors.

RATIFICATION OF AGREEMENTS

Both the local union and the local employer association in construction often require ratification of a proposed collective bargaining agreement by their memberships before it becomes binding. Failures to ratify by either side are not uncommon.

Disputes and Dispute Settlement

THE ROLE OF THE STRIKE

Construction is a strike-prone sector of the economy. During 1970–75, for example, construction, with only about 5 percent of the nation's total employment, contributed about 24 percent of all strikes and 19 percent of all workdays lost due to strikes.[29]

Why does construction have so many strikes? There are two primary reasons. First, with each trade negotiating a separate agreement in virtually every locality in the country, strikes follow strikes as one trade after another tries to settle a contract to its advantage.[30] Rather than one big strike, as in steel or automobiles, construction generates many strikes of short duration and limited impact. But these frequent strikes add up to a generally substantial strike record.

Second, strikes in construction occur for reasons that are uncommon in other sectors of the economy. For example, about one-fifth of all

[29] Bureau of Labor Statistics, "Analysis of Work Stoppages, 1975," Bulletin No. 1940 (Washington: U.S. Government Printing Office, 1977); see also Bureau of Labor Statistics, "Work Stoppages in Contract Construction, 1962–73," Bulletin No. 1847 (Washington: U.S. Government Printing Office, 1975).

[30] See Strauss, pp. 237–51.

strikes in construction occur because of jurisdictional disputes (i.e., disputes over which trade should be assigned work at a construction site). Also, grievances provide the motivation for many strikes since binding arbitration of grievances by neutrals is not as common in construction as elsewhere in American industry.[31]

Strikes are a historic as well as a current problem in construction, and there have been adjustments in the conduct of collective bargaining to lessen their impact. For example, some seasons are more favorable to one party in negotiations than to the other. The period just before peak activity is most favorable to the labor organization, for a strike at that time is most crippling to employers and least likely to result in a net loss of work to the union. Conversely, the slack season of the year is generally most favorable for the employers. Over many years a form of compromise has evolved in which negotiations occur just before the start of the season, a relatively neutral period of the year for both parties.[32]

Picketing by striking trades is not common in construction unless the strikers believe that other trades are doing their work. Picketing, of course, tends to deprive all trades of work on a project, since union men usually honor the pickets of any trade. However, the interdependence of the production process is such that after a few weeks a strike by a single trade will often cause work for the other crafts to cease, so that in terms of time lost that of the striking craft may represent only a small proportion of the total. Furthermore, when jobs are kept operating despite the absence of one or more trades, contractors' costs tend to rise because of the difficulty of scheduling work around the unfinished jobs of striking trades.

DISPUTE-SETTLEMENT PROCEDURES

Certain branches of construction have developed imaginative and effective methods of dispute resolution. The most sophisticated is the Council on Industrial Relations of the Electrical Construction Industry.

The CIR, a national bipartite tribunal of the International Brotherhood of Electrical Workers and the National Electrical Contractors Association,[33] renders final and binding decisions in both contract and grievance disputes, and it applies to virtually all agreements (95 percent) in the electrical branch of the industry. To date in its 50-year history, the CIR has made more than 2,500 decisions, with most rendered since 1947.

The Council clause, which is incorporated in local union agreements,

---

[31] See Lipsky and Farber, pp. 388–404.
[32] For a full discussion, see Ulman, pp. 440–53.
[33] White, pp. 16–24, is a major source for this material on the CIR.

specifies essentially that, "There shall be no stoppage of work either by strike or lockout because of any proposed changes in this agreement or disputes over matters relating to this agreement." It establishes a local labor-management committee consisting of three employer and three union representatives, respectively, and all matters in dispute are to be resolved by majority vote. The clause further provides that, should the committee fail to adjust the dispute, "such shall then be referred to the Council of Industrial Relations for the Electrical Contracting Industry. Its decision shall be final and binding on both parties without limitation of the time unless it is removed by agreement of the local union and its employing contractors. It may not be excised unilaterally."

The Council mechanism is supplemented by an informal arrangement between the NECA and the IBEW, under which in the instance of an unresolved dispute the chairman or secretary of the local committee is to notify the appropriate IBEW vice-president and regional director of NECA so that their representatives may assist the local committee toward reaching agreement. This procedure has resolved disputes in an unknown but significant number of cases. Those not resolved have gone to the council, which meets quarterly in Washington and operates with panels of 12 members, six appointed by the international president of the IBEW and six by the president of NECA; the two presidents serve as co-chairmen of the council. All decisions are by unanimous vote. The CIR has never utilized outside neutrals. With the exception of one case, council decisions have been respected, and there have been no strikes or lockouts.

JURISDICTIONAL DISPUTES

The concept of exclusive work jurisdiction is fundamental to unionism in the building and construction trades. At some point in its history, each international union received a charter from the AFL, granting it exclusive jurisdiction over specific work operations. These might involve either manual operations, designated materials, or designated industries. Each union asserts the right to control its work jurisdiction by obtaining recognition as the source of manpower for employers doing the work or by obtaining the affiliation of employees assigned to the work. Because of changes in materials, technology, and other aspects of construction, the jurisdictional claims of different unions often conflict and may become the source of disputes at the jobsite.[34] Jurisdictional disputes are a major source of friction in the industrial relations

---

[34] See Taft, pp. 185–210. For interpretations of the underlying reasons for the dependence of the American labor movement in general, and the building trades in particular, on the principle of exclusive work jurisdiction, see Perlman, and Whitney.

of the construction industry. Strikes over jurisdiction are common, even though collective bargaining agreements and federal law prohibit them. Jurisdictional disputes arise when two or more unions claim the assignment of men to a particular task. They are inevitable in an industry in which wage rates and other conditions of employment differ by occupation, in which mechanics are organized into labor unions on craft lines, and in which production processes and materials are continually changing.[35] Because work jurisdiction is central to industrial relations in construction, it is unlikely that disputes can ever be eliminated. Rather, the objective of the industry has been to develop means of resolving them in such a way as to minimize the disruption of production.

Jurisdictional strikes were made an unfair labor practice under the Taft-Hartley Act in 1947, and procedures for the handling of such cases by the National Labor Relations Board were spelled out in Section 10(k) of the act. Section 10(l) provides injunctive relief and opens the way for damage suits in federal courts. In adjusting a jurisdictional dispute, the NLRB is required to make a positive assignment of work to a particular craft. Unfortunately, the Board has little expertise in dealing with competing jurisdictional claims, and its procedures are lengthy and cumbersome. As a result, contractors and unions have sought to establish voluntary machinery internal to the industry to adjust these disputes. Federal law explicitly recognizes the value of private dispute settlement and allows the NLRB to dismiss unfair labor practice charges when voluntary adjustment is attempted.

The most important mechanism for voluntary adjustment of jurisdictional disputes is the Impartial Board for the Settlement of Jurisdictional Disputes, a panel of three neutral persons familiar with the industry. It has a full-time chairman and an office in Washington. The board was established in 1973 by the Plan for the Settlement of Jurisdictional Disputes in Construction, which was negotiated by the Building and Construction Trades Department and certain national employer associations. The form of the current plan, negotiated in 1975, follows previous plans in which there was a tripartite National Joint Board for the Settlement of Jurisdictional Disputes (1948–73), and an appellate board (abolished in 1975). No appellate board now exists, but the current plan has established the office of the impartial umpire to perform certain functions in support of the plan, including administering a resolution of the Building and Construction Trades Department regarding compliance with the plan. Previous alterations of the jurisdictional dispute machinery were necessitated in part because of the dissatisfaction of the contractors' associations and the international unions with

---

[35] See Dunlop, "Jurisdictional Disputes," p. 165; see also Strand.

the methods of settling disputes and the inability of the machinery to achieve enforcement of its awards in some cases.

The board's decisions are based primarily upon agreements between national unions allocating jurisdiction and upon so-called decisions of record. Prior to 1947, jurisdictional disputes were settled either by decision of the American Federation of Labor or, at a later date, by decision of the Building Trades Department of the AFL. These decisions constitute the record, along with certain agreements between unions recognized by the Federation or the Department. These decisions and agreements are published in the *Green Book*, construction's handbook of trade jurisdiction. Other agreements, for the most part recognized by the Impartial Board but not printed in the *Green Book*, are published by the Bureau of National Affairs in a book entitled *Construction Craft Jurisdiction Agreements*.

In recent years many employers have refused to be bound to the plan, so that decisions of the Impartial Board are not binding upon them. Also, several trades have begun to insist upon inclusion of jurisdictional claims in their collective bargaining agreements, and sometimes the agreements also provide for damages to be paid the union if the employer misassigns work. The formal position of the Building and Construction Trades Department and its affiliate national unions is in opposition to these trends. But they continue.

Outcome of Collective Bargaining

Wage Structure in Construction

Trades generally negotiate separately, and the relative position of each in wage and fringe benefits is a result of negotiations. The skilled vs. unskilled differential is as important in construction as it is in steel or automobiles, but it is determined not by a single industrial union and employers, but by decentralized bargaining. There is a tendency for differentials to be resistant to change,[36] but study of a long period reveals that significant changes do occur.

Table 5 lists the major building and construction trades in order of national average hourly compensation for 1950 and 1975. It can be seen that the plumber and pipefitter replaced the bricklayer as the highest paid trade, and that the plasterer and lather fell back considerably. In general the mechanical trades moved up over the period, due in part to the growing importance of industrial and power-plant construction which uses the skills of the mechanical trades in a disproportionately large amount.[37] The laborer remained at the low end of the distribution,

---

[36] Strauss, *Unions in the Building Trades.*
[37] See Mills, "Manpower in Construction."

but the percentage differential from bottom to top narrowed from 71.5 percent to 42.0 percent. Similarly, the differential between the carpenter and laborer (especially important since these two trades are numerous and work closely together in building construction) declined from 43.6 percent in 1950 to 29 percent in 1975. Thus, the table illustrates two major changes in the construction wage structure as developed in collective bargaining over the period 1950–75: (1) the movement to the top of the rate structure by the mechanical trades; and (2) the narrowing of the skill differential between the laborer and the skilled trades.

TABLE 5

Building Trades Ranked by Average Wage and Fringe Benefits Packages, 1950 and 1975 (Building Construction Rates Only)

1950[a]		1975	
Bricklayers	$2.83	Plumbers & pipefitters	$12.06
Plasterers	2.80	Structural ironworkers	11.34
Lathers	2.78	Electricians	11.31
Plumbers & pipefitters	2.57	Rodmen	11.29
Elevator constructors	2.56	Sheet metal workers	11.17
Electricians	2.54	Boilermakers	11.13
Structural ironworkers	2.53	Bricklayers	11.06
Boilermakers	2.50	Asbestos workers	11.01
Asbestos workers	2.48	Carpenters	10.99
Sheet metal workers	2.42	Elevator constructors	10.98
Rodmen	2.38	Lathers	10.58
Carpenters	2.37	Cement finishers	10.51
Cement finishers	2.37	Plasterers	10.35
Roofers	2.28	Roofers	10.33
Painters	2.02	Painters	9.81
Laborers	1.65	Laborers	8.49

Source: Bureau of Labor Statistics and Construction Services Division, U.S. Department of Labor.
[a] In 1950 fringe benefits were not a significant part of compensation.

CONSTRUCTION AND OTHER SECTORS OF THE ECONOMY

Construction traditionally has been a high-wage sector in the American economy. Its position abroad has not been as high because of the lesser proportion of the construction workforce who are skilled and the different structure of firms, occupations, and supervision. Hourly earnings in construction reflect the higher wage scales in the industry. In 1976, for example, average hourly earnings in construction exceeded those in manufacturing by some $2.50 per hour, a percentage differential of about 48 percent.

Relatively high wage levels and high hourly earnings are not necessarily translated into high annual earnings figures, however, because of considerable intermittency of work in construction. Table 6 demonstrates the impact of intermittency of employment on construction workers' annual earnings. In 1969 and 1970, average hourly earnings in construction exceed those in all other industrial sectors listed. However, median annual earnings in construction often lagged those in other industries. In 1969, only 59.7 percent of construction workers received 50 weeks or more of employment, causing annual earnings in construction to be far lower relative to those in other sectors than hourly earnings would suggest. For example, in 1969, hourly earnings in construction *exceeded* those in all manufacturing by some 56 percent, but median annual earnings in construction were *below* those in manufacturing.

DIFFERENTIALS WITH NONUNION CONSTRUCTION

Union trades persons in construction are generally paid more than nonunion trades persons. Surveys of earnings by union and nonunion workers show substantial differentials in favor of union mechanics for both hourly[38] and annual earnings (see Table 6, for example). It is not certain, however, exactly what these differentials measure. Nonunion construction is concentrated in homebuilding and small-scale commercial work, and geographically is largely in the southern states. For a variety of reasons it is to be expected that these branches of construction and these geographic areas would experience lower wages and hourly earnings than other branches and areas.

When union and nonunion contractors perform the same work in the same localities, differentials are likely to be smaller. Persons knowledgeable of construction believe that on comparable work, skilled nonunion mechanics receive as much hourly pay as union men, and perhaps even more. Fringe benefits are probably lower for nonunion mechanics, however. The structure of occupations and work tasks is probably considerably different on nonunion construction projects. Nonunion contractors appear to make far greater use of semiskilled workers and compensate them at rates nearer to those of a union laborer than of a union skilled journeyman.[39] The extensive use of semiskilled mechanics is also common to construction abroad. Often these workers are classified as helpers of the more skilled men, a classification which the building trades unions have sought to eliminate over the past several decades.

The result of these differences in job classifications is that nonunion contractors pay a small, highly skilled group of employees (so-called "lead men" or "key men") at or above the union scale, while a large proportion of semiskilled workers receive a lesser rate of pay. Unskilled

[38] Martin E. Personick, "Union and Nonunion Pay: Patterns in Construction," *Monthly Labor Review* 97 (August 1974), pp. 71–74; Bureau of Labor Statistics, *Employee Compensation and Payroll Hours, Construction-Special Trade Contractors, 1969,* Report No. 413 (1972); and Bureau of Labor Statistics, *Employee Compensation, Heavy Construction Industry, 1971* Report (1974).
[39] Northrup and Foster.

TABLE 6

Median Annual Earnings of Experienced Male Workers, by Industry of Longest Job, 1969 and 1970, and by Region, 1970

Industry longest job	1969			1970							
	Worked 50–52 weeks	Worked 1–49 weeks	Percent working 50–52 weeks	Northeast		North Central		South		West	
				Union	Non-union	Union	Non-union	Union	Non-union	Union	Non-union
Construction	$8,750	$7,647	59.7	$9,596	$6,168	$9,470	$5,476	$8,616	$4,635	$9,613	$6,889
Mining	8,741	7,231	76.3	[a]	[a]	[a]	[a]	[a]	8,097	[a]	[a]
Manufacturing	8,849	6,930	77.4	7,869	8,842	8,308	8,750	7,614	6,518	8,539	8,884
Durable	9,001	7,097	77.1	7,912	9,396	8,142	8,874	7,354	6,474	8,399	9,379
Nondurable	8,545	6,501	78.0	7,762	7,862	8,857	8,471	7,945	6,563	8,872	7,447
Transportation and public utilities	8,982	7,252	77.7	8,901	8,433	9,299	8,763	8,940	6,829	9,478	8,083
All industries	8,633	6,898	72.2	8,385	7,353	8,574	7,289	8,053	5,839	8,852	7,078

Source: 1970 Census of Population, Vol. PC(2)–7B, Table 13, p. 73; Selected Earnings and Demographic Characteristics of Union Members, 1970, BLS Report No. 417, 1972, Table 10, p. 23.

[a] Not available.

workers (i.e., laborers) on nonunion projects in most areas apparently receive considerably lower pay than union agreements provide.

INFLATION

As noted, construction has long been a high-wage sector of our economy, but it has not often been a wage leader in the economy as a whole. However, in the 1960s there were certain unusual circumstances involving the composition of construction demand and the condition of construction and related labor markets. The result was a very rapid escalation in wages and hourly earnings which peaked in the late 1960s and early 1970s (see Table 7).

TABLE 7

Average Union Hourly Wages and Benefits in Building Trades

Year	Wages	+ Benefits	= Total	Percent Change
1966	$4.59	$ .39	$ 4.98	
1967	4.83	.44	5.27	5.8
1968	5.14	.54	5.68	7.8
1969	5.54	.63	6.17	8.6
1970	6.18	.79	6.97	13.0
1971	6.88	.95	7.83	12.3
1972	7.27	1.06	8.33	6.4
1973	7.62	1.21	8.83	6.0
1974	8.14	1.45	9.59	8.6
1975	8.91	1.63	10.54	9.9
1976	9.47	1.91	11.38	8.0
Percent change:	1966–76			128.5
	1966–71			57.2
	1971–76			45.3

Source: Bureau of Labor Statistics.

In March 1971, President Nixon established a wage-control program for the construction industry only. The program, which operated until May 1974, was administered by the tripartite Construction Industry Stabilization Committee. During the major part of the program (1972–73), wage and benefit increases negotiated in collective bargaining agreements were substantially reduced.[40] In the aftermath of the controls, and in the context of a substantial consumer price inflation, earnings increases in construction rose, but were nonetheless below those in many other major industries (Table 8).

A substantial recession in construction, which raised construction unemployment rates for 1975 to as high as 18 percent on average in the nation as a whole, helped moderate wage increases and gave them a peculiar regional pattern. In 1976, the average wage and fringe-benefit

---

[40] See Mills, "Construction Wage Stabilization," pp. 350–65.

TABLE 8

Average Hourly Earnings in Selected Industries
Percentage Increase

	1965–70	1970–75	1965–75
Total private economy	31.8	40.2	84.9
Contract construction	41.6	38.2	95.7
Automobile manufacturing	30.3	53.1	98.2
Trucking & truck terminals	32.7	57.0	108.3

settlement for the first year in construction was 7.3 percent; the national average increase in major collective bargaining agreements in all sectors of the economy was 9.5 percent. The regional variation in construction was pronounced—from a low of 4.7 percent in New England and the Mid-Atlantic states, to a high of 11.4 percent in the Northwest. In some few isolated situations, local unions negotiated wage-rate reductions on certain types of work in the hope of attracting a greater volume of construction.

It would be too much to conclude that the inflationary problem in construction collective bargaining has disappeared. The recent levels of settlements nationally, while acclaimed as "moderate" by many economists, should be viewed in context. Settlements averaging 7 percent in an environment of massive unemployment do not augur well for the future, when the volume of construction activity accelerates. Also, the structure of compensation in construction, so laboriously straightened out in the period 1971–74, has again become distorted. Differentials between the East and Midwest vs. the West Coast are at historic highs. A resumption of construction activity in the East and Midwest threatens to set off a very rapid narrowing of existing differentials. Also, the absolute level of the wage and fringe-benefit package has reached high levels in certain leading agreements. A major United Association local in San Francisco has obtained a wage and fringe-benefit package of $19.66 per hour as of April 1, 1977, and existing agreements now call for $18.00 packages in the New York City area in 1978. Clearly, $20.00 per hour packages will not be unusual in construction by 1980. A decade ago, such settlements seemed impossible.

WORKING CONDITIONS

Construction unions have devoted considerable attention over the years to negotiating improvements in working conditions. These provisions are of great variety, and many are unique to a particular trade. Some of them have been discussed above. No general statistics about the form, prevalence, or costs of these provisions are available. However, among the most important conditions of somewhat general applicability in construction are those involving travel pay, show-up pay, foremen to journeymen ratios, and stand-by men.

Travel pay involves an employer's compensating employees for travel to the worksite. Since construction job sites often change and can be located in remote areas, travel can be a major expense. Travel-pay arrangements differ considerably in collective bargaining agreements. Some provide for reimbursement of out-of-pocket costs, such as gasoline and motel rooms. Others provide that all employees receive a standard amount of travel pay per hour or day, regardless of distance to the job site or of expenses incurred. In the western states, zones have been established around metropolitan areas, and the wage scale is determined by zone, rising the further one gets from the central city. The wage scale is thereby made to include a standard premium for travel, regardless of the actual travel or expenses incurred by workers. In some instances, travel-pay arrangements have become poorly disguised wage supplements.

Show-up pay is a liability, usually in the amount of two- to four-hours' pay, incurred by a contractor when mechanics are required to report to work, but are not in fact put to work. These situations may arise because of weather conditions, failure to materials to arrive, or similar occurrences. Ordinarily a contractor may cancel an order the previous night for men to report the following day, though some contracts provide longer notice periods. Show-up pay in certain trades customarily excludes a situation where inclement weather cancels work. In such an event, both the contractor and the worker share the loss of a day's profit and pay. In many contracts, the operating engineers have obtained a 40-hour week guarantee; that is, if a contractor assigns an engineer any work during a week, he must pay him for 40 hours. Other trades have not negotiated this type of provision.

Journeymen to foremen ratios are commonly negotiated in construction. The fact that foremen are commonly covered by the collective bargaining agreement and usually are union members reflects both the lack of stable employment in the industry, even at the foreman level, and the practice of journeymen working for different employers. A journeyman may serve as a mechanic on one job and as a foreman on the next. Unions often seek to minimize the journeymen to foreman ratio, while employers seek to increase it. Ratios range in construction from 3 to 1 to 20 to 1 or so.

Stand-by manning provisions are ordinarily related to the jurisdiction of a trade. Carpenters may seek to have a journeyman carpenter assigned to maintain forms during a concrete pour, or operating engineers may seek to have a journeyman engineer maintain small electric motors on a job. In both instances, ordinarily there is no work to be done, since the forms are set and the motors are fully automatic once they have been switched on.

Other working conditions may be negotiated in some instances. Some agreements give preference on certain types of work to older members of the workforce. Others provide that the employer must supply tools, and/or storage lockers, foul weather gear, portable toilets, cold drinking water, warm-up shacks, etc. Until the last few years, all such conditions as described above and sought by the unions seem to have been increasing in construction agreements.

The recent recession has caused employers to seek and often obtain a moratorium on the negotiation of additional improvements in working conditions, and in many instances employers have sought and obtained reductions. For example, an agreement negotiated in the Hudson River Valley of New York in 1976 eliminated all travel-expense provisions, the reporting-pay provision, the journeymen to foreman ratio, and the requirement that a carpenter must observe the forms during a concrete pour.

How extensive such changes are in construction, and the magnitude of their economic impact, are not known at this time.

Contract Administration

Grievances arise for workers in construction just as they do in other sectors of the economy. But grievances of certain types, common elsewhere, are unusual in construction. Grievances over promotions rarely arise in an environment in which there is virtually only the journeyman classification in each trade. Grievances about discharge are also unusual in an environment in which the employer is usually the sole judge of competence on a job, and in which job turnover is continual.

Grievances about hiring violations, uncommon elsewhere, are frequent in construction. Employers are often charged with violations of the contract as a result of hiring a particular worker directly, rather than notifying the union as a source of referral. Grievances alleging failure of the employer to pay wages or overtime, or to make fringe-benefit contributions, are also common.

Historically, construction has made little use of binding arbitration by neutrals as a means of settling grievances. Instead of the usually lengthy process of grievance handling and arbitration, there is the "instant justice" of construction. When the job steward and the employer's superintendent fail to settle a grievance, the business agent of the local union intervenes. If he is also unsuccessful, a strike is likely to be called on the spot. The grievance, and the strike, are then settled in some manner.

The strike has the advantage of usually bringing about a swift resolution of the matter. Lengthy delays in resolving disputes often result in the project being completed, and the worker laid off, before the controversy is settled. In recent years more construction agreements have included no-strike clauses and binding arbitration of grievances. Whether this importation of procedure from other sectors into construction will be successful is yet to be determined.

The Nonunion Challenge

DEVELOPMENT

There has always been a nonunion portion of construction, just as there has always been a struggle in construction over the role of the unions. The tide of union strength has ebbed and flowed. In the 1920s, the American Plan was directed at the building trades, as at other unions, and was successful in some areas.[41] The post-World War II decades brought a broadening of union strength which began to dissipate in the late 1960s. By the mid-1970s, a substantial open-shop movement was again challenging the building trades unions.

What was new, and particularly disturbing to the unionized portion of construction, about the open-shop challenge of the 1970s was its size and refinement. In the recent past, most nonunion contractors were small, lower technology firms operating in the less complex branches of construction. But in the 1960s and 1970s, a nonunion movement development that demonstrated considerable sophistication. A number of large nonunion firms grew up in the design-and-build aspects of industrial construction. By the mid-1970s, several nonunion companies operating from home offices in Texas and the Carolinas were among the largest such companies in the world. For the first time, unionized industrial construction firms confronted direct nonunion competition on a significant scale in their major markets.

Simultaneously, there developed among medium- and small-scale nonunion commercial builders, especially general contractors, a national association capable of providing staff support and programs to member firms. A major function of the association involves labor relations, including legal advice and support to member firms involved in disputes with the building trades unions. Called Associated Builders and Contractors, Inc. (ABC), this association has helped stimulate other associations to develop the capacity to service nonunion firms as well.

[41] See Haber.

ABC is a national association of nonunionized construction contractors that operates through some 45 chapters at the local or state level and involves some 8000 member firms. ABC is not the only association of nonunion contractors, nor is it the largest or the oldest (for example, the Associated General Contractors of America has a larger membership of nonunion firms), but it is notable in marking the most complete departure from past practice by nonunion employers in construction. Ordinarily, nonunion construction contractors have not provided fringe benefits, including health insurance and pension coverage, nor formal training to employees. Each firm operated independently, hiring and laying off employees at will, and at whatever wage rates were determined by bargaining with each workman individually. Nonunion firms were generally small and numerous in an industry that was, however, largely organized by the building trades unions.

ABC was established as an association of nonunion contractors, with a principal focus upon labor relations. The term "Merit Shop" was coined to represent a policy of hiring both union and nonunion men, but without the existence of a collective bargaining agreement. The local associations hired staff and supported individual companies in resisting union organizing efforts or other types of union pressure (such as exclusion of nonunion contractors from construction projects on which union contractors operated). But the associations had affirmative purposes as well. Apprenticeship and training plans, health and welfare plans, and pension plans were developed on an association (i.e., multiemployer) basis. This is the basis on which training and fringe benefits are ordinarily made available in the unionized sector of construction, but their development by an association of nonunion contractors was a major innovation. In a sense the "Merit Shop" associations have adopted many of the substantive industrial relations policies and procedures of the unionized segment of construction, but decision-making about labor relations and personnel policy remains under the control of a local or national contractors' association without union involvement or participation.

The combination of large nonunion industrial contractors and an association of smaller general and specialty contractors is formidable enough, but organization by the owners, or construction users, has added a third dimension to the challenge. Owner-involvement in construction labor relations is an old occurrence. For example, in the early 1900s, owners, material suppliers, and contractors joined forces to compel the Building Trades Council of Chicago to disband and to accept open-shop conditions on all projects. In the 1920s, the American Plan was spearheaded in construction by major manufacturers. And again in the 1960s, major industrial firms, concerned by what they perceived to be inflationary and inefficient practices in construction, became actively interested in the labor relations of construction. In the 1920s, much of the owners' interest in construction had been to limit the spread of unionism from the building trades to their own, unorganized, industrial workforces. In the 1960s and early 1970s, much of the owners' interest was to limit what they perceived as the spread of a wage inflation from construction to their own, now largely organized, industrial workforces.

The owners seek different options in purchasing construction. A project may be costed several ways and the least expensive alternative chosen. At meetings of large utilities and industrial firms in the 1970s, three alternative means of having construction done are commonly described: construction by a large national design-and-build construction firm that is unionized; construction by a similar, nonunion firm; construction with the owner acting as a general contractor and using its own employees to a greater or lesser degree (so-called "force account" construction).

ALLEGED ADVANTAGES OF NONUNION CONSTRUCTION

To attract the owners' interest, nonunion contractors advertise the open-shop as "a better way" to conduct construction. Calculations are offered showing that because of lower pay scales and allegedly more efficient operations, nonunion construction is less expensive than union construction.[42] Spokesmen for the nonunion contractors describe the cost advantages of nonunion construction to owners as resulting from the following factors: (1) the employment of helpers or learners at low rates of pay; (2) the use of laborers to do work that is journeymen work in the union portion of construction (especially the unloading of materials); (3) the absence of premium pay for such things as shift work, show-up, and the use of certain types of equipment; (4) payment of time-and-one-half for overtime, not double-time as is common in the union portion; (5) avoidance of interferences due to craft union jurisdictional demarcation lines; (6) absence of minimum-crew-size rules; (7) absence of stand-by men; and (8) absence of specific journeymen to foreman ratios.[43]

DOUBLE-BREASTED CONTRACTORS

Union contractors have two possible responses to the threat of nonunion competition. One is to become open-shop contractors themselves, either wholly or partially. A second response is to attempt to negotiate

---

[42] An example of such an exercise may be found in Northrup and Foster.
[43] Robert T. Thompson, "The Alternative of Open-Shop Construction," *Public Utilities Fortnightly* 98 (October 7, 1976), pp. 53–55.

arrangements with the unions that will improve their competitiveness.

Many union firms have countered the nonunion threat by joining it, to a degree. In the parlance of construction, these contractors have become "double-breasted." "Double-breasted" means that the same persons operate two businesses, one using union labor and one operating open-shop. Under United States law, the two companies can be separate and independent and entitled to all the protections available under our labor law to independent businesses. The unions and employers have been litigating the status of double-breasted contractors, with the unions attempting, with some success, to limit the practice legally.[44] However, double-breasted companies can operate successfully, and more and more are doing so. There are no data of a comprehensive nature on the frequency of double-breasted operations.

Many large nonunion companies have operated union subsidiaries for several years. In a development of major importance for construction, large union companies are, in the 1970s, beginning to operate nonunion subsidiaries. For decades the largest union industrial and utility contractors have been associated in the NCA, an association that has been fully union. This association and the projects that its member companies do have been at the heart of the union portion of construction. As nonunion firms began to get a larger share of their market, these firms began to threaten to go double-breasted. In recent years several NCA contractors have been acquired by conglomerates which also own nonunion construction firms, and NCA contractors that have preserved their independence have themselves purchased nonunion companies, which they apparently intend to operate nonunion. These and other acquisitions now in progress may presage a general movement of previously fully union national contractors to double-breasted status.

Finally, to accommodate the growing open-shop movement, several major contractor associations, especially AGC, have established separate labor committees and labor relations staffs to service their union and nonunion member firms.

THE RESPONSE OF THE UNIONS

The building trades unions have responded to the growth of the nonunion portion of construction in several ways. At the local level, unions and employers have attempted to improve the competitiveness of union construction by a variety of measures. Among these are reductions in wages and fringe benefits and relaxation of working conditions and premium pay arrangements. In some instances these changes have

---

[44] Robert V. Penfield, "The Double-Breasted Operation in the Construction Industry," *Labor Law Journal* 27 (February 1976), pp. 89–93.

been incorporated in local collective bargaining agreements. In other instances the changes have been made on an ad hoc basis. Some local collective bargaining agreements have been amended to set forth explicitly a procedure by which a local union and employers may hold a conference prior to the bidding of a construction job at which the particular standards to apply on that job may be established as is necessary to meet nonunion competition.

At the national level, the unions have greatly expanded the use of the project agreement as a method of helping to insure that large construction projects are performed on a union basis.

Finally, the trades have attempted in many instances to do a better job of organizing nonunion workers. The success of such efforts is hampered, however, by several factors. First, the traditional method of organizing in the industry has been to have contractors sign prehire agreements involving recognition of the unions, rather than organizing employees directly. Second, many employees of nonunion firms are actually union members working under open-shop conditions. The capacity of the unions to enforce their rules against such activities by their members is limited as a practical matter by political realities within the unions. Third, the development of labor law has been such as to preclude effectively the use of the unions' strongest weapon in organizing, the secondary boycott, and has substituted for it a process of little value in construction—the project-by-project election.

The recent controversy over the situs picketing bill in the U.S. Congress had, on one side, the unions attempting to obtain a relaxation of the legal restrictions under which they have been placed since the mid-1950s, opposed by management and owners determined to retain the legal advantages that they have gained. The failure of the unions to obtain relief through the passage of the situs picketing bill (formally entitled "equal treatment for construction workers") represents a setback in the attempt of the unions to develop an effective response to the growth of the nonunion portion of construction.

UNION VS. NONUNION CONSTRUCTION: HOW SHARP IS THE DISTINCTION?

Public discussion of construction's labor relations, and particularly the discussion about the situs picketing legislation, presumes a clear-cut distinction between union and nonunion construction. In most other sectors of the economy, a relatively unambiguous answer can be given to the inquiry whether the employee in a plant or store or government agency is represented by a union. In construction, it is less easy to make this distinction. The expansion of open-shop construction into geographic areas and branches of the industry previously fully unionized has required both open-shop contractors and the unions to develop certain methods of living together.

One such method allows a nonunion contractor to operate without reference to a collective bargaining agreement, except that the contractor must hire members of the local union and pay the wage rates and fringe benefits as negotiated between the local union and the association of union contractors. In some instances this arrangement is made verbally between the nonunion contractor and the local union; in others, it is tacit only. But in some instances, the arrangement is put in writing, in the form of a letter from the firm to the local union. Such a letter reads (the proper names are fictitious):

> Apex Construction agrees to employ members of Construction Workers Local Union No. 2 and agrees to pay the current wage rates and fringe benefits as negotiated between Local 2 and the Associated Contractors of Metropolis.
>
> This letter in no way is intended to be construed as the signing or acceptance of any collective bargaining agreement.

Neither the employers nor the unions, local or national, countenance such an arrangement as a matter of policy. For the employer, the arrangement is a violation of its policy of not dealing with trade unions. For the union, the arrangement represents the surrender of all protections of the collective bargaining agreement with respect to working conditions and all other matters save only the wage rate and fringe-benefit contributions. In consequence, both the company and the union would probably deny to outsiders the existence of the arrangement. There are also legal issues as to whether such a letter constitutes recognition of the union by the company, and whether it constitutes a binding contract. But such issues have not been litigated as yet, because it has been to the interests of both parties to avoid litigation. Arrangements of this nature are common enough in some geographic areas to have been given a name—a "one-liner," that is, a "one-line," or brief, deal.

Is a contractor that is party to a one-liner a union or a nonunion firm? Is a construction job worked under a one-liner a union or a nonunion job? Are employees working for a contractor party to a one-liner union or nonunion employees? Such issues of definition and classification are best left to those who insist on dividing the world into union and nonunion categories in order to compile data series. What is important in construction itself is the development of methods of doing business that do not rigidify the union-nonunion distinction, but instead blur it in order to make it of less practical significance.

Another method of reducing the significance of the union-nonunion distinction is for a contractor to subcontract parts of a project in such a way that some are done union and other parts are done nonunion. In many instances, the structure of subcontracting, and sometimes the firms themselves, are essentially merely legal arrangements arrived at in order to implement certain understandings about what is to be union, what is to be nonunion, and what is to be mixed on a particular project.

Collective Bargaining Reform

For a decade or more, labor and management leaders in construction and some government officials have worked toward reform of the collective bargaining process in the industry. Among the problems confronting the union sector are the frequency of strikes, the sometimes rapid inflation in construction, and the recent growth of the nonunion portion of the industry. It is not too much to say that there has been a general consensus that labor relations in construction require reform, and that central to the concern is the complex and decentralized structure of bargaining.

What has been lacking is any consensus on how bargaining should be reformed. At one extreme, some observers argue that the growth of the nonunion portion of construction should be encouraged as a device to control problems in the union portion by virtue of the competition of union and nonunion companies for construction projects. Others, believing in some instances that there are practical limits to what can be achieved through the promotion of nonunion construction, and also in some instances favoring collective bargaining as a positive goal in itself, have sought to bring about changes in the union portion of construction directly. But even among those of this viewpoint, there is considerable disagreement over what the solutions might be.

Beginning in the mid-1960s, the federal government established a series of committees composed of national union presidents and chief executives of national employer associations. While devoting attention to the problems of the moment, these committees also served as devices for discussions regarding reform in the industry. During the period of statutory wage control, 1971–74, the Construction Industry Stabilization Committee, a tripartite body, experimented with various means of reforming bargaining in construction—among them were regional bargaining, multitrade bargaining, and national level oversight of local collective bargaining. The abrupt termination of controls in May 1974 returned collective bargaining in construction to its 1960s' status.

In 1975 the Ford Administration proposed a bill to reform construction collective bargaining. In essence, the bill would have established a national tripartite committee with certain powers to intervene in local

96COLLECTIVE BARGAINING

negotiations and to promote, where feasible, such reforms as regional bargaining. The central concept of the bill was that a more active national involvement was necessary in local bargaining and that it should be done on a coordinated basis by the various trades and branches of construction. The national involvement was intended to introduce certain broader perspectives about the secondary impacts of local negotiations (including limitations on the leap-frogging process) and to coordinate the actions of various trades and localities.

Simultaneously, in 1975, the Building and Construction Trades Department of the AFL-CIO supported a bill in Congress to relax legal restrictions on picketing activities by the unions in construction (the situs picketing bill).[45] The unions indicated a willingness to accept both pieces of legislation. After some preliminary confusion, the employer associations generally (with some exceptions) took the position that they would oppose the situs picketing bill in any form and without regard to the provisions of any other piece of legislation. In essence, the employers made situs picketing a nonnegotiable issue. In the fall of 1975, Congress amended the situs picketing bill extensively, and thereafter passed both bills as a package. After intensive lobbying by the employer associations, and especially by broader employer groups (including, for example, the United States Chamber of Commerce), President Ford vetoed the package in December 1975.

In response to the veto, the national unions resigned from a national tripartite committee that had been functioning during 1975 as a forum for discussion and cooperative activities between government, management, and labor. In 1977, following the defeat of President Ford in the 1976 presidential election, the package measure, including situs picketing and collective bargaining reform, was reintroduced into Congress. Again the employer associations and employers generally actively opposed the bill, and it was defeated in the House of Representatives in the spring of 1977. As a result of these events, collective bargaining reform in construction has apparently been indefinitely postponed.

---

[45] U.S. Congress, House of Representatives, Committee on Education and Labor, Subcommittee on Labor-Management Relations, *Equal Treatment of Craft and Industrial Workers*, Hearings on H.R. 5900, 94th Congress, 1st Session (Washington: U.S. Government Printing Office, 1975).

List of References

Bourdon, Clinton C. "Demand Instability and the Construction Labor Force." Joint Center for Urban Studies, MIT and Harvard, Working Paper No. 37, 1976.
Christie, Robert A. *Empire in Wood: A History of the Carpenters Union.* Ithaca, N.Y.: Cornell University Press, 1956.

Dunlop, John T. "The Industrial Relations System in Construction." In *The Structure of Collective Bargaining*, ed. Arnold R. Weber. Chicago: University of Chicago Graduate School of Business, 1961.

————. "Jurisdictional Disputes: 10 Types." *Constructor* (Journal of the Associated General Contractors) (July 1953), p. 165.

Grimes, A. J. "Personnel Management in the Building Trades." *Personnel Journal* 47 (January 1968), pp. 37–47.

Haber, William. *Industrial Relations in the Construction Industry*. Cambridge, Mass.: Harvard University Press, 1930.

Lipsky, David B., and Henry S. Farber. "The Composition of Strike Activity in the Construction Industry." *Industrial and Labor Relations Review* 29 (April 1976), pp. 388–404.

Mills, D. Quinn. "Construction Wage Stabilization." *Industrial Relations* 11 (October 1972), pp. 350–65.

————. "Explaining Pay Increases in Construction: 1953–1972." *Industrial Relations* 13 (May 1974), pp. 196–201.

————. "Manpower in Construction: New Methods and Measures." In *Proceedings of the 20th Annual Winter Meeting: The Development and Use of Manpower*. Madison, Wis.: Industrial Relations Research Association, 1967.

Mooney, Booth. *Builders for Progress*. New York: McGraw-Hill Book Co., 1965.

Northrop, Herbert, and Howard G. Foster. *Open Shop Construction*. Philadelphia: Wharton School, University of Pennsylvania, 1975.

Perlman, Selig. *A Theory of the Labor Movement*. New York: Macmillan Co., 1928.

Perloff, Jeffrey M. "The Wage Change Process in the Construction Industry." Ph.D. thesis, Massachusetts Institute of Technology, 1976.

Ross, Clark. "Wage Determination in Construction." Ph.D. thesis, Boston College, 1975.

Sanford, Edward P. "Wage Rates and Hours of Labor in the Building Trades." *Monthly Labor Review* 45 (August 1937), pp. 281–300.

Segal, Martin. *The Rise of the United Association: National Unionism in the Pipe Trades, 1884–1924*. Cambridge, Mass.: Harvard University Press, 1970.

Shulenburger, David E. "Prior Identification of 'Key' Wage Determining Units." *Industrial Relations* 16 (February 1977), pp. 71–82.

Stokes, McNeil. *Collective Bargaining in Construction*. Washington: Bureau of National Affairs, Inc., 1977.

Strand, Kenneth T. *Jurisdictional Disputes in Construction*. Pullman: Washington State University Press, 1961.

Strauss, George. "Business Agents in the Building Trades." *Industrial and Labor Relations Review* 10 (January 1957), pp. 237–51.

————. *Unions in the Building Trades*. University of Buffalo Series 24, No. 2. Buffalo, N.Y.: 1958.

Taft, Philip. *The AFL in the Time of Gompers*. New York: Harper & Bros., 1957.

Ulman, Lloyd. *The Rise of the National Trade Union*, 2nd ed. Cambridge, Mass.: Harvard University Press, 1966.

White, Donald J. "The Council on Industrial Relations." In *Proceedings of the 24th Annual Winter Meeting, Industrial Relations Research Association*. Madison, Wis.: The Association, 1971.

Whitney, Nathaniel R. "Jurisdiction in American Building Trades Unions." Johns Hopkins University Studies in Historical and Political Science No. 1. Baltimore: 1914.

CHAPTER 3

Trucking*

HAROLD M. LEVINSON
University of Michigan

The Industry

As used in the following analysis, the "trucking industry" refers to those firms that are engaged in the movement of freight "for hire"—that is, who are in the business of transporting goods owned by others on a fee-for-service basis. This is in contrast to the use of trucks for "private carriage"—that is, as an adjunct to some other primary business such as manufacturing or trade.

For analytical purposes, it is also important to break down the operations of for-hire carriers in various ways. First, such companies may be common carriers, who offer their services to the public as a whole, or they may be contract carriers who handle the freight of one or more specific shippers under special contractual arrangements. Second, for-hire carriers may be broken down into three functional types— over-the-road (or intercity, or long-line), pickup and delivery, and local cartage. Intercity operations involve the movement of freight over distances usually from 200 miles up. Pickup and delivery is an adjunct to intercity movements, involving the pickup and delivery of long-line freight at its origin and destination, while local cartage is entirely a local service, involving the transfer of goods from one point to another within the same metropolitan area. Often the same firm will provide over-the-road and pickup-delivery services; local cartage firms are usually independent. Finally, a distinction is commonly made between for-hire carriers of general freight (sometimes called "dry freight") and specialized carriers of automobiles ("haulaway"), liquid products (tank-

* This analysis has depended critically on the generous cooperation of many union and employer representatives, who discussed the many issues involved with me, often at considerable length. Since these discussions were all "off the record," I can only express my sincere thanks to all of them collectively. Particular thanks are also due to the Research Department of the Eastern Conference of Teamsters for making available their extensive file of trucking contracts. Professors Charles Rehmus, Don Garnel, and Gerald Somers provided valuable comments on an earlier draft. Thanks are also due to JoAnn Sokkar and Mabel Webb of the Industrial Relations Library at the University of Michigan for much assistance in gathering basic data. The final analysis and interpretations are, of course, solely my own responsibility.

ers), refrigerated products ("reefers"), household goods, heavy machinery, and agricultural commodities. The following discussion will focus on collective bargaining in general freight, though brief reference will be made to the other sectors as well.

GOVERNMENT REGULATION

Since 1935, a large proportion of common and contract carriers operating in interstate commerce have been subject to extensive regulation by the Interstate Commerce Commission (ICC) under the Motor Carrier Act of 1935 (incorporated as Part II of the Interstate Commerce Act of 1887). Before a carrier can enter the industry, he must obtain a certificate of convenience and necessity which will specify the commodities to be handled, the routes to be used, and the cities to be serviced. In addition, the ICC regulates the rates charged: they must be reasonable, compensatory (i.e., not below costs), and not unjustly discriminatory.[1] Also, the Commission must approve all mergers or consolidations of existing firms as well as discontinuance of any service already provided. Exempted from these regulations are (1) carriers transporting certain classes of agricultural products, and (2) operations within defined commercial zones in and around large metropolitan areas.

Despite the ICC restrictions on entry, the trucking industry is still one that has a huge number of small firms. In 1974, after a period of nearly 40 years during which the ICC's policy has been to support the development of fewer and larger firms, there were still 14,600 *regulated* carriers engaged in interstate operations (down from 19,600 in 1950). Of these, more than 75 percent earned gross revenues under $500,000.[2] Moreover, thousands of carriers operate on an intrastate basis under state permits and at least an equally large number of companies operate their own private truck fleets.

An adequate picture of the character of the industry also requires that note be taken of the presence of an estimated 100,000 owner-operators, individuals who own and drive their own equipment but who have no ICC operating authority.[3] These operators may legally carry only nonregulated exempt commodities or may handle regulated freight only under a leasing arrangement to a certified common or contract carrier.

---

[1] The Commission does not set rates directly. Rate schedules are filed by regional rate bureaus representing most or all regulated carriers in the region. The Commission may affirm, deny, or modify these proposed rates as it sees fit. Also, individual carriers may file individual rate schedules or may "flag out" of particular rates filed by the bureaus. Such individual rates may be challenged on the grounds they are not compensatory.

[2] American Trucking Association, *American Trucking Trends*, 1975, p. 9.

[3] Wyckoff and Maister, p. 1. These authors estimate that owner-operators handled from 25 to 40 percent of total intercity truck transportation in the early 1970s. [The complete citations of all footnote references are listed at the end of the chapter.]

They are not legally permitted to operate their equipment for a private company since this would constitute noncertified for-hire carriage; nevertheless, this is a common practice in an industry so large and decentralized that prevention of such practices is extremely difficult.[4]

Thus, while the regulation of rates and entry by the ICC undoubtedly protects the carriers from what would otherwise be severe price competition, it by no means eliminates competitive pressures arising from a shift of customers to private trucks, from individual carriers filing their own rate schedules, or from the ubiquitous, though illegal, competition of owner-operators.

THE ECONOMIC BACKGROUND

By far the dominant economic factor that has characterized the trucking industry over the past quarter century or more has been its rapid rate of growth.[5] Several dimensions of this growth are briefly summarized in Tables 1 and 2. From 1950 to 1973–74, operating revenues of ICC-regulated intercity motor carriers increased more than 500 percent, intercity ton-miles rose by 230 percent, while total employment

TABLE 1

Operating Revenues, Ton-Miles, and Employment in
ICC-Regulated Intercity Motor Freight, 1950–1974

Year	Gross Operating Revenues (billions)[a]	Intercity Ton-Miles Carried (billions)[a]	Average Number Employees (thousands)[b]
1950	$ 3.7	65.6	224.2
1955	5.5	82.9	332.2
1960	7.2	104.4	389.8
1965	10.1	140.3	439.8
1970	14.6	167.0	549.2
1973	20.7	221.0	628.1
1974	22.7	218.0	NA

Source: Interstate Commerce Commission, Bureau of Accounts, *Transport Statistics of the United States* (annual), and ICC, *Annual Reports.*

a Class I, II, and III motor carriers of property.

b 1950 and 1955, Class I carriers; 1960–73, Class I and II carriers. These classification changes had no effect on the comparability of the entire series.

rose by 180 percent. These figures compare with increases of less than 400 percent in money GNP, 127 percent in real GNP, and 70 percent in total nonagricultural employment in the economy as a whole over the same period.[6] In terms of operating revenues from the movement of all

----

4 Wyckoff and Maister, pp. 4–8.

5 A full discussion of the major factors underlying this growth may be found in Levinson, Rehmus, Goldberg, and Kahn, chs. 1–6.

6 *Economic Report of the President* (January 1977), Tables B-1, B-2, B-32.

TABLE 2

Distribution of Operating Revenues of Federally
Regulated Freight Carriers, 1950–1975
(billions of dollars)

Year	Rail-roads		Motor Carr.		Water		Pipe-line		Air		Total
	$	%	$	%	$	%	$	%	$	%	$
1950	7.9	64	3.7	30	0.3	2	0.4	4	0.1	1	12.5
1955	8.9	57	5.5	36	0.3	2	0.7	4	0.1	1	15.5
1960	8.4	50	7.2	43	0.3	2	0.8	5	0.2	1	16.9
1965	9.3	44	10.1	48	0.3	1	0.9	4	0.4	2	21.0
1970	11.4	40	14.6	52	0.4	1	1.2	4	0.7	3	28.2
1975	15.6	38	22.0	53	0.8	2	1.8	4	1.3	3	41.2

Source: American Trucking Association, *American Trucking Trends, 1975*, p. 17, and 1976 *Statistical Supplement*, p. 3. Totals may not equal the sum of the parts because of rounding.

types of federally regulated intercity freight, Table 2 shows that the share of motor carriers has increased dramatically from 30 percent in 1950 to 53 percent by 1975, all at the expense of the railroads. Table 3 provides the most basic reflection of the favorable position of the industry, namely, its profit rates (profits as a percentage of investment). The first two columns, compiled by the ICC and the Federal Trade Commission, show motor carriers consistently doing better than all manufacturing firms over the entire 1950–75 period, with an after-tax profit rate of 12.6 vs. 11.3 percent. The superior experience of the largest common carriers is shown more sharply in the City Bank of New York

TABLE 3

Profit Rates and Profit Margins in Trucking
and Manufacturing, 1950–1975[a]

Years	Class I Motor Carriers (1)	All Mfg. (2)	Common Carrier Trucking (3)	All Mfg. (4)	Class I and II Motor Carriers (5)
1950–54	14.2%	11.6%	NA	NA	4.7%
1955–59	11.1	11.0	NA	NA	3.7
1960–64	10.6	10.0	14.1%	11.1%	3.9
1965–69	14.0	12.5	18.6	13.3	4.7
1970–75	15.5	13.8	19.0	15.1	5.5
1950–75	12.6	11.3			4.5
1960–75			17.2	13.2	

Sources: Columns 1 and 5:   Interstate Commerce Commission, *Annual Reports*. Column 2:   *Economic Report of the President*, January 1977, Table B–81. Columns 3 and 4: National City Bank of New York.

   [a] Columns 1–4 are profit rates; column 5 is profit margins. All figures are after taxes. See fn. 7 in text.

data in columns (3) and (4), with an average 17.2 percent return to common carriers from 1960 to 1975 compared to only 13.2 percent for large manufacturing firms. Clearly the rapid rise in the industry's revenues, output, and employment have been translated into favorable returns on investment as well.[7]

Collective Bargaining: The Parties[8]

THE UNION

Originally chartered by the AFL in 1899, the International Brotherhood of Teamsters (IBT) was for many years made up of strong, autonomous local unions in several large cities, representing drivers in local cartage, construction, and delivery trades (milk, coal, etc.). This situation changed dramatically with the rapid growth of intercity freight movement, particularly after World War II. From a total membership of only 75,000 in 1933, the Teamsters expanded to include approximately one million members in 1950 and to two million by 1974, making it the largest union in the country. Between 1974 and 1976, however, total membership declined to 1.9 million, the first drop in the past quarter-century.[9]

Of this total only an estimated 25 percent are in the freight division. The remainder are in warehousing, construction, trade, and various local delivery services, as well as a rising number in many sectors quite unrelated to "teamster" functions—for example, police, teachers, and others.[10] Employees within the freight division are organized into local unions on various bases. In smaller cities, all job classifications (line drivers, local drivers, platform men, etc.) are usually members of the same local. In larger cities, one or more of these groups may be in

[7] In view of the widely prevailing use of profit margins, or operating ratios (profits, or operating expenses, as a percent of *sales*), in describing the profit position of the trucking industry, these data are also included in Table 3. These are quite low, reflecting the high turnover of capital—i.e., the high ratio of sales revenues to investment dollars—in the industry. They are not an indication of poor profitability; however, they do indicate that relatively small increases in operating costs will greatly reduce profit margins and hence put more upward pressure on prices.

[8] Several studies have described the nature and growth of collective bargaining in trucking and will not be repeated here. The interested reader is referred to Hill; Leiter; Roper; James and James; Levinson, ch. 5; Levinson et al., ch. 3; and Garnel.

[9] U.S. Department of Labor, *Directory of National Unions and Employee Associations*, 1975 (Washington: 1977); and Bureau of National Affairs, *Daily Labor Report*, Sept. 2, 1977, p. B17.

[10] After being expelled from the AFL-CIO in 1957 on grounds of corrupt practices, the Teamsters amended their constitution in 1961 to assert jurisdiction over "all workers—without limitation." At the present time, the union recognizes no jurisdictional limits and is more properly considered to be a "general" than an industrial or craft union. Its members are organized into some 750 locals, 48 joint councils, and 5 area conferences.

separate locals. Overall, approximately 70 to 80 percent of freight membership is made up of employees handling freight within a local area, while 20 to 30 percent operate on an intercity basis.

All locals (in all industries) are required to affiliate with a Joint Council (largely an administrative unit) and to an area Conference, of which there are now five—Western, organized in 1937, Southern (1943), Central (1953), Eastern (1953), and Canadian (1976). Under the Teamster constitution, each conference is set up as a self-contained administrative unit, with its own trade divisions, organizing personnel, and professional staff (legal, research, etc.). All its activities, however, are under the complete control of the international president. He is empowered to appoint an international vice-president as conference director, and all conference activities "shall be at all times subject to the unqualified supervision, direction, and control of the General President." [11]

The ultimate governing body is, of course, the international convention, which meets every five years. The convention has the power to amend the constitution, to elect the international officers, and otherwise to establish the policies of the organization. Between conventions, the operations of the union are directed by its general president (now Frank Fitzsimmons), general secretary, and a general executive board of 16 vice-presidents.

THE EMPLOYERS

The highly fractionalized nature of the trucking industry, involving tens of thousands of firms engaged in diverse freight-moving operations, has had a profound impact on its bargaining structure. On the employer side, the basic problem has been that a large majority of these firms lack the financial resources to be able to resist a strike of more than a few days' duration without facing a financial crisis. As a result, the employers have long been weak and divided at the bargaining table despite continuing efforts over the years to develop an effective source of "countervailing power." They have attempted to develop a stronger negotiating position by establishing employers' associations to present a

[11] International Brotherhood of Teamsters, *Constitution*, Article XVI. The geographic areas covered by each conference are the following: *Central* (12): Ohio, Indiana, Illinois, Michigan, Wisconsin, Minnesota, Iowa, Missouri, North Dakota, South Dakota, Nebraska, Kansas; *Southern* (10): Georgia, Florida, Kentucky, Tennessee, Alabama, Mississippi, Arkansas, Louisiana, Oklahoma, Texas; *Western* (13): California, Oregon, Washington, Nevada, Idaho, Montana, Utah, Wyoming, Colorado, Arizona, New Mexico, Alaska, Hawaii; *Eastern* (15): Maine, New Hampshire, Vermont, Massachusetts, Connecticut, Rhode Island, New York, New Jersey, Pennsylvania, Delaware, Maryland, Virginia, West Virginia, North Carolina, South Carolina; *Canadian:* all provinces.

united front and to formulate a unified bargaining approach. In practice, however, when the "chips are down" in the final hours and minutes of negotiations, the union has almost invariably been able to convince one employer or group of employers to yield; once the united front was broken, others quickly followed. On the few occasions when unity was maintained to the deadline, a strike of only a few days' duration was usually sufficient to force agreement from the weakest carriers and the union's victory was again complete.

As freight carriage has expanded from local to regional movements, employers' associations have similarly expanded from city to state or multistate groupings. The most recent and most ambitious effort in this direction came in 1963 with the establishment of a national association, Trucking Employers Incorporated (TEI). In order to provide the highest degree of centralized power and responsibility, TEI was governed by an executive policy committee made up of chief executive officers of various trucking companies. In 1976, this committee had 102 members, elected by approximately 30 regional employers' associations who represented the formal membership of TEI; individual companies were, in turn, members of the regional association in which their home offices were located. Each regional association was assigned a number of votes for members of the policy committee in approximate relationship to the total number of employees of all ICC-regulated carriers of general freight headquartered in their respective areas.[12] The policy committee was authorized by individual carriers to act in their behalf in negotiating, ratifying, or rejecting collective bargaining agreements; to initiate lockouts; and to administer nationally established grievance procedures. In addition, a board of directors of 36 members, four national officers (chairman, vice-chairman, secretary-treasurer, and president), and a nine-man negotiating committee (the president plus two representatives from each of the four conference areas) were elected by the policy committee.

TEI continued to represent the trucking industry in its triennial negotiations from 1964 to 1976. The number of affiliated companies varied over time, numbering approximately 800 to 1,000 and employing about 300,000–500,000 unionized employees. In addition, a large number of smaller non-TEI employer associations became signatories to the same contract, though they did not participate directly in the negotiations.

---

[12] This led to some anomalous situations, particularly where only a few unionized carriers were headquartered in a predominantly nonunion area, as in the South. Under TEI's voting rule, the representation (and corresponding supporting assessments) of these companies were much larger than the size of each would justify.

Despite the changes introduced by TEI, it was not able to overcome the basic weakness inherent in the nature of the trucking industry. While it undoubtedly helped to provide greater continuity and perhaps unity among the larger firms, diversity of interests and slim financial resources continued to result in groups of carriers breaking away from the bargaining team and acceding to the union's demands. Because of these and other internal tensions, TEI was faced with a serious secessionist movement in late 1977, which led to the formation of another employers' association, Carrier Management, Inc. (CMI). In the face of this threat of even greater disunity, however, a reconciliation was effected in May 1978 with the merger of TEI and CMI into a new organization known as Trucking Management, Inc. These matters will be discussed fully in a subsequent section.

Development of Centralized Bargaining

As intercity freight movements grew in importance, the early structure of local autonomy and decentralized bargaining gradually gave way to broader regional contracts and ultimately to national negotiations. While there were a few earlier movements toward multistate bargaining in various regions, the chief architect of the drive toward full centralization and standardization was James R. Hoffa, president of the Teamsters from 1957 to 1967. Prior to his election to the presidency, he had led a successful drive to establish regional bargaining for over-the-road and local employees in the central (12 states) and southern (10 states) areas. He later extended this approach to the West (11 states) in 1958 and 1961, and consolidated several smaller area agreements in the remaining 15 eastern states. This process finally culminated with the signing of the first National Master Freight Agreement (NMFA) with TEI in 1964.

This drive toward centralization and standardization was not made without meeting strong resistance from several powerful local unions whose autonomy and superior benefits were threatened by Hoffa's program. To overcome this resistance, he obtained important changes in the Teamster constitution at the 1961 convention. These changes established the areawide conference as a formal organizational unit with broad powers to negotiate regional collective bargaining contracts. Moreover, the new constitution required all local units to affiliate with the area conference and provided that if a majority of local unions within an area voted to support areawide bargaining, all involved local unions would be required to participate in it and be bound by its terms. Since the constitution also stated that all conference activities were subject to the complete control of the general president, the clear effect of these changes was to force dissenting locals into conference-wide bargaining while centralizing power in Hoffa's hands.[13]

The 1964 NMFA, however, still fell short of Hoffa's ultimate objective of negotiating truly nationwide agreements establishing standardized wages, fringes, and working conditions for each occupational group (road drivers, local drivers, platform men, office employees, etc.). Except for a cost-of-living wage adjustment clause, the NMFA provided national standards only with respect to certain broad *noneconomic* provisions such as union security, grievance procedures, seniority, etc. Major *economic* provisions relating to wages, fringe benefits, and many others continued to be incorporated into a series of regional "supplements," following the same geographical lines previously in effect. Nevertheless, across-the-board *changes* in rates and fringe benefits were centrally negotiated, thereby shifting the effective locus of economic decision-making away from the regional to the national level. With respect to a whole host of other issues (pay practices, working rules, seniority applications, dispatch rules, starting time, etc.), literally hundreds of "local riders" continued to be attached to the various area supplements, thus providing a considerably greater degree of variability in these "noneconomic" dimensions than is suggested by the concept of "centralized bargaining."

Had Hoffa remained in power, there seems little doubt that further, and perhaps complete, standardization would ultimately have been achieved. Only three weeks before the 1967 negotiations were begun, however, he was imprisoned to serve a 13-year sentence for jury-tampering and misuse of union pension funds. Amid considerable confusion, negotiations were taken over by Frank Fitzsimmons, Hoffa's hand-picked successor,[14] who was subsequently elected to the presidency in 1971 and reelected in 1976.

Although the "momentum" of Hoffa's drive resulted in some further consolidation in 1967 and thereafter, Fitzsimmons has not had the desire —and perhaps not the power—to continue to press the issue. Since 1967, therefore, the basic structure of trucking negotiations has remained largely unchanged. Essentially, this has meant a National Master Freight Agreement centrally negotiated by the Teamsters and TEI on various noneconomic terms; centrally negotiated across-the-board wage-fringe

---

[13] For a fuller discussion of these conflicts, see James and James, ch. 13, and Levinson, *Determining Forces*, ch. 5. The latter discussion also emphasizes the conflicting interests of employer groups, with the local cartage companies resisting the encroachment of the growing long-line carriers into their negotiating flexibility.

[14] Recognizing his possible imprisonment, Hoffa had obtained a constitutional change at the 1966 convention which established a new post of general vice-president who was to take over upon the death, resignation, or removal of the general president. His choice was Fitzsimmons, from Hoffa's Detroit Local 299.

increases superimposed on existing regional differentials; several regional over-the-road and local cartage supplements, incorporating a wide range of economic and noneconomic provisions (subject to approval by the central IBT-TEI negotiators); and a number of riders incorporating specific working rules and practices, again subject to the NMFA and central approval.

The specific regional over-the-road and local cartage supplements in effect under the 1976–79 NMFA are listed in Table 4. Clearly, the greatest degree of consolidation is in the central, southern, and western areas, where negotiations are on a conference-wide basis. The role of the Eastern Conference is considerably less, with 21 contracts in 12 geographic areas reflecting more decentralized power and greater diversity of terms.[15]

Special-Commodity Riders

In addition to the "general commodity" supplements listed in Table 4, the parties also negotiate four conference-wide "Iron and Steel and Special Commodity" riders. This concept developed during the late 1950s and early 1960s in the central states, where a large volume of iron and steel products was moving from the Chicago-Gary and Pittsburgh areas within and through the midwest region. This was high-density, low-valued, truckload freight being moved by independent non-union owner-operators under contract-carrier certification and paid on the basis of a percentage of the gross revenues received by the carrier for the goods moved.

In an attempt to gain jurisdictional control over these operations while recognizing that this freight could not continue to move by highway if the union's normal wages and work practices were applied, the union adopted an alternative approach. Essentially, this involved the application of completely different standards to the movement of these specialized types of freight in order to permit unionized carriers of general commodities to compete effectively for them. Moreover, in order to provide the carriers with a backhaul, the list of allowable special commodities was expanded to include similar types of heavy, low-valued items—building materials, paper rolls and cartons, fertilizer, etc.—as well as exempt agricultural products.

---

[15] The only Teamster groups that have remained consistently outside the NMFA are local drivers and other local employees within the jurisdiction of Local Unions 705 and 710 in Chicago. Local 705 is made up entirely of local cartage groups; all line-drivers are in Local 710, plus additional local employees. Only the 710 line-drivers are under a separate NMFA supplement. The reason for this strange arrangement is the presence in Chicago of a strong rival independent union covering about half the local cartage workers in the area; hence the IBT locals wish to maintain full flexibility in their negotiations.

TABLE 4

Over-the-Road and Local Cartage Supplements
Under the 1976–1979 NMFA[a]

Area Covered	Over-the-Road	Local Cartage
Central Conference (12 states)	X	X
Southern Conference (10 states)	X	X
Western Conference (13 states)[b]	X	X
Eastern Conference		
Northern New England (3 states)	X	X
(Southern) New England (3 states)	X	X
Upstate New York	X	X
Local Union 707 (New York City)	X	
New Jersey–New York		X
Motor Transport Labor Relations/		X
Tri-Area Labor Relations[c]		
Central Pennsylvania	X	X
Joint Council 40 (Western PA)	X	X
Maryland-DC	X	X
Virginia	X	X
West Virginia	X	X
Carolina (2 states)	X	X
Local Union 710 (Chicago)	X	
Joint Council 7 (Calif. Bay Area)		X

[a] A few additional NMFA supplements cover office employees and garage employees in the western and southern states and in the states of Michigan, New Jersey, and the Carolinas.

[b] Including Hawaii and Alaska.

[c] Covering Philadelphia and three-county area in eastern Pennsylvania and southern New Jersey.

Although the specific provisions of the four area riders differ somewhat, their major approach is substantially the same. Essentially, each provides the following:

1. Any carrier wishing to operate under the Special Commodity Supplement is required to set up a separate special-commodity division, with terminals, equipment, etc., functioning completely independently of its general-commodities division. Only products specifically listed in the agreement may be handled under special commodities; others may be included only with the specific approval of a joint union-employer committee set up to police these contracts. In some areas, notably the East and South, every request for special-commodity handling requires approval, including designation of every origin-destination point to be served.

2. All freight is moved by owner-operators who are compensated by payment of a specified percentage of gross revenues (approximately 75 percent in 1976) as payment for wages, equipment-leasing, vacations, and holidays. Under a union-shop clause all operators (except those in "right to work" states) are required to become union members. The carrier also

pays the regular welfare and pension contributions plus social security taxes and various other costs. All maintenance and operating costs are paid by the owner-operator.

3. All shipments must be in truckload lots and may move directly from shipper's dock to consignee. This is a major concession on a working rule applicable to most general freight, which must move from terminal to terminal (see the section on Pay Practices and Working Rules, below).

The significance of the extreme precautions noted under item 1 is to prevent the carrier from diverting his regular freight to the special-commodity division. In effect, the union is acting as a discriminating monopolist by maintaining a high price (wage) to those buyers who can afford it (general commodities), while charging a lower price to those who cannot (special commodities), for the same product (transportation service). As in the monopoly case, the success of such a policy requires that the classes of buyers be effectively segmented; hence, the close controls over the commodities and localities involved.

It is precisely for this reason that the entire special-commodity concept has been viewed with much suspicion in many areas and has been adopted less than enthusiastically by many local unions. Although the approach was initiated in the Central Conference in 1961, it was not extended into the other conferences until nearly a decade later. Resistance is still strong from locals in the East and South, who distrust the entire approach and who believe (not without justification) that "cheating" (i.e., the movement of general commodities under the special-commodity provisions) does occur. In the central and western regions, special commodities are more widely accepted, though with an equal awareness of the problems involved.

Despite this reluctance and opposition, there is no doubt that the scope and importance of special-commodity divisions has grown very rapidly in recent years and will continue to do so in the future. The fundamental reason is simple: It represents a most important method by which the Teamsters union can attempt to retain its jurisdictional control over an increasing share of freight which would otherwise be moving under nonunion conditions.

OTHER MAJOR FREIGHT AGREEMENTS

Brief mention should be made of other important agreements covering various types of specialized freight not falling under the NMFA jurisdiction. Structurally similar to the NMFA is the National Master Automotive Transporters Agreement covering approximately 20,000 employees, with Eastern, Central, Southern, and Western Conference supplements. Conference-wide negotiations have also been established in all except the West for more than 50,000 employees of United Parcel Service (UPS), a nationwide common carrier providing door-to-door pickup and delivery of small packages. In each of these cases, wage *adjustments* are considerably influenced by the NMFA pattern; however, wage *levels* are keyed to local standards under several "riders" to the UPS agreements, while geographic differentials also exist under the Automobile National Master. Broadly based agreements are also in effect for tanker (primarily petroleum) products, usually on a statewide or small regional basis. Other types of freight agreements, such as household goods, are still negotiated on a local or companywide basis.

Centralized Bargaining and the Wage Structure

We have noted that the process of centralization and standardization, though already begun in a few areas during the late 1930s and 1940s, was aggressively pressed by Hoffa in the central and southern areas during the 1950s, was gradually extended into the West and East from 1958 to 1964, and reached its peak in the 1964 and 1967 national agreements. Full centralization and standardization was not achieved, however, particularly in the eastern states, and wage differentials have largely been maintained since 1967, though some further steps toward consolidations have been made.

LOCAL CARTAGE

The impact of these developments on the structure of local driver wages is reflected in Tables 5 and 6, covering the years 1950–74.[16] The summary data in Table 6 are particularly revealing. From 1950 to 1958, when Hoffa centered his attention on the central and southern areas, the very low southern rates were raised dramatically by an average of $1.26 per hour (107 percent) and those in the central area by $1.06 (65 percent). These compared to increases of 87 cents (62 percent) in the East and only 65 cents (39 percent) in the West. As a result, the central states replaced the West as the highest union paying region, and the South moved from a level far below both the West and East to a position well above them.[17] Finally, the overall spread of rates among all four regions was greatly reduced from 50 cents (on an average of $1.45) in 1950 to only 32 cents (on an average of $2.41) by 1958. By contrast, the relative position of the West and East improved from 1958 to 1967, as Hoffa

[16] For more details of developments during the earlier half of this period, see James and James, chs. 22 and 23; and Sheifer.

[17] This does not necessarily mean that the *average* southern wage exceeded that in the West and East, since the proportion of local employees under union contracts in the South was less than that in the other regions.

TABLE 5
Local Cartage Wage Rates, 1950–1974[a]

	1950	1958	1967	1974
Central Area				
Detroit	1.63–1.79	2.69–2.75	3.76–3.82	6.90–6.96
Chicago	1.55–1.85	2.36–2.66	3.48–3.78	6.77–6.92
Grand Rapids	1.59	2.60–2.66	3.67–3.73	6.81
Indianapolis	1.48–1.53	2.59–2.64	3.66–3.71	6.80–6.85
Cleveland	1.52–1.60	2.59	3.66	6.80
Columbus	1.48–1.55	2.59	3.66	6.80
Dayton	1.46	2.59	3.66	6.80
Toledo	1.57	2.59	3.66	6.80
Cincinnati	1.47	2.59	3.66	6.80
Milwaukee	1.53	2.58	3.66	6.80
Louisville	1.48	2.51	3.63	6.77
Peoria	1.40	2.44	3.56	6.70
Des Moines	1.38	2.44	3.56	6.81
Kansas City	1.38	2.44	3.56	6.70
Minneapolis	1.39–1.46	2.44	3.60	6.70
Omaha	1.28	2.44	3.56	6.70
St. Louis	1.50–1.60	2.44	3.56	6.70
Median	1.53	2.59	3.66	6.80
Range (MIN-MAX)	1.28–1.85(.57)	2.44–2.75(.31)	3.56–3.82(.26)	6.70–6.96(.26)
Range ÷ Median	37%	12%	7%	4%
Southern Area				
Dallas	1.26	2.44	3.58	6.72
Houston	1.23	2.44	3.58	6.72
San Antonio	1.26	2.44	3.58	6.72
Oklahoma City	1.20	2.44	3.58	6.72
Little Rock	1.14	2.47	3.58	6.72
Atlanta	1.12	2.40	3.56	6.72
Memphis	1.28–1.41	2.45	3.56	6.72
Knoxville	1.15	2.44	3.56	6.72
New Orleans	.84– .89	2.44	3.58	6.69
Jacksonville	.90	2.44	3.56	6.72
Median	1.18	2.44	3.58	6.72
Range (MIN-MAX)	.84–1.41(.57)	2.40–2.47(.07)	3.56–3.58(.02)	6.69–6.72(.03)
Range ÷ Median	48%	3%	0.6%	0.4%
Western Area				
San Fransico Oakland	1.56–2.00	2.28–2.65	3.77–4.02	6.96–7.21
Los Angeles	1.38–1.53	2.29–2.44	3.72–3.84	6.86–6.98
Seattle	1.55–1.80	2.35–2.44	3.62	6.76
Portland	1.53	2.30	3.55	6.76
Spokane	1.55–1.80	2.25	3.55	6.76
Denver	1.20	2.35	3.55	6.69–6.74
Salt Lake City	1.22–1.32	1.84–1.89	3.55–3.60	6.69–6.74
Median	1.68	2.33	3.58	6.76
Range (MIM-MAX)	1.20–2.00(.80)	1.84–2.65(.81)	3.55–4.02(.47)	6.69–7.21(.52)
Range ÷ Median	48%	35%	13%	8%

Table 5 (continued)

	1950	1958	1967	1974
Eastern Area				
Boston	1.41–1.51	2.27	3.56	6.56
Providence	1.35	2.27	3.56	6.56
New Haven	1.35	2.27	3.56	6.56
New York	1.65–1.86	2.19–2.37	3.37–3.47	6.62–6.72
Newark	1.71–1.85	2.36–2.52	3.37–3.47	6.62–6.72
Rochester	1.40–1.45	2.25–2.27	3.48	6.69
Buffalo	1.41–1.45	2.31	3.59	6.73
Philadelphia	1.50	2.35	3.66	6.67
Scranton	1.37	2.17	3.57	6.71
Pittsburgh	1.58–1.63	2.35–2.45	3.57	6.71
Erie	1.40	2.41	3.57	6.71
Baltimore	1.35	2.25	3.50	6.70
Washington, DC	1.32	2.17	3.50	6.70
Richmond	1.10	2.08	3.56	6.70
Charlotte	.96	2.08	3.56	6.70
Median	1.40	2.27	3.56	6.70
Range (MIN-MAX)	.96–1.86(.90)	2.08–2.52(.44)	3.37–3.66(.29)	6.56–6.73(.17)
Range ÷ Median	64%	19%	8%	3%

Sources: U.S. Department of Labor, Bureau of Labor Statistics, *Union Wages and Hours: Motortruck Drivers and Helpers,* Bulletins 1012 (1950), 1246 (1958), 1591 (1967), 1917 (1974).

ᵃ All rates are as of July 1; in a few instances, the timing of wage increases may distort the usual structural relationships.

TABLE 6

Dispersion of Local Cartage Rates, by Region

Region	Median Wage Rate				Index (Average = 100)			
	1950	1958	1967	1974	1950	1958	1967	1974
Central	$1.53	$2.59	$3.66	$6.80	106	107	102	101
Southern	1.18	2.44	3.58	6.72	81	101	99	100
Western	1.68	2.33	3.58	6.76	116	97	99	100
Eastern	1.40	2.27	3.56	6.70	97	94	99	99
Average	1.45	2.41	3.60	6.75	100	100	100	100
Spread	.50	.32	.10	.10				
% spread	34%	13%	3%	1%				

extended his influence into these areas. The overall result was the achievement of near uniformity among all areas by 1967, a situation which has continued to 1974 (the last date for which data are available).

A somewhat different and more detailed perspective of the developing local wage structure can be seen in Table 5, which reflects the progressive narrowing of differentials *within* each of the conference areas.

From 1950 to 1967, the range of rates fell sharply in all regions, from spreads of 60 to 90 cents in 1950 to virtual uniformity in the South and spreads of 25 to 50 cents elsewhere (on much higher wage levels). Even these latter figures tend to overstate the degree of diversity within regions, since they are greatly affected by high rates in a few key cities, particularly Detroit and San Francisco-Oakland. After 1967, however, differentials held approximately constant except in the East, where some further narrowing continued to 1974.

OVER-THE-ROAD

The effect of centralized bargaining on the structure of long-line driver wages is more difficult to evaluate because methods of payment are much more complex and in some cases have changed over time. There are three basic methods of payment—hourly rates, mileage rates, or trip rates (fixed sum per trip)—which are combined in a variety of ways.[18]

The prevailing system in the Central and Southern Conferences has for many years been based on a combination of mileage and hourly rates. The mileage rate is paid for all miles driven, but with a minimum guarantee of eight hours pay at the hourly rate, if greater. In addition, all time spent in nondriving activities—loading, unloading, road delays, etc.—are paid at the hourly rate. The applicable mileage rate varies with type of equipment: the larger or heavier the equipment, the higher the rate. The western area has a similar system, with two differences: mileage rates are the same for all types of single-man equipment, but a premium of one-half cent is paid for miles driven in excess of 250 on a single run.

Methods of payment in the several eastern agreements have changed considerably as a result of pressures from Hoffa during the 1958–67 period to conform to the Central Conference approach. Prior to that time, the prevailing system had been the trip rate, under which specific amounts were paid for specific runs. Although the methods of determining trip rates had usually originated from some reasonable formula relating distance to hours, improvements in highways and equipment had made many rates obsolete and created large differences in driver earnings, depending on the particular trips involved. These contracts also included a base hourly rate to cover unspecified runs or other contingencies.

Under these circumstances, a change from trip rates to the Central Conference miles-and-hours formula would result in a considerable drop in earnings of some drivers. The approach pressed by Hoffa was to

[18] For a full description of these methods, see Seidenberg.

freeze existing trip rates until the continually rising mileage-hourly rates would yield equivalent earnings. At that point, the trip rates were discontinued and the miles-hours formula took over.

These complexities must be kept in mind in discussing the data in Tables 7 and 8, which provide an overview of the movement of basic hourly and mileage rates in line-driver contracts from 1959 to 1977. They also indicate the gradual consolidation of Eastern Conference agreements from 21 separate areas in 1959 to 12 in 1972–77.[19]

TABLE 7

Over-the-Road Hourly Rates, 1959–1977

Area	Sept. 1959	Feb. 1966	Sept. 1972	April 1977
Central Conference	$2.50	$3.25	$5.68	$8.44
Southern Conference	2.50	3.25	5.68	8.44
Western Conference	2.57	3.25	5.68	8.44
Eastern Conference				
Carolinas	2.50	3.25	5.68	8.44
Virginia	2.50	3.25	5.68	8.44
West Virginia	2.53	3.25⎱	5.68	8.44
Bedford, Pa.	2.50	3.25⎰		
Western Pa.				
(Pittsburgh)	2.57⎱	3.32	5.75	8.51
Western Pa. (JC 40)	2.57⎰			
Central Pennsylvania	2.46⎱			
Northeastern		3.32	5.75	8.51
Pennsylvania	2.17⎰			
Motor Trans. Lab.				
Rel.; Tri-Area	NA⎱	3.41	5.81	No Contract[a]
South Jersey	2.55⎰			
Hagerstown, Md.	2.44⎱			
Cumberland, Md.	2.33⎰	3.28⎱		
Washington, D.C.	2.59⎱	3.28⎰	5.71	8.47
Baltimore	2.65⎰			
Mid-Jersey	2.65	3.45	Based on Destination[b]	
New York City	2.52	NA	5.60	8.36
Upstate New York	2.37	3.34	5.77	8.53
New England				
(Southern)	2.34	3.31	5.65	8.41
Maine	2.07–2.17	3.11⎱		
New Hampshire	2.24	3.25⎬	5.51–5.68	8.44
Vermont	2.19	3.25⎰		
Range (MIN–MAX)	$2.07–2.65 (.58)	$3.11–3.41 (.30)	$5.51–5.81 (.30)	$8.36–8.53 (.17)

Source: Survey reports by Research Department, Eastern Conference of Teamsters.

  [a] Because of high hourly and trip rates, very few line drivers are domiciled in area, hence no road contract in effect.

  [b] Contract provides that applicable rate will depend on driver destination.

[19] The data are from a series of reports on local cartage and over-the-road contract terms prepared by the Research Department of the Eastern Conference of Teamsters. They were initiated in 1959 to provide background for Hoffa's drive for greater standardization.

TABLE 8

Over-the-Road Mileage Rates (5-Axle Units)[a]

Area	Sept. 1959	Feb. 1966	Sept. 1972	April 1977
Central Conference	9.075¢	11.125¢	15.45¢	20.85¢
Southern Conference	9.075–9.20	11.125	15.45	20.85
Western Conference[b]	8.375–8.875	10.725–11.225	15.05–15.55	20.45–20.95
Eastern Conference				
Carolinas	8.95	11.125	15.45	20.85
Virginia	8.95	11.125	15.45	20.85
West Virginia	9.025	11.125⎫		
Bedford, Pa.	9.20	11.125⎬	15.45	20.85
Western Pa. (Pittsburgh)	Trip⎧			
Western Pa. (JC 40)	Trip⎨	11.050[e]	15.45[e]	20.85
Central Pennsylvania	Trip⎬			
Northeastern Pennsylvania	Trip⎭	11.500[e]	15.825[e]	21.225
Motor Transp. Labor Rel.; Tri-Area	Trip⎧			
South Jersey	Trip⎨	Trip	Trip	No Contract[d]
Hagerstown, Md.	Trip⎬			
Cumberland, Md.	Trip⎨	11.075[e]⎫		
Washington, D.C.	Trip⎧	⎬	15.40[e]	20.80
Baltimore, Md.	Trip⎭	11.075[e]⎭		
Mid-Jersey	10.25		Based on Destination[e]	
New York City	9.075	NA	15.00	20.40
Upstate New York	Trip	Trip	15.975[e]	21.375
New England	Trip	11.00[e]	15.375[e]	20.775
Maine	Trip	Trip		
New Hampshire	Trip	11.00[e]⎫	15.45[e]	20.85
Vermont	Trip	11.00[e]⎭		
Range (MIN-MAX)	8.375–9.20 (0.825)	10.725–11.50 (0.775)	15.05–15.975 (0.925)	20.45–21.375 (0.975)

Source: Survey reports by Research Department, Eastern Conference of Teamsters.

[a] To provide comparability, mileage rates apply to 5-axle trucks in all areas. In some areas, this rate also applies to other trucks; in other areas, different rates apply to other trucks.

[b] Lower rate applies to miles up to 250; higher rate applies to miles over 250.

[e] Applicable where total mileage earnings exceed trip-rate earnings.

[d] Because of high hourly and trip rates, very few line drivers are domiciled in area, hence no road contract in effect. Applicable rates are set by riders.

[e] Contract provides that applicable rate will depend on driver destination.

Both tables show a clear trend toward a narrowing of differentials, particularly from 1959 to 1966. In terms of hourly rates, the minimum-maximum range fell from 58 to 30 cents during this period, and to only 17 cents by 1977 despite rising absolute wage levels. The primary reason for this was the sharp realignment of northern New England rates in the 1964 negotiations, bringing them up to the Central Conference standard.

The basic trend in mileage rate differentials is substantially similar, though the shift from trip to mileage rates makes a consistent comparison difficult. The apparent widening of absolute differentials after 1966 is solely the result of newly converting areas (specifically the high rate introduced into Upstate New York). If the sample of areas is held constant throughout (i.e., the converting areas are excluded), the range declines from 0.825 cents in 1959 to a constant 0.5 cents from 1966 to 1977 (explained entirely by the system of payment in the Western Conference).

A longer period perspective of the evolving wage structure can be developed from regional data published by the Interstate Commerce Commission on total compensation and total hours paid for of line-haul drivers of Class I intercity common carriers of general freight. The resulting estimates of average hourly earnings of line drivers are shown in Table 9.[20]

TABLE 9

Average Hourly Earnings of Line-Haul Drivers, Class I
Intercity Common Carriers of General Freight

Region[a]	1950	1958	1967	1970	1973
Central	$1.75	2.79	4.91	4.88	6.46
Southern	1.54	2.92	4.02	4.91	6.60
Western	1.93	2.86	4.58	5.55	6.60
Eastern	1.59	2.53	3.80	4.77	6.71
Average	1.69	2.75	4.07	4.97	6.58
Indexes (Average=100)					
Central	104	101	99	98	98
Southern	91	106	99	99	100
Western	104	104	113	112	100
Eastern	94	92	93	96	102
Average	100	100	100	100	100
Range	23	14	20	16	4

Source: Interstate Commerce Commission, Bureau of Accounts, *Transport Statistics in the United States* (annual).

[a] The regional breakdowns used by the ICC are matched exactly to the conference regions with one exception: North and South Carolina are included in the ICC Southern Region (above), but are within the Teamster Eastern Conference.

As in the case with respect to local cartage rates, the most striking change during the 1950–58 period was the effect of Hoffa's extension of central states' wages into the South. The result was to bring southern line-driver earnings up dramatically from the lowest regional group in 1950 to the highest in 1958, reflecting the combined effects of higher

[20] These figures will be affected, of course, by many factors other than negotiated wage changes: hours paid at overtime rates, differences in highway and weather conditions, distances between major metropolitan areas, and traffic density are among the most important.

wages and favorable driving conditions. By contrast, the West suffered a sharp decline in its relative position, while the central and eastern regions declined by less; the *level* of eastern earnings, however, was considerably below the central level.

The extension of Hoffa's influence into the West and East after 1958 and the establishment of central negotiations after 1964 appears to have had somewhat disparate effects. In the West, earnings rebounded sharply in 1967 and 1970 to their previously high level, reflecting the favorable driving conditions in that area once their rates were again adjusted upward. In the East, however, earnings increased more slowly from 1958 to 1970, perhaps reflecting the depressing effects of the freeze on trip rates until the rising mileage-hourly rates became effective. Finally, the nearly complete equalization of earnings shown for 1973 is striking, though very difficult to explain in terms of bargaining developments. The improving position of eastern drivers may well have been a continuation of trends toward equalization developing earlier. However, the reason for the sudden decline in western driver earnings is not evident. Whatever the causes, line-driver hourly earnings in 1973 were closer to equality in all four regions than at any previous point.

Fringe Benefits

The degree of standardization of major fringe benefits has been even greater than that of wages; moreover, the same benefits apply to both local cartage and over-the-road employees. As of 1977, the fringe benefits provided in the several area contracts listed in Tables 7 and 8 were as follows:

Vacations: 1 week after 1 year, 2/2, 3/10, 4/15, 5/20; all agreements.

Holidays:
   Nine: Central, Southern, Eastern Pennsylvania, Carolinas, Virginia, West Virginia, Local 710 (Chicago)
   Ten: Maryland-D.C., JC 40 (Western Pennsylvania), Upstate New York
   Eleven: Western and Central Pennsylvania, New England, North New England
Thirteen: New York City
Sick Leave: 3 days; all agreements except JC 7 (9 days).
Health and Welfare/Pensions (employer payments):[21]
$50.78/wk: Western
54.68/wk: JC 40

---

[21] Although total weekly payments are nearly identical, contracts vary with respect to the standards of payment. Some require payment only on an hours-paid-for basis; others require a full weekly payment if more than some specified minimum number of hours are worked.

$55.50/wk: Central, Southern, Carolinas, Virginia, West Virginia, Local 710
55.60/wk: Maryland-D.C., Central Pennsylvania, Upstate New York
56.70/wk: New England, North New England, Eastern Pennsylvania
68.00/wk: New York City

The high degree of standardization is evident. Only New York City stands clearly above the rest, while the Western Conference welfare/pension contributions are somewhat below the general average.

The Relative Movement of Wage-Fringe Benefits

WAGES

The basic economic, political, and power factors impinging on the bargaining relationship in trucking—a rapidly expanding demand, Hoffa's drive for dominance, a powerful union facing weak and divided employers—would indicate that the industry's employees have enjoyed relatively favorable increases in wages and fringe benefits. The wage data in Table 10, comparing the trend of hourly earnings of unionized drivers in regulated trucking with those of production workers in several other quite strongly unionized industries, confirm this expectation. For the entire period 1950–73, local and line drivers obtained increases in hourly earnings of 300 percent as compared to increases of only 200 to 250 percent for employees in construction, coal, railroads, motor vehicles, and basic steel. It should be noted that this advantage was most marked during the early years from 1950 to 1964, the period of Hoffa's rise to power, the huge increases negotiated in the South from 1950 to 1958, and the extension of his influence into the West and East from 1958 to 1964. From 1964 to 1970, however, trucking earnings simply kept pace with other sectors, reflecting Hoffa's primary preoccupation with his legal problems, his dominant interest in achieving the framework of a true national agreement in 1964, and his sudden departure and the subsequent confusion just prior to the 1967 negotiations.

The contract periods 1970–73 and 1973–76 also present contrasting trends. The 1970–73 contract incorporated extraordinarily large wage increases as a result of a refusal by the strong local cartage unions in Chicago (who had never been under the NMFA) to accept the $1.10 negotiated by the national union with TEI. After a 13-week strike centered in Chicago, the local unions obtained a total increase of $1.65. To save face, the national union promptly raised this to $1.85, which was quickly agreed to by TEI. With respect to this outcome, it should be

TABLE 10

Average Hourly Earnings in Regulated Trucking and
Selected Industries, 1950–1976

Year	Base Hourly Rates[a] (1)	Line Drivers[b] (2)	P + D Drivers[b] (3)	Contract Constr. (4)	Bitum. Coal (5)	Rail- roads (6)	Motor Veh. & Equip. (7)	Basic Steel (8)
			Average Hourly Earnings					
1950	$1.55	$1.69	$1.50	$1.86	$1.94	$1.57	$1.78	$1.70
1955	2.07	2.31	2.09	2.45	2.47	1.96	2.29	2.39
1958	2.46	2.75	2.54	2.82	2.93	2.44	2.55	2.88
1961	2.73	3.12	2.87	3.20	3.14	2.67	2.86	3.16
1964	3.07	3.56	3.33	3.55	3.30	2.80	3.21	3.36
1967	3.50	4.07	3.73	4.11	3.75	3.24	3.55	3.57
1970	4.22	4.97	4.55	5.24	4.58	3.89	4.22	4.16
1973	6.23	6.58	6.44	6.37	5.75	5.40	5.46	5.45
1976	7.70	NA	NA	7.68	7.91	6.88	7.10	7.68
			Changes					
1950–64	98%	111%	122%	91%	70%	78%	80%	98%
1964–70	37	40	37	48	39	39	31	24
1970–73	48	32	42	22	26	39	29	31
1973–76	24	NA	NA	21	38	27	30	41
1950–73	302	289	329	242	196	244	207	221
1950–76	397	NA	NA	313	308	338	299	352

Source: Col. 1, Central Conference contracts, as of new contract dates (1950 rate, eff. 11/49); cols. 2 and 3, Interstate Commerce Commission, Bureau of Accounts, *Transport Statistics in the United States;* cols. 4–8, U.S. Bureau of Labor Statistics, Bulletin 1312-10, *Employment and Earnings in the United States.*

[a] Over-the-road drivers, central states area.

[b] Class I common carriers of general freight.

noted that local drivers gained considerably more than line drivers during the subsequent three years, reflecting the local cartage focus of the Chicago "revolt."

Finally, the 1973–76 contract was again more moderate, reflecting the political pressures on Fitzsimmons to support the Nixon Administration's wage-restraint program.[22] During those years, other sectors regained some ground. For the 1950–76 period as a whole, however, it is clear that the Teamsters have enjoyed superior wage gains.

FRINGE BENEFITS

The picture with respect to employer costs of privately financed fringe benefits is less clear, since comparative data are sparse. Table 11 shows the comparative employer costs of private welfare and pension programs as a percent of average hourly earnings for common-carrier trucking, primary metals, transportation equipment, and all manufacturing. In general, the data show a late start for Hoffa in negotiating a

---

[22] Fitzsimmons had supported Nixon in the 1972 election and was the sole labor representative on the Pay Board after four others had resigned.

TABLE 11

Employer Contributions to Private Welfare and
Pension Programs, 1951–1975

Year	All Manufacturing		Primary Metals		Transport Equipment		Central Conf.	
	¢	%	¢	%	¢	%	¢	%ᵃ
1951	6.7¢	3.8%	8.2¢	4.7%	5.7¢	3.1%	2.5¢	1.5%
1955	9.7	4.8	10.9	5.1	10.0	4.6	10.5	4.8
1961	16.2	6.4	22.0	8.1	16.4	5.9	20.0	6.7
1967	20.5	6.7	30.5	9.3	22.3	6.8	43.8	11.2
1973	44.3	9.6	59.2	12.3	52.9	11.0	83.8	12.9
1975	58.5	11.0	87.7	15.3	74.0	13.1	108.8	14.8

Sources: U.S. Chamber of Commerce, *Fringe Benefits* (biennial); Central contracts.

ᵃ Percentage computed on base of average hourly earnings of line and road drivers of Class I common carriers of general freight. See Table 10 for original data.

pension plan, which was not initiated in the Central Conference until 1955. Since that time, Central Conference employer contributions have increased approximately in step with metals and transport equipment, though more rapidly than in all manufacturing; each of these groups is too broad to provide reliable comparisons, however.

The trend of paid vacations and paid holidays in the central states has also tended to parallel those in most other industries. Hoffa negotiated six holidays in 1952, again somewhat behind the pace in metals and motor vehicles. These remained constant for 15 years until 1967, then increased gradually to nine in 1976 (plus three days of paid sick-leave in 1977). His vacation plan of 1 week after 1 year, 2 weeks after 5 years, which was relatively liberal in 1949, has developed slowly since then as follows: 1952—1 week after 1 year, 2 weeks after 3; 1955—1 week after 1 year, 2 weeks after 3, 3 weeks after 12; 1958—1 week after 1 year, 2 weeks after 3, 3 weeks after 12, 4 weeks after 20; 1961—1 week after 1 year, 2 weeks after 3, 3 weeks after 11, 4 weeks after 18; 1964—1 week after 1 year, 2 weeks after 3, 3 weeks after 11, 4 weeks after 16; 1967—1 week after 1 year, 2 weeks after 3, 3 weeks after 10, 4 weeks after 15; 1973—1 week after 1 year, 2 weeks after 2, 3 weeks after 10, 4 weeks after 15, 5 weeks after 20. Since 1955, vacation changes have been minor and now generally match, but do not exceed, the practices in other unionized industries.

In all, therefore, the Teamsters have obtained greater wage increases than other major unions. Their fringe benefits, however, have largely kept up with, but not exceeded, those of most unionized sectors.

Owner-Operators

Note has already been made of the estimated 100,000 owner-operators who own and operate their own trucks without possessing ICC operating authority. Under these circumstances, owner-operators are legally able to handle freight either (1) in exempt agricultural commodities, or (2) under a leasing agreement to a certified common carrier or contract carrier. Two legal leasing arrangements are available: a "permanent" lease (cancellable on 30-day notice) or a "trip lease" (one trip) basis. However, a trip lease is permissible only on a back haul— that is, the first leg of each trip must be done under a permanent lease or on an exempt commodity. The problems of policing such fine distinctions to prevent illegal movements are obvious. Moreover, an unknown (but substantial) amount of freight is illegally handled by individual owner-operators moving goods for private nontrucking firms on some type of fee-for-service basis.

For collective bargaining purposes, the legal status of the owner-operator is crucial in determining whether or not the provisions of the National Labor Relations Act apply. To the extent that owner-operators are considered to be "employees," they are able to organize and negotiate collectively. On the other hand, if they are considered to be independent entrepreneurs, such activity would violate the antitrust laws. The courts have held that each situation will depend on its own circumstances, with the most crucial factor being the extent to which the carrier exerts a "degree of control" over the individual owner's activity.[23] The terms of Teamster agreements clearly set forth the necessary conditions for such control so that an employer-employee relationship is thereby established. However, Teamster efforts to organize owner-operators of nonunion carriers have often been delayed or prevented if an employee status is not clearly shown.

Owner-operators are employed by unionized carriers in both their general-commodities and special-commodities divisions. The former operate under the NMFA and its road supplements, while the latter operate under the four conference-wide special-commodity riders. The terms of employment vary greatly between the two divisions, however. Under the NMFA and road supplements, the status of owner-operators is substantially the same as any other employee-driver. He is paid the established hourly or mileage rate, receives the same fringe benefits, and operates under the same pay practices, working rules, seniority standards, and other contract provisions. The only difference arises from the payment of an additional fee for the leasing of equipment. In order to prevent this arrangement from undermining the regular wage level, the contract specifies that separate checks must be issued for wages and equipment rental; responsibility for the payment of various other costs (maintenance and repair, license fees, highway tolls, etc.) is clearly de-

---

[23] See Wyckoff and Maister, ch. 6.

lineated; etc. The advantage of this system to the carriers is the availability of additional equipment with little or no investment or risk. On the other hand, it limits the carrier's control over the flexible use of equipment, since each driver insists upon using his own.

By contrast, the method of payment in the special-commodity divisions is based on a percentage of the revenue received by the carrier for the freight being moved; in addition, certain important working rules are eliminated or modified.[24] The purpose, of course, is to permit the unionized carriers to compete for truckload lots of high-volume, low-valued commodities which could not be profitably handled under general-commodity standards.

Clearly, the presence of such a large number of owner-operators poses a strong threat to the maintenance of union standards. In part, of course, this arises from the fact that nonunion common and contract carriers are free to compensate owner-operators at less than union scale, whether on an hourly or on a percentage-of-revenue basis. Equally important, however, is the relative ease with which such nonunion carriers can expand their operations, since a large portion of the capital investment and risk is undertaken by the individual operators.[25] Finally, of course, the illegal movement of freight also undermines both union wage standards and employment opportunities. Little wonder, therefore, that considerable antagonism exists between the union and the owner-operator, even when the latter is a (often reluctant) dues-paying member.

Pay Practices and Working Rules

As in most strongly unionized industries, particularly those with a history of local autonomy, trucking contracts contain a variety of working rules and pay practices that can be of considerable importance in affecting operating costs or productivity in the industry. Practices that are widely applied are incorporated into regional supplements; those of narrower application are in numerous riders. The following aspects of pay and rules deserve particular note.

HOURS OF WORK AND OVERTIME PAY

The provisions of the Fair Labor Standards Act (FLSA), requiring the payment of overtime for hours worked over 40 per week, does not apply to the great majority of trucking employees. Historically, this is explained by the fact that the industry was under ICC regulation at

[24] See the section on "Development of Centralized Bargaining," above.

[25] In fact, as Wyckoff and Maister point out, the average owner-operator could earn considerably more as a regular union road driver. He continues as an owner-operator in part because he gains utility from being "his own boss" and in part because he tends to underestimate his true costs of doing business. See especially ch. 10.

the time the FLSA was adopted. Since the ICC was responsible for insuring proper safety standards, including the maximum number of hours a driver was allowed to work and/or drive, Congress exempted trucking from FLSA standards.

In practice, government regulations at the present time prohibit a road driver from driving more than 10 hours per day or more than six days in every seven. No overtime premium is required, nor are they provided in collective bargaining contracts. As a result, many road drivers work 60 hours per week with no overtime pay; their annual earnings, of course, reflect these long hours.

The pay standards of local drivers and other local employees are markedly different. Although the FLSA does not apply, all negotiated contracts establish a standard 40-hour week, with time and one-half for hours worked over 8 per day and 40 per week.[26] Thus, although road drivers typically earn approximately $3,000 more per year than local drivers, the difference is based primarily on hours worked rather than on hourly rates. Table 12 provides some interesting data relevant to these differences. In 1970 and 1973, for example, hourly earnings of road drivers were only 9 and 2 percent, respectively, above those of local drivers, whereas hours worked were 17 and 19 percent greater for

TABLE 12

Average Annual Earnings, Average Hourly Earnings, and Average
Hours Worked Per Year, Over-the-Road and Local Drivers[a]

	Road Drivers			Local Drivers		
Year	Annual Earnings	Hourly Earnings	Hours Worked	Annual Earnings	Hourly Earnings	Hours Worked
1950	$ 4,410	$1.69	2609	$ 3,650	$1.50	2431
1955	6,029	2.31	2610	4,884	2.09	2335
1958	7,288	2.75	2650	5,688	2.54	2338
1961	8,323	3.12	2668	6,497	2.87	2260
1964	9,597	3.56	2696	7,580	3.33	2276
1967	10,610	4.07	2606	8,444	3.73	2266
1970	12,686	4.97	2555	9,923	4.55	2183
1973	17,249	6.58	2623	14,208	6.44	2205

Source: Interstate Commerce Commission, Bureau of Accounts, Transport Statistics in the United States.

[a] Data are for Class I common carriers of general freight. Figures may not be exact because of rounding in original data.

road drivers. The data are also of interest in evaluating the widely held view that over-the-road drivers have extraordinarily high earnings. While this is true for a small proportion, their overall average is not

[26] Some contracts, including the western states and several in the East, require premium pay for Saturday and Sunday as such. This is a costly rule for the large long-line carriers who must operate on regular six- and seven-day operations.

excessively high; more importantly, their total workyear is considerably higher than that of the great majority of industrial workers.

TERMINAL-TO-TERMINAL ROAD RUNS

This is the most widely applicable and probably the most costly work rule involving freight-moving operations. All over-the-road contracts covering the movement of general commodities[27] by common carriers provide that a road driver has jurisdiction only over the movement of freight from terminal to terminal; all other movement must be done by local drivers. With few exceptions,[28] this means that it is not possible for a road driver to make a single direct movement of a full truckload of freight from the shipper's dock to the receiver's dock. Rather, it is first necessary to dispatch a local driver to pick up the loaded trailer at the shipper's dock, and drive it to the carrier's terminal where a road driver takes it over the highway to the carrier's receiving terminal; at that point, a local driver delivers the trailer to the receiver's dock. This sequence usually involves unnecessary pickup and delivery labor as well as extra terminal delays and terminal labor.

FIXED STARTING TIMES

This rule is found in only a few large cities, most notably in the California Bay Area, the New York Metropolitan Area, Chicago, and St. Louis. Nevertheless, it is very costly to carriers—particularly short-haul carriers—operating in those cities and has been a major source of continuing friction in the West. As applied under Joint Council 7 (the Bay Area), the contract specifies a fixed workday shift from 8 a.m. to 5 p.m.; all other hours must be paid at overtime rates.

This rule is very costly in large city pickup and delivery because operations must normally begin at a very early hour to provide desired service schedules to local businesses, and because some "staggering" of loading and dispatching is required to accommodate a large fleet of trucks to fixed terminal facilities. Most of these problems are present in reverse at the end of the day. The result is a large volume of overtime payments which must be incurred to maintain efficient operations and provide adequate service. Where such rules are not in effect, of course, staggered 8-hour shifts permit flexibility with far less overtime.

---

[27] As noted in the section on "Development of Centralized Bargaining" above, this rule is not applied to freight moving under the special-commodities provisions. This is an important cost-saving concession to the carriers, resulting in a loss of employment to local drivers, who are thereby most resistive to the expansion of special-commodity coverage.

[28] An exception to this rule is permitted in some contracts if the pickup and/or delivery is *en route* between the two terminals. The issue of defining *en route* has been the subject of continuing grievance procedures. The rule also does not apply to contract carriers since they do not require or maintain central terminals.

Multiple-Run Payments

An issue confined largely to the central states involves "multiple-run" payments. As highways and equipment have improved, it has become increasingly feasible for drivers to complete more than one "tour of duty" within the maximum allowable 10 hours of driving time. This has been particularly true of "peddle" runs (pickup and delivery of freight within some specified distance from a home terminal) and "turnaround" runs (an over-the-road movement in which the driver moves an outbound trailer from A to B, exchanges it for an inbound trailer at B and returns to A). Since an hourly guarantee has normally applied to each of these runs (based on earlier standards of available equipment, highways, etc.), the union has pressed for a multiple guarantee when two or more runs can now be completed within one day. Accommodation has usually been reached by providing for the basic guarantee on the first run plus a smaller guarantee for subsequent runs or compensation on subsequent runs on a straight mileage and lower hourly rate basis.[29]

The Piggyback Overflow Rule

A widely cited rule, originally negotiated in 1961 and still in effect, is the so-called "overflow rule" relating to the use of trailer-on-flatcar (TOFC) or piggyback service. Article 29 of the 1976–79 NMFA provides that

> An employer shall not use piggyback . . . over the same route where he has established relay runs or through runs except to move overflow freight. If a driver is available . . . at point of origin when a trailer leaves the yard for the piggyback . . . such driver's runaround compensation shall start from the time the trailer leaves the yard. Available regular drivers at relay points shall be protected against runarounds if a violation occurred at point of origin.

Essentially, this clause permits a signatory employer to use TOFC only if a regular driver is not available to move the freight over the highway. If a driver is available when TOFC is used, he (as well as other drivers at subsequent relay points) must be compensated in any case.

A full analysis of the significance of this clause goes much beyond the scope of the present survey.[30] However, three important points should be stressed.

---

[29] There are many variants on the problem and on the compensation methods used to deal with it. For a more detailed discussion, see Seidenberg, pp. 61–63.

[30] A complete analysis may be found in Ainsworth, Keale, Liba, and Levinson, pp. 184–210. See also Levinson et al., chs. 4 and 5.

1. While this provision is an appropriate "work preservation" clause designed to prevent carriers *signatory to the NMFA* from substituting piggyback for regular established highway runs, it does *not* apply to TOFC service offered directly to shippers by railroads, where either the railroad or the shipper provides the necessary equipment and ancillary pickup and delivery service. Thus, if a shipper prefers to consign his freight to a railroad for a TOFC movement, this clause does not prevent him from doing so.

2. Should the Teamsters try to prevent the movement of TOFC freight by interfering in some way with the methods noted in point 1, such interference would almost surely (under current legal standards) be held to be in violation of the secondary-boycott provisions of the Taft-Hartley Act.

3. Insofar as the growth of TOFC over the past decade has been much below what its proponents have anticipated, the causes do not lie with any restrictive policies of the Teamsters union.[31] By the same token, should the relative efficiency and costs of TOFC improve in the future, the Teamsters cannot prevent such a shift in modal preference from being put into effect.

Seniority, Grievance Procedure, and Change of Operations

SENIORITY

The basic contract provisions regarding seniority are set forth in the NMFA and its supplements, though considerable deviations arise from the application of local riders to particular companies or local unions. The general standard for accumulating and exercising seniority is length of service at a particular terminal and within terminals by two occupational groups—namely, line drivers and city employees (local drivers, dockmen, etc.). Separate seniority boards are maintained for these job classifications and are used as the basis for determining the order of layoffs and recalls, in bidding for new runs and available job vacancies, in selection of preferred shifts and starting times, etc. No bumping normally occurs between seniority boards, nor has either group normally been eligible to exercise accumulated seniority in bidding for runs or vacancies in the other's jurisdiction.[32] In all conference areas except the

---

[31] Another contract provision still often cited in the literature refers to the fee of $5.00 per trailer or container moved by carriers by TOFC. Yet this provision, originally negotiated in 1961, was never seriously enforced and has been eliminated from the NMFA since 1973. See Levinson et al., pp. 66–69.

[32] Since adoption of the Civil Rights Act of 1964 and subsequent government pressures, some modification of these limitations has been introduced in various areas. See the section on "Current Developments," below.

South, there is no bumping across terminals as well. Under the Southern Road Agreement, however, laid-off line drivers can elect to bump lower seniority drivers at another southern terminal of the same company.

GRIEVANCE PROCEDURES

The formal structure of grievance procedure follows that of most multiemployer bargaining setups. Grievances are first dealt with at the company level. If not settled, they are appealed to a Joint State Committee,[33] then to a Joint Area (Conference) Committee, and finally to a National Grievance Committee set up under the NMFA. Committees at each level are made up of an equal number of union and employer representatives, with a majority vote deciding the issue. Matters involving interpretation of the NMFA itself must go to the National Committee for final adjudication.

Beyond this formal structure, however, are major differences between trucking grievance procedures and those in the great majority of other industries. Most striking is the absence of compulsory arbitration as a final step for settling deadlocked issues (except in discharge cases where local option is permitted and where some contracts so provide). Instead, either party is permitted to use "all lawful economic recourse to support its position," once all prior steps have been completed. Since the power relationships in the industry greatly favor the union, this "open end" procedure can provide a de facto mechanism under which the union's position on a disputed issue will prevail and can thus achieve favorable contract improvements through grievance procedures rather than negotiations.

The open-end procedure was originally introduced by Hoffa in the central and southern states and subsequently vigorously pressed by him into the West and East where arbitration had previously been commonly used. During these years, it was generally believed that Hoffa used the procedure not only to obtain favorable interpretations of contract language, but also to hold out the promise (threat) of favorable (unfavorable) treatment of grievances of individual carriers in response to their support (opposition) of his collective bargaining or other internal union objectives.[34]

A further dimension of these procedures at all committee levels, also traceable back to Hoffa's influence, is its lack of any formal explanation of the rationale behind any particular decision and hence the absence of any body of "common law" precedents to be developed and

---

[33] The Central Conference supplements permit optional local Road and local Cartage Committees to intervene between the company and state levels.

[34] James and James, ch. 11.

applied to subsequent grievances.[35] This "informality" is supported as providing a high degree of flexibility to the parties to consider each case on its particular merits and avoiding excessive "legalisms." It also lends itself, however, to favoritism among companies and among local unions (by employer as well as union representatives), as well as to getting rid of "troublemakers" and other such objectives. In the past, Hoffa's use of these "off the record" proceedings to gain such economic and political objectives was commonly recognized.

Despite these seeming drawbacks to the open-end procedures, there was general agreement among employers (as well as union representatives) that they were working reasonably well and that a shift to the far more prevalent arbitration system was not desirable. In part, this was due to the judgment of the employers that the abuses of the past were much less prevalent since Hoffa's departure and that decisions were fair and equitable. In addition, employers felt that arbitration was too costly, that the industry itself was too large and complex for any outsider to understand, and that the flexibility and informality of the decision-making process was an advantage to all parties concerned. This was not to deny that some "misuse" of these procedures still occurred, but rather to say it was not considered serious enough to counterbalance the perceived risks and costs of the alternative.[36]

CHANGE OF OPERATIONS

In terms of its potential effect on the efficiency of any carrier, or indeed on the well-being of the industry as a whole, an extremely important provision of the NMFA is concerned with a "change of operations." This clause states that

> Present terminals, breaking points, or domiciles shall not be transferred or changed without the approval of an appropriate Change of Operations Committee. Such Committee shall be appointed in each of the Conference Areas, equally composed of employer and union representatives.

---

[35] Official transcripts are made of the presentation of facts and of questions and answers made at committee hearings. However, no records are kept of subsequent discussions within the committee, and only a brief formal ruling is issued either supporting or denying the grievance. Over the years, the employers have accumulated a "black book" of past rulings on important issues which has been used informally in the presentation and discussion of grievances. It has no official standing, however, and may or may not be controlling in current questions.

[36] These views appear to contradict an oft-repeated assertion by employer representatives that they support grievance arbitration in order to reduce the imbalance of power. It was reliably reported and corroborated by various employer spokesmen, however, that in the 1976 negotiations, the union indicated it would be prepared to accept arbitration on all discharge grievances, but the offer was refused by the TEI policy committee.

Although the contract also specifies that this Committee "shall observe the employer's right to designate home domiciles and the operational requirements of the business," its net effect has been to give the union's representatives an effective veto power over any important change in operating procedures which a company might wish to introduce.

The overwhelming weight of available evidence in this area indicates that the union's policies with respect to such proposed changes have been consistently moderate and adaptive, reflecting Hoffa's recognition of the fact that operational flexibility (as well as acceptance of new techniques) was necessary to permit the industry to provide efficient service and maintain and improve its competitive position vis-à-vis the railroads.[37, 38]

Current Developments: The Civil Rights Act and ERISA

CIVIL RIGHTS

Along with construction, the trucking industry is probably the most widely criticized for policies of discrimination against blacks and other minorities in hiring, assignment, transfer, and promotion. Such discrimination arises first, of course, in the hiring process, where minorities have been excluded from entry into the better-paying and generally considered to be more desirable[39] over-the-road jobs and have instead been assigned to the lower-paying and less desirable city jobs as local drivers, dock workers, hostlers, or garage employees. Moreover, once hired and assigned, minority employees are then "locked in" to these

[37] For a full description and analysis of these policies, see Levinson et al., ch. 3. Ralph and Estelle James explain Hoffa's acceptance of proposed change of operations as simply another quid pro quo in return for political or economic favors received in return. No doubt this was the case in some situations; however, it can hardly explain his and the union's continuing and consistent record in this area as well as in the acceptance of a whole range of new technological improvements, often in the face of considerable opposition from local unions.

[38] The NMFA also gives the Change of Operations Committee responsibility for protecting the position of employees affected by the change. The employer is required to pay reasonable moving expenses for workers who must be redomiciled. If work is transferred from one terminal to another, displaced employees may bid for new jobs on the basis of seniority; if more than one terminal is affected, seniority lists are "dovetailed" to determine the order of bidding rights. Several other contingencies are specified; in addition, the agreement gives the committee broad flexibility to use its own discretion in the application of seniority rights under special circumstances.

[39] Despite this widely held view, it is by no means obvious that road-driver jobs are "better" than city jobs. While a road driver earns approximately $3,000 more per year, he works many more hours (with no overtime premium) and must be away from home a large portion of the time. City drivers work fewer hours, earn overtime, and return home every evening. None of this denies the basic point, of course, that every person should be free to choose irrespective of sex, race, or national origin.

jobs by strict seniority provisions which prevent any movement between the road and city seniority boards and which impose a positive burden on any employee who may wish to transfer because of the loss of all past accumulated seniority.

The evidence indicating the presence of such discrimination is substantial. According to Justice Department statistics for 1974 relating to companies operating under the NMFA, only 92 of a total of 2,767 line drivers (3.3 percent) employed by Consolidated Freightways—the second largest general-freight carrier in the country—were minorities. The comparable figure for Pacific Intermountain Express—the eighth largest carrier—was 3.0 percent out of a total of 1,747.[40] By contrast, the proportion of minorities in city classifications has been much larger.

Since adoption of Title VII of the Civil Rights Act of 1964, these hiring and seniority policies have been the subject of extensive negotiation and litigation by individuals and government agencies.[41] By far the most important of these was initiated by the Attorney General in January 1971 in a suit brought against T.I.M.E.-D.C. (T-DC), a nationwide motor freight carrier, and the Teamsters union (IBT) alleging a "pattern or practice" of racial discrimination in violation of Title VII. The suit claimed that T-DC had engaged in discriminatory hiring, assignment, and promotion practices against blacks and Chicanos, and that IBT had been a party to these actions by negotiating collective agreements which contained seniority provisions that perpetuated these practices. Clearly, since the practices being litigated were typical of virtually all trucking companies operating under the NMFA (as well as those outside its jurisdiction), the outcome of this case was of crucial importance to the industry and indeed to many collective bargaining situations outside the industry as well.

The case was ultimately heard by the Supreme Court, which issued its decision in May 1977.[42] The Court unanimously supported the findings of two lower courts that a statistical analysis of the company's hiring and employment patterns clearly indicated a "pattern or practice" of employment discrimination which violated the 1964 Civil Rights Act.[43]

---

[40] For additional statistical data as well as a complete discussion of all aspects of the issues involved, see Gould, especially p. 366. See also Leone; and fn. 43 below.

[41] Gould, chs. 3, 4, and 14.

[42] *T.I.M.E.-D.C.* v. *United States*, 14 FEP Cases 1514 (1977), reported in Bureau of National Affairs, *Daily Labor Report*, May 31, 1977, pp. D1 and D19.

[43] Considerable statistical material was introduced. Perhaps the most striking was the fact that with one exception—a single black man employed as a line driver from 1950–59—the company and its predecessors had never employed a black on a regular basis as a line driver until 1969. As late as 1971, only 13 of 1,828 line drivers were black or Chicano and of these, all eight blacks had been hired after the litigation had commenced.

Much more important for its longer-run significance for seniority provisions in many other collective agreements, the Court held (with Justices Marshall and Brennan dissenting) that the maintenance of separate seniority boards was a bona fide seniority system, created and maintained for a legitimate business purpose because of basic differences in the operating needs and characteristics of road and city drivers, and hence not per se in violation of Title VII. It could not, of course, continue to be *applied* in a discriminatory manner, nor could it be protected as a bona fide system if its original *intent* was to discriminate.[44]

Finally, in a further important extension of its bona fide ruling, the Court held that it was not illegal for employees with vested seniority rights to continue to exercise those rights with respect to *pre-Act* discrimination. Put alternatively, no relief need be granted to employees for the effects of discrimination suffered *prior to* the effective date of the 1964 Act (July 2, 1965). However, persons suffering the effects of discrimination after that date did need to be "made whole," insofar as those effects could reasonably be inferred from a reconstruction of past circumstances. The case was remanded to the district court for a resolution of this "difficult task."[45]

The issue of discrimination was by no means ended with this decision, however. In early 1974, a much broader industrywide suit had been brought by the government against 349 trucking companies employing some 225,000 workers (including 50,000 road drivers) alleging a "pattern and practice of unlawful discrimination" against blacks and Chicanos in the industry; other defendants included TEI, IBT, and the Machinists union. The government also proposed that affected companies agree to sign a "partial consent decree" under which they would adopt certain affirmative action hiring goals, facilitate the transfer of minority-group employees into road-driver jobs (including back-pay adjustments in some cases), and establish training programs to enable minority workers to qualify as road drivers.[46]

---

[44] The basis for the Court's ruling in this situation was Section 703(h) of Title VII, which provides in part that ". . . it shall not be an unfair employment practice for an employer to apply different standards of compensation, or different terms, conditions, or privileges of employment pursuant to a bona fide seniority . . . system . . . provided that such differences are not the result of an intention to discriminate because of race . . . or national origin . . . ."

[45] The implication of this landmark decision for seniority systems in a host of other industries is obvious. For the Court held, in effect, that such systems did not become unlawful per se because they had been used for discriminatory purposes in the past; that the Act was not retrospective beyond its effective date, so that previously acquired seniority rights would not be affected; and that retroactive correction of post-1965 discrimination would be based on the specific circumstances of specific discriminatees. Thus the fear of a major disruption of common seniority practices was eliminated.

[46] Bureau of National Affairs, *Daily Labor Report*, March 21, 1974, pp. A10, A11.

In part because of the pending litigation in the *T.I.M.E.-D.C.* case, negotiations concerning the exact terms of the consent decree extended over the subsequent three-year period. While the *T-DC* decision was generally favorable to the carriers and the union with respect to the legality of the seniority provisions and responsibility for back-pay adjustments, the Department of Labor has continued to press for adoption of affirmative action programs for motor carriers with 50 or more employees and government bills of lading totaling $50,000 or more in any one year. It seems probable, therefore, that more active minority hiring and training programs and some modifications of strict separate road and local seniority-board provisions will be introduced over the coming years.

ERISA

Another area in which recent legislation has had an important impact on bargaining has resulted from passage of the Employment Retirement and Income Security Act of 1974 (ERISA). This act established extensive regulatory standards for privately negotiated pension plans, including "prudent" investment practices, minimum funding and vesting of pension rights, and several others.

Under the aegis of this legislation, the government initiated an intensive investigation during 1975 into the operations of the huge Central and Southern States Pension Fund (CSPF), originally established by Hoffa in 1955 and reported to have total assets of $1.4 billion in 1977, while receiving employer contributions for some 380,000 working Teamsters and making monthly pension payments to more than 70,000 retirees.

The reason for the investigation flowed from the fact that the CSPF had for many years been the subject of widespread charges of mismanagement in its investment of funds, corruption and kickbacks in making questionable loans, tie-ins with organized crime, excessive disqualification of retirees, and others.[47] Yet it was not until 1976 that the government appeared willing and able to pursue the matter in any depth and not until early 1977 that the U.S. Department of Labor undertook aggressive action to force changes in its personnel and operating procedures. In March 1977, an agreement was reached under which all members of the Board of Trustees (including Teamster President Fitzsimmons and International Vice-President Roy Williams, director of the Central Conference) resigned, full control over the fund's assets was

---

[47] See especially James and James, ch. 24.

transferred to outside professional managers, and a full review of the fund's financial position was to be made.[48]

In addition to its impact on the administrative procedures and management of the fund, ERISA's stricter funding and vesting standards have also considerably increased the costs of all Teamster pension programs. Under the Central States agreement of 1976–79, employer contributions were increased from $22 to $31 per week over that three-year period; similar increases were negotiated elsewhere as well. Moreover, it is estimated that a further increase of from $4 to $8 per week will be required in the 1979 contract in order to meet ERISA's standards.

Finally, note should be taken of the fact that nothing in the 1977 agreement regarding the fund's administration precludes the government's taking additional legal action in the future, either to require further internal reforms or to bring actions against specific individuals for alleged misuse of funds or other unlawful activities.

Current Developments: Rising Internal Union Dissidence

Traditionally, the Teamsters union has been far from a model of union democracy. Despite Hoffa's wide popularity and strong support among the rank-and-file membership, he tolerated no criticism and repressed any opposition to his policies. In view of his considerable power, it is not surprising that dissident groups have been unable to establish any viable organization within the union's framework.

In recent years, however, two small organizations have been able to survive the antagonism of the leadership and indeed appear to be exerting an influence much beyond what their size would suggest. The largest is the Professional Drivers Council, Inc. (PROD), organized in 1973 and currently claiming some 7,000 members. PROD's primary focus is on the internal operations of the union, including the removal of top officials for alleged corruption and misuse of funds, reform of welfare and pension fund administration, elimination of excessive salaries to officers,[49] improved safety standards, etc.

The smaller organization, established in 1976 and claiming approximately 3,000 members, is Teamsters for a Democratic Union (TDU). While TDU also supports internal democratic reforms, it places greater emphasis on improved contract provisions, greater rank-and-file militancy, local control of strikes, more aggressive grievance handling, etc.

[48] An important power remaining within the control of the trustees involved questions of eligibility and review of claims for retirement benefits. This had been an area of earlier criticism, though some of the sources of earlier problems, especially lack of reciprocity across different pension plan jurisdictions, have been almost completely eliminated.

[49] An excellent and well-researched report on some of these matters is found in Fox and Sikorski.

In contrast to PROD's more national orientation, TDU's focus is primarily on the establishment of a network of local union centers of power.[50]

While these groups have thus far been too small to have had any perceptible effect on bargaining, they have added another highly visible source of criticism of the union's operations; even more important, the TDU has clearly been making small but steady gains in its drive to elect its candidates to local union offices. It seems clear that despite their small size, the Teamster leadership is both aware and sensitive to the potential threat which could develop from these dissident groups.[51]

Insofar as these trends have introduced a greater degree of democracy into the union, they are surely to be commended. An unfortunate corollary to this trend, however, is a rise in militancy which will put greater pressure on the union leadership to negotiate even higher wage-fringe benefits at a time when the unionized sector of the industry is facing increasingly difficult economic problems.

Current Developments: Rising Nonunion Competition

By far the most crucial collective bargaining problem facing the parties at the present time is a clear downward trend in the share of freight being moved over the highway by Teamster members. There is no disagreement by spokesmen on both sides of the table that this trend has been developing over a number of years, and that its impact is substantial and growing more serious. Although no precise data are available by which to measure the magnitudes involved, it was the judgment of many participants that the volume of freight being handled by the union had declined by approximately 20–25 percent over the decade 1967–77. In terms of union membership in the freight division (which is considerably broader than the coverage of the NMFA), rough estimates were a decline from about 500,000 in the mid-sixties to approximately 375,000–400,000 a decade later; of these totals, about 70–75 percent have been under the NMFA.[52]

Several factors have gone into the development of these trends— legal, economic, and political. By far the most basic element in the pic-

---

[50] *Constitution and By Laws* (Cleveland: Teamsters for a Democratic Union, 1976).

[51] See, for example, "Florida Local Reinstates Teamsters Expelled Over Dissident Literature," *New York Times*, February 8, 1977; "Teamsters Panel Agrees, Surprisingly, To Hear Charges Against Fitzsimmons," *Wall Street Journal*, September 15, 1977; and "Dissidents in the Teamsters are gaining clout," *Business Week*, November 13, 1978. Among the cities in which TDU candidates were elected are Oklahoma City, Green Bay, Wis., Flint, Mich., St. Louis, and Lynn, Mass.

[52] Estimates of the proportion of intercity freight being handled by Teamsters are even more difficult to come by. In one important conference area, it was estimated to have declined from 70 percent to "below 50"; this was not necessarily representative of the other areas, however.

ture has been a crucial change in the framework of labor law which has greatly restricted the ability of the union to resist the rise of non-union carriers. This change, introduced under the Taft-Hartley Act of 1947 and expanded under Landrum-Griffin in 1959, makes it an unfair labor practice for a union to engage in a secondary boycott or to enter into an agreement with an employer under which he agrees to cease doing business with a third person. In addition, the Taft-Hartley Act provides that anyone suffering business injury as a result of an unlawful secondary boycott may sue to recover damages.[53]

These restrictions represented a serious blow to the Teamsters, since the use of secondary pressures and "hot cargo" clauses had been an important method by which Hoffa had not only protected the jurisdiction of the union but also extended it to employers far removed from his primary locus of power;[54] even more important, they provided an impenetrable defense against encroachment of nonunion carriers into strongly held union areas.

It was not until the mid-1960s that the full impact of these legal changes began to be felt by the Teamsters union. By that time, however, several court decisions had made it clear that union members could no longer refuse to load or unload goods being shipped by or interlined with nonunion carriers, nor could union employers "voluntarily" do so; that it could not prevent nonunion drivers from making pickups or deliveries at customers' docks; that drivers (union or nonunion) were subject to discharge if they refused to cross secondary picket lines set up at a company's docks; that the right to picket a nonunion driver was strictly circumscribed as to time and place; and that the courts were prepared to award substantial damages to carriers adversely affected by such unlawful activities.[55] Over time, as the impact of these decisions has become clear, the union has become increasingly cautious in pressing its actions against nonunion firms, and the latter in turn have become more aggressive in extending their operations into strongly unionized areas and in seeking court injunctions quickly if the union takes unlawful retaliatory action.

---

[53] These provisions are incorporated as Sections 8(b)(4)(B) and 8(e) of the National Labor Relations Act and Section 303 of Taft-Hartley.

[54] An excellent description of these techniques may be found in James and James, ch. 9.

[55] The number of relevant cases is extensive: see particularly *Truck Drivers Local 413* v. *NLRB* (Brown Transport Corporation and Patton Warehouse, Inc.), 52 LRRM 1252 (1963) and 55 LRRM 2878 (1964); *Teamsters Local 695* (Madison Employers Council), 152 NLRB 577, 50 LRRM 1131 (1965); *Overnite Transportation Co.* v. *IBT*, 50 LRRM 2379 (1965); and *Teamsters Local 512* (AAA Motor Lines), 211 NLRB 94, 87 LRRM 1029 (1974). An extensive discussion of all these issues is found in Morris, Badle, and Siegel, and Annual Supplements thereto; and in Gorman.

While this basic change in legal framework was the major factor underlying the decline in the union's jurisdictional control, a further proximate cause was the sharp increase in Teamster labor costs initiated in 1970 with the refusal of the Chicago local to accept the centrally negotiated IBT-TEI package of approximately $1.35 over a three-year period, or about 9.0 percent per year. After a 13-week strike which ended in a total victory for the Chicago locals,[56] Fitzsimmons—under clear political pressure to assert his control over the bargaining process —insisted upon an even larger increase. The final agreement with TEI provided a total package of approximately $2.20 per hour over a 39-month period; on a wage-fringe base of about $4.50, this represented a rise approximating 12.5 percent per year.

The sharp upward movement was temporarily slowed during 1973–76, when Fitzsimmons was constrained by his political support of Nixon to abide by the Administration's "pay restraint" program.[57] Fitzsimmons entered the 1976–79 negotiations, however, with several strong pressures to negotiate another very favorable contract. The severe inflation of the previous period required both a large immediate "catch up" wage increase and an "uncapped COLA." In addition, his leadership role was being subjected to severe criticism on several fronts, including charges of corruption in the handling of the huge Central States Pension Fund and of undemocratic internal practices, pressed by the newly organized dissident groups within the union. Moreover, suspicion had been aroused by the disappearance and presumed murder of Hoffa in July 1975, after he had been released from jail and had initiated plans to oppose Fitzsimmons in the upcoming union convention in June 1976. All these pressures came to focus on the 1976 negotiations, only three months before the convention where Fitzsimmons wished to gain a clear and overwhelming vote in support of his reelection.

The outcome was predictable. After a series of largely pro forma negotiations and a brief three-day attempt by TEI to maintain a united front in the face of a called strike, the union's terms were met. The final package, assuming a 6 percent annual increase in the Consumer Price

---

[56] The Chicago locals negotiated a wage increase of $1.65 plus 37 cents in COLA and other fringes. Some insight into the power relationship of the parties may be gained from the fact that TEI attempted to bolster the employers' position by providing approximately 6 million dollars in financial aid, with no perceptible results except to lengthen the period of the strike. The financial aid was purely an ad hoc action, however; TEI has never attempted to develop any planned strike-insurance program, primarily because of the difficulty of gaining cooperation and contributions from so many firms.

[57] The 1973–76 contract provided for wage-fringe increases of $1.50 over a 33-month period, approximating a rise of 8.0 percent per year. Council on Wage and Price Stability, *An Analysis of the Master Freight Agreement* (September 1976).

Index, amounted to approximately $1.00 per hour per year, or an annual rate of 10.4 percent.[58]

The cumulative effect of these increases in labor costs under the 1976–79 contract, superimposed on those initiated in 1970–73, had the effect of increasing even further the motivation of shippers to seek out nonunion or non-Teamster transportation modes wherever possible.

The shift from union to nonunion freight movement has occurred in a number of ways. First, a number of nonunion common carriers whose operations have in the past been confined to the weakly organized southern region, have been expanding rapidly into the other conference areas by acquiring new operating rights, assigning nonunion drivers (often owner-operators) to newly established runs, and opening new terminals with nonunion personnel.[59] Although the Teamsters have at times made attempts to organize these employees, they have on the whole been quite unsuccessful. In part, this has been due to the basic changes in legal framework noted above. In addition, however, unionism is often perceived by these workers, and particularly by owner-operators, as a threat to their independence and employment opportunities; hence they are often not amenable to union organizing efforts.

Of greater importance in many areas has been the decision by large companies to shift to their own private trucking operations. In many instances, these companies are nonunion, able to operate effectively because of the legal barriers to union secondary actions. Even where companies are under collective agreements with some other union, the integration of new trucking positions into the regular wage structure results in wage levels considerably below the regular Teamster scale. Alternatively, some firms have been able to utilize owner-operators by negotiating for the services of a contract carrier and joining with him in obtaining the necessary operating authority from the ICC or state regulatory agency.[60]

A further manifestation of the nonunion threat, though reflected within the union's jurisdiction, has been a much more rapid rate of increase in the gross revenues from the special-commodities as compared

---

[58] *Ibid.*

[59] A question is commonly raised as to how nonunion carriers are able to attract business away from union carriers if their tariffs (prices) must be the same under ICC regulations. There are two major explanations. First, more efficient service may be provided by the avoidance of various working rules; and second, individual carriers can choose to file tariffs below those set by the regional rate bureaus and can successfully maintain them so long as they are "compensatory"—i.e., cover costs. In recent years, the ICC had been particularly amenable to independent rate-setting by individual carriers.

[60] Wyckoff and Maister point out that despite general views to the contrary, a large majority of petitions for new operating rights are approved by the ICC; see p. 4. Also, we are here omitting the not uncommon illegal use of owner-operators by private companies.

to the general-commodities divisions of large carriers, and a similar rise in the number of products approved by the union for movement under special-commodities conditions. As the union has been faced with the loss of general-commodity freight to nonunion carriers, it has responded in part by permitting more products to move under special-commodity concessions. However, various conferences and various locals have responded in various ways. In general, the central and western regions have been more receptive to recognizing the problem by granting the carriers more leeway in expanding the scope of their special-commodities divisions, either formally or by informal "understandings." By contrast, the eastern locals remain much more strongly opposed, perceiving special commodities as nothing more than an underhanded device to deprive them of "legitimate" work. An important consequence is that a large volume of truckload freight is moving nonunion in the eastern states (e.g., containerized freight moving inland from eastern ports) which would normally be under special commodities in other areas.

A final impact of the growing nonunion threat has been the spread of various "under the table" agreements made by local unions with many individual companies or groups of smaller companies under which the officially negotiated wage-fringe standards are being quietly undercut. Technically, such concessions can properly be negotiated only as riders to the major agreements and only with the approval of the international union; for obvious reasons, such riders are rarely approved. As a result, local union officials—with the consent of the employees affected—have simply done so without official approval (though often with official knowledge). These practices have usually been confined to smaller companies in financial difficulties; however, they have been reported as "common practice" in some large metropolitan areas as well and may be indicative of a growing recognition within the union that more broadly based policies of adjustment are necessary.

Current Developments: Employer Schism and Reorganization

THE EMPLOYERS

Trucking Employers Incorporated (TEI) was organized in 1963 to provide a more stable and cohesive association than had its various predecessors. While these objectives were achieved to some degree, the basic sources of disunity and internal tension remained and indeed became greatly exacerbated by the developing threat of nonunion competition.

The most basic source of tension arose from the diversity of firms coming under the broad umbrella of TEI negotiations. These included common, contract, and private carriers; long-haul, short-haul, and local-cartage firms; companies of varying financial strength and size, etc. The most serious source of internal conflict arose from differences in the interests and negotiating priorities of the smaller, generally financially weaker, short-haul carriers (roughly defined as those whose major operations involve runs of 300 miles or less) vs. the larger, generally better financed and more profitable long-haul carriers whose major operations are national or broadly regional in scope.

Existing contract provisions and the direction of negotiating policy can have important differential effects on these two broad groups of carriers. One crucial difference arises from the fact that short-line carriers expend approximately 65–75 percent of direct labor costs on local operations—that is, on the pickup and delivery of freight at each end of a run. By contrast, long-haul carriers spend about that same proportion on line-driver costs, since local operations are relatively less important. To compound the difference, local drivers are paid on an hourly basis while road drivers earn mileage rates; moreover, opportunities for productivity gains have generally favored road drivers through improved intercity highways and larger and faster equipment. The significance of these various factors for the negotiation of wage increases is obvious, since the tradeoffs between hourly and mileage increases can have a major differential effect on the costs of the different carrier groups involved.[61]

A second source of conflict involved the varying impact of various working rules on different carrier groups. Fixed starting times are extremely costly to short-haul carriers operating in the cities affected; yet these same rules are much less costly (relatively) to long-haul carriers in those same areas. Similar differences arise with respect to multiple-payment runs, to the requirement of a pickup and delivery leg at each end of full truckload shipments, and others. In these areas as well, it is noteworthy that the most costly of these rules provide greater benefits (and impose greater costs) on local-cartage and short-haul companies, reflecting the early history of strong local-cartage unions and the much larger proportion of union members in local occupations. This also has given the short-haul companies a much stronger interest than the long-haul companies in pressing for work-rule changes.

A final difference worth mention involves the financial position of these carrier groups. Though there are many exceptions, it is nevertheless true on average that the large line-haul carriers are financially stronger and more profitable than the smaller short-line firms.

---

[61] It should also be noted that the union is by no means indifferent to this tradeoff, since about 75 percent of its freight membership is in local cartage and only 20–25 percent in over-the-road movements.

Whether justified or not, these differences in the structure of operating costs, the impact of working rules, size and financial strength, and other considerations have generated a rising dissatisfaction, distrust, and resentment among the short-haul carriers who felt that their interests and concerns had not been adequately represented in TEI's negotiating policies. They perceived the major cause to be the domination of TEI by the national carriers and the nature of the highly centralized bargaining structure which made it virtually impossible to gain adequate consideration of the regional and local problems which were of major concern to them.

THE SIGNIFICANCE OF THE NEGOTIATING PROCESS

As noted, the structure of the negotiating process itself has contributed considerably to the degree of internal distrust and frustration. It will be recalled that the basic economic package of wage-fringe benefits is centrally negotiated at the highest level, with the general president and top conference freight officials on the one hand and the nine-member TEI negotiating team on the other. While this group is meeting, many meetings are taking place at various subsidiary levels, reflecting the large number of conference and other regional over-the-road and local cartage supplements, special-commodity agreements, and various "local riders" as well. Since working rules are incorporated into supplements or riders rather than the NMFA, desired modifications must be negotiated at those levels; however, if such issues remain deadlocked at supplementary levels, they are brought to the top negotiating team for a presentation of the issues by each side and a final discussion and settlement by the top negotiators. At least in theory, no agreement is final until all lower-level deadlocked issues are settled. In practice, however, at least the major terms of the wage-fringe package have been agreed to before the deadlocked matters are brought to the top level.

The effects of this process on negotiations below the top level are clear, for unless there is a quid pro quo available to be negotiated, there is little incentive for union representatives to agree to modifications of working rules, and the most important of these matters are consequently deadlocked. However, by the time they are subsequently heard "at the top," the major economic terms have been settled, the parties are tired, and the employers have little stomach to face a strike on issues which often affect only a few localities or a particular conference. Yet it is precisely these types of issues which can be extremely costly to particular short-haul carriers who are thus frustrated by the centralized structure from being able to negotiate their individual and local problems on a quid pro quo basis.

BREAKUP OF TEI AND EMPLOYER REORGANIZATION

These internal frictions within TEI have been present for many years. They have become increasingly acute, however, in response to the growing threat of nonunion competition. As already noted, this competition has particularly hurt the smaller short-haul carriers, who were seriously affected by the much greater proportionate increase in hourly as compared to mileage rates in the 1970–73 contract,[62] and who were increasingly frustrated by the failure of the centralized negotiating process to deal with their need for modifications in local and regional working rules.

This rising level of dissatisfaction also hurt the effectiveness of the negotiations for TEI, since the bargaining team was considerably hampered in its negotiations by distrust, delay, and internal bickering among the members of its too large executive policy committee of 102 members —or even its 36-member board of directors—who were responsible for ultimate ratification of any agreement.

These developing forces finally came to a head in September 1977 with the resignation of three top officers and seven other directors of TEI to form a new association called Carrier Management, Inc. (CMI).[63] In the first instance, CMI was made up of 10 companies claiming employment of 50,000 Teamster members; during subsequent months, additional defections from TEI developed. Moreover, since there had always been various other smaller employers' associations remaining outside TEI,[64] the TEI-CMI schism left the employers in a state of marked disarray, only some 18 months before the expiration of the existing contract on March 31, 1979.

Once an open break had developed, however, the employers were faced with an "agonizing reappraisal" as to how any dual system of negotiations should proceed and what its ultimate effects might be. Despite the widespread dissatisfaction with TEI's structure and performance, little serious thought had been given to how the differing problems of the short-haul and local carriers were to be dealt with. One suggested approach had been to establish a "two-tier" system of bargaining, with a second level of negotiations conducted for the short-haul and

---

[62] It will be recalled that the 1970–73 agreement grew out of a revolt by Chicago local-cartage drivers, which finally raised hourly rates by $1.85 instead of the $1.10 originally negotiated. However, mileage rates for road drivers never entered the picture and their original increases remained intact. Interestingly, increases in mileage rates are generally ignored when the value of trucking agreements is estimated. See, e.g., Council on Wage and Price Stability, September 1976.

[63] Bureau of National Affairs, *Daily Labor Report*, Sept. 2, 1977, p. A11.

[64] The most important of these is the Motor Carrier Labor Advisory Council, which has sometimes settled with the Teamsters before TEI and has thus set the pattern which TEI subsequently accepted.

local carriers, incorporating lower wages and some modifications of costly working rules. This second tier would be completely autonomous and independent, in the sense that regional work practices, etc., would be directly negotiable on a quid pro quo basis rather than handled as deadlocked "supplements" to be considered only after the overall economic package has been agreed upon. The geographic scope of the second tier would be on a conference-wide or smaller regional basis, largely along the lines of the current NMFA supplements.

While such a two-tier system could be theoretically feasible, it would in practice raise a crucial question as to the willingness of the union to accept a system in which certain groups of carriers (and their employees) would negotiate greater wage and fringe improvements than other groups of carriers and their employees. Quite aside from the very difficult problem of deciding which group any given carrier would fall into, since many would fall into a "gray area," the union would be faced with some of its members receiving different rates of pay or benefits while doing the same work in the same locality or over the same routes.[65]

A further danger facing the parties after the split was the possibility that greater decentalization might worsen the employers' situation by encouraging whipsawing and reintroducing regional and local union rivalries. Thus, while the leadership of the newly organized CMI may have hoped to create a stronger bargaining organization than TEI, it was not at all clear that the breakup would indeed yield any benefits for the defecting employers.

Whatever the underlying causes, discussions were initiated within a few months to heal the breach and bring the organizations back together. By April 1978, a tentative merger agreement had been reached, and in late May a new unified organization was formed, known as Trucking Management, Inc. (TMI). Despite some modifications, the basic organizational framework was quite similar to the previous TEI, with basic membership made up of 35 employer organizations representing in turn about 500–600 motor carriers.[66] A policy committee made up of 102 motor carrier executives chosen by the 35 organizations was responsible for ratification of contracts, while a 45-man board of directors provided more direct contact with the six top officers. Also as before, a negotiating committee of up to 10 members, led by an ap-

---

[65] For example, such a two-tier system would mean that line drivers operating over the Los Angeles–San Francisco run would receive different rates of pay, depending on whether they were employed by a large national carrier or a smaller short-haul carrier. Similarly, local drivers and dockmen within a city would be paid differently, depending on the "tier" within which their employer was negotiating.

[66] *Transport Times* (American Trucking Association), June 12, 1978, p. 1.

pointed president, had the responsibility for negotiating the NMFA.

In view of its continuing size and organizational complexity, the ability of TMI to overcome the problems of its predecessor remains to be seen. Its major hope undoubtedly lies in the appointment of a new president and chief negotiator, J. Curtis Counts, who had earlier accepted that position with TEI in November 1977. As a long-time management negotiator in various other industries, and as a former director of the Federal Mediation and Conciliation Service, Counts brought a considerably greater depth and breadth of experience to TMI than had any of the previous spokesmen for the trucking industry. In addition, some increase in funding for a more adequate TMI staff was provided.[67] There is nevertheless little doubt that the new employer organization would continue to be faced with the same problems as the old and that the new president would face a formidable task in holding together the diverse interest groups of the industry. Moreover, even assuming this could be accomplished, the threat of outside groups "breaking the line"—particularly the independent Chicago Truck Drivers Union and the Chicago-based Motor Carrier Labor Advisory Council (MCLAC)—was always present.[68]

The 1979 Negotiations and Beyond

The Union's Dilemma

Against this background of rising nonunion competition, declining union employment, and employer confusion and distrust, the union leadership is faced with some very difficult decisions, particularly whether to press its clear bargaining advantage or to modify its policies and reevaluate its longer-run approach. This dilemma is particularly clear in trucking, quite irrespective of the degree of success which TMI may have in developing a unified negotiating strategy, because the fundamentally superior power position of the union will in the end be the primary determinant of the bargaining outcome. As one employer representative aptly put it, "The union holds all the cards" (except, of course, the power to prevent nonunion entry).

---

[67] Prior to this time, TEI's total permanent staff was made up of the president, his administrative assistant, and a secretary! The rationale for this degree of penury was that TEI was free to call upon individual carriers to provide necessary staff work of various kinds as needed. However, this system had several drawbacks. Most important, it prevented the development of an independent staff that could provide continuity, independence, longer-run planning, and the development of a body of data and an expertise on all branches of the industry.

[68] The new TMI group has attempted to prevent this type of defection by integrating the MCLAC president into the top negotiating committee for the 1979 NMFA. The MCLAC companies are not in TMI, however, and the organization is still free to "go its own way" if it wishes.

In this situation, the counterbalancing pressures on the union leadership are equally difficult to evaluate and reconcile. In sharp contrast to Hoffa, who—despite his serious shortcomings—provided clear direction and control and held the complete confidence and allegiance of the membership, Fitzsimmons has decentralized power and control in order to retain the support of important union officials at the conference and local levels and does not have the membership's unquestioning support. Added to this is the rising influence of the dissidents who—while fully to be supported in their drive for internal democratic reforms—are also unfortunately prepared to shout "sellout" at any sign of concessions which the leadership might make to protect the union's position in the industry or to recognize the differing economic pressures on the various employer groups. The result is a degree of political insecurity at the top union level which makes it very much more difficult to negotiate and support a moderate settlement.

There are, however, important counterbalancing pressures as well. As noted earlier, there is widespread recognition among leading union representatives that some relief must be provided, particularly to the short-haul carriers, if they were to continue to operate under union conditions. Moreover, the union leadership would much prefer to maintain a unified structure of bargaining on the employers' side, both for negotiating efficiency and administrative simplicity.[69] It is in the better interests of the union, therefore, that the fledgling TMI be able to maintain its unity; such an objective would also best be served by a moderate settlement. Finally, the Teamsters are not insensitive to the adverse public "image" resulting from the legal actions undertaken by the government in connection with the financial handling of their pension and health care funds; here again, a course of moderation could be of some—though uncertain—help.

In light of these conflicting factors, it is most difficult to evaluate what the union's bargaining stance will be in the 1979 negotiations and beyond. One possible approach would be to ignore the problem by continuing to press for large wage-fringe increases, insist upon the same terms of settlement for all employer groups, and accept the continuing erosion of the union's jurisdiction. Such a policy can be feasible even in the long run since some volume of freight—long-distance, high-value LTL shipments—will probably continue to move under union control.

---

[69] Though there are a few sources of pressure within the union for a return to more decentralized bargaining, they are quite minor. Overall, the centralized structure is favored by over-the-road drivers who operate in many geographic areas, while a large majority of local drivers and other city employees have obtained considerable gains as a result of Hoffa's drive for standardization. Moreover, centralized bargaining on economic issues has still permitted considerable local variations in working rules, etc., through local riders.

In addition, the strong local unions in many large metropolitan areas would continue to handle much purely local cartage freight, though pickup and delivery of most intercity freight would be lost. By contrast, a moderate approach in 1979 could incorporate quite modest wage adjustments (in addition to existing COLA provisions), greater job security, improved financing and coverage of existing fringe benefits, and perhaps most important, some modifications in working rules which have been most burdensome to the short-haul carriers. The importance of this last concession is matched, however, by the difficulties of gaining its acceptance by the union members who would be most affected. Nevertheless, it is probably a sine qua non for maintaining employer acceptance of the existing bargaining structure and for giving both the IBT and TMI more time to develop a longer-run approach to the problems of the unionized sector of the industry.

UNION-MANAGEMENT COOPERATION?

A suggestive and at least potentially important development for future bargaining trends was the establishment in late 1977, by action of TEI and IBT, of a joint Teamster-Trucking Industry Labor Management Committee, under the chairmanship of John T. Dunlop, Professor of Economics at Harvard, former Secretary of Labor, and an extremely experienced participant in all aspects of collective bargaining. The committee was charged with studying four major issues with a view to making recommendations for possible action by the parties. The four were the erosion of business and of jobs from for-hire to private carriage; industry productivity; the impact of federal regulation, such as health and safety rules; and the impact of economic deregulation of the trucking industry.

The relationship between these issues and the course of collective bargaining is clear enough. The crucial question, of course, is the extent to which such joint consideration of problems away from the immediate pressures of the negotiating table can be effective in helping to achieve an acceptable accommodation in 1979 and in establishing the basis for more permanent efforts thereafter. As with the negotiations themselves, this will be a formidable task for an industry and union which have had no previous experience in joint consultation on problems and in developing joint recommendations for change. Nevertheless, the mere act of establishing such a committee and of participating in its deliberations by a union long accustomed to obtaining its objectives easily by the exercise of its own power is in itself a hopeful indication that the union is more fully prepared to accept the need for moderation. If so, the committee can develop into a meaningful adjunct to the negotiating process.

THE LONGER RUN: DEREGULATION?

In recent years, pressures for the introduction of varying degrees of deregulation of the interstate for-hire trucking industry have been set forth with increasing frequency. The extent and complexity of the issues involved in this matter go far beyond the scope of the present discussion.[70] Should any important modifications be made in the current regulatory framework, however, most particularly in the area of facilitating the entry of new firms into the industry, the impact on union jurisdictional strength would be serious indeed. Taken in conjunction with the impact of the secondary-boycott and "hot cargo" provisions of the Taft-Hartley Act already noted, the entry of large numbers of new carriers would surely reduce even further the share of freight moving under union contract and might well force a return to a much more decentralized bargaining structure. In this process, the strong local unions in the large metropolitan areas would probably be able to survive and even continue to grow. Certain segments of long-line movement might also remain under union jurisdiction. Nevertheless, a major portion of intercity freight and large sectors of local freight would very probably be handled by nonunion owner-operators or larger nonunion carriers. The extent of these effects will depend greatly, of course, on the exact nature of the deregulatory provisions, if indeed they are enacted.

THE LONGER RUN: RISING ENERGY COSTS

It is hardly possible to discuss the future of collective bargaining in trucking without some reference to the potential longer-run problems that may arise as a result of the anticipated rise in the costs of energy. As with deregulation, it is beyond the scope of the present analysis to address the issue of which transport mode is more "energy efficient," and hence to attempt to evaluate what the impact of rising energy costs might be on the movement of freight by various modes. At least at the present writing, there are few indications of any clear shift of traffic away from the highway to other transport modes and the service advantages of truck movement are still considerable. It is possible, however, that any such trends, if they are to develop, have not yet had time to become evident.

Assuming that rising energy costs were to have an adverse impact

---

[70] The relevant literature is extensive. A small sample of the opposing claims may be found in Moore, and in *A Cost and Benefit Evaluation of Surface Transport Regulation.*

on highway movement, it is generally presumed that an important aspect of such a shift would take the form of a movement away from all highway to an intermodal "piggyback" movement.[71] The *overall* impact of such a shift on Teamster employment, however, would be considerably less than is sometimes assumed, although the *distribution* of that effect among different Teamster groups would be highly unequal. The most serious impact would be on long-line drivers engaged in the movement of freight over distances of at least 300 miles or more. However, employment of local drivers and dockmen as well as intercity drivers on runs of up to 300 miles will be unaffected, and indeed local driver employment might well be increased. The essential point to be stressed, therefore, is that rising energy costs and (possible) shifting modes of freight traffic will not present a serious threat to the viability of the trucking industry or to the Teamsters union as a whole, though it could require the transfer of drivers from long-line to local operations.[72]

Problems and Prospects: A Concluding Comment

Considering the seriousness of the developing trends discussed above, it does not seem overly dramatic to suggest that collective bargaining in the trucking industry is "at the crossroads," and that how the parties deal with them over the next few years may well be crucial to the long-run viability of collective bargaining in that industry, at least in its present structure and strength. While strong leadership and imagination will be required on both sides if long-standing attitudes and policies are to be modified, the key variable will be the willingness of the top union leadership to accept the political risks of a move toward moderation in wage-fringe improvements and toward an easing of costly working rules. Whether this leadership will appear—and, indeed, whether the membership can be convinced to accept such a move—remain the crucial questions. On the basis of the available evidence discussed above, there appears to be at least some basis for "cautious

---

[71] Whether such savings in energy do in fact occur remains a matter of dispute; in addition, the service advantages of direct truck movements and the high capital outlays required for efficient intermodal service continue to present formidable barriers to any rapid expansion in piggyback use. Thus, over the period 1970–72 to 1978, the proportion of all rail freight carloadings moving by truck trailer or container increased from 5 to only 8 percent. *Yearbook of Railroad Facts* (Association of American Railroads), 1979. For a full discussion of these issues, see Ainsworth et al.

[72] A highly detailed analysis of the potential impact of an "advanced" intermodal system on the employment of Teamsters indicated that no more than 10 percent of *total* freight employees would be adversely affected by traffic diversion from highway to piggyback. Line-driver displacement was estimated to be as high as 30–40 percent; however, almost all of this would be counterbalanced by a large increase in local driver employment. For the detailed analysis, see Ainsworth et al., pp. 107–34 and 178–210. Since this study related to a specific traffic corridor, other corridors could yield different results.

optimism" concerning the ultimate outcome. One can only hope that these qualities and conditions will be forthcoming, and soon.

List of References

A Cost and Benefit Evaluation of Surface Transport Regulation. Washington: Interstate Commerce Commission, Bureau of Economics, 1976.

Ainsworth, D., M. Keale, C. Liba, and H. Levinson. *An Improved Truck-Rail Operation: Evaluation of a Selected Corridor: Final Report.* Washington: U.S. Department of Transportation, Federal Highway Administration, December 1975.

Fox, Arthur, II, and John Sikorski. *Teamsters Democracy and Financial Responsibility.* Washington: PROD, 1976.

Garnel, Donald. *The Rise of Teamster Power in the West.* Berkeley: University of California Press, 1972.

Gorman, Robert A. *Labor Law: Unionization and Collective Bargaining.* St. Paul: West Publishing Co., 1976.

Gould, William B. *Black Workers in White Unions.* Ithaca, N.Y.: Cornell University Press, 1977.

Hill, Samuel. *Teamsters and Transportation.* Washington: American Council on Public Affairs, 1942.

James, Ralph, and Estelle James. *Hoffa and the Teamsters.* Princeton, N.J.: D. Van Nostrand Co. Inc., 1965.

Leiter, Robert. *The Teamsters Union.* New York: Bookman Associates, 1957.

Leone, Richard. *The Negro in the Trucking Industry.* Philadelphia: University of Pennsylvania Press, 1970.

Levinson, Harold M. *Determining Forces in Collective Wage Bargaining.* New York: John Wiley & Sons, Inc., 1966.

Levinson, Harold M., Charles M. Rehmus, Joseph P. Goldberg, and Mark L. Kahn. *Collective Bargaining and Technological Change in American Transportation.* Evanston, Ill.: Northwestern University Transportation Center, 1971.

Moore, Thomas G. "Deregulating Surface Freight Transportation." In *Promoting Competition in Regulated Markets.* Washington: Brookings Institution, 1975.

Morris, C. J., G. E. Badle, and J. S. Siegel. *The Developing Labor Law.* Washington: Bureau of National Affairs, 1971.

Roper, Sam. *The International Brotherhood of Teamsters.* New York: John Wiley & Sons, Inc., 1962.

Seidenberg, Jacob. "Evolution of the Current Pay Practices and Fringe Benefits in the Over-the-Road Motor Freight Industry." In *Report of the Presidential Railroad Commission,* App. IV. Washington: 1962.

Sheifer, Victor J. "Bargaining and Wages in Local Cartage." *Monthly Labor Review* (October 1966), pp. 1076–84.

Wyckoff, D. Daryll, and David H. Maister. *The Owner Operator: Independent Trucker.* Lexington, Mass.: D.C. Heath and Co., 1976.

CHAPTER 4

Steel*

JACK STIEBER
Michigan State University

Collective bargaining agreements negotiated by the United Steelworkers of America and the major steel-producing companies have long been regarded as significant for the United States economy because the basic steel settlement is a "key bargain" which influences collective bargaining in other industries.[1] The impact of steel settlements on steel prices affects the overall price level in the economy because steel products are basic to the production of a large number of consumer and industrial products as well as armaments. Despite the shrinkage in steel hourly paid employment from over 570,000 in the early 1950s to less than 360,000 in recent years, steel negotiations, along with those in the automotive industry, set standards against which many other unions and companies measure their own agreements. Since 1973, interest in steel negotiations has been heightened by the introduction of the Experimental Negotiating Agreement (ENA) under which the parties have agreed to submit unresolved national bargaining issues to arbitration rather than resort to economic force when their contracts expire.

This chapter examines collective bargaining in basic steel in sections dealing with the industry, the union, the structure of bargaining, negotiations before and after 1962, the impact of bargaining on wages, and the major provisions of agreements. A final section focuses on the implications of the Experimental Negotiating Agreement for collective bargaining generally and for the economy.

---

* The author wishes to express his appreciation to Kent Murrmann, graduate assistant in the School of Labor and Industrial Relations, Michigan State University, who compiled much of the data and assisted in the research for this chapter. He also acknowledges the assistance and cooperation of Steelworker staff members and steel company executives who read and commented on a draft of this chapter. Finally, helpful comments were received from anonymous reviewers who read an earlier draft of the manuscript. The author alone, of course, is responsible for the chapter as published.

[1] Dunlop, pp. 3–31. [The complete citations of all footnote references are listed at the end of the chapter.]

The Steel Industry

In 1976, the American steel industry consisted of 89 companies with basic steel-making capacity, of which 25 had a capacity of at least one million tons and eight were capable of producing more than eight million ingot tons of steel a year; they accounted for 72 percent of total capacity. The largest, the United States Steel Corporation, produced 41 million tons in 1976, or 23 percent of the total industry capacity of 180 million tons, a much lower proportion than the two-thirds it accounted for at the turn of the century or even the 27 percent in 1960. The industry's basic steel capacity has increased by 66 percent since 1952 and 21 percent since 1960.[2]

Steel companies generally consist of fully integrated multiplant operations engaged in processing ranging from the coking of coal and the smelting of iron ore to the final output of an almost endless variety of shapes, sizes, and qualities of steel products in many stages of finishing. There is little opportunity for product differentiation among steel companies, so that purchasers may shift orders from one company to another or even to foreign producers without being concerned that their needs will not be met. This is a feature that distinguishes the steel industry from such industries as automobile manufacturing where name-identification and product-differentiation can have a significant effect on sales.

TECHNOLOGY

More important than raw capacity figures of ingot steel is the composition of that capacity in terms of steel-making technology. Until about 1960, some 90 percent of all steel in the U.S. was produced by the open-hearth process; most of the remainder was produced in electric furnaces. A tremendous change in the technology of steel production in the United States has occurred since 1960, with open-hearth steel being replaced by steel produced by the basic oxygen process and to a lesser extent by the electric furnace. By 1975, some 62 percent of all U.S. steel was produced using the basic oxygen process, with the remaining 38 percent about equally divided between open-hearth steel and electric-furnace steel. This change in steel technology is important for collective bargaining because of its effect on employment, productivity, and cost of production. The oxygen process sharply reduced the time required to obtain melting "heat" level to about 45 minutes as compared with nine to ten hours under the open-hearth process. In addition,

[2] Steel capacity data are from the American Iron and Steel Institute prior to 1960, the *Wall Street Journal* for 1961–72, and the Institute for Iron and Steel Studies for 1973–76; individual company capacity figures are from a Memorandum prepared by the Research Department, United Steelworkers of America, dated 3/17/76.

steel produced by the oxygen process requires roughly one-fifth the labor of open-hearth steel and uses mostly semiskilled operators, while the open-hearth process requires a higher proportion of unskilled laborers for physical jobs. The oxygen process also requires a smaller investment and results in lower production costs because of greater productivity.[3]

The electric arc furnace also has productivity advantages over the open hearth and is particularly suited to producing stainless and other specialty steels. Its major advantage over the oxygen process is that it can use 100 percent scrap or pellets in place of hot metal. The electric arc process requires less capital than the oxygen process and permits steel manufacture in smaller plants not associated with a blast-furnace complex. Electric steel-making is expected to account for about 25 percent of all steel capacity by 1980. Another important advance in technology is continuous casting, in which steel is poured directly from the furnace into the continuous caster, from which it emerges as a solid semifinished slab, billet, or bloom. Under the traditional method, steel was poured into ingot molds that had to be cooled, stripped, and reheated before being rolled into semifinished form. Manpower requirements are estimated at 10 to 15 percent less with continuous casting than with ingots. Currently, only 10 percent of steel is produced by this method, but it is expected to approach 50 percent by 1985. Other technological changes in steel-making include more automated and continuous rolling and finishing processes and the use of computers for processing data and controlling operations.[4]

LOCATION

Because of the large capital investment required for steel production, geographical distribution of steel-making plants shifts slowly. The major factors affecting the location of steel plants are technology of steel production, transportation costs, location of raw materials such as iron and coal, and the location of steel-consuming industries. Of these, the most important influence in recent years has been the location of markets for steel, while sources of raw materials are now of less importance than they once were. During the last decade the proportion of steel produced in older steel centers in Pennsylvania, Ohio, New York and several East Coast states has decreased, while production in the Southeast, Indiana, Michigan, and the central states has increased.[5]

[3] Heistand, pp. 13–19; Wogan, pp. 39–43; *Technological Change* . . . , pp. 21–33.
[4] *Technological Change* . . . , pp. 22–24.
[5] *Annual Statistical Report* (Washington: American Iron and Steel Institute, 1965–76); and Warren.

These shifts have not included large amounts of tonnage, but they indicate a trend that is likely to continue as old facilities are phased out and new mills are constructed. Recent shutdowns or curtailment of steel-plant operations in eastern states are an indication of an intensifying westward shift of steel production.

EMPLOYMENT

Steel employment has declined substantially during the last 25 years, although employment figures vary significantly from year to year depending upon the level of operations. Peak employment was attained in 1952 when 683,000 hourly paid and salaried employees were engaged in the production and distribution of basic steel and its products. This was a year in which the industry operated at 95 percent of capacity following a 59-day steel strike. From this peak, employment declined to 539,000 in 1959, the low point of the 1950s decade and the year in which the longest national Steelworker strike began. The operating rate that year was only 63 percent of capacity. Employment recovered from the 1959 nadir to a decade high of 593,000 in 1965, from which point it again declined to a low of 476,000 in 1977, when the industry operated at 71 percent of capacity.[6] Overall, steel employment decreased at a compound average rate of 1.4 percent per year between 1953 and 1977.

Production and maintenance employees, who are paid on an hourly basis, have been affected more quickly and more significantly by cutbacks than have the nonproduction salaried employees. The entire employment decrease since 1953 has been borne by production and maintenance workers, while salaried employees have experienced only minor fluctuations in absolute terms and significant increases as a proportion of total employment. By 1975, one out of every four employees in the steel industry was engaged in nonproduction work, as compared with one out of six in the early 1950s. Total production and maintenance employment in 1976 was 351,000; the total number of salaried employees in the industry in 1976 was 121,200.

The structure of employment has also changed in response to technological changes in the steel-making process. In addition to the growing proportion of office and technical employees, the more complex machinery and instruments introduced into the industry have required

---

[6] *Annual Statistical Report* . . . . Since these figures do not cover 100 percent of the industry, they have been adjusted per information from the Research Department of the United Steelworkers of America. In general, operating rates of 80 to 95 percent of capacity are most satisfactory for the American steel industry. Below 80 percent, plant, equipment, and workers are not fully employed, and above 95 percent inefficient equipment is drawn into use. Productivity suffers when operations are either too low or too high. *Employment and Earnings, 1909–1975*, Bureau of Labor Statistics Bull. No. 1312-10 (Washington: 1976).

more skilled and trained craft workers and fewer semiskilled, unskilled, and service hourly workers. The changing nature of steel work is reflected in the average job classification under the industry's job-evaluation system. The average production and maintenance job class has risen from about 8.5 in 1960 to nearly 10 in 1977.

PROFITS

The steel industry is not as profitable as manufacturing industries generally or some of the other major industries in the United States. Profits depend on demand for steel as reflected in shipments of finished steel products, the prices at which those products are sold, and the cost of production. Steel shipments are strongly influenced by cyclical trends in the national economy and are closely related to the production of raw steel. Generally, steel shipments range from 65 to 75 percent of raw steel production, depending on the mix of finished steel products required by steel consumers and the efficiency of the use of production materials. Shipments exceeded 90 million tons for the first time in 1965 and fell below that level in only three subsequent years before reaching an all-time high of 111 million tons in 1973. Shipments declined slightly to 109 million tons in 1974 and then plunged to 80 million tons in 1975, the lowest level in 12 years. In 1976, shipments picked up to 89 million tons and 1977 shipments were expected to exceed 90 million tons but to fall considerably short of the 1973–74 levels.[7]

In only nine of the last 27 years (1950–76) has return on net worth in the steel industry exceeded 10 percent. By comparison, profit rates in "all manufacturing" averaged more than 10 percent in 20 years during this period. Six of these relatively profitable years in steel occurred in the decade of the fifties, which was heavily influenced by the Korean War, and in the prosperous 1955–57 period. During the next 20 years, return on net worth exceeded 10 percent only in 1966, 1974, and 1975. Generally, the most profitable years were those in which capacity utilization and shipments were at high levels and steel prices were increasing. However, sharp price increases have sometimes boosted profits even when shipments were relatively low. Thus, the impetus of a 16 percent price increase in 1975, coming on top of an even larger price rise of 27 percent in 1974, enabled the industry to earn a 10.7 percent return on net worth even though 1975 shipments were at a very low level.

Although the top ten companies bargain through a single coordinating committee, they are not equally profitable.[8] U.S. Steel, the largest

---

[7] Memorandum on "Steel Industry Profits," Research Department, United Steelworkers of America, August 2, 1977.

[8] The "coordinating committee" has represented from 9 to 12 companies in various negotiations, but has recently consisted of 10 companies.

company and the acknowledged leader of the industry, has often been at or near the bottom in terms of return on net worth, as have Bethlehem and Republic, the second- and third-ranking companies. It is interesting to note that the top-level industry negotiating committee has drawn its four members from these three companies. In 1975 when a fifth member was added, he came from Jones and Laughlin, also one of the industry's less profitable companies.

STEEL IN THE WORLD MARKET

One of the most significant developments affecting collective bargaining in the steel industry has been the increase in steel imports. Before the 1959 steel strike, neither the industry nor the union paid much attention to steel imports. Indeed, up to 1958, the United States exported about three times as much steel as it imported. In 1958, the ratio was still about 1.5 to 1 in favor of American steel. Then came the 1959 steel strike when the industry was shut down for 116 days and steel users had to rely heavily on foreign steel. In that year, imports rose to 5.5 million tons compared to 2.1 million tons of iron and steel products exported. Although the gap narrowed when production was resumed after the strike, steel imports never again fell below the level of exports. Imports reached a peak of almost 20 million tons in 1968 and again in 1971 and 1972, while exports rose moderately. The year 1970, when 8.1 million tons were sold abroad, was our best export year, and even then exports came to only slightly more than half the level of imported iron and steel. After that, exports declined sharply to 4.1 million in 1975 and 3.9 million in 1976, while imports remained high.[9] Imports peaked at 18 percent of the U.S. market in 1971, then declined for several years. In 1977 there was an upsurge of imports which was expected to reach or exceed the former peak by the end of the year.[10]

During the last generation, the U.S. has shifted from a net exporter to a net importer of steel, and net imports have been running between 12 and 18 percent of U.S. steel consumption for the last decade. In terms of world raw steel production, the United States in 1974 accounted for 18.6 percent of the total as compared with close to 40 percent in 1955. During this same period, world production increased from about 500 million to 783 million ingot tons, while U.S. production rose from 111 to 145 million tons.[11] By 1980 world steel capacity is expected to increase to over one billion tons, while U.S. capacity will increase little over the present level of 180 million tons per year. At that time, Japan,

---

[9] Annual Statistical Report . . . .

[10] Business Week, September 26, 1977, p. 56.

[11] A Study of Steel Prices (Washington: Council on Wage Price Stability, 1975), p. 28.

the Soviet Union, and the combined European Common Market countries will be able to produce more steel than the United States.[12]

Until the last decade, the Steelworker leadership attributed the industry's inability to compete with foreign steel companies to unnecessarily high prices. In general, the union supported free trade and refused to join with the industry in demanding tariffs or quotas on steel imports. The union position changed officially in 1968 when the Steelworker convention passed a resolution urging quotas on steel imports and attacking dumping practices and government subsidization of foreign steel producers.[13] From that time on the union has worked closely with the industry to restrict imports and has refrained from criticizing price increases by steel companies. Indeed, in December 1976, only a few months before the opening of 1977 negotiations, Steelworker President I. W. Abel publicly supported the steel industry's move to increase prices, citing rising costs of materials, energy, and wages as justification.[14]

The Union

The United Steelworkers of America, unlike most unions which were spawned at the local or plant level, was organized from the top down. It was a product of the Congress of Industrial Organizations (CIO), the Wagner Act, and John L. Lewis, president of the United Mine Workers of America and the CIO in the 1930s. Prior to the formation of the Steelworkers Organizing Committee (SWOC) by the CIO in 1936, the Amalgamated Association of Iron, Steel and Tin Workers, the AFL union with jurisdiction over steel, represented less than 10 percent of the nation's steel workers. The Amalgamated had suffered defeats by the industry in strikes in 1892, 1901, 1909, and 1919. Although the Amalgamated maintained its identity during the organizing drive started in 1936, the SWOC had the exclusive right to direct the organization of all steel workers and control the revenues from its membership. In May 1937, the SWOC claimed over 300,000 members, about 63 percent of all production and maintenance steel workers. In 1942, the SWOC and the Amalgamated were folded into the United Steelworkers of America, an international affiliate of the CIO claiming 660,000 "enrolled" members, less than 500,000 of whom were paying dues.[15]

---

[12] *Mineral Facts and Problems—Bicentennial Edition,* Bureau of the Mines Bull. No. 667 (Washington: 1976), pp. 550–51.

[13] *Proceedings of the Fourteenth Constitutional Convention of the United Steelworkers of America* (Chicago: August 19–23, 1968), pp. 253–55.

[14] *John Herling's Labor Letter,* December 18, 1976.

[15] Ulman, ch. 1; Galenson, p. 119.

LEADERSHIP

The leadership of the Steelworkers during its formative years and through the mid-1960s drew heavily upon coal miners. John L. Lewis appointed Philip Murray, a vice-president of the United Mine Workers, chairman of the SWOC. Murray brought with him David J. McDonald, his personal secretary, as secretary-treasurer of the SWOC. Many of the district directors and international staff members during the early years of the union also came out of the Mine Workers. It was not until 1965 when I. W. Abel defeated McDonald for the presidency that the Steelworkers union had a bona fide steel worker at its head.

Given the influence and example of the Mine Workers and the way in which the Steelworkers came into being, it was not surprising that the union was highly centralized in its organization and structure. There were also other reasons why centralization of authority made sense for a union of steel workers. It faced stiff opposition from the industry during its formative years. Although the United States Steel Corporation unexpectedly signed an agreement with the SWOC in March 1937 without a strike, "Little Steel," which included Bethlehem, Republic, National, Armco, Inland, and Youngstown Sheet and Tube, fought the union bitterly and remained unorganized until 1941. Even then, the union did not have a union shop or checkoff in any major steel company, and there were many nonunion workers in the industry. Since it dealt with an industry dominated by one giant, U.S. Steel, and several mini-giants, whose policies were well coordinated, it was important for the union to speak with one voice. Success depended on a strong central organization and solidarity toward the industry. These factors were also important in representing the membership in the courts and the political arena as well as in relations with local, state, and national authorities, including the President of the United States.[16]

In order to succeed, the union had to fulfill its organizing-campaign promise to eliminate wage inequities within and between companies and to remove wages from competition in a national market for steel. To do this, it had to deal effectively with an oligopolistic industry operating in a national market, carry on active lobbying and public relations programs, and, if necessary, have the strength to shut down the entire industry by a national strike. Under the circumstances, a centralized structure was essential to successful organization and bargaining with the steel industry.

In its early years, when the United Mine Worker influence was predominant and, to a considerable degree, throughout Murray's presidency from 1942 to 1952, the union was tightly controlled from the top. Mur-

[16] *Ulman,* ch. 1.

ray's paternalistic attitude toward the union and its members was evident at its first Wage and Policy Convention in 1937 when he said: "Our union is young. . . . It is growing, and we must exercise care in the development of this child until it reaches maturity."[17] Thirteen years later when convention delegates were agitating for more local autonomy in contract approval, Murray's response continued to reflect the extent to which his Mine Worker background had molded his philosophy of leadership: "We don't do as a lot of organizations do . . . with respect to collective bargaining processes," he said. "The policy of the Steelworkers Union . . . is the policy of the United Mine Workers. . . . I happen to be one of those who assisted in that organization's policy for . . . 28 or 30 years and the mine workers never raised objections to the policy because they found out in the end that they were able to get more out of it."[18]

The veneration in which Murray was held enabled him to turn back demands for greater local autonomy and more democratic decision-making processes. Under his successors, numerous changes were made which had the effect of giving local unions and their leaders more of a voice in the union's affairs. However, despite many amendments, the Steelworker constitution has continued to reaffirm the authority of the international in such matters as hiring and firing of staff representatives, finances, mapping district jurisdictions, chartering locals, calling strikes, conducting negotiations, and placing administratorships over local unions for violating the constitution. The international exercises its authority through powers lodged in the president and the executive board, periodic audits of local union finances, and the staff of 1,125 field representatives and 469 headquarters personnel, who are hired, directed, and paid by the international office of the union.[19]

The union has five national officers: president, vice-president for administration, vice-president for human affairs, secretary, and treasurer. The 1976 convention established the position of vice-president for human affairs in response to pressure from black members and also split the office of secretary-treasurer into two positions. The international executive board consists of the five national officers, the national director for Canada, and 25 district directors. Under the union's constitution, a strong president has ample power to run the union and control collective bargaining policy. While subject to control by the executive

---

[17] *Proceedings, First Wage and Policy Convention,* 1937, p. 10, as quoted from Livernash and others, *Collective Bargaining in the Basic Steel Industry,* p. 80. (Hereafter cited as *Collective Bargaining in the Basic Steel Industry.*)

[18] *Proceedings of the Fifth Constitutional Convention of the United Steelworkers of America* (Atlantic City, N.J.: 1950), p. 275.

[19] Ulman, ch. 1; staff figures are from *Audit Report, July 1 to December 31, 1976* (Pittsburgh: United Steelworkers of America, 1977).

board, the president is able to exert considerable influence over that body through his constitutional powers and his authority to control the international staff and resources necessary to the political security of the district directors. Under the presidencies of McDonald and Abel, the executive board has exhibited more independence than it did under Murray, but the president is still the dominant figure in the union.

The international officers and the district directors are elected by membership referendum, with each director being chosen by members within his own district. As long as Murray was president, the referendum was merely an exercise in reaffirming confidence in his leadership. Except for a few district directors, Murray and his running-mates were never opposed for election. However, this was not true during the incumbency of Murray's successors. McDonald succeeded to the presidency upon Murray's death and his post of secretary-treasurer was filled by I. W. Abel, a district director from Canton, Ohio. In February 1953, they and Vice-President James Thimmes were elected without opposition. In 1955, McDonald's control was challenged within the executive board when a number of district directors refused to support his candidate for the vice-presidential vacancy caused by Thimmes's death. Dissident directors backed Joseph P. Molony, district director in Buffalo, against McDonald's administrative assistant, Howard Hague. Although Hague won with twice as many votes as Molony, this was the first of what was to become, in subsequent years, a series of contested elections for international office in the Steelworker union.

The first challenge to a Steelworker president occurred in 1957, when relatively unknown Donald Rarick, leader of a rank-and-file dues-protest movement, managed to poll a surprising 35 percent of the vote against McDonald. McDonald was unopposed in 1961 but, in 1965, almost half the district directors revolted against his leadership and supported a slate headed by Secretary-Treasurer Abel. Running on a campaign of returning the union to the membership, opposition to the Human Relations Committee[20] established as a part of the settlement of the 1959 steel strike, and dissatisfaction over unresolved local issues, Abel won by 10,000 votes out of 600,000 cast. Apart from substantive campaign issues, McDonald's image as a high-liver and a playboy suffered in comparison with Abel's reputation as a hard-working officer who had come up from the ranks. Along with Abel, the union elected a new vice-president and secretary-treasurer and 14 pro-Abel district directors, out of a total of 29. Despite the almost even split among district directors, the executive board united behind the new administration.

---

[20] See, pp. 168–70 of this chapter for a discussion of the Human Relations Committee.

Abel's defeat of an incumbent president demonstrated that it could be done, and in 1969, another unknown, a staff lawyer, Emil Narick, ran against him. Narick ran an even more surprising race than Rarick had run in 1957 against McDonald. Without any overt policy issues and against a president whose private and public life were unassailable, Narick, running on an "antiestablishment" program, polled 181,122 to Abel's 257,651. Even more surprising was Narick's showing in the large basic steel locals where he outpolled Abel by substantial margins. Although the three top officers were reelected, a number of incumbent district directors were defeated in 1969, giving the executive board a decidedly new look. This election, even more than the unsuccessful challenge to McDonald in 1957 and his defeat in 1965, indicated an underlying unrest among the membership that the officers and district directors could ignore only at their peril. All three elections were challenged by the losers and pointed up glaring defects in the union's election procedures.[21]

Abel was unopposed for reelection in 1973, but in 1977, when the Steelworker compulsory retirement at age 65 precluded his candidacy, the union experienced its first campaign involving two nonincumbent candidates. The administration ticket, supported by the officers and all but one of the district directors, was headed by Lloyd McBride, a 60-year-old director from St. Louis. He was opposed by Edward Sadlowski, 38 years old, director of the union's largest district covering the Chicago-Gary area. Sadlowski ran on a platform opposing the Experimental Negotiating Agreement (ENA), adopted by the union and the industry in 1973, and charging that the top leadership was working too closely with the steel companies and not paying enough attention to local issues. McBride generally supported Abel's policies, although he expressed an open mind regarding continuation of the ENA. Both candidates ran full slates for the top five offices. The campaign was hotly contested and acrimonious. McBride won, with 57 percent of the 578,000 votes cast, as did all of his running mates. There were contests in 15 of the 25 districts and for the position of National Director of Canada. Incumbents were defeated in three districts, and many directors did not seek reelection.[22] Something new was added to the union's leadership in the election of Lynn Williams, a Canadian, as secretary. This was the first time that Canada's 190,000 members were represented in the national leadership of the union. Only three other U.S. unions have a Canadian international officer.

[21] Herling, *Right to Challenge*, pp. 380–81.
[22] *Daily Labor Report No. 83*, April 28, 1977 (Washington: Bureau of National Affairs, Inc., date).

Shortly after taking office, McBride, in what may be indicative of his administrative style, reorganized headquarters' operations in Pittsburgh by allocating specific areas of responsibility to the other four officers. Previously, most departments reported directly to the president. Under the reorganization, the president will oversee the union's legal and legislative activities. The other 24 departments and operational sections were divided among the secretary, treasurer, and the two vice-presidents, each of whom will report to the president.[23]

NEGOTIATION PROCEDURES

Rank-and-file involvement in basic steel and other negotiations is exercised through the Wage Policy Committee (WPC) and 19 industry conferences. The WPC consists of the international officers, the district directors, and about 145 delegates elected on the basis of membership in each district.[24] The Wage Policy Committee is supposed to set bargaining policy for the entire union on the basis of local, district, and international convention resolutions. In practice, the committee acts on a statement prepared by the international staff from resolutions submitted by district conferences and local unions and suggestions of international officers and key staff members. The various negotiating committees have maximum flexibility in deciding the weight to be given to the demands incorporated in the policy statement. Until 1966, when the industry conferences were established, the WPC was also responsible for recommending strikes and ratifying or rejecting contracts and strike settlements in major negotiations.

Only four conferences, all of them in industries characterized by national bargaining—basic steel, aluminum, nonferrous metals, and containers—have been given full authority to draw up uniform bargaining proposals to present to companies in their industries. Conferences in industries in which bargaining is on a plant or individual-company basis continue to operate under general collective bargaining goals formulated by the Wage Policy Committee. The four bargaining conferences have responsibility for recommending strikes to the international executive board and for ratifying or rejecting contract settlements. A strike can be called only after a vote of the industry membership, but no such vote is required before conference rejection or ratification of a settlement.

Industry conferences, unlike the Wage Policy Committee which draws its members from the entire union, are restricted to members directly affected by negotiations in a given industry. Membership is

[23] *Steel Labor,* August 1977.
[24] *Report of the Officers of the Seventeenth Constitutional Convention of the United Steelworkers of America* (Atlantic City, N.J.: 1974), pp. 40–41.

drawn from local unions within the industry plus district directors and presiding officers designated by the international president. Staff members are assigned to provide technical assistance to each conference. Each local union has a single vote in the conference regardless of membership size.[25]

MEMBERSHIP

In December 1976, the Steelworkers had 1,400,000 members in 5,700 local unions, making it the largest union in the AFL-CIO and second only to the Teamsters in the nation.[26] The union has compensated for membership losses in basic steel, where employment has been declining, by intensified organizing efforts and mergers with other unions. In 1967, the Mine, Mill and Smelter Workers Union with 75,000 members, primarily in nonferrous metals, joined the Steelworkers; in 1971, about 20,000 members were added through merger of the United Stone and Allied Products Workers; and in 1972, District 50 Allied and Technical Workers voted to merge its 175,000 members with the Steelworkers. About 35 percent of the membership is in basic steel and iron mining; no other industry conference contains as much as 10 percent of the union's members. The union has had limited success in organizing office employees who constitute only 3 percent of the membership. Of some 15,000 organized office and technical employees, about half are employed by U.S. Steel.

FINANCES

Started with loans of over $1.5 million from the CIO and the United Mine Workers, the Steelworkers in 1976 had a net worth of $136 million including $94 million in the strike and defense fund. Additional monetary resources of about $65 million were held at the local union level, exclusive of Canada.[27] In keeping with the relatively high earnings of its members, Steelworker dues are also higher than those of most unions. Each member is assessed two hours' pay per month which, in 1977, amounted to at least $13 for the average steel worker and more than $20 for those in the top job classifications. The first $6 of each member's dues is divided equally between the international and the local union; of the remainder, 40 percent goes to the international, 40 percent to the local, and 20 percent to the union strike and defense fund. Local unions receive half of the $10 initiation fee; the other half goes to the international.[28]

---

[25] Ibid., pp. 37, 93.

[26] Audit Report . . . 1976, p. 1.

[27] A Ten-Year Record of Progress, 1965-1975 (Pittsburgh: United Steelworkers of America, 1976), p. 8; Audit Report . . . 1976.

[28] International Constitution of the United Steelworkers of America, 1974.

Dues increases and the distribution of dues between the international and local unions have always been a source of contention within the union. Despite frequent strikes prior to 1960, the leadership successfully opposed proposals to establish a national strike fund until 1968 on the ground that such a fund was impractical to meet workers' needs in an industrywide strike. Even Philip Murray had difficulty in getting convention delegates to vote dues increases and in putting down demands to allocate a higher proportion of dues to the local unions. In 1946 locals succeeded in increasing their share of dues from one-fourth to one-half, where it has remained.[29] By tying dues to earnings in 1968, first with a maximum of $10 which was dropped in 1974, the union eliminated the necessity for asking convention delegates to deal regularly with the thorny issue of dues increases. As long as wages continue to rise, dues will also go up.

The Steelworkers is one of the few major unions which has resisted the trend to move its headquarters office to Washington. The union headquarters has always been located in Pittsburgh and is housed in one of the new skyscrapers in the city's Golden Triangle at the confluence of the Allegheny and Monongahela rivers.

Bargaining Structure

During the 40 years since U.S. Steel recognized the Steel Workers Organizing Committee in 1937, the bargaining process has undergone major changes. The initial agreement to recognize the union, reached by CIO President John L. Lewis and U.S. Steel Chairman Myron C. Taylor, was not followed by most other steel companies, which held out until 1941. These first agreements with the union were reached separately by each company, and individual-company agreements have continued, even though the process whereby they have been arrived at has changed from bargaining on a company-by-company basis to what is in effect industrywide bargaining.[30]

FROM COMPANY TO INDUSTRY NEGOTIATIONS

Steel companies have always made a point of their individuality and the differences between them with respect to basic steel capacity, variety of finished steel products, degree of integration, differences in labor markets in which plants were located, profitability, and other factors. Despite these differences, there has been a strong tendency toward uniformity in wage scales and wage adjustments dating back to the late

---

[29] Ulman, pp. 45–51.

[30] The major agreement is between the union and the Coordinating Committee Steel Companies which, at different times, has represented from 9 to 12 companies with about three-fourths of the nation's steel-making capacity.

19th and early 20th centuries, long before the advent of the Steelworkers union. This insistence on individuality and company-by-company bargaining persisted until 1955, despite union efforts to bargain on an industrywide basis. Separate negotiating committees met at each company's principal location. But, in practice, the committees generally marked time until a settlement was reached between the union and U.S. Steel. This settlement was then followed, possibly with minor adaptations, by each of the major companies. The fact that the economic bargains were virtually identical did not deter the companies from refusing to negotiate jointly, let alone reach a common agreement applicable to all of them. During disputes in World War II and also in 1946, 1949, and 1952, the companies resisted requests by government-appointed boards that, in order to save time, they make a single industry presentation of their case. They did agree to a consolidated presentation by a coordinating committee supplemented by individual-company statements.

The first break in strict company-by-company bargaining came in 1955 when the top six companies agreed to a Steelworker proposal that their respective committees meet separately with the union in Pittsburgh, where the union and U.S. Steel were headquartered, rather than in the different cities where companies had their principal offices. While this may appear to have been only a minor departure from past practice, it was significant because it permitted Steelworker President McDonald to lead the negotiations of each committee, rather than having district directors head committees in locations outside of Pittsburgh. This change of venue insured against the possibility that a district director, chairing negotiations with a lesser company, might settle before McDonald and his committee reached agreement with U.S. Steel, thereby undercutting the first-term union president who was still trying to consolidate his position. It also enabled the union to make more efficient use of its limited number of technicians in negotiations and reduced the likelihood of deviations from the U.S. Steel pattern. The change was probably welcomed by U.S. Steel because it too did not like deviations from the pattern set in its own negotiations and wanted to eliminate the facade of individual-company bargaining which in fact did not exist. The other companies either could not or did not deem it worthwhile to resist the combined pressure of the two major forces in the industry's collective bargaining.

A second and more significant step toward industry bargaining occurred in 1956 when 12 major steel companies authorized a four-member committee to bargain on major issues on their behalf. Other issues were left to individual-company bargaining. The industry committee consisted of two representatives from U.S. Steel, and one each from Bethlehem and Republic. The union was represented by its three international officers and the general counsel.[31] The memorandum of agreement, reached after a 36-day strike, was signed by all 12 companies.

In 1959, the major companies went even further toward recognizing the precedence of their common over individual interests by authorizing a four-member committee to negotiate on their behalf on all issues. The union would have preferred to continue the previous arrangement whereby nonmajor issues were left to individual company-by-company bargaining. Indeed, when negotiations were found to be making no headway, the union wanted to return to individual bargaining as they had in 1956. The industry refused and intimated that any union strategy designed to divide them might result in a mutual-aid pact and a strike-insurance agreement. The industry's strong resistance to a return to company bargaining may have been influenced by the following factors:

1. Recognition that individual companies could not resist a strong centralized union which represented all steel workers.

2. Elimination or reduction of differences in wages, benefits, and other provisions between companies during previous negotiations, leaving little incentive for any company to want to bargain individually.

3. Defense against a possible union strategy of trying to avoid a Taft-Hartley injunction by striking companies on a selective basis rather than shutting down the entire industry.

4. Desire by other companies to have a voice in a final settlement rather than having to follow an agreement reached by the union with U.S. Steel or another pace-setting company.

5. Concern on the part of U.S. Steel that its leadership in industrial relations might be challenged by another company, particularly Bethlehem Steel, which had been the first company to settle with the union on pensions and insurance in 1949 and, in 1952, was prepared to grant a union shop against Big Steel's wishes. Furthermore, U.S. Steel was reasonably certain that it

---

[31] An interesting and unusual characteristic of the Steelworkers has been the extremely important role played by the general counsel, both in negotiations and the internal affairs of the union. Lee Pressman was general counsel from 1937 to 1948 when Murray forced him to resign because of his identification with communists in both the Steelworkers and the CIO. He was succeeded by Arthur J. Goldberg whose influence was even greater than Pressman's. Goldberg served from 1949 to 1961 when he was appointed Secretary of Labor by President John Kennedy. After Goldberg, the influence of the general counsel has diminished, although he is still a member of the union's top negotiating team. Ulman ascribes this unusual reliance on lawyers to the Steelworkers' continuing involvement with the federal government. The fact that Pressman and Goldberg were exceptionally talented undoubtedly also contributed to their influence on both the Steelworkers and the CIO (Ulman, pp. 73–75).

would be the prime choice for strike action if the union decided to follow a selective-strike strategy.[32]

As for the union, while a selective-strike strategy had some appeal, it also had certain risks and raised difficult questions: Which company or companies should be struck, and how would union solidarity be affected by some members walking picket lines while others in adjoining or nearby plants were working? In the absence of a strike fund, which was not established until 1968, how were striking workers to be cared for? Could the union win a strike against U.S. Steel or a combination of other companies without the prospect of government intervention which was unlikely unless the entire industry was shut down?

In view of these factors and unanswered questions, it is not surprising that both sides preferred to continue their movement toward industry bargaining rather than revert to individual company-by-company negotiations.[33] The 116-day 1959 strike helped to solidify industry bargaining and also marked a turning-point in the way in which bargaining was conducted. As a result of the strike, the parties recognized the need to maintain a continuing relationship between contract negotiations to deal with problems that did not lend themselves to resolution during periodic meetings. The 1960 settlement provided for the establishment of a Human Relations Research Committee "to plan and oversee studies and recommend solutions of mutual problems" in several specified areas: "Guides for the determination of equitable wage and benefit adjustments," the job-classification system, wage incentives, seniority especially as it relates to layoff and recall, medical care, and "such other overall problems as the parties, by mutual agreement, may from time to time refer to the Committee."[34]

Only the first of the above-noted "problems" was really new, since the industry and the union had had a long history of cooperation on job-classification and other day-to-day problems of contract administration. The name of the committee was changed in 1962 to the Human

---

[32] For a more detailed account of bargaining structure prior to 1960, see Stieber, "Company Cooperation . . . ," and Collective Bargaining in the Basic Steel Industry, ch. 6.

[33] Union and industry real positions and motivations on company-by-company vs. industry bargaining are difficult to ascertain. Prior to the 1959–60 strike and settlement, both sides were always maneuvering with an eye to government intervention and how it would affect the outcome of negotiations. Consequently public statements may have been bargaining ploys designed to induce or deter government intervention. The author's assessment is based on a careful reading of the record supplemented by personal discussions with top level union and company officials. (For other accounts, see the "Report of the Subcommittee on Labor Disputes in the Basic Steel Industry," American Bar Association, Section of Labor Relations Law, Program of the 1966 Annual Meeting, 1966 Committee Reports (Chicago: American Bar Center), pp. 367–74.)

[34] Healy, ch. 7.

Relations Committee (HRC) in recognition that its function went beyond fact-finding to include recommendations and negotiations in an effort to reach mutually acceptable solutions.

THE HUMAN RELATIONS COMMITTEE

The HRC initially provided for co-chairmen who were to be "two persons of outstanding qualifications and objectivity," one chosen by the companies and the other by the union. This allusion to neutral co-chairmen was soon abandoned and the chief negotiators for U.S. Steel and the union, R. Conrad Cooper and David McDonald, were named co-chairmen. The rest of the committee's membership consisted of the other three principal negotiators on each side. The study functions of the committee were performed by subcommittees made up of union and industry representatives.

The parties soon reached an impasse and gave up on the first and most ambitious objective of the HRC—establishing guides for the determination of equitable wage and benefit adjustments. However, the subcommittees dealing with more conventional subjects were highly productive. To the general public, the HRC was noteworthy, not for the accomplishments of its study committees which received little publicity, but for its success as a negotiating device to avoid strikes and achieve early settlements. The 1959 strike had convinced the parties that frequent steel strikes were too costly for both sides. The industry lost business to foreign steelmakers through increased imports and to producers of steel substitutes such as aluminum, plastics, glass, wood, and paper products. Buying habits were also changed, with consumers stocking up on steel inventories in anticipation of a strike, thus reducing demand even after settlements reached without a strike. The union recognized that work lost during a strike could become permanent because buyers became locked into long-term contracts with foreign suppliers or continued to use steel substitutes. Thus, strikes or the possibility of strikes caused irreplaceable losses in profits and jobs.

The HRC continuous study and negotiation approach was praised by industry, government, steel users, students of industrial relations, and the general public. The union and especially its president, David McDonald, were hailed for having learned a lesson from the 1959 strike and for following farsighted and statesmanlike policies. But what appeared as successes to outside observers were viewed differently within the union. The work of the HRC, which led to early and relatively modest settlements in 1962 and 1963, had the effect of diminishing the role of the district directors and local union leaders who served on negotiating committees. By the time contract negotiation time rolled around, international union staff members—lawyers, economists, pension experts, and other specialists—serving on subcommittees had reached agreement with their industry counterparts on most issues, leaving little for negotiating committees to do. McDonald was criticized for having turned negotiations over to the technicians.

In addition, the traditional union attitude was that employers came up with their best offer only at the last minute when a strike was imminent. Thus, an "early" settlement was, by definition, a "poor" settlement. As a result, McDonald, in 1965, faced a revolt which had as its campaign cry, "Give the Union back to the membership." This time the dissidents' candidate was not a nonentity like Donald Rarick who ran against McDonald in 1957, but the secretary-treasurer, I. W. Abel, running on a slate with two of the union's popular district directors, Walter Burke and Joseph Molony.

While the revolt against the HRC was not the only issue in the 1965 election, the narrow margin by which McDonald lost indicates that he would almost certainly have been reelected if he had not had this additional cross to bear into the campaign. In the first steel negotiations following the election, a strike was narrowly avoided by a last-minute settlement which resulted in sizable economic benefits and eliminated any reference to the HRC from the ensuing contracts. But while the HRC was gone, the contracts contained provisions for continued joint study of apprenticeship training, testing, grievance and arbitration procedures, and other problems which might arise during the term of the agreement. In addition, the study committees continued to meet under "Human Relations Rules," which meant that all discussions were off the record unless and until the parties reached agreement. Also continued were the meetings between the top industry and union negotiators who had the final say on agreements reached by study committees. However, the HRC's role in negotiations over contract renewals, which was most criticized during the Steelworker election campaign, was eliminated.

Within two years of his election, Abel tried to sell the union on a scheme designed to eliminate crisis bargaining in the industry with its attendant problems of inventory stockpiling, increased imports, and lost work for union members. In 1967, the top union and company negotiators who had been meeting periodically came up with the idea that, if a settlement could not be reached in 1968 negotiations, the parties should agree in advance to submit their dispute to arbitration and forgo economic action. HRC rules would govern negotiations and, if agreement was not reached on all issues, either party would be free to raise any issue in arbitration. This approach was designed to assure steel customers that there would be no strike and, at the same time, create maximum incentive for the parties to reach agreement in negotiations rather than risk reopening all issues in arbitration.

This was truly a new and novel approach to negotiations. But the union's international executive board refused to buy it. Some directors considered it "political suicide," coming only two years after McDonald's defeat for "taking the Union away from the membership." Others preferred to rely on old-fashioned bargaining which placed maximum pressure on the industry by threatening strike action if agreement was not reached.

Without executive board support, the idea was dropped and 1968 negotiations followed the traditional pattern. Inventories accumulated months before the strike deadline, imports reached a new high, a settlement was reached only minutes before the expiration of the contract, and steel production fell by 30 percent in the months after the agreement was signed. The idea of guaranteeing continued production by prior agreement to arbitration was ahead of its time. Five years later, it was revived, in modified form, and accepted by the union.[35]

The Experimental Negotiating Agreement

Negotiations in 1971 followed established procedures with the major companies and the union reaching a settlement on national issues, followed by individual-company agreements on local issues. Sixteen months before the expiration of this agreement, on March 29, 1973, the union and the industry coordinating committee startled the industrial relations world by announcing that they had adopted an Experimental Negotiating Agreement (ENA) that would govern negotiations on a new contract in 1974. The most significant provision of the ENA was an agreement not to strike or lockout at the expiration of the contract and to submit all national issues not resolved through collective bargaining to a panel of impartial arbitrators for final and binding decision. Thus the parties guaranteed that there would be no interruption of steel production the following year.

The no-strike–no-lockout guarantee of the 1973 agreement was similar to the proposal rejected by the union in 1967. However, the six years that had elapsed plus some significant additions made the ENA acceptable where its predecessor had failed. By 1973, I. W. Abel had been president of the Steelworkers for eight years and had established much greater control over the union than he commanded as a fledgling president in 1967. The 1968 and 1971 negotiations, though settled without

---

[35] For an "insider's" view of the Human Relations Committee, see Feller, pp. 152–59.

strikes, had been accompanied by substantial accumulation of inventories and by an upsurge of steel imports, followed by a drastic drop in production and employment after agreement was reached. By 1973, the union leadership had unequivocally accepted the industry's belief that drastic action was necessary to quell steel imports in order to maintain the domestic market for American steel and prevent postsettlement layoffs and unemployment.

But economic arguments alone would probably not have sufficed to persuade district directors to give up the right to strike had the industry not sweetened the agreement by the following concessions:

1. The no-strike agreement would not extend to local issues. For the first time in the history of steel negotiations, local unions were given the right to strike over local issues, subject to approval of the international president.

2. Each steel employee would be given a bonus of $150 "because economic advantages could accrue to the companies by elimination of the effects of hedge-buying and shutdowns."

3. A minimum wage increase of 3 percent per year would be granted at the beginning of each contract year, subject to additional increases which might be negotiated by the parties.

4. The cost-of-living agreement providing a 1 cent increase in wages for each .3 increase in the 1967 Consumer Price Index (instead of 1 cent for each .4 increase in the 1957–59 CPI provided in the 1971 contract) would be continued for the term of the new agreement.

5. If the parties went to arbitration, provisions dealing with local working conditions, union shop and checkoff, the principle of cost-of-living adjustments, wage increases and the bonus under ENA, management rights, and the no-strike–no-lockout commitment could not be changed.

Of the above, granting the right to strike on local issues after an industry settlement was most important. It was accepted by the companies with great reluctance and only because they were convinced that the union would not agree to the ENA without this provision. The right to strike on local issues is particularly objectionable to a company like Inland Steel, which produces all of its steel in a single plant. For Inland, a local strike is a company strike. Local strikes are also a threat to multiplant companies, because customers may shift orders from struck plants or plants in which local agreements have not been reached to others where settlements have been negotiated. Inland and other reluctant companies were persuaded to go along with the industry coordinating committee decision only by a detailed spelling-out of the local issues provision. The ENA defined a "local issue" and set forth a timetable for negotiations on such issues, the manner in which a strike vote was to be conducted, and, most important of all, the requirement that a local strike must be authorized by the international president of the union. In effect, the industry was depending on the Steelworker president to protect against a pattern of local strikes that could have the effect of shutting down all or a substantial portion of the industry.

The ENA provided the following time schedule for industry negotiations in 1974:

February 1:	Begin negotiations.
April 15:	Reach full agreement on all issues or agree on certain issues and submit remaining issues to an arbitration panel.
April 20:	If arbitration required, parties submit an agreed list of issues to panel; or, if unable to agree on issues, submit their respective formulations of such issues.
May 10:	Parties submit to panel and exchange detailed statements on issues.
May 20:	Parties submit to panel and exchange replies to each other's statements.
June 1:	Arbitration hearings begin.
July 10:	Panel renders decision.
July 20:	Parties reach agreement on contract language and other steps to implement panel decision.
July 31:	Panel decides unresolved questions on implementation of award.
August 1:	Effective date of panel award.

The ENA also provided a rigid schedule for negotiations on local issues:

April 1:	Deadline for beginning discussions at plant level. No additional issues may be submitted after this date, except as a result of changed conditions.
May 1:	Unresolved local issues referred to co-chairmen of union-company negotiating committee.
June 10:	Union chairman at each company decides whether to withdraw local issues or put them to secret ballot vote of all employees in plant.
June 30:	Deadline for local vote on issues.
July 8:	If majority vote for strike, dispute is referred to international president for permission to strike.
July 15:	President forwards decision on strike request to union co-chairman with copy to company co-chairman. If strike permission granted, president

specifies date strike must begin, which shall not be earlier than August 1.

August 1: Earliest date for strike over local issues. If strike does not begin on first scheduled turn of date specified by president, the right to strike is automatically canceled.

The same timetable starting June 10 applied to the right of a company to lock out on local issues.[36]

Should arbitration be required, ENA rules called for a five-member panel: one appointed by the union, one by the companies, and three neutrals appointed by agreement of the parties, of whom two "shall be persons who are thoroughly familiar with collective bargaining agreements in the steel industry." The panel membership, including a chairman designated by the parties, must be completed by February 1. Only the impartial members of the panel have a vote, and all decisions are to be by majority vote. Other rules governing the panel's deliberations are:

1. Hearings begin not later than June 1 at times and places agreed to by the parties.

2. Upon joint request of the parties made before June 30, the panel shall refer back issues for further negotiation.

3. Hearings are informal and not governed by statutory or common-law rules of evidence.

4. In order to encourage frank discussion during negotiations, conversations and proposals during such negotiations "shall not be referred to" in presentation to panel, except as parties agree otherwise.

5. Panel decision shall give facts and reasons for conclusions to enable parties to understand and implement decisions.

6. Decisions are effective August 1 and specific provisions shall become applicable as of dates provided in the award.

7. Decisions are final and binding on the parties.

8. Impartial member fees and expenses are shared equally by the parties.[37]

The years 1973 and 1974 set records for steel production with resulting high profits and employment. While factors other than ENA were operative during these years, the parties and outside observers credited the no-strike guarantee with contributing to steel industry prosperity. Negotiating under ENA conditions, the union and the industry coordinating committee reached agreement on a new contract

[36] "Steel Industry's Experimental Negotiating Agreement," 83 LRR 79, May 21, 1973.
[37] *Ibid.*

three and one-half months before the expiration date of the old contract. The new contract continued the ENA, guaranteeing labor peace in the steel industry until at least 1980. Industry concern over the ENA local-strike option was allayed when there were no strikes over local issues in 1974. The ENA had passed its first test with flying colors.

Under provisions of the 1974 agreement, ENA rules, with minor modifications in the time schedule, again governed 1977 negotiations. Formulation of union demands started, as usual, with a bargaining program, developed by the officers and staff members, based on resolutions adopted by the 1976 constitutional convention of the union. The next step was the Statement of the International Wage Policy Committee adopted in December 1976. This was followed by discussions and deliberations of the Basic Steel Industry Planning Committee in January and a meeting of the Basic Steel Industry Conference in February.[38] It is this latter group which adopts the broad outlines of the program to guide negotiators in their meetings with the industry.

Bargaining began in February 1977 with the usual mass meeting of hundreds of international union officers and staff, basic steel local union presidents, and a large number of company and plant representatives of the ten major steel companies. The first day of the two-day meeting was allotted to the union and the second to the companies in what are appropriately called "sound-off" sessions. The union presented its demands with supporting statements by officers, local representatives, and staff members. Industry spokesmen responded. This industrywide sound-off was followed by individual company "sound-off" meetings which, in 1977, started in mid-February and continued for the rest of the month.[39]

Industry negotiations started on February 16 under a modified ENA schedule, and settlement on a new three-year contract was reached on April 8. The new contract included agreement to continue the ENA during the 1980 negotiations, assuring that there would be no national steel strike until at least 1983.[40] However, unlike 1974 when there were

[38] In 1968, the union established an Eleven Company Negotiating Advisory Committee to make available a representative group of local union leaders in basic steel, whose views would reflect rank-and-file thinking, as an advisory body to the union's negotiating committee. This body was continued in subsequent negotiations and variously called the Policy Planning Committee and the Basic Steel Industry Planning Committee. In the 1977 negotiations, this committee was made up of 55 local union presidents, district directors, and headquarters technicians selected by the Steelworker president. It reviewed the Wage Policy Committee statement and drafted a working paper of basic steel bargaining objectives for consideration at the Basic Steel Industry Conference. (Resolution of the International Board adopted March 18, 1968, and letter to author from Otis Brubaker, Steelworker Research Director, dated November 15, 1977.)

[39] *Steel Labor*, March 1977.

[40] The terms of the ENA were readopted with one modification. The parties provided that the guaranteed minimum annual wage increase of 3 percent could, by mutual agreement, be applied to other wage or benefit items.

no strikes over local issues, 15,000 iron ore miners in 16 mines voted and received authorization to strike over local issues after agreement was reached on a national contract in 1977. The strikes started on August 1 and lasted four and one-half months before settlements were reached and ratified by all striking local unions. The major issue— incentive pay for iron miners—gave rise to a dispute over what constituted a local issue. The settlement included agreement to modify the ENA so that future disputes over the definition of local issues would be settled through arbitration.

The Strike-Prone Years

Strikes have been endemic to the steel industry since the late 19th century. In 1892, the Amalgamated Iron and Steel Workers struck the Homestead plant of the Carnegie-Illinois Corporation in response to the company's attempt to reduce wages and eliminate the union from its operation. Production continued during the strike under protection of the state militia and about 300 Pinkerton agents, and several workers were killed. The Amalgamated was driven from Homestead and Carnegie-Illinois plants and, by 1894, its membership had dropped from 29,000 before the strike to about 10,000.

The Amalgamated next struck U.S. Steel in 1901, in an attempt to secure a contract with the newly organized corporation that had resulted from the merger of numerous steel producers. Again strike-breakers were able to keep operations going and, after a month-long strike, the union was forced to accept terms less favorable than those originally offered by the corporation. A third strike occurred in 1909 when U.S. Steel tried to oust the Amalgamated from mills in which it had contracts with the corporation. After a 14-month strike, the corporation was successful in removing the union from all its plants, and by 1914 the Amalgamated represented workers in only a few independent steel companies accounting for about 20 percent of steel production.[41]

The next major confrontation between steel labor and management occurred in 1919. This time the strike was called by the National Committee for Organizing the Iron and Steel Workers led by William Z. Foster, a radical labor leader, formerly associated with the Industrial Workers of the World (IWW) and later a leader of the Communist Party in the United States. The committee, which represented only about 20 percent of steel employment, demanded the right to bargain collectively, an 8-hour day and a 6-day workweek, abolition of the 24-hour shift, increased wages, and the dissolution of company unions. Despite efforts by AFL President Samuel Gompers to discourage a

---

[41] Brody, *Steelworkers in America*, pp. 50–51, 62–68, 71–74; Hogan, pp. 231–33.

strike, 350,000 workers left the mills in September 1919. Though public opinion was initially favorable to the steel workers, the radical background of Foster and Gompers's initial disapproval of the stoppage eventually turned the public against the strike. The workers returned to the plants in January 1920 without having achieved their objectives.[42]

During the 1920s, unionization in the steel industry was at a very low level. Paternalism, welfare programs, and employee representation plans were pursued by the industry through the early 1930s. Unionism was resurrected by the Great Depression, the National Industry Recovery Act of 1933, followed by the National Labor Relations Act and the formation of the CIO and the Steel Workers Organizing Committee (SWOC) in 1935.[43] U.S. Steel's surprise recognition of the SWOC in March 1937 was followed only by the Jones and Laughlin Steel Corporation among the second rank of steel companies. In May and June of 1937, the union struck "Little Steel" in strikes marked by violence, bloodshed, and death. The companies succeeded in breaking the strike during the first two weeks in July, aided by a combination of poor economic conditions and inability of the fledgling union to maintain simultaneous strikes against so many companies on such a broad front. The fact that unfair-labor-practice charges against the companies were eventually sustained and cost them several million dollars in back pay was small comfort to the union in its drive to organize Little Steel. Four years later, the union won bargaining rights in Little Steel as a result of National Labor Relations Board elections.

Despite the 1938 recession, the SWOC was able to preserve existing wage rates in U.S. Steel but made little headway in organizing other companies. During the war years that followed, contracts were negotiated peacefully with the aid of the War Labor Board, except for a four-day strike in December 1943. Wages were increased 10 cents in 1941 and, in 1942, the War Labor Board's "Little Steel Formula" resulted in an additional increase of 5.5 cents. The union also gained maintenance of membership, dues checkoff, exclusive bargaining rights, and a start on fringe benefits on which to build in future years. In 1944, the War Labor Board rejected union demands for a wage increase, elimination of geographical differentials, and equal pay for equal work throughout the industry. The Board did, however, provide up to 5 cents an hour for elimination of intraplant wage-rate inequities, a decision which subsequently facilitated negotiation of an industrywide job-classification system. Take-home pay was increased by the introduction of shift differentials, and vacation provisions were also liberalized.

---

[42] Brody, *Labor in Crisis*, pp. 67–68.
[43] Galenson, pp. 75–122.

The end of the war found both sides adamant in their insistence on recouping perceived losses suffered during the war. From the union's viewpoint, steel workers had failed to keep up with increases in the cost of living, and take-home pay was expected to decline due to a postwar reduction in the workweek. The industry was chafing under price restraints imposed during the war which, in the steel companies' view, unfairly limited profits. A similar situation prevailed in many other industries. After five months of negotiations, fact-finding, and presidential intervention, the largest steel strike in history, involving 750,000 workers in basic steel and steel fabrication companies, started on January 21, 1946. Only Kaiser Steel, which accepted an 18.5-cent increase proposed by President Truman, continued to operate. After a month-long strike and following strike settlements in the automobile industry, a settlement was reached on the basis of an 18.5-cent wage increase and government agreement to permit the companies to raise steel prices by $5.00 per ton. This was the first of several steel strikes in which wages and prices were linked in settlements reached after three-way negotiations between the union, the industry, and the government.[44]

In January 1947, the industry and the union reached agreement, after two years of negotiation, on a job-classification program known as the Cooperative Wage Study (CWS), after the office set up by the companies to coordinate their negotiations. It covered approximately 180,000 jobs in 450 basic steel plants representing 90 percent of the industry. It went beyond the War Labor Board directive and dealt with interplant as well as intraplant inequities. This was the first in a series of joint efforts by the companies and the union in a relationship which has been marked by a high degree of mutuality and understanding on some matters at the same time that antagonism and strife were prevalent in contract negotiations.[45]

Shortly after announcement of the inequities agreement, the parties entered negotiations on a new contract. In relatively harmonious meetings, free of government intervention for the first time in many years, agreement was reached with U.S. Steel on a contract worth about 15 cents per hour—12.5 cents across the board plus a half-cent increase in the increment between job classes. In addition, vacations were increased, the southern wage differential was reduced, severance pay was introduced for plant closures, and a number of significant contract changes were made. Other companies followed U.S. Steel's lead with some modifications, except for Inland Steel where a week-long strike

---

[44] For a detailed account of negotiations in the steel industry 1937–60, see *Collective Bargaining in the Basic Steel Industry*, pp. 235–307.

[45] See Stieber, *The Steel Industry Wage Structure*, for a detailed analysis of the wage-inequity program.

was settled with language providing for protection against wildcat strikes which had been a particular problem in this company. The completion of the inequities program and the peaceful 1947 contract negotiations were a high-water mark in relations between the parties that was not to be duplicated for many years to come.

In 1948, the union's hands were tied by the 1947 agreement which permitted reopening the contract on wages but without the right to strike. After negotiations characterized by much vituperation and charges of bad faith, the union accepted a 13-cent average wage increase in a two-year contract with a one-year reopener on wages and social insurance over which the union could strike. This settlement set the stage for another round of negotiations in 1949 which included government intervention, fact-finding hearings and recommendations,[46] a six-week strike, and finally a settlement giving steel workers a noncontributory pension program and a contributory insurance plan. The contract, reached in a recession year and against the backdrop of a decline in the Consumer Price Index during the first six months, included no wage increase and was to last for two years with a wage reopener in December 1950. An unusual aspect of the 1949 negotiations was that the pattern was set by Bethlehem Steel which settled before the traditional industry leader, U.S. Steel.

In 1950, negotiations were again carried on under war conditions, the Korean War having started in June. With demand for steel booming and profits excellent, the parties had little difficulty reaching agreement on a substantial wage increase averaging 16 cents per hour before wage and price stabilization policies were put in place. Price increases were instituted immediately thereafter with tacit government approval.

Starting in October 1951 and ending in July 1952, there took place the most dramatic labor negotiations that had yet occurred in steel or any other industry. They were marked by a war which was not going well, mounting inflation only slightly contained by half-hearted wage and price controls, government intervention through the Wage Stabilization Board, and the resignation of the head of the Office of Defense Mobilization because of differences with the President over steel wage-price policies. Before the drama ended, a new factor not previously present in U.S. labor relations—presidential seizure of the steel industry, which was subsequently declared unconstitutional by the U.S. Supreme Court—played a major role in the final settlement.

The union's demands encompassed both major economic benefits and

---

[46] This fact-finding board was not appointed under the Taft-Hartley Act national emergency disputes provisions because President Truman strongly opposed this part of the Act. This board could make recommendations, a power which was not available to boards appointed under the Taft-Hartley Act.

the full union shop. Thus, money was joined with principle in these negotiations. In a thinly veiled allusion to the tie between wages and steel prices, U.S. Steel President Benjamin Fairless responded to union demands with the statement that the wage issue "probably cannot be determined by collective bargaining and will apparently have to be decided finally in Washington." [47] The dispute went to the Wage Stabilization Board, which, industry members dissenting, recommended a 17.5-cent wage increase over 18 months, substantial improvements in fringe benefits, and a union shop. The union accepted the recommendations; the steel companies rejected them.

Negotiations ensued both with the union on wages and benefits and with the government on an allowable steel price increase. Apart from money items, the industry was unalterably opposed to granting a union shop. Faced with the prospect of a steel strike during a war and unwilling to use the emergency injunction provisions of the Taft-Hartley Act, President Truman blamed the industry for the impasse in negotiations and seized the steel mills on April 8, 1952, under the "inherent powers" of the presidency. The union called off the strike and the mills continued to operate while the companies appealed the seizure to the Supreme Court of the United States. On June 2, the Supreme Court decided 6 to 3 that the President's action was unconstitutional. Within hours, 560,000 steel workers went out on strike.

The strike, originally considered unthinkable during wartime, lasted 59 days. When the stoppage was almost two months old, industry representatives, at the invitation of the union, made an unprecedented appearance before the Steelworkers' Wage Policy Committee to present their case, with particular attention to the union shop which at that point was holding up settlement. The Wage Policy Committee rejected the industry position and voted to hold out for the WSB recommendations. A few days later, with the steel shortage approaching catastrophic proportions for the war mobilization, the parties reached agreement in the White House on July 24. The cost of the package was estimated at 21 cents per hour—16 cents in wages and 5 cents in fringe benefits. The union-shop issue was compromised by permitting new employees to opt out of membership within 30 days after employment and any member to leave the union during the last 15 days of the contract. The industry was permitted to raise prices $5.20 per ton. The agreement was to run until June 30, 1954, with a reopening on wages in 1953.

In 1953 and 1954, negotiations were consummated without strikes and, in 1955, the mills were down for 11 hours pending a settlement reached the morning after expiration of the existing contract. The 1953

---

[47] *Collective Bargaining in the Basic Steel Industry*, p. 275.

settlement of a wage reopening came three weeks before the deadline and was strongly influenced by the General Motors–UAW "living document" agreement under a contract that still had two years to run.[48] The Steelworkers received an 18.5-cent general wage increase and agreement to eliminate the U.S. Steel southern wage differential. This was the first negotiation led by David J. McDonald, who had succeeded to the Steelworker presidency when Philip Murray died in November 1952. In 1954, another peaceful settlement was reached providing a 5-cent wage increase and improvements in pensions and insurance, again following a pattern previously set in the automobile industry. The union reopened on wages in 1955, a highly prosperous year for the industry and, after hard bargaining, a settlement was reached on the basis of a 15-cent average wage increase. Both the 1954 and 1955 agreements were followed by increases in steel prices.

In 1956, the parties reverted to their earlier postures in prenegotiation statements and during negotiations. U.S. Steel blamed competition among industrywide unions and the Steelworkers in particular for inflation. The union responded by accusing the industry of using wage adjustments as an excuse for excessive price increases. The industry set its sights on a long-term contract—it suggested five years—in order to avoid annual negotiations and possible strikes. The union demanded a substantial wage increase, institution of a Supplementary Unemployment Benefit Plan, which had been achieved by the UAW in autos in 1955 and also in the Steelworker-organized can industry, a full union shop, and significant increases in fringe benefits. The eventual settlement, reached after a month-long strike, was for a three-year contract without any reopenings but with annual wage increases and semiannual adjustments for increases in the cost of living. In addition to base-rate increases of about 26 cents spread over the life of the agreement, the union won an SUB plan, improvements in pensions and insurance, premium pay for Sunday and holiday work, other fringe improvements, and a modified union shop. During the three years of the contract, total employment costs increased by nearly 30 percent and steel prices went up by $21 per ton, leading to arguments among the industry, the union, and the government as to the cause-and-effect relationship between steel wages and prices and their impact upon the economy.

The next round of negotiations was noteworthy because it involved the longest postwar steel strike. It also turned out to be the last national

[48] In May 1953, General Motors acceded to the UAW request to reopen their five-year agreement negotiated in 1950, based on the union's argument that a labor contract was a "living document" which may be modified to take account of unforeseen developments—in this case, the Korean War, other settlements, and inflation.

stoppage for at least 24 years in an industry which had rarely been able to reach a major contract settlement without a strike. Thus, 1959 marked both a new low and gave rise to a new high in harmonious labor-management relations in this important industry.

Negotiations started in an atmosphere of concern over unemployment, rising employment costs, competition from substitute products and foreign steel producers, and inflation. Under the 1956 agreement, employment costs and steel worker earnings had risen far more than those in most industries, while productivity had lagged and employment declined by 10 percent. The union wanted substantial increases in wages and benefits as well as greater employment security. The industry set as its major objective contract changes that would give companies greater freedom to manage their operations efficiently and unburdened by limitations contained in local-working-conditions clauses of existing contracts.

The strike that started on July 15, 1959, shut down 87 percent of the nation's steel-producing capacity and led to layoffs in railroads, barge and truck lines, coal mines, and many other industries. Steel workers returned to work after 116 days under a Taft-Hartley injunction,[49] which was challenged by the union and sustained by the U.S. Supreme Court on the ground that the strike imperiled the national safety by stopping or slowing defense production even though the nation was not at war. It took another two months of negotiation involving the Secretary of Labor, the Vice-President of the United States, and industry and union representatives before agreement was reached on January 4, 1960.

The settlement gave the union about 16 cents in direct wage increases, continuation of the cost-of-living escalator with only two adjustments limited to a maximum of 3 cents each after offsetting insurance cost increases, improvements in pensions and insurance, and maintenance of the SUB plan. The industry failed in its effort to eliminate or change the local-working-conditions contract clause. That issue was referred to a joint committee for study, but no agreement was reached and Section 2-B continued unchanged. Though not recognized at the time, agreement to establish a joint Human Relations Research Committee to study various problems in the industry proved to be more significant than any other provision of the agreement.

Public apprehension over the frequency, length, and effects of strikes in the basic steel industry prompted Secretary of Labor James P. Mitchell, shortly after the onset of the 1959 strike, to appoint a five-member committee of university industrial relations specialists, chaired

---

[49] Unlike his predecessor in the White House, President Eisenhower had no compunction about invoking the national emergency disputes provisions of the Taft-Hartley Act.

by Professor E. Robert Livernash of Harvard University, to oversee a Department of Labor study of the collective bargaining process in steel. The report which resulted from that study concluded that the adverse effects of steel strikes on the economy had not been of serious magnitude because "when a strike approaches a critical stage, pressures upon the parties to settle become substantially irresistible."[50] The committee believed that early government intervention in steel negotiations had tended to frustrate and hinder the bargaining process and had neither secured settlements nor avoided strikes. In the economic sphere, the group found that steel settlements had only a minimal effect upon the overall price level in the economy. This finding differs from that of Eckstein and Fromm in their 1959 study of "Steel and the Postwar Inflation" for the Joint Economic Committee of Congress. They concluded that the impact of the increase of steel prices on other industrial prices is large and that "the wage and price behavior of the steel industry represents an important instance of inflation caused to a substantial degree by the exercise of market power."[51]

Looking to the future, the Livernash Committee said that a major problem confronting the union and the steel companies was the necessity of adjusting to an increasingly competitive environment in a manner best suited to protect their mutual longer-term interests. The next section indicates that the parties had apparently come to the same conclusion and details the effects on collective bargaining in the ensuing 15 years.

The Harmonious Years

In the 13-year period, 1946–59, strikes occurred in five of the ten negotiations on new or reopened contracts over which the union had the right to strike. This record stands in sharp contrast to the 15 years starting in 1962, during which the parties negotiated seven times under contract expirations or reopenings without losing a single day as a result of a national steel strike. This period of labor peace is guaranteed to continue until at least 1983 under terms of the Experimental Negotiating Agreement governing negotiations in 1974 and 1977, and to which the parties are bound in their 1980 negotiations.

In December 1960 and October 1961, wage rates and increments between job classifications were increased by a total of 16 cents per hour under deferred-increase provisions of the 1960 agreement. In addition, the cost-of-living escalator yielded 1.5 cents in wages, the remaining 4.5 cents allowable under this provision having been used to offset

---

[50] *Collective Bargaining in the Basic Steel Industry*, p. 18.
[51] Eckstein and Fromm, p. 34.

rising insurance costs. With the contract due to expire on June 30, 1962, the union and industry negotiating committees opened discussions in mid-February, leaving much more time to reach agreement than in previous negotiations. Actually, representatives of the parties and joint subcommittees had been exploring major issues prior to the start of formal negotiations under the aegis of the Human Relations Research Committee. A further difference between the 1962 negotiations and those in previous years was that both sides refrained from going public with their demands, offers, and arguments. On March 31, three months before expiration of their contract, the parties announced agreement on a two-year contract, reopenable after one year on wage rates, insurance, or pensions. There was no provision for a wage increase and the cost-of-living escalator was discontinued. This did not appear to be a major union concession at the time, since the Consumer Price Index had remained quite stable during the previous two years. The settlement improved the SUB plan, established moving allowances for long-service employees transferred to other plants within a company, liberalized holiday pay and vacation allowances, established a savings and vacation plan to provide supplemental vacation-retirement benefits, and encouraged early retirement by liberalizing eligibility requirements for employees 55 years or older.[52]

The 1962 settlement cost, estimated at 2.5 percent, was within the limits suggested by the wage guideposts set forth by the Council of Economic Advisers as consistent with stable unit costs. When U.S. Steel and several other companies, a week after the settlement, announced a general price increase of 3.5 percent on all steel products, it provoked a major confrontation with the Kennedy Administration which charged that no steel price increase was justified under the guideposts. Three days later, after Inland Steel and Kaiser Steel decided not to follow U.S. Steel's lead, the companies retracted the increases. The episode showed that the Administration was serious about its price stability policy. But the "victory" was bought at the price of arousing considerable concern in industry generally over government's involvement in pricing decisions.[53]

The following year, without a formal contract reopening, the parties announced on June 20 that they had reached agreement on contract provisions effective August 1, 1963, to improve income and job security. Again there was no wage increase. A major innovation was the pro-

---

[52] For details of this and other settlements through 1974, see *Wage Chronology, United States Steel Corporation and United Steelworkers of America (AFL-CIO) March 1937–April 1974*, Bureau of Labor Statistics Bull. No. 1814 (Washington: 1974).

[53] Sheehan, pp. 33–38.

vision for extended "sabbatical" vacations for workers with high seniority. Workers in the upper half of the seniority list in each company
were to receive 13 weeks' vacation once every five years in addition to
their usual vacation during the other four years.[54] Improvements were
also made in insurance, hospitalization, and sickness and accident benefits. Since the contract was to run until May 31, 1965, this meant that
steel workers would go without a wage increase for almost four consecutive years. The 1963 settlement, estimated to cost about 1.5 percent,
was preceded and followed by steel price increases totaling approximately 3.3 percent. Unlike the previous year, these price increases,
though they breached the guideposts, were not challenged by the Administration.[55]

In 1965, negotiations were conducted against a backdrop of the
Vietnam War, government wage-price guideposts, and new union leadership. David McDonald had become a casualty of two contracts widely
hailed as models of labor statesmanship, an approach to negotiations
which his opponents charged gave too much power to staff technicians,
and his own vanity and lifestyle. After the new president, I. W. Abel,
took over negotiations, the parties appeared to be reverting to the
previous hard-line attitudes which had led to strikes in the past. However, under strong pressure from President Lyndon Johnson, they
reached agreement on a three-year contract without a strike. It provided for wage increases totaling slightly less than 20 cents in two in-
stallments; increased pensions, insurance, and hospital-surgical-medical
benefits; and upgrading of trade and craft jobs by two job classes. There
was no provision for reestablishing the cost-of-living escalator which
had been discontinued in 1962.

Negotiations in 1968 were unusual in that plant-by-plant discussion
of local issues began on April 15, one-and-a-half months before the top-
level negotiating teams started to meet on basic economic issues. This
innovation as well as other changes in the union bargaining structure
were results of Abel's campaign promise to pay more attention to local
issues and to give local leaders a greater voice in negotiations. A major
issue was the coverage and yield of incentive pay plans which varied
widely among companies. The meetings were again conducted in secret,
and a week before contract expirations both sides started to prepare for
a strike. However, on the evening of July 30, a settlement was reached
which touched on almost every aspect of wages and benefits.

A general wage increase of 20 cents an hour in 1968 was supple-

---

[54] In U.S. Steel, this "senior group" included workers with approximately 17
years or more of service.
[55] Goodwin, pp. 171–86.

mented by deferred increases of 12 cents in 1969 and again in 1970, each time with widened increments between job classes, making a total wage impact of 51.5 cents over the contract period. This sizable wage concession was designed both to compensate for the significant rate of acceleration in the cost of living during the previous three years and possibly to protect against future price increases during the life of the three-year contract, since steel contracts did not contain a cost-of-living escalator. Improvements in the pension plan provided increased monthly allowances and initiated a surviving spouse's benefit. SUB benefits were increased and an earnings protection plan was instituted for employees subjected to a wage decrease due to automation or other technological change. Hospitalization benefits were improved, a new major medical plan was added, life insurance was increased, vacations and holiday pay provisions were liberalized, and shift differentials were increased. The contract made no changes in incentive-pay arrangements which had been a major union objective. However, a joint union-management committee was established with provision that if agreement could not be reached, the issue would be submitted to arbitration.

When the joint committee could not reach agreement after a year of negotiations, the incentives issue was submitted to an impartial three-member arbitration panel which made its award on August 1, 1969. The decision directed that each company provide incentive coverage in steel-producing operations to at least 85 percent of its production and maintenance employees on a companywide basis and not less than 65 percent in each plant. The award defined three categories of jobs and directed the following incentive earnings opportunity under new incentive plans for each category: direct incentive jobs, 35 percent above the "incentive calculation rate"; indirect, 23 percent; and secondary indirect, 12 percent.[56] The effect of the decision varied from company to company depending upon its existing incentive coverage and earnings opportunity.[57] In U.S. Steel, incentive coverage was extended to 90 percent of its employees as compared with 80 percent before the award. The award was more costly for some other companies that had smaller proportions of workers on incentive jobs. Both sides regarded the arbitration decision as a major victory for the union.[58]

[56] The award did not affect incentive yields on existing incentive plans. The "incentive calculation rate" is about 60 percent of the standard hourly wage rate received by a nonincentive worker. Thus workers on "direct" incentive jobs have earnings opportunity about 21 percent greater than nonincentive workers, 14 percent on "indirect" jobs, and 7 percent on "secondary indirect" jobs.

[57] Coordinating Committee, Steel Companies and United Steelworkers of America, 53 LA 145 (1969).

[58] Some union staff members believe that U.S. Steel was not unhappy with the arbitration decision because it required other companies to come closer to matching its own level of incentive coverage.

The parties entered 1971 negotiations with the Consumer Price Index rising at the unprecedented rate of more than 5 percent a year, steel production-worker employment down by over 50,000 from 1968 levels, steel imports at record high levels, and steel production and profits relatively low. The union sought to reinstitute the cost-of-living escalator that had been discontinued in 1962 and to provide further protection for its members against the hazards of layoff, retirement, and sickness. The companies were deeply concerned about the economic situation of the industry. Both sides wanted to avoid a strike and the consequences —lost production, further increases in steel imports, and lost work for steel workers.

Unlike 1968, national negotiations started earlier than plant meetings on local issues. Agreement was reached in the face of an imminent strike under a 24-hour contract extension. The contract gains closely resembled settlements the union had made a few days earlier with aluminum and can companies. Wage rates were increased 50 cents per hour for the first year and 12.5 cents in each of the next two years, and increments between job classifications were widened. The total impact on base rates was 85 cents per hour. For the first time since 1961, these increases were incorporated into the incentive calculation rates resulting in larger increases for workers on incentive jobs.[59] A cost-of-living escalator was reestablished starting with the second year of the three-year agreement. Pensions, insurance, medical care, SUB, and holiday and vacation provisions were all improved substantially. The parties' concern over competition and the health of the industry was reflected in an agreement to establish joint productivity committees at each basic steel plant.

Major changes were also made in the grievance and arbitration procedures. The revisions, based on the report of a joint union-industry study committee, compressed time limits between steps, made steps 1 and 2 oral, gave increased authority to grievance committeemen and foremen to settle or withdraw grievances, and introduced the concept of "expedited arbitration" on routine grievances for a two-year trial period. Expedited cases are heard by relatively inexperienced arbitrators paid at lower fees than regular steel arbitrators; hearings are informal with no transcript or posthearing briefs; presentations are made by plant-level representatives on both sides; hearings are held within 10

---

[59] Before September 1, 1965, employees on jobs covered by incentive plans in effect on April 22, 1947 ("old incentives") received percentage increases in total earnings (excluding overtime, shift and Sunday premiums, and cost-of-living adjustments) equal to the percentage increases in standard hourly wage rates for such jobs. But for most incentives ("new incentives") wage and increment increases had become part of employees' base rates in every settlement until "incentive calculation rates" were established in 1965.

days of appeal to arbitration; and decisions are rendered within 48 hours.[60]

Further evidence of the parties' ability to cooperate on mutual problems was provided by their response to government complaints alleging that the steel companies and the union had engaged in a pattern of discrimination against minorities. After complex negotiations, involving nine major steel companies, the union, the Equal Employment Opportunity Commission, and the Departments of Labor and Justice, agreement was reached on a consent decree which was approved by the court on April 4, 1974.[61] The decree provided:

1. Half of all trade and craft job openings to be filled by minority and women employees until their proportions in such jobs reached the percentage existing in the entire bargaining unit.

2. Back pay of about $40 million to be distributed to some 35,000 minority and 5,600 women employees. In order to receive back pay, an individual was required to sign a waiver barring recovery of further damages for discrimination occurring prior to the decree or for the continuing effects of such prior discrimination. [This waiver provision was attacked by the National Association for the Advancement of Colored People and others.]

3. Plant-wide seniority to replace unit or department seniority in determining promotions, step-ups, demotions, layoffs, and recalls.

4. Implementation committees consisting of at least two union (including at least one minority person) and two company members to be established at each plant. A government representative may serve as an observer on each such committee.[62]

Negotiations in 1974 were conducted for the first time under rules set forth in the Experimental Negotiating Agreement. The settlement,

---

[60] "Summary of USA of Streamlined Grievance Procedure and Expedited Arbitration Developed in 1971 Negotiations (Official Text)," *Daily Labor Report No. 9*, January 13, 1972, pp. E1–E3. See also Fischer, "Implementation of Arbitration Awards," pp. 126–34; and Fischer, "The Steel Industry's Expedited Arbitration. . . ."

[61] There were two consent decrees. Consent Decree I dealt with production and maintenance workers and involved both the union and the companies. Consent Decree II, to which the union was not a party, dealt with hiring of women and minorities—a management function. The second decree provided a first-year goal of 20 percent of all production and maintenance vacancies for hiring women, and of 25 percent of all supervisory vacancies and management trainees for hiring minorities and women.

[62] Ben Fischer, "Evaluating the Steel Industry Consent Decree," *Equal Employment Opportunity Symposium*, Rutgers University, November 28–29, 1975. For a critical view see *Daily Labor Report No. 115*, June 13, 1974.

reached three and one-half months before the contract expiration date of June 30, paralleled the aluminum and can agreements arrived at a few months earlier. Wages were increased by 60 cents over the three years of the contract and increments were also widened at a cost of an additional 7 cents. Incentive workers received larger increases because the wage adjustments were incorporated into "incentive calculation rates." These increases were in addition to the $150 bonus for each worker and quarterly cost-of-living adjustments provided for under the ENA. The agreements gave employees retiring after July 31, 1974, a 5 percent "inflation" adjustment beginning in August 1976. In addition, the minimum pension rate was raised and the alternate percentage formula for calculating pensions was improved. Other benefits included a tenth paid holiday, a fifth week of vacation after 25 years, adoption of a dental plan, increased sickness and accident benefits, and increased SUB levels and financing.[63]

As 1977 negotiations approached, there was much speculation as to whether ENA would be continued. The union was in the midst of a hotly contested election campaign conducted from the last half of 1976 to February 1977. Outright opposition to ENA was a major campaign theme of Edward Sadlowski, maverick district director from Chicago. His opponent, district director Lloyd McBride of St. Louis, though supported by retiring president Abel and the rest of the union's executive board, nonetheless promised to reexamine ENA with an open mind: "If it meets the test in 1977, it is quite likely it will be renewed. If it does not, it is positive that it will not be renewed."[64]

The industry, while normally standing aloof from internal union politics, was concerned that no matter who won the election, the ENA might become a casualty of the campaign. After carefully weighing the pros and cons, it was decided that Bruce Johnston, Vice-President of Industrial Relations for U.S. Steel and chairman of the companies' co-ordinating committee, should speak out, not to take sides in the election but to make clear the industry's position on ENA in the forthcoming negotiations. On December 16, 1976, Johnston addressed the Pittsburgh Personnel Association on "A Steel Negotiator Looks at Election Issues."[65] The speech was heralded to the media in advance and was preceded by a press conference in which Johnston expressed concern over the "dismal" performance by both candidates for the union presidency in discussing the major issues. He criticized their failure to lay out the

---

[63] *Monthly Labor Review*, vol. 97, no. 6 (June 1974), pp. 68–69.

[64] *The New York Times*, article by A. H. Raskin, September 27, 1976.

[65] *U.S. Steel News*, 77/1.

facts so that union members might better understand the real issues in
the steel industry.

Johnston concentrated on the Experimental Negotiating Agreement
and its purpose of reducing the flood of foreign steel that was en-
dangering both the union and the companies. He said that ENA had
been successful in blunting layoffs resulting from inventory buildup in
1974 by assuring American steel consumers of a continuous supply of
steel without resort to foreign suppliers. His main point was that the
bulk of the risk and cost of ENA was borne by the companies, not by
the union. The union's giving up the right to call a national strike was,
in Johnston's view, more than balanced by gaining the right to place a
final settlement in the hands of arbitrators. This means, he declared, that
"the company's assets, its cash flow, its financial resources—all of the
equity of the stockholders managed by the company—are placed on the
line and at the mercy of an arbitration panel." He further pointed out
that, for the first time, local unions were being given the right to strike
over purely local issues. Finally, he noted that even before sitting down
at the bargaining table, the union was already guaranteed under ENA
almost the total value of the major settlements already made in 1976.
Johnston warned that the steel industry was not tied irrevocably to the
ENA concept and neither candidate for the union presidency needed
to worry about renewing ENA if it did not do the job for which it was
designed.

The speech made headlines, particularly in steel centers where the
campaign for the union's top offices was being waged. This was what
U.S. Steel wanted and intended. The company believes that it helped
rank-and-file steel workers to evaluate better what was being said or
left unsaid by the candidates about the ENA. The Johnston speech also
served as an introductory broadside to negotiations scheduled to begin
within a few months. Whatever its intention or effect, McBride and his
slate were elected and ENA was continued in the 1977 contract. McBride
participated for the first time in the negotiations, which were led for
the union by outgoing President Abel. Afterwards, industry spokesmen
expressed confidence that they would be able to work with him as they
had with his predecessor.

Entering negotiations in 1977, the industry was in a downswing
after three very good years. Profits in 1974 had attained record high
levels, yielding a return on net worth of 17.0 percent, better than during
any previous postwar year. While 1975 and 1976 were not nearly as
profitable as 1974, rates of return at 10.7 and 9.0 were much better than
average for the steel industry. However, a downturn started during the
latter part of 1976 and by the end of the first quarter of 1977, when

negotiations were in process, the industry was operating at a deficit and five of the ten companies making up the coordinating bargaining committee were losing money. This was an atypical quarter because the extreme winter weather and energy shortages had forced curtailment of many operations. The economic situation of the industry improved during the second quarter of 1977, after negotiations were completed. However, despite increases in shipments and sales during the first half of 1977 over the comparable period in 1976, profits after taxes were down 64 percent.[66]

The union's major objective going into 1977 negotiations was "lifetime security" to counter declining steel employment and shutdowns of older steel facilities. The industry was reported to be willing to consider some job-guarantee approach in return for "realistic tradeoffs" which might take the form of greater control over work assignment and scheduling.[67]

The settlement as it eventually evolved fell short of the union's stated objective but made a start toward providing considerable security for the most senior group of workers in the steel mills. A new Employment and Income Security Program applicable to employees with 20 years or more of service (about 40 percent of the workforce) virtually guaranteed full income security for this group for two years in case of plant shutdowns, extended layoff, short workweeks, or sickness or accident, and also provided beefed-up early pensions for those whose age and years of service totaled 65. It is noteworthy, however, that the agreement provided income rather than employment security except insofar as companies might be deterred from closing plants and laying off senior workers by the substantial costs they would incur by such layoffs. Indeed, within a few months after the agreement was negotiated, several major companies announced shutdowns and reductions in steel-making capacity at aging high-cost plants, which resulted in a loss of about 24,000 production-worker jobs. The companies blamed foreign imports and high costs of meeting government antipollution standards for the shutdowns. Union officials predicted that many of these workers would be eligible for pensions, but union and industry spokesmen disagreed as to whether they would be eligible for benefits under the new income-security program which was to become effective January 1, 1978.[68] One union staff member said that if the company view prevailed, "it

[66] Memorandum prepared by Steelworker Research Department, September 30, 1977.

[67] The Wall Street Journal, December 11, 1976.

[68] Ibid., August 19, 1977.

would be obvious that they went through all this mostly to save on labor costs."[69]

It is interesting to note that the union was able to improve on the steel income-security package in negotiations with major aluminum producers only two months after the steel settlement. These agreements went beyond the steel contracts by establishing a three-tiered program providing the highest benefits for workers with 20 years or more of service, and decreasing benefits for workers with 10 to 20 years of service and 2 to 10 years of service.[70]

In addition to the income-security program, the steel settlement provided general wage increases of 80 cents and a 1-cent increase in the increment between job classes, spread over three years, making a total cost of 88 cents per hour exclusive of the impact on incentives, continuation of the COLA escalator, improvements in pensions, insurance, SUB, and an additional paid holiday. The total steel package was estimated by the Council on Wage and Price Stability to raise wage and fringe benefits by 30.6 percent over the three years of the contract, assuming an inflation rate of 6 percent a year. This is roughly comparable to the Council's estimate of the auto settlement in 1976.[71]

The 1977 negotiations differed in two major respects from 1974 bargaining. The agreement negotiated by the top-level negotiating committee was first rejected by the Basic Steel Industry Conference by a standing vote of 148 to 143. Only after a highly emotional speech by Abel explaining the consequences of rejection, with a supporting statement by McBride, was the agreement approved on a roll call vote 193 to 99.[72] Opposition was led by representatives from locals of iron ore miners and clerical and technical workers, who felt that their interests had been ignored in order to get a good settlement for production and maintenance workers. Iron miners were angry over the union's failure to obtain incentive coverage for them comparable to what prevailed for steel production workers. Clerical workers were concerned about the absence of protection against computerization which threatened their jobs. A union staff member explained the initial rejection by the fact that less than half of the 800 members of the conference voted. The "good guys," figuring that ratification was a certainty, had left early to be home for the Easter weekend. In addition, the conference voting procedure is not weighted by size of local, so that representatives from small iron mining and clerical and technical locals had disproportionate influence.

---

[69] *The New York Times,* September 25, 1977.
[70] *Daily Labor Report No. 104,* May 27, 1977.
[71] *Daily Labor Report No. 106,* June 1, 1977.
[72] *John Herling's Labor Letter,* April 16, 1977.

The second major difference between 1974 and 1977 was in developments surrounding local issues. The right to strike over local issues provided for in the original ENA had resulted in no strikes after the 1974 settlement. Following the 1977 settlement, however, some 15,000 iron miners and processing workers in 16 mines in Minnesota and northern Michigan struck over what they regarded as local issues, shutting down almost all production of iron ore used in steel-making. Strikes were also voted in several basic steel and fabricating plants, including the 18,000-worker Inland Steel plant, largest in the industry. Steelworker President McBride authorized strike action in every local that requested it, but the basic steel disputes were settled before the August 1 deadline. In Inland Steel where there were 247 alleged local issues in dispute, settlement was reached on the basis of incentive adjustments for some 2,000 to 3,000 workers.[73] Some steel fabricating plants were also struck.

The iron mining strike, led by Duluth-based district director Linus E. Wampler and initiated by an anti-McBride faction of the union, dragged on until mid-December before settlements were negotiated and ratified by all the striking local unions. The companies contended that the major issue—incentive pay for iron miners—did not meet the ENA definition of a "local issue" because it had been discussed in national negotiations, and they sued the union for contract violation. The union disagreed, arguing that many local issues were discussed but not necessarily resolved in national negotiations. The strike settlement provided an incentive-pay program for at least 75 percent of all iron miners, effective November 1, 1979. Workers not covered by the incentive-pay plan would continue to receive a 30-cent-per-hour bonus under an existing Attendance Bonus Program previously in effect for all miners. The settlement agreement also provided that future disputes over what constituted a local issue would be settled by arbitration and that company lawsuits against the union would be dropped.[74]

Impact on Wages

The single most important influence on the steel industry wage structure has been the national job-classification system, which became effective in February 1947. This program was designed primarily to eliminate intraplant inequities but, because of its industrywide nature and the subsequent negotiations over geographic differentials, differences in base

---

[73] The New York Times, August 11, 1977; Iron Age, vol. 220, no. 6 (August 8, 1977), p. 19.

[74] A. H. Raskin, "Mesabi Ore Strike Unraveling Steel Industry's Peace Hopes," The New York Times, November 30, 1977, pp. 60–61; Steel Labor, December 1977, p. 3; Daily Labor Report No. 244, December 19, 1977, p. A23.

rates for similar jobs throughout the industry have been virtually eliminated. The initial agreement did not deal with alleged inequities on
incentive jobs which were left for future consideration and have never
been resolved.[75]

The Cooperative Wage Study (CWS) program grouped all steel
jobs into 30 classes with rates starting at the plant "base common labor
rate" for job class 1 and proceeding upward to class 30 with increments
of 3.5 cents between classes. As a result of negotiations since 1947, job
classes 1 and 2 were combined and four new job classes were added
so that there are 33 job classes starting at 1-2 and going to 34. The
parties also negotiated increases in increments between job classes from
the original 3.5 cents to 11.7 cents, effective August 1, 1979. By combining general wage adjustments and increases in the increment between
job classes, the parties were able to keep base-rate skill differentials from
narrowing as rapidly as they would have under the impact of straight
across-the-board cents-per-hour increases. Thus, between 1947 and 1956
when the parties negotiated their first cost-of-living escalator, differentials between job classifications were maintained more or less intact.
For example, job class 16, which included most skilled craftsmen, was
55 percent above job class 1 in 1947 and 53 percent higher in 1955, and
the difference between job class 1 and 32 decreased from 114 to 110
percent. In most other industries, there was a much greater narrowing
in differentials between skilled and unskilled jobs.

With the advent of escalator clauses in the 1956 steel contracts,
providing for equal cents-per-hour adjustments for increases in the Consumer Price Index, differentials in steel started to narrow. By 1961, the
differential between most skilled craftsmen and the lowest paid jobs had
declined to 47 percent and, between job class 1-2 (which were combined in 1956) and 32, it had decreased to 100 percent. These decreases
would have been much larger had not the parties continued to increase
increments almost every time they negotiated general wage increases.
During the period 1962–71 when the escalator clauses were not in effect
in steel contracts, differentials were again maintained fairly well. However, the escalator clause was reestablished in the 1971 contracts and
by August 1, 1977, differentials had narrowed to 29 percent between
job classes 1-2 and 18 (all trade and craft jobs were increased by two
classes in 1966) and 57 percent between the lowest- and highest-rated
jobs. This contraction occurred because of the sharp rise in the Consumer Price Index during the 1970s and despite the continued linking
of general and increment increases.

The above discussion of differentials pertains only to base rates, or

[75] See 1969 Arbitration Decision, 53 LA 145.

standard hourly wage rates as they are called in the steel industry. However, base rates were much less important in 1977 than in 1947 or even in the 1960s, due to the extension of incentive coverage and the increased yield of incentives since the 1969 arbitration award. In 1947, less than half of all steel workers were employed on incentive jobs as compared with more than 85 percent in 1977.

The average job class in the industry has gravitated from about 8.5 to 10 over the years as a result of changing technology, job mix, the introduction of new and changed jobs, and the raising of all trade and craft jobs by two classes in 1966. Each job is evaluated by management in accordance with the CWS job-classification manual, but the union may contest evaluations through the grievance and arbitration procedure. While the CWS system is by far the major determinant of the steel industry wage structure, labor market pressures, negotiations, and arbitration decisions have undoubtedly had some influence on the upward trend of classifications.

Because of the extensive incentive coverage among steel production and maintenance workers, the general wage and increment adjustments, which are incorporated into incentive calculation rates, result in larger actual increases in earnings than the announced figures. Thus a worker employed on a job with an incentive yield of 20 percent will earn about 12 percent more than a nonincentive worker in the same job class who receives the standard hourly wage rate. For the average steel worker in job class 10, with a 20 percent incentive, the 88-cent general and increment increase over the three years of the 1977 contract will have been supplemented by an additional 13 cents in hourly earnings when the contract expires in 1980, exclusive of cost-of-living increases under the escalator clause. Unlike general and increment increases, cost-of-living adjustments are not put into the incentive calculation rate, but are made part of an "hourly additive" for incentive jobs. The incentive calculation rate plus the hourly additive equals the standard hourly wage rate for a nonincentive job in the same classification. Average hourly earnings in the steel industry reflect the fact that a high proportion of all steel workers are employed on incentive jobs.

After the 1977 settlement, a typical steel worker working a full year, classified in job class 10, and assigned to an incentive-rated job was earning about $7.85 an hour, $63 a day, $315 a week, and $16,400 a year. By May 1980 when the 1977 contract expires (assuming a 6 percent annual rate of inflation), he will be earning almost $10 per hour and more than $20,000 a year. Premium pay for overtime, Sunday, and holiday work will add about 10 percent to these figures.[76] This is sub-

---

[76] "1977 Steel Settlement," United Steelworkers of America, p. 13.

stantially more than the average earnings of manufacturing workers generally or of workers in almost any other industry. Only construction workers and petroleum workers earned more on an hourly basis in May 1977, and the former were certainly not earning as much as steel workers on an annual basis because of the greater instability of construction employment.

Why are steel workers' earnings so much higher than earnings of other manufacturing workers? Studies of wage determination have reached different and inconclusive results regarding factors affecting earnings.[77] Among the variables generally recognized as possibly influencing earnings are: cost of living, productivity, profits, industry concentration, value added, labor quality, and union power. Problems of definition, specification, measurement, and interrelationships between variables make the task of determining the independent effect of any single factor virtually impossible. In addition, the cause-and-effect relationship between earnings and individual factors is far from clear. Thus, increases in the Consumer Price Index are both a cause and a consequence of wage adjustments. This is also true of some other factors that influence wages.

Perhaps the factors most widely recognized as affecting wage adjustments are increases in the cost of living as measured by the Consumer Price Index, productivity, and profits. Unions entering negotiations demand at least a wage increase to maintain real earnings plus an additional adjustment to take account of the productivity increase in the national economy. Many companies and unions have institutionalized these adjustments by incorporating cost-of-living escalators and annual increases, variously called improvement factors, productivity increases, or deferred increases, into long-term collective bargaining agreements. In addition, unions in industries and companies with relatively high increases in productivity and/or profits argue, often with considerable success, that they are entitled to share the benefits of such increases. Employers argue the reverse when productivity and profits are relatively low.

Table 1 shows average annual changes in the Consumer Price Index, average hourly earnings and productivity, and average annual profit rates in iron and steel, automobiles, and all manufacturing for 1947–62 and 1962–76. The periods coincide with the years of labor strife and labor peace in the steel industry. The automobile industry is chosen for comparison purposes because, like steel, it is almost 100 percent organized by a strong union and its earnings rank next to steel in durable

---

[77] See, for example, Ashenfelter and Johnson; Eckstein and Wilson; Hildebrand; Howard and Tolles; Levinson; Lewis; Livernash; Reder; Rosen; Sawheny and Herrnstadt; and Schweitzer.

TABLE 1

Average Annual Rate of Change in Consumer Price Index, Average Hourly Earnings, and Output Per Manhour, and Average Annual Return on Net Worth in Iron and Steel, Motor Vehicles and Equipment, and All Manufacturing, 1947–1962 and 1962–1976[a]

Industry	1947–62				1962–76			
	CPI	Average Hourly Earnings	Output per Manhour	Return on Net Worth	CPI	Average Hourly Earnings	Output per Manhour	Return on Net Worth
All manufacturing	2.0	4.6	2.8	11.5	4.6	5.7	2.7	11.7
Iron and steel	2.0	5.6	2.2	10.1	4.6	6.3	1.9	8.3
Motor vehicles and equipment	2.0	4.8	5.2[b]	15.8	4.6	6.4	3.5	13.6

Sources: CPI: BLS Handbook of Labor Statistics 1976 and Monthly Labor Review, various issues in 1976–77. Average hourly earnings: Employment and Earnings 1947–75 from BLS Bulletin 1312-10, 1976; 1976 from "Employment and Earnings," Vol. 24, No. 3 (March 1977). Output per manhour: BLS Productivity Indices: Selected Industries, various years; Employment and Training Report of the President, 1977. Return on net worth: Federal Trade Commission, Quarterly Financial Report on Manufacturing, Mining, and Trade Corporations 1947–1977.

[a] Changes in CPI, average hourly earnings, and output per hour computed by compound interest formula, terminal-years method.

[b] Computed on basis of data for 1957–62; data not available prior to 1957.

goods manufacturing. All manufacturing data serve as a bench mark against which to compare these two industries.

Average hourly earnings in iron and steel increased more, on an annual basis, during the 1962–76 period than during 1947–62. But the difference in the average annual increase in the Consumer Price Index during the two periods was so great that, in terms of real earnings, steel workers fared much better during 1947–62 than during 1962–76. When earnings are adjusted for increases in the Consumer Price Index, steel workers' real average hourly earnings increased 3.4 percent per year in the earlier period as compared with 1.6 percent per year in the latter period. The average annual increase in output per man hour and the return on net worth in the steel industry were also higher in 1947–62 than in 1962–76.

Steel workers' earnings increased more per year than earnings of either automobile workers or all manufacturing workers during 1947–62. This is surprising in view of the larger average annual increases in output per manhour and return on net worth in both industry categories than in steel. In 1962–76, average hourly earnings of steel workers increased annually at about the same rate as earnings of automobile workers, despite much larger increases in productivity and substantially higher profit rates of auto companies as compared with companies in the steel industry. Increases in all manufacturing earnings lagged behind both steel and autos in 1962–76, although productivity increases and profit rates were much larger than in steel but lower than in the automobile industry.

In terms of gross hourly earnings, steel workers and auto workers were about even in 1947 ($1.45 and $1.47, respectively). By 1962, steel workers were making $3.25 per hour or 26 cents more than auto workers, and by 1976 the gap had widened to 58 cents per hour, $7.68 as compared with $7.10. The largest factor in the differential hourly earnings of the two groups of employees was undoubtedly the incentive earnings opportunity available to almost all steel workers. The automobile industry has very few incentive jobs. Steel workers also widened their differential with all manufacturing workers: from 23 cents per hour in 1947 to 86 cents in 1962 and $2.49 in 1976.[78]

The increased cost of labor has been passed on to consumers of steel products. Wholesale prices of finished steel products went up by 360 percent between 1947 and 1976: 111 percent during 1947–62 and 119

---

[78] Because auto workers have generally had a longer workweek than steel workers, their average weekly earnings exceeded those in steel by $2.12 in 1947, were about the same as earnings of steel workers in 1962, and were only $1.90 less than steel workers' earnings in 1976. There has been little difference between the average workweek in steel and in all manufacturing.

percent between 1962 and 1976. By comparison, the BLS Wholesale Price Index (Industrial Commodities) increased by 157 percent between 1947 and 1976; 34 percent in 1947–62 and 92 percent during 1962–76.[79] Until 1967, the union was critical of steel price increases, especially when they followed contract settlements and were ascribed to wage and benefit increases. The union position was that the settlements were merited by increases in the cost of living and productivity, and that they were noninflationary. In 1968, the union changed course when Steelworker President Abel criticized the Johnson Administration for its attack on steel price increases coming shortly after the settlement that year. Abel said it was inappropriate to single out steel for postnegotiation price increases when other industries followed the same practice without criticism.[80] After 1968, the industry generally refrained from blaming the union for price increases. The union was either silent or, as in 1976, supported the industry when it raised prices.[81]

The Steelworkers' union boasts that no other industrial union in the United States has matched its record of wage gains.[82] The record certainly supports the view that steel workers have fared well under collective bargaining. Most students of industrial relations believe that "union power" exerts a significant influence on wage determination and helps to explain interindustry wage differentials.[83] Given the relatively poor productivity record and low profitability of the steel industry, union power must be accorded substantial weight in any explanation of Steelworker wage gains during the postwar period.

There is also research support for other factors as possibly contributing to relatively large wage increases in steel. These include the large value added in processing steel, the quality of steel labor as measured by training and skill requirements, and high capital investment per worker. Industry concentration has also been found to be positively correlated with wage changes because it enhances the ability of companies to pass on increases in labor costs through higher prices.[84] There is little evidence that unemployment, either in the nation or in the in-

---

[79] *Handbook of Labor Statistics, 1975* (Washington: Bureau of Labor Statistics, 1975); *Monthly Labor Review*, vol. 99, no. 7 (July 1976); vol. 100, no. 7 (July 1977); vol. 100, no. 9 (September 1977).

[80] *Daily Labor Report No. 162*, August 19, 1968.

[81] *John Herling's Labor Letter*, December 18, 1976. In internal documents, the union has criticized steel and other price increases. A research department memorandum on "U.S. Steel's 1970 Annual and Fourth Quarter Financial Survey" said that steel companies were not "using much restraint" in pricing; and the "Report of Officers" to the 1976 Steelworker Convention characterized corporations' price behavior as "anti-social."

[82] "1977 Steel Settlement," p. 7.

[83] See fn. 66.

[84] *Ibid.*

dustry, has had much effect on steel wages. Settlements in 1960, 1971, 1974, and 1977, all years of relatively high national and industry (except 1974) unemployment, were substantial, as they were also in 1965 and 1968 when the nation was at or close to full employment and steel unemployment was low. Only in 1949, 1962, and 1963 did Steelworkers go without a wage increase, reflecting in some degree the depressed state of the national economy and/or the industry. On the other hand, there is little doubt that rising steel labor costs have accelerated technological change in the industry with a resultant reduction in steel employment. It might be argued that this was inevitable and even desirable in order to enable the industry to compete in the international market. Bad as the import situation is in steel, it would doubtless be worse if the American companies had lagged even further behind competing nations in steel technology.[85]

Employee Benefits

Wages are the most important but not the sole element in assessing the economic status of steel workers and employment costs to steel employers. Almost every steel negotiation has included benefits other than wage increases in the total settlement package. As wages have gone up, other benefits have assumed increased importance to steel workers. They have also become a more significant element in total employment cost.

In 1976 total employment cost per hour was almost 50 percent higher than average hourly earnings of production workers in steel companies. The additional cost was made up of pay for time not worked on holidays and vacations; various allowances and adjustments; employee benefits including pensions, insurance, supplementary unemployment payments; and employer taxes for social security, unemployment compensation, and workers' compensation. In 1976, according to the American Iron and Steel Institute, employee benefits cost steel companies $2.61 per hour and pay for time not worked $1.13 per hour, the former having increased more rapidly than the latter since 1960.[86] The 1977 settlement improvements were estimated by the Council on Wage and Price Stability as adding 94 cents per hour to the cost of employee benefits over the life of the contract.[87]

---

[85] "Steel's Sea of Troubles," *Business Week*, September 19, 1977, pp. 65–88.

[86] "Total Employment Cost Per Hour—Wage Employees in the Iron and Steel Industry," *Annual Statistical Report 1976* (Washington: American Iron and Steel Institute, 1977).

[87] "Analysis of Steel Settlement by Council on Wage and Price Stability," *Daily Labor Report No. 106*, June 1, 1977.

There follows a summary of the major economic benefits enjoyed by steel workers under the 1977 contract:[88]

Holidays and Vacations. In 1979 steel workers will have 11 paid holidays including United Nations Day which was added in 1977. Regular vacations range from one week for employees with one to three years of service to five weeks for those with 25 or more years of service. In addition, employees in the upper half of the seniority list of each company receive a total of 13 weeks vacation once every five years.

Pensions. As of August 1979, minimum monthly pensions, exclusive of social security, will range from $135 for the lowest paid employee with 10 years of service to $675 for an employee with 45 years of service at the top of the wage scale. Employees retiring under an alternate basic formula may receive higher benefits. The alternate formula provides for a benefit equal to 1.1 percent of earnings for each of the first 30 years of service and 1.2 percent for each additional year.

Insurance. Effective August 1979, life insurance for active employees will range from $10,000 to $12,500, depending upon an employee's hourly wage rate. Retired employees are insured for $3,000. Sickness and accident benefits range from $153 to $211 per week, depending on earnings, for 26 weeks for all employees, and an additional 26 weeks for employees with two years or more of service.

Supplementary Unemployment Benefits. An employee on layoff receives a maximum of $125 per week while eligible for state benefits and $170 for all other weeks, plus $1.50 for each dependent up to four. These benefits are subject to reduction or elimination depending upon the position of a company's SUB fund. There are also provisions for payment of short-week benefits and payments during shutdowns resulting from government pollution controls, energy shortage, or coal strikes.

Health Care. Effective in 1979, active employees and their dependents will have comprehensive hospital-medical-surgical coverage plus major medical insurance of $30,000 annually and $50,000 lifetime per individual, a dental plan, and a vision-care plan.

Moving Allowance. Employees transferring from one plant to another because of plant shutdowns or long-term layoffs receive relocation allowances ranging from $600 to $1450 for married employees and $200 to $550 for single employees, depending upon the distance between the two plants.

Severance Allowance. Employees terminated as a result of a plant closure or permanent discontinuance of a department, who are not en-

---

[88] Agreement between United States Steel Corporation and the United Steelworkers of America, Production and Maintenance Employees, August 1, 1977; "1977 Steel Settlement," United Steelworkers of America; "Developments in Industrial Relations," *Monthly Labor Review,* vol. 100, no. 6 (June 1977), pp. 62–63.

titled to other employment with the company, are eligible for severance pay ranging from four weeks for three to five years of service to eight weeks for ten years or more of service.

Employment and Income Security. This program, effective January 1, 1978, applies only to employees with 20 or more years of service and provides the following benefits:

a. Such an employee becomes eligible for a "Rule of 65 Pension" if: (1) he is off work because of a shutdown, extended layoff, or disability, (2) his age plus service equals 65 or more, and (3) his company fails to provide him with suitable long-term employment. In addition to a regular pension, such an employee will receive a $300 per month supplement until eligible for social security or until he obtains suitable long-term employment.

b. The regular 52-week Supplemental Unemployment Benefit duration is extended by up to an additional 52 weeks, provided the employee is not offered appropriate work at his home plant or suitable long-term employment at another location. An employee affected by a plant shutdown receives the extended SUB only until he becomes eligible for an immediate unreduced pension. Unlike SUB benefits for other employees, benefits for employees covered by this program are not subject to reduction or elimination because of the financial position of a company's SUB fund. Nor can payment of such benefits operate to reduce benefits payable to other employees.

c. The short-week benefits for covered employees will be calculated on the basis of average straight-time hourly earnings, including incentive earnings and shift premiums, instead of on the basis of the standard hourly wage rate. These benefits will be guaranteed and are not subject to the financial position of the SUB fund.

d. The protected level of hourly earnings for covered employees, who are reduced to lower-paid jobs in an economic layoff, will be 90 percent of the base-period rate instead of the 85 percent for other employees. The "base period" will be the higher earning rate of the two calendar years preceding the benefit quarter instead of the immediate preceding calendar year.

e. Covered employees suffering long-term but not permanent disability will be eligible for 104 weeks of sickness and accident benefits instead of 52 weeks as are other employees.

f. All insurance coverage will continue for 104 weeks for covered employees instead of the 52 weeks for other employees.

Conditions of Employment

In addition to wages and benefits, steel industry collective bargaining agreements contain many other provisions which govern relationships between the parties. While not measurable, these provisions represent the heart of the agreement and are often considered more important than the economic aspects of the contract in that they affect both the day-to-day and the long-term relationship of the union and the company. The basic provisions of the steel contracts have been in place for many years and do not change with each contract renewal. They include the usual provisions dealing with recognition, management rights, union security, grievance and arbitration procedures, and seniority. These provisions may vary from company to company though, for the most part, the language is similar or even identical. Other provisions of steel contracts which are more unusual or deserving of special attention are summarized below.

Purpose and Intent of the Parties. Some parts of this section take on special significance in view of the Experimental Negotiating Agreement negotiated in 1973 and continued in 1974 and 1977. For example, the following paragraph:

> The parties are concerned that the future for the industry in terms of employment security and return on substantial capital expenditures will rest heavily upon the ability of the parties to work cooperatively to achieve significantly higher productivity trends than have occurred in the recent past. The parties are acutely aware of the impact upon the industry and its employees of the sizable penetration of the domestic steel market by foreign producers. The parties have joined their efforts in seeking relief from the problem of massive importation of foreign steel manufactured in low-wage countries. Thus, it is incumbent upon the parties to work cooperatively to meet the challenge posed by principal foreign competitors in recent years. It is also important that the parties cooperate in promoting the use of American-made steel.[89]

Local Working Conditions. Section 2-B, which the companies tried unsuccessfully to eliminate in the 1959 steel dispute, defines local working conditions as "specific practices or customs which reflect detailed application of the subject matter within the scope of wages, hours of work, or other conditions of employment and includes local agreements, written or oral, on such matters." It further provides that: (a) an employee does not have the right to have a local working condition established where such condition has not previously existed or to have

[89] U.S. Steel Agreement, Section 1, paragraph 1.4.

an existing condition changed or eliminated except as specifically provided by agreement; (b) local working conditions may not deprive an employee of rights granted under the Agreement; (c) local working conditions providing benefits in excess of or in addition to benefits in the Agreement must remain in effect for the term of the Agreement unless changed or eliminated by mutual agreement or in accordance with paragraph (d); (d) the Company has the right to change or eliminate a local working condition if the basis for the existence of the condition is changed or eliminated, thereby making it unnecessary to continue such local working condition.

Contracting-Out. Decreasing employment and layoffs have made steel workers increasingly sensitive to contracting-out work which the union believes could be done by its members. The contract has contained some limitation on the company's right to contract-out work since 1963. The 1977 Agreement established a Joint Steel Industry-Union Contracting-Out Review Commission composed of three industry and three union representatives and an impartial chairman. The commission is charged with investigating contracting-out practices at steel plants and making recommendations to the parties. The commission will submit quarterly progress reports and a final report by September 1, 1979, covering contracting-out practices of steel plants and their impact on bargaining units, the economic consequences to the companies of contracting-out decisions, and "such further recommendations as it considers appropriate."

During the commission's work, trade and craft workers are given an interim guarantee of 40-hours pay whenever outside contractors perform work in a craft in which steel craftsmen are laid off or working less than 40 hours per week. To receive this guarantee, an employee must be willing to accept assignments in his own craft in a seniority or work unit other than his own. Joint contracting-out committees, previously established in steel plants, must receive advance notice of work to be contracted-out, and the union may initiate grievances on such work in accordance with the agreement.

Although the findings and recommendations of the Review Commission are to be only advisory, the fact that the body is being chaired by a neutral member indicates the serious view taken by the parties of this issue and opens up the possibility that the neutral's views may be determinative should the union and industry members not be able to reach agreement.

Grievance Administration and Arbitration. Steel companies and the Steelworkers union have developed sophisticated and orderly procedures to process grievances arising in day-to-day operations. The prevailing practice is for the agreement between the union and each major company to provide for a permanent arbitrator, who serves under contract, subject to termination by either party, and renders final and binding decisions on all grievances appealed to arbitration. Some agreements permit the appointment of assistants to the chief arbitrator to expedite the adjudication of cases. The U.S. Steel Agreement provides for a Board of Arbitration whose chairman submits draft decisions prepared by himself and his aides to union and company designees before they are issued in final form. This procedure provides an opportunity for the parties to consult with the chairman on decisions that they believe may present problems in the administration of the agreement. The union issues the full text and summaries of all significant decisions for use by staff representatives, local unions, and others who wish to purchase them.

Expedited arbitration for routine cases was introduced in 1971 and continued in subsequent agreements. By 1977 more than 2,400 cases had been decided by expedited arbitration. Initially either party could veto referral of a case to expedited arbitration. The 1977 Agreement provided that, except for grievances involving concerted activity or multiple grievances arising out of the same event, all grievances including written reprimands or suspensions of five days or less are to be processed through expedited arbitration. All other disciplinary grievances and discharges are to be processed through regular arbitration (unless the parties agree to use expedited arbitration) and decisions rendered within 60 days, unless the arbitrator finds that circumstances require otherwise. It is estimated that 90 percent of all disciplinary grievances appealed to arbitration will now go through expedited arbitration procedures.

Safety and Health. The agreements include detailed provisions designed to eliminate accidents and health hazards. Employees must be informed of hazards and precautions to take in working with toxic materials. The company has a program for periodic in-plant air-sampling and noise-testing. Grievances alleging unsafe or unhealthy conditions start in the third step and, in an emergency, may be referred to immediate arbitration. Alcoholism and drug abuse are recognized to be "treatable conditions" and the parties agree to cooperate in encouraging afflicted employees to undergo a coordinated program designed to rehabilitate them. Plant and company joint safety and health committees have been established to facilitate implementation of this section of the agreement.

Joint Union-Management Committees. Recognizing that some matters require intensive and continuing study, the parties have established a number of joint committees at the industry, company, and/or plant level. Such committees in existence under the 1977 Agreement and memoranda of understanding deal with the following subjects: contracting-out, civil rights, safety and health, job classifications, incentives, grievance and arbitration procedures, apprenticeship, employment security, and plant productivity; there is also a committee to study ways to contain future health-care costs.

Summary and Conclusions

With some noteworthy exceptions, American industrial relations have generally evolved from highly antagonistic relationships, characterized by mutual distrust and frequent strife, to more accommodative, sophisticated relationships in which the parties understand each others' needs, motives, and problems and, more often than not, are able to resolve their differences amicably. In no industry is this more true than in basic steel. National steel strikes, which were routine during the first two decades of collective bargaining, have been avoided since 1960 and are ruled out by agreement until 1983. Communication through joint committees to deal with specific problem areas, and frequent meetings and informal discussions between union and company officials at all levels, have replaced the arm's-length negotiating sessions which were pretty much limited to periods of contract expiration and renewal. Government intervention, considered almost inevitable during steel negotiations through the mid-sixties, has not been a major factor in settlements reached during the last decade.

A number of factors have contributed to the changed climate of labor-management relations in steel: (1) As the framework of the parties' relationship has been spelled out in contractual provisions which are accepted by both sides as relatively permanent, economic considerations and a more realistic assessment of the necessary parameters of settlements have become more important than "principle" in negotiations. (2) Government has become reconciled to the view that labor peace in steel cannot be achieved without sizable steel price increases which contribute to inflationary pressures in the economy. While voicing concern over inflationary settlements, recent administrations have not intervened in negotiations or tried very hard to block price increases, even when deemed excessive in relation to increased costs of production. (3) Long-term contracts, with built-in adjustments to compensate for increases in the cost of living and productivity, have replaced one-year agreements with the attendant pressures on both sides to reevaluate their positions and take advantage of changing economic conditions. (4) Concern by the steel companies and the union over the impact of steel imports on the long-term health of the industry and on employment of steel workers has led the parties to seek solutions to this mutual problem through joint action.

The major vehicle that the industry and the union have chosen to effectuate their individual and joint interests is the Experimental Negotiating Agreement, the major innovation in labor-management relations of the 1970s. Attention has focused on two questions pertaining to the ENA: Is it transferable to other industries, and how long will it continue in steel?

The first question has been answered, to a degree, by the fact that no other parties to a major agreement have seen fit to adopt an ENA-type provision, despite the apparent positive experience in the steel industry. This is not surprising in view of the particular circumstances motivating the parties to the steel agreement: industry bargaining leading to an industrywide strike if no agreement is reached in negotiations; virtual certainty of government intervention with unpredictable results if a national strike occurs and continues for more than a few weeks; and fear of foreign imports and consumer shifts to substitute products in anticipation of a strike or during an actual stoppage. Companies tempted to go the ENA route must also consider the high cost necessary to persuade a union to give up the right to strike, and union leaders must take account of the almost certain internal opposition to such an agreement within their organizations.

Within the steel industry itself, ENA is likely to continue to be controversial. Favoring continuation of ENA is the likelihood that steel imports will remain a threat to the American steel industry and employment for a long time. Steelmakers in Japan and the European Economic Community have expanded production capacity far beyond the needs of their domestic markets. The United States is and will continue to be the largest and most open market for their products. American steel producers welcome the support of the Steelworkers union in trying to persuade the government to limit the flow of steel imports and also appreciate the hands-off policy followed in recent years by the union with regard to steel price increases. While these policies flow from an identity of interest of the parties, scrapping the ENA is likely to put strains on joint efforts in these areas.

On the other hand, ENA poses problems for both sides. The industry pays a high price for the national no-strike guarantee, and the union leadership, by giving up the right to strike for six years at a time, provides a ready-made issue for an opposition movement. In addition, there is always the possibility of strikes over local issues, such as occurred in the iron mines in 1977, which may make the industry wonder about loopholes in the no-strike guarantee. Finally, the efficacy of ENA in stemming steel imports is doubtful, since foreign steel sales have continued at high levels during the years that ENA has been in effect. There is, of course, the likelihood that without ENA, steel imports would have been even higher. But the record indicates that the problem is more fundamental and that, while ENA can eliminate a sharp rise in imports during contract negotiations, it is not the answer to the basic threat posed by foreign-made steel to the American steel industry. Steel technology, productivity, and prices all play important roles in determining whether the industry can compete with foreign steel producers.[90]

On the national scene, ENA both assists and hinders government efforts to reduce the rate of inflation. ENA helps to combat inflation by guaranteeing an uninterrupted supply of a product that is basic to many industries, and to the entire economy. On the other hand, ENA settlements have provided a costly target for other unions to shoot for in their own negotiations, thus adding to inflationary pressures in the economy. Observers of labor-management relations in the United States have often decried the adversarial posture taken by unions and management and have expressed a preference for a more cooperative relationship between the parties. The ENA represents an important step in this direction. The question is whether it comes at too high a price.

---

[90] In response to demands from the steel industry and the Steelworkers' union that the government act to curb imports, allegedly being sold in the United States at prices below production costs of foreign producers, the Carter Administration has developed a "reference price" plan to become effective February 1, 1978. Reference prices are minimum sales prices. Steel products priced below reference levels will be subject to penalties by the imposition of "dumping" duties. It will be some time before the effects of this plan, which also includes other forms of assistance to the steel industry, will become evident. (*The New York Times*, November 25, 1977, and January 7, 1978.)

List of References

Ashenfelter, Orley, and George E. Johnson. "Unionism, Relative Wages, and Labor Quality." *International Economic Review* 13 (October 1972).

Brody, David. *Labor in Crisis, The Steel Strike of 1919.* Philadelphia and New York: J. P. Lippincott Co., 1965.

———. *Steelworkers in America, The Nonunion Era.* Cambridge, Mass.: Harvard University Press, 1960.

Dunlop, John T. "The Task of Contemporary Wage Theory." In *The Theory of Wage Determination, Proceedings of a Conference held by the International Economic Association*, ed. John T. Dunlop. London: Macmillan & Co., Ltd., 1957.

Eckstein, Otto, and Gary Fromm. "Study Paper No. 2, Steel and the Postwar Inflation." In *Study of Employment, Growth and Price Levels.* Washington: Joint Economic Committee, Congress of the United States, 1959.

Eckstein, Otto, and T. A. Wilson. "The Determination of Money Wages in American Industry." *Quarterly Journal of Economics* 76 (August 1962).

Feller, David E. "The Steel Experience: Myth and Reality." In *Proceedings of the 21st Annual Winter Meeting, Industrial Relations Research Association.* Madison, Wis.: The Association, 1968.

Fischer, Ben. "Implementation of Arbitration Awards." In *Arbitration and the Public Interest*, Proceedings of the 24th Annual Meeting, National Academy of Arbitrators. Washington: Bureau of National Affairs, Inc., 1971.
──────. "The Steel Industry's Expedited Arbitration: A Judgment After Two Years." *Arbitration Journal* 28 (September 1973), pp. 185–91.
Galenson, Walter. *The CIO Challenge to the AFL, A History of the American Labor Movement 1935–41*. Cambridge, Mass.: Harvard University Press, 1960.
Goodwin, C. D., ed. *Exhortation and Controls: The Search for a Wage-Price Policy 1947–1971*. Washington: Brookings Institution, 1975.
Healy, James J., ed. *Creative Collective Bargaining*. Englewood Cliffs, N.J.: Prentice-Hall, 1965.
Herling, John. *Right to Challenge*. New York: Harper and Row, 1972.
Hiestand, D. L. *High Level Manpower and Technological Change in the Steel Industry*. New York: Praeger Publishers, 1974.
Hildebrand, George H. "The Economic Effects of Unionism." In *A Decade of Industrial Relations Research, 1946–1956*, eds. Neil W. Chamberlain, Frank C. Pierson, and Theresa Wolfson. New York: Harper & Bros., 1958.
Hogan, William T. *Economic History of the Iron and Steel Industry in the United States*. Lexington, Mass.: D. C. Heath and Co., 1971.
Howard, William A., and N. Arnold Tolles. "Wage Determination in Key Manufacturing Industries." *Industrial and Labor Relations Review* 27 (July 1974).
Levinson, Harold M. "Unionism, Concentration, and Wage Changes: Toward a Unified Theory." *Industrial and Labor Relations Review* 20 (January 1967).
Lewis, H. Gregg. *Unionism and Relative Wages in the United States*. Chicago: University of Chicago Press, 1963.
Livernash, E. Robert. "Wages and Benefits." In *A Review of Industrial Relations Research*, Vol. 1, eds. W. L. Ginsburg, E. Robert Livernash, Herbert S. Parnes, and George Strauss. Madison, Wis.: Industrial Relations Research Association, 1970.
Livernash, E. Robert, and others. *Collective Bargaining in the Basic Steel Industry*. Washington: U.S. Department of Labor, January 1961.
Reder, Melvin. "Wage Determination in Theory and Practice." In *A Decade of Industrial Relations Research, 1946–1956*, eds. Neil W. Chamberlain, Frank C. Pierson, and Theresa Wolfson. New York: Harper & Bros., 1958.
Rosen, Sherwin. "On the Interindustry Wage and Hours Structure." *Journal of Political Economy* 77 (March/April 1969).
Sawhney, Pawan K., and Irwin L. Herrnstadt. "Interindustry Wage Structure Variation in Manufacturing." *Industrial and Labor Relations Review* 24 (April 1971).
Schweitzer, Stuart O. "Factors Determining the Interindustry Structure of Wages." *Industrial and Labor Relations Review* 22 (January 1969).
Sheehan, John. *The Wage-Price Guideposts*. Washington: Brookings Institution, 1967.
Stieber, Jack. "Company Cooperation in Collective Bargaining in the Basic Steel Industry." *Labor Law Journal* 11 (July 1960), pp. 614–21.
──────. *The Steel Industry Wage Structure*. Cambridge, Mass.: Harvard University Press, 1959.
Technological Change and Manpower Trends in Five Industries. Bull No. 1856. Washington: U.S. Department of Labor, Bureau of Labor Statistics, 1975.
Ulman, Lloyd. *The Government of the Steelworkers' Union*. New York: John Wiley & Sons, Inc., 1962.
Warren, Kenneth. *The American Steel Industry, 1850–1970: A Geographical Interpretation*. Oxford: Clarendon Press, 1973.
Wogan, William. *The 1970's: Critical Years for Steel*. Lexington, Mass.: D. C. Heath and Co., 1972.

CHAPTER 5

Electrical Products

JAMES KUHN
Columbia University

Collective bargaining in the electrical products industry does not easily lend itself to a full description nor a comprehensive analysis; it is conducted by many different unions and a diverse group of firms producing a wide range of goods. The bargainers handle grievances and negotiate agreements not only for workers who manufacture giant generators, transformers, and switches in huge factories housing thousands of employees, but also for those who fabricate tiny, delicate components for radios, TV sets, communications equipment, and electrical components in small laboratory-like plants. Some are employed by great industrial conglomerates, while others work for companies that may provide jobs for only a few hundred people.

Officials of many companies point out that they cannot practically separate their industrial relations experience in electrical products from that in other areas. The vice-president of industrial relations, The Bendix Corporation, noted that his corporation is "a multi-national, diversified company and does not conveniently slot into a single [industrial] category. . . . We deal with over 30 different major unions and negotiate and administer 108 separate collective bargaining agreements. [We are] a major supplier to the automotive market; [are] deeply involved in aerospace electronics work; and [are] also a recognized leader in the industrial and energy fields." Over 2,000 of Bendix's 80,600 employees are classified as electrical equipment employees, but the Machinists (IAM) represents them rather than any of the electrical unions. Even small firms producing only electrical products find their industrial relations influenced by developments in other industries. Franklin Electric, a small company with about 2,200 workers in three plants, negotiates with three different unions—the International Union of Electrical, Radio and Machine Workers (IUE), the Allied Industrial Workers, and the United Auto Workers (UAW). Bargaining and industrial relations in each are markedly different.

The Bureau of Labor Statistics records 17 unions that bargain in the

209

industry labeled "electrical machinery, equipment and supplies." They range from the IUE and the International Brotherhood of Electrical Workers (IBEW), that together enroll about 60 percent of the over one million members in the industry, to the American Federation of Musicians and the International Federation of Professional and Technical Engineers that account for only a few thousand workers in a scattering of bargaining units (see Table 1). Some of the unions and firms regularly negotiate nationwide agreements. Among the most prominent are

TABLE 1

Number and Share of Union Members in the Electrical
Machinery Industry, by Union Organization, 1974

Union	Total Membership 000's	Share of Members in Industry, %	Members of Industry 000's	Members in Industry as Share of Industry Total, %
IBEW	991	45	446	42
IUE	298	73	218	20
UE	163	75–80[a]	122–130[a]	11–12[a]
UAW	1,545	7	108	10
IAM	943	9	85	8
CWA	499	10[a]	50[a]	5[a]
Ind. Workers	97	20[a]	20[a]	2[a]
TE	19.5	45	9	1
Others	—	—	8–16	.5–1
Total			1,074	100

Source: U.S. Department of Labor, Bureau of Labor Statistics, *Directory of National Unions and Employee Associations*, Bulletin 1937, 1975.
[a]Estimated, based on 1972 data estimates of union officers.

those reached by General Electric separately with the IUE and its onetime bitter rival, the United Electrical, Radio and Machine Workers of America (UE); Westinghouse's agreements with the IUE, the UE, and its employees' independent union; and RCA's national contract with the IBEW. Western Electric still negotiates separate local agreements with the IBEW, and the other large companies also negotiate local agreements with many different unions.

Enough industry employees are concentrated in the several large corporations and the few big electrical-equipment unions represent a sufficient portion of them, however, that collective bargaining tends to follow their patterns. Certainly the industrial relations policies and practices of General Electric, Westinghouse, the IUE, and the UE have dominated the labor scene in the industry for a generation or more. Since the late forties, the disputes among these four organizations, the strikes that have involved them, and the settlements reached have regularly made newspaper headlines throughout the United States. The two rival unions, along with the IBEW, account for nearly three-fourths of all union members in the industry. General Electric and Westinghouse probably employ one-sixth to one-fifth of the industry's union members and, with Western Electric and RCA, they encompass roughly a third of the total (see Table 2).

TABLE 2

Number of Workers, in Units of 1,000 or More, Covered by Agreements and Share of Industry Union Members, by Selected Companies

	Number	Share
General Electric	117,300	11%
Westinghouse	64,750	6
RCA	37,550	4
Western Electric	85,500	8

Source: U.S. Department of Labor, Bureau of Labor Statistics, Wage Calendar, 1970, 1971, 1972.

Despite the concentration of employment and union membership, the industry is heterogeneous enough that differential trends in employment, shifts in occupational mix, and changes in plant location and product can change and, as will be shown, have changed and are changing the impact and thrust of collective bargaining among companies and unions in the electrical equipment industry.

Economic Changes in Industry and Unions, 1960–76

Employment gains in the electrical-equipment industry since 1960, and even more so since the end of World War II, appear to have provided favorable conditions for union growth and successful collective bargaining. The number of industry employees increased almost half again as much as those in durable manufacturing, accounting for about one-quarter of the net increase in jobs in the larger sector (see Table 3). In the earlier, postwar period, 1947–60, employment in electrical equipment increased more than three times faster than in durable manufacturing, and made up 40 percent of the total net gain in jobs there.

TABLE 3

Employment Changes, Durable Manufacturing and Electrical-Equipment Industries, 1947–1976 (000's and %)

Industry	Employees No.	%	Production Workers No.	%	Nonproduction Workers No.	%
Durable manufacturing						
1947–60	1,074	13	0	0	1,074	79
1960–76	1,567	17	838	12	729	30
Electrical equipment						
1947–60	432	42	183	23	246	109
1960–76	364	25	214	21	150	32

Source: Employment and Training Report of the President, 1977, Tables C-4 and C-5, pp. 273–74.

The unions' main strength continues to lie in their membership among production workers. The proportion of nonproduction workers in the industry, however, has risen sharply. From 1947 to 1960, it rose from 22 to 32 percent, but it has not changed much since. By 1976 it was just under 34 percent. Over those same years, the number of production workers increased markedly and, in absolute number, as fast as the number of nonproduction workers.

The changes in union membership from 1960 on, and the relatively slow growth of workers' earnings in the electrical-equipment industry indicate, though, that the unions were not able to capitalize on the upward employment trend and the continued high demand for labor that it implies. For example, from 1958 to 1968 the number of production workers increased by 462,000, but the three major unions in the industry reported membership gains of only 200,000. Since an unknown but sizable portion (probably more than two-fifths) of the gains were in other industries, these unions succeeded in adding to their rolls about one production worker for every four new jobs created in electrical equipment. The record is not an impressive one (see Table 4).

TABLE 4

Membership in Selected Unions Organizing the
Electrical-Equipment Industry, 1958–1974
(000's)

Year	IBEW	IUE	UE
1958	740	278	160
1960	771	288	160
1962	793	285	163
1964	806	271	165
1966	875	320	167
1968	897	324	167
1970	922	300	163
1972	957	290	165
1974	991	298	163

Source: U.S. Department of Labor, Bureau of Labor Statistics, *Directory of National Unions and Employee Associations,* for various years.

The record of the IUE and UE worsened after 1968; both showed declines in total membership. The IUE in particular suffered losses of members from 1968 to 1970, when its membership declined by over 10 percent, almost twice the rate of drop in employment of production workers in the industry. By 1974 it had recovered somewhat. The IBEW, in contrast, continued to add members at a modest rate. For neither union do the data indicate what portion of the recent gains have been in the electrical-equipment industry.

Table 4a suggests that none of the three electrical unions has made important membership gains through winning representational rights in

TABLE 4a

Single-Union Representational Elections in the Electrical-Equipment Industry Elections Won and Lost by Selected Unions and by Number of Employees Eligible to Vote, Fiscal Years 1972–1976

	Wins		Losses		Total	
	No. Elections	Emps. Eligible	No. Elections	Emps. Eligible	No. Elections	Emps. Eligible
IBEW	103	7,373	104	12,522	207	19,895
Southern states only[a]	20	2,917	18	5,870	38	8,787
IUE	42	4,713	95	20,704	137	25,417
Southern states only[a]	13	2,937	30	10,285	43	13,222
UE	21	2,400	11	984	32	3,384
Southern states only[a]	1	906	1	38	2	944

Source: NLRB monthly records of representational elections.

[a] Alabama, Arkansas, Florida, Georgia, Kentucky, Mississippi, North Carolina, South Carolina, Tennessee, Texas, Virginia, and West Virginia.

NLRB elections over the past five years, 1972–76. The three unions—IBEW, IUE, and UE—won elections in which 14,000 workers were eligible to vote; the IBEW claimed more than half of them. But the three unions lost elections in which 34,000 workers were eligible to vote, the IUE's losses accounting for two-thirds of the workers eligible.

The IBEW is the most active organizer of the three, both conducting and winning more elections than the other two unions together. In the South, however, the IUE has conducted more elections than the IBEW. Its wins, though, were fewer and the number of eligible workers in those wins was barely larger than those of the IBEW. Neither the IBEW nor the IUE appears to have increased its organizing efforts appreciably in the South even though a far larger portion of the industry's employment is now located there. In 1960, for example, they conducted a total of only 14 representation elections, winning six and losing eight. In the last five years, they have averaged 16, winning seven of them.

The unions show a significant difference in the size of the units they successfully organize (see Table 4b). Both the IBEW and IUE tend to lose the larger and win the smaller units, in the South as well as in other sections of the country; one-third of the eligible employees in the IBEW's wins were in units of 10 or under and more than two-thirds in units of 50 and under. The IUE apparently concentrates its efforts on larger units than does the IBEW, with the average number of employees eligible per election larger in both its wins and losses.

TABLE 4b

Average Number of Employees Eligible in Single-Union Representational Elections, Electrical-Equipment Industry, by Wins and Losses and by Selected Unions, Fiscal Years 1972–1976

	Wins	Losses
IBEW	72	120
Southern states only[a]	146	326
IUE	112	218
Southern states only[a]	226	343
UE	114	90
Southern states only[a]	906	38

Source: See Table 4a.
[a] See Table 4a.

The data indicate that if present trends continue, the IBEW, already enrolling 100,000 more workers in the industry than the IUE and the UE together, will slowly increase its lead. Should its leaders decide to play a more militant, visible bargaining role than in the past, the structure and conduct of collective bargaining in the industry could change markedly.

Not only is the balance of membership weight among the unions shifting, and possibly the weight of union members in the industry's workforce, but the outcome of bargaining is changing in ways disturbing to the unions' leaders. Increases in hourly earnings in the electrical-equipment industry have lagged behind those in durable manufacturing since 1960. Especially noticeable to politically sensitive union officers is the growing gap between electrical workers' earnings and those secured by workers in the aircraft and steel industries in recent years (see Table 5). Some company negotiators, such as those at Maytag, point to the GE-IUE wage settlement as a pattern that their workers should follow. The UAW, which negotiates for Maytag's electrical-equipment workers, rejects it, of course, preferring to model their demand at higher settlements of autos and agricultural implements.

TABLE 5

Ratios of Average Hourly Earnings in Electrical
Equipment to Those of Other Selected Industries

	Elect. Equip/ Dur. Mfg.	Elect. Equip/ Aircraft	Elect. Equip/ Steel
1960	93.8	84.4	75.0
1965	92.5	82.2	75.4
1970	92.4	79.8	78.8
1975	89.1	76.5	65.9
1976	88.6	76.1	63.9

Source: Employment and Training Report of the President, 1977, Table C-8, p. 277.

The electrical-equipment industry confronts market conditions as well as occupational structures and production processes so different from those of the aircraft and steel industries that such earning comparisons are not economically appropriate. However, electrical union leaders are aware of the relative decline since 1947—and invidiously compare their wage gains with those of the Machinists (IAM), the UAW, and Steelworkers (USW). They fear that the poorer wage record of their unions provides a persuasive reason for members or unorganized employees in the industry to opt for one of the other unions.

Though employment shows a steeper upward trend in electrical equipment than in the whole of the durable goods industry, it has risen most erratically. The demand for electrical workers has fluctuated widely. At the extreme, the number of production workers jumped in a single year, 1965–66, by 185,000, an increase of more than 16 percent. Less than a decade later the number fell in a year's time, 1974–75, by over a quarter of a million, 233,000, a drop of nearly 17 percent! Since 1960 the number of production workers dropped in seven years by an average amount of 5 percent and increased in nine years by an average of nearly 7 percent.

Such employment swings are larger than those in steel, a notoriously cyclical industry. Workers and unions in it have had to contend with employment declines as large as 13 percent, 1974–75, and an overall downward trend. Despite the problem of maintaining union membership under such conditions, the Steelworkers union has managed to increase the size of its organization. From 1966 to 1972, the number of production workers in steel dropped by over 74,000, but the USW increased its membership by 332,000. At the same time average hourly earnings in steel, already a third larger than those in electrical equipment, increased their lead. One may conclude that though instability of employment has not made organizing easy for unions in the electrical-equipment industry, there are probably other problems that have produced the mediocre performance of the IUE and the UE.

Union officials in both the IUE and UE explain the slow growth of their organizations through the sixties and the fall-off in membership in the seventies, as well as the relative decline in industry wages, on two changes: the loss of product markets and jobs to imports and the move of the industry to the South. The extent of the job losses due to imports is not readily measured with available data and thus can only be guessed. There is no doubt, though, that the industry's move to the South is massive. Since employment has continued to grow, although fitfully, as both changes have taken place, the union problems are not due to a decline in the number of workers available to be organized, but rather to the difficulties of enrolling workers in new plants as old, well-established locals shrink and even disappear.

From 1960 to 1968, imports of electrical apparatus, correcting for price inflation, rose almost fourfold to $1.8 billion. This rise was far greater than the increase of U.S. exports of the same kinds of goods. Even with the sharply increased flow of imports, however, domestic employment in the industry rose by over half a million, pushing up the total by over a third. Nor did the flooding tide of imports stop union growth. Membership increased modestly. Since 1968 and up to 1975, real imports have increased by only 44 percent, while exports were rising by 73 percent. In 1975 real exports of electrical apparatus were 1¾ times larger than imports, and if "electronic computers, accessories and parts" were added to them, the total was 2¼ times greater than the imports. These figures indicate that overall the industry gains from international trade. If imports hurt a part of the industry, expanding exports certainly help other parts.

The gains distribute themselves unevenly across the industry, however, causing severe dislocations. That part of the industry producing the heavy electrical power machinery and switch-gear equipment has

TABLE 6

Imports and Exports of Electrical Apparatus and Selected Electrical Equipment, 1968–1975
(Millions of 1972 Dollars)

Year	Imports					Exports				
	Total	Power Mach. & Switch Gear	Telecommunications Apparatus	Electron Tubes, Transistors, Semiconductor Devices, & Parts	Other	Total	Power Mach. & Switch Gear	Telecommunications Apparatus Including Radio & TV	Domestic Electrical Equip.	Other
1968	1848	208	911	174	555	2678	623	627	142	1286
1969	2339	235	1208	209	687	3046	639	703	150	1554
1970	2549	277	1237	251	784	3221	656	709	128	1728
1971	2733	281	1400	276	776	3175	703	703	129	1640
1972	3377	356	1672	396	953	5698	787	836	158	3917
1973	3806	390	1751	596	1069	4330	917	895	192	2326
1974	3194	340	1365	616	873	4723	1004	916	254	2549
1975	2653	308	1120	486	739	4643	1045	963	222	2413
Average Change/ Year	115	14	30	45	26	281	60	48	11	161

Source: *Statistical Abstract of the U.S.*, 1976, Table 1415, p. 847, and Table 1421, p. 851; and *Statistical Abstract of the U.S.*, 1971, Table 1242, p. 773, and Table 1247, p. 778.

enjoyed a net real balance of exports for a long time, and exports have continued to rise faster than imports from 1968 to 1975. The rise in imports of telecommunications apparatus has been matched by a rise in exports over the same period, though imports are considerably larger. The industry sector most hurt by imports is electronic equipment, semiconductor devices, and transistors. Imports have exceeded exports by a wide and growing margin (see Table 6). Workers who have been producing these goods are being displaced in large numbers; their job losses in the industry are losses for the union, too, seriously impairing its strength in membership and revenues.

The movement of some part of the industry to the South is large and no doubt sustained, though recent employment data are not available. Old plants closing in the Northeast and new ones opening in the South can pose major organizational problems for unions. From 1963 to 1972, the Northeast (New England and the Middle Atlantic states) lost more than 49,000 jobs and the South gained 118,000 (see Table 7). As a result, where the South accounted for only one out of eight production workers in 1963, by today, if the shift has continued, as seems likely, it now provides jobs for at least one out of four workers and perhaps an even higher proportion.

TABLE 7

Production Workers in the Electrical-Equipment Industry by Number and Share for Major Regions, Selected Years

Year/ Region	Northeast		North Central		South		West		Total	
	No.	%	No.	%	No.	%	No.	%	No.	%
1963	394	38	394	38	134	13	127	12	1048	100[a]
1967	458	35	494	37	210	16	159	12	1322	100[a]
1972	345	30	426	37	252	22	136	12	1160	100[a]

Source: U.S. Department of Commerce, Bureau of the Census, Census of Manufacturers, Vol. 3, 1963, 1967, and 1972.

[a] Percentages do not add to 100 because of rounding.

The largest employment shifts have taken place in that part of the industry producing communications equipment. The Northeast lost nearly 57,000 jobs during 1963–72 and the South gained 38,000, while the nation lost a net of 31,000. By 1972 more than a quarter of employees in communications equipment were working in the South. Only nine years before, 15 percent had worked there.

A pronounced shift in employment has taken place also in the part of the industry producing transmission and distribution equipment. The IUE and UE have long organized the northern workers in the plants that manufacture this equipment, and they form the very core of their organizations. In 1963 the Northeast accounted for 44 percent of the employment in this heavy-equipment work and the South but 10 percent. By 1972 the Northeast had lost 10,500 employees and the South gained nearly 22,000. The Northeast's share dropped to 38 percent and the South's jumped to 28 percent. Moreover, employment in the South, for every part of the industry, has increased significantly.

The Share of Women Workers and the Relative Decline in Wages

A factor that has not affected union organizing, but may have influenced the decline in the relative earnings of electrical workers over recent years, is the changing proportion of women in the industry's labor force. The share of women employed in electrical-equipment work has long been approximately double the share in the whole of the durable goods industries. In its share of women workers, electrical equipment resembles the nondurable industries which average about twice the proportion in the durables. Since women's earnings are almost always below those of men, the greater the share of women workers, the lower an industry's earnings usually are.

Within the electrical-equipment industry, the sectors with the highest proportion of women employees show the lowest earnings.[1] These sectors have grown faster than the whole industry, thus now exerting a larger downward pressure on earnings than 15 or more years ago. Such casual association cannot be assumed to be a causal one, however. Closer examination of the downward drift of relative earnings in the industry with the changes in proportion of women, compared to those in all durables, reveals a more complex relationship.

The share of women in durable industries has been increasing so that, while from 1959 to 1966, relative earnings tended to decline as the relative share of women employees in electrical equipment rose ($\bar{r} = -.988$), from 1967 to 1974 the two variables show a modest positive relationship ($\bar{r} = 0.58$). In the latter period relative earnings declined, but so did the relative share of women employees. The changing correlation indices suggest that other forces were probably also affecting earnings. With technological change continually making obsolete established production processes, products, and skills, both employers and workers are subject to new and unexpected competition. It arises from outside as well as within the industry and from both domestic and foreign sources; the lack of stability in all the industry's markets with the ever-

---

[1] They are three: radio and television equipment, electronic components, and lighting and wiring equipment. In 1975, considerably more than half the employees were women; their earnings were 15 to 26 percent below the industry average. The four sectors with the lowest proportion of women, 38 percent, were miscellaneous, electrical test and distributing equipment, electrical industrial apparatus, and household appliances; workers' earnings were at the industry average or above.

present pressures on costs and wages probably explains the continued downward slide of relative earnings since 1967, and no doubt contributed to their decline from 1959 as well.

The Industry Record of Work Stoppages

Historically, the electrical-equipment industry has not been strike-prone. In recent years its losses due to work stoppages averaged less than three-quarters those of all manufacturing industries. The number of stoppages annually, adjusted for employment changes, also shows about the same or a slightly higher ratio to those in manufacturing. With less than 1 percent of working time lost through stoppages and less than one stoppage for every 10,000 employees in 1971–75, the industry presents a quiet labor scene. Producers of electrical equipment lost 10 to 16 times as many workdays due to injuries[2] as from all work stoppages.

A close inspection of the data on work stoppages reveals some significant changes in the industry's number and incidence of strikes since the late fifties and early sixties—changes reflecting important developments in the industry's collective bargaining and shifts in industrial relations. First, both the number of strikes and the share of workers involved increased sharply after 1965, reaching a peak in the great 1969 GE strike (see Table 8). Since then these indices have declined, but not to their former levels of the early sixties. A graph of the indices resembles a chart of a fever victim's temperature, rising to a crisis stage and then dropping quickly, but to a level still too elevated to be considered healthy by past records.

Accompanying the fever-like symptoms of work stoppages is a recent increase in the number of short stoppages, those of one to three days in length. They account for a larger share of all stoppages in the industry than similar stoppages in either the transportation-equipment or the rubber industries, long plagued by short-walkouts—"wildcat" strikes (see Table 9). In the fifties such strikes were thought to be uncommon in electrical equipment and contrasted sharply with the record in the other two industries.[3] Since 1956 the trend in the *duration* of work stoppages has been upward in transportation equipment and rubber, but down in electrical equipment.

The work-stoppage data point to continuing difficulties in the industrial relations of companies and unions that the parties have not been able to dissipate through their collective bargaining. Further, neither the passing of time nor the strike of 1969 resolved the problems or changed

---

[2] U.S. Department of Labor, Bureau of Labor Statistics, "Occupational Injuries and Illnesses in the United States, By Industry," *BLS Bulletins,* recent years.

[3] Kuhn, *Bargaining in Grievance Settlement,* pp. 53–57. [The complete citations of all footnote references are listed at the end of the chapter.]

TABLE 8

Measures of Work Stoppages in Electrical Equipment, 1960–1975

	Av. Number[a]	Index	Av. Worker Participation[b]	Index	Av. Duration[c]	Index	Av. Working Time Lost[d]	Index
1956–60	5.8	100	4.2	100	21.2	100	.45	100
1961–65	7.1	122	3.7	88	13.7	65	.19	42
1966–70	11.1	191	9.4	224	21.2(13.0)[e]	61	.74	164
1971–75	9.0	155	5.3	126	16.1	62	.33	73

Source: U.S. Department of Labor, Bureau of Labor Statistics, Analysis of Work Stoppages, various years.

[a] Number of strikes per 100,000 employees.

[b] Workers involved as a percent of employment.

[c] Workdays lost divided by workers involved.

[d] Workdays lost.

[e] Omitting 1969, the year of the long strike, average duration was 13.0.

TABLE 9

Numbers of Workers Involved in Short Work Stoppages, 1-3 Days,
as Share of Totals for Selected Industries, 1968–1975

	Electrical Equipment		Transportation Equipment		Rubber	
	No.	WI[a]	No.	WI[a]	No.	WI[a]
1968	34%	29%	14%	29%	19%	20%
1969	33	41	27	23	19	22
1970	22	17	28	21	7	5
1971	31	33	20	11	6.5	14
1972	39	47	21	16	25	31
1973	23	26	21	21	12	29
1974	16	7	11	14	7	10
1975	18	28	14	9	7	20

Source: U.S. Department of Labor, Bureau of Labor Statistics, *Analysis of Work Stoppages*, various years.

[a] Workers involved.

the conditions that have encouraged workers to resort to short strikes. Whatever those problems are, they seem to have increased and the conditions that created the problems have either continued or worsened.

From Boulwarism to Coordinated Bargaining

The analysis in the rest of this chapter focuses upon the approach to collective bargaining taken by General Electric (GE) and the eventual union response, led by the IUE. Other companies such as Westinghouse, Western Electric, and RCA, as well as other unions, including the UE, IBEW, and United Automobile Workers (UAW), have contributed to the development of the bargaining in the industry, but in many cases they played ancillary roles, following the lead of GE and the IUE.

That GE officials might take the lead and command the attention of the industry is understandable, given the dominating size of their company. It is one of the industrial giants of American business, in 1976 ranking ninth on *Fortune's* list of The Five Hundred Largest Industrial Corporations. The number of its employees is equal to over a fifth of all those in the electrical-equipment industry, and larger than the combined employment of Westinghouse and Western Electric. Not only is GE a big, nationwide company, it also produces so wide a range of goods that its output is a cross-section of industry. No other single electrical producer competes and sells in as many markets as does GE.

The managers of the other electrical products firms have long followed GE's lead in bargaining. For example, GE's national labor agreements have usually expired two weeks before those of the next largest company, Westinghouse. Negotiators for the latter thus almost always knew the outcome of GE's bargaining and its settlements before they completed their own. With minor variations, they usually sought, and received, the terms to which GE had already agreed. The Director of Personnel Relations, Westinghouse Electric Corporation, explains, "Since GE normally sets the 'pattern' of bargaining in the Electrical Industry, obviously their bargaining approaches have affected those of our Company. . . . [We have] followed GE's lead in national agreements. GE bargains before we do and the GE settlement quickly becomes the basis for union demands in the follow-up bargaining. The pattern set by GE clearly has a substantial impact on our bargaining."

As bargaining agent for the largest share—about 60 percent—of all the union members in GE, the IUE became the key union in the industry even if, in recent years, it has not boasted the largest number of members. The IBEW reports twice as many members in electrical-equipment plants as the IUE, but they are mostly scattered among many small bargaining units. It negotiates a *national* contract for only 17,500 RCA workers; its contracts with Western Electric, covering about 70,000 workers, are negotiated locally and usually follow GE's pattern.

IBEW's sheer bulk and its leaders' interest in extending their influence may make it a more influential union in the industry in the future than it has been in the past. It has not been in the forefront of developments in collective bargaining over the past 20 years, however. RCA officials assert that the IBEW, which represents over two-thirds of its organized workers, as well as the IUE, the other large membership union with whom they negotiate, make much of the GE settlement as a pattern to be followed. "Though we deal with the same unions as GE and Westinghouse and of course hear a great deal about the GE pattern, we point out we don't produce the same products. . . . They can't seriously expect us to follow them."

The UE has played the second most important union role in the industry. Its membership ranks a poor third to the other two leading unions, but it has enjoyed excellent leadership, representational rights for workers in a number of key production plants of the large companies, and the distinction of being the original CIO union organizing electrical workers successfully and aggressively in the thirties and forties. Nevertheless, its size and isolation from the AFL-CIO unions has allowed it limited scope for bargaining initiative; whether in dispute or in cooperation with the IUE, it has largely been able only to respond.

The Prelude to Collective Bargaining in the Sixties

Collective bargaining during the sixties was punctuated by two important strikes: the first opened the decade by appearing to demonstrate the success of GE's labor relations program developed by Lemuel R. Boulware, and the second in 1969–70 closed it by demonstrating the strength of cooperating unions coordinating their efforts. The causes of the strikes, their outcomes, and the slow, evolving changes in collective bargaining during the decade and since cannot be well explained without an understanding of the major internal forces and conditions that helped shape the values, policies, and practices of GE and the IUE—and UE—in the years prior to 1960.

The union leaders who emerged in the thirties from the early organizational efforts brought with them the seeds of disunity that later, in sprouting and rank growth, were to split and weaken the electrical workers in their bargaining. The large companies, which were among their chief targets, did not resist the coming of unions with the fierceness found among those in autos, steel, and rubber.

James B. Carey won the presidency of the newly formed United Electrical and Radio Workers of America. He had risen from among the workers in the large battery works of Philco Radio in Philadelphia, winning a national reputation when, after a short strike, the company signed an agreement in 1933 with his local union. He was 21 years old. Carey early showed a flair for boldness (or rashness), invective, and dramatic speech-making, but he developed little competence as an administrator. Making best use of his talents, he concentrated on public relations activities and left the day-to-day running of the union to the other officers. While popular with many of the rank-and-file members, his fellow officers then found him, as other union leaders in different circumstances later were to find him, both tactless and irritating.[4]

His chief associate in the union was Julius Emspak, who had been elected secretary-treasurer. He was a leader from the independent union in GE's big Schenectady plant. The local later became one of the largest in the union, exerting great influence upon the conduct of collective bargaining in the company. James Matles became director of organization, having joined the UE in 1937 with 15,000 workers who had been members of the Machinists union. Both Emspak and Matles were "left-wing stalwarts"[5] who carefully followed the political twists and turns of the Communist Party. Their influence in the union and their political activities in the wider labor movement began to create dissension in the UE by 1939; they also exacerbated the organizational disputes that the industrially organized, CIO-supported UE had long had with the IBEW. The cleavage within the union over politics became a line of fracture

---

[4] See Northrup, ch. 5, pp. 39–49; and Galenson, ch. 5, pp. 239–65.
[5] Galenson, p. 256.

that finally split the union, with far-reaching and long-lasting consequences for collective bargaining in the industry.

Carey's unwillingness to support the political stands of Emspak and Matles led to a widening of the split. In the union election of 1941, Carey lost his office to Albert J. Fitzgerald, a local leader from the big GE local at West Lynn, Massachusetts, who had the backing of Emspak and Matles. Carey continued ineffectually to oppose the Communist stands of the union as secretary-treasurer of the CIO, but he was by then too much an outsider to be effective in determining union policy or influencing union activities.

The UE continued to win representational elections and to increase its membership through World War II. By the end of the war, it had enrolled at least 400,000 workers, and in testing its strength, as did most of the rest of American unions in 1946, it struck for a better settlement than GE managers were at first willing to make. The nationwide company strike lasted nine weeks, the largest and longest labor dispute in which GE had ever been involved. The wave of strikes in almost every industry throughout 1946 that had involved, in sum, more than 10 percent of the labor force alarmed many Americans.

Congress began to investigate the powerful unions that were blamed for the unprecedented strikes. Not only did many in the electorate seek legislative curbs on unions' concerted activities, but public concern over Communist-dominated unions also mounted swiftly. Inclusion in the Taft-Hartley Act of provisions to rid unions of Communist officers was a clumsy device, but it indicated a widespread and particular antipathy to Communists in control of unions. Philip Murray, president of the CIO, and the other leaders of the major industrial unions moved toward purging their organizations of Communist officers. At its 1949 convention, the CIO broke with the UE, which had ceased paying its per capita tax. At the same time the CIO established a rival union, the IUE. The president, James B. Carey, for the second time in less than 20 years had the task of organizing the electrical-equipment workers. The UAW, Machinists, and IBEW, as well as a number of other unions had already begun to raid the outcast UE. With strong support from Murray and the CIO, however, in a few year's time the IUE succeeded in winning away three-quarters of the UE's members in representational elections conducted by the National Labor Relations Board.

The elections were hard fought, sometimes refought, and a few locals passed back and forth between the rivals. In many cases the fights left embittered and strong, militant factions to be dealt with by the winning union. At the Erie, Pennsylvania, plant of GE, for example, the IUE won the salaried staff, but the UE retained the production workers; in the next year, the UE won the salaried staff back in a re-election.[6] In the large and important Local 255, Pittsfield, Massachusetts, the IUE won the 1950 election, but the local members indicated to Carey that they were voting more against the Communist leadership of the UE than for him. When he shortly called for an endorsement of a strike as a bargaining threat, they turned him down as did several other new IUE locals at GE plants.[7]

The IUE did not win all its big locals quickly or easily. The largest local, in the Schenectady plant of GE, did not switch to the IUE until 1954. And in GE's big Lynn plant, the UE and IUE struggled for years to see which union would represent the workers. In the first election, in 1950, the IUE won by 900 votes out of 12,000; the following year the UE challenged the IUE and lost by a larger margin of 1,100 votes. In 1953, the UE again secured an election, but lost by 1,450 votes.[8]

The widespread interunion fighting, campaigning, and agitation drained budgets, pulled leaders away from virgin organizing, and concentrated attention of members and leaders on union issues and problems rather than on those posed by employing firms. In such an unstable and competitive situation, responsible union leadership was not always encouraged, and the furthering of reasonable collective bargaining was difficult.

At the very time the UE was splitting apart and fighting with the IUE for the support of the locals, the managers at GE began to develop a new program of industrial relations. The development added another and a new dimension to the challenges faced by the officers of both unions. As they saw it, the company challenged their role as leaders of the workers and their function as negotiators for their members.

The nine-week strike conducted by the UE in 1946 had shocked the top managers of GE. They had pictured themselves as generous employers, in touch with their workers and responsive to their needs. The company had long followed a program that attempted to recognize workers' on-the-job interests and to promote two-way communication between employers and employees. The length of the strike, the violence at some plants, particularly in Philadelphia, and the way in which settlement finally came—the president of the company, Charles E. Wilson, meeting with the union leader, James Matles, to approve the terms—convinced company managers that the time had come for a thorough review and reevaluation of GE labor relations and approach to employees.

<hr/>

[6] Northrup, pp. 46–47.
[7] *The Berkshire Eagle*, September 12, 1960.
[8] *Business Week*, April 2, 1960, p. 73.

Wilson asked one of his vice-presidents, Lemuel R. Boulware, to examine the strike and the company's employee program. His managerial record during the strike had commended him as the person to reexamine GE's approach to employees. At that time he had been in charge of seven "affiliated companies" that were owned by GE but bargained locally rather than under the national agreement. What impressed Wilson was the fact that none of the 16,000 employees in the affiliated companies had joined the strike, though a number of them were enrolled in three UE locals.

Boulware concluded from his examination that the strike had been "little short of a debacle" and a "somber event" for the company.[9] "General Electric simply had to correct the ridiculous situation where— despite the best of intentions and the best practices known—the company was distrusted and disapproved by employees and neighbors in some very important matters."[10] He urged a new approach to collective bargaining, for under the old and existing approach "every improvement in employee welfare was getting to be regarded as something which we had greedily and viciously resisted, and which had had to be *forced* out of us *unwillingly.*"[11] Henceforth, the company should, he insisted, make a firm, fair offer at the negotiating table and assure itself that both employees and people in the communities where they lived recognized and appreciated the company's efforts on their behalf. Such assurance could be secured only if the terms in fact were fair, and if the company had helped everyone understand, long before negotiations began as well as long after, the values GE was upholding and the problems with which it was wrestling.

Boulware had his new employee and community program operating effectively from the time of the 1948 and 1949 negotiations. The UE accepted the terms he offered on behalf of the company with almost no change or adjustments. It was riven by internal dissension, on the defensive within the labor movement, and thus in no position to bargain hard. In the following years, as GE negotiated separately with the IUE and UE, the unions were seldom able to win any significant improvements in wages, fringes, or working conditions above those offered by the company.

From its inception, the IUE could not secure membership approval of a strike authorization from enough locals to make the threat of a

---

[9] Matles and Higgins, pp. 245–46.

[10] Boulware, p. 3.

[11] "Year-End Review: Where We Were, Where We Are, Where We Are Trying to Go in Employee Plant Community and Union Relations," *General Electric Company Employee Relations Newsletter,* December 3, 1954, p. 2, quoted in Northrup, p. 27.

walkout a convincing bargaining ploy. And all too often, if the IUE rejected a company offer, the UE or other unions in GE would accept; the result on occasion was the denial for months to IUE members of wage increases enjoyed by all other GE employees. In 1955, however, the company and union signed a five-year agreement that Carey called "a splendid settlement,"[12] but relations between the IUE and GE did not take a turn for the better. Nor did relationships improve with other large companies. The IUE struck Westinghouse for 156 days in 1955–56 and, after government pressure had been applied, settled for terms that no one described as a win. The militancy of its Westinghouse locals declined markedly for some time.

As the decade of the fifties drew to a close, Boulware began to end his involvement in labor relations at General Electric. In 1957, he turned over his operating responsibilities to others, though retaining his title as vice-president and consultant. He retired in 1960. The policies he had formulated and followed had generated enough controversy that arguments about their usefulness and legality were to dominate national-level collective bargaining until after the 1969 strike.

The Effect of Boulwarism on Collective Bargaining

The programs and policies of GE that were popularly called "Boulwarism" became a great issue of controversy among labor scholars, in the law courts, and on picket lines, especially after Boulware had left active direction of them. Without a careful analysis of what was accomplished at what cost, or even with slight reference to any particular experience, the merits of Boulware's programs were lauded by apologists and the dangers were decried by critics. Both assumed the important issue to be the ideology underlying the program. The debates then focused on the values that informed the ideology. All too few of the debaters examined the bargaining situations or the negotiated settlements carefully to identify how—or if—the ideology, its values, and the Boulware program was causally related to them.

In supporting Boulware and his program, the officers of GE and those in other companies were attempting more than merely strengthening their hand at the bargaining table; they meant to persuade workers and the whole industrial community that business could, to sum up in GE's slogan, "do good voluntarily in the balanced best interest of all." Those who followed the Boulware programs took upon themselves a difficult task. It was, first, finding out what needed to be done for employees and the community and of doing it voluntarily and responsibly. Second, it was persuading others, in particular employees and those

---

[12] Northrup, p. 64.

who lived in the communities where GE was a major producer, of the rightness of the managerial decisions.

The heart of the Boulware program, if one accepted the assumption that management could and would work in the best interests of all, was deciding what to do. The selling of the decision followed as an ancillary activity, needed because people were bombarded with much misinformation from other sources and often simply misunderstood management's rationale. To those who were skeptical of managers' ability to comprehend and adequately respond to the multitude of interests that claim a stake in business decisions, the heart of the Boulware program was the flood of propaganda (or "communications," to use GE's term) that accompanied the company offer. The massive use of all communications media to sell the company terms as the best possible ones raised fears among many people for the well-being and continued effectiveness of collective bargaining. Proponents and opponents of Boulwarism thus usually talked past each other, frustrated in understanding each other and in being misunderstood. Neither could nor would grant the assumptions of the other.

GE's direct appeal to its employees at the same time it presented its offer to union negotiators had not been a part of the usual rules by which the game of collective bargaining had been played. But Boulware, given his assumptions, found that the old rules forced him and his company into a false position; he objected. The success of his job marketing depended upon a company-made offer, worthy of acceptance on its own terms. He had no need of union help in presenting the offer, though it might contribute in the information stage; and he certainly had no reason to support the political leaders in either union. Neither Carey in the IUE nor Matles and Emspak in the UE were likely to help achieve any of the goals he and other company officials had in mind.

Those who supported and furthered Boulware's programs derided "the traditional give and take of the so-called auction bargaining as 'flea bitten eastern type of cunning and dishonest but pointless haggling.' "[13] Herbert Northrup, who had served on GE's negotiating team in 1960, approved, pointing out that the Boulware approach put "negotiations on a more factual and less emotional basis."[14]

The denigration of give-and-take bargaining and the decrying of emotion, the emphasis on facts and "sound reason" by all those involved in GE's negotiations, may reflect a presumptuous and arrogant approach to collective bargaining; it may also reflect, though, their special, unpleasant negotiating experience with Carey of the IUE. In hearings

---

[13] *NLRB* v. *General Electric Co.*, 418 F.2d 736, 72 LRRM 2530, at 2533 (1969).
[14] Northrup, p. 29.

before the NLRB, the company made much of his behavior.[15] One can guess that his volatile personality, erratic, irritating, vituperative, and exasperating negotiating style scarred company officials, giving them a peculiarly warped view of bargaining.

The open espousal by GE managers of Boulwarism, their full use of corporate resources to "sell" company positions, and their disparagement of the usual haggling at the bargaining table alarmed many people who saw both unionism and collective bargaining threatened. The threats were exaggerated. After all GE had bargained with the IUE since 1950 and with its predecessor union since the thirties. In each year that the union had brought charges of bad-faith bargaining against the company, GE had negotiated comprehensive agreements with the hundred or so unions designated as bargaining agents for its workers. There had been only two strikes in the postwar period, 1946 and 1960. In reaching a settlement to end the latter strike, GE had not sought additional concessions from the union, "despite the strength of its position," as one member of the NLRB put it.[16]

Of course, a negotiating party may involve itself in specific "bad-faith" bargaining in an otherwise good relationship. If it should refuse to bargain over a mandatory subject or refuse information lawfully due the other party, it can be found not to be bargaining in good faith. The NLRB and the court, however, did not limit their findings to specific charges; they concluded that through the practices of Boulwarism, GE had manifested an *"overall* failure to bargain in good faith,"[17] had developed a *pattern* of conduct inconsistent with good-faith bargaining,[18] and demonstrated "an absence of subjective good faith."[19] By viewing the overall pattern of negotiating, a "mosaic of many pieces, but depending not on any one alone,"[20] the Board and court had concluded that "the state of mind"[21] of the company officials did not allow good-faith bargaining.

The negotiating pattern was composed of three parts, of which the last one was the most important and the most innovative. That "linchpin" part, as the court designated it, was the selling to the employees and the general public the fully formed bargaining proposals. In the preparation of the proposals the company first solicited comments from

---

[15] *Respondent's Brief for Trial Examiner,* Pt. 1, Before the NLRB 2nd Region, Case Nos. 2-CA-7581, 2, 4; 7864 (Post 10-CA-1682), pp. 32–37 and Appendix B, pp. 1–42.

[16] Quoted in Northrup, p. 90.

[17] 72 LRRM at 2545, italics added.

[18] 72 LRRM at 2546, italics added.

[19] 72 LRRM at 2551.

[20] 72 LRRB at 2545.

[21] 72 LRRM at 2550.

its local management personnel on the desires of the workforce and the type and level of benefits that they expected over the forthcoming contract term. It then translated these comments into specific proposals, with careful research into their cost and effectiveness for, and attractiveness to, employees. With the first two parts of the programs, the Board and court had no complaints and therefore hardly examined them.

The selling of the proposals impressed both the Board and court because of the size of the effort and the company's insistence upon characterizing its proposals as a firm, fair offer.

> Through a veritable avalanche of publicity, reaching awesome proportions prior to and during negotiations, GE sought to tell its side of the issue to employees. . . . To bring its position home to its employees, GE utilized a vast network of plant newspapers, bulletins, letters, television and radio announcements, and personal contacts through management personnel.[22]

The court contrasted the aggressive selling of the company proposals with the union's limited and lame advertising effort. "The IUE also tried its hand at publicity, including an 'IUE Caravan' that traveled from city to city, and occasional articles in the International Union's newspaper. In scope and effectiveness, however, they were far outshadowed by the Company's massive campaign."[23] The Board had illustrated the scale of GE's publicity. During the negotiations and strike in 1960, the company had directed 277 different written communications to employees at its Pittsfield, Massachusetts, plant and 246 such items to its employees at the Schenectady, New York, plant.[24]

Neither the Board nor the court found the company's communications, advertising, or other publicity to be illegal, untruthful, or unreasonable per se. The consequences of the selling, nevertheless, were detrimental, they concluded, to good-faith bargaining. It was, they said, designed and executed to derogate the union in the eyes of its members and the public at large. The take-it-or-leave-it approach to negotiations in general emphasized both the powerlessness and uselessness of the union to its members, while at the same time picturing "the Company as the true defender of the employees' interest, further denigrating the Union, and sharply curbing the Company's ability to change its own position."[25]

The Board saw in the company's firm offer "an attempt to bypass the Union and an attempt to disparage its importance and usefulness

---

[22] 72 LRRM at 2533.
[23] 72 LRRM at 2534.
[24] General Electric Co. and IUE, 150 NLRB 219 and n. 19 (1965).
[25] 72 LRRM at 2546.

in the eyes of its members."[26] The court held that "the Board could
appropriately infer the presence of anti-Union animus and . . . could
reasonably discern a pattern of illegal activity designed primarily to
subvert the Union. . . . [GE] negotiated, to the greatest possible extent,
by ignoring the legitimacy and relevance of the Union's position as
statutory representative of its members."[27] "GE displayed a patronizing
attitude towards Union negotiators inconsistent with a genuine desire
to reach a mutually satisfactory accord."[28] The court summed up its
and the NLRB objections to GE's approach:

> We have already indicated that one of the central tenets of
> "the Boulware approach" is that the "product" or "firm, fair
> offer" must be marketed vigorously to the "consumers" or em-
> ployees, to convince them that the Company and not the Union
> is their true representative. GE, the Trial Examiner found,
> chose to rely "entirely" on its communications program to the
> virtual exclusion of genuine negotiations, which it sought to
> evade by any means possible. . . . The aim, in a word, was to
> deal with the Union through the employees, rather than with
> the employees through the Union.[29]

The Board and court based their judgment of GE's illegality on a
narrow and conservative definition of collective bargaining. The Boulware approach, they feared, "devitalizes negotiations and collective bargaining and robs them of their *commonly accepted meaning.*"[30] Commonly accepted by those who may perceive only a small part of the
whole intricate process? As practitioners in, and scholars of, industrial
relations well know, collective bargaining is far more then the periodic,
publicized high-level negotiations over the terms of the labor agreement.
To treat those activities as the whole of collective bargaining or even
the larger part so narrows the term that it excludes the bulk of it. The
national negotiations and agreement, after all, are the hangers and hooks
on which local unions and plant managers drape the full form and
shape of collective bargaining.

Collective bargaining is thus far wider than the Board and court
recognized. Unions and companies devote the greater part of their industrial relations efforts to the continuous, daily work of administering,

---

[26] 72 LRRM at 2546.

[27] 72 LRRM at 2546.

[28] 72 LRRM at 2546.

[29] 72 LRRM at 2548. The trial examiner penned the last sentence and both the
Board and the court echoed it.

[30] *General Electric Co.*, 150 NLRB 192, 57 LRRM 1491, at 1500 (1964), italics
added; quoted by James A. Gross, Donald E. Cullen, and Kurt L. Hanslowe, "Good
Faith in Labor Negotiations: Tests and Remedies," 53 *Cornell Law Review* 1029
(1968). Italics added.

interpreting, and negotiating the terms of the agreement, cutting, stretching, and generally fitting their general wording to the multitudinous, complex circumstances that apply at the place of work. The efforts are those involved in the grievance processes. What is not accomplished in the general negotiations can frequently be won by a skillful foreman or supervisor for the company, or for the union by an adept shop steward or divisional representative. Gains under the overall agreement can also be lost through the negotiating and bargaining in the shop.

Given the high level of industrial relations activity at the local and shop level, the continuous interaction of union and management representatives, and daily communicating, negotiating, and bargaining found in most organized workplaces, one can hardly reach a conclusion about how union prestige is faring and collective bargaining is flourishing without examining its vitality at the lower levels as well as at the top.

The success of GE's "selling" of its bargaining position rested upon a thorough and honest preparation. If union members did not find the firm offer a fair one or if it disappointed their expectations, there is no reason to believe that they would find it acceptable, whatever the magnitude of GE's efforts to persuade them otherwise. Workers can quickly and perceptively judge the quality of an employer's offer and understand its implications and rewards for their own particular interests. Within the industry, GE's offers were not usually characterized as poor, cheap, or low either before or after it took the Boulware approach. Union leaders, of course, did not agree with such characterization; they wanted higher wages than they were offered, and since the GE offers excluded the union shop, unionists considered the offers substandard. The packages usually compared well with those won elsewhere in the industry, and only marginally over a long period of time did earnings slip behind those in other related industries such as machinery and automobiles. That slippage may well be the result of changing economic conditions, not Boulwarism.

Outside observers, with no partiality for GE's unions, may skeptically wonder if the company could truly discover the needs and desires of employees, and then always respond to them, however carefully it conducted its research and fully examined its data sources. The skepticism is well placed. Seriously to entertain the conceit that one group can reliably, equitably, and freely serve not only its organization's interests, but also the interests of others, demands of the group a breadth of view, a depth of perception, a clarity of purpose, and steadfast honesty that has yet to be found for any length of time among American business persons or unionists—or any other group, for that matter.

However one may judge the qualities GE officials brought to their employee relations program, one could view the program itself as an innovative development of collective bargaining. The Board and court overlooked the innovation, for they defined collective bargaining conservatively, as they had known or become familiar with its practice in most other situations. They were also led to overlook the innovation because they implicitly assumed, first, that unions play a passive, dependent, and responding role in bargaining, and second, that union members know and hold to their own interests so slightly that a massive propaganda barrage can persuade them to ignore and weaken their union leaders. If the IUE, UE, and other unions, as well as their members, acted in accordance with these assumptions, proof of the Board's and court's assumption is not necessarily provided. Such acts are subject to other explanations that the chapter will shortly explore.

Boulware, for reasons of both strategy and tactics, sought to change the locus of give-and-take bargaining from the national negotiating table to an earlier stage and in more local, decentralized settings—the company plants. Insofar as the industrial relations personnel sounded the needs and expectations of workers on the job, shop stewards, and local union officers, they offered the unions an opportunity to engage in bargaining and to haggle over the terms of the yet-to-be-determined proposal. National officers may find such an early and low-level locus of bargaining both inconvenient and difficult to manage. Their decision not to try to influence the negotiation at that time and place may be taken because of internal weakness, poor administration, and lack of resources, or as a matter of policy. But in either case, the decision is the union leaders'; it is a weak response to a company challenge. Their weakness should not be blamed on the company, nor should the company be charged with unlawful action.

For many of the same reasons Boulware and his associates found the new locus favorable to them, the IUE and UE found it unfavorable. That the unions were not able to pull themselves together, coordinate policies, planning, and programs among their locals, flexibly responding to GE's innovative style, passes a severe judgment upon them. In time they slowly were able to respond to the challenge, generating innovations of their own.

The history of Boulwarism before the NLRB and the courts, however, is as sorry as the unions' response to it. The Board members and judges reveal all too little understanding of collective bargaining in practice, and all too little faith in unions' strength to respond to innovation and challenge. Fortunately, the slow, winding path of the cases through the mazes of the various forums, consuming nine years in total, allowed the parties to continue their bargaining. The company challenge finally produced union response, which in turn has challenged the company. The forums saw at stake only weak and threatened collective bargaining in the electrical-equipment industry; history revealed strong and responsive collective bargaining in that industry.

DIVIDED UNIONS: THE UNDERLYING STRENGTH OF BOULWARISM

GE developed and pursued its approach to industrial relations and collective bargaining in circumstances that brought forth few challenges from the unions with whom it dealt. Its efforts were completely managed by a staff that was talented, innovative, unified, and tough; the efforts of the unions opposite contrasted unfavorably in almost every way. They were directed by uncertain leadership, particularly in the key organization, the IUE, which was also weakened by divisiveness at all levels.

The primary responsibility for union conditions lay with the IUE president, James B. Carey. Despite, or because of, his early organizing successes and his talents as a publicist and union orator, he never unified the unions he headed nor did he ever persuade many other persons of ability and position to work with him cooperatively, in or out of his own organization. He saw himself as one of the pioneers of industrial unions, a person of prestige and standing. In an exchange during the 1960 negotiations, he compared his role in the labor movement with that accorded to the then presidents of the Steelworkers and the Auto Workers. Clearly, he felt he received all too little recognition:

> You know it is hard for me to hold my head up when I meet with Reuther and McDonald. Reuther has been able to get things that we haven't been able to get in our industry. He is looked at with great envy. I was elected in 1933 to a National Office and he wasn't until 1946. It hurts me deeply to see them get these things and when I met McDonald he was typing agreements, not negotiating. It's embarrassing to me. . . .[31]

Carey's relationships with the leaders of the larger locals in the IUE had never been easy. As he and the IUE entered the 1960 negotiations, there were many signs that the union was anything but unified. At the 1958 convention Carey secured changes in the union constitution that increased his nominal authority as president. He would no longer have to bow to the adverse votes of the large locals, which had plagued him and prevented any GE-wide strike since the founding of the IUE. Of course, to change the rules but not the realities of power and consent was a dangerous move. In 1960, Carey received a majority vote legally

---

[31] *Respondent's Brief for Trial Examiner*, Appendix B, p. 16.

authorizing a strike, but four large locals and a few others decisively voted against it. The Pittsfield local voted 2 to 1 against a strike, and in Schenectady the margin against was 5 to 3. The strike vote carried in the second largest local, West Lynn, but Carey still had to contend with chronic and vocal opposition.

It may well have been out of his realization of union disunity that he advocated a strike: somehow, the ranks would pull together if he could only get them involved in a strike. He had told a reporter for *Steel Magazine* the previous year that "I owe G.E. a strike." He later denied the comment, but indicated during the negotiations that he thought a strike necessary or inevitable. He told the company officials, "Even if the offer was good, I still would not accept it."[32] And a member of the IUE-GE Conference Board reflected the union's—or Carey's—need for a strike, against all odds, when he said, in apparent resignation, "We've got to take on GE some time. I guess this has to be the time." He may have been resigned to a strike, but not all the locals were.

Under the union constitution all locals were bound to accept the decision of the Conference Board, but the members of Local 301, Schenectady, and its president, Leo Jandreau, delayed and protested. They did not join the strike when it began at midnight, October 2, 1960. Shop stewards later began circulating petitions calling for the local to join the other GE members of IUE, and both national and local union leaders exerted pressure on Jandreau. Three days after the strike had begun, the local president announced that a majority of members had signed the petition, and therefore he would authorize the strike to begin.

Strong local opposition to the strike continued, however, and within a week the members of the Schenectady local authorized their officers and executive board "to suspend or extend the strike locally at any time they feel their acting is in the best interests of the membership."[33] In defiance of the international, the local signed a truce arranged with GE, and the members returned to work.

The loss of the IUE's largest local in the strike was a serious blow to Carey. He had gambled that a strike under way would rally workers; he lost. As the strike moved into its third week, almost 40 percent of all workers under IUE agreements had returned to their jobs.[34] The outcome had generated even more divisiveness among the locals and within the union than before the strike.

In addition to exacerbating the conflicts that already existed among the local unions and with local officials, the strike also badly split the

---

[32] *The Berkshire Eagle,* October 17, 1960.
[33] *The Berkshire Eagle,* October 13, 1960.
[34] *Business Week,* October 29, 1960, p. 82.

international officers. As disaffection grew among the GE locals after Schenectady's return to work, Carey and his supporters pinned their faint hopes upon the IUE negotiations with Westinghouse. The union's secretary-treasurer, Al Hartnett, headed the negotiating team; they hoped that he and other negotiators would refuse the company's offer, almost a duplicate of GE's, and call the members out on strike. It was the only possible way to salvage the union from the deteriorating position at GE.

Hartnett declined to extend the strike. He reached agreement with Westinghouse just as the strike at GE was finishing its third week, accepting less than the IUE was demanding from GE. Hartnett had realistically evaluated the situation. Even before the IUE had struck, the IAM local at the GE jet engine plant in Evendale, Ohio, approved the company's offer by a 12 to 1 majority. Within the first week of the strike, the UAW's local at GE's Evendale plant also voted to accept the offer, and 33 locals of other unions, including the IBEW, had signed agreements with GE. With IUE's fellow members in the Industrial Union Department (IUD) of the AFL-CIO refusing to back the strike, defeat was sure; only the date of capitulation was unresolved.

Without the support of the IUD unions and the reinforcement from the Westinghouse locals, the GE strikers had to quit. The union called off the strike two days later. A. H. Raskin of *The New York Times* called the abortive strike "the worst setback any union has received in a nationwide strike since World War II." [35]

Carey blamed Hartnett for undermining the strike at a critical time, and the two men showed mounting hostility toward each other over the next three years. Both appealed to local unions around the country, campaigning to rally supporters. The IUE executive board finally ousted Hartnett, but by the time negotiations began in 1963, many IUE officials recognized that Carey's effectiveness as a leader was so diminished that he was not likely ever to recover it. He took part in no more than half a dozen negotiating sessions with GE and militantly opposed the company's offers. The IUE-GE Conference Board soundly rejected his opposition, and many unionists saw the rebuff as a greater personal blow than the strike debacle of 1960.[36]

By 1964, internal disputes had become so serious that the powerful Schenectady local began to negotiate changes for itself in the national agreement. GE officials claimed that the 60-year-old incentive system no longer worked and wanted to change it. The international fiercely resisted any change, but local officials negotiated an agreement grad-

[35] "GE's Labor Formula," *The New York Times*, October 25, 1960.
[36] *Business Week*, October 5, 1963, p. 118.

ually to remove 3,000 production workers from incentives. The IUE-GE Conference Board, at the behest of Carey, condemned the action to no avail. The local action was a dangerous sign that the IUE was fragmenting on a crucial item—company-wide wage standards. Both the integrity of the union and its labor agreements were in peril.

An increasing number of IUE officials had become convinced that Carey could never still the dissension wracking the union nor unite the many unions bargaining with GE into an effective negotiating team. None publicly expressed himself as the UE leaders did, but privately they may well have agreed. As the 1960 strike ended, Albert J. Fitzgerald, president of the UE, told members of a district council that the strike came "at the wrong time and the wrong place and certainly the wrong leadership. . . . [The leaders] are guilty of irresponsibility and stupidity." [37] Further, the UE had long insisted that GE's success rested not on its persuasive power and generous offers, but the fragmented approach of the hundred-odd unions to bargaining with the company. Disunity among the workers, not employee communications, powered Boulwarism.[38]

Despite the constitutional difficulties, carefully written in, to prevent a challenge to incumbents, many union officers in both local and international positions decided to oppose Carey. They backed Paul Jennings, executive secretary of District 3 (New York–New Jersey), for president in 1964, and he won, though only after the Labor Department intervened under the Labor-Management Reporting and Disclosure Act of 1959, and found that the initial count had been fraudulently rigged for Carey.

Before the outcome of the election was clarified, Walter Reuther proposed a merger with the UAW. He noted that the industry's diversification had cut across union jurisdictional lines so that IUE and UAW "more and more are dealing with the same corporations at the bargaining table." Since the IUE's internal dissension was disturbing to the UAW and "causing great damage to the IUE and its members and . . . weakening the entire labor movement," he suggested that equal numbers of representatives from each union should meet to agree on "a sound, workable and equitable" merger.[39] Gordon Freeman, president of the IBEW, strongly objected to the UAW's unilateral move. He intended that his union should be in on any division of the IUE. The Machinists also pointed out that it enrolled more members in the industry than the

[37] *The Berkshire Eagle*, October 22, 1960.
[38] Matles and Higgins, p. 252.
[39] *Business Week*, February 13, 1965, p. 28.

Auto Workers; and the Communications Workers found fault with the UAW's entering an already cluttered field.[40]

Jennings was faced with an urgent task of pulling the IUE together if it were to survive, while avoiding dismemberment by rival unions. At the same time, he needed to work with those same rivals to establish a joint bargaining strategy in negotiating with the major employers in the industry. Only by joining together might they hope fully to test and counter successfully the strength of Boulwarism.

Coordinated Bargaining: The Union Response to Boulwarism

Many union leaders in the electrical-equipment industry understood the desirability of joining together to confront GE and Westinghouse. Both companies were large enough to cover most of the industry, and even unions representing a small portion of their workforce could count many thousands of members in the two firms. As long as the IUE, with Carey as president, continued as the dominant union in GE, however, no one could see any feasible way of securing joint action. Unions had worked with Carey in the formulation of joint terms for negotiating in both 1958 and 1960, but the efforts had come to naught.

In October 1958, representatives of the IUE, the Machinists, and the IBEW met together under the aegis of the IUD to plan a campaign to "obtain meaningful job security for all GE and Westinghouse employees." [41] Other unions joined them, but the campaign did not proceed far with the GE negotiations. At Westinghouse, however, an informal coordination of bargaining approaches had developed and continued up into the sixties. All the national agreements expired at the same time, after GE's, and the company usually offered the same essential terms to all the unions, patterned on GE's. With most of the union representatives staying in the same hotel, they early found meeting together for discussions both natural and easy. "Evidence tends to indicate that all phases of contract settlement have been thoroughly discussed by all of the involved unions," [42] wrote one scholar who interviewed the principal negotiators.

The IUD unions involved in the electrical-equipment industry formally met again before the 1960 negotiations to discuss how they should approach GE and Westinghouse. The IAM insisted, as it had before, that it did "not intend to cede to anyone bargaining responsibilities for its members." [43] The group excluded the UE, of course, since it was not

[40] *Business Week*, February 20, 1965, p. 128.

[41] *Business Week*, July 16, 1960, p. 47.

[42] Chernish, p. 106.

[43] *Business Week*, August 16, 1960, p. 47.

a member of the AFL-CIO and thus the IUD. The unions involved agreed that they, at least, would present common demands to GE and coordinate their prenegotiating activities. They did not follow through, however, for Carey began to take the IUE in the direction of a strike, a destination none of the other unions cared to reach. He made much of the coordination that had taken place, offering it as evidence that the "combined strength and unity of the AFL-CIO unions . . . are standing in the wings, pledged to aid and support the just demand of the IUE." [44]

Just before the IUE broke off negotiations with GE, and when a strike clearly loomed ahead, the excluded leaders of the UE proposed that all unions with GE agreements join together and, in solidarity, pledge not to sign separately, but to coordinate bargaining and to strike together. Further, the UE proposed that together they agree upon a set of priority items for which they would bargain.[45] The other unions were not willing to work closely with the UE, the IUE strike was ready to begin, and in any case Carey was not about to be upstaged by his rivals in the UE. Nothing came of the proposal.

And nothing came of other early efforts at interunion coordination. The unions settled as they could, at times convenient to each, while the IUE stumbled into defeat. The IUD member unions had settled with GE before the IUE gave up the 1960 strike. Coordinated bargaining had failed badly and was not apt to be tried again with Carey as the leader and spokesperson. No coordinating meetings took place in the 1963 negotiations. The UE settled early, as did the big Sheet Metal Workers' local at the Hotpoint plants in Chicago. The IUD member unions settled, each by itself, as in former times.

With Carey's removal from office in 1965, the opportunity for a new start towards unity in bargaining offered itself, if Jennings could supply the needed leadership. In his first statement after taking office, he pledged that "diverse voices" would be heard in the union.[46] His pledge suggested that cooperation with other unions would be possible, for Jennings had a reputation as a union leader who had a knack for composing fights and working out acceptable compromises. George Meany saw the time as right to realize a dream of his—unity among the electrical-equipment unions.

A decade earlier, in the year the AFL and CIO merged, he had suggested the consolidation of the IBEW, IUE, the Utility Workers, and the CWA. So large a union in an important industry would greatly strengthen organized labor. He was, thus, pleased to give his support

[44] Quoted from the *IUE News* in Northrup, p. 74.
[45] *Business Week*, October 15, 1960, p. 31.
[46] *Business Week*, April 17, 1965, p. 54.

to the formation of a Committee on Collective Bargaining (CCB) in 1965. The seven-union members of the CCB were "to coordinate activities with reference to negotiations with the General Electric Company and the Westinghouse Electric Corporation to take place in 1966." [47] Walter Reuther, president of the UAW and the IUD, also heartily supported the CCB.

The CCB established a steering committee with responsibility for implementing approved policies. Jennings recognized one serious omission from the CCB, the UE. In a speech to an IUD conference in November 1965, he made a strong plea for "every other union that has any contract with Westinghouse or GE to join the committee . . . to participate with us in this collective bargaining program." [48] Still an outcast independent union, the UE was not formally eligible as a CCB member. Apparently and with no criticism for other members, the IUE informally shared information with its leaders and may well have discussed strategy and bargaining issues.

On several occasions in late 1965 and early 1966, the steering committee offered to meet with GE negotiators. The CCB pointed out that "since our eight unions have a jointly developed approach on how to create the most successful type of meetings and since your management has a national policy on this matter, the simplest and most effective solution is a conference between us." [49] The company rejected such a conference. It made clear that it "would not recognize the committee on collective bargaining as a 'merged negotiating body.' " [50]

The IUE then replied that it had not intended any formal request for joint bargaining and would abandon any such suggestions. Abandonment was sensible, for an NLRB trial examiner had just ruled that the bargaining alliance in the copper strike of 1968 violated the Taft-Hartley Act. It appeared to be a blow to coalition bargaining. The unions involved had insisted on a common contract expiration date, a settlement to be applied alike to each union and each bargaining unit, and company acceptance of the principle that no agreement became effective until all settlements had been reached. [51]

When the IUE negotiating team met with GE representatives in early May 1966, however, it had seven additional but nonvoting members, one

---

[47] Chernish, p. 83. The seven unions were the IUE, the Machinists, UAW, Allied Industrial Workers, IBEW, Sheet Metal Workers, and American Federation of Technical Employees.

[48] Chernish, p. 85.

[49] *General Electric Co.* v. *NLRB*, 412 F.2d 512, 71 LRRM 2418, at 2419-20 (1969). The American Flint Glass Workers had joined the CCB in March 1966.

[50] *General Electric Company and IUE*, 173 NLRB No. 46, 69 LRRM 1305, at 1309 (1968).

[51] *Business Week*, February 22, 1969, p. 108.

for each of the CCB members. The GE negotiators refused to engage in any discussions and left the meeting; they insisted they would meet only with IUE people. After directed by a federal court, four and a half months later they met, under protest, with the IUE committee, including the additional members. Negotiations continued, while the union and company made various legal moves in the courts and with the NLRB to test the lawfulness of the unions' unified approach. The company denounced it as coalition bargaining, illegally obliterating bargaining units certified by the NLRB and locking the various unions into a conspiratorial understanding. The union upheld the approach as mere coordination of bargaining, by having selected representatives of its own choosing from other unions to help in the lawful and desirable purpose of furthering collective bargaining.

The legal cases made their ways through the forums of NLRB panels and courts too slowly to provide a decision for the 1966 negotiations. The bargaining between the IUE and GE that year was tough, and as the expiration date of the old agreement approached, an impasse loomed. The CCB members met to denounce the company's offer as "completely unacceptable," and they then set up a review committee, with Meany as chairman, "to evaluate" any new offer from GE. Inside observers analyzed the situation as one in which the IUE could not budge GE. If Meany could persuade the federal government to intervene, additional pressure could be put on GE without the risk of a strike.[52] At any rate, President Johnson did intervene shortly afterwards and the negotiators moved to Washington with three Cabinet secretaries paying close attention. Over the next two weeks, during which the old contract was extended, the parties made some changes in the new cost-of-living provision, and they finally reached an agreement.

The UE had been negotiating with GE along a parallel track. It did not settle, however, until two days after IUE and GE announced their settlement. Provisions of the agreements for both unions were essentially the same. The Machinist and UAW locals at Evendale struck over local issues (and because of their defense work were enjoined under Taft-Hartley), as did a UE local at Ashland, Massachusetts, and the IUE's Schenectady local.

The contrast with previous negotiations was startling. The unions had held together, coordinating their strategy and tactics throughout the months of negotiating. The UE had not formally joined the CCB, but its staff people had worked closely with the IUE's staff. No union settled early or by itself; the CCB had used the prestige of the AFL-CIO to bless its efforts at the beginning and in the midst of the negotiations.

[52] *Wall Street Journal*, August 6, 1969.

The blessing added little in substance, but it spoke strongly of the unity and resolve on the unions' part.

GE had offered initially more than the CCB had expected and thus had dissipated much of the worker militancy on which some member-union leaders had counted. Without a major issue around which to rally workers, few believed that the old splits and cleavages in the IUE were so well repaired that a strike could be chanced. The GE negotiators on the other side could be reasonably satisfied with their performance. They had moved a bit from their original offer, but they had maintained for the company the initiative in bargaining. They also had a three-year contract, largely to their liking.

The editors of *Business Week* concluded that all parties involved had made gains.[53] From a longer perspective, it appeared that the IUE had gained the most, if the Board and the courts upheld the principle of coordinated bargaining. After nearly a generation of disunity, dissension, internal fights, and external quarrels, it had managed major negotiations with apparent peace and harmony on its side of the table. If coordinated bargaining continued, GE's use of the Boulware approach to collective bargaining would be truly tested.

Company officials were not happy at the prospects of confronting a coordinated group of unions at the bargaining table. Like those who earlier had examined Boulwarism with a jaundiced eye and predicted bad results, on the basis of theory alone, so GE examined coordinated bargaining, insisted on the invidious title "coalition bargaining" and predicted dire consequences for unions, the public, and the company. Its spokespeople argued that such bargaining would escalate disputes into industry-crippling strikes and thereby create national emergencies.[54] Further, they expressed concern that employee disaffection might appear as locally elected union representatives lost their authority to make their own bargaining decisions.[55] Quoting Leo Teplow of the American Iron and Steel Institute, they pointed out that "rank and file restiveness will not be helped by bargaining in larger units resulting from coalition or merger. Quite the contrary. The larger the unit, the more the individual employees feel that their needs and their demands have been lost or overlooked in the national bargain." [56]

Before the court the company asserted that NLRB approval of the unions' behavior would sustain "an improper effort to adjust economic power." [57] The court rejected the assertion, pointing out, "Of course,

---

[53] *Business Week*, October 22, 1966, p. 149.
[54] *General Electric Employee Relations Newsletter*, December 19, 1960, p. 10.
[55] *General Electric Employee Relations Newsletter*, December 19, 1960.
[56] *Ibid.*
[57] 71 LRRM at 2423.

it would be nonsense to pretend that IUE's purpose was not to increase its bargaining strength but that goal is a normal one for unions or employers." [58] In general, the NLRB and court recognized that coordinated bargaining was subject to abuse and that untoward consequences could appear. But the majority in each forum did not believe that the possibility of abuse indicated inherent abuse in the new bargaining arrangements. Both found for the union. They pointed out that GE had, in fact, invited the arrangements:

> [The] practice is to formulate a set of national company proposals for presentation to the IUE and the UE, two of the three unions with which there is bargaining on a national scale. . . . [GE's] mode of centralized administration, despite the multiplicity of bargaining units and representatives, is rendered feasible in part because the Company's collective agreements, with an insignificant number of exceptions, have uniform expiration dates.
>
> IUE claims that having members of the other unions on its committee increases communications between all of them and to that extent reduces the ability of the Company to play one off against the other. In any event the plain facts are that the IUE proposed negotiating technique is a response to the Company's past bargaining practices, that it is designed to strengthen the IUE's bargaining position, and that both sides know it.[59]

While the coordinating unions maintained their unity in the negotiations with GE, they broke apart in the bargaining with Westinghouse later the same year, 1966. The IBEW represented about one-fifth of the company's unionized workers, a larger proportion than it represented in GE. Heretofore, it had contented itself with the pattern settlements of the IUE or UE and, as a member of CCB, everyone expected it to go along with the CCB negotiations. As the unions and company bargainers moved toward an agreement, however, the IBEW announced that it had to resolve 13 special problems at Westinghouse. Unable to gain a quick resolution, the union called out workers in 20 plants. The strike spread, but it did not stop all production. Within two weeks the parties reached a settlement not significantly different from those reached with the IUE, UE, and Federation of Westinghouse Independent Salaried Unions.

Observers explained the IBEW's break with CCB as an attempt to lay claim to a larger role in industry bargaining. If Jennings did not succeed in pulling the IUE together and Meany should push for a consolidation among the unions, the officers of the IBEW wanted to be

[58] *Ibid.*
[59] *Ibid.*

able to assert a strong claim to both members and bargaining leadership in the industry. The IBEW's willingness to assert its independence underlined the precarious position the IUE occupied in the CCB. The larger union was ready to take over the IUE and the UE—or any fragment that became available.

The leaders of the two smaller unions realized that they had to pull together if they were to deal effectively with GE and to maintain their roles in the union movement. They met early in 1969, the year in which the big national agreements were to expire, to discuss the upcoming negotiations with GE and Westinghouse. They agreed "to undertake steps to establish joint cooperation." Shortly thereafter, Walter Reuther of the UAW and Frank Fitzsimmons of the Teamsters, on behalf of their Alliance for Labor Action, promised "the achievement of maximum cooperation and coordination . . . as they relate to the forthcoming GE negotiations." [60] Meany realized the wisdom of relaxing the AFL-CIO's policy of noncollaboration with outside, independent unions. He therefore allowed representatives of the Teamsters and Auto Workers to sit with the IUE negotiators and others from the CCB unions. Never before had the unions in the electrical-equipment industry shown such unity and cooperation.

The IUE already had shown itself unified and strengthened. Jennings had been reelected by acclamation at the IUE's national convention the year before, and enthusiasm ran so high that the local unions easily and quickly ratified a 25 percent increase in dues to swell the strike fund. The CCB members, with the IUE leading, had no difficulty in agreeing to the proposals they were to present to both GE and Westinghouse in the fall.

GE approached the negotiations much as it had prepared for bargaining since 1948. After early discussions with the unions, it finally presented its terms with the usual fanfare and publicity. Matles, of the UE, who had responsibility for the economic package, tried to persuade the GE negotiators to keep their offer secret and to allow a longer time to discuss and bargain before committing the company to a particular offer. They refused; later, some at GE believed the company had made a serious mistake, given the union bargainers' conviction that the offer was too low as well as the strength of unity among CCB members.

The unions rejected the company offer and a strike became a certainty. The threat of a strike had been apparent for many months. The issue was far deeper, though, than the amount or timing of wage increases over the following three years. The showdown over Boulwarism was at hand.

---

[60] Matles and Higgins, p. 261.

As the strike began, a company spokesman accused the union leaders of conducting "ideological warfare." [61] Union leaders retorted that GE's demands were "union busting moves by the one major employer in the U.S. that persists in strike breaking as a matter of policy." George Meany, speaking for the AFL-CIO, declared the strike was "a fight for survival by the American trade union movement." [62]

The strong feelings on both sides as reflected in these words promised a long, intractable strike: both were defending principle, something that neither could easily compromise nor trade off. One arbitrator, at the time, warned that when both parties walk with God, they produce the hardest disputes to settle.

As the strike continued, Meany indicated his strong backing of the unions by calling upon unionists across the country to boycott GE products. The response to his call was hardly enthusiastic, and given GE's low inventories probably would not have helped in any case. Of a bit more significance, both as symbol and substance, were the funds raised for the strikers. The AFL-CIO contributed more than $2 million and the UAW gave $1 million to the IUE and UE. The most significant act was the giving to the UE its proportional share of these contributions. That act indicated the degree of unity the unions had achieved.[63]

The strike continued for 101 days, and settlement was reached only after the company brought Virgil Day back to the negotiating table. Day was the GE official who had held the primary responsibility for bargaining since Boulware's day, but had been shifted to another, higher post in the company shortly before negotiations began. To reach an agreement, he adjusted GE's offer, and the union, in give-and-take, settled for less than its original proposals. Some company officials argued that this adjustment had been the normal, flexible reshuffling GE had always been willing to make. *Business Week's* labor editor concluded, though, that "the new 40-month contract, costing more than GE put on the table in two previous offers, was a product of realistic negotiations." [64] Union leaders were pleased with the outcome. One remarked that "the most outstanding thing about this [settlement] is that it is the first fully negotiated contract with General Electric in 20 years." [65]

In the two negotiations since the "Great 1969–70 Strike," as union leaders referred to it, in 1973 and 1976, collective bargaining at GE proceeded much as negotiations do in most American industries where large companies and strong unions deal with each other. In the 1973

[61] Quoted in Kuhn, "General Electric and Union Rights," p. 317.
[62] Kuhn, "General Electric and Union Rights."
[63] Matles and Higgins, p. 285.
[64] *Business Week*, January 31, 1970, p. 28.
[65] *Ibid.*

negotiations the parties had not yet reached agreement when the expiration date arrived; they extended the old agreement. The IUE and UE negotiators worked together closely, spearheading the coordinated bargaining of all the involved unions. In the settlement, GE appeared to give more ground than in any of its negotiations since 1946. Matles remarked that "there is no question about it; this was a negotiated agreement in every sense of the word." And Jennings declared that "GE has now entered the Twentieth Century." [66]

In the 1976 negotiations the talks between GE and the IUE, with its coordinating union representatives, were conducted in strictest secrecy, and the parties reached settlement ten days before the IUE could legally have struck. A sign that collective bargaining had changed since 1969–70, or that at least a new spirit had manifested itself, was the absence during the nine weeks of any union accusation that GE was involved in Boulwarism. One top union negotiator reflected on the experience and said, "The lion and the lamb are still not in the same bed, but there was no real bitterness or rancor in the talks. It was a healthy, pretty open relationship." [67]

Time and experience had tested both Boulwarism and coordinated bargaining. On the one hand the former had turned out to be hardly as fearsome as its detractors had proclaimed; it also turned out to offer a good deal less than its advocates imagined, except under the special circumstances of poor union leadership and divided unions. On the other hand, unionists found that coordinated bargaining hardly solved all the problems whose causes many had attributed to their divisions of earlier years. Despite the increased union pressure for wage gains, electrical workers' earnings continued to slip behind those of workers in autos and steel. In Pittsburgh, where steel and electrical-equipment workers live close together, the invidious comparisons made by the workers have produced unrest among union members and contributed to interunion difficulties and the IBEW strike at Westinghouse in mid-1976.

IBEW negotiators had long felt at a disadvantage in the company, since only 1,100 of its 12,800 members were covered by a national agreement. A nationwide agreement, the unionists argued, would strengthen their bargaining power, enabling the union better to press for higher rates for skilled workers, an especially sore issue, and better terms generally. Member feeling ran so strong that the IBEW officials felt obliged to allow a strike of their members. The action broke their agreement to act together with the other CCB unions. Dissident members of the IUE

---

[66] *Ibid.*, June 16, 1973, p. 92.
[67] *Ibid.*, July 12, 1976, p. 26.

then broke ranks and joined the IBEW, closing Westinghouse's large East Pittsburgh plant and seven other company plants.

In addition to the problem of workers' discontent at Westinghouse over relative union gains, the electrical unions found coordination among themselves more difficult than in their negotiations with GE. The IBEW struck at Westinghouse in 1966 after the other members of the CCB had settled. In 1976 the IBEW again broke ranks and struck after the CCB had agreed to extend the old agreement past its July 11 expiration date. Rivalries among the unions prevented them from choosing a negotiating subcommittee until after the 11th; until then each union met separately with Westinghouse officials. The IUE and UE belatedly followed the IBEW in striking, and not until after Secretary of Labor W. J. Usery entered negotiations did the unions pare down their bargaining team to three representatives, one each from the IBEW, IUE, and UE. Only then were the unions able to reach agreements among themselves and move toward settlement.

At RCA the unions asked for coordinated bargaining at the same times they sought it at GE and Westinghouse, but their requests appear to have been pro forma. The company did not favor dealings with the CCB, and since the unions showed no enthusiasm for coordination, bargaining has continued much as before. The unions probably would have even more difficulties in working together at RCA than at Westinghouse. In the latter, the IBEW claims about a fifth of all union members; at RCA it has enrolled about two-thirds.

The varying strengths of the unions, as measured by membership, among the several large companies in the industry apparently created problems for the unions. The makeup of the CCB and division of responsibilities among the negotiators appropriate for GE have not been satisfactory for Westinghouse, and not even attempted at RCA. One informed manager in a large company concluded that "from the standpoint of employers, employees and, in many cases, the unions themselves, the CCB has not produced constructive change. The bargaining has become more complicated, more cumbersome with less dependable leadership, and rife with uncertainties. It is highly doubtful that the CCB has produced a net gain over the type of Industry bargaining that preceded 1966."

Coordinated bargaining does not appear to be an innovation that either side can be expected to extend throughout the industry. Managers do not like it, and the unions have run into difficulties in working together not only because their membership rank in different companies varies greatly, but also because their organizational style, leadership, and approach to bargaining differs significantly. Managers who negotiate with both the IUE and the IBEW, for example, find the latter union much more formal and more "businesslike" than the former. The industrial relations officer of one large company said:

> The IBEW is formally decentralized. The Washington [national] office does not get involved in plant affairs, except through formal channels. The International rep pays little attention to day-to-day plant activities. The local rep and business agent run the show. On the whole the IBEW has stronger local leadership than the IUE—such leaders are now rare in the IUE. The national leaders of the IUE are strong though; you always know where you stand with them. Unfortunately, that is not necessarily true at the local levels.

Daily Collective Bargaining: The Dilemma of Grievance Settlement by Either Arbitration or Strikes

The most persistent forces molding collective bargaining in the electrical-equipment industry for at least a quarter of a century has been, first, the fragmentation of union leadership, and second, the companies' insistence, particularly acute in GE, upon maintaining the initiative in all matters of employee relations. Few, if any, managers in electrical product firms outside of GE adopted Boulwarism as an industrial relations program, and some managers considered it inappropriate for their situation and style. However, many managers learned from GE and adopted Boulware's assertiveness, if not the whole program he devised for his company.

One example was given by the industrial relations officer of a large corporation: "We did not adopt Boulwarism in form or substance, but we did selectively find advantageous portions of that approach such as employee communication, employee economic education, bargaining research and bargaining tactics." Another example was provided by the industrial relations manager of Franklin Electric, a small electrical producer. While his company did not follow the GE settlements in its negotiations with the IUE, UAW, and Allied Industrial Workers, it has "resisted many restrictions on management that could have crept in under 'good intentions.' Since [the IUE organized us], the Company has resisted any creeping restrictions that may inhibit its ability to manage the business."

The fragmenting of the unions was rooted in the strong ideological commitment of the UE leaders to a class unionism whose ultimate aim was to change the economic system. As James J. Matles of the UE summed it: ". . . organizing the millions of workers still unorganized, developing a strong, independent political movement, redistributing the national wealth and income. . . ." [68] If unions were ever to realize such changes, they had to maintain full control and use of strikes and other concerted activities. Relinquishing control would sacrifice the one effective source of strength enjoyed by industrial workers.

A whole generation of local leaders in the UE, many of whom later joined the IUE, rejected the ideology of radical economic change, but they held tightly to the premise that a union could not wisely surrender its right to strike over terms of work deemed unsatisfactory. Once they had given up the ideology, many local leaders continued to insist upon the unfettered use of the strike out of an appreciation of its practical uses. A political reputation could be built upon the skillful direction of such strikes, and a power-base independent of the international could be established and continued when the locus of strike decisions remained at the local level.

Managers who believed that they must always maintain their initiative could use that belief to argue against arbitration. To accept that process was to surrender independence of judgment, allowing third parties to supplant, supplement, or modify managerial decisions. As long as the unions with whom they dealt were divided and unable strongly to oppose those decisions, common sense alone, without any necessary backing from ideology, did not recommend arbitration. It would only offer the unions another forum in which to plead their case, a case management could safely ignore.

The two antithetical ideologies produced a curious identity of policy for the unionists and the managers; neither wanted arbitration and a limitation on grievance strikes. Those on both sides who cared little for the ideological issue soon discovered practical reasons, peculiar to their interests and positions, for continuing the policy. Thus, the national officers of the IUE made slow headway in extending grievance arbitration and curbing local strike action. The companies opposed them and the local leaders did not strongly support them.

On this issue Boulware and his successors skillfully sided with the local leaders and the UE, elevating the unions' right to strike over grievances to a high principle of a free society. Of course, Boulware also added that the unions' right was merely the obverse of management's rights.[69] He did not publicly note what he privately recognized, that the company position on arbitration and strikes strengthened the local unions at the expense of the international, adding to the factionalism and disunity of the union and thus sharpening the thrust of his employee relations program.

---

[68] Matles and Higgins, p. 304.
[69] Northrup, p. 139.

Neither the union nor management advocates have tried to justify the workers' right to strike over grievances by examining the record of costs and gains involved. Managers believed that the right contributed to union weakness, and many union leaders asserted it was a vital ingredient of worker militancy. What workers may have won through local strikes to offset the cost of lost wages has not been a matter of union discussion, and few managers have questioned their policy by asking what the company won in refusing arbitration and accepting local strikes over grievances. A review of GE's changing approach to, and grudging gradual acceptance of, arbitration suggests that whatever the ideological difficulties posed by arbitration, grievance strikes create practical problems exceedingly troublesome and perhaps too costly to allow to continue.

THE PROPER ROLE OF GRIEVANCE ARBITRATION

The IUE and GE in their initial 1950 agreement established a conventional three-step grievance procedure now found in most agreements in the industry. The first step involved the employees' foreman and steward; the second step was an appeal to local representatives and plant managers; while the third step was an appeal to headquarters, that is, national union officers and company executive officers or their designated representatives. The parties agreed that grievances would offer no occasion for strikes, or other concerted action, or for lockouts, until they had been processed, unresolved, through all the steps. Either party could ask for arbitration of such grievances, but the agreement limited the arbitrator. He had no "authority to establish a wage rate or job classification," or to rule on insurance and pension issues. Further, the arbitrator was to have "no authority to add to, detract from, or in any way alter" any provision.

Beginning with the 1951 negotiations and steadily since then, the IUE sought to widen the ambit of arbitration. It proposed the right to take to arbitration—as a matter of right and not on company sufferance —any unsettled, fully processed grievance dealing with wages, hours, and working conditions. GE refused, though it agreed to minor changes in the procedures for selecting arbitrators. In 1955 it accepted an IUE proposal that disciplinary penalties, including discharges, should, as a matter of right, be subject to arbitration.

GE recognized what had become clear to most persons in industrial relations, by the mid-fifties, that discipline and discharge involved judicial issues properly to be accorded due process. In return for its agreement to extend judicial arbitration, however, GE insisted upon a provision to limit arbitration of other kinds of issues. Arbitrators were forbidden to decide the arbitrability of any case, if either party objected, until a court had rendered final judgment. It also added to the list of specific issues excluded from arbitration, "salary," "piece rate," and "the appropriate classification of any employee."

The next major change in the arbitration provisions of the GE agreements came in 1963 at the demand of the company and in response to the sweeping endorsement given by the Supreme Court to arbitration in the *Trilogy* decisions three years earlier.[70]

Through a long and complex new provision of the agreement, GE sought to limit the scope of arbitration and, in particular, to exclude any broadening of arbitration as a matter of right, on the basis of implication or interpretation. The company negotiators wanted doubts to be resolved against coverage, opposite to the court's ruling. Judge Feinberg, writing for a majority of the Second Circuit Court of Appeals, noted that the 1963 provisions were "more detailed and limited than the typically general language of an ordinary arbitration clause." With some impatience he remarked that the detailed provisions posed difficult problems for the court—and he suspected for the parties themselves. Indeed, "when an arbitration clause begins to resemble a trust indenture, one wonders what gain there is for either party in agreeing to arbitrate at all, other than the questionable joys of litigation." [71]

Litigation there was; the IUE brought eight unsettled grievances, two of which had arisen under the 1960 agreement and the others under the 1963 agreement, to the federal courts asking for judgment that they be arbitrated. Final rulings did not come until 1969; the court held that four of the grievances were arbitrable and three were not; the remaining case involved the layoff of a worker out of seniority. The parties agreed to a resolution without appealing it.

Shortly thereafter, the IUE again brought suit to compel arbitration of another set of grievances that had arisen under the 1963 and 1966 agreements. Thirty-nine grievances were included, and the District Court found 37 of them arbitrable. The Appeals Court upheld the lower court decision, and included in its decision a stern warning to the parties. Judge Kaufman told them he was

> constrained to comment on the distressing history of [their] litigation. . . . The availability of the courts is essential to labor peace and the strike-free operation of industry. But by continually and regularly falling back on the courts, these

---

[70] See *United Steelworkers of America* v. *American Mfg. Co.*, 363 U.S. 564, 46 LRRM 2414 (1960); *United Steelworkers of America* v. *Warrior & Gulf Navigation Co.*, 363 U.S. 574, 46 LRRM 2416 (1960); *United Steelworkers of America* v. *Enterprise Wheel & Car Corp.*, 363 U.S. 593, 42 LRRM 2423 (1960).

[71] *IUE* v. *General Electric Co.*, 407 F.2d 253, at 258, 70 LRRM 2082 (1968).

parties have largely abdicated their responsibilities to such peaceful, voluntary resolution of their own problems and have thus abused the judicial process. We hesitate to consider the consequences if more employers and unions adopted the stringent contractual arbitration language involved here and then foisted on the federal courts . . . the responsibility for directing when and when not to arbitrate each time a dispute concerning one of thousands of employees survived the grievance machinery.[72]

The courts declared that public policy insisted upon a wider scope for arbitration than GE managers liked and wanted, though they recognized the right of the company to restrict coverage more than the IUE desired. The first group of disputed grievances had involved issues of lateral transfer, layoff by seniority, disciplinary penalties, rate determination, and discharge for engaging in grievance strikes. The second group of grievances included 25 pay-rate cases on which the union wanted more freedom for the arbitrator than the company believed the agreement authorized. The court found for the company. The other cases involved rates of standard and temporary pay. The court upheld the company argument that two grievances over overtime pay and work schedules were not arbitrable because the agreement excluded them. In sum, the court declared that two criteria determined arbitrability under the agreement: first, there must be a claimed violation of a specific provision, and second, there must be no specific exclusion from arbitration for the claimed violation.

In the seventies, conditions had changed sufficiently for both parties that voluntary resolution of further arbitration issues had become more possible than ever before. Both had learned much from the strike of 1969–70, and the leaders and officers in both organizations who conducted affairs were people differently attuned to industrial relations from those who had dealt with each other through the decades of the fifties and sixties. Among the newer officers, the ideological values of the past were less compelling than the practical benefits of reasonable mutual adjustments to their respective needs and sensible compromises of the requests and offers of both.

A high official of the IUE asserted that prior to the court cases, the company had often stalled effective use of the arbitration process by claiming nonarbitrability. After the court decisions—and the strike—the union had been able to get matters to arbitration without resort to the court. Also, since 1971, he said,

---

[72] IUE v. *General Electric Co.*, 250 F.2d 1295, at 1298, 78 LRRM 2867 (1971).

> There has been a more effective use of the arbitrability confer-
> ence [that meets three times a year at the headquarters levels]
> . . . to get agreement on arbitration requests. . . . Moreover,
> the Company [in 1973] has even agreed to submit the issue of
> substantive arbitration to an arbitrator in one case on which we
> could not reach agreement.[73]

In that case,[74] the parties used an arbitrator rather than an appeal to
the courts to interpret the agreement. The case involved work by out-
of-classification employees, performed on a regular and overtime basis,
while other employees within the classification were on a layoff status.
The arbitrator finally found that the criteria for compulsory arbitration
were satisfied.

In 1971, during the term of the 1970 agreement, the IUE and GE
undertook a major change in the arbitration procedures to expedite the
resolution of unsettled grievances over discharges and upgrading. In
recent years these have accounted for more than a third of all cases
submitted to arbitration. The change achieved its purposes of both reducing costs and speeding decisions. The expedited procedures cost
about half as much as the usual arbitration decision and processing time
declined by almost six months. So successful were the results that the
parties incorporated the new procedures into the 1976 agreement.

In reviewing the collective bargaining between the union and GE
over the past six years, an international officer of the IUE said that the
grievance and arbitration procedures have worked more effectively than
at any other time. He perceives arbitration as an effective problem-
solving mechanism; along with the conditional strike provision, it can
provide a stability in industrial relations in the electrical-equipment industry that in the past has been all too rare and intermittent.

Westinghouse and the union have also changed their arbitration and
grievance procedures to speed settlement of disputes. Company officials,
however, characterize the provision for "quickie arbitration" as a relatively minor change; it allows summary oral argument in a hearing and
a decision without opinion or transcript. "While the purpose of the
change has been met," one manager said, "accelerated arbitration has
not been used very often." A more constructive change, he found, was
the early introduction of top plant industrial relations officers into discipline and discharge disputes. It has expedited processing to the greater
satisfaction of both union and management.

If there has been a trend in changes in grievance procedures and
arbitration in the industry, it has probably been toward more expedi-

[73] In a letter to the author, March 1976.
[74] *General Electric Co. and IUE*, #16049, AAA Case No. 1330-642-73, Peter
Seitz, arbitrator.

tious handling of cases and broader use of arbitration. Sprague Electric Company and IUE agreed to reduce the number of grievance steps from five to three for over 1,000 workers involved. They also agreed in 1970 to "full and binding arbitration," after having tried out limited arbitration under their 1967 agreement. Franklin Electric Company has also sought arbitration provisions that provide for terminal decisions on all grievances. The industrial relations manager reports that without the change, "the union [could] strike or delay processing a grievance at their discretion. . . . The new provision has accomplished its purpose of an orderly grievance procedure and removed the blackmail aspect from the union."

McGraw-Edison and the Steelworkers, who represent over 2,000 electrical-equipment workers in the company, have recently included expedited arbitration in three contracts. The managers report that

> in some cases [the speeded-up procedure] has worked to the advantage of both the company and the union in getting non-precedent type grievances heard by an impartial third party, and an award within twenty-four (24) hours after the hearing itself. The hearings therefore are also less formal.

Generalizations cannot easily be made, however. Bendix managers reported that they have changed arbitration toward "quickie" hearings. "Another change in the arbitration process has been a *move away from hearings at which there is no testimony taken,* with only briefs and statements by the parties and evidentiary material being offered. *More comprehensive hearings are now being held*" (italics added). Nevertheless, Bendix follows the trend toward greater use of arbitration.

> Over the past years, the arbitration provisions in our collective bargaining agreements have been broadened to include more items of possible dispute, with fewer items excluded from the arbitration process. This has worked to the mutual advantage of the parties by greatly reducing the possibility of mid-term work stoppages.
>
> There has been a move away from corporate staff evident in pre-arbitration screenings with the International Union representatives. This has encouraged the parties at the local level to settle disputes and not rely on outside help.

Many companies, some large and most small, have made no changes in either arbitration provisions or grievance procedures. Where strong, stable leadership develops on both sides, grievance handling can often be quite informal, making formal changes superfluous. An example is in Allen-Bradley where, beginning in 1942, both UE and company industrial relations were handled by the same two men. Though leadership has changed since, the informal style and stable relationships have continued. In the last nine years, there have been only four arbitration cases, and grievances continue to be handled as earlier. There are no provisions for reducing grievances to writing, and there are no time limits on processing them.

Where limited arbitration exists in the industry, and especially in GE, it has been accompanied by the provision for strikes over fully processed but unresolved grievances. Workers and union members are tempted to use such strikes to win gains above and beyond those granted through the agreement. Despite restrictions on the use of grievance strikes, ingenious shop stewards and local union officials have found ways to evade them.

THE PROPER ROLE OF GRIEVANCE STRIKES

Over the past 20 years, the number of strikes in the electrical-equipment industry, after adjusting for changes in production employment, has increased significantly as has the share of production workers involved in strikes. The industry experienced about 40 percent more strikes between 1965 and 1975 than during the period 1957-64; the share of workers involved has increased by about 50 percent. Given the large proportion of short strikes recorded for the industry by the Bureau of Labor Statistics, one may presume that the quickie grievance strike has become an increasingly common and disruptive feature of collective bargaining. Incomplete and often fragmentary data from several of the companies support that presumption. G. P. Irwin of Maytag believes "that the trend of a high rate of work stoppages in the industry is caused by General Electric's labor contract language which permits any number of employees to stage a legal strike any time employees are not satisfied with how a particular job is rated. This unique clause has caused a number of short work stoppages at all locations over the years." Insofar as this belief is valid, the parties are turning to arbitration none too soon if they seek more peaceful, less disruptive, and perhaps more stable industrial relations.

Under the initial IUE-GE agreement, negotiated in 1950, and until at least 1958, three conditions legitimated any local work stoppage. The matter at issue had to be subject to the grievance procedure, it must have been cleared through all the grievance steps, and there could be no decision to arbitrate the specific issue. Even if a grievance could be appealed to arbitration, absent an agreement with the company for such an appeal, a local union was free to strike over it. Further, there was no time limit imposed; if the union had not accepted the company's third-level answer and if the matter had not been referred to arbitration, it continued as an open grievance, available for the union local as a strike issue.

GE workers began to take advantage of their opportunities to strike over grievances. In 1957, at the Syracuse plant they used the strike to such advantage that GE imposed disciplinary penalties in retaliation. Skilled craftsmen decided to protest the company's refusal to adjust a number of wage rates that had been processed through the grievance steps. Workers on each of the three shifts left the plant for two hours to attend union meetings; they repeated the meetings on two following days. Finally, on the third day the entire skilled group struck, and the company responded by disciplining them. The arbitrator who heard the case decided that the workers' actions were not allowable under the contract. In his decision, he found that, by attending the meetings, the workers had struck, and then had returned to work, only to begin the strike again the following day. Thus, in effect, they were striking more than once over the same grievance.

The arbitrator's decision proved to be no serious barrier to multiple, disruptive strikes, however. In late 1962, at the same location, workers engaged in a series of harassing strikes. They repeated the pattern in early 1963, and the company imposed a disciplinary penalty of one day's suspension on each striker. The union appealed to arbitration; in this case the arbitrator found that each of the repeated short walkouts had been conducted in support of separate grievances, with each worker participating only once for each grievance. The company protested that the formal separation of the strikes was not significant and that the economic effect was the same as the earlier strike series. The arbitrator to whom the second case was appealed ruled that the formalities were significant, that the union had acted within the terms of the agreement, and that it was a situation of tit for tat. Local union leaders discovered that they could use the letter of the agreement to widen the ambit of their grievance strikes as well as GE could use the letter to restrict the ambit of arbitration.

Locals became increasingly adept at using multiple grievances to justify many short strikes, which if properly orchestrated could squeeze production schedules and interfere with shipments and sales to the detriment of the company. To restrict the grievance strike, GE secured the IUE's approval in 1966 of a provision that members may strike only during the subsequent 12 months over any grievance to which the company has given a third-level answer. The effect of this condition was to restrict the "bank" of grievances over which a union could strike to relatively recent ones.

How effective and widespread these strikes could be was illustrated in a case that arose at GE's Rome, Georgia, plant. In 1966 and 1967, the local filed some 200 wage-rate grievances, each one over a different job classification. All were processed through the grievance procedures and remained unsettled. Thereafter, the local began a series of shift, overtime, and weekend strikes; each strike was separate, involving a different "exhausted" or unresolved grievance. After eight weeks of harassment, the company sought a state injunction against the local; ultimately unsuccessful in that approach, it charged unfair labor practices before the NLRB, arguing the local had attempted to obtain a general wage increase during the mid-term of the contract without proper statutory notice. In addition, the company disciplined 1,100 employees who had participated in the strikes.

The courts and the NLRB upheld the local, and an arbitrator sustained the local's right to strike for part of a shift, a whole shift, or during overtime periods, as long as each strike was over a separate grievance. He wrote in 1968: "As I read the parties' Collective Bargaining Agreement it does not impose any limitation upon the Union's right to strike at any time, in any manner, and for whatever duration it desires so long as it complies with the limitations and conditions therein specifically set forth . . . ."[75]

In 1970 the parties agreed to a further condition for locals to meet before engaging in grievance strikes. Union leaders were to provide the company with more than 24 hours' prior notice of a strike. Upon receipt of such a notice by the company, it and the union were to meet. The negotiators were not eager to accept this further restriction upon grievance strikes. However, the locals have discovered that it works well for them in practice. In effect, it added a last step to the grievance procedures, giving the company an opportunity to resolve a grievance for which the union has given a strike notice. Moreover, with some careful union managing, the restriction offers plenty of room and time for artful maneuver and bargaining. Once notice is given, the local does not have to strike immediately upon the expiration of the 24-hour period, but may strike at any time after that as long as it is within the subsequent 12-month period.

Management has tried to limit the locals' use of grievance strikes by insisting that the grievance on which the workers base a strike is actually the one they seek to resolve. All too often they have good reason to believe that workers ostensibly striking over an "exhausted" grievance are in fact protesting another matter—perhaps a recent dis-

---

[75] *General Electric Co. and IUE*, #17806, 17999, 18166, AAA Case Nos. 32-30-0139-68, 32-30-0140-68, 32-30-0142-68, September 15, 1971, Sidney Cohn, arbitrator, p. 34.

pute that has arisen and may not yet be formulated as a grievance or else a grievance still in the midst of processing. Proof of such a situation is not easy to discover and even harder to provide for an arbitrator. As knowledgeable as arbitrators are about the realities of the workshop, grievances and strike situations so complexly intertwine with the usual confusions of daily production activity that able local union leaders can often through subterfuge cover a strike over a current "hot" dispute with a legitimating exhausted grievance whose strike notice has been given.

Company plant managers, as well as stewards and other local officials, freely describe such cases in private. A foreman at one plant gave an example: He recommended for discharge a worker caught sleeping for the third time. The man was a popular senior worker in his workgroup, and the union members were aggrieved he had received such harsh treatment. The steward identified a grievance already cleared through the third step and on which strike notice had been given. The group walked out, making clear to the foreman informally that the real issue was a reduction of the penalty and reinstatement of the worker. The foreman remarked, "In the strikes that last two or three days, most frequently a weekend and a day, it is difficult, to a degree, to identify the real issue."

A business agent for one large local assured the researcher that the union sees that the appropriate company officials find out quickly what a strike is about. He explained:

> If I want the toilets painted pink, then I'll strike because the aisles are too narrow. I won't change the narrowness of the aisles, but the toilets will be painted. I'll harass them on the issue over there till we get what we really want over here. The managers always know what it is the union wants. . . . There is good communications. Whenever the Union goes on strike I call my counterpart in the Company. The communications is always by telephone, and it is always informal. Nothing is ever written. The content of the discussion concerns the real positions of both the Company and the Union. Both sides confront to the other what their real object is in taking action.
>
> In one instance I blackballed the union relations manager; it was because he had violated the informal agreement by testifying publicly [in an arbitration hearing] to the contents of his informal telephone conversation. The day after the manager testified I contacted his boss and indicated that I would never again speak to [that] . . . manager. Several weeks later the manager was, in fact, reassigned.

The accuracy of the example cannot be determined, but so many people in both union and company positions in large plants related similar cases that one may believe the informal settlement of grievances under cover of "legal," unrelated strikes is not at all uncommon among the big locals.

The use of subterfuge to mount strikes in support of informally presented grievances explains how the unions have undermined GE's policy of never "giving in" on a grievance to end a strike. Local union officials of every rank and in every location where interviewed—that is, among the large plants—agreed that GE managers were completely predictable in their response to grievance strikes: they refused to change their decision on the grievance formally in dispute. The officials were just as unanimous, however, in agreeing that under cover of the formal grievance, other disputes could often be resolved, compromised, or won; indirectly, usually after some delay, the managers would quietly respond, bringing remedy to all or part of the workers' complaint.

A chief steward at one large plant, who had handled grievances for 15 years, explained how grievance strikes affected the managers he dealt with:

> Strikes serve a useful purpose. . . . [They] will force the Company to move slower in the future than they would otherwise have moved. Instead of increasing the line speed by 20 units an hour, we may be successful in forcing the Company to limit the increase to only 2 units per hour.
>
> The best strategy for the union to pursue is to function like a pest, like a hornet-stinging. Frequent use of short half-shift strikes, makeshift strikes, maximizes the cost to the Company and minimizes the cost to the union membership. It minimizes the cost to the union membership because workers are not off the job for long periods of time. On the other hand, it maximizes the cost to management since costs [go up] . . . in constantly starting up and shutting down the production line.
>
> Frequent job actions of short duration are thus more effective than a single protracted action for that reason. They have a bigger impact. In a long strike the company simply shuts down production completely thereby achieving a certain cost saving.

Both plant managers and local union officials agreed that grievance strikes often were not important in and of themselves, but served the necessary and useful purpose of validating threats of such strikes in the future. Strategic work groups—maintenance crews in one plant, crane operators in another, shippers in a third—can use their strike threats at times that offer the possibility of maximum disruption to production and high costs upon the company. Before the walkout is under way and while the parties are discussing the matter—that is, during the penulti-mate step—the company is free to adjust, change, or modify its former decisions. Union officials strongly believe that it does so, and few com-pany managers deny that they do.

Conclusions

GE, as the industrial relations pace-setter and pattern-maker for the electric-equipment industry, has long assumed a strict, stern, and de-manding role for itself: to maintain the initiative in bargaining and to protect wherever possible its ability to manage its workforce and deter-mine its workrules unilaterally. It played that role with no little skill and considerable success as long as the unions with whom it negotiated failed to work together and suffered from inept leadership.

Dissatisfied with the response allowed them, as management fulfilled its role, in the early sixties the unions began to coordinate their efforts and jointly confronted the major companies with whom they dealt. They made the companies' role more and more difficult to realize. At the same time that the unions strengthened themselves at the companywide ne-gotiating table, the locals were becoming increasingly adept at evading the restrictions and conditions on grievance strikes and turning them to their own advantage.

Discouraged by GE from using arbitration for peaceful resolution of many disputes under the agreement, local UE and IUE unionists followed their traditional ideological bent: strike for local gains when bargaining power is strongest. Local leaders became expert at manip-ulating plant managers through strike threats and strikes. Company policy on grievance strikes and arbitration forced local union leaders over the years to develop managerial and administrative skills that have well supplemented the political competence that any popularly elected union official must demonstrate. One result of GE's formal and rigid industrial relations program, therefore, has been to educate the union leaders who work with it in bargaining subtleties and abilities that an easier-going, less insistent program would not have required.

When asked to evaluate the development of overall collective bar-gaining in the industry over the past 20 or so years, experienced officials in both company and union positions responded in the following way: union-management relationships at both plant and company levels have matured. "There is," said one company officer, "a more logical flow in negotiations than there used to be." Another remarked that his company was now more sophisticated in its approach to labor problems, not view-ing them as simply black or white. Not only is the company more sophisticated but so are the unions, according to the managers. They all agreed that with the newer, more professional bargainers on both sides, negotiations are probably tougher than before—or least as tough—but there is less emotion and less rhetoric. Both sides deal more carefully in facts and will not only consider data, but will analyze them critically and sensibly.

Again and again, men on both sides mentioned their long experience in working with each other. Through their on-the-job training, they have learned what is possible and probable. Leaders on both sides have come up through grievance bargaining at plant and local levels. They know each other well and the whole bargaining process from its roots. They did not come into the profession having to fight for recognition and a particular place in which to serve and to work. Both are members of ongoing, well-established organizations, fulfilling their respective responsibilities as professionals should always do. Both sides understand well the desires that push, and the limits and requirements that constrain, the other.

As earlier noted in the chapter, the apparent rise in local work stoppages resembles the tracings on a fever chart in which the crisis of peak temperature was passed in 1969–70. The level of the tracing is still too high to indicate a return to normal health, however. If the unions and the companies continue to change their bargaining relationships as they have been doing over the past seven years, though, the public can expect collective bargaining in the industry increasingly to resemble and reflect negotiating procedures, approaches to arbitration, and policies of accommodation found in most other large, organized durable-goods industries. The changes will signal the giving way of ideologies that clash with the requirements of American-developed collective bargaining; they will demonstrate the pragmatic and practical adjustments that typify industrial relations in the United States.

List of References

Boulware, Lemuel R. *The Truth About Boulwarism.* Washington: Bureau of National Affairs, 1969.
Chernish, William N. *Coalition Bargaining.* Philadelphia: University of Pennsylvania Press, 1969.
Galenson, Walter. *The CIO Challenge to the AFL.* Cambridge, Mass.: Harvard University Press, 1960.
Kuhn, James W. *Bargaining in Grievance Settlement.* New York: Columbia University Press, 1964.
Kuhn, James W. "General Electric and Union Rights." *Christianity and Crisis* (December 8, 1969).
Matles, James J., and James Higgins. *Them and Us: Struggle of a Rank and File Union.* Englewood Cliffs, N.J.: Prentice-Hall, Inc., 1974.
Northrop, Herbert R. *Boulwarism.* Ann Arbor: Bureau of Industrial Relations, Graduate School of Business Administration, University of Michigan, 1964.

CHAPTER 6

Agriculture

KAREN S. KOZIARA
Temple University

Introduction

Collective bargaining in agriculture, virtually nonexistent until the recent past, now seems on its way to becoming established. This chapter attempts to provide some insight into this formative period for agricultural labor relations. First, the nature of the industry and labor market are discussed, and then the historic and public policy background of collective bargaining in agriculture is presented. Additionally, current labor relations trends, including participants, tactics, issues, and outcomes are analyzed. Finally, an attempt is made to forecast possible future directions in organizing and collective bargaining.

THE INDUSTRY

Agriculture is a major United States industry in terms of employment, number of producing units, and essentiality of output. About 5.5 million people worked on 2.75 million operating farms during 1977, and virtually everyone living in the United States as well as many people in other countries depend on their output. It is also an industry in which collective bargaining has been rare. A number of industry characteristics help explain both the slow development of collective bargaining and the nature of the bargaining that does exist.

One of agriculture's essential characteristics is that it comes closer to pure competition than does any other industry. There are many more production units in agriculture than in any other U.S. industry. Almost every agricultural product has thousands of producers. Partly due to sheer numbers, and partly because agricultural products of a given grade or quality are usually indistinguishable, no one producer affects market price.

Another important industry characteristic is that agricultural prices and incomes fluctuate considerably from one time period to another. One reason for the fluctuation is that product supply depends on a number of factors, such as weather conditions and pests. Although quantities supplied to the market vary due to growing conditions, public demand for agricultural produce is relatively constant and not particularly responsive to changes in product price. Because of elastic supply and relatively inelastic demand, agricultural products are priced after production, unlike manufactured products which are usually priced before they are produced. Thus, not only do prices and incomes fluctuate with changes in supply quantities, but also prediction of price and income movements is difficult, and there is no guarantee that prices will reflect costs. Poor growing conditions may result in high prices for some growers and low incomes for adversely affected growers, while good conditions may mean large crops, low prices, and low incomes for all growers.[1]

Industry competition also provides growers with a continuing incentive to make use of new technology to reduce costs whenever feasible. As a result, productivity has risen rapidly in agriculture. Between 1965 and 1975, output per worker hour rose by 58 percent in the industry, as compared to 13.9 percent in manufacturing.[2]

Another characteristic of agriculture is that much of its production is seasonal, particularly in labor-intensive crops such as fruits and vegetables. A result of seasonality is both fluctuating labor needs and the need for adequate supplies of labor during seasonal highs if crop spoilage is to be avoided.

It is hardly surprising that producers in a competitive industry with seasonal labor demands and unpredictable income streams are resistant to collective bargaining. Industry competition means that any grower who raises wages because of a collective bargaining contract will be at a competitive disadvantage vis-à-vis other growers. Seasonal labor demands make growers vulnerable to economic action when a season's output can be jeopardized, and collectively bargained wage rates increase stability of production costs while prices remain erratic.

A further industry factor inhibiting collective bargaining is the relatively small size of most farms. Average farm size in 1977 was estimated at 393 acres.[3] Many small farms use few, if any, hired workers, and small groups of workers are generally difficult to organize. However, the potentially inhibiting impact on unionization on many small farms is somewhat mitigated by production concentration on large farms. In 1974, farms with annual product sales value of $100,000 or more consti-

---

[1] Suits, pp. 1–39. [The complete citations for all footnote references are listed at the end of the chapter.]

[2] U.S. Department of Commerce, *Statistical Abstract of the United States,* 1975, p. 851.

[3] U.S. Department of Agriculture, Crop Reporting Board, *Farm Numbers* (December 1976), p. 1.

tuted only 4.1 percent of total farms, but accounted for 47.4 percent of total farm sales. In contrast, the 25 percent of all farms that had annual sales value of $2,500 or less a year accounted for less than 1 percent of total farm sales.[4]

In addition, there is an ongoing trend, encouraged by increased mechanization, toward further production concentration on large farms. Between 1940 and 1970 average farm acreage doubled, and from 1966 to 1976 there was a 15 percent drop in the number of farms, while farm acreage declined by only 4 percent.[5] Large-scale farming is not equally dispersed geographically, suggesting that some states will be more attractive targets than others for unionization efforts. Production concentration is highest in Nevada, California, Arizona, New Mexico, and Florida. In these states, more than half of total agricultural output comes from farms with annual sales of $100,000 or more.[6]

Another feature of agriculture, due to the large numbers of producers and industry competitiveness, is an enormous variety of ownership, financing, and marketing arrangements. Some growers, true to popular image, own their own land, finance and raise their own crops, and sell their crops to food processors. Others are financed by food processors who contract to take crops when harvested. Still others belong to cooperatives, which may provide information, harvesting, marketing, and other services. Some growing operations are part of larger firms that process and market the product as well as grow it, and some land owners contract out their land to tenant farmers.

The number and variety of grower associations is yet another result of the large numbers of producers and the relatively small size of many of them. There are far more of these associations in agriculture than in any other industry. Generally, these associations were formed to provide growers collectively with services that would have been difficult for them to obtain individually. Some, such as the American Farm Bureau Federation, made up of member farm bureaus from 49 states and Puerto Rico, concentrate on political action; so also do the state bureaus. Others, such as the California Strawberry Advisory Board, the North American Blueberry Council, and Florida Citrus Mutual, represent growers in only one crop and can provide research, marketing, and public relations services as well as political representation. Some associations engage in worker recruitment either on a regular basis or when needed.

---

[4] U.S. Department of Agriculture, Economic Research Service, *Farm Income Statistics*, Statistical Bulletin No. 547 (July 1975).

[5] U.S. Department of Agriculture, *Farm Numbers*, p. 1.

[6] U.S. Department of Agriculture, *Farm Income Statistics*, 1975.

A few grower associations are actively involved in labor relations. For example, the Western Growers Association, which represents fresh fruit and vegetable growers in California and Arizona, was organized during the 1920s to handle insurance and transportation matters. It became involved in collective bargaining in packing houses and trucking several decades ago, and its labor relations responsibilities have increased with the growth of collective bargaining in agriculture. In addition, there are a few associations, such as the Independent Growers' Association in Central California, which came into existence because of organizing efforts among farm workers and now concentrate on labor relations matters.

Competition, price and income instability, production concentration, diversity in ownership and marketing arrangements, and seasonality all have important ramifications for agricultural labor relations. Price and income instability increases grower reluctance to engage in collective bargaining, diversity in ownership and production concentration affects bargaining structure, and seasonality results in special problems for collective bargaining and public policy. Finally, some grower associations play an important and ongoing role in farm labor relations.

THE AGRICULTURAL LABOR FORCE

Although industry characteristics have slowed development of collective bargaining in agriculture, the nature of its labor force has also discouraged unionization. Agriculture's labor force, unlike those of most industries, is made up of both family and hired farm workers. The percentage of family workers has decreased slightly with increases in average farm size, but family workers still make up about 70 percent of the farm labor force. This means that less than one-third of the labor force is potentially organizable.

There are about 2.6 million hired farm workers, defined as people who do any farm work for a cash wage or salary. Although the farm labor force has been declining during much of this century and is about 20 percent smaller than it was ten years ago, its average size has stabilized during the 1970s because mechanization in some crops has been offset by increased production in other labor-intensive crops. However, not all hired farm workers are equally attached to agricultural work.

Because of agriculture's seasonal nature, year-round workers (those who work 250 days or more a year) and regular farm workers (those who work from 150 to 249 days a year) account for about 70 percent of farm work in terms of days actually worked. However, these two groups make up only 22 percent of the labor force. Seasonal workers, who work from 25 to 149 days, make up about 33 percent of the labor force and account for 25 percent of the work. Casual workers, who work less than 25 days, account for 45 percent of the labor force, although they do only 5 percent of the work.[7] Many seasonal and casual workers are students, housewives, and others wanting temporary work. Because of their limited labor force commitment, they are often poor prospects for unionization.

Migratory workers who either leave home at least overnight to do farm work, or do hired farm work and have no permanent residence, comprise about 7 percent of hired farm workers. Although migrant numbers have declined since 1965 when about 11 percent of the labor force was migratory, migrant numbers appear to have stabilized during the 1970s.[8] Traditionally, their mobility made them difficult to find and organize and, if organized, to keep within a union.

The farm labor force also has large numbers of foreign workers. Between 1951 and 1964, importation of foreign workers for temporary farm work was authorized under Public Law 78, which was permitted to expire at the end of 1964. As a result of that policy change, legal importation of foreign farm workers dropped from 200,000 in 1964 to 36,000 in 1965.[9]

However, although the legal importation of workers to do farm labor has been sharply curtailed, there are large numbers of illegal aliens in the hired farm labor force. Obvious questions can be raised about the accuracy of estimates of actual numbers of illegal aliens. During 1975 the Immigration and Naturalization Service located about 680,000 deportable Mexican aliens in the U.S., many of whom were agricultural workers. The actual number of illegal aliens from Mexico is much higher and probably totals several million.[10] Recent research indicates that flows of illegal aliens from Mexico are related to the vigor of movements in agricultural output and wages in the two countries, with trends in Mexican agriculture being somewhat more important than U.S. agricultural trends.[11]

President Carter's proposals with respect to the problem of illegal immigrants have implications for the number of foreign workers employed in farming. In addition to the amnesty provisions, his proposals would make it illegal to hire illegal aliens. They also provide for expanded enforcement efforts. These measures, if enacted, would probably reduce the numbers of illegal aliens in the farm labor force.

---

[7] Rowe and Smith, pp. 1–11.
[8] Ibid.
[9] U.S. Department of Labor, Manpower Report of the President, 1966, p. 133.
[10] U.S. Department of Justice, Immigration and Naturalization Service, Annual Report, 1975, pp. 13–14.
[11] Frisbee, pp. 3–14.

In terms of demographic characteristics, the hired farm labor force is predominantly young, with a median age of 23. This relative youth is another factor mitigating against unionization. Although 70 percent of the hired farm labor force is white, black and Spanish-origin workers are overrepresented relative to their numbers in the general population. They are also more likely than white workers to be dependent on agricultural employment and to spend in excess of 150 days a year in farm work. Thirty percent of Spanish-origin and 24 percent of black farm workers work 150 days or more in agriculture, while only 21 percent of white farm workers are employed in agriculture 150 days or more a year.[12]

The hired farm labor force is not distributed evenly geographically. Three states—California, Texas, and Florida—account for about half of hired farm workers (see Table 1).[13] These states are important producers of fresh fruits and vegetables, which require large amounts of hand labor. They are also among the five states with highest production concentration on large farms.

TABLE 1

Five Most Important States by Hired Employment
Field and Livestock Workers
Four Quarter Average
(July 1977, October 1977, January 1978, and April 1978)

State	Rank	Number of Hired Field and Livestock Workers (in thousands)
California	1	184.7
Texas	2	62.7
North Carolina	3	58.4
Florida	4	34.5
Washington	5	29.1

Source: U.S. Department of Agriculture, Statistical Reporting Service, Crop Reporting Board, Farm Labor, May 1978, p. 15.

The nature of the farm labor force makes unionization difficult. Workers are scattered geographically and, even when not migratory, operate in a casual and seasonal labor market. Many farm workers have only a temporary involvement in farm labor, and thus have little interest in joining unions.

THE NONUNION LABOR MARKET

The agricultural labor market's operation is somewhat different than that of most other labor markets. Because most agricultural production

[12] Rowe and Smith, pp. 1–3, 16.
[13] Ibid., p. 1.

is seasonal, a large portion of the labor force is composed of migratory and temporary workers. Resulting employment relationships are predominantly casual, with neither employees nor employers expecting them to become formalized or permanent.

Thus, growers are faced with a recurring necessity to recruit seasonal workers efficiently. Some growers do their own recruiting. Some recruit employees through cooperative associations. Most, however, rely on labor contractors to supply seasonal workers. Migratory labor contractors assemble crews that travel as groups, working on crops with progressive harvest dates. Other labor contractors recruit in local labor markets, sometimes on a daily basis.

Contractors usually make agreements with growers to harvest crops at a given price. Besides recruitment, labor contractors generally perform other functions such as providing transportation, keeping production and payroll records, paying wages, and sometimes supervising workers. Because contractors often perform important employer functions, many crew members regard them as employers.

The labor contractors' role gives them significant control over their crews, and some leaders abuse that control by engaging in practices such as underpaying workers, failing to report wages for income tax and social security purposes, and charging exorbitant prices for goods supplied to workers. As a result, the labor contractor system has been a particular target of the United Farm Workers of America, AFL-CIO (UFW), which seeks to replace it with hiring halls.

Abuses of the labor-contractor system resulted in passage of the 1964 Farm Labor Contractor Registration Act, which requires crew leaders to have and carry a certificate of registration; to inform workers of each job's terms and conditions, including existence of any labor dispute; and, when they pay workers, to keep payroll records. Growers also must maintain the same payroll records required of contractors, and they must make sure that contractors have valid registrations before using their services.

Some grower associations also become involved in recruitment. When recruitment is done through an employer association, supervision, payment, and employee housing may be either arranged by the association or left to individual growers. In addition, some employer associations make available pension and health plans for members' employees even though they have no other employment functions.

In the absence of a union, wages are usually based on informal agreements among area growers of a crop as to what piece rates are appropriate. Wage-determining considerations include supply of labor, crop condition, comparable area wages, and the economic state of the industry. The resulting wage rate is understood to be the "going wage" by both growers and workers.

Average wages in agriculture vary considerably both by region and among different labor force segments. In 1976, hired farm workers earned an average of $19.25 daily and $1,652 annually for 86 days of farm work. Year-round workers averaged $6,392 yearly, or $20.95 a day for 305 days of work. Average daily earnings were highest in the West and lowest in the Northeast as a result of production structure and the nature of the labor market.[14]

Until the mid-1960s there was little government regulation of the agricultural labor market. Since that time there has been a trend toward covering agricultural employment under the same legislation that applies to other industries. Treatment of agricultural workers under the Fair Labor Standards Act (FLSA) provides an example of this trend. Agricultural workers were excluded from FLSA coverage until 1967, when employees of farms using 500 or more days of hired labor in any calendar quarter of the previous year were brought under the FLSA's minimum-wage provisions. Originally, the agricultural minimums were set lower than those for general industry, but the 1974 amendments erased that distinction. These amendments set 1978 hourly minimums at $2.65 an hour with scheduled increases to $3.35 in 1981. Average hourly wages have been above legislated minimums in every geographic region. The greatest potential wage and employment impact of minimum wages is in relatively low-wage areas, particularly the South. However, in these areas a majority of workers are employed on small, and thus uncovered farms. Proportions of covered workers are highest in the West, particularly California, where agricultural wages are highest.[15]

Agricultural workers are also covered by several recently enacted statutes regulating employment relationships—Title VII of the 1964 Civil Rights Act, the 1970 Occupational Safety and Health Act, the 1974 Employee Retirement Income Security Act, and the federal Hazardous Occupations Order. However, as will be discussed later, agricultural workers are not covered by the National Labor Relations Act (NLRA) or similar federal legislation. In addition, much of the legislation regulating agricultural employment faces enforcement problems due to the large numbers of employers, the small size of many farms, their geographic dispersion, and employees' lack of knowledge about their rights.

In the absence of collective bargaining, employment relationships in agriculture continue to be relatively unstructured in comparison to other industries. There are few, if any, barriers to entry and employment re-

---

[14] *Ibid.*, p. 2.
[15] Fuller and Mason, pp. 75–76.

lationships have only temporary definition. Although there is a trend toward increasing government regulation of agricultural employment, less government regulation exists in agriculture than in most industries, and the effectiveness of existing policy is somewhat limited by enforcement problems.

Union History

EARLY EFFORTS

Agricultural worker unionism in the United States has a long, colorful, and repetitious history in that few efforts to organize farm labor have been successful. Early unionization attempts date back to the 1880s when there were strikes among Oriental farm workers in California. In 1890, the first stable union of agricultural workers, the Sheep Shearers Union of North America, was formed.

The Industrial Workers of the World (IWW) made the earliest extended effort to organize farm workers, focusing on West Coast and Midwest areas where there had been strikes and unrest. Although the IWW was responsible for a number of wage increases in the Midwest grain belt, it concentrated on educational activities, and many of the famous free-speech fights involved farm workers. Collective activity among farm workers slowed with the IWW's decline, and the 1920s were relatively calm for farm workers, as well as for the rest of the U.S. labor force.

The turmoil, endemic unemployment, and low wages of the Depression years brought about a number of serious attempts to organize farm workers. Where strikes and unionism had been limited and widely scattered in earlier years, during the 1930s organizing efforts became numerous and widespread geographically. The American Federation of Labor, the Congress of Industrial Organizations, and the Cannery and Agricultural Workers Industrial Union all organized actively, and various local unions were founded, such as the Beet Workers Union of Blissfield, Michigan, the Cranberry Pickers Union of Massachusetts, and the Southern Tenant Farmers Union.[16] Numerous strikes occurred during this period, many of them resulting in agreements. Because of these successes, some growers organized to meet the threat of unionization. For example, the Associated Farmers of California, established with the support of the Chamber of Commerce and the Farm Bureau, worked politically on antilabor policies, and occasionally formed vigilante groups to deal directly with unions.[17] Although the widespread labor unrest

---

[16] Jamieson, pp. 401–21.
[17] Chambers, p. 200.

characteristic of the 1930s resulted in few permanent gains for field workers, a number of bargaining relationships developed in related areas such as packing sheds and canneries.

Efforts to organize Hawaiian agricultural workers were equally unsuccessful prior to the 1940s. As on the mainland, growers used political power to slow organizing efforts, and Hawaiian farm workers were often foreign workers who were physically and culturally remote from the labor force's mainstream. Sporadic organizing efforts and strikes had little permanent impact on wages and working conditions.

Much of the credit for successful organization of Hawaiian agricultural workers is given to Jack Hall of the International Longshoremen's and Warehousemen's Union (ILWU). His organizing efforts began in the late 1930s, but were suspended during World War II. He became ILWU's regional director in Hawaii in 1944 and organized a voter registration drive which produced enough new voters to change the political composition of the territorial legislature. In 1945 that legislature passed the Hawaii Employment Relations Act.[18]

The Hawaii Employment Relations Act is tailored after the NLRA. However, it does not contain the NLRA's exemption of agricultural workers. Thus, Hawaii farm workers have the same collective bargaining protections as industrial workers, substantially easing the difficulty of organizing them. It helped the ILWU to organize the bulk of Hawaii's agricultural workers by the end of the 1940s.

The National Farm Labor Union (NFLU), an outgrowth of the Southern Tenant Farmers Union, was chartered by the AFL in 1946 to continue organizing efforts among agricultural workers. Its efforts centered originally in California and it was involved in several major strikes, but, as before, little progress was made in negotiating contracts. Organized labor, frustrated by the NFLU's lack of success, reduced its funding. Nonetheless, the NFLU continued organizing efforts in the South, again with little success, under its new name, the National Agricultural Workers' Union.

No further sustained efforts were made to unionize field workers until the AFL-CIO chartered the Agricultural Workers Organizing Committee (AWOC) in 1960. In its attempt to recruit workers, the AWOC used traditional trade union methods, which in some instances meant approaching workers through labor contractors because of the difficulty in reaching them in other ways. This approach, given the relationships between contractors and workers and the inappropriateness of standard organizing methods, did little to build lasting farm-worker commitment to trade unionism.

---

[18] Meister and Loftis, p. 63.

By the early 1960s the AWOC was floundering, and there were only a few widely scattered groups of agricultural workers with collective bargaining contracts. The workers at Seabrook Farms, in New Jersey, were represented by the Amalgamated Meat Cutters and Butcher Workmen; workers at Bud Antle, Inc., a large California lettuce grower, were represented by the Western Conference of the International Brotherhood of Teamsters (WCT); and the International Longshoremen's and Warehousemen's Union (ILWU) represented virtually all Hawaiian agricultural workers. Workers at a handful of other sites, such as a few dairy workers, were under contract, but the vast bulk of agricultural labor remained unorganized.

Efforts to organize farm workers up until the early 1960s share common elements that explain their general lack of success. As indicated earlier, the composition of the farm labor force makes unionization difficult. In addition, agricultural workers have little contact with labor's mainstream and concepts of unionization, and they generally did not have the resources necessary for self-organization. Finally, general oversupplies of farm workers permitted the use of strikebreakers to undercut strike efforts.

These difficulties are complicated by the societal complex surrounding agricultural labor relations. Growers have been determined opponents of unionization, both because of ideology and because of fears of increasing costs and destructive strikes at harvest-time. They are politically important on a national basis and in their local communities, and they used their political power effectively. Grower organizations have opposed coverage for farm workers under most protective labor legislation, and historically they have been a major force preventing NLRA protections from being extended to agricultural workers. Locally, their political power has enabled them to use police and other government officials to their advantage when combating strikes.

Thus, although some strikes resulted in immediate wage gains, the environment surrounding farm labor relations made it difficult for labor unions to build and sustain a firm organizational basis for ongoing collective bargaining. The one exception was in Hawaii where ILWU Local 142's actions got a change in public policy which, in turn, changed the surrounding societal complex.

The lessons to be learned from repeated failures to organize farm workers were not lost on César Chavez and his lieutenants. The strategies developed by the National Farm Workers' Association (NFWA), which evolved into the United Farm Workers of America, AFL-CIO (UFW), were tailored to overcome barriers to organizing agricultural workers.

Contemporary Unionism

Chavez organized farm workers with Saul Alinsky's Community Service Organization (CSO) for about a decade before leaving it in 1962 to found the NFWA. Using techniques learned at the CSO, he concentrated on developing a strong community-based organization, which required a response to farm-worker needs that went beyond traditional trade union organizing tactics. The NFWA was called an association rather than a union because no economic action was planned until an organizational structure existed that could support economic action. The NFWA followed this plan until 1965.

The Agricultural Workers Organizing Committee was still actively organizing farm workers, and in 1965 a Filipino local called a strike against Delano, California, wine-grape growers. Although the NFWA leadership thought strike action was organizationally premature, it decided that support for this strike was necessary. The strike lasted slightly more than two years, and it revealed elements of agricultural labor relations that were to be repeated over and over during the next decade. First, growers made apparent their reluctance to engage in collective bargaining by responding to this strike as they had in the past—by using strikebreakers, government policy, and police officers to offset the strike's impact.

Second, the strike revealed the NFWA's philosophy and tactics. From the beginning, the NFWA was committed to nonviolence, and during this strike it developed its boycott weapon. Initially, the boycott was effectuated by sympathetic unions refusing to handle struck grapes, but consumer boycotts were implemented when these unions ran afoul of NLRA secondary-boycott restrictions. Another important NFWA tactic, involvement of sympathetic individuals and organizations, also became apparent as volunteers worked on picket lines and provided some financial support.

Other strike results were cooperative actions between, and the eventual merger of, the AWOC and NFWA. In 1966, the NFWA joined the AFL-CIO as an organizing committee, the United Farm Workers Organizing Committee (UFWOC). In 1972 it became the United Farm Workers of America, AFL-CIO.

The most important consequences of the strike, however, were the initial contracts signed during 1967 and 1968 with ten wine-grape growers, a result of boycott pressure. Boycotts against Schenley Industries and DiGiorgio Fruit Corporation products were actually put into effect, and threats of boycotts enabled the UFWOC to gain recognition from the other growers. These wine-grape growers were vulnerable to boycotts because of their product's identifiability and substitutability.

After negotiating the original wine-grape contracts, the UFWOC had to decide whether to continue organizing efforts against wine-grape growers or to branch out into other crops. Although other growers of wine grapes would have been susceptible to boycott pressure, the UFWOC began organizing efforts in table grapes because of accumulated worker grievances and dissatisfactions.[19]

The UFWOC began its organizing of table-grape workers in 1967, concentrating in particular on workers at Giumarra Vineyards, a major U.S. grower. When a strike proved to have little effect in terms of curtailing production, the UFWOC began a boycott against Giumarra grapes. However, consumers do not distinguish between table grapes on the basis of producer, and the UFWOC found it necessary to strike and boycott all U.S. table-grape growers. The boycott continued until 1970 when growers representing about 85 percent of the table-grape industry signed UFWOC contracts.

The table-grape boycott was marked by bitterness. The UFW organized boycott committees in major cities, and growers responded by shipping grapes under many labels and requesting sympathetic private and governmental agencies to increase grape purchases. There were a number of violent incidents, the result of which was internal UFW friction over the advisability of continuing the commitment to nonviolence. Chavez used a 25-day religious fast to solidify UFW's members' belief in nonviolence.

While the table-grape contracts were being negotiated, the UFWOC began organizing lettuce workers. Almost immediately, Salinas Valley lettuce growers signed contracts with the Western Conference of Teamsters. The UFWOC responded by stepping up its organizing efforts and implementing a boycott against California lettuce. The subsequent jurisdictional battle between the two unions brought seven years of violence and unrest to California agriculture. Several efforts were made to establish a jurisdictional agreement between them, but none endured and the dispute continued.

The lettuce boycott was less effective than the grape boycotts, as consumers were less willing to forgo buying lettuce than they had been to substitute for boycotted wines and table grapes. In addition, some consumers, believing that they were supporting the UFW boycott, bought lettuce picked under WTC contracts. Only a few lettuce growers, vulnerable to boycott pressure because of conglomerate affiliations, signed UFW contracts.

In 1973, a number of grape growers signed contracts with the WCT rather than to renegotiate expired UFW contracts. Prospects for UFW

---

[19] Taylor, p. 214.

survival appeared dim because the grape workers were the heart of the UFW organizational strength, and this loss made it difficult for the UFW to function as a union.

The following year, the UFW developed a legislative proposal that would have provided California farm workers with protected bargaining rights, while not limiting the right to engage in strikes or boycotts; it failed to become law by a narrow margin. A similar piece of legislation, the California Agricultural Labor Relations Act (CALRA), which is discussed in more detail in a later section, was enacted in 1975 with sponsorship by the newly elected governor, Jerry Brown, who had active UFW support during his campaign.

CALRA had a dramatic impact on the fortunes of the UFW and WCT. In elections held under its auspices through early 1977, the WCT won 41 and the UFW won 151, including a number in established WCT bargaining units. These WCT losses, accumulated bad publicity generated by its role in the jurisdictional battle, and threats of UFW damage suits for violence prompted the Teamsters to sign a jurisdictional agreement in March 1977.

Under the five-year agreement, the UFW has jurisdiction over employees, including truck drivers, of employers engaged primarily in agriculture, and thus covered by CALRA. WCT jurisdiction is confined to employers covered by the NLRA. Workers under existing WCT contracts who fall into UFW's jurisdiction have Teamster representation until the contracts expire. They then come under UFW jurisdiction. Jurisdiction over workers covered by WCT contracts negotiated prior to 1960 will be settled between the unions on a case-by-case basis. Questions over agreement terms are subject to compulsory binding arbitration.[20]

EXTENT OF ORGANIZATION

CALRA gave new impetus to UFW organizing, and by the end of 1977 it had about 30,000 members.[21] Although membership was concentrated in fruits and vegetables, such as lettuce, grapes, and tomatoes, the UFW represents a wide cross-section of California agricultural workers, including people in flower-raising. It also has between 1,000 and 2,000 members under contract in Florida citrus groves owned by the Coca Cola Company, producer of Minute Maid products.

The Texas Farmworkers Union has attempted to organize workers in Texas, the Farm Labor Organizing Committee organized Ohio tomato

---

[20] The New York Times, March 10, 1977, pp. A-1, A-9.

[21] Philadelphia Newsletter of the United Farm Workers, AFL-CIO, November-December 1977.

workers in 1978, and the Asociación de Trabajadores de Puerto Rico, which merged with UFW in 1976, has actively organized in Delaware, New York, New Jersey, and Connecticut. None of these efforts has yet resulted in a collective bargaining contract. However, the Maricopa County Organizing Project, which concentrated on onion and citrus workers, won concessions from several Arizona citrus growers in 1978.

Because of election losses and the jurisdictional agreement with the UFW, numbers of field workers represented by the Teamsters are declining. The WCT expects to lose between 10,000 and 12,000 members as a result of the jurisdictional agreement. However, they still represent many workers in row crops and dairies in California, as well as a few agricultural workers in Arizona.

Local 142 of the International Longshoremen's and Warehousemen's Union, which will be discussed more fully in a later section, represents over 90 percent of Hawaii's agricultural workers. Its membership includes about 7,500 sugar workers, 4,500 pineapple workers, and a few hundred workers each in macadamia nut and papaya operations.

Public Policy

FEDERAL POLICY

Agricultural workers, or any individual employed as an agricultural laborer, have been specifically excluded from National Labor Relations Act protection since its passage in 1935. This exclusion probably can be attributed to the politically powerful position of agricultural growers vis-à-vis agricultural workers and the resulting reluctance of both President Roosevelt and organized labor to jeopardize congressional approval of the Wagner Act by insisting on farm-worker coverage.

There are similar exclusions in all but two of the 14 state laws regulating private-sector collective bargaining. Before 1970 only two states, Hawaii and Wisconsin, provided agricultural workers with protected bargaining rights. Hawaii law specifically includes agricultural workers, while Wisconsin law does not exclude them.

The impact of this policy vacuum became apparent with UFWOC's organizing efforts in the mid-1960s. The chaotic situation resulting from these drives, grower resistance, and the UFW-WCT jurisdictional battle was exacerbated by lack of mechanisms to resolve representation questions and define unfair labor practices.

Because of the turmoil, several proposals to regulate agricultural collective bargaining were introduced into Congress in the late 1960s and early 1970s. Some of these bills would have extended NLRA coverage to farm workers, while others developed separate laws for farm-worker bargaining. Although all proposals provided for elections and protected bargaining rights, they had marked differences, particularly with respect to limitations on harvest strikes, legality of boycotts, and whether administrative responsibility should be given to the National Labor Relations Board (NLRB) or the Department of Agriculture.

Disagreement over these issues shows a basic lack of consensus about appropriate public policy for collective bargaining in agriculture. In addition, the policy positions of many involved participants have shifted greatly over the last decade. Currently, growers confronted by collective bargaining want protection from secondary boycotts and harvest strikes, while growers who have not been exposed to collective bargaining do not want to encourage it by any form of NLRA coverage. The AFL-CIO supports NLRA coverage for agriculture workers because of its political feasibility compared to other federal policy options. The UFW would prefer NLRA coverage without the 1947 Taft-Hartley amendments, particularly those limiting secondary pressure.

This lack of agreement was a major factor preventing extension of NLRA coverage to farm workers, and it continues to be an important impediment to development of an agricultural bargaining policy. Besides disputes over the treatment of strikes and boycotts, questions about appropriate units, voter eligibility, election timing, and whether administration should be by an agricultural labor board or the NLRB raise policy problems.

STATE POLICY

Four states have passed laws regulating collective bargaining in agriculture since 1970. The Arizona Agricultural Employment Relations Act, the Idaho Agricultural Labor Act, and the Kansas Agricultural Employment Act all became law in 1972. Although California's law was not passed until 1975, the California Agricultural Labor Relations Board (ALRB) has handled many more cases than have the other state boards.

No cases have been filed under either the Kansas or Idaho laws, and there have been fewer than a dozen total representation and unfair labor practice cases in Arizona. Hawaii had a number of agricultural representation cases filed soon after passage of its general labor relations statute in 1946, and in recent years it has occasionally processed unfair labor practice cases from agriculture, but there have been no recent representation cases. There have been only three agricultural cases in Wisconsin. Thus, CALRA is of major importance for gaining an insight into the impact of one form of public policy on agricultural labor relations.

CALRA, modeled very closely after the National Labor Relations Act, provides for representation elections and outlines unfair labor practices for employers and unions. Much of the wording in the two laws is similar, and the ALRB is required to follow the National Labor Relations Board (NLRB) precedent when feasible. However, there are differences between the two statutes, the most important being in the treatment of secondary boycotts, appropriate unit determination, voter eligibility, and election administration. The following sections discuss CALRA's treatment of both these issues and strikes, and compares the California legislation with the NLRA and the other state laws.

Harvest Strikes. A major policy dilemma in designing collective bargaining policy for agriculture is what limitations, if any, should be placed on strikes during critical growing periods, such as harvests, when growers are especially vulnerable to strike pressure. The basis of the dilemma is that any effort to lessen grower vulnerability reduces union bargaining power, which is limited during much of the year by the seasonal nature of the industry.

Existing state law handles the issue of seasonally critical strikes in two distinct ways. California law, like that of Idaho, Wisconsin, and Hawaii, reflects the philosophy that strikes and strike threats are an important component of the bargaining process because they provide incentives for labor and management to reach agreement. Mediation and conciliation are the only impasse procedures available in these states, although the mediation process differs slightly among the statutes. NLRA treatment of the issue is similar, providing that strikes can be enjoined only under limited circumstances, such as when they create a national emergency or result from a jurisdictional dispute.

In contrast, Arizona and Kansas law attempts to protect growers and the public by placing extensive limitations on strikes. In Kansas, it is an unfair labor practice to strike during livestock marketing, harvesting, or critical production periods; compulsory arbitration is provided for the impasses unresolved after 40 days.[22] Both parties have access to the dispute-resolution process, but agriculture's seasonality makes the 40-day period more advantageous to growers than to unions.

Arizona employers can get ten-day injunctions in the case of a strike or boycott, or threat of a strike or boycott, by agreeing to submit the dispute to binding arbitration. There is no parallel way for unions to request either injunctions or compulsory arbitration. Thus, because of the way the law is structured, growers in a disadvantageous bargaining position can use the law to protect them, while unions cannot.

Secondary Boycotts. Although it is exceedingly difficult to distinguish legitimate primary pressure from illegitimate secondary pressure, the legislative history and wording of the Taft-Hartley Act (LMRA)

---

[22] 3A Kan. Stat. Ann. §§44-826 (1973).

clearly show that it was intended to protect neutral employers from economic pressure by making secondary boycotts illegal. However, because of NLRA's farm-worker exclusion, the UFW used secondary boycotts, or total boycotts of retail stores handling nonunion wine and grapes, as its major tool to gain recognition and contracts until 1972. That year, the NLRB brought suit against the UFW, charging that although agricultural workers were not protected by NLRA provisions, the UFW was a labor organization within the meaning of the Act and, as such, it was subject to its limitations on use of secondary pressure. The union and the NLRB settled the matter informally when the UFW agreed to stop its secondary-boycott activities.[23] Since that time, the union has confined its activities to limited, and thus permissible, boycotts of retail establishments.[24]

CALRA presents an interesting contrast to NLRA treatment of secondary pressure. Rather than making it illegal, CALRA states that publicity and picketing that request the public not to patronize secondary employers are permissible as long as the union is a certified representative of the primary employer's employees.[25]

CALRA specifically treats picketing supporting a boycott differently than does the LMRA. Taft-Hartley permits publicity other than picketing when a union wishes to inform the public that it has a dispute with an employer whose products are being distributed by another employer. Picketing may be used, but if it has a coercive impact on the secondary employer, it is an unfair labor practice.[26] In the parallel section of CALRA, labor unions are explicitly given the right to use picketing and other publicity to let the public know that products of an employer with whom they have a primary dispute are being distributed by other employers. Apparently, this picketing may continue even if it results in the secondary employer's being coerced into not dealing with the primary employer.[27]

CALRA's intent is somewhat obscure; its wording is general, and its meaning will not be clear until there is considerably more implementation and interpretation. However, the law does not appear to put as many limitations on boycotts and secondary pressure as does the NLRA. It seems likely that the UFW, which originally used boycotts to achieve recognition, will be able to use consumer boycotts as a bargaining tactic under CALRA.

[23] Bureau of National Affairs, *Daily Labor Report*, April 4, 1972, p. A13.
[24] Limited boycotts aimed at specific products carried by retail establishments are legitimate primary pressure rather than illegal secondary pressure. *NLRB v. Fruit & Vegetable Packers & Warehousemen, Local 760, et al.*, 377 U.S. 58 (1964).
[25] Cal. Labor Code §§1154.4 (West. Supp. 1976).
[26] 29 U.S.C. §§158 (b)(4).
[27] Cal. Labor Code §§1154.4.

The other state laws more clearly share with the NLRA the intent to outlaw secondary boycotts. Their wording generally parallels NLRA wording, although a few of them have more stringent restrictions on secondary pressure. In Idaho, for example, it is an unfair labor practice to refuse to handle or to encourage employees to refuse to handle agricultural commodities once they leave the original farm except in cases of primary strikes,[28] and in Kansas employers may sue for damages resulting from secondary boycotts.[29]

Elections. Because much agricultural work is seasonal, the time-lag between filing an election petition and an actual representation election is important in determining whether seasonal workers will have an opportunity to vote. California law attempts to maximize election participation of seasonal workers by specifying that this time period will normally be seven days or less. Expedited elections can be held within 48 hours in cases of a strike. Although Hawaii and Wisconsin allow for immediate elections in emergencies, neither the NLRA nor the other state laws facilitate seasonal workers voting in the same way.

The California law's show-of-interest requirement also provides voting opportunities for seasonal workers. Election petitions must be signed by a majority of agricultural employees currently working for an employer. For an election to be held, the number of employees may not be less than half the employer's peak agricultural employment in the current calendar year,[30] thus preventing elections from being decided by a small number of a grower's total employees during seasonal lags in employment. In contrast, the other states and the NLRA require a 30 percent show of interest among current employees, which makes it possible to have elections when no seasonal workers are on the payroll; however, the NLRB does not hold elections under these circumstances.

Appropriate Bargaining Units. Under the NLRA, employer, craft, plant, and plant-subdivision units are all potentially appropriate.[31] Similar treatment for agricultural workers would result in many questions about appropriate units, such as circumstances in which craft and departmental units could be created, and whether seasonal and permanent workers belong in the same units.

CALRA precludes many of these questions by requiring all of an employer's agricultural employees working in one location to be included in one bargaining unit. An employer's employees working in two or more noncontiguous geographic areas may be included in one unit.

---

[28] 5 Idaho Code §§22-4107, 4108 (1972, Supp. 1975).
[29] 3A Kan. Stat. Ann. §§44-828.
[30] Cal. Labor Code §§1156.3.
[31] 29 U.S.C. §§159.

This provision simplifies some, although certainly not all, unit-determination problems.[32]

Unit-determination guidelines are quite broad in the other states. The one exception is that Arizona law assumes that seasonal and permanent workers do not have a community of interest, and it requires that they be in separate units. Given the time period between petition filing and elections, this requirement makes it difficult for units of seasonal workers to be certified.

CALIFORNIA EXPERIENCE

Administering CALRA has proved difficult, and the ALRB has alternately been charged with having pro-UFW, pro-Teamster, and pro-grower bias. Many criticisms leveled at the Board result from its having had to begin operations two weeks after CALRA became law, with relatively untrained personnel attempting to function under extremely difficult conditions. Even trained and experienced people would have found it daunting to conduct elections when faced with two intensely competitive unions, reluctant and sometimes hostile employers, a casual labor force, seasonal and migratory workers, a workforce containing illegal aliens and many people who do not speak English, and an ongoing climate of mistrust and violence.

The initial caseload was much heavier than anticipated, and after six months of operation, the ALRB had spent its original appropriation and had to ask the state legislature for emergency funding. A major reason why the ALRB depleted its funds is that CALRA permits employers to bargain only with bargaining representatives certified by the ALRB. Thus, elections had to be held in each bargaining unit before negotiations could begin. During CALRA's first five months of operation, the ALRB conducted 429 elections. Because of the UFW-WCT jurisdictional dispute and questions over voter eligibility, many elections were disputed, further adding to the ALRB's caseload.

Funding was delayed for six months while growers attempted to get the state legislature to amend CALRA. Grower criticism focused on the access rule, which permitted union organizers to meet with workers on grower property for three nonworking hours a day. The Board promulgated this rule because of the difficulty in reaching migratory farm workers living on grower property anywhere but on that property. Growers claimed that the rule interfered with their property rights. They also feel that the make-whole remedy the law provides for unfair labor practices is ambiguous and that secondary boycotts should be illegal. Finally, some growers believe the law should contain more ex-

[32] Grodin.

tensive impasse procedures in order to reduce the likelihood of harvest strikes.

The UFW responded by having Proposition 14, which would have made CALRA part of California's constitution, placed on the November 1975 ballot. Because it would have guaranteed funding and prevented changes in CALRA except by constitutional amendment, Proposition 14 would have ended funding battles aimed at changing the law. Although rejected by the voters, Proposition 14 ended the deadlock over Board funding because growers agreed to refunding the ALRB without CALRA amendments in order to lessen some of the backing for Proposition 14.

ALRB operations ceased completely for six months. They resumed partially in July 1976, but elections did not begin again until December 1976. The Board's membership, as well as a large portion of its administrative staff, changed prior to resumption of operations.

After reactivation, the Board amended the access rule. The revised version changes the number of days during which union organizers have access to grower property from year round to four 30-day periods in a calendar year. Each of these periods begins when a labor union files in one of the ALRB's regional offices; it ends ten days after a disputed election, and five days after an undisputed election. The UFW was critical of these changes in the access rule and used them to support its contention that, although the law is well designed, its administration has been biased.

The California law had an enormous impact on agricultural labor relations. Although many growers felt that their workers neither needed nor wanted union representation, and although there were many delays in certification due to lack of ALRB funding, disputed elections, and unfair labor practice charges, election results show workers to be overwhelmingly in favor of it (see Table 2). The hectic early election pace leveled off in 1977, largely because the UFW was trying to negotiate contracts in bargaining units already certified before extending its organizing efforts further.

Unfair labor practice charges and questions about voter eligibility delayed certification of a number of elections. Even with these delays, UFW officials believe that the law has aided them in actual bargaining. They feel the requirement to bargain in good faith and the threat of the make-whole remedy have influenced employer attitudes and enabled the union to win contracts with much less reliance on boycotts than was necessary previously.

The impetus that CALRA gives to organizing and collective bargaining is particularly evident when California and Arizona experiences are

TABLE 2

Elections and Results:
California Agricultural Labor Relations Board

Election Category	7/1/1975 to 6/30/1976	7/1/1976 to 6/30/1977	7/1/1977 to 6/30/1978	7/1/1978 to 11/28/1978	Total
Total elections	423	188	122	35	768
Total certifications	276	172	106	17	571
United Farm Workers of America	202	30	28	5	265
Western Conference of Teamsters	39	—	—	—	39
Other[a]	28	130	64	7	229
No union	9	12	14	5	40

Source: Telephone conversations with ALRB administrator Linda Salinas, November 1978.

[a] Most of the "other" category elections were won by the Christian Labor Association in dairy operations.

compared. Agricultural production in the two states is similar. Many crops raised in California also grow in Arizona, and some growers raise the same crops in both states. The labor force is similar and sometimes interchangeable; some workers, such as those on lettuce crews, work in both states. Despite these similarities, there has been little organizing activity in Arizona, and the Arizona Agricultural Labor Relations Board has handled very few cases. The difference in the level of organizing is directly related to the nature of public policy in the two states. The time span between the filing of petitions and elections, the requirement of separate bargaining units for seasonal and permanent workers, and the restrictions on boycotts and strikes inhibit the development of collective bargaining in Arizona. The UFW, critical of Arizona law, has made little effort to organize workers in that state because it believed it would be futile. It has made several attacks on the law, including an unsuccessful effort to recall the governor. That was followed by a challenge of the law's constitutionality. The statute was declared unconstitutional in federal district court in 1978 due to its broad prohibitions on union activity.[33] It is likely that this decision will be appealed.

PROSPECTS FOR FEDERAL POLICY

Just as state regulation of public employee bargaining has provided fertile opportunities for policy experimentation, state agricultural bargaining laws provide the chance to analyze the impact of several different policy models on agricultural labor relations. Theoretically, this

---

[33] United Farm Workers National Union v. Babbitt, 449 F.Supp. 449 (1978).

experience will be helpful in designing future policy. It can also be argued that another advantage of allowing states to develop policy individually is that policy can be tailored to fit local, rather than national, needs and conditions.

However, there are several problems inherent in relying on state law rather than national policy to define rights and obligations in agriculture. One is that questions of equity arise when some people's bargaining rights are protected while the rights of others are not, merely because of accident of location. Second, the argument for developing policy to fit conditions in individual states neglects the fact that, unlike the public sector, the bulk of the product market and some of the labor market is interstate. As the number of states with collective bargaining in agriculture grows, the potential for confusion from overlapping or conflicting statutes also increases. Finally, and perhaps most importantly, much of the turmoil characteristic of agricultural labor relations in California since the early 1960s could have been avoided if there had been a policy framework to handle representation and jurisdiction questions. A federal law could prevent other states from reliving the California experience. This consideration is particularly important given the high priority placed on industrial peace by our national labor policy as expressed in both the National Labor Relations Act and the Railway Labor Act.

There is little likelihood that the concerned parties will reach a consensus in the near future as to what form agricultural bargaining policy should take. Until that consensus develops, there is little reason to expect enactment of a federal agricultural bargaining law.

Unions in Agriculture

The United Farm Workers of America, AFL-CIO

Philosophy and Objectives. The stated objective of the UFW is to bring dignity, justice, and better living and working conditions to farm workers. Collective bargaining is a major vehicle for achievement of these goals, but for collective bargaining to become feasible, it was viewed as necessary to build a strong organization capable of economic action.[34]

The UFW's original organizing units were built from small house meetings. These meetings were used to define farm-worker needs and concerns and to provide the UFW with direction as well as rudiments of an organization for addressing and dealing with some of the problems

---

[34] Analysis in this and the following section is based on interviews with growers, grower representatives, union officials, government officials, representatives of other involved organizations, and arbitrators during 1976 and 1977.

facing agricultural workers. These meetings provided the impetus for the union's first self-help projects, such as a credit union and a gas and oil cooperative.

These projects, and the requirement that members pay dues to stay in good standing, were designed to build rank-and-file involvement and commitment and to develop a sense of communality of interests. It is usually difficult for unskilled workers employed by different employers to perceive mutual interests and needs, but this recognition is often of fundamental importance to successful unionization, particularly in an industry as difficult to organize and geographically scattered as is agriculture.

Nonviolence is an underlying tenet of UFW philosophy. This commitment stems both from the belief that organizations dedicated to advancing human rights cannot legitimately abridge rights of other human beings by using violence, and from recognition that violent actions provoke even more violent and destructive reactions as well as alienate sympathizers. Although some union members became involved in violent activities, the commitment was felt to be important enough to be written into the UFW's constitution. It is used to explain the concepts of self-help and union service centers. UFW leaders feel that disenfranchised and hungry people are more likely to be tempted to use violence than people with alternative means of dealing with problems.

Because the agricultural labor force is made up of transient, local, permanent, temporary, and foreign workers, some of whom are illegal aliens, no single organizing approach can be effective. The UFW stresses community-based organizing and uses it most successfully with local workers who are permanently part of the farm labor force. To enlist migrants, it has often been necessary for UFW organizers to follow workers from location to location. Organizing illegal aliens is even more difficult, for they are hard to find and, once found, fearful of becoming involved in any activity that might result in deportation. Nonetheless, if left out of the union, they have the potential to undercut the union's bargaining position. Given the variety of situations faced, considerable flexibility is needed in the organizing process. Appeals to nationalism have been important in organizing because Chavez is viewed as a hero by both U.S. Chicanos and Mexicans.

It is sometimes asked whether the UFW is a union or a social movement. There can be little doubt that it is a union. It engages in collective bargaining; bargaining issues are wages and working conditions, and its weapons, like those of the rest of the labor movement, are primarily economic. However, in order to become a functioning organization, it has had to develop and expand techniques only sometimes associated with the labor movement. In addition, its successes, both at the bargaining table and with community organizing and all its ramifications, are beginning to have an impact not only on the economic position of farm workers, but also on the political and social structure of agricultural communities.

Organizational Structure. The National Level. The UFW has two major organizational levels: national headquarters and local ranch committees. National responsibilities include planning and directing negotiations, organizing, boycotts, legal support, finances, publications, lobbying, and fringe-benefit program administration. Because the UFW is a young and growing union, organizational responsibilities are subject to change. Currently, however, directors of most of the above activities are executive board members. General union policy comes from biennial conventions, and it is implemented on a daily basis by the executive board and the president.

Collective bargaining is handled by the administration and negotiations department, which also functions as the link between workers at each ranch and national headquarters. Staff members provide general guidance for ranch committees and communicate policy between ranch committees and the national office.

Several executive board members have training responsibilities. Included in the organizing department is a separate unit responsible for training recruits for both boycott committees and organizing. The administration and negotiations department trains rank-and-file workers in both negotiations and contract administration. The legal department trains paralegal assistants, and it also has at least one apprentice reading law while preparing to be an attorney.

Ranch Committees. The UFW puts high priority on encouraging worker involvement in all phases of union operations. Democracy is seen as a value in and of itself, and active worker participation is also viewed as a way to ensure commitment to the union and, in turn, union responsiveness to worker needs. Ranch committees were developed as a mechanism to ensure worker input into decision-making at the time when the UFW signed its first contracts.

There is at least one ranch committee at each ranch under contract; each committee is made up of five people elected by union members at that ranch. On some large grower operations there is more than one committee.

The UFW does not have local unions, and ranch committees perform many functions that local union officers and shop stewards are responsible for in other labor organizations. They handle the first two steps of the grievance procedure, provide advice and information for union negotiators, and supervise elections of representatives to negotiating committees and union conventions, and they can help administer hiring halls. They also are responsible for implementing contracts on a daily basis, communicating union policy to workers, and communicating worker needs and concerns back to the national headquarters.

In addition, ranch committees have a responsibility for developing among rank-and-file members an understanding and appreciation for the concept of collective bargaining, the meaning and application of collectively bargained contracts, and UFW philosophy. This concern with education stems partially from the fact that the UFW is a new union, and believes it necessary to make workers aware of the possibilities and limitations of collective bargaining if the organization is to function. It is also felt that workers must be responsible for their own contracts if the UFW is to continue to grow. The national union is heavily involved in organizing and negotiating, making it imperative that ranch committees handle contract administration, particularly given the geographic dispersion of bargaining units.

Few ranch committee members have had labor relations experience prior to their election. Although the reliance placed on ranch committees is understandable given the nature of the union and industry, it produces some short-run inefficiencies in contract administration. The union provides training and general guidance, but much that committee members need to know has to be learned through practice. This learning by experience, as well as the union's reliance on committee rather than individual decision-making, is a source of frustration to many growers who want rapid and consistent solutions to problems.

Inexperienced union representatives in combination with the UFW commitment to democracy have created some serious negotiating problems as well. Bargaining and settlements have been delayed by shifts in union position as a result of ongoing rank-and-file input. Sometimes this input has resulted in spurious demands and, on occasion, increases in the number of demands and disputed issues far into the negotiating process.

It is likely that this grower frustration will be an ongoing problem. Each time the UFW wins representation rights for bargaining units which have not previously been under contract, a new ranch committee must be elected, trained, and given responsibility. Many of these committees will need substantial on-the-job experience before smooth contract administration can be expected.

However, the ranch committee concept does have potential long-run advantages for the union, union members, and perhaps even the growers. Strong ranch committees will enable the national union to devote its energies to organizing and collective bargaining, while at the same time making possible worker input into union policy. Once established, ranch committees could also provide growers with an accessible, and possibly even rapid, mechanism for joint decisions.

Boycott Committees. The UFW's successful use of the boycott weapon is unique in the history of the American labor movement. The responsibility for implementing boycotts was given to local boycott committees. Boycott committees were supposed both to develop boycott support at the local level and to generate financial contributions sufficient to operate their own offices and to add to the union's general treasury.

These boycott committees existed from the late 1960s through early 1978. Their size and number varied with staff availability, but there were committees with permanent staff members in most large cities. Local volunteers assisted permanent staff in planning and effectuating programs.

UFW reliance on community-based organizing was apparent in the methods used by these committees. Boycott committees operated on the premise that effective community support could be achieved only through education and organization. Contact was made with unions, churches, and other potentially sympathetic organizations. Initial contacts were followed by meetings at which boycott staff members explained UFW goals and enlisted recruits and support. Volunteers contacted stores, leafleted, picketed, engaged in letter-writing campaigns to employers and government officials, and took part in a variety of fund-raising events. Although permanent staffing was controlled from UFW headquarters, individual committees were of necessity fairly autonomous in planning policies appropriate for local communities. For example, in some places it is possible to appeal to individual liquor stores not to carry a boycotted product. However, in some states alcoholic beverages are sold only by state-operated stores, making it necessary for the committees to concentrate on developing consumer awareness rather than appealing directly to retail stores.

Boycott committees had several ongoing problems. One problem inherent in using boycotts is the necessity of constantly communicating changes in policy while avoiding consumer confusion and maintaining support for the boycott. For example, the boycott of Gallo products was implemented in 1973, rescinded during the summer of 1976, and reinstituted during 1977. Its length led some consumers to assume that it had ended long before it did. Others reasoned that recognitional boycotts were no longer necessary after CALRA's passage. Some consumers did not know of the 1976 cancellation of the boycott, and, of those who did, there were many who did not know that it had been revived in 1977. Confusion was so widespread that in one instance a UFW board member announced at a public meeting in an eastern city that the UFW was no longer boycotting Gallo. At that same time, that city's boycott committee was publicizing the boycott.

Another problem for the union was boycott staff turnover, partially a consequence of reliance on volunteers to do frustrating work with results that are often difficult to see. Some turnover occurred because staff members tired of communal living arrangements and limited funds. Finally, turnover also occurred as staff members were shifted from one activity to another as UFW needs changed.

During early 1978 the permanent staff members of local boycott committees were recalled to UFW headquarters, and the local boycott offices were closed. UFW's representation election victories gave the union large numbers of new bargaining units to service, and the boycott staff was needed to help negotiate and administer new contracts. Adequate servicing of these new units was seen as being fundamental in developing UFW's organizational stability.

When the local boycott offices were closed, it was announced that the closings were temporary. Whether or not they will ever be used again is unclear because it depends on UFW's future goals and needs.

Union Personnel. The UFW is staffed from César Chavez on down to the boycott committees by volunteers who work for $10.00 a week and union-provided subsistence. The union emphasizes recruitment of farm workers to work on the UFW staff in the belief that the union is central to their life, and some volunteers are Chicanos who have been farm workers. However, there is also a large number of nonfarm-worker volunteers, generally Anglo, engaged in all phases of union operations. These volunteers became important to the UFW during early struggles in wine grapes when they joined picket lines. From there, they became active as organizers, boycott staff, and field-office administrators. Some early nonfarm-worker volunteers have important staff positions in the union hierarchy. Most nonfarm-worker volunteers are recent college graduates with an interest in civil rights and social reform. Others are interested in labor relations or labor law careers and see working with the UFW as a way to get valuable experience.

In general, new volunteers, regardless of source, are inexperienced in organizing, union administration, and collective bargaining and, although the UFW provides training programs for them, it is difficult to develop industrial relations expertise in a relatively short time. Thus, many volunteers leave training inadequately prepared for the labor relations problems that they encounter.

A problem resulting from reliance on volunteers is relatively high staff turnover, particularly at middle and lower organizational levels, making implementation of consistent policy difficult. In an effort to reduce turnover, the UFW currently requires at least a year's commitment from recruits.

For the present, the UFW appears committed to ongoing use of volunteers as union administrators. There are, however, critics of this policy who suggest that a paid professional staff would make union administration more efficient.[35] As the union grows, it may turn to supplementing volunteers with professionals.

Relationships with Other Organizations. One factor explaining the UFW's survival is its ability to attract support and assistance from a potpourri of organizations. Some are labor organizations; others are church, civil rights, neighborhood, and ad hoc groups. Although the AFL-CIO has given the UFW varying amounts of financial assistance, technical help for organizing and negotiations, and boycott support, the federation no longer donates money to the UFW. Technical advisers from the Industrial Union Department are occasionally made available.

The alliance between the UFW and the AFL-CIO has not always been an easy one and has been strained at times by their differing philosophies and goals. Some UFW methods have seemed unorthodox to AFL-CIO leadership, and even at odds with federation practice. The UFW's calling for a boycott without prior approval of, and sometimes to the disapproval of, the AFL-CIO has been a particular problem when an employer, such as Gallo, has contracts with other AFL-CIO affiliates. There is also a difference, as noted earlier, between the two organizations with respect to NLRA coverage for agricultural workers.

At the state level, the California Federation of Labor, AFL-CIO, while not giving funds directly to the union, has made it a practice to return the UFW's per capita tax. It also backed the UFW efforts to get passage of CALRA, and it publishes a monthly list of boycotted growers. Many state AFL-CIO members have been active boycott supporters. However, the UFW does not yet make a practice of attending AFL-CIO city central meetings, and members of the California Federation of Labor are somewhat less sympathetic to the UFW than they once were.

Help has come to the UFW from individual unions as well. City boycott committees have found many local unions to be friendly, helpful, and indispensable boycott allies. The United Automobile Workers contributed money, technical assistance, and continuing moral support both while a member of the AFL-CIO and after leaving the federation. In turn, the UFW has given help to other labor organizations, when

---

[35] Taylor, p. 322.

feasible. For example, the boycott machinery has given publicity to the Amalgamated Clothing and Textile Workers' drive against J. P. Stevens.

A number of churches and religiously affiliated organizations also have been active in the UFW's struggle. Some groups, such as the American Friends Service Committee (AFSC) and the California Migrant Ministry, were actively trying to improve conditions for farm workers prior to the UFW's origin, and they quickly identified with its efforts. Because many of the UFW's Chicano members are Roman Catholic, Catholic Church support has had emotional meaning as well as real practical significance. The National Council of Churches and many individual Jewish and Protestant leaders and congregations also have been invaluable to the UFW.

The American Friends Service Committee has had a particularly interesting arrangement with the UFW that stems from their shared commitment to nonviolence. The UFW leadership feels that negotiations have great potential for violence because of the possibility that employers may be hostile or that employees may become disgruntled when progress is slow. In addition, what goes on outside the bargaining room is often influenced by how negotiations are conducted, especially since some negotiating committees are quite large. The current director of negotiations was chosen over more experienced people partially because of his steadfast commitment to nonviolence. In sympathy with the objective of keeping negotiations peaceful, the AFSC provides for his living and traveling expenses.

Other liberal organizations, such as Americans for Democratic Action and the Student Nonviolent Coordinating Committee, have been important in the UFW's efforts, and contributions have come from many individual sources as well. The funds to buy the UFW headquarters at La Paz, California, came from an individual donor and, on one memorable occasion early in the UFW's history, Chavez went to Berkeley's Sproul Plaza at noon, explained the farm workers' plight, and asked students who gathered there for their lunch money. He returned to Delano with several thousand dollars.

These groups have been of fundamental importance to the UFW. They enabled it to survive financially, they were a major element in the success of boycott and letter-writing campaigns, and they have provided the UFW with political power vastly greater than its membership alone could muster. It is also a curiosity in the history of American labor. No other union has built a similar student-liberal-labor coalition, nor been able to use outside help to the same degree and with the same effectiveness.

The question is, of course, why has the UFW been able to marshall this level of support over such a long period of time, while other unions have not had this capability? Problems in agriculture labor are not new ones, and other unions that organized farm workers sought similar support without much success. One answer is that the UFW recognized it had to develop methods not used by other unions if it were to survive. These methods had to have the capability of changing basic power relationships in the industry, particularly given the limited role of law until 1975.

There are other possible explanations. One is that the successes of civil rights groups in influencing public policy awoke other organizations to the potential for creating social change, and thus increased their willingness to engage in change-oriented activities. Another is that the UFW success was made possible by changes in the political environment and development of more sympathetic attitudes toward farm workers by public and governmental agencies.[36] These explanations, however, fail to emphasize fully the UFW's unique circumstances and response to those circumstances. Relying on history, the UFW recognized that it had to develop new tactics if it were to be successful and that getting outside support would have to be among those tactics.

As a result, groundwork for outside support is laid as carefully as is that for bringing farm workers into the union. Both the UFW leadership and local boycott committees worked hard at developing these relationships, and, once established, they were carefully fostered. Cooperative relationships with mass media have been encouraged, and sympathetic media treatment has helped create a favorable public image of the UFW. In contrast, media treatment of growers and the Teamsters has generally been unsympathetic. The UFW efforts clearly indicate a realization that farm-worker strikes alone would have limited effectiveness in establishing collective bargaining.

Although the UFW has used support from many sources in achieving its goals, external supporters have had virtually no role in the union's decision-making. As explained by one long-time UFW supporter, "Supporters have expressed their views to the union on a number of issues and will continue to do so. But in the final analysis, supporters are stuck with their limited role as supporters."[37]

LOCAL 142 OF THE INTERNATIONAL LONGSHOREMEN'S AND WAREHOUSEMEN'S UNION

Objectives and Strategy. Local 142 had somewhat fewer problems in organizing farm workers than were originally faced by the UFW because

---

[36] Jenkins and Perrow, pp. 249–68.
[37] Hartmire, p. 13.

of the Hawaii Employment Relations Act and the smaller proportion of migratory workers in the Hawaiian farm labor market. However, they both confronted powerful grower opposition and the problems involved in organizing low-income workers with little prior labor movement contact. In addition, Local 142 faced an ethnically heterogeneous labor force which had previously inhibited unionization. Given the similarities in the extent and nature of the barriers to unionization faced by these unions, it is not surprising to find similarities in their tactics.

Like the UFW, Local 142 believed that in order to establish collective bargaining, an organizational strategy to create union loyalty and worker solidarity was needed. To build this solidarity, it emphasized that the union's function was to serve workers, and that this could be best accomplished through democratic decision-making.

Since its earliest organizing days, Local 142 has attempted to build member allegiance by meeting worker needs both at and away from the workplace. There is a shop steward system that handles work-related problems and grievances. In addition, there is a parallel membership-service system that provides workers with assistance on nonwork matters such as eligibility for government compensation programs, health matters, legal problems, community welfare, assistance in travel to foreign countries and foreign monetary exchange, and counseling on personal and family problems. This system is similar to UFW service centers in terms of objectives and problems handled. In both instances, they appear to have been important organizing devices.

Both unions also stress democracy. Local 142's conventions, held every two years, are considered the major source of union policy. Delegates to conventions are selected from and by each bargaining unit. Before becoming official union policy, convention resolutions must be approved by a referendum, in which every rank-and-file member can vote.

Unlike the UFW, Local 142 did not use ethnic appeals while organizing. Hawaiian farm workers come from a diversity of ethnic backgrounds, making it necessary for the union to stress similarities in their problems as workers as a tool in overcoming ethnic divisions. To ensure that all workers feel that they are part of the union, Local 142 uses interpreters at meetings when necessary. In addition, an effort is made to recruit people from different national backgrounds for leadership positions so that the union does not become identified with any one nationality group.

Organizational Structure. Local 142, with about 22,000 members, is a major force in Hawaii's labor movement and politics. In addition to agricultural workers, it has organized about 200 different types of workers in hundreds of bargaining units, including auto mechanics, hospital workers, cemetery workers, hotel and restaurant workers, retail clerks, and longshore workers. Because of its size, occupational diversity, and geographic dispersion, the local functions more like a regional body or district council than a traditional local union. It employs full-time staff for organizing, negotiating, legislative affairs, membership service, social work, and education. It also has a regular radio program and a monthly newspaper.

Local 142 is composed of about 200 different units, each consisting of members working for the same employer. Each unit has its own executive board and shop stewards and performs functions normally associated with a local union, such as formulating contract demands, negotiating (sometimes with Local 142 assistance), and handling grievances. Membership meetings are held at the unit, rather than the local, level.

Because much of the union's operation is at the unit level, Local 142 has extensive training programs. There are training programs for new union officers, shop stewards, and service-system representatives.

WESTERN CONFERENCE OF TEAMSTERS

Organizational Structure. The Western Conference of Teamsters is the oldest of the International Brotherhood of Teamsters' five area conferences that serve as intermediary bodies between locals and the international. Area conferences have sometimes been likened to internationals within an international, for they perform many functions normally associated with an international, such as collective bargaining, organizing, and research. They have a great deal of autonomy in decision-making vis-à-vis both local unions and the international.

The Western Conference covers 13 western states, but most of its membership is in California. It includes a number of locals representing processing workers, as well as locals set up to represent and organize field workers.

Philosophy and Tactics. Prior to UFW organizing among field workers, the Teamsters had established bargaining relationships with a number of growers covering truck drivers and packing-shed workers. Some of these agreements were negotiated on a multiemployer basis, while others involved single growers. In addition, the Teamsters had a few contracts covering farm laborers, but their interest in organizing field workers was extremely limited prior to the UFW's initial strike against wine-grape growers.

In 1966, the DiGiorgio Fruit Corporation, a wine-grape producer, agreed as a result of boycott activity to hold elections to determine if the UFW (then the NFWA) represented their workers. When election conditions were discussed, DiGiorgio announced that the Teamsters would be on the ballot. The UFW felt that Teamsters inclusion on the ballot was uncalled for, and it refused to take part in the subsequent election, which the Teamsters won. However, public pressure compelled DiGiorgio to negotiate terms for a new election, which was won by the UFW. Although the Teamsters lost the second election, they had indicated their interest in representing field workers.

The Teamsters did not actively try to organize lettuce field workers, but sporadically between 1967 and 1970 they did express an interest in representing them to a number of Santa Maria Valley growers. During 1970 negotiations with Salinas Valley lettuce growers over contracts covering truck drivers and shed workers, WCT officials indicated their willingness to represent field workers as well and, with the conclusion of negotiations, the growers met and agreed to recognize the Teamsters as the bargaining agent for field workers. Contracts covering field workers were signed. Shortly thereafter, Santa Maria growers agreed to a Teamster demand, presented in negotiations over driver, stitcher, and loader contracts, that the Teamsters be designated as bargaining representative for field workers as well.

The UFW reacted to the lettuce agreements with strikes and boycotts. Although the Teamsters and the UFW tried to frame a jurisdictional agreement, the results were inconclusive, and most of the growers continued to honor their Teamster contracts. As a result, the UFW, believing that workers preferred it to the Teamsters, continued the strikes and boycotts.

In an effort to bring these activities to a halt, growers brought suit against the UFW under California's Jurisdictional Strike Act. At that time, California had no general labor relations statute, but its Jurisdictional Strike Act provided for injunctions against concerted activities of competing unions in jurisdictional disputes unless one of the involved unions was financed, in whole or part, dominated, controlled, or interfered with by the employer seeking injunctive relief. In deciding the case, *Englund* v. *Chavez*, the California State Supreme Court acknowledged that there was no state-provided mechanism for determining the wishes of employees in representation cases.[38] However, it pointed out that the Teamsters made no claim of being the choice of a majority, or even any, of the involved workers, and the growers had made no effort to determine their employees' wishes. Available evidence indicated

---

[38] *Englund* v. *Chavez*, 8 C.2d 572, 105 Cal. Rep. 521, 504 P.2d 457 (1972).

that many, and perhaps a majority, of the concerned workers would have chosen the UFW as their bargaining agent if given an opportunity. Thus the court concluded that the UFW's activities were not enjoinable because the growers had interfered with the Teamsters by giving it exclusive bargaining rights when they knew that the Teamsters did not have support of a majority of their workers. The result of the decision was that the UFW could continue its actions directed at the growers and the Teamsters, but existing contracts remained in effect.

The case is interesting for several reasons. It makes clear that Teamster efforts to gain recognition in lettuce were directed at growers rather than field workers. Second, its description of events indicates little grower resistance to the Teamsters. The lettuce contracts marked the beginning of a mutually acceptable alliance between the growers and the Teamsters.

The forces at work when grape growers decided to sign Teamster contracts rather than renegotiate UFW contracts in 1973 are somewhat less clear. It appears, however, that negotiations between growers and the UFW had become stalled prior to grower recognition of the Teamsters.

There are several versions of why negotiations broke down. Issues at impasse were the hiring hall, seniority arrangements, and union security. The first two, hiring halls and extent of seniority units, are controversial because they are related to control of the workforce and, as such, they have implications for the union's security as an institution and management's ability to control and direct the labor force.

Thus, bargaining impasses may have resulted in outright differences over new contract terms. They may also have been fostered by grower expectations of a Teamster accord if negotiations with the UFW were unsuccessful. It has also been suggested that the inability of UFW negotiators to make decisions and union administrative inefficiency inhibited bargaining. Growers described the UFW's attempts at negotiating as "half-hearted at best, sullen, obstinate, uncooperative and completely irresponsible at worst." [39] Finally, delays in reaching agreement caused some frustration among workers, particularly since the disagreements concerned noneconomic issues, and at least some of them were tempted to consider the Teamsters as an alternative representative.

The resulting contracts between the grape growers and the Teamsters, like the lettuce contracts, were roughly equivalent to UFW contracts in terms of economic benefits. The major difference was that Teamster contracts did not provide for hiring halls. The absence of

---

[39] South Central Farmers League, *Summary of Significant Labor Relations Activity in the Table Grape Industry*, undated, p. 1.

hiring-hall provisions permitted continued use of labor contractors and made seniority issues unimportant because seniority was not a factor in the hiring process.

There are several possible explanations for grower willingness to bargain with the Teamsters. One explanation advanced by growers in *Englund* v. *Chavez* credits the Teamsters' strategic position and the resulting effectiveness of strikes. However, in many instances, other factors apparently were at work. Some growers foresaw a problem with having different organizations represent their field workers and their truck drivers and processing workers because a strike involving either bargaining unit would shut down operations.

In addition, many growers, when presented with the choice of bargaining with either the Teamsters or the UFW, preferred the Teamsters as an organization. In contrast to the UFW, the Teamsters seemed business-like and efficient. Finally, the Teamsters did not raise issues about control of the workforce and social reform, as the UFW did. The UFW's philosophy is an anathema to some growers who see it as being radical and irresponsible at best, and Communist-dominated at worst. Behind this view of the UFW may lie an uneasiness about its potential for changing existing Anglo-Chicano power relationships in local communities where political power had long been concentrated in Anglo hands.

In recognizing the Teamsters, growers acknowledged that collective bargaining involving field workers could no longer be avoided altogether. Given the inevitability of collective bargaining, they preferred to deal with an internally efficient organization which confined itself to economic issues, while accepting the status quo with respect to labor market operations and community power relationships. Only a few growers continued to deal with the UFW, either because of boycott pressure or the belief that allowing field workers to choose their own representatives would make for more cooperative employment relationships.

There are several interrelated reasons for Teamster interest in representing field workers. One explanation is that, because organizing field workers was difficult and did little to increase the bargaining power of truck drivers and processing workers already represented by the Teamsters, it became important to make the attempt only when another union began organizing them, thus making the Teamster-represented workers vulnerable to strikes called by another union.[40] It has also been

---

[40] Glass, pp. 24–27.

suggested that the WCT was interested in acquiring jurisdiction over the higher paid equipment operators as mechanization of farm work advanced.

Some observers have suggested political explanations, both internal and external. One theory is that Teamster interest in field workers resulted from a power struggle within the Western Conference, with field-worker units potentially important as a power base. The external political explanation credits Teamster interest to the close relationship between former President Nixon and the International Brotherhood of Teamsters and the equally close relationship between Nixon and California growers. The best explanation of Teamster motivation in representing field workers probably is some combination of these theories. Whatever the reasons, growers and the Teamsters found that their alliance served each other's needs very well until CALRA provided for representation elections.

As indicated earlier, election losses were one factor encouraging the Teamster-UFW jurisdictional accord. The success of this agreement and effective CALRA administration are fundamental to peaceful and orderly agricultural labor relations. The high incidence of violence and coercion during the struggle between the two unions is incompatible with free choice of bargaining representatives and meaningful collective bargaining.

The Collective Bargaining Process

BARGAINING STRUCTURE

Because of diversity in ranch size, ownership, and crops, agriculture provides examples of a wide range of alternative bargaining structures. Some negotiations are conducted on a single-employer basis, some on a multiemployer basis; in other instances, they involve a primary grower while other growers attend bargaining sessions and use the resulting agreement as a key settlement.

When Teamsters represented the bulk of California's organized field workers, most bargaining was done on a multiemployer basis. There were several large units, each restricted to a specific geographic area. A master agreement was signed by all unit growers, and wage supplements were developed for individual crops. These multiemployer agreements ended with passage of CALRA and its requirement that employers bargain only with certified bargaining representatives.

In Hawaii, sugar and pineapple contracts are negotiated on a multiemployer basis and then signed by individual growers. Macadamia nut and papaya growers bargain on an individual basis.

The UFW prefers to bargain on a multiemployer basis when growers agree. Although California law requires that only single-employer bargaining units be certified, there has been some movement back to multiemployer bargaining with the mutual consent of growers and the union. Several wine-grape growers led this trend shortly after the UFW was certified as bargaining agent for their employees.

Not all growers are willing to bargain on a multiemployer basis. Some reluctant ones have large operations or special growing or marketing conditions, or are owned by large corporations. They neither want someone else to bargain for them, nor do they wish to bargain for anyone else. However, some large growers do bargain on a multiemployer basis. In addition, there are some growers who insist on single-employer units as a way of making collective bargaining more difficult for the UFW.

It is likely that the number of multiemployer units in agriculture will increase, as multiemployer bargaining has advantages for both unions and growers. For unions, it greatly simplifies bargaining by reducing the number of individual negotiations. Particularly for small and medium-sized growers, it reduces negotiating costs, enables cooperative use of consultants, and provides protection against whipsaw strikes. For both parties it has the advantage of stabilizing wages over one industry segment. Because multiemployer bargaining raises the costs of disagreement for both parties, it will probably reduce the number of work stoppages to which the public is subject. However, this means it also increases the potential impact of impasses involving entire multiemployer units.

This potential may be mitigated if most multiemployer arrangements are limited to one growing area. Crops grown in different regions, even within relatively close proximity in one state, are harvested and come to market at slightly different times. Fruits and vegetables harvested early are usually more expensive to grow, but they have a higher market price than the same crops produced in other areas later in the season. Resulting differences in cost and pricing conditions reduce the likelihood of interregional multiemployer bargaining arrangements. Effective multiemployer bargaining could be limited by growing region, particularly since many of agriculture's grower-shipper and cooperative arrangements which provide a natural basis for multiemployer bargaining are similarly limited. Another alternative is that multiemployer units would include growers from more than one region, and that contracts would contain local-issue supplements.

Composition of Negotiating Teams

The major determinants of the composition of grower negotiating teams are ownership structure and size of growing operations. Large and corporate-owned operations are usually represented by their own labor relations staff, supervisory staff representatives, and legal advisers. However, grower associations play a very important role in negotiating agricultural contracts, and even some of the largest growers rely on them to negotiate on their behalf, although concerned growers are represented on negotiating committees. Smaller growers and growers involved in multiemployer units are even more likely to rely heavily on the assistance provided by grower associations and legal consultants.

Although the general makeup of employer negotiating teams is similar to that found in many industries, the composition of the UFW's bargaining teams is unusual. These teams are usually headed by the union's negotiations director and include necessary legal and research support staff. Sometimes the director is not available, and other staff members direct negotiations. However, because of the UFW's emphasis on democratic procedures, negotiations committees also include either the involved grower's ranch committee members or other elected rank-and-file members. Consequently, when the UFW is bargaining with large growers or multiemployer bargaining units, its bargaining team can consist of 100 or more members! Many growers found the size of the UFW's negotiating committee to be distracting initially, even though most union committee members take little part in actual bargaining.

In contrast, the Teamsters make little use of rank-and-file members during negotiations. Negotiations were conducted by representatives of the Western Conference and officers from individual locals.

ILWU's Local 142's initial contract demands come from individual units. In sugar, negotiations are conducted by a committee made up of unit representatives and at least one Local 142 representative. Geographic diversity is stipulated, and the spokesperson for negotiations is an ILWU vice-president. Pineapple negotiators are also chosen to provide broad representation. The spokesperson, however, is from Local 142 rather than from ILWU headquarters.

Bargaining Strategy

Union Negotiating Tactics. Because of difficulties involved in mounting effective strikes, particularly during nonpeak periods of labor demand, the UFW supplements strike threats with other forms of pressure. As one UFW official put it, "In a nonviolent movement there is a lot of opportunity to be creative." Thus, when negotiations slow or reach the impasse stage, the UFW turns to tactics originally developed to bring growers to the bargaining table.

Tactics chosen from the UFW's arsenal depend on the situation and the union's perception of grower vulnerability. Boycott threats are used frequently, as are letter-writing and phone-call campaigns. These campaigns are most common when grower operations are controlled by a conglomerate enterprise. When necessary, boycotts are instituted. Since CALRA's passage, the UFW has tried to use the make-whole remedy's ambiguity to its advantage in discouraging bad-faith bargaining. Because of CALRA, the UFW feels that it has been less necessary than previously to rely on economic pressure, and that the entire process of reaching settlements has been made easier.

In contrast to the UFW, the Teamsters and ILWU's Local 142 rely almost entirely on strikes and strike threats to gain bargaining concessions. Both unions are in a position to institute strikes more effectively than is the UFW.

The Teamsters' vertical integration provides them with a strategic position which the UFW does not have. Although the Teamsters have bargained new contracts with little recourse to the strike weapon, they did call strikes during the 1975–77 period of rivalry with the UFW to gain wage adjustments under their existing contracts to match wage levels being achieved in UFW negotiations. Theoretically, these strikes were spontaneous indications of worker displeasure at being paid inferior wages, but their widespread nature and the failure of Teamster leadership to condemn them led many growers to believe they were part of an overall strategy. The UFW engaged in similar stoppages to force employers with whom it had contracts to match Teamster wage gains, and the resulting wage spiral dismayed growers.

ILWU's Local 142 is able to use the strike weapon because of the Hawaiian agricultural labor force's relative stability. There are few seasonal workers in sugar production, and even in pineapple operations only about one-fifth of the labor force is seasonal during peak demand periods.

Strikes have frequently resulted from bargaining impasses. Since 1946, there have been about a dozen strikes in sugar and four in pineapples. Because of the fears of many mainland growers of harvest strikes, it is interesting to note that ILWU contracts terminate between seasonal peaks. This timing came about because the initial pineapple strike occurred during a critical seasonal period and was marked with strikebreaking, violence, and the ILWU's eventual capitulation. Seasonal workers were the major strikebreakers, and now Local 142 times strikes for winter periods when seasonal workers are not a problem.

This timing increases strike effectiveness, but it also increases their length. Strikes tend to last a month or more before operations are affected, but they are run in a business-like fashion. Growing operations are readied prior to strikes so that work can be resumed in an orderly fashion when impasses are resolved. Even during strikes, growers will call the union to ask for help in tending plants. The union cooperates, for future wages depend on what happens to crops during strikes.

Bargaining tactics used by these three unions provide an interesting contrast. In each instance, tactics are designed to capitalize on natural advantages and minimize inherent weaknesses in bargaining positions. Because of Teamster vertical integration, processing workers buttressed the relatively weak bargaining position of field workers. The strike was a more effective weapon for them than for the UFW, which represents only field workers.

Both the UFW and Local 142 have to be cognizant of potential strikebreakers. Local 142 avoids their impact by not striking during seasonal highs in labor demand. Because California agriculture is much more seasonal than is Hawaiian agriculture, strikes directed at growers during periods of low labor demand would have little effectiveness for the UFW. As a result, it supplements strike threats with a variety of other weapons.

It may be that at some future point the UFW will not have to rely on strike alternatives as major bargaining weapons—if or when growers become reluctant to endanger relationships with the union by using strikebreakers, and if or when the UFW has organized enough of any given labor force segment so that strikebreakers are not a threat. This condition prevails in a few of the UFW's bargaining relationships, but it is a long way from being characteristic of negotiations.

Grower Tactics. Grower responses to collective bargaining fall into three distinct evolutionary stages: avoidance, reluctant acceptance, and accommodation. Few growers arrive at accommodation without going through the initial stages; many are currently in one of the first two phases and are slowly making progress toward the third.

Avoidance. Avoidance was characteristic of almost all California growers until the very recent past, and it is still characteristic of many of them, as well as of growers in virtually every other region. Avoidance follows a predictable pattern, although it is not usually part of a carefully worked out strategy. When labor unrest becomes evident, growers in the avoidance phase use a number of measures to bring the concerted activities to an end and to find more tractable replacements for discontented workers. Among the tactics used are verbal threats, ejection from grower-owned housing, enlistment of police assistance, requests for injunctions, recruitment of strikebreakers, and refusals to negotiate. Growers countered UFW boycotts with publicity, advertising campaigns, and requests to government officials to increase purchases of boycotted produce. Several new grower associations with a primary interest in labor relations were created as a direct result of the union's organizing efforts.

Avoidance of collective bargaining traditionally involved opposition to NLRA coverage or similar legislation. A current refined variant to that tactic is grower support for NLRA coverage. This approach recognizes that NLRA coverage would have general political palatability, provide some protection against boycotts, and forestall enactment of state laws, such as the one in California, designed to foster collective bargaining in agriculture. Many California growers support NLRA coverage because it would make organizing more difficult than under current California law. They have also tried to get CALRA amended.

Some grower associations support NLRA coverage because the benefits of even a favorable state law would be limited to that state. For example, several Florida grower organizations, such as Florida Citrus Mutual, which represents many of the state's citrus growers, and the Florida Fruit and Vegetable Association, another major representative of Florida growers, support NLRA coverage because about 90 percent of Florida produce is shipped out of state and thus is vulnerable to national boycotts against which state law could provide no protection. However, most growers in states other than Florida and California still feel their interests are best served by opposing NLRA coverage for farm workers.

A new and relatively sophisticated avoidance mechanism has recently been recommended by some grower associations. Recognizing that good personnel relations and wages at least comparable to those collectively bargained take away some of unionization's impetus, these organizations offer suggestions about ways of improving personnel practices and provide regular information on comparative wage rates.

Reluctant Acceptance. Growers in this response stage realize that collective bargaining is inevitable for either legal or economic reasons, but they hope to limit its impact and even to outlast it and return to a nonunionized status. They engage in tactics such as shifting from labor-intensive crops to crops that require less field labor, delaying negotiations sometimes to the point of bad-faith bargaining, and attempting to choose, or influence the choice of, the union which represents their workers. The Teamster-grower alliance is a classic example of use of this latter tactic.

Accommodation. Growers who reach this stage of response recognize not only that collective bargaining is an inevitable and perhaps even a permanent condition, but also that developing good labor relations policies will be in their long-run best interests in terms of production and employee relationships. The first growers to arrive at this stage typically were part of conglomerate operations, vulnerable to boycott pressure and experienced with collective bargaining in other parts of their operations. Growers who appear to have most difficulty arriving at this phase are relatively small and independent operators who have had little experience with unions and who are emotionally as well as financially involved in farming.

There are a number of steps growers take when establishing the groundwork for a good collective bargaining contract and their responsibility for adhering to its provisions. For many supervisors in agriculture, collective bargaining requires enormous adaptation. Prior to unionization, there were few restrictions on supervisory power, and personnel concepts, such as progressive discipline, were virtually unknown. Recognizing the important role of supervisors in contract administration, some growers, such as Inter Harvest, Inc., a large Salinas Valley lettuce grower, and the Coca Cola Company instituted training programs for their supervisory personnel. Both companies also have professional labor relations staffs that stress communication with supervisory people. Communication between labor relations staffs and supervisors is often a problem in newly organized industries, but in agriculture communication problems are often intensified by geographic separation.

Inter Harvest also instituted monthly meetings at which foremen and union representatives meet informally to handle problems. The company gives foremen considerable autonomy in these meetings in the belief that as long as management rights are not being given away, there are benefits to be gained through encouraging harmonious working relationships.

In general, employers who reach accommodation express it as much through attitude as through explicit practices. Some indications of attitude are willingness to bargain in good faith, respect for contractual hiring hall and seniority arrangements, and a cooperative approach to the union in daily matters.

Grower progress toward accommodation tends to be slow. One reason is that many growers are still unwilling to accept collective bargaining. However, the willingness of some to recognize the Teamsters, although they were reluctant to bargain with the UFW, suggests that strained relationships and lack of trust between growers and the UFW may be a major problem. Ironically, these strained relationships are partially a result of the UFW's organizing tactics, which did much to alienate growers. However, without these tactics, it is unlikely that either the UFW or its more palatable alternative, the Teamsters, would have been successful, given the industry's historical imperviousness to collective bargaining. The UFW's commitment to democracy, which slows grievance administration and negotiation, also places a strain on progress toward grower acceptance of the concept.

Growers who reach accommodation levels of response acknowledge that both they and the UFW have gone through a learning process which makes their present relatively harmonious relationship possible. In one grower's words, "Initially, UFW felt that everyone was against them. Now they are more relaxed and they act like a professional union." This change has also been noted by some arbitrators and government officials.

Representatives of grower organizations are somewhat more cognizant than growers generally of the union's maturation. Some even mentioned that the UFW was beginning to indicate its recognition that the industry's economic well-being was important to the union as well as to growers. However, there are still many complaints that the UFW does not instruct its workers in the meaning of collective bargaining contracts. Work stoppages, rather than recourse to the grievance procedure, have been a problem, as has been maintenance of product quality.

Given their view of the UFW as well as their importance in agriculture, grower organizations could play an important role in easing grower progress toward the accommodation phase. Without outside guidance and reassurance, it may be that every grower will have to go through this learning period by itself, rather than learning from the experiences of others.

Administration of CALRA has influenced grower response to collective bargaining and possibly encouraged accommodation. Although it is often said that legislation does not change attitudes, laws can require behavior to be within acceptable bounds, and legal definitions of what is acceptable paves the way for attitude change.

BARGAINING ISSUES

Hiring halls and union- rather than grower-based seniority have been the most difficult issues in UFW negotiations. UFW contracts require that growers request workers from union-run hiring halls when they are adding to their workforces. There are a number of hiring halls throughout growing areas in California, as well as some in Florida for citrus workers covered by UFW contracts. In general, growers are supposed to provide a two-week preliminary notice, followed by an exact two-day notice, prior to starting time when workers are needed. If the union is unable to supply needed workers through the hiring hall, growers are free to recruit from other sources. In substance, these arrangements are similar to those in other casual industries where hiring halls are used.

However, hiring-hall arrangements have been a major source of contention between the UFW and many growers. For one thing, they make significant structural changes in labor market operations. Prior to collective bargaining, many growers relied heavily on labor contractors to supply seasonal workers. With hiring halls, labor contractors are redundant, and the burden of performing all employer functions is on the growers themselves.

Secondly, many growers have complained about administration of the hiring halls. Referrals are made according to union seniority rather than ranch seniority; thus it is difficult for growers to rehire employees who had worked for them in previous seasons, as well as for family groups to work together. The latter creates transportation problems and some displeasure among workers accustomed to traveling and working in family units. Other problems can be attributed to the inexperience of hiring-hall personnel, as when job orders are processed inadequately, and people are sent out for positions, such as truck driver, for which they are not qualified.

Finally, some growers feel that either the contract language outlining hiring-hall procedures or the hiring-hall concept itself is inadequate. It has been suggested that the required lead-time is unrealistic in agriculture because demand for labor depends on picking conditions that may change rapidly depending on weather. Even among growers who have become accustomed to hiring-hall requirements, there is a recognition that they are not a panacea for all problems inherent in a labor market characterized by rapidly shifting labor demands. As one grower put it, "The hiring hall works fine as long as workers are available. The problems occur when seasonal demands are high and workers are in insufficient supply."

However, even given problems in operating hiring halls, it is an important part of UFW operations. It is a way of protecting the union's security as an institution, for it ensures that available jobs go to union members in good standing. It is also a mechanism for building worker loyalty to the union rather than to growers or labor contractors. As a result, it is a very important and controversial item in negotiations, and it was one of the issues that encouraged growers to sign Teamster contracts that did not contain hiring-hall provisions.

The UFW is aware of past operational problems and is working to improve the way the hiring halls function. However, even though some growers are reluctant to agree to use them, the hiring-hall system remains a high priority bargaining item. However, some contracts have been signed which either do not contain hiring-hall provisions, or which modify hiring-hall arrangements to reflect grower and worker criticism.

Because hiring halls have established a new way for the employment relationship to function, they have changed the structure of the labor markets where they operate. With increases in the number of grower operations covered by collective bargaining contracts, hiring halls will have continuing importance in adding structure to the agricultural labor market.

Neither Local 142 nor Teamster contracts contain hiring-hall provisions. Economic issues have been of major importance to both unions in recent negotiations. Local 142 has been particularly interested in getting cost-of-living escalator clauses written into its contracts, but it has not been successful in achieving this goal.

BARGAINING OUTCOMES

Wages. Because of the range of agricultural operations, there are a variety of wages as well as different payment arrangements at any point in time. Hand-harvesting operations usually are paid for on a piece-rate basis, with a specified hourly minimum. Operations in which productivity is more difficult to measure are more commonly paid for on an hourly basis.

Although both hourly and piece rates are found in most farm-worker contracts, there are some exceptions to this pattern. For example, in Florida citrus prior to collective bargaining, piece rates were determined on a grove-by-grove basis, depending on crop and picking conditions. This method of setting wages developed because of the relatively long picking season for citrus crops, during which many factors, such as yield and weather, change.

This approach serves as a backdrop for the UFW-Coca Cola Company contract, which provides for a minimum hourly wage and a committee of union and management representatives to visit individual groves and negotiate piece rates as frequently as necessary. When the joint committee cannot reach agreement, the picking crews are free to strike.

Both the union and the company recognize some shortcomings in this approach. Because wages are not established in advance, neither the company nor individual workers know what future wage rates will be. As a result, the UFW and the company have experimented with a formula to set piece rates, using a grove's current output as compared to output in a base year as the major wage-determining criterion. All parties were satisfied with this formula, but it had to be dropped, at least temporarily, when a freeze affecting production made formula comparisons impossible. Given the nature of the industry, it is very likely that other innovative arrangements will develop to take into account peculiar crop or regional conditions.

Collective bargaining has already had an impact on wage levels in areas where there has been active unionization. Wages rose particularly rapidly in California during the period of UFW and Teamster rivalry for certification in elections from 1975 through early 1977, when the jurisdictional pact was signed. Whatever wages one union won, the other felt compelled to surpass. Unorganized growers responded by making similar wage increases in order to remain competitive in the labor market. The WCT contractual hourly minimum was $2.95 for July 1976. However, the actual hourly minimum for both unions was $3.45.

In 1966 farm workers had an average annual hourly wage of $1.23. By 1976 it had risen by 116 percent, to $2.66 an hour.[41] The minimum wage for workers covered by WCT and UFW contracts was $3.45 in 1976, a 140 percent increase over $1.40 an hour, the estimated 1966 wages of workers covered by the first UFW contracts prior to the advent of collective bargaining.[42] Because of collective bargaining's impact on wages, many California growers are concerned about the cost of California produce compared to produce from unorganized areas, such as Arizona, Texas, and Colorado.

Other Provisions. Collective bargaining contracts in agriculture are similar to those in most industries in that they specify union security and management rights, wage and effort bargains, individual security, and contract administration. They also include a number of provisions that reflect the industry's special needs and the union's character.

Seasonality is common in agriculture. The UFW handles some problems inherent in a seasonal workforce by making benefit levels contingent on hours worked. In similar fashion, Local 142 contracts divide the workforce into regular, intermittent, and seasonal workers. Regular workers are year-round workers. Intermittent employees remain on the payroll all year as long as they are available for work during seasonal highs and occasional work between seasons. Seasonal workers are employed for only a few days a year during peak demand. A worker's classification affects both benefit levels and his competitive status for

---

[41] U.S. Department of Agriculture, Crop Reporting Board, *Farm Labor* (February 1977), p. 9.

[42] Taylor, p. 120.

layoffs and recalls. Intermittent employees are eligible for regular jobs as they become available. Seasonal workers are less attached to agricultural work and rarely move into ranks of intermittent employees.

The UFW contracts also limit the use of some specific pesticides by making their use a contract violation. Pesticide limitation was originally a very emotional issue for many growers because of its potential for infringement on management rights. However, pesticide clauses have not been a serious problem in contract administration.

UFW and Local 142 contracts provide for unpaid leaves of absence, to allow workers to visit their country or island of origin. In addition, Local 142 permits short leaves, if necessary, to enable parents to travel to see their children's graduations. Both unions also have contract language regulating disposition and condition of grower-provided housing.

Both the UFW and Local 142 honor people historically important to them in their contracts. The UFW's pension plan is named after Juan De La Cruz, a worker shot during a jurisdictional strike. Its medical plan, which it operates out of its own clinics, is named for Robert F. Kennedy, a strong UFW supporter. The Martin Luther King fund, operated by the Farm Workers Service Center, makes expenditures for a variety of educational and charitable purposes. Local 142's contracts honor Jack Hall, its initial organizer, with a paid holiday named for him.

A program called Citizenship Participation Day is found in some UFW contracts. It is a paid holiday, and individual employees can designate wages paid for that day to be used by the UFW for educational purposes. One function of these donations is to support an information and lobbying office in Sacramento.

Current contracts contain no restrictions on mechanization, but this may be an issue in future negotiations. The UFW is also very concerned with child labor, and it too is a potential subject for bargaining. Local 142 already has extensive layoff and severance provisions in its contracts; these may become increasingly important in negotiations if the emerging trend for pineapple production to be shifted from Hawaii to Thailand and the Philippines continues.

CONTRACT ADMINISTRATION

UFW and Teamster contracts generally provide for three-step grievance procedures, while ILWU contracts usually provide for four steps. In each instance, binding arbitration is the final step.

Because of its relatively long-standing bargaining relationships, the ILWU has had more experience with grievances in agriculture than has either the Teamsters or the UFW. Grievance handling is not a major problem in ILWU's relationship with growers, and most grievance cases involve discipline and discharge issues.

Experience with grievances under Teamster and UFW contracts is much less extensive, particularly because very few growers have had ongoing bargaining relationships with the UFW. However, growers with Teamster contracts found the union business-like and concerned primarily with making sure that contract terms were enforced.

In contrast, the UFW directed itself more toward servicing individual workers, and was somewhat less concerned than the Teamsters with specific contract terms. Growers with experience with UFW contracts felt that many grievances were unfounded complaints concerning personal matters rather than questions of contract interpretation. This type of grievance on occasion led to work stoppages that created production problems.

Worker inexperience with collective bargaining and the UFW's emphasis on worker involvement in contract administration provides much of the explanation for the problems that did occur. Many workers had high expectations for collective bargaining and little understanding of what contracts actually meant. In addition, some UFW members preferred direct economic action and work stoppages to filing grievances because they were unconvinced that the grievance procedure would produce fair results. They reasoned that anyone who understood the industry well enough to be an arbitrator would have either a prounion or promanagement bias.

Contract administration was further complicated by supervisors inexperienced with collective bargaining. Many supervisors have trouble adjusting to limitations on their traditional prerogatives when they have to adhere to contract terms and follow fair and orderly discipline procedures. In some instances, their adjustment was further slowed by grower reluctance to accept collective bargaining even after contracts had been signed.

There are some indications that these problems moderate as bargaining relationships mature. As both parties gain experience with collective bargaining, they are better able to work together in resolving difficulties. However, initial adjustment periods seem unavoidable. Mutual acceptance is necessary before harmonious relationships can develop, and such acceptance seems almost impossible to achieve during the early stages of agricultural bargaining relationships.

FUTURE ORGANIZING

Predicting future events is perilous at best, and making meaningful generalizations about future organization of agricultural workers is fraught with difficulty. Many relevant factors are in a state of flux, including union and industry structure, technology, labor force composition, and public policy. Because all of these variables are capable of affecting trends in farm-worker unionization, they complicate prediction problems.

Recent events indicate that the UFW will be the union having the greatest continuing interest in organizing farm workers. Although the 1977 Teamster jurisdictional agreement covers only western states, the unions have informally agreed to its extension to other areas and to aid and assist each other when possible. ILWU's Local 142 is unlikely to become involved in organizing mainland workers, and Hawaiian agricultural workers are almost completely organized.

Given the UFW's emphasis on preparing a strong organizational base from which to launch economic action and its desire to take advantage of the favorable organizing climate provided by the Teamster accord and CALRA, its short-run efforts will be directed at consolidating its successes among California field workers.

As of late 1978, the UFW had negotiated about 125 contracts. This represents less than half of the bargaining units for which it had certified bargaining-agent status. Before organizing efforts are extended, the additional contracts must be negotiated if the UFW is not to lose ground already won. Thus, union officials will have to shift their focus from organizing to administration. However, the UFW does have a philosophic commitment to organize unorganized farm workers. In fact, organizing will probably be necessary in some crops in order to protect unionized workers from competitive pressures on wages from nonunion workers.

The question remains whether or not the UFW will be able to organize successfully in other states. Although competition with other unions should not be a problem, many barriers to organizing encountered in California still exist elsewhere. Employer attitude, labor market structure, and labor force composition will all contribute to making organization in new crops and areas slow and costly.

The fact that workers are organized in California will not be of much help in organizing other states. Thus, for organizing to be successful, the UFW will have to invest large quantities of human and financial resources and to continue to rely on other organizations for support. There is no way of knowing how many resources the UFW will have available for these efforts, and what level of assistance will be forthcoming from other sources. Nor is it clear, even if future organizing is limited, when the UFW will become a self-supporting union.

Organizing efforts most likely will be directed at medium- to large-sized growers of labor-intensive crops. Reliance on boycotts to gain recognition may be necessary, making identifiable growers in crops with elastic demand most vulnerable. Elastic demands are characteristic of many fresh fruits and vegetables, with a few exceptions such as lettuce. Agriculture in Texas, Arizona, and a number of states in the Southeast has many growers fitting this description.

It is interesting to note that the states which are natural targets for organizing are also states in which public attitude and policy are not particularly conducive to collective bargaining in general and farm-worker unionization in particular. Thus, public policy developments at state and federal levels will be a major factor affecting growth in agricultural bargaining. Federal policy is probably essential to future organizing success.

Increasing technology is a very real problem to the UFW. It hopes to reduce government-sponsored research which results in rapid mechanization and to discourage growers from using new technology, because technological change could well reduce both the union's appeal and the number of potential members.[43]

A final question is whether César Chavez will have the same charismatic impact on farm workers in other areas that he has had on California workers. There is no doubt that Chavez's philosophy, his understanding of the forces aligned against farm-worker unionization, and his heroic image have had incalculable importance to UFW success. Some observers think his appeal is basically nationalistic and will be limited to Chicanos living in the Southwest. Others feel that it is universal to agricultural workers. There are some who feel that the UFW's very existence depends on his continued leadership and that, without him, the union will either stagnate or disappear altogether.

It is hard to guess the extent to which Chavez's success will be transferable. Certainly, UFW gains in California enhance possibilities of its message appealing to currently unorganized workers in other areas.

Other labor unions have sprung from efforts of a dedicated person or group of persons. Once established, they have almost always survived leadership change and continued to function. The UFW is becoming firmly established in California. With that as its base, it will undoubtedly move into other areas, but its success in those areas will depend on factors such as financing, public policy, and public support. At most, however, organizing in agriculture will be slow and limited for some time to labor-intensive segments of the industry.

Conclusions

There have been few instances of easy transition from an industry's introduction to unionization to the establishment of stable collective

---

[43] *Guardian*, October 19, 1977, p. 9.

bargaining relationships. Organizing periods are generally volatile, accompanied by a great deal of hostility between employers and unions. Leadership, both union and management, tends to be in the hands of those who are best at battling the opposition. Prerequisites to collective bargaining stability include trained union and employer administrators, employer acceptance of collective bargaining, union concern with the industry's economic viability, and development of mutual trust. An important related factor is competent and rapid grievance handling in order to reduce the incidence of work stoppages.

During the next decade, agricultural labor relations will be characterized by continued organizing and the transition from organizing to orderly collective bargaining relationships. Because of ongoing organization and large numbers of individual growers, the transition to collective bargaining stability will be slower than in more concentrated industries. However, there are indications that the transition is under way. Increasing numbers of growers are reaching the accommodation stage of response to collective bargaining; experienced union and grower administrators are emerging; reliance on the grievance procedure is increasing; and there are some relatively cooperative union-employer relationships. CALRA has been an important factor encouraging transition. Experience with it indicates the importance of future policy design to the evolution of collective bargaining in agriculture.

List of References

Chambers, Clarke A. *California Farm Organization.* Berkeley and Los Angeles: University of California Press, 1952.

Frisbee, Parker. "Illegal Migration from Mexico to the United States: A Longitudinal Analysis." *International Migration Review* 1 (Spring 1975).

Fuller, Varden, and Bert Mason. "Farm Labor." *Annals of the American Academy of Political and Social Science* 429 (January 1977).

Glass, Judith Chanin. "Organization in Salinas." *Monthly Labor Review* (June 1968).

Grodin, Joseph R. "California Agricultural Labor Act: Early Experience." *Industrial Relations* 15 (October 1976).

Hartmire, Chris. "UFW Update." *Fellowship* 44 (September 1978).

Jamieson, Stuart. *Labor Unionism in American Agriculture.* Bulletin No. 836. Washington: U.S. Department of Labor, Bureau of Labor Statistics, 1945.

Jenkins, Craig J., and Charles Perrow. "Insurgency of the Powerless: Farm Worker Movements (1946–1972)." *American Sociological Review* 42 (April 1977).

Meister, Dick, and Anne Loftis. *A Long Time Coming.* New York: Macmillan Co., 1977.

Rowe, Gene, and Leslie Whitener Smith. *The Hired Farm Working Force of 1975.* Agricultural Economic Report No. 405. Washington: U.S. Department of Agriculture, Economic Research Service, July 1978.

Suits, Daniel B. "Agriculture." In *The Structure of American Industry,* ed. Walter Adams. New York: Macmillan Co., 1977.

Taylor, Ronald B. *Chavez and the Farm Workers.* Boston: Beacon Press, 1975.

CHAPTER 7

Airlines

MARK L. KAHN
Wayne State University

The dynamic and unstable airline industry, always the object of substantial government support and concern but also of intensive economic and safety regulation, has provided an environment for collective bargaining beset by many difficulties. Originally a public enterprise—it was inaugurated in May 1918 by the Post Office to accelerate mail delivery—scheduled air transportation was first turned over to private firms, as Post Office contractors, under terms established in the Air Mail Act of 1925 (Kelly Act). Scheduled passenger transportation began the following year for a total of 1.3 million passenger-miles in 1926, about 6,000 passengers averaging just over 200 miles per trip. It was another ten years before the number of passengers exceeded one million, as compared with 240 million passengers enplaned in 1977. The remarkable growth of commercial air transportation in the United States since 1936, at least until 1970, is illustrated by the data in Table 1.

Passenger traffic rapidly became the primary focus of airline activity,

TABLE 1

Traffic and Employment on U.S. Certificated Air Carriers
(Selected Years—Domestic and International Service)

Year	Passenger Miles (billions)	Freight & Express	U.S. Mail	Aircraft Miles (millions)	Employment (December)
		(millions of ton-miles)			
1936	0.4	1.9[a]	5.7[a]	74	9,995
1946	7.0	53.7	41.1	369	97,191
1956	27.6	633.9	160.4	869	143,514
1966	79.9	3,048.4	774.9	1,482	244,028
1969	125.4	4,437.2	1,566.1	2,385	311,922
1970	131.7	3,514.0	1,470.1	2,418	297,374
1976	179.0	5,096.2	1,114.2	2,320	303,006
1977	193.2	5,426.5	1,147.3	2,419	308,068

Sources: Civil Aeronautics Board, *Handbook of Airline Statistics*, 1973 Edition, Part II, Tables 15, 27, 40, 49, and 55. The 1976 and 1977 data are from Air Transport Association of America, *Air Transport 1978*, pp. 12 and 33.

[a] Domestic only; international not available.

315

and remains so at present. During 1977, 82 percent of airline industry revenues were derived from regular passenger travel. Within the United States, the airlines aggressively displaced other common carriers of intercity passengers (railroads and buses): the airlines' share rose from 11.4 percent in 1949 to 43.6 percent in 1959, 61.8 percent in 1966, and 81.3 percent in 1977. In overseas travel, the ocean liner has been largely displaced by the airplane, with the air share, which passed the halfway mark in 1950, exceeding 93 percent in 1976 of all travel between the United States and other countries. U.S. air carriers provided just over half of this overseas passenger traffic. On the other hand, the market for air cargo, although expanding, remains highly specialized: in 1976, less than two-tenths of 1 percent of all U.S. intercity freight traffic was moved by air.[1]

The form and substance of collective bargaining in this dynamic industry derived from and today reflect its technology and its economics. Government, through specialized statutes and agencies, has impacted substantially on airline labor-management relations. Industry structure and pricing are dictated by the Civil Aeronautics Board (CAB). Safety regulations are designed and enforced by the Federal Aviation Administration (FAA). Accidents are investigated and their causes determined by the National Transportation Safety Board (NTSB). Labor relations are within the jurisdiction of the Railway Labor Act, under which the National Mediation Board (NMB) deals with representation issues and dispute settlement.

As essential background, we look first at the combination of public promotion and regulation under which air transportation has developed, the relevant economic and technological characteristics of the industry, and the kind of labor force it requires. We then examine the evolution and present state of public policy and regulation in regard to airline labor relations, a unique story in itself. Against this backdrop, the chapter reviews the growth and structure of union and management organization for collective bargaining, bargaining procedures and their substantive results, and the influence of the Railway Labor Act's dispute-settlement procedures. The chapter concludes with a discussion of some current issues and the policy conclusions derived from this body of collective bargaining experience.

---

[1] Historical data through 1972 appear in Civil Aeronautics Board (CAB), *Handbook of Airline Statistics*, 1973 ed. (Washington: March 1974), Part II, Tables 1-94. Recent airline data, derived from carrier "Form 41" reports to the CAB, are available in Air Transport Association of America (ATA), *Air Transport 1977* (Washington: ATA, 1977).

Public Policy: Support and Control[2]

Airline growth and flight safety are closely interrelated. Although the 1925 Kelly Act authorized the Postmaster General to contract with private firms for the transportation of air mail, little interest was displayed by private capital because of the obvious hazards of such ventures. Congress's appreciation of this concern led to the Air Commerce Act of 1926, which directed the Secretary of Commerce to establish lighted civil airways and air traffic regulations, and to certificate as "safe" both the pilots and the aircraft flying in interstate commerce. With this reassurance, the Post Office was able in 1927 to obtain bids from private contractors and thus establish the first private transcontinental air mail route. Air mail proved to be a popular novelty with the public, but mounting Post Office deficits and economic difficulties experienced by many carriers (including some who had undertaken passenger transportation without government support) led Congress to believe that the Postmaster General required more authority and discretion if the development of air transportation were to be promoted by means of air mail pay. Accordingly, the 1930 Watres Act authorized him to pay carriers for air mail transportation by space reserved instead of weight flown, to change contract rates, to revise routes in "the public interest" without competitive bids, and to adjust air mail operations in light of "advances in the art of flying and passenger transportation."

Postmaster General Brown implemented the Watres Act with vigor, but his Democratic successor, James Farley, charged fraud and collusion between the air mail carriers and the previous Post Office administration. Farley canceled all air mail contracts on February 9, 1934, and a presidential Executive Order directed the Army to take on the task. The Army's service, although abridged and less reliable, proved to be three times as costly per plane-mile. The hastily enacted Air Mail Act of 1934 tried a new approach. Now it would be the Interstate Commerce Commission (ICC) that would determine the rates to be paid by the Post Office for air mail on each route, although the Postmaster General would continue to let the contracts. The Act also barred airline companies from certain kinds of interlocking relationships and from the manufacture of aircraft, and contained provisions, which will be described later, designed to promote the economic welfare of pilots and other airline employees.

Improved aircraft—notably, the inauguration of the DC-3 in 1936—and moderate economic recovery encouraged strong growth in the airline market. There were problems, however:

[2] Kahn, "Collective Bargaining . . . ," esp. pp. 428–36. [The complete citations for all footnote references are listed at the end of the chapter.]

Divided responsibility for air transportation produced considerable friction between the Post Office and the ICC, especially when revenue from passenger travel displaced air mail payments as the major source of carrier income. Bidding for new routes became a scramble for *anticipated* passenger traffic, and thus became increasingly unrelated to costs. This process reached a climax when Eastern Air Lines bid zero cents per mile in June, 1938, for the mail contract on the Houston-San Antonio route.[3]

There was a national consensus that unified economic and safety regulation had become imperative, with the only major question being whether the airlines would be placed under ICC jurisdiction or assigned to a new independent federal agency.

The Civil Aeronautics Act, enacted on June 23, 1938, established the pattern of public regulation that remained essentially unchanged for 40 years. As modified pursuant to an executive reorganization plan effective June 20, 1940, a new regulatory commission, the Civil Aeronautics Board (CAB), was granted wide-ranging authority over air transportation. Competitive bidding was abolished. Instead, the CAB was now to determine route structure by issuing certificates "of public convenience and necessity." Subsidization, completely at the CAB's discretion, was to be accomplished by way of air mail rates, established separately for each carrier, on any basis preferred by the CAB. As its guide, the CAB was directed to consider:

. . . the need of each such air carrier for compensation for the transportation of mail sufficient to insure the performance of such service and, together with all other revenue of the air carrier, to enable such carrier under honest, economical and efficient management, to maintain and continue the development of air transportation to the extent and of the character and quality required for the commerce of the United States, the Postal Service, and the national defense.[4]

The CAB could and usually did alter each carrier's initially established air mail rate on a retroactive basis in order to ensure the fulfillment of its conception of these objectives. The CAB was also empowered to regulate fares, to control and monitor all interairline agreements and mergers, to promote air safety and national defense by formulating appropriate Civil Air Regulations, and to handle aircraft accident investigation. A new agency, the Civil Aeronautics Administration (CAA), became responsible for maintenance of the airways, implementation of the safety regulations established by the CAB, and subsequently (under the Federal Airport Act of 1946) for airport development.

[3] *Ibid.*, p. 431. See Ballard, p. 251.
[4] Civil Aeronautics Act, Sec. 406(b).

Although many particular decisions of the CAB were unavoidably controversial, the regulatory framework established in 1938 gained general public acceptance as it facilitated substantial airline growth along with a good safety record. The next major legislative action did not take place for 20 years, prompted by Congress's concern for the safety of aviation as a whole. By 1958, more than half of the activity at the 128 CAA-operated control towers, located at the nation's busiest airports, was associated not with the airlines but with general aviation.[5] Under the Federal Aviation Act of 1958, the CAA was renamed the Federal Aviation Agency (FAA). The making of safety rules (the Federal Aviation Regulations or "FARs") was shifted from the CAB to the FAA, thus consolidating the formulation and implementation of safety regulation for all categories of flying: airline, military, and general. The CAB retained all of the powers and duties it had exercised under the 1938 Act in regard to economic regulation and accident investigation.

On October 15, 1966, Public Law 89-670 created a new federal Department of Transportation (DOT). The FAA was renamed the Federal Aviation Administration, thus leaving its initials unaltered. Aircraft accident investigation was taken from the CAB and assigned to a new National Transportation Safety Board (NTSB) with jurisdiction over all interstate common-carrier accidents. The CAB's economic role was unaffected and so remained essentially the same as in 1938.

We will see, in the next section, how the politics of the CAB shaped the structure and operation of the airline industry. Although the CAB has been credited with facilitating the rapid growth of an effective and safe system of air transportation, it was subjected to increasing criticism beginning in the early 1960s (see below, pp. 334-38), based on charges that CAB policies were excessively anticompetitive and detrimental to consumer interests. Considerable bipartisan support developed in the 1970s for new legislation that would promote freedom of entry and price competition, a view that was endorsed by President Carter and his activist 1977 appointee to the CAB chairmanship, Alfred Kahn (no relation to the author).

On October 24, 1978, President Carter signed into law the Airline Deregulation Act of 1978. This is a complex 52-page law, characterized by the House-Senate Conference Committee as "new, comprehensive legislation, which entirely overhauls the aviation regulatory system." [6] The major provisions of this 1978 Act, especially as they appear to affect

[5] Federal Aviation Agency, *FAA Statistical Handbook of Aviation*, 1967 ed., ch. V, "General Aviation."

[6] Conference Report, "Airline Deregulation Act of 1978" [to accompany S. 2493], House of Representatives, 95th Congress, 2d Session, Report No. 95-1779, October 12, 1978, p. 56.

the collective bargaining context, will be summarized later. It is already clear, in any event, that the industry has entered a period of intense congressionally-mandated competition that will inevitably be an unsettling factor in airline union-management relations. The 1978 Act even contains "sunset" provisions under which the CAB itself will be phased out by 1985 unless Congress should change its mind prior to then.

Technology and Economics

INDUSTRY STRUCTURE[7]

The CAB, upon its creation in 1938, certificated 24 carriers in accordance with the "grandfather" clause of Section 401(a) of the Civil Aeronautics Act, under which any airline then operating on a regular basis was entitled to automatic certification. No other company has since been permitted to enter the industry as a trunk line. Twelve mergers and one abandonment reduced the number of trunks to 11 as of August 1, 1972, when Northeast was absorbed by Delta. These trunk lines furnished, during 1976, 82.5 percent of the revenue ton-miles (passengers and cargo) and 92.5 percent of the revenue passenger miles of the scheduled industry. The trunks' share of total 1976 scheduled industry operating revenue was 86.8 percent. Table 2 provides some illustrative 1976 data for each of the trunk airlines.

Ten of the 11 trunk lines—all except United, an exclusively domestic carrier—fly on both domestic and "international and territorial" routes. The data in Table 2 cover each trunk carrier's total (i.e., "system") operations. During 1976, 21.8 percent of trunk carrier revenues came from "international and territorial" operations. The trunk airlines, while certificated for scheduled service, also provide charter service. During 1976, 6.2 percent of their revenue ton-miles (passenger and cargo) were on a nonscheduled basis.

Local service carriers, originally called "feeders," were first authorized by the CAB in 1946 in order to determine, on an experimental basis, the kind of scheduled service they could provide to communities not served by trunks. Temporary certificates of convenience and necessity were granted to 23 companies. Thirteen managed to survive beyond January 1, 1953, and were granted permanent route certificates under Public Law 38, approved May 19, 1955. Subsequent mergers eliminated five of these carriers by April 12, 1972, when Mohawk was absorbed by Allegheny. On January 25, 1975, however, the CAB certificated Air New England as a local service carrier, raising their number to nine. Table 2 provides their names and some illustrative data. Local service carriers

---

[7] Kahn, "Collective Bargaining . . . ," pp. 436–41; ATA, *Air Transport 1977.*

TABLE 2
U.S. Air Carriers: Selected Data, 1976

	Revenue Passenger Miles (Millions)	Operating Revenue ($ millions)	Number of Employees (4th Qu.)
Trunk Lines (System Operation)			
United	32,392	2,633	49,849
American	24,613	2,094	36,080
Trans World	24,221	2,039	35,396
Pan Am	20,063	1,731	26,793
Eastern	19,520	1,825	34,684
Delta	17,930	1,629	29,091
Northwest	11,272	971	11,208
Western	7,834	605	10,221
Braniff	7,170	675	10,636
Continental	6,296	552	9,608
National	5,271	439	7,571
	176,572	15,193	260,137
Local Service Carriers			
Allegheny	3,610	439	7,794
Air West	1,702	211	4,004
Frontier	1,680	204	3,838
Ozark	1,184	164	3,177
North Central	1,179	191	3,587
Piedmont	1,178	155	3,146
Southern	1,125	140	2,787
Texas International	1,009	126	2,317
Air New England	53	15	423
	12,720	1,645	31,073

Source: CAB Form 41, as computed by Air Line Pilots Association, Research Department, *Trunk and Local Service Carrier, Financial and Traffic Rankings*, Calendar Year 1976 (Washington: 1977), processed.

collected, during 1976, 9.3 percent of total scheduled industry operating revenues.

The remaining 3.9 percent of scheduled industry operating revenues was distributed among the following airline categories: two intra-Hawaiian (Aloha and Hawaiian), five intra-Alaskan (Alaska, Kodiak-W. Alaska, Munz Northwestern, Reeve Aleutian, and Wien Air Alaska), three all-cargo carriers (Airlift International, Flying Tiger, and Seaboard World), and three helicopter companies providing local service (in, respectively, the New York, Chicago, and San Francisco-Oakland areas).

In addition to the scheduled industry, there is one category of certificated nonscheduled carrier: the supplemental. These airlines operate large aircraft on long-distance trips. On July 10, 1962, Public Law 87-528 authorized the CAB to grant certificates for such supplemental transportation, primarily on a charter basis. The operating revenue obtained by the eight supplemental carriers which operated during 1976 was 2.5 percent of scheduled industry operating revenues.

Finally, there are two categories of scheduled service not subject to economic regulation by the CAB (although they must, of course, meet FAA safety requirements). Scheduled carriers functioning exclusively within a single state (e.g., Pacific Southwest in California, Texas Southern in Texas) are subject to economic regulation only by that state. Commuter air carriers—air-taxi operators that offer regular scheduled passenger and/or mail transportation—are not subject to economic regulation provided their aircraft do not exceed 12,500 pounds maximum gross take-off weight. An estimated 5.5 million passengers were enplaned during 1975 by commuter carriers in the U.S. and Puerto Rico.[8] Unless otherwise noted, data on the "scheduled industry" or the "certificated industry" (scheduled plus supplemental) do not include the intrastate or commuter airlines.

This chapter will focus on the collective bargaining experience of the trunk lines, although pertinent incidents or examples at other carriers will be cited. The trunk lines not only provide the bulk of air transportation, but have historically been the locus of pattern-setting developments in union-management relations.

TECHNOLOGY AND THE MARKET[9]

The rapid growth of the airline market depicted in Table 1 was the result of a combination of factors, all related to an aggressive and intensive use of progressive technology: continuing improvements in speed, reliability, comfort, and safety, and declining "real" air fares. The demand for air transportation has been highly responsive to increases in disposable national income, to changes in air fares, and to the relative costs of other transport media.

It has been the policy of the CAB to certify at least two carriers, and up to as many as five, on each trunk line domestic route. Foreign-flag air carriers provide aggressive competition on international routes and, under CAB policies, are getting direct access to more U.S. cities (including Atlanta, Houston, Los Angeles, Miami, and San Francisco). Charter flights operated by the supplemental carriers compete with scheduled and charter flights by the trunks. The commuter lines provide alternatives on some trunk and local service routes. The nonair means of transportation—passenger cars, buses, trucks, railroads, and shipping —offer alternatives to passengers and to shippers of cargo. Hence, each carrier in fact views its market as highly competitive, in spite of the restrictions on entry imposed by the CAB and the declining number of

[8] *Aviation Daily* (Washington: Ziff-Davis Publishing Company, Inc.), May 25, 1977, p. 142: "Study Says Commuter Passengers Will Reach 14 Million by 1988."

[9] Kahn, "Collective Bargaining . . . ," pp. 441-51, provides a more extensive discussion of this topic.

trunk and local service carriers. Moreover, the 17 mergers and one abandonment among the trunks and local service lines were all associated with severe economic difficulties.

Another CAB policy has been to enforce uniformity of price for any given class of service on each route. Price uniformity has been attained on international routes through negotiations under the aegis of the International Air Transport Association (IATA). Intercarrier competition has therefore been compelled to emphasize nonprice features, such as the availability and quality of meals, the efficiency and charm of in-flight service, en route music, motion pictures on long hops, and schedule frequency and convenience. Each carrier has also been concerned about its reputation for reliability and seeks to minimize weather, traffic, and mechanical delays. Nonflight services and facilities are also part of the competitive picture: information, reservation and ticketing arrangements, accessibility of airports, and the quality and adequacy of terminal facilities.[10]

The single most important means of nonprice competition, however, has been the airplane itself. Each airline soon realized that the surest way to acquire a larger share of the traffic on any given route was to deploy a better aircraft than its rivals. As the CAB explained it to a congressional committee in 1957:

> The history of equipment [i.e., aircraft] purchases leaves little doubt that the stimulus of competition has been in the forefront of the factors influencing airline management in its constant search for new equipment. Thus, new equipment has traditionally been placed into operation on the most competitive segments; and the introduction by one company on such a route has been followed by a scramble on the part of competitors to introduce with the greatest possible speed comparable or more advanced types. . . . What might be termed "luxury" equipment has been introduced at times and under conditions

---

[10] But see Kahn, "Collective Bargaining . . . ," p. 442: "Not all of these factors are the direct and exclusive function of the air carriers. Weather and traffic delays are problems that are in part the responsibility of government-sponsored facilities for air traffic control and for landing capabilities under adverse weather conditions. Airport location, construction and operation, and transportation between airports and city centers, are primarily state and local government decisions, with considerable federal financial aid available. Airport user charges paid by airlines cover only a portion of total airport costs. But terminal facilities for handling passengers and cargo are investments that must be undertaken by the airlines themselves. . . ." The airline industry, despite competition among carriers for large market shares, has also cooperated effectively, through agreements approved by the CAB, to facilitate public access to information and reservations on a uniform industrywide basis. See Paul R. Ignatius, President, ATA, Statement before the Subcommittee on Aviation of the Committee on Commerce, Science and Transportation, U.S. Senate, on S. 292 and S. 689, April 7, 1977. Such cooperative activity has contributed to the ability of the airlines to wrest a larger market share from other transport media.

that virtually precluded a conclusion that economic considerations other than competitive ones warranted or prompted the action.[11]

Older models, prior to being sold, would be retained on the least competitive segments.

Four major rounds of aircraft innovation swept through the industry.[12] The first was epitomized by and consisted primarily of the Douglas DC-3, a well-designed and highly efficient propeller plane with two piston engines, introduced in 1936. Capable of carrying from 21 to 27 passengers up to 1,685 miles at a cruise speed of 188 miles per hour, the DC-3 dominated the airways until after World War II. Round 2 witnessed the activation and dominance, starting in the late 1940s and lasting throughout the 1950s, of much larger and faster propeller aircraft with four piston engines. One important example was the DC-6, activated in 1947, that could carry 58 passengers up to 2,520 miles at a cruise speed of 300 miles per hour.

Round 3 involved the industry's swift conversion from piston to turbojet propulsion. The Boeing 707-120, introduced on October 26, 1958, by Pan American, carried about 120 passengers (more or less, depending upon configuration) at a cruise speed of about 570 miles per hour for distances up to about 2,500 miles. The Douglas DC-8 had its debut on September 18, 1959. Similar to the B-707, the DC-8 carried about 122 passengers at 530 miles per hour up to 3,680 miles. Each of these long-range jets was powered by four turbojet engines. A smaller and highly successful three-engine turbojet, the Boeing 727, appeared in 1963. More economical for shorter route segments, the B-727 carried 96 passengers at a cruise speed of 555 miles per hour.

Round 4, which is not yet completed, began in 1970 with the wide-bodied and huge Boeing 747. Cruising at 600 miles per hour, the B-747

[11] U.S. Congress, Committee on the Judiciary, Antitrust Subcommittee, *The Airlines Industry*, 85th Congress, 1st Session (1957), pp. 788–89.

[12] CAB, *Handbook . . . 1973*, Part VIII, Item 5, pp. 546–54 "Introduction of New Aircraft Types into U.S. Airline Service, 1914–1972," provides brief descriptions of 128 aircraft types and modifications, but with this caveat:

Note: This item . . . has been difficult to compile. Literally dozens of sources have been consulted, but multiplicity of sources often produced a multiplicity of answers to the same question. Part of the difficulty lies in the fact that any given plane model could and did vary as customer specifications varied. Thus, for a given model, engines can vary as to manufacturer and power, and power ratings seem to be in constant flux; number of seats can differ astonishingly; "normal cruising speed" is a most ticklish item to nail down; "range" is even more difficult; "cargo capacity" is often just not obtainable; "price", understandably, varies with quantities purchased, and even more with date of purchase; and "date of first introduction into airline service" makes one wonder if accurate history can ever be written. . . .

can carry up to 450 passengers for 6,000 miles. It is 231 feet long (86 more than the B-707). In its all-cargo version, the B-747 carries up to 127 tons of freight. Ninety-nine were in use (and 12 on order) at the end of 1977. Two other somewhat smaller widebodied models appeared in 1971, the McDonnell Douglas DC-10 and the Lockheed L-1011. Each is about 180 feet long and has a maximum passenger capacity of 345. One hundred and ninety-nine were in use by the end of 1977, and 20 more were then on order.

A rough indication of the technological impact of these successive waves of aircraft technology is furnished by the changes in payload (ton-miles per hour), which was 396 for the DC-3. The DC-6 had five times the DC-3's payload, while the DC-8's payload was almost five times that of the DC-6. Although a "stretched" DC-8-61 (1966) was good for double the payload of the original DC-8, the DC-8-61 was "redoubled" by the B-747, with its payload of 37,500 ton-miles per hour.[13]

Of course, it is a fair generalization that larger aircraft are most economical on longer trips. Accompanying the major changes described above, a variety of aircraft types suited to shorter trip-lengths have been activated. These have included twin-engine piston propeller planes larger and faster than the DC-3, notably the Martin 202 (1947) and 404 (1951), and the Convair 240 (1948), 340 (1952), and 440 (1956); a number of twin-engine jets equipped with propellers (prop-jets), including the Viscount (1955), the Fairchild F-27 (1958), and the Convair 540 (1959); and medium-range twin-engine turbojets, particularly the DC-9 (1965) and the B-737 (1967).

Each successful basic jet transport aircraft type subsequently appeared in versions offering desirable combinations of improved capacity and/or range, utilizing more powerful engines. The original DC-9, for example, was 104.4 feet long and carried 80 passengers. Later models, essentially the same except for fuselage extensions and engines with greater thrust, provided increased capacity as follows: 1967—105 passengers (119.3 feet long), 1968—115 passengers (125.6 feet long), 1975—135 passengers (133.5 feet long), and 1980 (projected)—155 passengers (147.8 feet long).[14]

The pace of the displacement of piston propulsion among the certificated carriers was remarkable. In terms of passenger-miles flown, the jet percentage increased from 5.1 percent in 1959 to 73.3 in 1961, 82.6 in 1963, 94.7 in 1966, and 99.8 percent in 1969 (fourth-quarter data). As

[13] Kahn, "Collective Bargaining. . . ," p. 445.
[14] "A Revamped Jet Confounds the Plane Makers," *Business Week*, November 14, 1977, pp. 95–96.

of the end of 1977, the scheduled airlines had a total of 2,226 aircraft in service: 2,030 pure jets (including 298 widebody), 168 turboprops, and 28 piston. Three helicopters (turbine-powered Sikorsky S-61s) were also in use for scheduled service.[15] The employment impact of these changes in airline technology along with airline market growth are to be considered later.

Costs and Profits

From 1938 until 1955, the CAB used its mail-rate authority to assure each carrier a reasonable rate of return. The fraction of total revenue supplied by this direct subsidy (over and above an appropriate service rate for transporting mail) was significant, declining from a high of 22.7 percent in 1938 to 6.9 percent in 1945 and moving unevenly from 1946 through 1954 between 7.1 percent (in 1948) and 3.1 percent.[16] As this writer has previously commented:

> It is essential, for our purposes, to recognize that such a virtual guarantee of an adequate return on investment encouraged airline managements, until after 1954, to attach a low priority to immediate or short-term cost considerations. When arguing vigorously for new route certificates, making decisions about new aircraft acquisitions, or bargaining collectively with labor organizations, the effects on pre-subsidy profits were not, within a reasonable range, a major decision criterion as long as the CAB stood by to bail each carrier out.[17]

The relationship of subsidy adjustments to losses caused by strikes will be taken up below. In any event, the major carriers have received only a service rate for air mail since 1955. Local service carriers continued to draw substantial subsidy support, but only on a uniform "class rate" since 1961. Caves has observed:

> From 1951 on, as more and more trunklines went off subsidy, their behavior in seeking route extensions was confined to entry into currently and potentially profitable markets of dense traffic or long hauls. At the same time, they began an elaborate process of sloughing off money-losing cities and segments. By one count, trunk service has been replaced by local-service airlines in ninety-four cities. . . .[18]

---

[15] CAB, *Handbook . . . 1973*, p. 444 (Table 10e); also, 1967 edition, p. 412; ATA, *Air Transport 1978*, p. 26. The major features of U.S. commercial transport aircraft in use today are summarized in *Aviation Week & Space Technology* 106 (March 21, 1977), p. 95. This listing contains 53 passenger and 16 cargo aircraft types, including (for example) seven variations of the B-747.

[16] Caves, p. 413.

[17] Kahn, "Collective Bargaining . . . ," p. 453.

[18] Caves, p. 328.

A similar concern for costs was encouraged in other areas of decision-making by the removal of the trunks from air mail rate subsidization.

Rates of return on investment (equity plus debt), or "ROI," have fluctuated greatly since 1954. These swings have been partly a response to the impact of national economic conditions on passenger and cargo load factors (i.e., the percent of seat-mile and ton-mile capacity flown that is actually utilized). Their amplitudes have been magnified, however, by the duration of each reequipment cycle to which the industry committed itself at a prosperous (high load factor) time but which extended into a period of cyclical contraction. Since 1965, for example, the scheduled industry's ROI declined rather steadily from a 1965 high of 12.0 percent to a 1970 low of 1.2 percent, crawled back up to 6.4 percent in 1974, fell to 2.5 percent in 1975, and rebounded to 8.0 percent in 1976 and 10.9 percent in 1977.[19] Since long-term debt exceeds stockholder equity, and interest obligations have priority, equity rates of return swing even more precipitously.

The year 1970, characterized by ATA as having given the airlines "the worst financial results in their history," [20] involved the simultaneous appearance of a major economic recession (with passenger traffic actually declining after July 1970) and the beginning of "Round 4" of reequipment; not only were 78 enormous B-747s activated in 1970, but 26 new "stretched" B-727s came into service. No general fare increases were authorized by the CAB in 1970, while unit costs rose 9 percent (including, according to ATA, a 15 percent increase in average wages).

A significant characteristic of the airlines' profitability situation is that there has consistently been a huge variation in ROI among the carriers at any given time as well as from year to year. Table 3 shows, for each trunk airline, the ROI and the return on equity capital for 1975 and 1976. The extreme variability is self-evident. There also exists a wide range in the ratio of debt to equity: from 0.18 (Northwest) to 2.34 (Trans World) in 1976. And operating profit as a percent of total revenue varied in 1976, among the trunks alone, from 10.6 (Northwest) to 0.8 (National).[21]

---

[19] ATA, *Air Transport 1970* and *Air Transport 1978*. These are ATA "actual corporate ROI" figures, which run smaller than the CAB's calculations because of certain expenses disallowed by the CAB. See ATA, *The Sixty Billion Dollar Question*, p. 6; CAB, *Supplement to the Handbook of Airline Statistics* (Washington: November 1975), Pt. VI, Table 4, "Explanation of Corporate Rate of Return Elements," p. 111.

[20] ATA, *Air Transport* 1971, p. 6.

[21] Air Line Pilots Association (ALPA), Research Department, *Trunk and Local Service Carrier Financial and Traffic Rankings*, Calendar Year 1976 (Washington: ALPA, 1977, processed), p. 6. Computed from CAB Form 41 data.

TABLE 3

Return on Investment and Return on Equity Capital, Trunklines, 1975 and 1976

Trunk Carrier (System)	Overall Return on Investment (ROI)				Return on Equity			
	1976	Rank	1975	Rank	1976	Rank	1975	Rank
Pan Am	13.6[a]	1	0.0	10	32.1[a]	1	−19.8	10
Delta	12.2	2	7.9	3	15.7	2	7.7	3
Braniff	10.9	3	9.8	1	15.4	3	13.4	1
Western	9.5	4	7.9	2	12.1	5	9.1	2
Eastern	9.0	5	0.1	9	14.4	4	−16.2	9
Northwest	7.9	6	7.4	4	8.1	8	7.2	4
American	7.6	7	0.5	8	9.8	7	−3.8	7
Trans World	7.6	8	−1.7	11	10.8	6	−24.0	11
Continental	7.0	9	4.2	6	6.1	9	6.3	8
United	4.1	10	2.3	7	3.4	10	−0.7	6
National	4.1	11	7.3	5	1.8	11	5.5	5

Source: Air Line Pilots Association (ALPA), Research Department, Trunk and Local Service Carrier Financial and Traffic Rankings, Calendar Year 1976 (Washington: ALPA, 1977), p. 6.

[a] A 1976 restructuring of debt increased Pan Am's 1976 income by $102.9 million. Excluding this adjustment, Pan Am's 1976 ROI would have been 4.0 percent (11th ranked) and its return on equity would have been −2.4 percent (11th ranked).

The various airlines also differ substantially in their operational characteristics: route structure (especially, long vs. short haul), composition (and age) of the aircraft fleet, extent of competition (route by route), and many less tangible elements, such as management effectiveness. Longer flights, for example, have (other things equal) lower seat-mile costs. Table 4 presents some of the substantial operational differences among the trunks in 1976.

The major capital investments of the air carriers have been in their aircraft, which constitute (after depreciation) about half of the industry's assets. Given the substantial growth of the industry, it has had to raise enormous sums of capital. For example, the airlines' assets rose from $2.8 billion in 1959 to $9.3 billion in 1967 and $16.9 billion in 1977. The value of flight equipment (after reserves for depreciation and airworthiness) was, respectively, $1.5 billion, $5.2 billion, and (in 1976) $8.2 billion.[22]

The airline industry and its supporters, including the aircraft manufacturers, have been expressing much concern that the ROI—consistently far below the 12 percent ROI considered reasonable by the CAB —will not enable the carriers to meet their substantial equipment needs as anticipated between now and 1989. The ATA estimate is that from 1976 through 1989, the airlines will require $65 billion to meet their capital needs, of which all but $5 billion will be needed during the 1980s.[23] The Air Line Pilots Association (ALPA) concurs, predicting that the trunks alone will have to spend $59 billion on aircraft, for both replacement and growth, through 1989, or 2,233 aircraft.[24] Boeing sees the need for a capital cost approaching $50 billion by 1986, and observes:

> The air transport industry simply cannot attract this much capital under present conditions. The Civil Aeronautics Board has found that a 12% rate of return on investment "should be sufficient to compensate the carriers for their costs of capital, provide the equity owners with returns comparable to returns on investments in enterprises having comparable risks, and enable the carriers to maintain their credit and to attract capital." However, as previously shown, the U.S. air transport industry hasn't come close to this performance in a decade and in the last seven years the industry fell five billion dollars short of earning a full return.[25]

[22] ATA, *Air Transport 1970* and *Air Transport 1978*.
[23] ATA, *The Sixty Billion Dollar Question*, p. 2.
[24] ALPA, *Presidents' Report 1976* (undated), Tables 3 and 4, pp. 16–17.
[25] Boeing Commercial Airplane Company, p. 62.

COLLECTIVE BARGAINING

TABLE 4

Trunk Carriers (System), Selected Operating Characteristics, 1976

Trunk Carrier (System)	Average Stage (Flt.) Length (miles)	Rank	Average Daily Aircraft Utilization (hours)	Rank	Average Daily Departures per Aircraft	Rank	Average "Block to Block" Time (hours)	Rank
American	787	3	9.0	7	4.4	7	2.0	3
Braniff	549	8	9.7	2	6.5	3	1.5	7
Continental	566	7	10.0	1	6.8	2	1.5	8
Delta	444	11	9.3	3	7.2	1	1.3	11
Eastern	518	10	9.1	5	6.1	5	1.5	9
National	526	9	9.0	9	6.2	4	1.5	10
Northwest	651	5	7.5	10	4.2	8	1.8	5
Pan Am	1,470	1	9.2	4	2.7	11	3.4	1
Trans World	921	2	8.2	8	3.6	10	2.3	2
United	672	4	7.2	11	4.0	9	1.8	4
Western	613	6	9.0	6	5.8	6	1.6	6

Source: Air Line Pilots Association (ALPA), Research Department, *Trunk and Local Service Carrier Financial and Traffic Rankings, Calendar Year 1976* (Washington: ALPA, 1977), pp. 24, 26, 28.

PRODUCTIVITY AND EMPLOYMENT[26]

In an industry experiencing high rates of innovation and substantial growth in capital per employee, employment naturally depends upon the relationship between changes in productivity (output per manhour or per employee) and changes in output. Airline productivity studies have generally used revenue ton-miles (RTM) as the measure of output, assuming that the average passenger with luggage weighs 200 pounds, and have counted labor input in terms of employees because suitable information on hours worked has not been available for flight personnel.

An aircraft delivers seat-miles and cargo space, which can be measured together as "available" ton-miles. The load factor determines the relationship between "available" ton-miles and RTM. Hence, short-term changes in productivity are more sensitive to changes in demand than would be indicated by changes in "available" ton-miles. Thus, airline productivity increased by 8.7 percent from 1975 to 1976, when RTMs rose 9.2 percent, but available ton-miles increased only 4.9 percent.

Business was excellent during World War II, but technology, based on the DC-3, was static and manhour output relatively stable. From 1947 to 1955, however, as the industry converted heavily to larger and faster four-engine piston aircraft, output per employee increased at an annual average rate of 11 percent. Fortunately, output (RTM) increased at an annual average of 17 percent during this period, so that employment increased by 44 percent, equal to an annual average growth of just under 5 percent. From 1955 to 1957, with fairly stable technology, output per employee grew annually at only about 3 percent while RTM grew at a 14 percent rate, causing employment to increase by 11 percent annually. Table 5 shows the annual percent changes in productivity— i.e., RTM/employee—from 1957 through 1976. Output per employee grew about 11 percent annually from 1961 to 1966. Since RTMs were again increasing about 17 percent a year for this period, employment rose from 170,000 to 244,000 over these five years: about 7 percent per year.

Employment peaked at the end of 1969, when it reached 311,922, but fell to less than 300,000 when the 1970 economic recession kept RTMs from increasing more than 1 percent from 1969 to 1970 (calendar-year figures). Employment has seesawed gently since then, accommodating to the negative impact of the widebodied aircraft and to the vicissitudes of the economy—falling further to 292,185 in 1971, increasing to 311,499

---

[26] Kahn, "Collective Bargaining . . . ," pp. 457–58; CAB, *Handbook . . . 1973*, Pt. VII, Table 16; CAB, *Supplement . . . (1975)*, p. 149; and CAB, "Productivity and Employment Costs in System Operations of the Trunk Carriers and Pan American" (see Table 5), June 1977. Recent data from ATA, *Air Transport 1977*.

TABLE 5
Average Employment Cost, Productivity, Unit Labor Cost, and Annual Percent
Change U.S. Trunk Airlines, 1957–1976

Year	Employment Cost per Employee $	Percent Change	RTMs per Employee	Percent Change	Employment Cost per RTM ¢	Percent Change
1957	6,239		26,387		23.6	
1958	6,538	4.8	26,869	1.8	24.2	2.5
1959	7,160	9.5	29,767	10.8	24.1	− 0.4
1960	7,412	3.5	30,241	1.6	24.5	1.7
1961	7,880	6.3	32,300	6.8	24.4	− 0.4
1962	8,224	4.4	35,901	11.1	22.9	− 6.1
1963	8,617	4.8	39,657	10.5	21.7	− 5.2
1964	8,994	4.4	43,696	10.2	20.6	− 5.1
1965	9,358	4.0	49,779	13.9	18.8	− 8.7
1966	9,680	3.4	55,001	10.5	17.6	− 6.4
1967	10,464	8.1	60,836	10.6	17.2	− 2.3
1968	11,176	6.8	63,295	4.0	17.7	2.9
1969	12,189	9.1	64,439	1.8	18.9	6.8
1970	13,805	13.3	65,932	2.3	20.9	10.6
1971	15,000	8.7	70,747	7.3	21.2	1.4
1972	16,557	10.4	77,395	9.4	21.4	0.9
1973	17,591	6.2	77,544	0.2	22.7	6.1
1974	19,338	9.9	79,225	2.2	24.4	7.5
1975	21,094	9.1	79,818	0.7	26.4	8.2
1976	23,272	10.3	86,791	8.7	26.8	1.5

Source: CAB, "Productivity and Employment Costs in System Operations of the Trunk Airlines and Pan American from 1957 through 1976," prepared by H. T. K. Paxson, Economic Analysis Division, June 1977. Processed.

by the end of 1973, slipping back to 303,006 at the close of 1976, and rising to 308,068 during a prosperous 1977.

The airline industry requires categories of employees with a wide diversity of career patterns and skills: those who operate the aircraft, who handle passenger services during flight, who provide reliable communications, who maintain the flight and other equipment, who service the aircraft, who deal with passengers before and after they fly, who handle the usual multitude of office functions, and who provide supervision and general management. Table 6 provides employment data for these major categories (which bear a close relationship, as we shall see, to the structure of collective bargaining) for selected years since World War II.

Although the persistent upward trend in airline employment until 1970 made many adjustments to changing conditions easier to achieve, technological progress has eliminated or threatened the survival of various crafts. On the flight deck, nonpilot radio operators and navigators have disappeared, while the nonpilot flight engineer—after a period of substantial industrial relations strife in the early 1960s—has been largely displaced by the "second officer" who is a pilot.[27] Improved

[27] Kahn, "Collective Bargaining . . . ," ch. 27, "Adjustments to Technological Change on the Flight Deck," pp. 502–36.

TABLE 6
Employment on U.S. Scheduled Air Carriers, Selected Years
(End of Year Data)

Category	1947 No.	1947 Percent	1957 No.	1957 Percent	1969 No.	1969 Percent	1977 No.	1977 Percent
Pilots & copilots	6,637	7.8	13,286	9.0	26,262	8.4	26,991	8.8
Other flight deck	1,333	1.6	3,797	2.6	8,387	2.7	6,985	2.3
Flight attendants	4,077	4.8	9,450	6.4	33,621	10.8	44,579	14.5
Communications	3,829	4.5	4,004	2.7	3,264	1.0	1,226	0.4
Mechanics & related	21,140	24.8	31,162	21.2	52,886	17.0	45,054	14.6
Aircraft & traffic service	11,610	13.6	36,052	24.5	86,462	27.7	90,445	29.4
Office employees	32,691	38.4	31,799	21.6	63,743	20.4	60,363	19.6
All others	3,835	4.5	17,640	12.0	37,297	11.0	32,425	10.5
Total	85,152	100.0	147,190	100.0	311,922	100.0	303,068	100.0

Source: Compiled from Air Transport Association of America (ATA), *Air Transport* (called *Facts and Figures* prior to 1970), various editions through 1978.

applications of electronics have sharply reduced the number of communications employees, whereas the large jets have effected a dramatic increase in flight-attendant employment (see Table 6). Of course, employment at each carrier (see Table 2) is closely related to the magnitude of its revenues and output.

At present, labor costs represent about 42 percent of the industry's operating expenses. This is a decline from about 50 percent in 1947 and about 44 percent in the late 1960s, caused primarily by the substantial growth that has taken place in capital investment and, therefore, in depreciation charges. Unit labor costs are, of course, a reflection of both output per employee and of rates of employee compensation. We defer until later an examination of how airline employees have fared under collective bargaining in terms of pay levels and changes. Unit labor costs, as measured by the CAB in cents per RTM, declined from about 24 or 24.5 cents during the 1957–61 period to a low of 17.2 cents in 1967. Since then, as shown in Table 5, they have increased every year, reaching 26.8 cents in 1976.

THE OUTLOOK

Until 1970, the U.S. airline industry was blessed, as a whole, by persistent and dramatic market growth facilitated by radical improvements in technology and declining real air fares. The environment for collective bargaining, in spite of many particular problems affecting some carriers and some employee groups, benefited from substantial direct subsidies (until 1955), large increases in employment (through 1969), declining unit labor costs (until 1967), and deep-seated optimism (until 1970).

The 1970s witnessed two significant shifts. High rates of both inflation and unemployment in the national economy, enormous increases in fuel prices, fuel shortages in 1973–74, and increasing unit labor costs adversely affected rates of return through 1975. Moreover, and of great importance to our central interest in collective bargaining, is the fact that the age of dynamic technological progress is over for the foreseeable future. Aircraft technology has stabilized on turbojet propulsion. All turbojets fly at roughly the same speed and provide (or can provide, given the passenger configuration) about the same degree of passenger comfort and reliability of service. The abandonment of the American supersonic effort and the extremely limited role of the Anglo-French Concorde[28] indicate that the "SST" will not significantly affect commercial air transportation for many years. There will, of course, be con-

---

[28] "Output of Concorde Seen Ending in 1978 with 16 Planes Built," *Wall Street Journal*, September 22, 1977, p. 12.

tinual "gentle" refinements of present aircraft types, and some new variations, aimed at filling gaps in the present varieties of jet equipment.[29]
But the enormous growth rate of output per employee experienced in
the decades prior to 1970 would appear to be over.

The airline market remains a growth market, however. A healthier
economic environment since 1975, together with increasingly vigorous
price competition (involving a multitude of discount fare arrangements
encouraged by the CAB since mid-1977) produced an increase in revenue passenger miles (RPMs) for the scheduled industry of 8.0 percent
in 1977 over 1976. For the first 11 months of 1978, RPMs were a remarkable 18.1 percent above the comparable 1977 period, with passenger
load factors rising from 55.8 percent to 61.9 percent.[30] The year 1978
will obviously record a substantial increase in ROI. As *Aviation Daily*,
an authoritative publication, commented on November 7, 1978:

> The nation's 11 trunk airlines already have surpassed the
> one billion dollar mark in earnings with the first nine months
> results almost double those of the same period last year. Every
> carrier except Northwest Airlines, which was on strike for most
> of the third quarter, reported record quarterly earnings. Car-
> riers attributed record profits to sharply higher traffic, the result
> of deeply discounted fares, continued strength in business
> travel and investment tax credits.
>
> Based on heavy advance reservations, some airline execu-
> tives see the growth continuing for the balance of the year and
> into the first quarter of 1979. However, after that, the economic
> picture is questionable. Continued traffic growth could be se-
> verely impacted by the continuing inflationary pressures, rising
> prime rate and uncertainty concerning deregulation, according
> to some carrier executives. Although many carriers have or-
> dered large, more fuel efficient aircraft to help counter the
> pressures of inflation, most of the new orders will not be avail-
> able until the 1980s.[31]

Meanwhile, the industry's current financial health will reinforce its ability to meet essential capital needs.

It is too soon (January 1979), of course, to predict the impact of the
Airline Deregulation Act of 1978 on the long-range economic condition
of the industry. Critics of the previous regulatory framework had long
argued that it produced, in Caves's words, "unnecessarily high costs and

---

[29] For an excellent survey of aircraft technology in process, see "Transport Designs
Taking Shape," *Aviation Week & Space Technology* 106 (March 21, 1977), pp.
141–56.

[30] ATA, *Air Transport 1978*, inside front cover; and *Aviation Daily*, December 29,
1978, p. 307 and table behind p. 307.

[31] *Aviation Daily*, November 7, 1978, p. 33.

restrictions on the responsiveness of the industry to expressions of consumer choice." [32] Jordan observed that the [then] status quo benefited customers who preferred high quality service and who were not concerned about price, but added:

> . . . It is difficult, however, to see how the majority of passengers have been benefited by being charged substantially higher fares, by being discriminated against when they fail to qualify for promotional fares, and by being required to purchase high quality service despite their demonstrated preferences for lower quality service if it is provided at significantly lower fares.[33]

Congressional consideration of "deregulation" legislation was initiated in October 1975 by President Gerald Ford. It acquired broad support from organizations and individuals representing a wide political spectrum and was strongly endorsed by President Carter and by the CAB itself. The case for change was well expressed by President Carter's 1977 appointee to the chairmanship of the CAB:

> . . . First, the industry has, under regulation, experienced a very satisfactory growth. Airline service, both passenger and freight, has been widely extended, and has made a major contribution toward knitting together the people of this country and of the world. The quality of service is good, and the price has declined in real terms over these last four decades. This has been a very satisfactory record.
>
> But, second . . . regulation has also had a constricting and rigidifying effect. Understandably, in view of its mission to nurture and promote the growth of what was once a weak, infant industry, regulation has had a strong tendency to protect the established carriers against competition, both among themselves and from newer aspiring entrants seeking to offer the public new and more diversified choices in service quality and price. By discouraging competition in price, it has tended to channel rivalry among existing carriers along service lines—more frequent scheduling at the expense of load factors, advertising and other forms of sales promotion, wider seating and provision of various in-flight services. This kind of rivalry in itself can be highly desirable, but not when its tendency to inflate costs and rates goes unchecked by the free opportunity of existing carriers and new entrants to offer lower service quality/price combinations. It takes price competition to encourage air travel among ever lower income strata, to expand the availability of air service to ever-increasing proportions of our population. . . .

[32] Caves, p. 442.
[33] Jordan, p. 226

It is on the basis of considerations such as these that the Board has come now to endorse the taking of decisive steps toward opening the airline industry to a fuller measure of competition. Air transportation shows all the signs of being, potentially, a naturally competitive industry. But for government restrictions, entry would be relatively easy. So would exit. This is one of the few industries in which the physical capital employed can itself move readily out of crowded into empty markets. In these circumstances, it is extremely difficult to envisage competition becoming destructive.[34]

The CAB chairman added, however, that "The Board has concluded that it cannot do all it believes desirable without a new mandate from Congress."

The ATA, most airlines, and the airline labor organizations were actively opposed to "deregulation." The chairman of Delta Airlines termed the pending legislative proposal sponsored by Senators Kennedy (Massachusetts) and Cannon (Nevada) "an ill-conceived and potentially ruinous bill." [35] On the other hand, several air carriers endorsed such action, including Frontier, Hughes Air West, Pan American, and United.

Organized labor created an "Airline Labor Coordinating Committee of the AFL-CIO" composed of five unions (ALPA, BRAC, FEIA, IAMAW, and TWU). This committee, in a statement to members of Congress dated April 18, 1977, concluded:

. . . [T]his proposed experiment in free market economics would be of no measurable benefit to the traveling and shipping public, but would cause irreparable harm to airline employees. Stronger carriers would seize this opportunity to abandon their public service responsibilities and to prey upon their weaker competitors in their profitable markets. Cut-throat price competition would undoubtedly ensue resulting in a bloodbath of financially-depressed airlines and a reorganization of the industry into an oligopolistic structure insensitive to the interests of consumers. To invite such consequences would be shortsighted and foolhardy.

Accordingly, as representatives of virtually all organized airline employees, we are united in our purpose to oppose any changes in the market entry and exit provisions of the Federal

---

[34] Testimony of Alfred E. Kahn, Chairman, CAB, before the House Budget Committee Task Force on Tax Expenditures, Government Organization, and Regulation, July 14, 1977 (prepared text, processed), pp. 1–3.

[35] Winston Williams, "Two Airlines Hit Deregulation Bill," *The New York Times*, August 24, 1977, p. 43.

Aviation Act of 1958 as proposed in the various bills pending in the Congress today. . . .

Despite such opposition and much controversy, the Airline Deregulation Act of 1978 was enacted in October 1978.[36] A new "Declaration of Policy" amends Section 102 of the Federal Aviation Act of 1958 to instruct the CAB that, among other considerations, the following are in the public interest:

> (9) The encouragement, development, and maintenance of an air transportation system relying on actual and potential competition to provide efficiency, innovation and low prices, and to determine the variety, quality, and price of air transportation services.
> (10) The encouragement of entry into air transportation markets by new carriers, the encouragement of entry into additional air transportation markets by existing air carriers, and the continued strengthening of small air carriers so as to assure a more effective, competitive airline industry.

The 1978 Act provides for automatic entry of any airline (including any intrastate air carrier that operated more than 100 million available seat-miles during the preceding calendar year) onto one route per year during 1979 and through 1981. It also permits any carrier to designate service it is already certified to provide between any one pair of points as immune from automatic entry during each of these calendar years. As to fares, the Act establishes a discretionary suspension-free flexibility zone: 5 percent above the industry standard (effective July 1, 1979) unless the carrier transports 70 percent of the passengers in that market; and up to 50 percent below the industry standard (effective immediately) unless the CAB determines the decrease to be predatory. Many other provisions, some extremely complex, implement the objective of greater reliance on competition to serve the public interest. Three significant provisions relating to labor relations—dealing with the industry's Mutual Aid Pact, with employee dislocation primarily caused by the regulatory changes contained in the Act, and with a protracted pilot strike at Wien Air Alaska Airlines—will be reviewed later in this chapter.

Public Policy and Airline Labor

Today's legal framework for airline industrial relations evolved during the 1930s, primarily as a consequence of effective lobbying by the Air Line Pilots Association (ALPA) and prior to any collective bargaining experience. This unique framework includes a minimum-wage

---

[36] Public Law 95-504. For an excellent collection of analytical papers strongly supportive of deregulation legislation, see MacAvoy and Snow.

formula for pilots (1935), coverage of the airline industry within the Railway Labor Act (1936), and special labor provisions in the Civil Aeronautics Act (1938), all of which are still in effect. We now look briefly at the origins of this framework and examine its content.[37]

THE PILOTS ORGANIZE

Those pilots fortunate enough to be employed by the airlines showed no interest in unionizing during the 1920s. They had been well paid as Post Office employees (1918–25), and the private contractors who took over air mail delivery retained the same pay formula. Earnings, under this approach, depended on three factors: seniority, measured by cockpit hours in air-mail service; miles flown per month; and hazard, as indicated by the proportion of night flying and the terrain. Pilots enjoyed a public "mystique" blending skill, courage, and professional dedication. Most of the industry's entrepreneurs were fellow pilots, the firms were small with relatively close personal relations, and optimism about the industry's prospects was pervasive.[38]

Post Office funding enabled airline traffic and employment to keep growing even after the October 1929 stock market crash. Unsubsidized aviation activities could not withstand the impact of the depression, however, and hordes of unemployed pilots assiduously sought airline jobs. By late 1930, rumors were widespread that carriers intended to replace the Post Office formula with straight monthly salaries. One major carrier, T&WA, announced a switch early in 1931 to a straight hourly basis of pay. To scuttle any slowdown among pilots, pay was to be determined by each run's average duration, not its actual time. Soon thereafter, in the spring of 1931, all of the scheduled carriers placed a pilot pay cut into effect. These developments prompted the early and rapid formation of ALPA, which soon counted a majority of the regular airline pilots among its members.[39]

Meanwhile, E. L. Cord, an aggressive businessman, had decided to take advantage of the pilot surplus. His Century Air Lines, which began operations in March 1931, provided substantially lower pilot pay than Century's subsidized competitors. Later that year, Cord announced that Century was prepared to carry air mail at exactly half the established rate. Soon after, while his offer was under serious consideration in Washington, Cord announced a pilot pay cut of $200 per month, effective February 1, 1932. Century's pilots were ordered to resign and then reapply for work at the new rates, thus provoking ALPA's first strike. Al-

---

[37] Kahn, "Collective Bargaining . . . ," pp. 461–82, offers a more elaborate treatment of this topic.

[38] Hopkins, ch. 1, "The Pilot Mystique," pp. 5–18.

[39] David, p. 29. See also Hopkins, ch. 3, "Impact of the Depression," pp. 35–51.

though Cord advertised for and found replacement pilots, Century encountered serious difficulties when ALPA's leadership, the following month, transformed hearings before the House Post Office Committee into a forum on the merits of the Century dispute. As a consequence of these revelations and the publicity they engendered, as well as the news that three of Century's pilots were killed and two injured while practicing night flying, Cord not only failed to get the air mail contracts he sought but saw his passenger traffic decline as well. Cord's two airline subsidiaries were liquidated. As Hopkins later observed:

> [ALPA President] Behncke and his ALPA emerged from the Century strike with a national reputation and several influential new friends in Washington. . . . This kind of support offered enormous opportunities for the pilots to pursue their goals in Washington, and from the Century strike until the passage of the Civil Aeronautics Act of 1938, gaining protection for pilots by lobbying in Washington for federal legislation was almost ALPA's only concern. . . .[40]

In fact, ALPA did not turn to the bargaining table until after mid-1938. Its first collective bargaining agreement was signed on May 15, 1939, with American Airlines.

One outgrowth of the Century strike was the idea, contained in a bill submitted on April 1, 1933, to amend the Railway Labor Act to include air transport. This proposal encountered strong opposition from the Aeronautical Chamber of Commerce and was considered unnecessary by the Postmaster General. The bill failed to pass, but the legislative experience thus acquired by ALPA proved useful when it switched to a different immediate objective: legislative prescription of the terms of employment.[41]

NLB DECISION No. 83

It was evident, in 1933, that larger and faster aircraft were on the way. Not surprisingly, ALPA and the carriers were at odds over whether pilot pay should depend upon hours flown or on mileage. ALPA, on September 21, filed charges with the National Labor Board (NLB), recently created under the National Industrial Recovery Act, that the carriers intended to force the pilots into a national strike by means of unreasonable wage cuts. When five major carriers announced salary changes effective October 1, ALPA set a strike date of September 30.

---

[40] Hopkins, p. 111.
[41] Kahn, "Industrial Relations . . . ," pp. 135–37. H.R. 11053 and H.R. 11867 (identical to S. 4565), 72nd Congress, were the first two versions of bills intended to effect Railway Labor Act coverage of the airlines.

ALPA President Behncke, with some well-placed telephone calls, persuaded the NLB to take jurisdiction of the dispute. The carriers, meanwhile, agreed to accept the decision of the NLB on a fully retroactive
basis.[42]

This decision, announced on May 10, 1934, as No. 83, held that the
pilots and carriers were both entitled to share the benefits of improving
aircraft technology. The NLB therefore incorporated as pay elements the
proposals of both parties:

> The rate of base pay shall be $1,600 a year with an increase
> of $200 for each year of service up to a maximum of $3,000.
> Air-line pilots shall be paid the base rate plus an hourly rate
> of $4, $4.20, $4.40, $4.60, $4.80, and $5 for day flying and $6,
> $6.30, $6.60, $6.90, $7.20, and $7.50 for night flying at hourly
> speeds of under 125 miles, 125 miles, 140 miles, 155 miles, 175
> miles, and 200 or more miles, respectively.
> In addition, at monthly mileages of under 10,000, 10,000 to
> 11,999 miles, and 12,000 miles and more, respectively, the pilots
> shall be paid 2 cents, 1½ cents, and 1 cent a mile for all miles
> per hour flown at an hourly speed of more than 100 miles.
> The differential existing on October 1, 1933, for copilots and
> for flying over hazardous terrain shall be maintained.

ALPA had urged the NLB to impose either a monthly flight time limitation of 80 hours or a monthly mileage limitation of 12,000 miles. The
NLB rejected a mileage constraint on the basis of insufficient experience,
but recommended 85 hours as the maximum monthly flying time for
pilots. Finally, the NLB stipulated: "This award shall remain in effect
for a period of one year." [43]

ALPA was pleased with the NLB's award but soon discovered that
no carrier intended to comply with it. No effort at enforcement was
undertaken by the NLB. Technically, none of the five original carrier
parties to the dispute was still in existence—their corporate identities
having been changed as a consequence of the cancellation of all air mail
contracts on February 9, 1934—so judicial enforcement seemed unlikely.
ALPA concluded that legislative enactment was the only device by
which it could secure for its members the wage formula established by
the NLB.

On March 7, 1934, even before Decision No. 83 was published, President Roosevelt had sent identical letters on air mail legislation to
Senator McKellar and Representative Mead, the appropriate committee
chairmen, including this suggestion: "Public safety calls for pilots of

---

[42] Kahn, "Collective Bargaining . . . ," p. 463.
[43] National Labor Board, *Decisions*, Pt. II, p. 20.

high character and skill. The occupation is a hazardous one. Therefore the law should provide for a method to fix maximum flying hours, minimum pay and a system for retirement or annuity benefits." [44] ALPA, in this spirit, sought to have Congress specify that compliance with NLB decisions must be a condition of holding any air mail contract. The Air Mail Act of 1934, enacted on June 12, contained two labor provisions: Section 12, which authorized and directed the Secretary of Commerce to prescribe maximum pilot flying hours and safe operation methods on air mail lines; and Section 13, under which holders of air mail contracts were required to "conform to decisions of the National Labor Board." [45] Section 13 was amended in August 1935, again at ALPA's urging, to read:

> Sec. 13. It shall be a condition upon the holding of any air mail contract that the rate of compensation and the working conditions and relations for all pilots and other employees of the holder of such contract shall conform to decisions heretofore or hereafter made by the National Labor Board, or its successor in authority, notwithstanding any limitation as to the period of its effectiveness included in any decision heretofore rendered. This section shall not be construed as restricting the right of any such employees by collective bargaining to obtain higher rates of compensation or more favorable working conditions and relations. [46]

Neither the NLB, nor its 1935 successor (the National Labor Relations Board) ever issued any decision relating to airline employee pay or working conditions except NLB Decision No. 83.

The Railway Labor Act, Title II

ALPA, soon after the passage of the 1934 Air Mail Act, resumed its campaign to have air transportation brought within the jurisdiction of the Railway Labor Act. Strong support for this proposal was expressed by the Railway Brotherhoods, the International Association of Machinists, and the Federal Coordinator of Transportation. This time, in contrast to the previous year, the airlines decided not to oppose this idea, apparently on the theory that such coverage would provide a rationale for eliminating the mandatory application of Decision No. 83. [47] Thus,

---

[44] *Revision of Air Mail Laws*, Hearings on S. 3012, etc., Senate Committee on Interstate and Foreign Commerce, March 12, 1934, p. 2.

[45] *U.S. Statutes at Large*, Vol. 48, Public No. 308, 1933–34.

[46] *U.S. Statutes at Large*, Vol. 49, Public No. 270, 1935–36.

[47] Kahn, "Collective Bargaining . . . ," p. 467. More detail concerning the legislative history of Title II of the Railway Labor Act appears in Kahn, "Industrial Relations . . . ," pp. 149–52.

with strong support and little opposition, Title II of the Railway Labor Act, signed on April 10, 1936, brought the airlines within the Act's jurisdiction.

The Railway Labor Act of 1926 had been enacted against a background of substantial legislative experimentation and collective bargaining experience in the railroad industry. Moreover, it had been drafted by and was jointly supported by the railroads and the well-established railroad unions.[48] Title II, in contrast, applied the Act to an infant industry of vastly differing characteristics in which only the pilots had organized and which was devoid of any collective bargaining experience.

The Act (as amended in 1934) established a three-member National Mediation Board (NMB). Its members, not more than two of whom may be from the same political party, are appointed by the President for staggered three-year terms. The NMB (which has a staff of professional mediators) provides mediation services. It also handles representation questions, will interpret the meaning of agreements reached in mediation, and, on request, appoints neutral arbitrators for grievance disputes. The Railway Labor Act (RLA) contains (Section 2) a statement of General Purposes and Duties which, in substance, obligates the carriers and unions to bargain collectively in good faith with each other's chosen representatives. A 1951 amendment (Section 2, Tenth) permits compulsory union membership under negotiated union-shop provisions. Unlike the National Labor Relations Board, the NMB does not investigate and adjudicate charges that a party has violated its "duties" under the RLA. The validity of such charges must be determined either by the federal courts or, conceivably, by the Civil Aeronautics Board (see below).

Section 2, Fourth, of the RLA provides: "Employees shall have the right to organize and bargain collectively through representatives of their own choosing. The majority of any craft or class of employees shall have the right to determine who shall be the representative of the craft or class for purposes of this Act. . . ." Railroad bargaining units had been well established prior to 1926. On the airlines, however, the authority and responsibility of the NMB to define "craft or class" has had a substantial impact, for some employee categories, on the growth and structure of unionism.[49]

Section 6 requires carriers and unions to "give at least thirty days' notice of an intended change in agreements affecting rates of pay, rules, or working conditions. . . ." When the parties to a dispute over the making or amending of an agreement fail to reach a settlement in

[48] Rehmus, pp. 7–8.
[49] Some examples will be cited later. See Eischen, ch. II, pp. 23–70.

344 COLLECTIVE BARGAINING

direct negotiations, they are obligated by the RLA to comply with a sequential procedure before resorting to self-help. First, mediation may be invoked by either party or initiated by the NMB. Second, if no agreement is reached under mediation, the NMB must invite the parties to accept voluntary (but, of course, binding) arbitration. Third, if arbitration is rejected by either party or by both, the status quo must be maintained for a 30-day period. Fourth, either before or after the expiration of this status quo period, if the unsettled dispute threatens "to deprive any section of the country of essential transportation service" (Section 10), the President of the United States may, in his discretion, appoint an emergency board to investigate the dispute and issue non-binding public recommendations for its settlement. Finally, when the President has created an emergency board and for 30 days following its report, "no change, except by agreement, shall be made by the parties to the controversy in the conditions out of which the dispute arose." Thirty-three airline emergency boards were appointed from 1946 through 1966 (and none between 1966 and November 1978).

A unique feature of the RLA is that mediation is obligatory. Although the parties to a dispute over contract terms cannot be required to reach an agreement while in mediation, they are prohibited under the RLA from proceeding to the next sequential step—and therefore from engaging in strikes or lockouts—until, *in the judgment of the NMB,* they have bargained to a genuine impasse. The NMB exercises this authority firmly, and in some instances has kept parties in mediation for extended periods, even well beyond a year. The U.S. Court of Appeals, responding in 1970 to a challenge of this authority instituted by the International Association of Machinists, observed:

> What is voluntary about mediation, including mediation under this [Railway Labor] Act, is the decision to accept or reject the result available from the mediation process. What is involuntary about mediation under this Act is the obligation to engage in the mediation process even though a party is not unreasonable from his point of view in his conviction that further mediation is futile. The court's inquiry cannot go beyond an examination of the objective facts and determination thereon whether there is a reasonable possibility of conditions and circumstances (including attitudes and developments) available to the Board, consistent with the objective facts, sufficient to justify the Board's judgment that the possibility of settlement is strong enough to warrant continuation of the mediation process. . . .[50]

---

[50] *Machinists* v. *National Mediation Board,* 425 F.2d 527, 73 LRRM 2278 (1970).

We will consider, below, the effects of such obligatory mediation on the collective bargaining process in the airline industry.[51]

Title II of the RLA also refers to grievances, or disputes concerning the interpretation or application of existing agreements. Section 204 requires that such disputes, if unsettled, be submitted for binding determination to boards of adjustment established at the system (carrier) or multicarrier level. The NMB is granted the discretion to order the creation of a National Air Transport Adjustment Board (in Section 205), but this has not occurred. Work stoppages over "minor" disputes—i.e., grievances—are prohibited by the RLA. How the RLA has affected the handling of grievances in the airlines is examined later.

INDUSTRIAL RELATIONS AND THE CAB

Congress undertook, in 1937, the development of permanent and comprehensive air transport legislation. ALPA, against considerable opposition, sought to perpetuate the minimum standards of NLB Decision No. 83 and also to make carrier compliance with the Railway Labor Act a condition of holding a route certificate. Except for a strong endorsement from Chairman Mead of the House Post Office Committee, ALPA had to fight this legislative battle largely unaided. ALPA failed to obtain a provision that would have compelled the CAB to revoke the route certificate of any carrier found to have violated the RLA, but its lobbying efforts were otherwise a complete success.[52] Section 401(1) of the Civil Aeronautics Act of 1938, which was retained unchanged as Section 401(k) of the Federal Aviation Act of 1958 (and is still the law today), provides:

> (1) Every air carrier shall maintain rates of compensation, maximum hours, and other working conditions and relations of all of its pilots and copilots who are engaged in interstate air transportation within the United States (not including Alaska) so as to conform with Decision numbered 83 made by the Na-

---

[51] See Krislov, pp. 310–15. Krislov observed that mediation under the RLA is more than merely mandatory because "[i]t requires that the parties make a 'satisfactory' effort during the sessions before they can proceed with other steps and then ultimately resort to self-help" (p. 311). Krislov suggests the name "quasi-judicial mediation" for this process, and he also suggests that its applicability to the public sector should be seriously considered.

[52] Col. E. S. Gorrell, president of the Air Transport Association, protested in vain that retention of Decision No. 83 would "impose forever upon every person [sic] now or in the future engaged in air transportation the wage scale and the hour limitations which were adopted in an extralegal arbitration proceeding in a dispute between the pilots and five airlines . . . and, in May of 1934, decided in light of conditions then prevailing and on the basis of a study of only these five companies." *To Create a Civil Aeronautics Authority*, Hearing on H.R. 9738, House Committee on Interstate and Foreign Commerce, March and April 1938, p. 243. Quoted in Kahn, "Collective Bargaining . . . ," p. 469.

tional Labor Board on May 10, 1934, notwithstanding any limitation therein as to its period of effectiveness.

(2) . . . [Requires compliance with Decision No. 83, but on an annual basis, in overseas or foreign or territorial air transportation.]

(3) Nothing herein contained shall be construed as restricting the right of any such pilots or copilots, or other employees, of any such air carrier to obtain by collective bargaining higher rates of compensation or more favorable working conditions or relations.

(4) It shall be a condition upon the holding of a certificate by any air carrier that such carrier shall comply with title II of the Railway Labor Act, as amended.

Compliance with Decision No. 83 has been essentially self-enforcing. Moreover, pilot labor agreements have, since 1946, improved considerably upon these minimum standards. As for compliance with the RLA, the CAB has reluctantly concluded that in some instances it must determine whether a carrier has violated the RLA, and it has done so.[53] Although such determinations are more commonly made in the courts, the CAB's ultimate authority to revoke a carrier's right to operate makes Section 401(k)(4) of the Federal Aviation Act a powerful constraint on carrier conduct, especially during work stoppages.[54] More generally, the CAB's economic powers have inevitably affected the relative bargaining power of carriers and unions. Thus, the unions' leverage was strengthened, in strike situations, by the elimination of direct subsidies to major carriers after 1954 and by the placing of local service carriers on a uniform class-rate subsidy. On the other hand, the decision of the CAB to approve the airlines' Mutual Aid Pact—under which, as will be explained below, struck carriers obtain monetary payments from other carriers—tended to strengthen the employers' bargaining position.

All airline unions continue to devote substantial resources to their dealings with the CAB and the FAA. This writer pointed out, in 1952, that

. . . the CAB has entered into and materially influenced every major aspect of airline personnel and industrial relations. On safety grounds, this agency prescribes employee qualifications, complements for skilled personnel, and many working conditions; it has acted to protect employees against the adverse

---

[53] Kahn, "Collective Bargaining . . . ," pp. 477–78.

[54] For a classic example, see Kahn, "The National Airlines Strike," p. 24. Although National in 1948 had replaced all of its striking pilots, a CAB threat to dismember this carrier (ostensibly, as part of a general program to improve the nation's airline route structure) compelled National to reach a settlement with ALPA.

effects of mergers and acquisitions, route sales, and the joint use or interchange of equipment and personnel, and to accomplish this has even prescribed a formula for integrating seniority lists; it has substantially affected union bargaining power by evolving a subsidy policy under which strike losses are not offset; and it has induced employer compliance with the Railway Labor Act by the actual or threatened exercise of its economic powers. To effectuate its labor role, the agency has employed dispute settlement techniques which run the gamut from voluntary mediation to the equivalent of compulsory arbitration.[55]

This situation remains essentially unchanged to this day, except for the transfer in 1958 of safety policy formulation from the CAB to the FAA. The CAB does prefer to minimize its direct role in labor issues, however, and often requires the parties to arbitrate disputes involving the application of CAB rulings. For example, the CAB on April 1, 1975, issued Order No. 75-4-4 approving a route swap between Pan American and Trans World Airlines. A seven-page Appendix, entitled "Labor Protective Provisions," obligates each carrier to compensate any employee who is "placed in a worse position" as a result of the swap and to provide a "dismissal allowance" to any employee who becomes unemployed because of the swap. Section 12 of this Appendix requires that "any dispute or controversy . . . with respect to the protections provided herein" must be determined either by a method established by the parties or by an arbitrator selected from a panel furnished by the NMB. The airline unions appear before the CAB at hearings on such proposed interairline arrangements, of course, in order to press for the most generous protective provisions the CAB can be persuaded to impose.

The CAB has long pursued a policy of attaching labor protective provisions (LLPs) as conditions to its approval of airline acquisitions and mergers. As the CAB itself recently observed:

> The Board's policy of imposing labor protective provisions pursuant to the public interest obligations imposed by the Act rests on the need to obtain a degree of stability in air transportation that freedom from industrial strife will provide. The public interest in imposing labor conditions does not, under court interpretation and Board precedent, rest broadly on consideration of general employee welfare.[56]

The CAB has not ordinarily attached LPPs to its approval of route

---

[55] Kahn, "Regulatory Agencies . . . ," p. 697.

[56] CAB Docket 27114 et al., Pan American-Trans World Route Agreement, decided November 16, 1976, Opinion, p. 20 (processed).

transfers, suspensions, or deletions (the above-cited Pan American-TWA case being an exception), because it requires a showing of a "widespread and systemwide impact" on employees as a precondition to the imposition of LPPs.[57]

The principle of employee protection is implemented by Section 43 of the Airline Deregulation Act of 1978, which calls for a comprehensive program of financial benefits for any airline employee who suffers a "qualifying dislocation" caused by the bankruptcy or major contraction of an air carrier resulting from the regulatory changes provided by the Act. The benefits are to be provided by the Secretary of Labor from federal funds, however, in contrast to the payment of LPPs by the carriers.

The 1978 Deregulation Act does appear to have generated a new wave of merger activity among air carriers, although it is too early to predict how many mergers will actually take place in the near future. Accordingly, employee protection under CAB-required LPPs as well as under Section 43 of the Deregulation Act will be an economic consideration of substantial continuing importance.[58]

Collective Bargaining

Unlike such industries as basic steel, bituminous coal, and automobile manufacturing, in which a single industrial union exercises a dominant role, airline bargaining is fragmented according to the "craft or class" representation formula of the Railway Labor Act and is conducted on a single-carrier basis as well. This section will examine, first, the extent and nature of airline labor organization and the bargaining power of these unions; second, the carriers' countervailing response, notably the now defunct Mutual Aid Pact (MAP); and third, the bargaining process and its substantive results, with particular reference to pilots, flight attendants, and maintenance employees.

AIRLINE UNIONISM

The airlines have been highly unionized since the late 1940s. Most carriers negotiate separate contracts with labor organizations represent-

---

[57] CAB Docket 26245, American-Pan American Route Exchange Agreement, Order Denying Petition served August 26, 1977, pp. 4–5 (processed).

[58] One effect of "deregulation" has been to generate considerable interest on the part of many airlines in merger possibilities. See, for example, the following reports in *Aviation Daily*: September 1, 1978, "Continental-Western Announce Merger," p. 2; September 13, 1978, "Texas International Will Fight Pan Am-National Merger," p. 57; November 3, 1978, "TXI Eyes Mergers With Southern, Western and Pan Am," p. 19; November 20, 1978, "Ozark Opposes North Central-Southern Merger"; December 5, 1978, "TXI A Potential Big Winner Even If Pan Am Gets National," p. 172; and December 6, 1978, "Economists See Little Problem With Future Airline Mergers," p. 181. See also, *The New York Times*, December 24, 1978, Section 3, "They're Just Wild About National," pp. 1–2.

ing pilots, flight attendants, "mechanics and related" employees, and dispatchers. About half of the airlines have their "clerical, office, fleet and passenger service employees" represented by unions. Although "stock and stores" employees were originally considered by the NMB as part of the latter "clerical" unit,[59] many carriers granted voluntary recognition to such units. Nonpilot flight engineers are still independently represented at three trunk lines (AA, NA, and PA), but have been largely replaced in the "third seat" by second officers who are qualified pilots.[60] Additionally, there exists a variety of small bargaining units—meteorologists, flight-kitchen personnel, guards, nurses, communications employees, etc.—primarily at the large carriers.

Table 7 summarizes the representation picture for the 20 trunk and local service carriers, which (as of mid-1977) had a total of 134 collective bargaining contracts in effect, eight of which had been executed during March-June 1977. Most contracts have a duration of two to three years, although protracted negotiations frequently produce a good deal of retroactive application. Often, several bargaining units of ground employees have elected to be represented by the same union at a given carrier, and when this occurs there is a tendency toward multiunit bargaining with common contract expiration dates for these units. The situation at American Airlines, shown in Table 8, is illustrative. The Transport Workers Union of America (TWU) represents six bargaining units covering virtually all of American's unionized ground personnel, and five of the TWU contracts with American show a common expiration date of August 31, 1977.

Space limitations preclude, here, a proper coverage of the history of airline unionization.[61] ALPA has represented virtually all airline pilots since the 1930s except at American, where the independent Allied Pilots Association was established in 1963 as the consequence of a dispute over ALPA's mandatory policy of requiring three pilots in turbojet cockpits.[62] Maintenance employees began to organize in 1937; dispatchers in 1939; communications employees, navigators, and flight engineers during World War II;[63] flight attendants, stores, and others during the late 1940s. As Table 7 suggests, there is a good deal of interunion rivalry

---

[59] See Eischen.

[60] For a thorough examination of the protracted jurisdictional dispute involving the flight engineer's seat, see Baitsell, chs. 7 and 8.

[61] Kahn, "Industrial Relations . . . ," ch. 4, covers the development of airline unionism in detail through 1949.

[62] Kahn, "Collective Bargaining . . . ," pp. 526–27.

[63] Flight radio operators and flight navigators were once required as cockpit crew members on overseas flights but lost their jobs to improved technology. Flight engineers have been virtually eliminated among U.S. carriers. See Kahn, "Collective Bargaining . . . ," ch. 27, "Adjustments to Technological Change on the Flight Deck."

TABLE 7
Union Representation on U.S. Trunk and Local Service Carriers,[a] June 1977

Craft or Class[b]	No. of Carriers Unionized	Labor Organizations Involved	No. of Carriers Unionized
Pilots	20	Air Line Pilots Association (ALPA)	19
		Allied Pilots Association (APA)	1
Flight attendants	19	Association of Flight Attendants/ ALPA (AFA)	10
		Transport Workers Union of America (TWU)	4
		Service Employees Int'l. Union (SEIU)	1
		Int'l. Brotherhood of Teamsters (IBT)	1
		Independents	3
Mechanics and related	18	Int'l. Association of Machinists (IAM)	13
		Transport Workers Union of America (TWU)	2
		Aircraft Mechanics Fraternal Assn. (AMFA)	2
		Int'l. Brotherhood of Teamsters (IBT)	1
Dispatchers	18	Transport Workers Union of America (TWU)	13
		Int'l. Association of Machinists (IAM)	2
		Independents	3
Clerical, office, fleet, and passenger service	10	Air Line Employees Association/ ALPA (ALEA)	5
		Brotherhood of Railway & Airline Clerks (BRAC)	2
		Int'l. Brotherhood of Teamsters (IBT)	2
		Int'l. Association of Machinists (IAM)	1
Communications	7	Int'l. Association of Machinists (IAM)	3
		Transport Workers Union of America (TWU)	2
		Int'l. Brotherhood of Teamsters (IBT)	2
Stock/supply clerks	7	Int'l. Brotherhood of Teamsters (IBT)	4
		Int'l. Association of Machinists (IAM)	2
		Transport Workers Union of America (TWU)	1
Meteorologists	5	Transport Workers Union of America (TWU)	5
Guards	4	Int'l. Association of Machinists (IAM)	4
Flight engineers[c]	3	Flight Engineers International Assn. (FEIA)	3

Source: Assembled from information supplied by NMB, AIRConference, and unions.

[a] These are the eleven trunk and nine local service carriers listed in Table 2.

[b] In addition, there are 23 contracts (mostly at Eastern, Northwest, Pan American, and United) for miscellaneous units, e.g., nurses, foremen, and a number of technical specialties.

[c] There are no nonrepresented flight engineers. All remaining flight engineers not represented by FEIA are part of the flight deck crew represented by ALPA.

TABLE 8

Union Representation at American Airlines, December 31, 1976

At year end, American's employees numbered 35,984. Approximately 60 percent are represented by labor unions. Shown here is a list of the unions, their membership, and the expiration dates of existing contracts. Nonunion employees include management specialist 5,601, agent 5,919, clerical 2,206, and other 1,044.

Craft or Class	No. of Employees	Union[a]	Contract Expires
Pilots	3,580	APA (Indep.)	March 31, 1977
Flight engineers	509	FEIA	March 31, 1977
Flight attendants	5,162	TWU	August 31, 1978
Maintenance	11,319	TWU	August 31, 1977
Stores	614	TWU	August 31, 1977
Dispatchers & assistants	94	TWU	August 31, 1977
Communications	74	TWU	August 31, 1977
Meteorologists	27	TWU	August 31, 1977
Guards	15	IAM	June 30, 1979

Source: American Airlines, *1976 Annual Report*, p. 8.

Note: The flight attendants, in 1977, shifted their affiliation from the TWU to a new independent union, the Association of Professional Flight Attendants (APFA).

[a] See Table 6 for full names of unions. All of the above unions except the APA are affiliates of the AFL-CIO.

except in the pilot bargaining unit. The only major airline which remains an exception to substantial unionization today is Delta, where only the pilots and dispatchers are organized.

The "craft or class" basis of representation under the RLA has been a frequent source of controversy, although it is difficult to estimate whether less fragmentation would have occurred if the airlines had remained under the National Labor Relations Act. The NMB has traditionally supported the principle "that well-recognized crafts or classes are of prime importance in facilitating stability in carrier-employee relations" (NMB Case No. R-2783, April 15, 1959). It has not been easy to implement this principle, however, in the face of the myriad changes in job content and in the scale of employment over the years as well as the variety at any given time among the airlines in their size and operational methods. An excellent examination of this topic has recently been written by Eischen.[64] Currently, controversy centers on whether the long-established but least-organized "clerical, office, fleet and passenger service" representation unit should be splintered. On March 23, 1977, the NMB determined (in Case No. 4550) that United's passenger service employees should constitute a "craft or class" for the purposes of an election sought by ALEA. In the ensuing election, only 2160 of 8140 eligible employees voted. ALEA's representation claim was therefore dismissed by the NMB on June 14, 1977, on the basis that less than a

---

[64] See Eischen.

majority of the unit (actually, only 26.5 percent) had cast ballots. The industry, which strongly opposes such splintering, has formally asked the NMB to reconsider its position.[65]

Since the typical airline negotiates with unions representing perhaps four major groups of employees—each of which is essential to airline operation—and sometimes with several additional bargaining units; since the bargaining process under the aegis of the RLA has often been quite protracted, especially because of the ability of the NMB to extend the mediation phase; because the industry is sensitive to the condition of the general economy but also extremely uneven among the carriers in economic performance and condition; and because representation disputes and competitive unionism are not uncommon—the industry has rarely been free from significant union-management tensions and potential (if not actual) work stoppages. As this writer has noted:

> The economic characteristics of air transportation make the airlines relatively vulnerable to strikes. Considerations of safety (and the Federal Aviation Regulations or FAR's), reinforced by public relations considerations for a safety-conscious passenger market, make it impractical in most instances for any carrier to attempt to operate in the face of a strike by any major bargaining unit. An airline cannot produce extra product in anticipation of or after a strike, as can a factory, nor can it provide service mechanically, during a strike, like a highly automated public utility. Strike-lost traffic is simply handled by competing airlines or does not move by air. Substantial fixed costs continue during any strike. Moreover, it may take a long while after the resumption of operations for traffic to return to pre-strike levels. Not only have hitherto loyal customers (for cargo as well as passenger transportation) discovered the virtues of the competition, but a flood of precautionary transfers of future reservations to non-struck carriers inevitably occurs.[66]

MANAGEMENT ORGANIZATION

The carriers have demonstrated, at times, a wish to confront some unions, especially ALPA, on a multiemployer if not an industry-wide basis. Thus, when facing pilot demands in 1945–46 to improve the Decision No. 83 pay formula on the faster and larger four-engine propeller aircraft, the industry created an Airlines Negotiating Conference (ANC). ALPA refused to recognize or deal with ANC, even as the

---

[65] Before the U.S. National Mediation Board, "Brief and Motion on Behalf of the Airline Industrial Relations Conference and Concerned Carriers," October 17, 1977. Of counsel: Poletti, Freidin, Prashker, Feldman & Gartner, by Herbert Prashker, New York City.

[66] Kahn, "Labor-Management Relations . . . ," p. 110.

representative of any single carrier. Instead, ALPA struck TWA on October 21, 1946, after rejecting the recommendations of a presidential emergency board (No. 36) appointed pursuant to the RLA. This 26-day strike, the first since the 1932 Century stoppage, ended with an agreement to arbitrate pilot pay on the DC-4 and the Constellation. Under the award, the speed brackets of Decision No. 83 were extended to "300 mph and over," base pay was raised by $50 per month, and mileage pay was also improved. ALPA was pleased with this outcome, which it was able to use as a bench mark throughout the industry. The carriers, having no success with ANC, abandoned it on February 28, 1947.

Although the arbitration award reflected increased aircraft speed to ALPA's satisfaction, it took no account of aircraft size as a pay criterion. ALPA kept searching for a carrier that would grant such a concession, and on April 19, 1947, it obtained a novel "gross weight pay" at Eastern. Under this additional pay element, each captain was to receive 1¾ cents per hour for each 1,000 pounds of his aircraft's maximum certificated gross take-off weight. For the DC-6, this meant an extra $1.26 per hour. The subsequent extension of Decision No. 83's "incremental" pay approach plus gross weight pay to jet aircraft, for which ALPA successfully bargained, provided the basis for major increases in pilot pay levels.[67]

Apart from two short-lived exceptions (in 1953 and 1966), when the IAM and five carriers agreed to joint bargaining, single-carrier bargaining has remained the rule.[68] The NMB has never directed the creation of a multicarrier unit, and it seems clear that multicarrier bargaining could develop only in the unlikely event of mutual agreement by all parties. Not only do the unions see no virtue in such an arrangement, but the airlines on their part would find it difficult to implement, given their great diversity in operating and in economic characteristics. The ANC was succeeded by an industry clearing house, the Airline Personnel Relations Conference (APRC), to assist each carrier in keeping up to date on labor relations and personnel developments. Another effort to invigorate carrier coordination at the bargaining table was initiated in 1971, when APRC was replaced by the Airline Industrial Relations Conference (AIRCon). Although AIRCon often served as the industry spokesman on general matters of labor policy and facilitated the sharing of ideas and the distribution of information, it was never able to make

---

[67] Kahn, "Collective Bargaining . . . ," p. 557. Gross weight pay is now commonly set at three cents per hour, yielding (for example) $3.24 per hour on the DC-9, $12.27 per hour on the L-1011, $21.45 on the B-747. See 1977 Eastern-ALPA Agreement, Section 5.

[68] Kahn, "Collective Bargaining . . . ," pp. 493–94, fn. 83.

a significant dent in the tradition of single-carrier autonomy in union relations.[69]

In December 1978, AIRCon's Executive Board, composed of the chief executive officers of its 22 member airlines, concluded that "certain of AIRCon's efforts had been futile, and that benefits gained have not justified the costs incurred by member carriers." Accordingly, its Executive Board voted unanimously to convert AIRCon from its original mission into a two-person unit, housed in the Air Transportation Association's offices, "responsible only for the collection and dissemination of industry collective bargaining data. . . ."[70]

With the airlines thus unable to present a unified industry position in collective bargaining, the stronger airline unions have been able to exert considerable bargaining-table leverage, capitalizing upon pattern-spreading and "whipsaw" techniques among the generally strike-fearful carriers. The airlines, casting about for some kind of economic device to offset their inability to achieve bargaining table solidarity, initiated in 1958 a Mutual Aid Pact (MAP) under which member-carriers on strike receive substantial benefits from other airlines that are MAP members.

As originally established by six major airlines in October 1958, the Pact applied to the shutdown of any member-carrier by a strike called to obtain demands "in excess of or opposed to" the recommendation of a presidential emergency board or by a strike initiated before the exhaustion of RLA procedures "or which is otherwise unlawful."[71] Each member, in this situation, was to pay to the struck member all of its net income from strike-diverted traffic. The Pact was amended on March 7, 1960, to cover strikes called in the absence of any emergency board appointment, and more carriers enrolled. MAP was revised again on March 26, 1962, in order to guarantee to any carrier shut down by a strike benefits equal to at least one-quarter of its "normal air transport operating expense." These benefits were to be derived from a combination of "windfall" payments (based on net income from strike-diverted traffic) as before, plus "supplemental" payments based on each carrier's share of all of the members' total air transport revenue. The next revision, effective October 31, 1969, established a far higher level of benefits. Windfall plus supplemental payments as a percent of the struck carrier's normal air transport operating expenses were set at: 50 percent

---

[69] The interairline agreement establishing AIR Conference was approved, with certain modifications, in CAB Order 73-6-96, dated June 22, 1973.

[70] *Aviation Daily*, December 8, 1978, p. 193: "Air Conference Reduced to Information Exchange."

[71] Kahn, "Mutual Strike Aid . . . ," pp. 595-606. The text of the original Pact and its amendment through March 7, 1960, are in an Appendix.

for the first two weeks of the strike, 45 percent for the third week, 40 percent for the fourth week, and 35 percent thereafter (until the end of the strike). The maximum liability on each member for supplemental payments was doubled to 1 percent of its prior year's operating revenue. And the local service carriers were invited to join MAP as of January 1, 1971.[72] As of 1977, MAP membership included every trunk and local service carrier except Delta, Allegheny, Southern, and Pan American (which withdrew in 1975 after a contract settlement with ALPA containing a one-year wage freeze).

The Pact, like any intercarrier agreement, required CAB approval. The original 1958 MAP and each subsequent revision was vigorously and vehemently contested before the CAB by the airline unions. The CAB's own administrative law judge recommended in 1972 that MAP benefits should be limited to the 25 percent level in effect during 1962–69 and the local service carriers excluded from membership.[73] Nevertheless, on February 27, 1973, a majority of the CAB approved the Pact without modification for another five-year period.[74]

The financial solace provided to a struck carrier was obviously considerable. From the Pact's inception through 1975, a total of $482 million in MAP payments have been made by its members. Because strike experience has varied considerably among the carriers, some have obtained large net gains while others have incurred substantial losses.[75] One prominent example of the Pact's operation was the 160-day BRAC strike against Northwest Airlines in 1970. Northwest's MAP receipts amounted to $47.3 million, a sum which converted an income loss for 1970 of $1.8 million (before taxes) into a net income (before taxes) of $44.6 million and a return on investment of 5.4 percent, third highest in the industry that year.[76]

Space does not permit here a detailed review of the experience under MAP and the controversy that has surrounded it. ALPA went

---

[72] Unterberger and Koziara, pp. 26–45, is an excellent exposition of MAP's development and operation.

[73] CAB Docket 9977, Airlines Mutual Aid Pact, Initial Decision of Arthur S. Present, Hearing Examiner, Served: March 27, 1972 (processed). Mr. Present commented (p. 17): "The evidence indicates that during a full shutdown a struck carrier can limit its operating expenses to 29.2 percent of its normal level."

[74] CAB Docket 9977, Order No. 73-2-110, February 27, 1973.

[75] John J. O'Donnell, President, ALPA, "Statement before the Subcommittee on Aviation, Committee on Public Works and Transportation, U.S. House of Representatives, Concerning Airlines' Mutual Aid Pact," March 9, 1976, Appendix 3. From 1958 through 1975, the largest "net gainers" were National ($121.3 million through January 5, 1976) and Northwest ($85.5 million). The largest "net losers" were American ($68.5 million), Pan American ($56.1 million), Eastern ($46.4 million), and United ($46.0 million).

[76] CAB Hearings on Mutual Aid Pact, 1971, Docket 9977, ALPA Exhibit No. 6, derived from Trunk Carrier Exhibits, Vol. 1.

into court to challenge the legality of the CAB's 1973 approval of the Pact. On August 8, 1974, the U.S. Court of Appeals, D.C. Circuit (No. 73-1214), dismissed ALPA's contentions that MAP as approved by the CAB violated national labor policy, the RLA, the antitrust laws, and the public interest. Chief Justice Bazelon said:

> Despite the CAB's experience with the Pact, we would not affirm, of course, if issues of employee welfare had been ignored or slighted. . . . But in a finding that the unions do not dispute, the Board in this case declared[:]
> that the employees retain substantial and effective bargaining power regardless of the Mutual Aid Agreement. Thus, the record shows that air carrier wages . . . are higher than, and . . . have increased faster than, wages in other industries, including other transportation industries.

Actually, there is no evidence that settlements under the Pact were lower because of its benefits, or that Pact members welcomed work stoppages. The record does indicate that strikes, once started, tended to last longer because of the Pact. Perhaps the most important function of MAP was emphasized by ATA's President Paul Ignatius in 1976:

> The major point, which unions never challenge, is that Mutual Aid is vital to preserving the financial viability of a struck carrier. Airline strikes can be devastating. And in the uncertain financial circumstances our industry currently faces, a strike could cripple an airline or even push it into insolvency. Mutual Aid protects against that catastrophic risk.[77]

Nevertheless, persistent union opposition—manifested both at the collective bargaining table and in congressional lobbying—together with the 1978 legislative climate favoring more intensive competition in the increasingly prosperous industry, led to the Pact's undoing. Another factor was Northwest Airlines' shutdown on April 29, 1978, by an ALPA strike that lasted for 109 days. Northwest collected $105 million in MAP benefits during this strike, which ended on August 15, 1978, thereby unbalancing even more the distribution of payments and benefits among the member carriers.[78]

On July 14, 1978, Eastern Airlines announced that it would withdraw

---

[77] Paul R. Ignatius, ATA President, statement prepared for Subcommittee on Aviation, House Committee on Public Works and Transportation, on H.R. 1234, April 1, 1976 (Processed), p. 3. For a vigorous debate on the merits of the Pact, see Herbert R. Northrup, "Comment" on the Unterberger-Koziara article and "Reply" by Unterberger and Koziara, *Industrial and Labor Relations Review* 30 (April 1977), pp. 364–79.

[78] *Wall Street Journal*, August 16, 1978, p. 4: "Pilot Strike Ends at Northwest as Pact Is Signed."

from the Pact at the end of 1979. Eastern's President Frank Borman, noting that Eastern had collected $26.1 million in MAP benefits but had paid out $74 million, stated: "At one time, Eastern considered Mutual Aid to be a 'dread disease' insurance policy, but with the excellent attitude of our employees and their outstanding contributions to current wage programs, the cost of the insurance premiums exceeds the value of the benefits." [79]

On August 28, 1978, *Aviation Daily* revealed that American Airlines Chairman Albert Casey, in a letter to the 14 other airline members of the Pact, "noted recent congressional and CAB opposition to the air agreement, and said it was 'questionable whether the Mutual Aid Agreement in its current form will be reapproved by the CAB in the aftermath of the Northwest strike.'" Casey proposed a September meeting to consider modification of MAP that "would best serve to enhance our chances of renewed approval." [80] On September 12, 1978, the Pact members unanimously agreed to changes "to eliminate the possibility that an airline could show a profit while on strike." Effective January 1, 1979, benefits to a struck carrier would be limited to 35 percent of its normal operating expenses for two weeks and to 25 percent for the next eight weeks. Only the "windfall" payments based on net income to other members from strike-diverted traffic would continue beyond ten weeks for the duration of any strike. [81]

This attempt to save the Pact from total destruction was not successful. The Airline Deregulation Act of 1978, adopted by Congress on October 15 and signed by President Carter on October 24, 1978, amended Section 412 of the Federal Aviation Act of 1958 by declaring any previously approved mutual aid agreement "disapproved and not in effect," and adding:

(2) No carrier shall enter into any mutual aid agreement with any other air carrier . . . unless such agreement provides (A) that any air carrier will not receive payments for any period which exceed 60 percentum of the direct operating expenses during such period, (B) that benefits under the agreement are not payable for more than eight weeks during any labor strike and that such benefits may not be for losses incurred during the first thirty days of any labor strike, and (C)

[79] *Daily Labor Report* (Washington: Bureau of National Affairs, Inc.), July 17, 1978, Pp. A2 and A3.

[80] *Aviation Daily*, August 28, 1978, p. 307: "American Chairman Seeks Meeting to Salvage Mutual Aid Pact."

[81] *Aviation Daily*, September 13, 1978, pp. 57–58; letter to Civil Aeronautics Board Re Docket 9977 dated September 13, 1978, from Charles A. Miller, Esq., Covington & Burling, Washington, D.C., Counsel for the Airline Members of the Mutual Aid Agreement.

that any party to such agreement will agree to submit the issues causing any labor strike to binding arbitration pursuant to the Railway Labor Act if the striking employees request such binding arbitration.

There does not appear to be any likelihood that the airlines will establish a new mutual aid arrangement subject to such restrictions.[82]

EARNINGS AND WORKING CONDITIONS

Airline employees have fared well under collective bargaining. The ATA, in its defense of MAP, had emphasized that airline employees are better paid than U.S. industry as a whole and have consistently obtained large pay increases. From 1967 to 1973, the ATA notes, average employee compensation (including fringe benefits) rose from $9,733 to $17,005, or by 75.4 percent, while average compensation in U.S. industry rose from $6,880 to $10,349, or by 50.4 percent.[83] Since 1973, as calculated by the CAB, "Employment Cost per Employee" rose on the trunk lines by 9.9 percent in 1974, 9.1 percent in 1975, and 10.3 percent in 1976, when it reached $23,272 (see Table 5).

It would require an essay as long as this chapter merely to describe and explain pilot pay and related working rules.[84] ALPA has successfully insisted, at the bargaining table, on retaining the "increment" pay system of Decision No. 83 plus the gross weight pay element added in 1947, although each pay element has now been converted into a rate per flight hour. At Trans World in mid-1977, for example, a captain with 12 or more years of service received *base pay* of $15.00 per hour; *hourly pay* of $26.00 on the B-727, $30.00 on the B-747, with $4.00 per hour extra at "night" (between 6:00 P.M. and 6:00 A.M.); *mileage pay* of three cents per mile flown; and *gross weight pay* of three cents per 1,000 pounds of the aircraft's maximum certificated gross weight. The TWA-ALPA contract provides that 600 mph shall be the speed for flight pay computation purposes, and that an additional $4.78 per hour is to be paid for all international flying. Mileage pay (at three cents) thus amounts to $18.00 per hour. For the captain in domestic day flying, this yields $85.14 per hour on the B-747, $64.28 on the B-727. Copilots (first officers) are paid 67.1 percent of 12th-year captain pay after 12 years of service. Flight engineers (second officers) obtain an increasing percent of captain pay up to a maximum, after 12 years of service, of 60.3 percent of 12th-year captain pay. In other words, all pilots are paid a

---

[82] *Aviation Daily*, October 13, 1978, p. 225: "Death of Mutual Aid Is Predicted."

[83] Ignatius, p. 7 and Table 6.

[84] See Kahn, "Collective Bargaining . . . ," chs. 28–30, pp. 537–95; Baitsell, ch. 4, "The Methods of Compensating Flight Crew Members," pp. 57–110.

negotiated rate per flying hour that varies with length of service, type of aircraft, and status (captain, copilot, or second officer).

Why, then, the "increment" system? As this writer has observed:

> From ALPA's viewpoint, this adherence to increment pay has been a shrewd policy. Emergency Boards have always been ready to accept the desirability of building upon the "established" method of wage determination, given their wish, or compulsion, to express recommendations in terms of "rational" criteria. Moreover, in an industry that is the beneficiary of much public interest and concern, it is far more acceptable for the pilots to seek extensions of mileage and hourly pay schedules, revisions in the gross weight pay formula, and changes in pegged speeds [e.g., the negotiated 600 mph at TWA], than to demand explicit direct pay increases. Similarly, ALPA found that it was more effective, during the 1950's, to obtain shorter hours indirectly by way of a complex package of new work and pay rules, than to demand open reductions in working hours or monthly mileage limits.[85]

ALPA's membership (27,953 on 35 carriers) earned an average during 1976 of $41,411. Captains averaged $53,541, first officers $35,388, and second officers $29,033.[86] Fringe benefits including pensions represent about 25 percent of payroll cost. With pilot employment no longer growing as in the past, it takes much longer today to advance from second officer to captain and to move up, by seniority, from the smaller to the better-paying larger aircraft. For this reason, the once tolerable dispersion in earnings between junior and senior pilots is no longer acceptable to impatient junior pilots, and recent negotiations are continuing a trend toward less unequal incomes.

The flight attendant group has not only grown tremendously in numbers and in the share of airline employment (see Table 6), but has changed since the mid-1960s from a virtually all-female "stewardess" group, averaging about two years of service and subject to termination upon marriage, to a group containing increasing numbers of males, averaging more than seven years of seniority and giving priority to such career-oriented objectives as pensions. At Pan Am in 1968, only 5 percent of the flight attendants were married, only 600 were over 30, only 15 percent participated in the elective pension plan, and 90 percent were female. By early 1977, 40 percent were married, 2,200 were over 30, 40 percent were in the pension plan, and the proportion of males had in-

---

[85] Kahn, "Collective Bargaining . . . ," p. 603.

[86] ALPA, Research Department Report, June 1977, Age-Wage Analysis, ALPA Pilot Membership 1976, p. 1.

creased from 10 to 15 percent.[87] Such changes in numbers and in characteristics, along with the influence of the 1964 Civil Rights Act and
organized demands for equal rights for women, generated considerable
unrest among flight attendants. Many were discontented with their prior
union representation, whatever union it happened to be. There have
been three prolonged strikes by flight attendants in and since 1973 (see
Table 9) and changes in representation have taken place at six trunk
lines in and since 1976: American (TWU to independent), Continental
(AFA to independent), National (AFA to TWU), Northwest (AFA to
IBT), Pan American (TWU to independent) and Trans World (TWU
to independent). Union rivalries and the underlying employee unrest
have tended, of course, to increase bargaining table militancy. At the
end of 1976, the average annual salary of U.S.-based trunk-line flight
attendants was $12,714, an increase of 10.6 percent over the end of 1975.
Flight attendants on local service carriers averaged $11,102 at the end
of 1976.[88]

Flight attendants earn a minimum base pay applicable to a specified
number of monthly flying hours which increases with length of service
usually through the 12th year plus "incentive pay" for each hour flown
per month above that minimum. Maximum monthly flying hours range
from 75 to 85 on the trunks, and is higher on some other carriers. At
American, for example, a flight attendant's maximum earnings for 77
hours in domestic service (as of mid-1977) rises from $801.70 in his/her
first six months of service to $1,336.90 per month in and after the 12th
year. Conditions previously obtained by the pilots serve as appealing
targets for the flight attendants: as one example, single-room accom-
modations on overnight layovers—a benefit enjoyed by pilots for many
years—were obtained by most flight attendants only in 1976. Recent
bargaining has contained more emphasis on benefits associated with the
greater length of service and the long-term career outlook of this group,
such as improved pensions and early retirement. Their collective agreements contain substantial provisions relating to working rules and conditions, impossible to summarize here.[89]

The labor agreements covering nonflight personnel tend to resemble
in approach and content the agreements that cover similar categories of
employees in other industries, in part because some of the unions
(BRAC, IAM, IBT, SEIU, and TWU) have substantial nonairline mem-

[87] Pan Am In-Flight Services, *Monthly Operational Bulletin*, Vol. VII Issue 3
(March 1977), pp. 5-6. From highlights of address by Kenneth Meinen, Vice
President-Personnel.

[88] AVMARK Management Report, p. 13.

[89] ALPA, Research Department, *Summary of Flight Attendant Agreements* (Washington: July 1977), Table 10, pp. 48-50. This 71-page document provides a comprehensive summary of the substance of flight attendant contracts.

berships. Mechanic and related employees on the trunk lines earned, as of the end of 1976, average salaries of $19,573, up 7.8 percent from the end of 1975. Top increment pay for the key "mechanic" classification (including license and line premiums) was generally between $9.00 and $10.00 per hour in mid-1977. Their contracts are usually from two to three years in duration, with general wage increases scheduled at six-month intervals and with protection against inflation provided by annual "escalator" adjustments geared to the Consumer Price Index. One informed observer suggests that a tendency toward common expiration dates of IAM agreements and similar "pattern" settlements by IAM for its many "mechanic and related" and other ground-employee bargaining units is having a stabilizing impact that "has ameliorated the abuses of whipsawing." Whether this will persist under improving economic conditions in the face of rivalry from the TWU, the AMFA, and the IBT remains to be seen.

Small, specialized bargaining units, such as those composed of dispatchers or meteorologists, tend to follow the patterns of change obtained by other ground employees, especially because, where unionized, they are most often represented by the IAM or the TWU. At American, a dispatcher with ten or more years of service had a monthly base pay, at the end of 1977, of $2,427. American's meteorologists with ten or more years of service had base pay of $2,212. Both are represented by TWU and their fringe benefits and working conditions are similar to those in the American-TWU mechanics' agreement. Other trunk line average salaries at the end of 1976 were: aircraft and traffic service, $17,028; reservations and sales, $14,640. Fringe benefits, for the industry as a whole, averaged $4,808 per employee in 1976, or 26 percent of earnings.[90]

One common thread that runs through all airline collective bargaining agreements is a heavy reliance on carrier seniority within each bargaining unit, not merely as a means of relative protection against layoffs, but as the principal criterion for access to promotional opportunities and to preferable working conditions. For pilots, seniority determines not only one's order of entry into a higher job classification (i.e., from second officer to first officer to captain), but also the order in which a pilot may be trained for and fly larger and higher-paying aircraft, his choice of domicile, and his monthly flying schedule. Because of the importance of one's seniority, each employee has a vital stake in the survival and growth of his/her employing carrier. For the unions, this translates into a strong preference for the structural status quo.

It is clear that unionized airline employees, against the historical

---

[90] AVMARK, pp. 8–10

background of a federally supported and regulated industry, expanding markets, progressive technology, declining unit labor costs (until 1967), and single-carrier "craft or class" bargaining, have fared well as a whole in terms of earnings and working conditions. Some airline managers—although not most—would today support legislation imposing some variation of compulsory arbitration for unsettled interest disputes because of their concern about the economics of air transportation in the face of increasing labor-cost trends.[91] The unions not only oppose any imposition of compulsory arbitration, but also, as noted earlier, vigorously objected to "deregulation." [92] Obviously, greater ease of entry and exit under the terms of the 1978 Deregulation Act, if they should lead to significant changes in the distribution of traffic among carriers, will disturb vested employee rights rooted in airline seniority within each class or craft.

Dispute Settlement Under the RLA

This section, before noting some recent constructive developments, examines the dispute-settlement procedures of the Railway Labor Act in relation to their impact on airline collective bargaining and grievance handling.

NEGOTIATION

Airline collective bargaining agreements are invariably for a fixed term, usually two to three years. As this writer recently pointed out:

> . . . Whether because of the complexity of airline contract provisions, the dynamic character of the industry in terms of economics and technology, and/or the awareness of the parties that mediation is mandatory, collective bargaining usually commences with "Section 6" proposals on many, perhaps hundreds, of items. Clearly, the parties do not normally anticipate that such a rich menu can be digested within the thirty-day notice period required by Section 6.[93]

Nevertheless, although settlements prior to mediation used to be rare, more than half of all airline contract negotiations in recent years have been successfully concluded prior to the involvement of the mediator.

MEDIATION

Since a strike is unlawful until the RLA's procedures have been exhausted, the negotiating parties—unless they have a realistic expectation

---

[91] Kahn, "Labor-Management Relations . . . ," p. 122.

[92] See above, pp. 337–38.

[93] Kahn, "Labor-Management Relations . . . ," p. 119.

of reaching a prompt settlement in direct negotiations—anticipate the participation of a mediator assigned by the NMB. Because the ensuing step of the RLA procedures does not commence until the NMB determines that an impasse has been reached (see above, pp. 343-44), the negotiating parties are normally motivated to make effective use of the mediation phase. Moreover, the effectiveness of mediation has been enhanced by the fact that presidential emergency boards have not been appointed for airline disputes between 1966 and 1978 (for reasons to be noted below), thus eliminating an earlier tendency of each party to use the mediation period as a convenient opportunity in which to prepare for its presentation to the emergency board.

Experienced airline union and management negotiators generally express respect for the mediation process, although in particular instances they may criticize the NMB's delay in declaring an impasse or the tactics employed by a mediator. Mediation statistics are abundant but not very helpful to an attempt to evaluate the value of the process, since one cannot know what would have happened in its absence.[94] Shrewd use by the NMB of its authority to control the duration of mediation undoubtedly serves to reduce the number of airline strikes and may also avoid the cumulative impact on bargaining and on the traveling public of simultaneous strikes on major carriers serving given routes.

Active mediation does not end with the proffer of arbitration, except in the rare case that the proffer is accepted.[95] Now that airline emergency boards can no longer be expected, it is at this critical time that a member of the NMB may enter the situation in cooperation with the staff mediator to exert maximum leverage on the parties. Many settlements have taken place in this period.

EMERGENCY BOARDS

The theory of the RLA's presidential emergency board was, of course, that its findings and recommendations would provide a basis for settlement that the disputing parties would find difficult to reject, especially because of the public's interest in avoiding any stoppage that would "deprive a section of the country of essential transportation service" (Section 10). Although no strike on a single carrier actually satisfies this criterion, 33 emergency boards were routinely appointed between 1947 and 1966 in almost every instance that a strike deadline had been set. In six of these instances, the parties reached a settlement before their

[94] Cemini, ch. IV, provides and discusses NMB mediation data for 1936–69. The NMB Annual Reports furnish more recent data.

[95] Cemini, p. 23, notes that arbitration was usually rejected by the carriers prior to the 1950s, and usually by the unions since then.

emergency board issued its report. Of the other 27 cases, the board's recommendations were accepted by both parties only twice, while eight of the settlements reached after a board's report were preceded by strikes. A comprehensive survey of the airline emergency-board experience has been prepared by Cemini, who noted that the relative ineffectiveness of these boards was explained by the NMB on the ground "that the complicated and technical issues precipitating these disputes were given little publicity and that they were somewhat incomprehensible to the public." [96]

Cullen assigns primary credit to George P. Shultz, Secretary of Labor in 1969, for the decision that the President should no longer appoint emergency boards in single-carrier labor disputes.[97] It is significant that this policy, to which no exception was made until 1978, has the strong support of union and management officials. The appointment of an airline emergency board in November 1978 by President Carter was compelled by a peculiar excursion of Congress into executive authority contained in the 1978 Deregulation Act:

> Sec. 44. Within ten days after the date of enactment of this section the President, pursuant to section 10 of the Railway Labor Act, shall create a board to investigate and report on the dispute between Wien Air Alaska, Incorporated, and the Air Line Pilots Association. Such board shall report its findings to the President within thirty days from the date of its creation.

The outcome of this intervention into a strike that had been continuing since May 8, 1977, is not yet known.[98]

There remains a substantial consensus, however, that airline bargaining tends to be more effective when the parties are not tempted to treat direct negotiations and the mediation phase as periods in which they should prepare for emergency board hearings, while the public has accepted the inconvenience of airline strikes that have occurred in the absence of emergency boards.

STRIKES

Considering the variety of bargaining units and the large numbers of airline contracts to be periodically negotiated (the NMB's Annual Re-

---

[96] Cemini, p. 24.

[97] Cullen, p. 174.

[98] The stickiest issue in the protracted Wien Air Alaska pilots' strike involves whether two or three pilots will man the cockpits of Wien's B-737s. The carrier has been flying its B-737s with nonunion pilots trained by Boeing and has subcontracted many bush routes in Alaska. See, for example: "Alaskan pilots carry strike to Detroit," *Detroit Free Press*, October 2, 1978. Section 44 of the 1978 Deregulation Act was primarily a product of effective lobbying by ALPA.

port says that there were 986 on file), strikes have been relatively infrequent, although costly to the parties and troublesome to the affected public when they did occur. From January 1, 1970, through December 31, 1978, a total of 31 strikes took place on all certificated U.S. carriers, or an average of about four per year. Some were very brief. Sixteen of the strikes, listed in Table 9, lasted more than 15 days. Twelve different carriers were involved in these longer strikes, which were called by

TABLE 9

Strikes on Scheduled U.S. Airlines, January 1970–December 1978
(Excluding Strikes of Less Than 16 Days)

Carrier	Started	Ended	Duration (days)	Union (Unit)
National	1–31–70	4–24–70	187	ALEA (Clerks)
Northwest	7– 8–70	12–14–70	160	BRAC (Clerks)
Mohawk	11–12–70	4–14–71	154	ALPA (Pilots)
Hughes Air-West	12–15–71	4–10–72	118	AMFA (Mechanics)
Northwest	6–30–72	10– 2–72	95	ALPA (Pilots)
Ozark	4–19–73	6–30–73	73	AMFA (Mechanics)
Trans World	11– 5–73	12–18–73	44	TWU (Flight Attendants)
National	7–14–74	10–30–74	110	IAM (Mechanics & Related)
Texas Int'l.	12– 1–74	4– 4–75	125	ALEA (Clerks & Stn. Agents)
National	9– 1–75	1– 5–76	127	ALPA/AFA (Flt. Attendants)
Airlift	11–14–75	3– 2–76	109	ALPA (Pilots)
United	12– 6–75	12–21–75	16	IAM (Mechanics & Related)
Alaska	9–28–76	10–21–76	24	AFA (Flight Attendants)
Continental	10–23–76	11–16–76	24	ALPA (Pilots)
Wien Air Alaska	5– 8–77	a	a	ALPA (Pilots)
Northwest	4–29–78	8–15–78	109	ALPA (Pilots)

Sources: Airline Industrial Relations Conference (AIRCon), National Mediation Board, Carriers, and Unions.

a Still in progress as of December 31, 1978.

seven different unions. Six of these strikes were by pilots, four by mechanics, three by flight attendants, and three by clerks and station agents. National suffered three long strikes, each by a different union. Northwest also had three long strikes, two by its pilots. No other carrier listed had more than one long strike. Obviously, there has been a substantial dispersion of the incidence of long strikes during these years. As already noted, it is likely that MAP served to increase the number of long strikes (although not the total number of strikes), but there is no evidence that the magnitude of settlements had been significantly dampened by MAP. An interesting perspective on the role of MAP in providing economic underpinning to a struck carrier was voiced by ALPA President John J. O'Donnell—a long-time MAP critic and opponent—at the end of 1976 in an *Aviation Daily* interview: "I am concerned about going off mutual aid until all airline unions recognize their responsibility to the industry. It would have a tremendously adverse impact on younger pilots if a strike occurs and we have no way to preserve the carrier. If we kill mutual aid now, I could have a lot of pilots on the street who are forty years old. They would not get hired anyplace." O'Donnell expressed hope that more unions and carriers could agree on processes to help achieve final settlements without compulsory arbitration.[99] This chapter will look at some recent developments of this type after a brief treatment of the impact of the RLA on grievance handling.

AIRLINE GRIEVANCE MACHINERY

The drafters of Title II of the RLA naively empowered the NMB (in Section 205) to order the establishment, at its discretion, of a "National Air Transport Adjustment Board" of four members, two to be appointed by the air carriers, two by the labor organizations "national in scope," to hear and decide all otherwise unsettled grievances or disputes involving the interpretation and application of agreements. The NMB, fortunately, has never seen fit to direct the creation of such a national board. It is self-evident that no such bipartite organization could satisfactorily represent the multitude of diverse carriers and unions in the adjudication of grievances.

Section 204 of the RLA, however, directs each air carrier and union (pending the implementation of Section 205) to establish their own adjustment board. This mandate led to the inclusion, in all labor contracts, of provisions establishing a four-member "System Board of Adjustment" to decide grievances under that contract and for the addition of a fifth member, usually called the referee, to break any deadlock of the four-member board. Although some unions and carriers have begun, in recent years, to utilize three-member system boards and even (usually, only by mutual agreement for the particular case) sole arbitrators, the use of five-member arbitration boards is still prevalent. Since most arbitration machinery in other industries relies on sole arbitrators, the persistent use of boards in the airlines deserves further study. This writer has commented, in relation to the airlines' experience:

> A tripartite arbitration board has advantages. . . . A referee's colleagues on the board often help to clarify the facts and issues. Moreover, the partisan members can serve as an avenue of communication and education for their respective parties that will contribute to their understanding of the process and its results. It is also true that the five-man board and its procedures constitute a relatively elaborate, expensive and slow process for the arbitration of grievances. On large carriers, where increas-

---

[99] *Aviation Daily*, December 30, 1976, p. 329.

ing numbers of grievances are referred to a single board, bottlenecks have developed at the board level. The advantages of
a system board have to be balanced against the cost and the
time involved.[100]

Under the American-TWU contract, six regional system boards hear and
decide discipline grievances while three specialized system boards handle contract interpretation cases. Many parties are regularly modifying
their grievance machinery in light of experience and their own needs.
It is fortunate that the precedent of the National Railroad Adjustment
Board created by the RLA did not lead to the imposition of legislatively
prescribed grievance arbitration machinery in the airlines.[101]

RECENT DEVELOPMENTS

The transformation of the airlines after the 1960s—from an era of
dynamic technology, enormous market growth, and increasing employment, into a period of economic uncertainty, relatively stable technology,
modest market growth, and erratic changes in employment—radically
changed the environment in which collective bargaining operates. The
improving economic picture since 1975, obviously a positive factor, has
been offset by uncertainties associated with the 1978 Deregulation Act.
There are many indications that some airlines unions are concerned
about the economic health of their employers and about the costs associated with strikes. Carriers and unions alike would also prefer to
avoid the often protracted periods of bargaining traditional under the
RLA. Here, briefly noted, are some of the relevant actions and procedures that have recently taken place.

Postponement of Pay Increases. Because Eastern and Pan American
were both undergoing financial crises in 1975, ALPA and IAM at Eastern, and ALPA and FEIA at Pan Am, agreed to postpone pay increases
for that year, while TWU agreed to accept later effective dates than the
industry pattern for pay increases at Pan Am.

Eastern's "Variable Earnings Program" (VEP). Eastern, during 1976
and 1977, persuaded all of the unions representing its employees to
accept a VEP based on a target profit rate of 2 percent of gross revenue,
or about $40 million for 1977. Each employee is being paid 3.5 percent
less than the amount called for in the pertinent labor agreement, with
this deduction placed in a "Variable Earnings Account." If at the end
of the fiscal year (December 31) Eastern's profits should equal precisely
the target rate, the 3.5 percent of withheld employee earnings would be
distributed in full. To the extent that Eastern's profits fall short of this

---

[100] Kahn, "Airline Grievance Procedures," p. 319.
[101] For the railroad experience, see Seidenberg.

target, the funds in the Variable Earnings Account are to be applied toward that target up to the full amount deducted, as required, with any difference not required to meet the target to be distributed to the employees. On the other hand, if Eastern's profit target is exceeded, one-third of the excess up to a maximum equal to 3.5 percent of payroll is to be distributed among the employees in proportion to earnings. In substance, then, Eastern's VEP creates a 7 percent range in employee earnings—3.5 percent below and above the contract rates—contingent on this carrier's profit position. This innovative profit-sharing plan has obvious significance in relation to collective bargaining, not only because it relates employee earnings to profits in a general sense, but in particular because the initial costs of a strike by any of Eastern's unions will be borne by Eastern's employees up to as much (if Eastern were prosperous) of 7 percent of payroll.

Expedited Bargaining Timetables. Several carriers and unions have executed letters of agreement establishing stringent time-limits on negotiations, although without any other device for encouraging or ensuring settlement. In some instances, such timetables have led to expeditiously negotiated agreements. Early settlements can backfire, however, especially where rank-and-file ratification is the rule (as among flight attendants) and if the membership interprets the quick deal as implying that its negotiators could have held out for more. For example, United and ALPA/AFA agreed on March 8, 1977, to exchange "Section 6" notices on May 27, 1977; to engage in direct negotiations from June 20 through July 29, 1977; to jointly request (if no agreement had been reached) mediation by the NMB, to be provided from August 1 through 31, 1977; to jointly request a proffer of arbitration by the NMB on September 1, 1977, if no agreement were signed by that time; and to "respond to the proffer within 72 hours." The NMB was also requested to assign a mediator full time to observe the direct negotiations and then to assign the same mediator, if need be, during the August mediation phase. United and ALPA/AFA proceeded according to this timetable and did reach agreement while in mediation on August 31, 1977, the day before the expiration of their prior contract. This contract, which provided for a 27.1 percent general increase in pay over its two-and-one-half-year term and many substantial improvements in pay and workrules, was submitted for ratification with a "For" vote recommended by the Negotiating Committee and the MEC chairperson. Although the vote was conducted by mail, only 4,826 of the 7,174 members of the bargaining unit responded. The contract was rejected by a vote of 2,613 against, 2,011 for (with 17 void ballots). The same ALPA/AFA negotiators returned to the bargaining table; the NMB made its proffer of arbitration on October 19, 1977, thereby "starting the clock" for the 30-day status quo; a strike deadline was set for 0001 on November 19, 1977; a new contract, containing all of the previously obtained improvements plus additional gains in work and pay rules, was reached just five minutes before this strike was scheduled to start; and, with 5,954 ballots returned this time, the renegotiated contract was ratified by 4,937 "Yes" votes. It would appear that membership ratification can upset the outcome of expedited bargaining arrangements.

Expedited Bargaining with Fact-Finding. On September 10, 1976, United and ALPA agreed to use the services of a private "fact-finder" to observe and mediate during their direct negotiations according to an expedited timetable. ALPA's constitution does not call for membership ratification of new contracts, which require only the endorsement of the ALPA Master Executive Council for that carrier. They appointed, as fact-finder, Professor Benjamin Aaron of the University of California. Negotiations began early in October 1977; a settlement was reached in direct negotiations on November 1, 1977, six weeks prior to the Section 6 deadline; and the contract was ratified by ALPA's United Master Executive Council 12 days later.[102] A similarly successful experience took place at TWA which, on April 1, 1977, agreed with ALPA to use former Secretary of Labor William J. Usery as a private fact-finder. An agreement, effective October 1, 1977, was negotiated in August during six days of bargaining within a two-week period.

Expedited Bargaining with Arbitration. On February 19, 1976, National agreed with ALEA to exchange Section 6 proposals 120 days prior to the expiration of their current contract, or February 1, 1977; to engage in direct negotiations limited to ten issues from each party through April 30, 1977; to request the NMB on March 15, 1977, to provide mediation for 30 days commencing May 1, 1977; to *accept* a proffer of arbitration by the NMB on June 1, 1977, if no settlement had yet been reached; to select the arbitrator by June 5, 1977, either directly or from a list presented by the NMB; and to require the arbitrator to conduct hearings and render an award on unresolved economic issues by July 15, 1977. National and ALEA also agreed that no strike or lockout could take place over any unresolved noneconomic issues. Pursuant to this schedule, a new contract was consummated on May 31, 1977, the day before the arbitration proffer (and ratified by 3,002 to 119 three weeks later). Because arbitration was not utilized, this machinery remains in force for the next National-ALEA contract negotiation.[103] A similar

[102] "Reach Early Agreements on Pilots' Contract," *Friendly Times* (Chicago: United Air Lines, December 1976), pp. 1, 9.

[103] "Peace Pact Worked!" *The Air Line Employee* (Chicago: ALEA, July-August 1977), pp. 3-4.

agreement was negotiated on July 7, 1976, between Braniff and ALPA and resulted in a new contract also reached just before going into arbitration.

The specifics of all such arrangements are less important, of course, than the motivations that gave rise to them. Such arrangements short of a firm commitment to arbitrate can be successful only in the presence of a jointly held determination to make them work. And prior commitments to arbitrate won't be made or repeated if there is excessive mistrust or animosity or if a previous experience produced a result unacceptable to either party. Moreover, although innovative approaches to obtaining prompt and acceptable contract settlements demonstrate that the parties, under the RLA umbrella, are free to improvise, these devices have been contrived and tried only at a small fraction of airline bargaining tables. The public, nevertheless, can hope that they represent the beginning of a trend that will not be upset by traumatic economic events or reactions to changing regulatory policies.

Conclusions

Much has necessarily been omitted from this brief examination of collective bargaining in the airlines that is relevant to a thoroughgoing appraisal of how the process has functioned in this highly regulated transportation industry. Because of the multiplicity of crafts and classes and unions, and of the substantial differences among the carriers, little could be said about the substance of collective agreements (most of which are longer than this chapter), about the structure and government of the unions with their highly dispersed memberships, about job content and working conditions, or about the substantial role of the Federal Aviation Agency and its "FARs" in shaping the work environment. Our references to interesting illustrative incidents have been minimal. This writer believes, however, that the following conclusions can be legitimately inferred from the airline collective bargaining experience on the basis of this overview.

1. Collective bargaining has worked reasonably well, and undoubtedly better than any viable alternative, especially when one considers the enormous technological, structural, and economic changes in the industry during its 40 years of collective bargaining experience.

2. The Railway Labor Act, on balance, has provided a suitable legislative framework for collective bargaining. Its most positive contribution has been the feature of mandatory mediation, buttressed by the right of the NMB to keep the bargainers in the mediation phase until, in the NMB's judgment, genuine and sufficient bargaining has occurred. Another desirable feature is its prohibition of strikes over

grievances and its encouragement of tripartite grievance arbitration. Although the NMB has made some questionable bargaining-unit decisions among ground employees, such problems would have been difficult for any labor relations agency to avoid in an industry experiencing great employment growth and with tremendous disparity in size among the carriers.

3. Single-carrier airline strikes can clearly be tolerated by the public and do not ordinarily justify public action to prevent or terminate them in the absence of an agreement between the disputants. Airline strikes, in retrospect, have not been frequent, considering the large number of collective bargaining agreements involved.

4. A trend toward the selection of the same union by different employee units at the same carrier, such as has taken place with the TWU at American and the IAM at United, is a contribution toward labor relations stability and should be encouraged.

5. Airline employees, as a whole, have obtained good earnings levels and working conditions under collective bargaining. There does exist a possibility, now that productivity growth is less than in the past and unit labor costs are rising, that uninhibited union pressures—with labor costs about 42 percent of total operating costs—could generate imprudent cost increases. This possibility is far from a certainty, however, especially in light of recent indications of concern by labor organizations for the industry's economic health. Accordingly, there does not appear to be any present need for a public policy change that would inhibit in this industry the ultimate right to strike or that would actually impose compulsory arbitration to resolve unsettled disputes over the terms and conditions of employment.

List of References

Air Transport Association of America. *The Sixty Billion Dollar Question.* Washington: ATA, September 1976.
AVMARK Management Report. *Employee Productivity—A Key to Airline Profits—1976.* Washington: AVMARK, Inc., June 30, 1977.
Baitsell, John M. *Airline Industrial Relations.* Boston: Harvard University Press, 1966.
Ballard, Frederick A. "Federal Regulation of Aviation." *Harvard Law Review* 60 (1947).
Boeing Commercial Airplane Company. *Importance of Adequate Near Term U.S. Airline Earnings to Continued Leadership by U.S. Commercial Aircraft.* Seattle: Boeing, revised September 1976.
Caves, Richard E. *Air Transport and Its Regulators.* Cambridge, Mass.: Harvard University Press, 1962.
Cemini, Michael. *Airline Experience under the Railway Labor Act.* Bull. 1683. Washington: U.S. Department of Labor, Bureau of Labor Statistics, 1971.
Cullen, Donald E. "Emergency Boards under the Railway Labor Act." Ch. VI in *The Railway Labor Act at Fifty,* ed. Charles M. Rehmus. Washington: National Mediation Board, 1977.
David, Paul. T. *The Economics of Air Mail Transportation.* Washington: Brookings Institution, 1934.

Eischen, Dana E. "Representation Disputes and Their Resolution in the Railroad and Airline Industries." Ch. III in *The Railway Labor Act at Fifty*, ed. Charles M. Rehmus. Washington: National Mediation Board, 1977.

Hopkins, George E. *The Airline Pilots—A Study in Elite Unionization*. Cambridge, Mass.: Harvard University Press, 1970.

Jordan, William A. *Airline Regulation in America—Effects and Imperfections*. Baltimore: Johns Hopkins University Press, 1970.

Kahn, Mark L. "Airline Grievance Procedures: Some Observations and Questions." *Journal of Air Law and Commerce* 25 (Summer 1969).

———. "Collective Bargaining on the Airline Flight Deck." Part IV in *Collective Bargaining and Technological Change*, Harold M. Levinson et al. Evanston, Ill.: The Transportation Center at Northwestern University, 1971, pp. 421–607.

———. "Industrial Relations in the Airlines." Doctoral dissertation, Harvard University, 1950.

———. "Labor-Management Relations in the Airline Industry." Ch. IV in *The Railway Labor Act at Fifty*, ed. Charles M. Rehmus. Washington: National Mediation Board, 1977.

———. "Mutual Strike Aid in the Airlines." *Labor Law Journal* 11 (July 1960), pp. 595–606.

———. "The National Airlines Strike: A Case Study." *Journal of Air Law and Commerce* 19 (Winter 1952).

———. "Regulatory Agencies and Industrial Relations: The Airline Case." *American Economic Review* 42 (May 1952).

Krislov, Joseph. "Mediation Under the Railway Labor Act: A Process in Search of a Name." *Labor Law Journal* 27 (May 1976).

MacAvoy, Paul W., and John W. Snow, eds. *Regulation of Passenger Fares and Competition Among the Airlines*. Washington: American Enterprise Institute for Public Policy Research, 1977.

Rehmus, Charles M., ed. *The Railway Labor Act at Fifty*. Washington: National Mediation Board, 1977.

Seidenberg, Jacob. "Grievance Adjustment in the Railroad Industry." Ch. VIII in *The Railway Labor Act at Fifty*, ed. Charles M. Rehmus. Washington: National Mediation Board, 1977.

Unterberger, S. Herbert, and Edward C. Koziara. "Airline Strike Insurance: A Study in Escalation." *Industrial and Labor Relations Review* 29 (October 1975), pp. 26–45.

CHAPTER 8

Hospitals*

RICHARD U. MILLER
University of Wisconsin

Introduction

Collective bargaining is a contemporary development in the employee relations of American hospitals, unlike the long history of labor-management relations in such industries as construction, coal mining, steel, or trucking. For example, the number of hospital workers represented by labor organizations in the late 1960s was approximately 9 percent.[1] By mid-1977 the proportion of hospital employees under union contract generally exceeded 20 percent,[2] and was significantly higher in certain geographical areas of the United States.[3] If health care were less important socially, politically, or economically, it would probably not be worth the trouble incurred in attempting to understand either the complexities of this industry or the labor-management issues which have emerged as collective bargaining has become established. Yet, as Table 1 shows, it is hard to ignore the impact of an industry which consumes an increasing share of the gross national product, accounting for more than $162 billion in expenditures in 1977 and predicted to reach a spending level of $280 billion by 1982. How rapidly expenditures for the delivery of health-care services have grown in the last two decades is underlined by reference to the statistics on per capita spending which

---

* The author wishes to express his appreciation for the assistance received from health-care labor and management who, during the course of numerous contacts and interviews supplied much of the basic data for the chapter. A special sense of gratitude is felt to Norman Solomon of the Industrial Relations Research Institute of the University of Wisconsin, who assisted in the research and who provided valuable comments on an earlier draft; to Lu Dewey Tanner, formerly of the Federal Mediation and Conciliation Service, who painstakingly reviewed the chapter in its early states; and to Barbara Dennis of IRRI who not only read and edited the manuscript as it evolved but also contributed substantively to its final form. Errors of omission and interpretation remain solely mine.

[1] Freeman and Medoff, Table 1, p. 153. [The complete citations for all footnote references are listed at the end of the chapter.]

[2] Communication from the Office of Wages and Industrial Relations, Bureau of Labor Statistics, December 12, 1978.

[3] See pages 391–94 of this chapter.

approximated $142 in 1960 compared with $737 for health care expended
in 1977 for each person in the United States.

TABLE 1

Aggregate and Per Capita Health-Care Expenditures,
Selected Years 1929–1977

	Total Expenditures for Health Care (billions of dollars)	Percent of GNP	Per Capita Expenditures
1929	$ 3.6	3.5%	$ 29.16
1935	2.8	4.1	22.04
1940	3.9	4.1	29.98
1950	12.0	4.5	78.35
1955	17.3	4.5	103.76
1960	25.9	5.2	141.63
1965	38.9	5.9	197.75
1970	69.2	7.2	333.57
1975	123.7	8.5	571.21
1976	141.0	8.7	645.76
1977[a]	162.6	8.8	736.92

Source: Robert M. Gibson and Charles R. Fisher, "National Health Expenditures, Fiscal Year 1977," *Social Security Bulletin* 41 (July 1978), Table 1, p. 5.

[a] New federal fiscal year ending September.

Beyond its size and growth, it is also important to keep in mind that organizations that provide health-care services are found in a variety of political and legal jurisdictions. For example, of the 7,082 hospitals in operation in 1976, 5.4 percent were under federal government control, and 26 percent were units of state or local government. Thus, while the public sector is significantly involved in the delivery of health care, the majority of institutions are operated by private parties either for profit (10.6 percent) or nonprofit (47.5 percent).

In addition, unlike the typical manufacturing or service industry, direct payments from those who purchase the product or service play a very minor role in the income of hospitals. Direct payments from patients, for example, constituted only 6.0 percent of all income received in 1977; the major sources of income were private insurers (35.8 percent) and public agencies (55.7 percent).[4] As so-called third-party payers have acquired an increasingly larger role in the financial structure of the health-care industry, their potential for intrusion into the industry's bargaining relations has grown commensurately.

Finally, a brief overview of current health-care issues would be remiss if it omitted the widespread controversy surrounding the rising cost of health-care services. Except for the period of the economic stabilization programs (August 1971 to April 1974), prices of health services have tended to rise much faster than the general consumer price

---

[4] Gibson and Fisher, p. 6. By comparison, consumers paid 34.2 percent of their hospital bills in 1950.

index; on a base of 1967, the November 1978 CPI (all items less medical services) registered 199.4, while the medical services index was 244.1.[5] Given the structure of financing in the industry, the role of the public sector both as an employer and as a source of funds, and the priority attached to accessible, quality health care, cost containment has become an issue at all levels of government. Price ceilings have been advocated, cost controls implemented, services cut back, institutions merged, and the industry generally threatened with stringent regulation of every facet of operation.

Collective bargaining, therefore, clearly has an important role in such an industry for a number of reasons. First, the structure of collective bargaining and the efficiency with which it functions are primarily determined by the general characteristics of the industry. Second, since labor cost constitutes upwards of 60 percent of total cost, negotiated settlements often have an unsettling effect on cost-containment efforts. Third, the need for continuous delivery of health-care services places a premium on the maintenance of the labor-management relationship and the availability of mechanisms for conflict resolution. Finally, given its status as a service industry of mixed public and private ownership, no single existing industrial relations model will be adequate either for describing health-care collective bargaining or for formulating and evaluating policies to deal with its problems.

In order to make the task of this chapter more manageable, the discussion of collective bargaining will be restricted to hospitals, thus excluding nursing homes, clinics, and related institutions. The financial and organizational structures, missions, patient-care mixes, and workforces of the latter are different, and therefore their exclusion necessarily limits the extent to which generalizations can be made across such diverse segments of the health-care industry. The hospital, however, exists at the center of the health-care delivery system, employing 72 percent of the industry's workforce of 4.3 million people.[6] In addition, it is also the source of more than $65 billion of total health-care expenditures. Hospitals obviously are the dominant sector in the health-care industry and therefore are a legitimate focus for the study of collective bargaining in their own right.

The Hospital Industry: Structure, Characteristics, and Trends

Although its roots can be traced to the Middle Ages, in its present

[5] U.S. Department of Labor, Bureau of Labor Statistics. "The Consumer Price Index—November 1978." News, December 22, 1978. Since 1950 the cost of a day of hospital care had risen by more than 1,000 percent as contrasted with the general level of prices which was up 125 percent. Council on Wage and Price Stability, The Rapid Rise of Hospital Costs, p. 11.

[6] American Hospital Association, Hospital Statistics, 1977 Edition, pp. xi–xii.

form the hospital is largely a product of this century. In 1873, for example, there were only 178 hospitals in the entire country, the majority being detention centers for the mentally ill. Sick individuals who could support themselves preferred to remain at home, and hospitals existed primarily as "places where the homeless and poverty stricken went to die." [7] However, with the advent of surgical anesthesia, asepsis, and general hygiene at the end of the nineteenth century, a technological and scientific health-care revolution began which continues to the present time. Thus, by 1909 the number of hospitals exceeded 4,300, and the institution itself had evolved into a multiphase center incorporating teaching and research as well as health-care services.

Although the absolute numbers of hospitals have not increased significantly in the last 25 years, a radical change in hospital structure, control, and administration has occurred. Gross assets have increased eightfold, public health care has shifted from federal to state and local government, and nongovernment, not-for-profit hospitals have displaced investor-owned institutions.

These trends are a further consequence of the continuing impact of new developments in medical care and science. For example, diseases such as tuberculosis and polio which formerly required long periods of confined treatment have largely been eradicated, and mental illness has increasingly become subject to treatment through outpatient approaches rather than long-term hospitalization. Also, technological innovations often have required large capital investment and highly trained specialized personnel. Thus, as the short-term, general-care community hospital emerged as the major source of the delivery of health care, it also underwent important modifications in its characteristics and methods of operation.

Associated with the trend toward the general-care community hospital is the increasing size of such health-care institutions. The number of small community hospitals (less than 100 beds) declined by 18 percent between 1965 and 1976 and, although the number of moderate-sized hospitals (100–399 beds) increased by 26 percent, the greatest expansion by size of hospital (85 percent) occurred among those with 400 or more beds. As a consequence, the average community hospital in the United States had 163 beds in 1976, up from 129 12 years earlier.[8] Hospital size, in turn, is highly correlated with salary level, personnel per bed, ratio of full-time to part-time employees, and availability of specialized services. More shall be said about this in the following sections of the chapter.

---

[7] "Working in Hospitals: Then and Now," *1199 News* (September 1976, special issue), p. 5. See also Enright and Jonas, pp. 165–66.

[8] AHA, *Hospital Statistics*, 1977 Edition, p. viii.

THE HOSPITAL LABOR FORCE

The rapid growth in the demand for health-care services has stimulated the expansion of employment generally, but particularly in the hospital sector. Total hospital employment grew 194 percent from 1950 to 1976 and by more than 50 percent from 1965 to 1976.[9] Community hospitals, in turn, show even greater gains in personnel during the same periods: 275 percent (1950–75) and 79 percent (1966–75). Thus, while the total U.S. labor force has grown at an annual rate of 1.7 percent over the past 15 years, hospital employment has expanded at a 5.5 percent rate.[10]

Demographic Characteristics. That health-care employment is predominantly female is well known. According to the Bureau of Labor Statistics, 76 percent of all hospital workers were female in 1977.[11] This not only compares with an average of 40.5 percent for all workers, but is an increase from the percentage that characterized the industry in 1960. It should also be noted that nearly 25 percent of the males in the health industry are self-employed. The relevant figure for females is less than 2 percent.[12]

Minorities also tend to be "overrepresented" in health occupations. Blacks, for example, constituted 18.9 percent of total hospital employment, compared to 10.8 percent of all workers in 1977.[13] As with females, the relative proportion of blacks in the industry has been increasing since the 1960s. The "ghettoization" of certain health-care occupations is clearly evident from the figures in Table 2. Females have only token

TABLE 2

Selected Health-Care Occupations by Percent Female and Minority
1977

Occupation	Percent Female	Percent Minority
Licensed practical nurse	96.8	21.6
Registered nurse	96.7	11.3
Nurse's aide, orderly and attendant	86.5	26.5
Laboratory technician	74.2	15.5
Radiologic technician	71.8	7.1
Therapist	68.5	9.6
Social worker	61.2	19.1
Health administrator	45.1	5.1
Pharmacist	17.4	4.3
Physician (MD & DO)	11.2	9.2

Source: BLS, *Employment and Earnings* 25 (January 1978), Table 23, pp. 153–54.

[9] *Ibid.*, pp. 3–5.
[10] U.S. Bureau of Labor Statistics, *Employment and Earnings*, Bulletin 1312.
[11] U.S. Bureau of Labor Statistics, *Employment and Earnings* 25 (January 1978), Table 30, p. 161.
[12] National Commission for Manpower Policy, *Employment Impacts of Health Policy Developments*, p. 24.
[13] U.S. BLS, *Employment and Earnings* 25 (January 1978), Table 30, p. 161.

representation among physicians, dentists, and pharmacists; their highest proportion is in the nursing services, therapy, and social work. Moreover, the more highly skilled the "female" occupations, the less likely it is that blacks and other minorities will be found in those occupations.

Although there are few relevant statistics, anecdotal information also suggests that within many urban areas, minority employment is much higher in health-care institutions than general industry figures indicate. In such cities as New York, Boston, Detroit, and Chicago, nearly all housekeeping, kitchen, aide, and orderly positions are held by minority males and females.

Hospital Internal Labor Markets. Rather than the pyramidal structure usually associated with organizations, the hospital's occupational structure can be described as an "hourglass" [14] with large numbers of high-wage, skilled workers at the upper end of the structure, equal numbers of low-wage, low-skilled at the other end, and little in between. For example, of the more than 3,100,000 hospital workers employed in 1976, 54,231 were physicians, 538,141 were registered nurses (RNs), and 243,586 were licensed practical nurses (LPNs).[15] The remaining 2.1 million employees were primarily aides and orderlies, or performing such tasks as housekeeping, kitchen, and other services. Persons in skilled occupations or professions such as pharmacists, X-ray technicians, therapists, and building maintenance workers ordinarily make up only a small proportion of the total hospital workforce.

Although a great deal of interdependence exists among hospital occupations—the registered nurse and the physician, the LPN and the nurse, and so on—the structure itself is a mosaic of job clusters so compartmentalized by licensing, training, and custom that movement by personnel between them is difficult, if not impossible. Moreover, within the job compartments, progression ladders typically are short. Hence, the upward mobility often possible in industrial organizations is generally absent because of the extreme fragmentation of hospital occupational structures. Workers at low skill levels quickly reach deadends and, to achieve mobility, must leave the hospital for alternative employment. The growth in hospital size with its accompanying increase in specialized services has tended to reinforce the fragmented occupational structure as each new service frequently generates new and highly specialized occupations.

Associated also with the hospital's occupational structure is a clearly delineated status hierarchy. Status based on job skill is reinforced by the social status of the individuals occupying the positions. Thus, in

---

[14] See Metzger and Pointer, p. 12.
[15] AHA, *Hospital Statistics,* 1977 Edition, Table 5A, p. 19.

the words of one author, "the traditional occupational hierarchy within a hospital is designed to promote conflict." [16] As social values and role expectations have changed, occupational groups have begun to compete with one another in intraorganizational maneuvering for power and authority. While the conflict may come to resemble the jurisdictional battles of building trade unions, the added dimensions of sex, race, and professional status aspirations may sharpen the struggles.

Wage Structures and Levels. The trend toward larger hospitals has contributed not only to the general growth of the industry's employment, but also to modification of its utilization and remuneration. As noted above, more specialized services tend to be associated with larger health-care institutions, and these specialized services often require highly complex equipment, large capital investment, and skilled personnel. Second, there is also a tendency for the ratio of personnel to bed size to increase with the number of beds in the hospital. For example, American Hospital Association statistics (see Table 3) indicate that the category of largest hospitals (500 plus) utilized nearly twice as many full-time-equivalent personnel per bed as did the group of smallest hospitals (24 or less beds). Third, as also shown in Table 3, the proportion of full-time to part-time personnel is much higher in the larger than in the smaller community hospitals. Even in the very largest hospitals, however, one worker in five continues to be employed only part time.

Finally, as can be seen in Table 3, salary level is highly correlated with hospital size. This, of course, is not only a function of higher skill levels and more full-time work, but also a consequence of the fact that

TABLE 3
Community Hospital Employment and Salaries[a]
1976

Bed Size	Full Time	Part Time	FTE/Bd	FT/Tot. Per.	Average Annual Salary
6–24	7,727	5,066	1.69	60.4	$ 6,994
25– 49	60,710	28,057	1.76	68.4	7,202
50– 99	188,061	69,962	2.06	72.9	7,727
100–199	391,584	133,385	2.36	74.6	8,575
200–299	369,312	122,518	2.69	75.1	9,366
300–399	303,552	100,092	2.71	75.2	9,691
400–499	253,198	67,223	2.91	79.0	9,787
500 plus	539,729	117,230	3.10	82.2	10,205
	2,114,376	643,537	2.61	76.7	$ 9,336

Source: Hospitals, JAHA, 51, September 16, 1977, Table 2, p. 70.
[a] Excludes interns, residents, and other trainees.

[16] Bloom, p. 168.

the larger hospitals tend to be located in areas in which wage levels are generally higher, cost of living greater, unions more active, and so on.

Despite significant wage increases over the last ten years, hospital wage levels continue to be low. In 1968, BLS statistics ranked the industry next to last of ten major industries.[17] Following eight years of very rapid expansion, the industry has moved up only one position. Average weekly earnings for nonsupervisory hospital workers were reported in 1977 to be $165.31 which, when converted to an annual figure, would place the average hospital worker only slightly above the poverty level, defined by the Community Services Administration as $6,200 for an urban family of four.[18] When these weekly earnings are compared with averages for other types of workers, the differences are striking: total private workers, $199.38; manufacturing workers, $236.00; and transportation workers, $286.38. Only in retail trade, with average weekly earnings of $146.73 do earnings appear to be lower.

Not only are wages low, but fringe benefits also suffer by comparison with other industries. The U.S. Chamber of Commerce, for example, reported that for 1977 an average of 36.7 percent of all private industry's payroll costs were accounted for by fringe benefit expenditures. Hospital fringe benefit costs were 25.7 percent on the average, the lowest for the 21 industries surveyed.[19]

Unionization at all levels of the hospital is a key to the magnitude and rapidity of change in the economic and social status of the industry's employees. The incidence of unions and their collective bargaining power in turn is a function of the legal framework setting forth employees' rights to organize, bargain, and engage in collective job actions. The next section of this chapter will provide a brief overview of the evolution of legal frameworks for hospital bargaining, including developments since the 1974 health-care amendments to the Taft-Hartley Act. In addition, to the extent possible, comparisons will be made between hospitals under federal or nonfederal public-sector control and those under private ownership.

The Legal Framework for Hospital Collective Bargaining

The diversity of political jurisdictions within which various sectors of the hospital industry operate has its clearest impact on the legal system for regulating the industry's labor-management relations. In many respects, it is more accurate to speak of legal systems in the plural, since one can identify at least three such systems and often more:

[17] Rosmann, "One Year Under Taft-Hartley," p. 64.
[18] U.S. BLS, *Employment and Earnings* 25 (January 1978), Table 30, p. 161. See *Federal Register*, Vol. 43, No. 66 (Wednesday, April 5, 1978), p. 14316.
[19] BNA, *Daily Labor Report*, December 18, 1978, pp. B1–B20.

those hospitals under federal public-sector law; those under state and local public-sector jurisdiction; and those private health-care institutions subject to regulation through the Taft-Hartley Act and its various amendments.

FEDERAL HOSPITALS

Until the advent of President John Kennedy's Executive Order 10988 in 1962, federal employees, including approximately 190,000 hospital workers, were without the legal right to unionize or bargain. Under the Executive Order, procedures were established for recognition based on the proportion of employees in the bargaining unit represented by the union, and a limited number of items became subject to bargaining. The inadequacies of E.O. 10988, particularly those related to conflict resolution, soon became apparent. Thus, in 1970 Richard Nixon issued a new Executive Order, 11491, which made major changes in the earlier E.O. Among other provisions, it created a three-member Federal Labor Relations Council to administer E.O. 11491, placed the authority to handle recognition issues within the U.S. Department of Labor, and established the Federal Services Impasses Panel to settle disputes over new contracts.[20]

It should be noted that the prohibitions on federal employee strikes were not relaxed by either of the Executive Orders. Section 305 of E.O. 11491 specifically bans strikes and specifies the following penalties for violation of the ban: discharge, loss of civil service status, and ineligibility for reemployment by the federal government for three years. Moreover, under the Order, it is an unfair labor practice for labor organizations to initiate or condone strikes of federal employees.

The importance of the Executive Orders is readily seen in the growth of unionization among federal hospital employees. In 1961, there were no federal hospitals in which at least one union had negotiated a contract.[21] Slightly in excess of one in five such hospitals had contracts in 1967 and for 1970, the relevant figure was 52.0 percent. By 1975, three-fourths of all federal hospitals had one or more collective bargaining agreements with their employees, compared with 19.8 percent for the hospital industry as a whole.[22]

NONFEDERAL GOVERNMENT HOSPITALS

Until Wisconsin took the step in 1959, no basis existed in any state law for nonfederal public employees to unionize, bargain, or strike, and

---

[20] See Nesbitt, pp. 130–33.

[21] "AHA Research Capsules—No. 6." p. 217.

[22] Employee Relations and Training Department, American Hospital Association, January 5, 1977.

few state or local government workers of any kind were covered by collective agreements. In 1961, for example, only 1 percent of the hospitals under state or local control reported union contracts.[23]

Perhaps in emulation of the federal Executive Orders, the number of states with some form of legal framework for public-employee bargaining rose rapidly during the 1960s, reaching a total of 36 by the end of the decade.[24] As a consequence, the rate of unionization of state and local government hospitals increased to 14.1 percent in 1970 and to 19.0 percent in 1975.

When the percentage of unionized workers rather than the percentage of hospitals is compared, the extent of unionization among nonfederal government hospital workers is the lowest of any category of public employees. Thus, the rate of organization of state and local public hospital employees was 33.1 percent in 1975 in contrast to 72.4 percent for firefighters, 68.6 percent for teachers, and an average of 49.9 percent for all nonfederal government employees.[25]

The comparatively low level of organization of local public hospital workers is directly traceable to the character of the various state public-sector legal frameworks. In 14 states, no public employee is covered directly by statute.[26] Restrictive laws that apply only to categories of workers such as firefighters and teachers exist in another nine states. Thus, in only slightly more than half of the states are there laws under which hospital workers can organize and bargain without question.

Within those states with statutes, a variety of legal configurations for collective bargaining have been created. Illustrative is the situation in Wisconsin in 1978 in which a State Employee Relations Act provided for full rights to organize and bargain, no right to strike or to arbitrate interest disputes, and state-wide bargaining units.[27] On the other hand, there was also a local government bargaining law which provided the same rights but also permitted a limited opportunity to strike while not prescribing either bargaining-unit structure or coverage.[28] The complexities of public-sector labor relations in such states as California, New York, and Washington are well known, rivaling Wisconsin in large measure.

---

[23] "AHA Research Capsules—No. 6," p. 217.

[24] Pointer and Metzger, pp. 73–76.

[25] BNA, *Daily Labor Report*, March 1, 1977, p. B1.

[26] See American Bar Association, *Report of the Committee on State Law*, as reproduced in BNA, *Government Employment Relations Report*, RF, September 19, 1977, p. 148.

[27] State Employment Labor Relations Act, WIS 111.80–111.97, Laws of Wisconsin, 1971.

[28] Municipal Employment Relations Act 111.70 Wisconsin Statutes, as amended January 1, 1979.

PRIVATE-SECTOR HOSPITALS

Pre-1974 Legal Frameworks. Not until August 1974 was the federal private-sector labor law (Taft-Hartley Act) amended to bring under its jurisdiction the more than 3,300 private nonprofit hospitals in operation at that time. Although this segment of the health-care industry comprised nearly half the hospitals and two-thirds of the personnel for the entire hospital industry, it had been specifically exempted from Taft-Hartley coverage.[29] Private investor-owned hospitals also were not subject to the federal collective bargaining laws during most of this period.

The National Labor Relations Act, the original collective bargaining statute enacted in 1935, was silent concerning coverage of private hospitals, and it was left to the National Labor Relations Board and the courts to determine the intent of Congress. Although it was concluded that private hospitals were within the Act's jurisdiction, the NLRB generally declined to act in such cases.[30]

Any doubt about the status of private, nonprofit hospitals was removed in 1947 with the passage of the Taft-Hartley Act which exempted in Section 2(2) "any corporation or association operating a hospital, if no part of the net earnings inures to the benefit of any private shareholder or individual." [31] The justification for the exemption hinged on the premise that nonprofit hospitals were "eleemosynary" institutions and, if subject to federal law, would experience difficulty in continuing to serve patients who lacked "the means to pay for hospital service." [32]

Private nonprofit hospitals seemed to exist in a legal vacuum. In 39 states there was no legal framework, and the legal presumption was that "nonprofit hospitals [were] in no way required to recognize or bargain collectively with their employees." [33] The Illinois Supreme Court admonished its legislature to take action, if only to control what was becoming an epidemic of labor-management conflict in the hospitals of the state.[34] The problem was exacerbated by the fact that Illinois had an anti-injunction law (a little Norris-LaGuardia Act), which apparently precluded the state courts from interfering in private-sector labor disputes.[35] By the early 1970s, only eight states—Connecticut, Massachu-

---

[29] See Pointer.
[30] Farkas, p. 259.
[31] Labor Management Relations Act, Public Law 101, 80th Congress, 1947.
[32] See the comments of Senator Millard Tydings during the Senate floor debate over the proposed nonprofit hospital exemption in *Congressional Record*, Vol. 93, Part 4, p. 4997.
[33] Metzger and Pointer, p. 63.
[34] *Peters v. South Chicago Community Hospital*, 44 Ill. 2d 22, 253 N.E.2d 375 (1969).
[35] Illinois Revised Statutes, Ch. 48, sec. 2 (a), Amended 1973.

setts, Michigan, Minnesota, Montana, New York, Oregon, and Pennsylvania—had statutes covering some or all hospital employees; coverage was implied in three additional states—Idaho, New Jersey, and Wisconsin.[36]

Wisconsin was one of the first states to regulate private hospital collective bargaining when the Peace Act of 1939, a general labor code, was extended by court decision to include employees of private hospitals.[37] The court found no distinction in the law between hospitals and other private employers with the result that lockouts, strikes, and other forms of concerted action were without constraints. In this respect, Wisconsin's Peace Act was apparently unique among state statutes.[38]

Although private hospital employees apparently were covered under Minnesota's "little" Wagner Act, also passed in 1939, that state chose in 1947 to amend its general labor code with the Charitable Hospitals Act,[39] which prohibited strikes, established compulsory arbitration of disputes, and limited the scope of bargaining to issues of "maximum hours of work and minimum hourly wage." Subsequently, the Minnesota Supreme Court interpreted the scope to exclude union shop, union security, and internal management of the hospital.[40]

The Michigan law was first enacted in 1949, although its application to hospital employees was not constitutionally tested for another ten years. In other states, specific hospital legislation did not appear until some years after the Minnesota and Michigan laws. New York, following Minnesota, amended its State Labor Relations law in 1963 to expressly cover the employees of nonprofit hospitals in New York City; the remaining areas of the state were brought under the law two years later.[41] Pennsylvania created a labor code to cover nonprofit hospitals just four years before it was to be pre-empted by the health-care amendments to Taft-Hartley.

In retrospect, the years before 1974 were a laboratory within which a good deal of experimentation in regulating hospital collective bargaining was carried on. Many states preferred a repressive stance, believing health-care bargaining was in conflict with the nonprofit and charitable image of hospitals and was as well an invitation to disastrous disruptions of the delivery of health-care services. A small number of states accepted

[36] Metzger and Pointer, Table IV-1, p. 62. For a comprehensive description of state private hospital labor law to 1972, see especially pp. 61–79.

[37] See Richard U. Miller and others, The Impact of Collective Bargaining on Hospitals: A Three State Study, pp. 26–28.

[38] Ronald L. Miller, "Collective Bargaining in Non-Profit Hospitals," pp. 254–55.

[39] See Richard U. Miller and others, The Impact . . . , pp. 28–30.

[40] Fairview Hospital Association v. Public Building Service Union, 241 Minn. 523, 64 N.W.2d 16 (1954).

[41] Metzger and Pointer, pp. 64–66.

collective bargaining for hospital employees but refused to give them the right to strike. In some instances the rights to organize and bargain were extended to only a select few hospital workers, notably registered or licensed practical nurses or other professionals. At the other extreme was Wisconsin where there was no differentiation between hospitals and other private-sector employers in any dimension of collective bargaining.

A legacy thus existed that would affect the way in which the 1974 amendments would be applied and the extent to which their objectives could be achieved. In cities such as New York, Cleveland, Chicago, Minneapolis, and San Francisco, labor and management already had many years of experience in dealing with each other. Bargaining units had been designated, contracts were in place, and the conventional weapons of collective bargaining warfare including strikes, picketing, and boycotts had been tested. New or novel patterns of labor-management relations thus could not be created under the Taft-Hartley amendments, nor were pre-1974 problems entirely solved by transfer to federal jurisdiction.

The Origin of Public Law 93-360. During the years before the health-care amendments were enacted, a series of events foreshadowed federal control. First, there was the momentum initiated in the 1960s with the Executive Orders of Presidents Kennedy and Nixon. Then, the NLRB reversed its policy with regard to investor-owned hospitals and nursing homes and assumed jurisdiction over them in 1967.[42] Three years later, the Board added nonprofit nursing homes to its jurisdictional list.[43]

In spite of obstacles, unionization in the industry expanded gradually, and by 1973, unions had achieved recognition at 14 percent of the nation's nonprofit hospitals, nearly twice the percentage of just six years earlier.[44] However, such recognition often was accompanied by highly publicized conflict and disruption. Analysis of data compiled by the U.S. Department of Labor for the period of 1962 to 1972 for the Health Care Industry (SIC 80) shows that 248 work stoppages took place, half of which (125) were for the purpose of recognition.[45] Absent or inadequate state legislation was often cited by both labor and management as a major ingredient in the bargaining conflict.

Finally, the basic premises of the Section 2(2) exclusion for nonprofit

[42] *Butte Medical Properties,* 168 NLRB 266 (1967); and *University Nursing Home, Inc.,* 168 NLRB 53 (1967).

[43] *Drexel Homes,* 194 NLRB 63 (1970).

[44] AHA, "Research Capsules—No. 6," p. 217, and Employee Relations and Training Department, AHA.

[45] *Coverage of Nonprofit Hospitals Under National Labor Relations Act,* pp. 158–285.

hospitals came under full attack by labor and management alike.[46] With more than 1.5 million employees and assets in excess of $25 billion (1973), it was no longer possible to argue that nonprofit hospitals had no impact on interstate commerce. Moreover, charity as a source of revenue was a negligible fraction of income. Federal regulation was thus inevitable.

Public Law 93-360. Despite efforts to limit the amendments to a mere deletion of the Section 2(2) exclusion of nonprofit hospitals from the Taft-Hartley Act, special conditions unique to health-care institutions were specified by Congress when the law took effect in August 1974. Among the more important stipulations are:[47]

1. A 90-day notice is required of parties intending to modify or terminate existing contracts. For parties in other industries, only a 60-day notice is required.
2. The Federal Mediation and Conciliation Service must be notified 60 days in advance in the event of modification or termination of existing agreements. For parties in other industries, the notification period is 30 days.
3. Notice of intent to strike or picket *must* be made ten days before such action takes place.
4. In the event of a dispute, the parties *are required* to participate in mediation efforts offered by FMCS.
5. If, in the opinion of the Director of the FMCS, a strike or lockout will "substantially interrupt the delivery of health care in a locality concerned," a Board of Inquiry may be convened. Fifteen days after its establishment by the Director, the BOI must issue a nonbinding report.

The thrust of the amendments is to minimize disruptions in the delivery of health care while at the same time extending to profit and private nonprofit health-care employees rights to engage in collective bargaining, strikes, picketing, and related forms of concerted action. Thus Congress sought to provide, through the extended notification periods, more opportunity to reach agreement than might exist otherwise and also to give mediation an early start. Moreover, the provision for mandatory mediation is also unique to the health-care industry. Should mediation fail, under special circumstances a Board of Inquiry could be set up to issue a fact-finding report before a strike could be scheduled. Finally, the stipulation of a ten-day notice in advance of a strike or picketing would enable hospitals, nursing homes, and other health-care institutions

---

[46] See especially the testimony of Norman Metzger, Vice President for Personnel, Mount Sinai Medical Center, New York City, as quoted in *Extension of NLRA to Nonprofit Hospital Employees,* p. 173.

[47] Labor Management Relations Act, as amended by Public Laws 86-257, 1959 and 93-360, 1974. See also Pointer and Metzger, pp. 41–55.

to make general preparations, so that the safety and well-being of patients would be ensured. The so-called "ally" doctrine of the NLRB was not to be applied to hospitals receiving patients from threatened or struck institutions.

Unit Determination Issues Under the Amendments. A major concern of Congress in removing the 2(2) exemption of Taft-Hartley was to avoid the development of bargaining fragmentation which had grown up under state law. Thus, at the time of passage of P.L. 93-360, the NLRB was instructed to avoid a "proliferation" of bargaining units in health-care institutions.[48]

Nearly a year passed before the Board announced its bargaining unit policy for hospitals. Finally, on May 8, 1975, the NLRB decreed in a series of cases that there were to be five basic units:[49] registered nurses, other health-care professionals, technical employees, service and maintenance employees, and business office clericals. To these units was added a sixth, employee physicians, in July 1977.[50]

Few policies enunciated by the Board in its 45-year history have been greeted with less enthusiasm. On the one hand, hospital management accused the Board of permitting unit proliferation to occur despite the instructions of Congress.[51] Hospital industry representatives argue that separate units for nurses, physicians, and other professionals are inappropriate; and they also contend that service, maintenance, and technical employees should be placed in a single unit.

The management position thus supports a policy of units severely limited in numbers, but "wall to wall" in coverage. As a consequence, it is not surprising that initial misgivings about the Board's unit policy have increased in the face of what appears to be a growing trend toward separate units for maintenance or other craft workers. Analysis of monthly NLRB election reports suggests these fears may not be groundless. For example, despite the professed policy against such units, from August 1974 through December 1977 the Board designated more than 50 craft or maintenance units. The large majority were for boiler operations (35) on the basis of petitions from the International Union of Operating Engineers (IUOE). Other unions whose petitions were accepted were plumbers, painters, carpenters, and electricians, among others.

[48] *Hospitals Under the National Labor Relations Act*, pp. 6–7.

[49] *Mercy Hospital of Sacramento, Inc.*, 217 NLRB 131 (1975); *Barnert Memorial Hospital Association*, 217 NLRB 132 (1975); *St. Catherine's Hospital of Dominican Sisters*, 217 NLRB 133 (1975); *Newington Children's Hospital*, 217 NLRB 134 (1975); *Sisters of St. Joseph of Peace*, 217 NLRB 135 (1975); *Duke University*, 217 NLRB 136 (1975); *Mount Airy Foundation*, 217 NLRB 137 (1975); and *Shriners Hospital for Crippled Children*, 217 NLRB 138 (1975).

[50] *Ohio Valley Hospital Association*, 230 NLRB No. 84 (1977).

[51] See the remarks of William Emanuel as reported in BNA, *Daily Labor Report*, May 3, 1977, p. A12.

It is noteworthy that in December 1977, seven representation elections were held in hospital craft units; of the seven elections conducted, six resulted from IUOE petitions.[52] The irony is that in the same month, the Third Circuit Court of Appeals strongly attacked the Board's unit policy in rejecting a unit of four boiler attendants certified by the NLRB:[53]

> The legislative history of the health care amendments, however, makes it quite clear that Congress directed the Board to apply a standard in the field that was not traditional. Proliferation of units in industrial settings has not been the subject of congressional attention but fragmentation in the health care field has aroused legislative apprehension. The Board should recognize that the contours of a bargaining unit in other industries do not follow the blueprint Congress desired in a hospital. . . . A mechanical reliance on traditional patterns based on licensing, supervision, skills and employee joint activity simply does not comply with congressional intent to treat this unique field in a special manner.

In a similar vein, Board unit policy which perpetuated fragmentation of bargaining whose origin lay under state policies of the preamendment years was also overturned by federal courts. Acting on a dispute arising from a unit of maintenance and engineering employees certified by the New York State Labor Relations Board in 1964, a federal Circuit Court of Appeals concluded that such units "[ran] counter to the 1974 legislative history stressing the dangers of overcompartmentalization in the health care industry." [54] Should the court decision stand, it would imply that hundreds of units organized by such groups as pharmacists, X-ray technicians, LPNs, and like employees under the former state jurisdiction will be of questionable legitimacy.

Major criticism of the NLRB's unit policy in the early years of the amendments also centered on its decision that hospital residents and interns, so-called housestaff, were students and not employees and, therefore, not covered by the amendments.[55] In an effort to circumvent the Board's ruling, the Physician's National Housestaff Association sought bargaining rights through state labor relations boards. The attempts

---

[52] National Labor Relations Board, *Election Report*, Cases Closed December 1977.

[53] *St. Vincent's Hospital* v. *NLRB*, CA No. 77-1027, December 15, 1977.

[54] As reported in *Hospitals*, *JAHA* 52 (January 1, 1978), pp. 18–19.

[55] *Cedars-Sinai Medical Center*, 223 NLRB No. 57 (1976). See also *Physicians National Housestaff Association, et al.* v. *Murphy*, USDC, DC (1978), in which the U.S. District Court for the District of Columbia refused to enjoin the Board from implementing its decision that housestaff were students.

proved futile when it was ruled that the states had no jurisdiction to
act, having been pre-empted by the federal law.[56]

The NLRB itself was divided on the issue with its newly appointed
chairman, John H. Fanning, declaring that the Board's decision was "untenable" and an "aberration" from 40 years of Board precedent![57] In
response to the protest over the *Cedars-Sinai* case, bills were introduced
into both houses of Congress to nullify the Board's decision.[58] In contrast
to the stance adopted by the American Hospital Association, the American Medical Association strongly supported the bills.

The Board, in the years immediately following the 1974 amendments,
also found itself struggling with other unit or representation issues, particularly as these related to registered nurses. In the first place, the
existence of hospital nursing supervision personnel among the officials of
national and state nurses associations was a signal to hospital management that the ANA and its state affiliates did not meet the definition of
labor organizations for purposes of certification. Although the NLRB
accepted a policy by which bargaining functions might be delegated to
local hospital chapters or related organizations, this did not find acceptance with appellate courts.[59]

Second, the Board also encountered difficulty in distinguishing between supervisory and nonsupervisory personnel.[60] Their responsibilities
for patient care often involve registered nurses in overseeing the activities of aides, orderlies, and LPNs. In addition the RN may be in charge
of wards or floors on evening or graveyard shifts. Thus, the standard
criteria historically used by the NLRB for judging supervisory status at
times have not been easily applied. Moreover, the parties themselves
have confused the issue through changes in assigned duties or titles in
an attempt to have nurses excluded from bargaining units. While the
Board has attempted to clarify its policies, the apparent inconsistency of
its position on unit determination points up the limitations for service
and professional workers of labor law procedures based in industrial or
manual blue-collar experience.

The Boards of Inquiry and the Role of the FMCS. The NLRB has

[56] *NLRB* v. *Committee of Interns and Residents, et al.,* CA-2 (1977).

[57] See Fanning's statement of April 28, 1977, before the American Bar Associa-
tion's National Institute on Hospitals and Health Care Facilities as reported in BNA,
Daily Labor Report, May 3, 1977, p. D3, and his dissent in *St. Claire's Hospital and
Health Center,* 223 NLRB 1002 (1976).

[58] Companion measures were introduced into the Senate (S. 1884) in July 1977
and the House (H.R. 2222) in January 1977 which would define professional employees to include interns and residents. BNA, *Daily Labor Report,* July 20, 1977,
pp. A2–A3.

[59] See *NLRB* v. *Annapolis Emergency Hospital Association d/b/a, Anne Arundel
General Hospital,* CA 4, No. 76-1166, August 31, 1977.

[60] Farkas, p. 263.

not been alone as an object of criticism in the application of the 1974 amendments. The Federal Mediation and Conciliation Service has responsibility for the notification, mediation, and Board of Inquiry section of P.L. 93-360, and of these activities, the BOI has engendered the strongest negative reactions, with labor complaining that boards are not appointed frequently enough, while management has attacked the timing of BOI appointments.[61]

Perhaps the greatest litigation over FMCS's role has occurred in conjunction with the issue of the time frame in which the BOI is to be appointed. The crux of the disagreement is the interpretation of the Section 213 which provides

> . . . the Director [of FMCS] may further assist in the resolution of the impasse by establishing within 30 days after the notice to the Federal Mediation and Conciliation Service under Clause (A) of the last sentence of Section 8(d) which is required by clause (3) of such Section 8(d), or within 10 days after the notice under clause (B) an impartial Board of Inquiry to investigate the issues involved in the dispute and to make a written report thereon to the parties within fifteen (15) days after the establishment of such a Board.

The FMCS has taken the position that the appointment of BOIs should be made no later than 30 days before the contract is to expire or within 30 days of receipt of the 60-day notice to FMCS, whichever is later. Hospitals, on the other hand, have argued that the 30-day period of appointment begins when FMCS actually receives the notice.[62] If the employers' premise were correct, a notification made to FMCS considerably in advance of the 60-day period prior to contract expiration would require a decision on the appointment of a BOI even before bargaining may have begun.

After a split in opinions between the California and Maryland federal district courts, the Court of Appeals for the Fourth Circuit ruled against FMCS.[63] Should this decision constitute the final word on Section 213, Congress may have to amend the section to revitalize the procedure as a dispute-settlement mechanism.

Employee Organization in the Hospital Industry

Apart from a description of the procedural aspects of the health-care amendments recounted here, it is important that an assessment of the

---

[61] See the comments of Herb Fishgold, former General Counsel for FMCS, and Nicholas Fidandis, then health-care sector coordinator of FMCS, in BNA, *Daily Labor Report*, May 3, 1977, pp. A14–A17.

[62] *Ibid.*

[63] *Sinai Hospital* v. *Searce*, CA 4 (1977).

impact of specific provisions be undertaken. In this section such an assessment will be made from the standpoint of trade unionism in the industry. How the amendments relate to collective bargaining practice and conflict will be discussed in the following section.

GENERAL DEVELOPMENT OF HOSPITAL UNIONISM

Although union activity in hospitals was reported as early as 1919, the development of collective bargaining for the industry is basically a phenomenon of the past 20 years.[64] For the most part, the mass organizing drives of the 1930s and 1940s bypassed hospital employees, leaving the industry largely untouched well into the 1960s. Major exceptions, however, were San Francisco and Minneapolis-St. Paul. As Table 4 indicates, growth came rapidly during the decade of the 1960s but has yet to reach the nationwide level of unionization.

The uneven distribution of unionism is apparent from Tables 4 and 5. The largest category with labor contracts is the federal hospitals, and the private investor-owned hospitals category is the smallest. The latter figures are particularly interesting given the fact that such hospitals have been under the jurisdiction of the National Labor Relations Act since 1967.

It is not difficult to explain the incidence of hospital unionism. In the first place, the states with the highest rates tend to be those where there was a legal framework conducive to both public and private hospital collective bargaining in the pre-1974 amendment period. Second, these states generally are also characterized by larger hospitals, more urbanization, and greater overall rates of unionization.

On the one hand, the continuing growth in the size of hospitals in the long run should be a force for greater unionization. On the other

TABLE 4

Percent of Hospitals With One or More Union Contracts,
by Control of Hospital,
1961–1975

	All Hospitals	Federal	State and Local Government	Private Nonprofit	Investor Owned/ Profit
1975	19.8	75.4	19.0	16.9	9.8
1973	16.8	63.2	16.6	13.9	8.0
1970	14.7	52.0	14.1	12.4	8.0
1967	7.7	22.6	5.3	8.2	4.9
1961	3.0	0.0	1.0	4.3	4.3

Source: Employee Relations and Training Department, American Hospital Association, January 5, 1977.

[64] Metzger and Pointer, pp. 22–24. See also Ronald L. Miller, "Collective Bargaining in Nonprofit Hospitals," pp. 17–18.

TABLE 5

Percent of Hospitals Reporting One or More
Collective Bargaining Contracts
by Bed Size, Location, and Census Division,
1976

Bed-Size Category	Percent of Hospitals[a]
Small (6–99)	12.1
Moderate (100–399)	26.5
Large (400 or more)	49.6
Location	
Metropolitan (SMSA)	30.8
Nonmetropolitan	14.2
Census Division	
New England	32.8
Middle Atlantic	44.3
South Atlantic	12.3
East North Central	27.1
East South Central	7.5
West North Central	18.2
West South Central	6.0
Mountain	14.7
Pacific	41.7

Source: Paul D. Frenzen, "Survey Updates Unionization Activities," *Hospitals, JAHA,* 52, August 1, 1978, Table 1, p. 94.

[a] Calculated by the ratio of hospitals reporting labor contracts to the total number of hospitals responding to a special survey conducted in September 1976 by the Hospital Data Center, American Hospital Association. Readers should note that because of change in computation methods by AHA, the 1976 survey results are not comparable to those published in earlier years.

hand, hospital unionization must break out of its isolated pockets in the Northeast, Upper Midwest, and Pacific Coast if the geographical distribution of unionization is going to be significantly different. This is a feat, however, largely unaccomplished by the labor movement generally.

One indication of the extent to which the future distribution of hospital unionism may change can be gleaned from a review of the rate of union success in NLRB elections in the period August 1974–December 1977.[65] In the first place, the states in which the most elections occurred are precisely those which already possess the highest rate of hospital unionization. Four states—New York, California, Pennsylvania, and Michigan—accounted for 48.6 percent of the elections. These same four states had 41 percent of the hospitals with labor contracts at the time the health-care amendments became effective.[66]

[65] Unless otherwise indicated, the data on representation elections were derived from the Monthly Elections Report published by the National Labor Relations Board. It should be noted that since the NLRB reports election data for the health-care industry as a whole (SIC 80), it was necessary to eliminate those cases not involving hospitals. This was undertaken by comparing the name of institution listed in the case with that contained in the AHA, *Hospital Guidebook for 1977.*

[66] Calculated from data supplied courtesy of the Employee Relations and Training Department, American Hospital Association.

The uneven geographical distribution of both contracts and union organizing activity would seem to reflect a strategy of enhancing organizing investments by consolidating existing membership bases rather than attempting to open new areas. Thus, for example, union organizing activity is reported to be twice as likely to occur at hospitals with labor contracts than at those without.[67]

Whether in tandem with existing bargaining units or as an attempt to establish an initial foothold within a hospital, union organizing success as measured by representation election victories also appears unevenly distributed over time. In the first months after the amendments became effective, unions were victorious in 61.3 percent of the representation elections held. The rate declined to 52 percent for the next 24 months (January 1975 to December 1976), and in the most recent period for which election information is available, calendar 1977, the unions' success rate of 45.8 percent fell below the national average of 48.0 percent.[68] It should be noted, however, that the total number of hospital elections held in 1977 increased by 31.6 percent, from 250 to 329.

The decline in the percentage of union elections won can be attributed to a number of causes. In the first place, it is reasonable to assume that those hospitals most vulnerable were organized in the remaining months of 1974 following the enactment of the amendments. Second, as hospital managements became more sophisticated in countering organizing drives, unions' success rate would be expected to fall.[69] Third, with many of the larger, urban hospitals of the Northeast and Pacific regions already organized, labor groups have had to turn increasingly to hospitals in areas more hostile to unions—the South and Southeast, or the suburban and nonmetropolitan areas.

The unions place part of the blame for their failure to reap the benefits of the health-care amendments on the NLRB. Describing the Board as "the graveyard of union aspirations," Leon Davis, president of District 1199 of the Retail, Wholesale and Department Store Workers Union, ascribed many of labor's problems to "endless hearings and interminable delays." [70] As a consequence, "management takes advantages of these delays by conducting anti-union campaigns and destroying the will of the workers for a union. Even if the union wins, the Board has no power or will to compel management to bargain collectively in good faith or to sign a contract with the union." [71]

[67] Frenzen, p. 104.

[68] National Labor Relations Board, *Forty Second Annual Report*, fiscal year ending September 30, 1977, p. 17.

[69] See Rosmann, "One Year Under Taft-Hartley," p. 66.

[70] BNA, *White Collar Report*, December 19, 1975, p. A2.

[71] *Ibid.*

The labor reform bills under debate in Congress during the winter of 1977–78 were in large part aimed at the alleged inadequacies of the NLRB and its administration of the Taft-Hartley Act. It is clear, however, that the lack of growth in hospital union membership is more than just a function of the NLRB; it is also a consequence of the nature of the industry and the characteristics of the unions themselves.

PREDOMINANCE AND CHARACTERISTICS OF EMPLOYEE ORGANIZATIONS

Few industries reveal a greater number and variety of labor organizations than health care generally and hospitals in particular. For example, analysis of NLRB representation elections conducted between August 1974 and December 1977 reveals that at least 34 different employee organizations have participated in organizing activity. Moreover, this figure understates the actual participation since, on the one hand, the Board then lumped together in one undifferentiated category, "Local Independent Union," unaffiliated blue-collar unions, professional associations including the American Nurses Association, and any technical or clerical group independent of the AFL-CIO. On the other hand, there continue to be many bargaining units of employees such as pharmacists, radiologic technicians, LPNs, and stationary engineers whose associations obtained recognition under state law. Under present NLRB unit policy, these organizations would probably be precluded from acquiring separate recognition.

No single union has received a charter from the AFL-CIO to represent hospital workers, and given the activity of independents, such a charter would be meaningless. Further, as unionization in the industry grows, the likelihood that the AFL-CIO could grant exclusive jurisdiction to any single organization diminishes. Thus, unions such as the American Federation of State, County, and Municipal Employees (AFSCME) seek representation among private hospital workers, the Service Employees Union does the same among public workers, District 1199 attempts to cover both professionals and nonprofessionals in vertical organizations, and a multitude of other unions even more remote from health occupations find their way into the industry. Among unions with hospital bargaining units one finds Teamsters (IBT), Laborers (LIUNA), Communications Workers (CWA), Hotel and Restaurant (HREBILL), Steelworkers (USWA), Paperworkers (UPIU), Meatcutters (AMCBWNA), and Retail Clerks (RCIA). Not all of these unions are equally active, however, in pursuing hospital bargaining units. The majority have acquired members in hospitals or other health-care institutions only as a response to inquiries from the employees themselves rather than from any grand organizing design.

The unions most aggressively seeking hospital members are the Service Employees, District 1199, AFSCME, and the American Nurses Association. These four organizations not only accounted for 75 percent of all hospital representation elections held from the date of the Taft-Hartley amendments through December 1977, but also have as members the bulk of public or private hospital employees. Thus, our analysis of the current state of hospital collective bargaining requires that we examine the activities of these four unions in some detail.

Service Employees International Union. The union with both the longest history and largest membership in the hospital industry is the SEIU. Its first bargaining unit was organized in San Francisco in the mid-1930s in the city's largest municipal hospital.[72] The private, non-profit, and other public hospitals in San Francisco were brought under union contract at the beginning of World War II.

Thus, with a 25-year head start, SEIU has become the dominant union in the private health-care field. Nearly half the union's 550,000 members are employed in health-related occupations, with 140,000 in hospitals alone. It is important to note also that 30,000 of the latter members are organized in public hospitals at both the federal and non-federal government levels.

Although the Service Employees Union is basically concerned with nonprofessional hospital workers—aides, orderlies, kitchen help, and maintenance—it has also organized significant numbers of technical and professional employees including registered nurses.

SEIU is strong in West Coast and upper Midwest hospitals, but it has been less successful in the Northeast and Atlantic Coast. It is virtually without hospital membership in Baltimore and Philadelphia and in New York City SEIU trails substantially behind District 1199 and AFSCME.

In many respects the Northeast hospital industry has been a battle-ground since the early 1960s in which the main contestants variously have been AFSCME, Teamsters, 1199, and SEIU. In the private sector, the victor more often than not has been 1199; in the public sector, AFSCME has usually emerged on top. In recent years also, the American Nurses Association has been drawn into the conflict as 1199 and others have sought bargaining rights among RNs. Although SEIU's conflict with 1199 in New York City was resolved through an agreement, organizing confrontations continue in Massachusetts and Connecticut.

The pattern of bargaining that characterizes a union is often a product of its structure, history, and leadership. Again, the parallels and contrasts with its chief rival, 1199, are striking. In the first place, no single charismatic figure of the stature of Leon Davis has emerged, at

---

[72] Denton, pp. 140–47.

least in terms of health-care activities. Second, as an old-line AFL union which had its start as the Building Service Employees Union, SEIU is distinguished by what Chamberlain and Cullen label as "dispersed" local unions.[73] In contrast to a plant or local industrial union, a "dispersed" union may cover many workers employed across a large number of companies and organizations, often encompassing a variety of industries and occupations. For example, of the 23,000 members of Local 250, with jurisdiction in San Francisco, 11,500 are in hospital bargaining units, 6,000 in nursing homes, and the remainder in nonhealth-care institutions including race tracks and ball parks. On the other hand, the counterpart local in Los Angeles, 399, has nearly as many members as Local 250, but a much smaller proportion of them are hospital workers.

In the SEIU structure, a local union may be associated with a Joint Council, which is composed of a minimum of 15 local unions. Typical are the Bay Area Joint Council, the Southern California Joint Council, the Pacific Northwest Research and Negotiating Department, and so on. The function of the Joint Council is to provide back-up for negotiations, assist with arbitration cases, and generally provide research and other expert services for affiliated locals.[74]

Several implications of this structural configuration need to be explored. First, the existence of the Joint Council enables the individual locals to pool their resources to ensure that expert bargaining help is locally available as the need arises. Second, the business representatives appointed to the locals, with the backing of the research specialists from the Joint Councils, are able to bring to bear on individual negotiations the knowledge of wage levels, working conditions, and contract settlements prevailing in competing health-care institutions as well as in similar occupations in nonhealth industries. The possibilities this creates for "whipsawing" individual hospitals has prompted management to move to multihospital bargaining in several locations including Minneapolis-St. Paul, Oakland-San Francisco, and New York City.

The vertical integration of hospital bargaining units attached to a dispersed local union which in turn is a unit within a Joint Council also may generate problems of emphasis in bargaining and "reactive" organizing. For example, in a large local encompassing thousands of members, only a minority of whom are hospital workers, priorities may be placed elsewhere, or the expertise needed to deal with the relatively specialized attributes of hospitals may not be available. In addition, union resources may be spread thinly across a multiplicity of demands.

---

[73] See Chamberlain and Cullen, pp. 180–82.

[74] Communication from Richard Liebes, Research Director, Bay Area Joint Council, SEIU, San Francisco, May 17, 1978.

The consequences may be that hospital members do not receive the attention they feel appropriate, and organizing may be largely haphazard, limited to responding or reacting to outside requests for unionizing help.

Although the SEIU is becoming increasingly a union of health-care workers, its structure for dealing with this industry's special problems is quite limited. Apart from annual conferences that may focus on hospital bargaining issues, the committees, councils, departments, or other specialized units present in comparable, large multi-industrial labor organizations are largely absent. The exception is the National Conference of Physician's Unions created in January 1973 to coordinate ten local unions of physicians chiefly affiliated to the Service Employees Union.[75] Since 1974 no new health-care units have been created within SEIU's structure.

In the meantime, the special case of the Health Employees Labor Program (HELP), a joint effort in Chicago of Service Employees Local 73 and Teamsters Local 743, provides an indication of the possibilities for interunion structural innovation in hospital bargaining. In 1959–60, AFSCME Local 1657 launched an organizing drive in several private Chicago hospitals. The failure of these attempts prompted bitter recriminations against the Teamsters for refusal to honor picket lines, while Service Employees Local 73 "was accused of trying behind the scenes to prevent some hospitals from recognizing (either) Teamsters, Local 743 or AFSCME, Local 1657." [76] Following a disastrous strike against two of the hospitals it was trying to organize, AFSCME withdrew from the Chicago private hospital scene. Although no new hospital organizing efforts were to be made until 1966, the lesson that more could be gained through interunion cooperation than conflict was not lost to the Teamsters and Service Employees unions.

Therefore, in the summer of 1966, the two unions, acting jointly under the umbrella of the Health Employees Labor Program, launched an organizing drive that by 1975 would bring 23 Chicago hospitals employing 7,000 workers under HELP contracts.[77] It should also be noted that much of this success was achieved in the first few years of HELP's existence, and despite the presumed benefits of coverage under federal labor law, almost no new hospital bargaining units have been organized since the early 1970s.

Given a high proportion of minority workers in nonprofessional jobs in Chicago hospitals and the social climate when organizing began in

---

[75] Bognanno and others, p. 33.
[76] Osterhaus, p. 152.
[77] Chicago Hospital Council, p. 2.

1960, it would be expected that a major tool in the unionizing drives of the decade would have been civil rights. Although this issue was injected by AFSCME in its drives, HELP did not employ it to the same magnitude in 1966 as it was used earlier nor clearly as ardently as 1199 was to do in New York City. Perhaps, as Metzger and Pointer contend, this was a function of HELP's "white middle class" leadership and the fact that neither the parent Teamsters nor SEIU had much connection with the civil rights movement.[78]

The coalition between the Teamsters and SEIU has not been repeated in private hospitals beyond Chicago. Although agreements do exist in several cases involving public employees, little joint hospital activity is in evidence. At the moment, unions and associations seem content to operate in isolation, often at each others' expense.

American Federation of State, County, and Municipal Employees. Although SEIU can claim the distinction of having organized the largest absolute number of health-care employees, AFSCME with 200,000 members in health care is not far behind. The April 1978 affiliation of the New York Civil Service Employees Association, which counted among 263,000 members some 60,000 mental health workers, may have relegated the Service Employees to second place.[79] Until its election victory over the Teamsters in December 1965 in New York City, however, AFSCME hospital bargaining units tended to be concentrated in state mental hospitals and, as a consequence, in rural areas often separated from other types of health-care facilities.[80]

The rise of more militant national leadership in conjunction with the gradual spread of permissive state public employee laws provided the catalyst for the organization of urban public hospitals and, in turn, reoriented AFSCME's participation in state and local health-care collective bargaining. The key role in this transformation played by the union's District Council 37 compels a brief examination of collective bargaining in the municipal hospitals of New York City.

In the 1930s and 1940s, limited success in organizing the public hospitals of New York City was achieved by the State, County, and Municipal Workers of America and its successor, the United Public Workers. Accused of Communist domination, the UPW was expelled

---

[78] Metzger and Pointer, p. 34.

[79] *New York Times,* April 22, 1978. A charge of raiding, however, was later filed by the Public Employees Federation, an organization jointly created by the American Federation of Teachers and the Service Employees Union, which claimed bargaining rights for 45,000 members of the former Civil Service Employees. See Jerry Flint, "Jurisdictional War Periled by New York Labor Dispute," *New York Times,* May 2, 1978. The Executive Council of the AFL-CIO ultimately upheld the position of the Public Employees Federation. BNA, *Government Employee Relations Report,* November 6, 1978, pp. 9–10.

[80] Denton, p. 174.

from the CIO in 1950, losing its hospital membership in the process. As the United Public Workers faded from the New York public employees' scene, two AFL unions, AFSCME and the Teamsters, sought to achieve hegemony among the workers at the city's municipal hospitals. Interestingly, the impetus for the Teamsters' public-employee organizing arose from two disaffected AFSCME District Council 37 leaders who left the council in 1952 following a disagreement with Jerry Wurf over organizing and bargaining philosophy.[81] The dissidents joined the Teamsters, receiving a charter for Local 237 and taking nearly half District Council 37's membership, including most of the hospitals.

From 1952 to 1965, the Teamster and AFSCME affiliates in New York City faced each other in a standoff among the municipality's employees. Each grew somewhat, but neither managed to become dominant. By the mid-1960s, however, it had become clear that if either union were to prevail among New York City's employees, the 18,000 employees of the hospital division would have to be organized. Thus, in 1965, the rivalry shifted to the hospitals and intensified, coming to a head in December 1965 in a representation election conducted by the New York City Department of Labor. AFSCME's District Council 37 received 6,134 votes, giving it a margin of victory of approximately 1,000 votes over the Teamster local and, thereby, gaining control over nearly 18,000 municipal hospital workers.

By the late 1970s, over 20,000 public hospital employees in New York City were within the ranks of AFSCME. This figure was not the peak, but in fact represented a substantial decline from the beginning of the decade. As the financial woes of New York accelerated, the City's Health and Hospital Corporation was forced to lay off 6,700 employees between October 1975 and May 1976.[82] A threat to lay off an additional 1,700 in August resulted in a four-day strike by District Council 37 against 16 of the HHC's hospitals. The strike was the first in New York City's public hospital history and was in violation of the state's public-sector labor legislation, the Taylor Law.

The ultimate settlement was a patchwork compromise which, in exchange for relinquishing cost-of-living increases estimated at $10 million dollars for 1976 and 1977, the union obtained the reimbursement of approximately 1,000 jobs.[83] For District Council 37, this was a Pyrrhic victory in every sense of the term. Moreover, continuing state and city

---

[81] The material relating to the organizing of New York City Municipal Hospital Employees is largely taken, unless otherwise noted, from Alana Sue Cohen.

[82] *Hospital Labor Relations Reports*, October 26, 1976, pp. 11–12. These layoffs came on the heels of a reduction in HHC employment through attrition and dismissal of 4,420 between June 30 and November 29, 1975. See Wolfe, pp. 15–16.

[83] *Hospital Labor Relations Reports*, October 26, 1976, p. 11.

economic pressures on the Health and Hospitals Corporation indicate that future negotiation rounds will be no easier.

While the problems faced by AFSCME in bargaining for New York City's public hospital employees are extreme, they are by no means unique. Urban financial disorder is epidemic among the large cities of the United States and efforts by local governments to restrain runaway deficits in the face of taxpayer rebellion often depend for their success on state and federal agencies. For the municipal-hospital sector, the bargain may depend on Medicaid and Blue Cross payments as well as direct budgeting subsidies. Thus, an appreciation of the complexities of hospital labor relations requires an examination of the role of the so-called "third-party payer," the subject of a later section.

AFSCME not only shares with other public-sector labor organizations the burden of governmental fiscal dislocation, but also the weight of a state or local public policy in opposition to trade unions and collective bargaining. Thus, legal frameworks in such states as Georgia, Alabama, Mississippi, North and South Carolina, and Texas pose major obstacles to the extension of AFSCME's bargaining units to southern public hospitals. Until state legal barriers are lowered, public hospital unionism will be an exception rather than the rule.

National Union of Hospital and Health Care Employees, District 1199 (Retail, Wholesale and Department Store Workers Union). Until 1957, District 1199 was a small union of some 5,000 pharmacists and drugstore employees limited geographically to certain boroughs of New York City.[84] At that time, only one nonprofit hospital, Maimonides, was organized and that by the Teamsters. Having no interest in nonprofit hospitals, the Teamsters, however, preferred to focus its efforts on the city's public employees. Reminiscent of the departure of several former AFSCME District Council 37 leaders to assume positions with a Teamsters' local, Elliot Godoff, a Teamster organizer, moved to 1199 with the union's blessing, taking the single nonprofit-hospital unit with him.[85] Godoff, who had also been an organizer for the Socialist-inclined United Public Workers, almost immediately launched 1199 into an organizing drive against 25 of the city's nonprofit hospitals. Combining an intellectual fervor harking back to the "sitdown" days of the CIO with a willingness to employ political action, strikes, and public appeals, 1199 gradually expanded its geographical range while at the same time bringing increasing numbers of hospitals under contract. In 1961, it had 5,000 hospital workers under contract; by 1966, 1199 had raised this amount fourfold and was active in New Jersey, Pennsylvania, and West Virginia

---

[84] Nash, pp. 48–55.
[85] For a detailed discussion of these events, see Nash, pp. 48–55.

as well as upstate New York. In fact, its growth was such by 1966 that the former name of Drug and Hospital Employees Union was discarded in favor of its present title, National Union of Hospital and Health Care Employees, District 1199. Although the connection with the Retail, Wholesale, and Department Store Union was continued, 1199's almost total autonomy was assured.

A nearly geometric growth of membership characterized the latter half of the 1960s and entire decade of the seventies. Between 1966 and 1970, membership doubled to 40,000 and more than doubled again to 80,197 in 1971. As the 1970s were drawing to a close, 1199's membership was above the 100,000 mark.

A breakdown of this membership reveals that, significant growth notwithstanding, 1199 remains firmly anchored in metropolitan New York with an estimated 60,000 members on Long Island and the boroughs of New York City. Although organizing efforts have carried it into the Midwest and South, the major focus of 1199 remains the northeastern states.

The intensity of its activities in the New York City area is further suggested by the fact that some 36,000 members are covered in one master agreement negotiated with the League of Voluntary Hospitals. The League, in turn, represents 14 hospitals. An additional 10,000 workers under contract with approximately 60 other health-care institutions customarily follow the pattern set in the League's master contract.

If 1199 remains a union with its roots deep in New York City, it also remains an organization of nonprofessional health-care employees, most of whom are black or Puerto Rican. Moreover, in 1978 some 70 percent of the membership was employed in unskilled or semiskilled service occupations and three of every four members worked in a hospital as opposed to a nursing home. In contrast to AFSCME and the SEIU, 1199 holds few public-sector health-care contracts.

The limited future of remaining confined to New York and the Northeast was recognized early in its transformation to a hospital and health-care union with the creation of a national organizing committee in 1968. In the same vein, 1199 has also sought to become a true "industrial union" by expanding its coverage vertically in an attempt to encompass technical, clerical, and professional health-care workers. As a vehicle to accomplish this, four divisions have been created: Hospital Employees; Drug Employees; Guild of Professional, Technical, and Office Employees; and League of Registered Nurses. The latter grouping for RNs is the most recent, coming into existence in 1977.

In the second half of the 1970s, 1199 in fact turned its attention specifically to the professional and technical employees. A review of those members assigned to each of the four divisions suggests the results as yet have been limited, with less than 1 percent of the members with RN status and approximately 20 percent in the technical and clerical categories. The union continues to represent 6,000 drugstore employees.

As a final point, it is appropriate to review briefly 1199's tradition of left-wing militance and strong civil rights orientation. Both value dimensions have significantly shaped its organizing and bargaining strategies and its public image. Thus, much more so than its rivals, 1199 has projected the image of a radical, minority-oriented nonprofessional workers' union.

In many respects, this image is accurate, having its inception almost with the birth of the union in 1932 as the Pharmacists Guild. Originally associated with the Trade Union Unity League, the Guild aligned itself with the CIO, becoming Local 1199 of RWDSU in 1937. Over the next 20 years, it gained a reputation as a strong proponent of social and political causes, including the elimination of racial discrimination in Harlem drugstores.[86]

In the absence of a legal framework for obtaining recognition in New York State, the union's strategy involved the careful selection of targeted hospitals, the building of community support through a public image as the champion of the underdog, and strong internal organizations within hospitals.[87] The strategy was the creation of a health "crisis" in which simultaneous work stoppages would be carried out across a number of hospitals with the intent not of shutting them down completely but, rather, to disrupt patient services sufficiently "to bring about political intervention and ultimately to secure legislated or voluntary recognition."[88] A second important element was to associate 1199 with the budding civil rights movement of the late 1950s and early sixties. As one author observes in this connection, the union was not reluctant to quote Dr. Martin Luther King's statement, "I consider myself a fellow 1199-er."[89]

Evidence abounds that the strategy was successful. Strikes elicited almost immediate political intervention from both the mayor and the governor. A special amendment to the New York state labor law to cover New York City hospitals was passed in 1963 and later broadened in 1965 to cover all private hospitals in the state.

In Philadelphia, Baltimore, and Washington, as well as in New York, organizing drives centered on civil rights issues with such slogans as

---

[86] Ronald L. Miller, "Collective Bargaining in Nonprofit Hospitals," pp. 82–83.
[87] Ibid., p. 81.
[88] Ibid., p. 82.
[89] Denton, p. 193.

"we think that hospitals are run like plantations: the administrators are white. . . ." [90] The highwater mark for 1199's mixing of civil rights and union organizing occurred not in any of the cities of the Northeast, but in the unlikely location of Charleston, South Carolina. In 1969 a group of black nonprofessional workers at two public hospitals in Charleston sought 1199's assistance in having their union recognized. Hospital administrators rejected the union's demands, arguing that South Carolina law did not permit public employee bargaining. A four-month strike ensued which ultimately attracted widespread publicity and the support of national labor and civil rights leaders. Although official recognition was not obtained, an informal agreement raised wages and established a grievance procedure. The settlement was hailed by the union as a major victory.

In projecting 1199's path in the future, three factors seem to constitute obstacles to the union's continued growth. First, the civil rights issues of the 1960s have lost their force as a rallying point. Government antidiscrimination legislation, increasing minority affluence, and the dormancy of the former radical movements have taken their toll. Second, the efforts of 1199 to become an industrial union through the inclusion of all categories of workers, whether professional, technical, or unskilled, must successfully confront the extreme occupational fragmentation of the hospital industry. As indicated earlier, the modern hospital has a highly compartmentalized workforce, each group often having a clearcut identity as a consequence of specialized training, licensing, and activities of an occupational association. Moreover, the higher one travels in the occupational hierarchy, the smaller becomes the proportion of minority employees.

Finally, the fragmentation of the union movement seeking organizational rights in hospitals is also an important consideration to 1199's growth. Although it considers itself *the* hospital union, even in New York City it shares the industry with AFSCME in the public hospitals, SEIU in the private proprietary hospitals, and such groups as the New York State Nurses Association across all classes of health-care institutions. Outside the Northeast, in addition to the above-mentioned unions, such organizations as the Laborers and Retail Clerks have acquired a strong presence in nursing homes and hospitals, often using blacks and other minorities as organizers.

Unless these obstacles can be surmounted in the next few years, 1199 may well permanently remain a geographically and occupationally narrow labor organization rather than the national industrial union for health-care employees to which it aspires.

---

[90] *Ibid.*

American Nurses Association. Beyond public-school teaching, nursing is one of the few professions which has historically been accessible to females in the United States. Thus in 1972, approximately 1,128,000 registered nurses were licensed to practice, 98 percent of whom were female.[91] In fact, as the profession developed in the nineteenth century, nursing came to epitomize the culturally idealized woman in its public image. Unswerving in her devotion to caring for her patients, the nurse carried into the hospital the roles of mother and wife: submissive, supportive, obedient, and self-sacrificing. In turn, these roles were reinforced by the hospitals which provided the training for young women who sought careers in nursing. Hospital nursing schools emphasized hierarchical relationships, strongly suggestive of military organizations in which uniforms identified rank; rules, often of a paternalistic nature, strictly governed behavior; and deference and respect for authority were instilled.[92] The nurse's cap symbolized a way of life without whose self-effacing dedication nursing could not be considered a profession.

Under the circumstances, it is not surprising to find that registered nurses often hesitate to support collective bargaining or to join organizations which do. Apart from any question of male retribution, collective action would be at best "unladylike" and at worst unprofessional. Strikes, picketing, and other forms of union activity would pose a threat to the safety of patients and a denial of selfless devotion to duty. The nurse's historical role of mother-surrogate prompted one author, writing in 1938 in the main publication of the American Nurses Association, to observe, "a nurses' union would be almost, if not quite as absurd as a mother's union." [93]

The force of economic and social events in the immediate pre-World War II period, however, called into question the wisdom of total reliance on hospital administrators for satisfaction of the nurse's job and economic needs. As a consequence of the mass unemployment of the 1930s, the inflation of the forties, and the demonstration effect of widespread trade union organization and militance, isolated groups of nurses began to turn to collective bargaining as a *supplement* to traditional forms of joint activity. Among the first to do this were the state nursing associations in California, which had its first contract by 1946, and the Minnesota Nurses Association which had 50 hospitals under contract by the close of 1948.

At about the same time the American Nurses Association itself began to move away from its previous opposition to collective bargaining with

[91] Barhydt, pp. 105–6.
[92] Wilson, p. 217.
[93] Ronald L. Miller, "Development and Structure of Collective Bargaining Among Registered Nurses (Part I)," pp. 134–40.

the adoption of the concept of an economic security program for RNs. The program was to guarantee reasonable and satisfactory conditions of employment while at the same time assure the public of professional nursing service of high quality and quantity. The concept spread rapidly among the state associations; 22 states had economic security programs by 1947 and 43 by 1957.

But old values fade slowly. The ANA felt compelled in 1948 to instruct the state associations not to work out their economic security programs with the state hospital associations, and in 1950 it reaffirmed a no-strike policy along with neutrality in nonnurse disputes. The no-strike policy, however, carried an obligation of fair treatment in employment conditions from hospital administrators. Implied was the possibility that should the obligation not be met, the no-strike policy would become inoperative.[94] The national no-strike policy was withdrawn in 1968, leaving the matter to the discretion of the individual state nurses' associations.

For reasons to be discussed below, the number of registered nurses under collective contracts grew very slowly after 1946, reaching about 9,000 in 1964 and 30,000 in 1969.[95] Two-thirds of the RNs under contract in the latter year were in four states: California (6,805), New York (5,597), Minnesota (4,103), and Washington (3,713).

The unionization of nurses has been affected by many factors including the small budget and staff provided for collective bargaining by the national and state associations, the high hospital turnover rates of younger RNs, the willingness of nurses generally to accept the decisions and authority of hospital administrators in employment matters, lack of agreement and coordination among national and state associations over appropriate positions vis-à-vis collective bargaining, and the low participation rate of general duty nurses in the national and state associations.

In many respects all of the above factors continued to operate throughout the 1970s. Thus, in April 1978 only 70,000 registered nurses were under contracts administered by state affiliates of the ANA, with an additional 25,000–30,000 covered by contracts of independent nurses associations or trade unions including 1199, Retail Clerks, Service Employees, and Teamsters. Interestingly enough, the ANA has fared significantly better than other labor organizations with the NLRB's representation machinery, winning nearly 80 percent of the 176 elections it has contested over the period 1973 to 1977.[96] However, these victories

---

[94] See Seidman, pp. 335–51.
[95] Ronald L. Miller, "Development and Structure of Collective Bargaining Among Registered Nurses (Part II)," p. 220.
[96] BNA, *White Collar Report*, May 5, 1978, pp. B5–B6.

added only 10,655 nurses to the total under contract over the five years. Moreover, the geographical distribution of unionized RNs continues, as ten years ago, to be concentrated in the Northeast, West Coast, and Great Lakes areas. With the exception of Florida, collective bargaining contracts for RNs are virtually nonexistent in the southeastern and southwestern states.

In an effort to provide a more focused and sustained basis for bargaining, the ANA created a Commission on Economic and General Welfare in 1969. Labeling the program as the "new approach," the national association sought to develop a means by which direct financial and staff assistance could be made available to local units and/or state associations. The objectives of the approach, according to one observer, were similar to those of the organizing committees of the industrial unions in the private sector.[97]

As the bargaining and membership growth results discussed above indicate, the economic and general welfare programs have not affected appreciably the extent of collective bargaining among registered nurses. By comparison with expenditures of similar sized organizations, the budget for the programs remains inadequate for the task. These inadequacies, however, reflect both the individual nurse's perception that collective bargaining is incompatible with nursing as a profession and the view of the ANA's leadership which sees collective bargaining as important but only as a supplement to more basic programs such as education. As a group largely drawn from the ranks of nursing administrators and educators, the leaders may consider collective bargaining a threat to their managerial positions.

Nursing as an occupation is being subjected to pressures for far-reaching changes which may well place the collective bargaining activities of RNs in a substantially different light. In the first place, college-trained nurses are gradually replacing hospital-program diploma graduates, and if ANA has its way, all nurses will have bachelor's degrees. Gone with the diploma programs will be the military atmosphere, segregation, and inculcation of passive obedience to administrative authority. Important also to the individual nurse's receptivity to collective bargaining will be the role models provided by other professions including teachers, doctors, and social workers. Thus, to the extent these occupations legitimately unionize, bargain, and strike, the less unprofessional this behavior will appear to nurses.

While changes in attitudes and roles will occur over many years, the most immediate issue for the ANA is its structure. At the state level the

⁹⁷ Ronald L. Miller, "Development and Structure of Collective Bargaining Among Registered Nurses (Part II)," p. 219.

association is a three-tiered pyramid composed of a board of directors and statewide officers at the pinnacle; districts organized on a geographical basis at the middle level; and a number of professional chapters within each district at the lowest stratum. The chapters are usually associated with individual hospitals and correspond roughly to the locals of a national labor union.

The practice of the ANA has been for the state nurses' association to petition for a representation election and, if successful, to receive the certification even though the actual election district or bargaining unit is the hospital chapter. The National Labor Relations Board has accepted the practice, conditioning its certification on the delegation of the actual bargaining activities to the hospital chapter.[98] The delegation was required on the assumption that since the state association officers are so frequently employed as nursing supervisors or administrators, they could not avoid allegations of management domination or interference. In 1977, the Fourth Circuit Court of Appeals ruled in the *Anne Arundel Hospital* case, however, that it was illogical and illegal "to certify a bargaining agent on the condition that it not bargain." [99] If the *Anne Arundel* decision were to prevail, several hundred bargaining certifications held by state nurses' associations among private-sector hospitals will become invalid. In addition, even if the Fourth Circuit's position were ultimately overturned, years would likely pass during which the ANA's right to bargain was in limbo. Hospital employers would feel no compulsion to bargain, and many bargaining units would cease to exist.

In response to *Anne Arundel*, the ANA's Economic and Welfare Commission convened a "blue ribbon" committee to assess the impact of the decision on the association's collective bargaining activities. At the end of September 1977 the committee made its report, essentially recommending no major structural changes in ANA unless "subsequent adverse litigation" were to make internal adjustments necessary.

Several months later the Commission itself suggested that a restricted supervisory membership category might be a way out of the legal bind brought about by the Fourth Circuit's decision. Individuals holding "restricted supervisory membership" would be excluded from the Association's Board of Directors and finance committees but could serve in other official positions. The recommendation was rejected by the

---

[98] See, for example, *Sisters of Charity Providence, St. Ignatius Province d/b/a St. Patrick Hospital*, 225 NLRB 110 (1976); and *Sierra Vista Hospital*, 225 NLRB 155 (1976).

[99] *NLRB* v. *Annapolis Emergency Hospital Association d/b/a Anne Arundel General Hospital*, CA 4, No. 76-1166, August 31, 1977.

ANA's Board of Directors amidst a storm of protest from other Association commissions and individual members.

The action of the federal court and the inaction of the ANA reinforced two sets of developments which had been in progress before the *Anne Arundel* decision. The first was the growth of independent registered nurse groups which exclude supervisors and exist almost solely for collective bargaining activities. Illustrative of this trend is the United Nurses Association of California with nearly 2,000 members in the Los Angeles area and the Connecticut Health Care Association representing 3,300 nurses, technical workers, and other hospital professionals. The latter group broke from the Connecticut Nurses Association in 1976 and by May 1978 had won 13 of 16 representation elections.[100] Similar developments also have occurred in Wisconsin, Massachusetts, Pennsylvania, and Michigan. Moreover, should the ANA either drop collective bargaining entirely or attempt to resist any significant structural change, the existing ANA bargaining units, perhaps under the umbrella of the economic and general welfare programs, may spin off to form a totally new nurses' labor organization.[101]

The second major development is the increasing incursion of such unions as the Service Employees, Retail Clerks, and 1199 into the nursing field. The change made in 1977 by 1199 to accommodate registered nurses through a new division, the League for Registered Nurses, has already been mentioned. In California the American Federation of Nursing, a unit of the Service Employees International Union Local 535, has been chartered, and in Massachusetts SEIU displaced the Massachusetts Nurses Association as the bargaining agent for RNs in several hospitals in Boston.[102]

Given the above circumstances, it seems apparent that the issue of structure which has haunted the ANA since the 1940s can no longer be circumvented. If it is to continue with its collective bargaining activities, it must reorganize. The internal politics of the association, however, seem to suggest it won't.

Other Unions in the Health-Care Industry. Although the bulk of the

[100] BNA, *White Collar Report*, May 5, 1978, pp. B5–B6.

[101] Illustrative of the possibility was the creation of an independent group in Wisconsin called the United Professionals for Quality Health Care. The UP was established in December 1978 following a decision at a special convention of the Wisconsin Nurses Association in that same month to phase out its collective bargaining activities. See Junkerman, p. 1.

[102] In November 1978 Albert Shanker, President of the American Federation of Teachers, announced the creation of a new division to be called the American Federation of Nurses-AFT and the commitment of $1 million to organize nurses and other health-care employees. See "Teacher Union Seeks to Organize Workers in Health Professions," *New York Times*, November 30, 1978, p. A-15; and *Health Labor Relations Reports* 2 (December 11, 1978), pp. 1–2.

workers covered by collective bargaining agreements are represented by SEIU, AFSCME, 1199, and the ANA, a number of additional unions have achieved substantial membership in the health industry. Retail Clerks International Union, for example, has an estimated 50,000 members in bargaining units spread across hospitals, nursing homes, pharmacies, and health maintenance organizations as of June 1978.[103]

Next is the Physicians National Housestaff Association with 12,000 members.[104] The PNHA was created in 1975 and represents interns and residents in cities such as New York, Chicago, and Los Angeles. The objectives and strategies of the Housestaff Association, including strikes, have been supported by the American Medical Association, although opposed by hospital and allied associations.[105] Finally, as the analysis of NLRB representation election data suggests, many other international unions have acquired bargaining units among health-care employees, but the nature of these unions' role in health care generally and hospitals specifically remains to be determined.

With considerably fewer numbers, although still quite active, is the Laborers International Union. In mid-1978, the LIU claimed representation rights for 7,200 health-care employees, approximately 6,000 of whom were working in hospitals.[106] Finally, as the analysis of NLRB representation election data suggests, many other international unions have acquired bargaining units among health-care employees. However, the nature of these unions' role in health care generally and hospitals specifically remains to be determined.

COLLECTIVE BARGAINING STRUCTURES

Hospitals are a complex arrangement of bureaucratic structures and administrative systems in which "management" is a composite of administrators, medical staff, and trustees, each exercising varying amounts of authority. In addition, the administrative process has become increasingly subject in recent years to review and control by numerous external bodies including accreditation and licensing agencies, rate-review commissions, and health planning organizations. Moreover, as already noted, the delivery of health care is an industry which derives 80 percent or more of its income from so-called third-party payers. Thus, hospital collective bargaining is much more a system of multilateral or multiparty relationships than of bilateral or joint decision-making.[107]

[103] Letter from Richard Perry, Director, Professional and Health Care Division, RCIA, June 19, 1978.

[104] Andrews, p. 30.

[105] Frederick, pp. 16–17.

[106] Letter from Louis D. Elesie, Director, Health Care Division, Laborers International Union of North America, July 18, 1978.

[107] See Ronald L. Miller, "The Hospital-Union Relationship, (Part I)," pp. 49–54.

The Issue of Unit Proliferation. Under state regulation, hospital bargaining units tended to follow occupational boundaries, not unlike those on construction worksites and with similar adverse consequences. Depending on the particular situation, such fragmentation can be a potential source of jurisdictional conflict over job tasks, "unbalanced" wage structures, barriers to the flexible use of hospital manpower, and frequent work interruptions as picketing and job actions which began in one group spread to the entire hospital workforce.

In Minnesota, for example, as an outgrowth of the policies followed by the state's labor relations agency, multiple bargaining units became the norm for many of the hospitals. Among those certified were units for pharmacists, radiologic technicians, LPNs, RNs, stationary engineers, maintenance employees, clerical workers, and unskilled nonprofessionals. New York State, in another example, sought initially to limit bargaining units to five occupations, but eventually accepted as many as 12, including units of supervisors.

With the cases of Minnesota and New York in mind, Congress specifically directed the NLRB at the time of passage of the health-care amendments to Taft-Hartley to avoid a proliferation of bargaining units. After extensive deliberations the Board initially adopted the five-unit policy, but, as pointed out earlier, this policy has not been strictly followed when conditions warranting separate units of maintenance and operating engineers have, in the Board's view, been justifiable.

Although the possibility of negative consequences from unlimited unit proliferation does exist, the available evidence does not support a conclusion that such problems have arisen. In the first place, unionization under both state or federal law has most frequently been limited to one or two units per hospital. Thus, the AHA found in an analysis of 1,157 hospitals with collective bargaining agreements in 1976 that 49 percent had only one contract and an additional 23 percent had two contracts. Some 17 percent had four contracts or more.[108] It is important to note that the private-sector hospitals, on the average, had fewer contracts per hospital than those under federal, state, or local government control.

Second, as will be discussed in more detail, even where unit proliferation has existed in hospitals, contractual restraints on manpower utilization thus far have been relatively unimportant, particularly when compared with the constraints on management flexibility imposed by prevalent systems of state licensing or certifying occupations.[109] Unions

---

[108] Frenzen, p. 96.

[109] On this point, see Hershey, pp. 224–25.

such as SEIU and 1199 in fact have sought to increase employee mobility through a reduction in internal labor market balkanization.

Finally, the conflict hypothesized to be associated with multiple bargaining units within hospitals also has not come to pass. Since the subject will be examined more extensively below, it is sufficient to note here only the policy of neutrality in nonnursing disputes adopted by the ANA. This policy has resulted in a general refusal by RNs to honor the picket lines of other hospital employees and, short of filling the jobs of striking workers, to make certain that patient care continues without interruption. As might be expected, nonnursing employees therefore have felt no obligation to honor RN picket lines.

Multiemployer Bargaining. Up to this point we have been talking about units established for administrative purposes so that public agencies could conduct representation elections. In practice, the actual negotiation unit may be smaller than the election unit as with fractional bargaining or larger as exemplified by a multienterprise or multiemployer bargaining unit.[110] In the hospital industry, the boundaries of the election units have typically been analagous with those for the negotiation unit. That is, the average hospital employee is covered by a collective bargaining contract whose geographic scope is limited to that worker's hospital. Multihospital bargaining is the exception rather than the rule. The exceptions are important, however, and could become the norm, at least for urban hospitals.

Formal multiemployer units, for example, are characteristic of nearly all hospital bargaining in Minneapolis-St. Paul and one contract may cover as many as 23 hospitals and 5,000 workers. In the San Francisco Bay area, master contracts tend to predominate and have been customarily negotiated with three separate groups of hospitals: Oakland-Eastbay with eight hospitals; San Francisco-Westbay with 8–10 hospitals depending on the union involved; and the Kaiser system with 14 hospitals and clinics in Northern California generally. Multiemployer negotiating units also have come into existence in Seattle with such employee groups as RNs, LPNs, and operating engineers. Seattle, however, continues with a system of single-hospital contracts for the large numbers of unionized hospital service workers.

The largest multiemployer hospital negotiating unit in the private sector involves some 55 members of the League of Voluntary Hospitals in New York City and District 1199, which represents more than 35,000 service workers. Multihospital units also exist in New York City between SEIU's Local 144 and approximately 23 proprietary hospitals. In con-

---

[110] The standard reference on bargaining structure and its variations is Weber, ed., pp. xviii–xx.

trast to Seattle, however, single-hospital units are the rule for unionized RNs, LPNs, and other employee groups.

Beyond the exceptions to the general pattern of single-hospital negotiating units noted above, in a number of other cities, Portland, Oregon for example, bargaining may be concurrent for a number of hospitals even though separate contracts are signed, or as is the case in Chicago where there is highly coordinated but no concurrent negotiations.

A review of those instances in which multihospital bargaining has occurred suggests several factors at work.[111] Such a bargaining structure tends to evolve in urban areas and in association with homogeneity of hospitals, when a union has achieved substantial organization of the hospital employees in a given area, where bargaining histories are similar, and where the employee unions or associations are able to exert significant bargaining power. While most of these factors seem to be sufficient for multihospital bargaining structures to appear, the one necessary condition is union power. In the words of one hospital negotiator, the multiemployer unit becomes the "countersaw" to the "whipsaw."[112] The latter term refers to a strategy sometimes employed in collective bargaining in which weaker employers are played off against the stronger in a divide-and-conquer maneuver.

The role of power in affecting structures is visible both in instances where multiemployer units were abandoned as well as in those where units most recently were established. Thus, when New York City hospitals affiliated with the League of Voluntary Hospitals concluded that the NLRB's adverse ruling on the bargaining status of interns and residents had significantly weakened the housestaff association, the master agreement disintegrated. Individual hospitals continued to bargain with the Committee of Interns and Residents, but only in those instances where the Committee could force the hospitals to do so. The breakdown of the CIR master contract in New York City was paralleled by the return to single-hospital bargaining for registered nurses.[113]

It seems logical to conclude that the reversions from multihospital bargaining described above are a short-run phenomenon rather than a permanent change in bargaining structure. On the contrary, the cost pressures alone to share activities, to standardize wages and employment conditions, and to consolidate hospital functions across metropolitan areas are compelling a much greater degree of integration in hospital management than heretofore. As analysis of statistical trends in the industry suggests diversity is giving way as the "modern" hospital is in-

---

[111] Feuille and others, pp. 98–115. See also Abelow and Metzger, pp. 390–409.
[112] Corbett.
[113] Feuille and others, p. 112.

creasingly epitomized by the large, urban, medical center. However, until such time as hospital unions are able to generate more power, it is doubtful that hospital bargainers will be willing to relinquish their individual discretion in exchange for group protection.

Pattern Bargaining: Leaders and Followers. As with many other industries, "orbits of coercive comparison" exist in health-care labor relations which extend the impact of agreements beyond the actual negotiation units. Illustrative of this point are settlements reached in the 1199–League of Voluntary Hospitals master agreement which then became a bench mark for the union in its bargaining with some 60 other New York metropolitan health-care institutions. Moreover, 1199 also exists in an orbit across which are carried the contract settlements of AFSCME's bargaining with the public hospitals and those of SEIU with the proprietary hospitals. While the bargaining outcome which is to be the source of the coercive comparison may shift because of special circumstances, in general the hospital sector of New York City is one interconnected bargaining unit. What is achieved by one union will not go unnoticed by the other two for very long.

Orbits of comparison also carry the settlements to the nonunion sectors of the hospital industry. Given the relatively low incidence of unionization, a form of pattern bargaining exists in which the "satellites" are either unorganized employees of an otherwise unionized hospital or those hospitals in which none of the workers is covered by a collective bargaining contract. In the former case, settlements may be said to "spillover" from the unionized to the nonunion employees within the same hospital.

The most critical effect of negotiated settlements may be on nonunion hospitals as they attempt to keep abreast or ahead of negotiated settlements as a response to the possibility—or threat—of being unionized themselves. The industry's organizational structure facilitates the responses to these so-called "threat" effects. While hospital employers may not engage in actual price-fixing, cartelization is nevertheless characteristic among these organizations. For example, there are in excess of 5,500 hospitals, and 75–80 percent of them are affiliated with the American Hospital Association. The AHA is further structured into state associations which as well may have among their organizational units more limited regional associations including city or metropolitan hospital councils.[114]

---

[114] Other hospital organizations have also come into existence in response to specialized needs or circumstances. Examples are the Council of Teaching Hospitals, the Federation of American Hospitals (which serves primarily private proprietary organizations), the American Osteopathic Hospital Association, the Catholic Hospital Association, and the American Protestant Hospital Association.

Although the AHA provides important legal, technical, and related assistance for the affiliated hospitals, the key source of help for labor relations activities is supplied by the local hospital councils, particularly in those areas where multiemployer bargaining is the norm. In addition, even though the local council may not conduct the actual bargaining, its role as the cockpit for the coordination of strategy and the exchanging of information provides the basis for a unified response to organizing drives, contract negotiations, and employee job actions.

An additional source of structure which brings together hospital employers is the American Society for Hospital Personnel Administration. Ostensibly an arm of the AHA's central office in Chicago, the Hospital Personnel Association is comprised of state and local groups. Although the availability of technical services through this association is limited, it still provides an important focal point for the exchange of information and the coordination of labor relations activities.

A final point with regard to management structures for bargaining is the prevalence of attorneys. Most frequently these lawyers are not employees of the hospital as such but rather are members of firms specializing in providing legal services to employers with labor problems. These services range from advice during union organizing drives, representation before arbitrators and state or federal labor agencies, and direct participation in bargaining. The frequent resort by hospital administrators to outside attorneys stems from many sources, not the least of which is the conviction that hospital services can best be delivered in a nonunion climate. Moreover, the inexperience of most hospital managers in confronting labor relations issues as well as the complexity of the legal framework have reinforced the tendency to hire consultants. Finally, the system of "cost-pass-through" has provided a mechanism by which wages and benefits could be raised in the face of union "threats" and labor relations advice and service could be purchased as a normal item of doing business subject to later reimbursement.

Thus the high incidence of hospital employer organization as well as dependence on outside legal services has created channels through which bargaining comparisons can be made and settlements transmitted. This structure links one election unit to another within and between hospitals, establishes a basis for integrating a number of election units into a broader system, and also carries settlements to nonunion hospitals as well.

Third-Party Payers and Hospital Labor Relations

The income of the average private hospital has grown enormously over the past 20 years. The advent of such government programs as

Medicare and Medicaid as well as the widespread use of health-care insurance has established the base for the significant growth experienced by the industry. A major characteristic, however, of the influx of these funds has been a shift in revenue sources from patients and charity to private insurance companies and government agencies. By the mid-1970s more than 90 percent of health-care expenditures were financed by third-party payers.

This transformation of health-care financing occurred simultaneously with the unionization of the industry's employees. In the early years, the expansion of external funds provided strong leverage by which budding hospital unions could persuade—or compel—public authorities to intervene in bargaining situations. For example, Nash recounts how Leon Davis, president of District 1199, is alleged as early as 1959 to have pressured Mayor Wagner of New York City into increasing the public subsidies to the private hospitals with which 1199 bargained.[115]

The form by which the external funds were received also had important implications for labor relations in the industry. Thus when paid as subsidies to cover operating deficits on the one hand, or as charges to be reimbursed by insurance rate increases on the other, costs could be "passed through." Expenses incurred in countering union organizing drives as well as paying increased wages as a consequence of a contract settlement thus could be shifted to the third-party payer. One can speculate that the high rates of hospital labor-management conflict which characterized recognition issues but *not* contract negotiations were a result of the prevailing financial systems of cost-pass-through.

The acceleration of general inflation at the end of the decade of the 1960s brought federal price controls and an end to automatic price increases for hospitals. Thus, President Nixon, acting under authority previously granted by Congress, set in motion the so-called Economic Stabilization Program in August 1971.[116] Although wage and price controls over nearly all other industries were modified soon after their promulgation, controls in health care were continued up to the termination of the stabilization program in the spring of 1974. The fact that this industry was singled out for special government action was a portent of a drastically modified policy for dealing with health costs which was soon to come.

Heightened public concern with the costs of health care in the 1970s arose from two sources. First, although the rate of increase in the general level of prices had moderated by 1975, such was not the case for

---

[115] Nash, p. 79.
[116] See Mitchell and Weber, pp. 88–92.

health costs. In 1976 alone, health-care prices rose twice as fast as the general consumer price index. As the burden for the third parties grew, their financial ability to support the increases declined. Hence a second major factor for public concern was the financial crisis in which many city and state governments found themselves during the same period.

Health cost containment, the byword of the 1970s, was to be achieved in a number of ways including health planning, health maintenance organizations, rate-review procedures, and controls over hospital investment. Perhaps the most far-reaching methods adopted were to freeze or severely limit Medicaid/Medicare payments to hospitals and to shift the system of payment from the traditional cost-pass-through to prospective reimbursement. In the latter system, the rate of reimbursement is established *before* the costs or charges are incurred. As Rosmann points out, the purpose is ". . . to create an incentive to provide care more efficiently and to control costs since costs in excess of the established rate of reimbursement for any type of care or group of beneficiaries will not be covered, but must be absorbed by the hospital." [117] Between 1968 and 1977, 25 states adopted rate-review procedures nearly all of which were prospective in nature.

Outside the Northeast, the impact of these changes on private-sector hospital collective bargaining is yet to be felt to any significant degree. Although the reasons for this are not clear, they may be associated with the comparatively better financial condition of both public agencies and the hospitals in other parts of the U.S. as well as the conservative bargaining stance assumed by unions in those areas.

In the Northeast and particularly New York, however, the new reimbursement policies have significantly affected the structure of bargaining and the behavior of the parties, leading to a hardening of positions and an increase in conflict.[118] According to Yager, labor and management, in seeking leverage at the table, draw the third-party payer into the negotiations in a variation of multilateral bargaining typical of the public sector. The difference is that in health care the bargaining is not multilateral, but a series of bilateral negotiations: employer and union, employer and public authority, union and public authority, and perhaps union acting jointly with employer against public authority. A more descriptive term might be "serial bargaining." The end result of the public authority's intervention in whatever form has been to "chill" bargaining between the parties, necessitating that the

---

[117] Rosmann, "Hospital Revenue Controls—Their Labor Relations and Labor Force Utilization Implications for the Hospital Industry."

[118] See Yager.

settlement be fashioned either by an outside arbitrator or less directly by the rate decisions of the public authorities themselves.

A case in point is the agreement reached by 1199 and the League of Voluntary Hospitals in early July 1978 in which it was acknowledged that the crucial negotiations took place with the state public health department. Settlement between the hospitals and the union apparently was only possible after state authorities gave assurances to League hospitals that reimbursement rates would be increased commensurately with the new contract.[119] The importance of the state's role in the negotiations is underscored by the fact that state health and budget officials were directed by the governor to stand by as 1199's strike deadline was approached. Acceptance by the state of the parties' settlement avoided what would have been the third strike of the city's nonprofit hospitals in as many negotiations.

The intervention of public authorities can also be a source of strikes as well as settlements. New York, again, is illustrative. Work stoppages have occurred among the city's hospitals on at least three occasions between 1973 and 1976. The first of the disputes began on November 5, 1973, and involved some 30,000 members of 1199. The eight-day strike, although directed at affiliates of the League of Voluntary Hospitals, was in reality against a decision by the Cost of Living Council. Acting under the federal economic stabilization program, the CLC indicated it would roll back to 5.5 percent the second-year wage increase of the union's contract with the League.[120] Work stoppages also occurred in 1976 involving both the private hospitals under contract to 1199 and New York City's public hospitals organized by District 37 of AFSCME. In each case a key role was played by the New York State Department of Health.[121]

It does not seem unreasonable to conclude that as federal and state efforts to regulate hospital costs continue, the experience of New York will become more generalized. This, in turn, bodes ill for the labor relations climate in the nation's health-care industry.

Collective Bargaining Patterns and Issues

In 1976 an estimated 2,500 collective bargaining agreements were in effect at hospitals across the United States.[122] As such, these contracts reflect the personal and institutional objectives of all the parties who

---

[119] "Higher State Rates Avert Major Strike in New York City," p. 23.

[120] *Health Labor-Management Report*, Vol. 1, No. 7, November 1973, (Special Issue.)

[121] See Schramm, pp. 521–22. A description of the strike by AFSCME District Council 37 against the public hospitals is contained in Bird, p. 1.

[122] BNA, *Daily Labor Report*, June 15, 1976, pp. A3–A4.

participate in the negotiations. Since more often than not objectives sought by one party may be in conflict with those of other parties, contracts also are a concrete measure of bargaining power. Although precise measures of hospitals' bargaining outcomes are not available, sufficient descriptive evidence has been gathered to provide a basis for reaching tentative generalizations.

The most extensive examination of hospital contracts to date is that carried out by Juris and associates.[123] After analyzing more than 800 collective agreements, Juris concluded "the contracts in [the hospital] industry are developing in a way indistinguishable from steel, auto, meatpacking, police and fire." This finding is surprising in view of the uniqueness often ascribed to the industry. In specific instances, however, hospital contracts are in fact quite different from those in other industries, pointing not to the assumed uniqueness but rather to the inability of hospital unions to generate the bargaining power of their counterparts in other industries.

UNION SECURITY, JOB CONTROL, AND INCOME PROTECTION

In the first place, a major objective of health-care labor organizations would be to obtain contract provisions that strengthen the union institutionally. By most measures, hospital contracts have a way to go to provide the institutional security achieved by other unions. Not only has the union shop been achieved half as frequently as in other industries (30 percent vs. 63 percent), but hospital contracts are twice as likely to be without any form of union security (34 percent vs. 18 percent).[124]

A second concern for hospital labor organizations in their bargaining would be contractually provided job and income security for their members. Unions customarily seek restrictions on subcontracting, crew size, and supervisors performing work in bargaining units; stipulations that length of service will govern layoff, recall, transfer, and promotion; and provisions for severance pay and supplemental unemployment benefits. Table 6 gives a picture of the frequency of occurrence of job- and income-related contract clauses, using data from Juris and the Bureau of National Affairs. Here again hospital agreements not only provide less union security but also less job security to individual members. From the hospital's standpoint, however, the relative absence of traditional work rules means that management retains a good deal of discretion in the utilization of its employees. These hospital contracts gen-

---

[123] Juris and others, "Nationwide Survey . . . ," pp. 122–30, 192; Juris and others, "Employee Discipline . . . ," pp. 67–69, 70–72, 74; and Juris, pp. 504–11.

[124] Juris and others, "Nationwide Survey Shows Growth in Union Contracts," p. 192, and BNA, *Basic Patterns in Union Contracts*, 8th Edition, May 1975.

TABLE 6
Contractual Restraints on Management Rights,
Selected Provisions
1974–1975

Contract Provision	Percent of Total Contracts with Provision	
	Hospitals[a] N = 817	All Industries[b] N = 400
Seniority		
Layoff	75.0	85.0
Recall	66.0	75.0
Transfer	44.0	48.0
Promotion	66.0	69.0
Supplemental unemployment benefits	*	17.0
Severance pay	9.0	39.0
Subcontracting	9.0	40.0
Crew size	5.0	NA
Work by supervisors	NA	57.0

* Less than 1 percent.

NA – not available

[a] Hervey Juris, "Labor Agreements in the Hospital Industry: A Study of Collective Bargaining Outputs," *Labor Law Journal* (August 1977), pp. 504–11.

[b] Bureau of National Affairs, *Basic Patterns in Union Contracts* (Washington, 1975).

erally do not seem to pose the impediments to productivity that have been historically true of other industries.[125]

WAGE LEVELS AND FRINGE BENEFITS

Through their attention to salaries and fringe benefits, labor-management agreements also directly affect the employee's income and standard of living. One author observes, for example, that as a consequence of the bargaining activities of 1199 in New York City the wages of nonprofessional hospital workers tripled between 1959 and 1969.[126] Wage bargaining results for hospital unions generally, however, have been far less spectacular. Thus, Fottler, using data from the BLS Area Wage Surveys, found that unions had an impact on hospital wage levels of between 4.5 and 8.2 percent.[127] When compared with effects estimated at upwards of 15 percent for unions in other industries, the contrasts are striking.[128] Table 7 presents additional data on collective bargaining provisions relating to wages and fringes which are consistent with those for wages generally. Only in the area of sick leave do hos-

[125] See also Richard U. Miller and others, "Union Effects on Hospital Administration: Preliminary Results of a Three State Study," pp. 517–18.

[126] Raskin, p. 24.

[127] Fottler, p. 54. See also Richard U. Miller and others, "Union Effects on Hospital Administration: Preliminary Results of a Three State Study," p. 649.

[128] A useful review of studies on the impact of unions on wages is contained in Johnson, pp. 23–28.

pital agreements exceed the standards of other industries. Thus, for example, in the case of holidays, hospital contracts not only provide fewer holidays but at considerably lesser rates of pay.

TABLE 7

Frequency of Contract Provisions Containing Selected
Wage and Fringe Benefit Items
1973–1974

Percent of Contracts Mentioning Provision	Hospitals	All Industries
Cost-of-living adjustment	6.0	36.0
Shift differential	58.0	82.0
Reporting pay	29.0	71.0
Call back pay	48.0	62.0
Premium pay for		
Saturday	11.0	52.0
Sunday	14.0	68.0

Source: Bureau of National Affairs, *Daily Labor Report*, No. 116, June 15, 1976, p. A4.

It could be argued that with employment expanding rapidly in the 1960s and early 1970s, hospital employees would feel few pressures to protect either their job or income security. Moreover, with ample financial resources and cost-pass-through, management would have little incentive for cost-cutting efficiency measures. Hence the absence of work rules, severance pay, SUB, and the like may not reflect a lack of union bargaining power. If this were true, however, we should also see higher wages, better fringe benefits, and stronger union security.

An alternative explanation which could be postulated is that since the contract data discussed above were largely obtained from agreements negotiated before the health-care amendments, they are no longer representative of labor relations in the industry. Unfortunately, more recent information has not been published to support or refute this conclusion. Inferentially, we can speculate that given the change to prospective reimbursement systems, the strong political pressure to control hospital costs, and the lack of organizing success by hospital unions, the picture portrayed by the 1973–74 contract data is still applicable. It is small consolation for hospital labor unions to say that at least they are not responsible for the rapid rise in health-care costs.

PATIENT-CARE ISSUES IN BARGAINING

From the hospital administrator's standpoint, few issues seem to have less of a place at the bargaining table than those concerned directly with the substance, form, and control of decisions affecting patient care. Hospital management's views in this regard are represented by the position taken by the Executive Committee of the American

Hospital Association:[129] "The staffing of a hospital must be an objective process and should not be controlled by a group with special interests. . . . Nurses as an organized group are not legally responsible for patient care. Only management has the responsibility to determine the number of employees, their qualifications, and their assignment within the institution so as to be consistent with the best patient care and the most effective utilization of personnel."

The AHA's policy statement is directed at what has often constituted a major source of conflict between registered nurses and hospitals: the minimum number of RNs assigned by a hospital to a ward, department, or specialized task. Such staffing issues have arisen also in disputes between hospitals and their housestaff when the latter have sought through bargaining to increase the employment not only of RNs, but also LPNs and nurses aides.

Related to staffing is the question of out-of-title work. Nurses, in demanding the right to refuse specialized work assignments when training was felt to be inadequate, have cited the ANA's *Code for Nurses* which reads in part:

Provision 3—The nurse maintains individual competence in nursing practice, recognizing and accepting responsibility for individual actions and judgements.

Provision 5—The nurse uses individual competence as a criteria in accepting delegated responsibilities and assigning nursing activities to others.

Attempts to incorporate the Nursing Code in contracts have been staunchly resisted by hospitals, resulting, as in the case of Youngstown, Ohio, in long and bitter strikes.[130]

The Youngstown strike of registered nurses as an example of conflict over out-of-title work has been duplicated in such cities as Chicago, Seattle, San Francisco, and St. Louis. In addition, it has also been a focal point for collective bargaining between hospitals and their committees of interns and residents when housestaff organizations have sought to limit such assignments as drawing blood, clerical tasks, and setting up I.V. systems. At times demands have also been made that nurses and paramedics be trained to handle work formerly assigned to interns and residents.

Although out-of-title work and staffing have been the primary collective bargaining issues, union demands have included other subjects related to patient care: length of workday and week, scheduling of hours and weekends, number of allied workers employed, guarantees

---

[129] *Health Labor-Management Report*, July 1974, p. 3.
[130] Lewis, p. 49.

of laboratory equipment improvement, the purchase of emergency medical supplies, and reactivation of previously closed patient-care units. In a dispute involving Cook County Hospital of Chicago, for example, interns and residents presented more than 100 patient-care demands.[131]

Beyond the substantive decisions concerning patient care, hospital labor organizations have also attempted to negotiate the procedures by which employees would participate formally in such decisions. Thus health-care advisory committees have been sought by interns and residents, and registered nurses have proposed a variety of joint committees carrying such titles as professional staffing, professional performance, or joint study, to name a few.

Whether it be procedural or substantive issues related to patient care, hospitals have resisted such efforts as, at best, attempts "by unions to mask economic demands in the form of patient care and quality of care issues," [132] and at worst, as evidence of a desire by employees and their organizations to take control of the hospitals.

Analysis of hospital labor contracts reveals little in the way of provisions relating to patient care. Agreements seem to be silent on staffing, out-of-title assignments, and related working-condition issues.[133] Although joint-participation committees are prevalent for both professional and technical employees (73 and 52 percent, respectively),[134] the authority and scope of the committees in dealing with patient-care questions are unclear. Moreover, if we note that joint committees occur in only 16 percent of nonprofessional employees' contracts according to Juris, the fear that participation in hospital management decision-making by professional employees will lead inevitably to demands for similar participation by nonprofessional unions seems unsupported.

The absence of patient-care-related clauses from hospital labor contracts may be explained by several factors. First, channels for resolving patient-care issues may continue to be informal and individual in orientation, or formal mechanisms may exist under extra-contractual conditions. Particularly in the nurse's mind, the role conflict of professional vs. union member may be a deterrent to mixing patient-care questions with collective bargaining.

Second, the attitudes of hospital administrators are also important in limiting the scope of collective bargaining to "traditional issues." The willingness of administrators to "buy-off" patient-care demands with economic counterproposals places health-care professionals in an

[131] *Health Labor-Management Report*, November 28, 1975, p. 1.
[132] *Ibid.*, July 1974, p. 3.
[133] Richard U. Miller and others, "Union Effects on Hospital Administration: Preliminary Results of a Three State Study," p. 518.
[134] Juris, p. 511.

obvious quandary. With salaries and fringe benefits comparatively low and the likelihood also low that patient-care demands will be conceded without strikes, the bargaining outcomes are predictable.

Finally, the general weakness of the bargaining position coupled with the professional hesitancy to engage in work stoppages reinforces the logic of the situation. Thus, hospital professionals' collective agreements in fact may, as Juris contends, be nearly indistinguishable in principle from those of union contracts in other industries both by design and by circumstance.

Labor-Management Conflict in Hospitals

A major point of controversy surrounding the passage of the health-care amendments of 1974 was the effect such legislation would have on strikes and other forms of labor-management conflict. Proponents of the amendments argued that coverage of hospitals and related institutions under Taft-Hartley would reduce the incidence of conflict, citing statistics that showed that of 248 strikes in the private health-care sector between 1962 and 1972, nearly half were caused by disputes over union recognition.[135] Fewer recognition strikes occurred in those states in which representational machinery was present and union organizing was regulated. Thus it was expected that the availability of the NLRB together with such devices as secret-ballot representation elections and majority rule in all state jurisdictions would remove a significant issue from resolution by force.

Those against the amendments saw legislative efforts to encourage collective bargaining as an open invitation to further strikes in the industry, which the public would not tolerate. In the words of one management representative,

> [An] extremely high price will be exacted if strikes occur in the hospital setting. Not an economic cost, but a human cost. The human cost of suffering or loss of life. The human cost resulting from an inability to restore vital life functions because of delay in bringing apprepriate [sic] skills to bear. A second, a minute, an hour, a day—each of these can be the critical time span which determines success or failure in treatment of a sick or injured person.[136]

While the advocates of expanding Taft-Hartley to include all private health-care employees prevailed, the amendments ultimately reflected congressional misgivings over granting full rights to strike and to en-

---

[135] *Coverage of Nonprofit Hospitals Under the National Labor Relations Act, 1973,* pp. 158–285.
[136] *Ibid.,* p. 165.

gage in related concerted activity. Hence came the ten-day notice of intent to strike or picket, the stipulation of compulsory mediation, the extended periods allowed for mediation and negotiation, and the provision for Boards of Inquiry. The strike was not forbidden, but it also was not to be a weapon used capriciously or punitively.

THE INCIDENCE OF HOSPITAL STRIKES

From Table 8 we see that the number of work stoppages registered for private health-service employees generally and hospitals in particular was almost identical in 1977 to the figures for 1973 and 1969. Thus, despite a significant increase in collective bargaining contracts in the industry, the number of work stoppages has not increased proportionately.

TABLE 8

Work Stoppages in the Private Health-Care Industry
1962–1977

	Total Work Stoppages (SIC 80)	Private Hospitals (SIC 806)	Percent of Total
1962	6	NA	—
1963	13	NA	—
1964	14	NA	—
1965	13	NA	—
1966	19	10	52.6
1967	27	17	62.9
1968	28	17	60.7
1969	43	30	69.7
1970	49	23	46.9
1971	36	19	52.7
1972	47	19	40.4
1973	56	32	57.1
1974	44	27	61.4
1975	63	25	39.7
1976	71	40	56.3
1977	56	30	53.6

NA – Data not available

Source: U.S. Department of Labor, Bureau of Labor Statistics, Division of Industrial Relations.

Other measures of strike activity also support the conclusion that the incidence and severity of labor disputes in health care are less than in other industries. For example, in 1977 the average number of workers involved in strikes in all industries was 411 compared with 259 for all private health care and 367 for private hospitals. The same BLS figures also show that the mean duration of health-care strikes was approximately half that of industry generally—15 days as opposed to 28 days.[137]

---

[137] FMCS, Minutes, of the Third Meeting, Health Care Labor Management Advisory Committee, December 6, 1976, p. 3.

Explanations for the patterns of health-care work stoppages are not difficult to find. In the first place, the shift from state to federal coverage for the private sector of the industry removed the necessity for strikes as a mechanism to achieve recognition and made the employment of work stoppages in contract disputes more difficult. Secondly, major credit has also been given for a "relatively strike-free environment" in hospitals to the 10-day strike notice requirement.[138] According to one observer, this "provides a sizeable period of time for emotions to cool off and for a mediator to do his job." [139]

In addition, the availability of the Boards of Inquiry has also played a role. The picture with regard to the effect of the BOIs, however, is not entirely clear. They have been criticized by the parties on a number of issues, most particularly on timing, and their use has declined over the years. For example, 24 boards were appointed during the first four months following passage of the amendments and an additional 31 were named in the subsequent six-month period. In 1975–76, 50 boards were created; in 1976–77, only 37 boards were named. From August 1977 through August 1978, there were only 34.[140]

The attitudes of the parties also have an effect on the number of work stoppages. Neither labor nor management supports use of the strike except as a last resort, and they have used interest arbitration for the resolution of disputes to a much greater degree than have other industries. Formal provisions for third-party resolution of disputes often have been incorporated directly into contracts. Illustrative are the so-called "pre-election" agreements negotiated by labor and management in Chicago and the stipulations to arbitrate new contract terms which have long been a part of the hospital agreements in Minneapolis-St. Paul. It should also be noted that provisions for arbitrating grievance disputes are also widespread, appearing in approximately 88 percent of all hospital contracts.[141]

Professional health-care employees such as nurses have a particularly strong aversion to walking off en masse. The American Nurses Association carried a prohibition against strikes in its constitution for 20 years after the Economic Security Program had been launched, and even though the national association was to discard the ban in 1968, many state associations including New York continued such provisions for nearly a decade thereafter. The ANA also followed closely a policy

[138] BNA, *Daily Labor Report*, September 25, 1978, p. A10.
[139] *Ibid.*
[140] Department of Research, Federal Mediation and Conciliation Service, personal communication, September 26, 1978.
[141] Juris, p. 508.

of neutrality in the labor disputes of other health-care unions, most notably declining to honor others' picket lines.

Given the lower perceived utility of strikes for health-care workers, other weapons of concerted activity often have been substituted. Thus, at times, job actions have taken the form of mass resignation, sickouts, work-to-rule, and noon-hour and off-time demonstrations. One of the more creative approaches employed on occasion by interns and residents has been to refuse to bill patients.

Conflict also may be individualized in the sense that workers may have excessive rates of absenteeism and turnover, file large numbers of grievances, and constitute a continuing series of disciplinary problems for theft, drug and alcohol abuse, and poor work performance. The nature of the workforce and its working conditions are such, however, that behavior described above gives a very mixed picture of conflict, particularly as a substitute for strikes. While turnover and absenteeism often are high, research suggests this is less a problem for unionized hospitals.[142] Further, the usage of grievance machinery and resort to arbitration also seem to be low by the standards of other industries.[143]

In general, labor-management relations in health care at the present time give little evidence of the conflict which was feared would accompany the unionization of the industry. While there are exceptions, strikes tend to be fewer, smaller, and shorter than in other industries. Compared to the situation in other newly organized industries, "the lack of intense, violent conflict in hospitals is perplexing."[144]

However few hospital strikes occur or however short their duration, those that do may have severe repercussions on the delivery of health-care services in a community and on a hospital's patients in particular. Therefore it would be useful to examine, to the extent possible, the impact of hospital strikes. A first point to consider is that it appears to be an exceptional case when a hospital is forced to cease operations completely when a work stoppage occurs. In the first 12 months following the enactment of the amendments, for example, 20 strikes occurred, only three of which caused the hospital to close down.[145] Rather, elective surgery is curtailed, outpatient services reduced, and all but the acutely ill discharged or transferred. Although picket lines may be set up, supplies usually continue to be delivered and nonstriking employees work. In the case of a strike by nurses, supervisory nursing personnel,

---

[142] Richard U. Miller and others, *The Impact of Collective Bargaining on Hospitals: A Three State Study*, pp. 182–183.

[143] See Nash on this point, pp. 98–105; and R. U. Miller and others, *The Impact of Collective Bargaining on Hospitals: A Three State Study.*

[144] Nash, p. 7.

[145] Rosmann, "One Year Under Taft-Hartley," p. 67.

licensed practical nurses, and nurses aides may be available to provide patient care.

Not all outcomes associated with strikes may in fact be negative from the hospital's standpoint. At the conclusion of a lengthy work stoppage of RNs in Seattle hospitals, benefits perceived by administrators from taking the strike were reassessment of staffing patterns and more economical use of personnel, intense press coverage which was a means of informing the public of the hospital's services as well as generating support for their position in the strike, and "most importantly," according to a management representative, "the firmness with which the hospitals resisted the nurses' demands will be noted by other bargaining units."[146]

Thus, hospital work stoppages do not appear to threaten the health and safety of patients and in this respect are no longer categorized by any of the parties involved in hospital bargaining as unthinkable. On the contrary, it appears that at times they can be considered as not an unwelcome outcome in bargaining. Even from the standpoint of public authorities, such action may be one means of forced economizing and cost control in an industry reluctant or unable to deal with its surplus beds and redundant personnel.

Collective Bargaining in Hospitals: Concluding Thoughts

It is clear from the foregoing that as a late arrival to the health-care industry, collective bargaining is still in its formative stages. Unlike the majority of industries discussed in this book, labor market structures are fluid, unionization uneven, and bargaining outcomes often uncertain. Amidst this turbulence the outlines of a structure for the industry's system of labor relations now seems to be discernable and with it, the basis for a forecast of things to come. In this concluding section of the chapter we shall sum up collective bargaining in hospitals, paying particular attention to current issues and problems. In this way perhaps we shall be better able to see what lies ahead for labor relations in the industry.

GROWTH AND CHANGE OF HOSPITAL BARGAINING

Taken from the vantage point of two decades, the level of unionization in hospitals has increased significantly. The momentum of the early years was not maintained in the 1970s, however, even with the enactment of the 1974 Taft-Hartley amendments. Although individual unions, such as District 1199, have achieved important numerical gains

---

[146] See a description of a ten-week strike of 1,200 RNs at 15 Seattle hospitals in Roach and others, pp. 49–51.

in members, overall the rate of growth has been slow and quite limited geographically.

In many respects consolidation seems to characterize the organizing of labor organizations in health care. More often than not unionization is directed at hospitals already possessing bargaining units and comes as a consequence of initiatives arising within the employer's workforce. In the face of frequent strong and bitter opposition from management, this is a rational policy calculated to economize on scarce union resources. It is also a policy of gradualism which forecloses any great breakthroughs or profound changes in the incidence of hospital bargaining in the coming years.

HOSPITAL BARGAINING STRUCTURES

The current patterns of collective bargaining reveal strong tendencies of centralization for both labor and management. The latter, working through urban or regional councils, is well structured both to counter organizing drives and to present unified or coordinated strategies for bargaining. The unions in the hospital field, on the other hand, tend to subsume their hospital members in large, so-called "dispersed" locals or state associations in which hospital negotiating policy is made with an eye to other kinds of workers within the local or to other health-care bargaining units administered by the local.

The structural problems of bargaining in health care are intensified by the occupationally fragmented nature of the hospital workforce and by the multitude of potential union rivals seeking hospital members. In the former situation, the possibility for competition and conflict is great between negotiating units within hospitals; and in the latter case the likelihood of raiding or organizational battles also exists.

At the present moment the amount of within-hospital unit proliferation is low. As pointed out above, the average hospital has only one labor contract. Moreover, the NLRB has, for the most part, followed the dictates of Congress in this regard. If for no other reason, however, than union organizing strategies of consolidation, the average number of bargaining units will gradually increase. Whether this will have negative consequences for bargaining is dependent on several factors including the extent to which different unions have title to the hospital's units or all are held by the same union. If the latter situation prevails, one would predict less interunit conflict. On the other hand, multiple union presence within the hospital may lead to an initial increase in conflict which later subsides. As has occurred in other industries, coalition bargaining may arise as unions seek to coordinate their efforts and to avoid being "whipsawed."

On the employer side, the gradual increase in union bargaining power will reinforce the existing tendencies already working to expand the scope of units. Thus in addition to the labor activity of the hospital councils, the economics of health-care delivery which are compelling coordination and sharing of technology and services provide a strong rationale for multiemployer negotiating units and pattern bargaining. As a consequence, bargaining may become increasingly remote from the individual hospital worker as units expand and administration is centralized.

THE IMPACT OF HOSPITAL BARGAINING

In terms of increased labor cost, the effects of collective bargaining on hospitals remain to be felt. Wages and fringes have tended to rise slowly, offset at times by decreased employee turnover. Moreover, as compared to unions in other industries, hospital labor organizations have yet to seek contractual restraints on management discretion in its utilization of certain groups of registered nurses and housestaff physicians. But even here the successes in achieving demands related to such issues as out-of-title work, staffing, or joint control have been outweighed by the failures. In either case, win or lose, efforts to obtain so-called patient-care demands have been accompanied by long and bitter conflict.

A related aspect of bargaining impact is the role of the strike and the availability of substitutes. Traditional in the context of private-sector labor relations, the work stoppage in hospitals was long held to be untenable. Experience has proven, however, and especially since 1974 that strikes have not grown concomitantly with unionization. By comparison with other industries, hospitals have enjoyed a relatively strike-free environment. The impediments posed by the legal framework have reduced the utility of the strike, but as much as anything the parties' own willingness to substitute such devices as interest arbitration have played an important role.

It would be unwise, however, to assume that in the future labor-management harmony will prevail. On the contrary, the ingredients for significantly increased levels of conflict in hospitals appear at hand. In the first place, the urgencies of cost control confront directly the goals of employees and their unions. Management efforts to raise productivity and restrain expenditures bring it on a collision course with worker needs for income security, job control, and a constantly improving standard of living. As has already happened in the public hospitals of many urban areas, both professional and nonprofessional employees have engaged in militant job actions in protest against layoffs, "low" staffing levels, and poor working conditions.

Other factors which are likely to be a source of future conflict are the attitudes of management and workers. Hospital administrators in the 1970s, perhaps reflecting more conservative trends in the general society, have adopted strong anti-union stances, apparently contesting unions at every turn and on every issue. Such a policy, while holding unions at bay for a time, is productive of both short-term and long-term conflict. The end results may be a climate of hostility and mistrust which may not be undone for many years into the future.

THE THIRD-PARTY PAYER ONCE AGAIN

How much conflict and with what consequences are questions whose answers lie in good part with the so-called third-party payers. Those who control the financial condition of health-care delivery also are in a position to influence the structure and behavior of hospital labor and management. Although the actual intervention of third parties is still quite limited geographically, the potential is increasing rapidly. Further, where the intervention has occurred, its effects have been profound. Bargaining has been chilled, settlements left to arbitrators or public authorities, and the process itself increasingly politicized. As private hospitals more and more have taken on the characteristics of a regulated utility, the distinction between private and public-sector institutions has become blurred. Given the role of the third-party payers, the fact that often the same unions operate in both sectors, and the commonality of technology and labor markets to private and public-sector hospitals alike, the significant distinctions may disappear altogether.

In sum, one has a vision of the future in which the large urban hospitals contain a complex of interrelated bargaining units, some professional and some not, in which much of the negotiation is carried on by councils of unions acting as a coalition. The hospital in turn will be but one unit in a network of other health-care institutions encompassed by a master contract. Much of the bargaining may consist of joint labor-management presentations to public authorities and their arbitrators.

Strikes will be few but potentially devastating as the hospitals of large geographical areas are shut down. Moreover, more often than not, while the objectives of the work stoppage may be economic, the actual thrust may be political—to force the public authorities to accept the agreements already reached by labor and management.

While the scenario presented above is imaginary, the foundation by which the events prophesied can occur is already in place. What implications these effects have for the future quality and accessibility of health-care in the United States can only be guessed. It does not seem unreasonable to conclude that in any case the results will not be positive.

List of References

Abelow, William J., and Norman Metzger. "Multi-Employer Bargaining for Health Care Institutions." *Employee Relations Law Journal* 1 (Winter 1976).

"AHA Research Capsules—No. 6." *Hospitals, JAHA* 46 (April 1, 1972).

American Hospital Association. *Hospital Guidebook for 1977.* Chicago: AHA, 1977.

————. *Hospital Statistics,* 1977 Edition. Chicago: AHA, 1977.

Andrews, Mary A. "Housestaff Physicians and Interns Press for Bargaining Rights." *Monthly Labor Review* 101 (August 1978).

Barhydt, Nancy R. "Nursing." In *Health Care Delivery in the United States,* Steven Jonas and contributors. New York: Saringer Publishing Company, 1977.

Bird, David. "Hospital Talks Are Intensified: Cut in Aid Cited." *New York Times,* August 7, 1976.

Bloom, Barbara I. "Collective Action by Professionals Poses Problems for Administrators." *Hospitals, JAHA* 51 (March 16, 1977).

Bognanno, Mario F., James B. Dworkin, and Omotayo Fashoyin. "Physicians and Dentists Bargaining Organizations: A Preliminary Look." *Monthly Labor Review* 98 (June 1975).

Bureau of National Affairs. *Basic Patterns in Union Contracts,* 8th Edition. Washington: BNA, May 1975.

Chamberlain, Neil, and Donald Cullen. *The Labor Sector,* 2nd edition. New York: McGraw-Hill Book Co., 1971.

Chicago Hospital Council. *Analysis of Collective Bargaining Agreements in Chicago Area Hospitals, 1975–76.* CHC Employer/Labor Relations Services Department, November 1, 1975.

Cohen, Alana Sue. "Organizing Hospital Workers: The New York Experience." Master's thesis, Massachusetts Institute of Technology, June 1973.

Corbett, Laurence P. "Countersaw to Whipsaw: Group Bargaining by Hospitals Meets Unions on Equal Terms." Unpublished paper, American Hospital Association, May 1976.

Council on Wage and Price Stability. *The Rapid Rise of Hospital Costs.* Staff Report. Washington: January 1977.

Coverage of Nonprofit Hospitals Under National Labor Relations Act. Hearings before the Subcommittee on Labor and Public Welfare, United States Senate, 93rd Congress, 1st Session, on S. 794 and S. 2292, July 31, August 1, 2, and October 4, 1973.

Denton, David R. "The Union Movement in American Hospitals, 1847–1976." Ph.D. dissertation, Boston University, 1976.

Enright, Michael, and Steven Jonas. "Hospitals." In *Health Care Delivery in the United States,* Steven Jonas and contributors. New York: Saringer Publishing Company, 1977.

Extension of NLRA to Nonprofit Hospital Employees. Hearings before the Special Subcommittee on Education and Labor, U.S. House of Representatives, 92nd Congress, 1st and 2nd Sessions, on H.R. 11357, 1972.

Farkas, Emil C. "The National Labor Relations Act: The Health Care Amendments." *Labor Law Journal* (May 1978).

Feuille, Peter, Charles Maxey, Hervey Juris, and Margret Levi. "Determinants of Multi-Employer Bargaining in Metropolitan Hospitals." *Employee Relations Law Journal* 4 (Summer 1978).

Fottler, Myron D. "The Union Impact on Hospital Wages." *Industrial and Labor Relations Review* 30 (April 1977).

Frederick, Larry D. "New Image for the AMA." *Modern Health Care* (February 1976).

Freeman, Richard B., and James L. Medoff. "New Estimates of Private Sector Unionism in the United States." *Industrial and Labor Relations Review* 32 (January 1979).

Frenzen, Paul D. "Survey Updates Unionization Activities." *Hospitals, JAHA* 52 (August 1, 1978).

Gibson, Robert R., and Charles R. Fisher. "National Health Expenditures, Fiscal Year 1977." *Social Security Bulletin* 41 (July 1978).

Hershey, Nathan. "Labor Relations in Hospitals in the Private Sector." *Proceedings* of the 22nd Annual Meeting, Industrial Relations Research Association, 1970.

"Higher State Rates Avert Major Strike in New York City." *Hospitals, JAHA* 52 (August 16, 1978).

Hospitals Under the National Labor Relations Act. Report submitted by the Committee on Education and Labor, 93rd Congress, 2nd Session, House of Representatives, May 20, 1974.

Johnson, George E. "Economic Analysis of Trade Unionism." *American Economic Review* 65 (May 1975).

Junkerman, John. "Area Nurses Forge New Union." *Madison Press Connection*, December 11, 1978.

Juris, Hervey. "Labor Agreements in the Hospital Industry: A Study of Collective Bargaining Outputs." *Labor Law Journal* 28 (August 1977).

Juris, Hervey, Joseph Rosmann, Charles Maxey, and Gail Bentivegna. "Employee Discipline No Longer Management Prerogative Only." *Hospitals, JAHA* 51 (May 1, 1977).

————. "Nation-wide Survey Shows Growth in Union Contracts." *Hospitals, JAHA* 51 (March 16, 1977).

Lewis, Howard L. "Nurse: How Much Like Doctors?" *Modern Health Care* (June 1975).

Link, Charles, and John Landen. "Monopsony and Union Power in the Market for Nurses." *Southern Economic Journal* (April 1977).

Metzger, Norman, and Dennis D. Pointer. *Labor Management Practices in the Health Services Industry: Theory and Practice.* Washington: Science and Health Publications, Inc., 1972.

Miller, Richard U., Brian E. Becker, and Edward B. Krinsky. "Union Effects on Hospital Administration: Preliminary Results from a Three State Study." *Labor Law Journal* 28 (August 1977).

Miller, Richard U., Brian E. Becker, Edward B. Krinsky, and Glen Cain. *The Impact of Collective Bargaining on Hospitals: A Three State Study.* Madison: Industrial Relations Research Institute, University of Wisconsin-Madison, 1977.

Miller, Ronald L. "Collective Bargaining in Non-Profit Hospitals." Ph.D. dissertation, University of Pennsylvania, 1969.

————. "Development and Structure of Collective Bargaining Among Registered Nurses." *Personnel Journal*, Part I, 50 (February 1971); Part II, 50 (March 1971).

————. "The Hospital-Union Relationship." *Hospitals, JAHA*, Part I (May 1, 1971); Part II (May 16, 1971).

Mitchell, Daniel J.B., and Arnold Weber. "Wages and the Pay Board." *American Economic Review* 64 (May 1974).

Nash, Abraham. "Labor Management Conflict in a Voluntary Hospital." Ph.D. dissertation, New York University, 1972.

National Commission for Manpower Policy. *Employment Impacts of Health Policy Developments.* Special Report No. 11. Washington: October 1976.

National Labor Relations Board. *Election Report.* "Cases Closed December 1977." Washington: NLRB, April 14, 1978.

————. *Forty Second Annual Report.* Washington: U.S. Government Printing Office, 1977.

Nesbitt, Murray B. *Labor Relations in the Federal Government Service.* Washington: Bureau of National Affairs, 1976.

Osterhaus, Leo B. "Labor Unions in the Hospital and Their Effect on Management." Ph.D. dissertation, University of Texas at Austin, 1966.

Pointer, Dennis. *Unionization, Collective Bargaining, and the Nonprofit Hospital.* Monograph Series No. 13. Iowa City: Center for Labor and Management, University of Iowa, 1969.

Pointer, Dennis D., and Norman Metzger. *The National Labor Relations Act: A Guide Book for Health Care Facility Administrators.* New York: Spectrum Publications, 1975.

Raskin, A. H. "Union with a Soul." *New York Times Sunday Magazine,* March 22, 1970.

Roach, David L. "Hospitals Stand Firm, Ensure Care in Lengthy Areawide Nurses Strike." *Hospitals, JAHA* 51 (August 1977).

Rosmann, Joseph. "Hospital Revenue Controls—Their Labor Relations and Labor Force Utilization Implications for the Hospital Industry." Paper presented at the 30th National Conference on Labor, New York University Institute of Labor Relations, May 17, 1977.

———. "One Year Under Taft-Hartley." *Hospitals, JAHA* 49 (December 16, 1975).

Schramm, Carl J. "The Role of Hospital Cost-Regulating Agencies in Collective Bargaining." *Labor Law Journal* 28 (August 1977).

Seidman, Joel. "Nurses and Collective Bargaining." *Industrial and Labor Relations Review* 33 (April 1970).

"Teachers Union Seeks to Organize Workers in Health Professions." *New York Times,* November 30, 1978.

U.S. Department of Labor, Bureau of Labor Statistics. "The Consumer Price Index —November 1978." *News,* December 22, 1978.

———. *Employment and Earnings.* Various issues.

Weber, Arnold R., ed. *The Structure of Collective Bargaining.* New York: Free Press of Glencoe, 1961.

Wilson, Victoria. "An Analysis of Femininity in Nursing." *American Behavioral Scientist* 15 (November-December 1971).

Wolfe, Samuel. "A Policy Overview of the Municipal Hospitals in Relation to the City's Other Hospitals." Unpublished report, January 1976.

"Working in Hospitals: Then and Now." *1199 News,* Special Edition (December 1976).

Yager, Paul. "The Mediator's Dilemma." Paper presented at the 30th National Conference on Labor, New York University Institute of Labor Relations, May 17, 1977.

CHAPTER 9

The U.S. Postal Service*

J. JOSEPH LOEWENBERG
Temple University

Collective bargaining in the United States Postal Service represents a compendium of philosophies about bargaining in the public sector. Within a decade the Postal Service transversed the route of no bargaining for its employees to limited bargaining to bargaining not unlike that found in the private sector of the economy. The changing character of collective bargaining in the Postal Service, compressed into a relatively short time span and applicable to a large organization, has not been easy. Nor is the future course of collective bargaining in the Postal Service assured. The development of collective bargaining in the Postal Service is significant in its own right and as a possible model for other federal government agencies.

From the founding days of the United States, postal service has been operated by government. Over the years Congress has granted a limited monopoly of postal matters to the Post Office.

For a long period the Post Office Department was a government agency operated and treated as other agencies. The chief of the department, the Postmaster General, was a member of the President's cabinet. Congress played a significant role in the affairs of the department by setting postal rates, determining employee compensation, and allocating annual appropriations. Other agencies affecting postal operations were the Bureau of the Budget, the Civil Service Commission, the General Accounting Office, the General Services Administration, the Interstate Commerce Commission, the Civil Aeronautics Board, and the Treasury.[1]

The Post Office Department was somewhat different from other federal government agencies, however. The number and dispersion of

---

* The author acknowledges the cooperation of the U.S. Postal Service and the postal unions in this study. Special thanks are due to the 36 officials who were interviewed. The findings and conclusions are the author's alone; so, too, are any errors of omission or commission.

[1] *Towards Postal Excellence; The Report of the President's Commission on Postal Organization*, Annex, Vol. 1, Report of the General Contractor (Washington: U.S. Government Printing Office, 1968) p. 122.

employees made the department visible throughout the country. Its importance to commerce, culture, family, and other institutions enhanced the significance of the service. Unlike many agencies, the Post Office Department collected fees from users of postal services.

Postal Reorganization

By the mid-1960s postal service in the United States was in trouble. Large increases in mail volume, mounting operating deficits, and exposés of tardy deliveries led the Postmaster General to proclaim that the postal system was in "a race with catastrophe" and to urge its reorganization as a public nonprofit corporation. The President appointed a Commission on Postal Organization that endorsed the views of the Postmaster General.[2]

The commission's recommendations encountered resistance. Postal employees and the postal unions, used to dealing with Congress, were wary about their relationships with a corporation. Only the National Association of Letter Carriers supported the basic concept of the reorganization.

The controversy surrounding postal reorganization contributed to the largest federal employee walkout to date.[3] The President had predicated any raise in postal employee wages on congressional approval of the reorganization bill. Antipathy to the concept of reorganization, frustration with delay in passage of wage increases, and complaints about deteriorating working conditions led to a nine-day wildcat strike. Over 200,000 postal employees participated at the height of the strike. Despite legal injunctions and token efforts to have the armed forces handle the mail, postal service in most parts of the country ground to a standstill.

To facilitate the end of the strike, the government and the postal unions negotiated on a number of topics. On April 2, 1970, the parties signed a memorandum of agreement on wage increases, a "jointly bargained and sponsored reorganization of the Post Office Department," and delay of disciplinary action against strikers until the department and the unions had formulated a joint policy. Part of the wage increase was contingent upon postal reorganization being enacted. The President signed the effective legislation on August 12, 1970.[4]

The Postal Reorganization Act established the United States Postal Service (USPS) as an independent agency of the federal government as of July 1, 1971. Overall direction was vested in an 11-member Board

---

[2] Ibid.

[3] Loewenberg, pp. 192–202. [The complete citations for all footnote references are listed at the end of the chapter.]

[4] Postal Reorganization Act, Public Law 81-375, 91st Congress, H.R. 17070.

of Governors; nine members appointed by the President selected the Postmaster General, and these ten selected the Deputy Postmaster General who completed the Board. An independent five-member Postal Rate Commission recommended postal rates and classifications to the Board of Governors.

The act envisioned that the Postal Service would be self-sustaining by 1985. Fiscal subsidies equivalent to 10 percent of 1971 appropriations would be provided through 1979 and would decrease by 1 percent annually through 1984. The act also authorized the USPS to borrow up to $10 billion.

Political patronage in appointments within the USPS was prohibited. The Postal Service was to "achieve and maintain compensation for its officers and employees comparable to the rates and types of compensation paid in the private sector of the economy of the United States." To determine employee compensation and working conditions, the Postal Service would bargain collectively with employee representatives and consult with supervisory organizations.

All in all, the Postal Reorganization Act marked a major turning point in the structure, philosophy, and operation of postal services in the United States. In labor relations, as in many other aspects, the Postal Service was to be an experiment if private-sector experiences could be adapted to the public sector. The new format of the Postal Service did not alter its basic function, however, or eliminate many of the ingredients that shaped the operations and character of the Post Office Department.

The Postal Service Today

The Postal Service is a large organization by almost any standard. In 1977 it employed more than 660,000 employees in over 40,000 postal facilities throughout the country. Almost 90 billion pieces of mail were moved in 1977 at a cost of nearly $14 billion. Although there are a few larger private corporations in the United States, the Postal Service is the largest public employer and the most widespread organization.

For many years the Postal Service enjoyed increases in mail volume and employment. Volume has fluctuated in recent years, but reached a record of over 92 billion pieces in fiscal 1977. Peak employment of 741,200 occurred in 1970, however.

The Postal Service is organized geographically and functionally. Reporting to the headquarters staff in Washington are five regional offices. The regions are further divided into approximately 50 districts and 300 management sectional centers, which are primarily mail-processing centers. Mail flows into these centers from 30,500 post offices.

The largest post offices, approximately 5,000 in number, employ about 85 percent of all postal employees. Other postal installations include bulk-mail centers, mail-equipment shops, mail-bag depositories, repair centers, and supply centers.

Functional responsibilities are evident in the headquarters organization: administration, employee and labor relations, operations, finance, and manpower and cost control. The operations group has long been considered dominant because it is responsible for the collection, processing, and distribution of the mails. The functional division is continued through region, district, and management sectional center offices along somewhat different designations: mail processing, customer service, finance, and employee and labor relations.

A chronic problem faced by the Postal Service has been turnover of top officials. Four postmasters general were appointed in the period 1960–71, and four have served from the reorganization until late 1978. Turnover has also occurred in other senior offices. Four persons, for instance, have filled the position of Senior Assistant Postmaster General for Employee and Labor Relations since 1971. A 1974 Senate report attributed the high turnover of top personnel to frequent reorganizations at headquarters.[5]

Postal reorganization reduced the impact of outside interference in postal management but did not eliminate it. In 1976, for instance, the General Accounting office urged that the Postal Service drop the Carrier Technician Program, which granted incumbents a higher grade than other letter carriers, because the program "was an expensive failure."

A notable change since the Postal Reorganization Act has been the availability and expenditure of capital funds for modernizing the Postal Service. In the five-year period 1967–71, approximately $1 billion was spent on buildings and equipment; in the following five-year period, more than $3 billion was invested.

Two major investments were for the addition of letter-sorting machines and the construction of bulk-mail centers. One operator on a letter-sorting machine can distribute the same volume of mail as ten clerks working manually.[6] The percentage of letter mail processed mechanically increased from 25 percent in 1971 to 63 percent in 1976. The 21 bulk-mail centers were designed to provide a nationally integrated mechanized system for processing parcel post, publications, and other bulk mailings. The $1 billion system, built between 1973 and

[5] Report of the Committee on Post Office and Civil Service, *Investigation of the Postal Service*, 93rd Cong., 2d Sess., March 7, 1974, Senate Report 93-727 (Washington: U.S. Government Printing Office), p. 14.
[6] Blomstedt, p. 148.

1976, utilizes containerization, conveyor movement, and computer-directed sorting machines.

Despite these and other forms of mechanization, the Postal Service is far from a fully automated or mechanized system. Even in bulk-mail centers, employees perform duties that involve human judgment and handling. The delivery of the mails to individual addressees continues to be a largely manual operation.

Increase in mechanization has not reduced the proportion of operating costs devoted to labor. On the contrary, total compensation as a percentage of all operating costs rose from 82.9 percent in 1970 to 86.1 percent in 1976, but fell to 85.7 percent in 1977.

Operating revenues also rose after 1971, but not always at the same rate as operating expenses. Annual operating deficits that averaged $1.5 billion in the four years prior to the Postal Service increased to an average of $2.2 billion in the first four years following the reorganization. Government appropriations reduced the annual deficit from $13 billion in 1973 to $700 million in 1977. The accumulated deficit of the Postal Service was $3.5 billion by the end of fiscal 1977.

Employees and Employment

Total employment in June 1977 was 661,391. The total was almost 80,000 (or 10.7 percent) less than the total in 1970 (Table 1). Except for 1974, employment had decreased steadily; the decreases in 1976 and 1977 were sharper than in other years.

Employees are classified in several ways in the Postal Service: by job title, grade level, and career status. These classifications have existed for many years, but have found new meaning since the advent of collective bargaining in the Postal Service.

The Postal Service has employees with innumerable skills and competencies. The overwhelming majority of persons are employed in field installations, however, and here job titles are more limited. Managerial functions are carried out by postmasters and supervisors. Processing of mail in postal installations is performed by clerks and mail handlers, the latter traditionally being assigned to bulk mail, letter sacks, and the like. Mail is delivered by city carriers, rural carriers, and special delivery messengers. Other functions are assigned to mail truck drivers, building and equipment maintenance personnel, and vehicle maintenance mechanics.

The change in employment for nonsupervisory workers in postal field installations was more severe than for other categories. In every year since 1970 such employment has been less than in the previous

TABLE 1

U.S. Postal Service Number of Paid Employees, 1970–1977

	FY 70	FY 71	FY 72	FY 73	FY 74	FY 75	FY 76	FY 77[a]
Postmasters	29,679	29,945	30,731	29,490	30,288	30,050	29,273	29,032
Supervisors	37,638	37,433	38,139	34,482	37,430	39,429	40,414	38,235
Clerks	314,528	303,350	286,347	284,846	284,002	282,208	263,836	261,884
Mail handlers	47,447	45,803	43,303	44,712	42,782	42,878	40,210	38,079
City delivery carriers	206,255	206,503	200,947	202,684	203,367	197,076	190,374	186,005
Drivers	6,902	6,690	6,466	6,281	6,368	6,352	6,387	6,174
Special delivery	5,871	5,744	5,148	4,376	4,198	3,991	3,581	3,163
Rural carriers	49,060	49,756	50,309	50,440	51,218	51,638	52,346	52,290
Maintenance	26,258	26,580	26,483	25,760	26,821	29,456	29,373	28,789
Vehicle maintenance facility	5,920	6,224	6,050	5,641	5,488	5,179	5,019	4,913
Total, postal field installations	729,558	718,028	693,923	688,712	691,962	688,257	665,813	648,564
Other, including headquarters, regional, and other field units, and inspection units	11,658	10,883	12,477	12,339	18,471	14,000	13,136	12,827
Total employees	741,216	728,911	706,400	701,051	710,433	702,257	678,949	661,391

Source: U.S. Postal Service.

[a] Fiscal Year 1977 data as of June 17, 1977.

year. The total decline was from 662,241 in 1970 to 581,297 in 1977, or 12.2 percent.

Analysis of employment changes by job title reveals that some classifications have been affected more than others. Special delivery messengers have experienced the greatest proportional reduction. In the occupations with larger numbers of employees, relatively more severe reductions occurred among clerks and mail handlers. Rural carriers and maintenance groups resisted the overall employment trends for a time, but recently these classifications have also proven vulnerable to lower employment.

The Postal Service maintains several pay systems. Most job classifications in field installations below that of supervisor are in one system covering grades 1 to 10, which is now subject to bargaining. Supervisors are paid according to the Postal Management Schedule, with steps through grade 16. A separate Professional, Technical, Administrative and Clerical pay system was instituted in 1976. The Postal Executive System applies to higher ranked members of the organization in grades 17 to 42.

The compression of Postal Service grades is noteworthy. Over 95 percent of bargaining-unit employees are at grades 4, 5, and 6 of the ten-level Postal Service schedule; over three-fourths are at level 5. Most letter carriers and clerks have been classified as grade level 5 and mail handlers as grade level 4. Since these three job classifications constitute the major occupations in postal operations, the monetary spread between these occupations is minimal, and opportunity for advancement is limited.

Postal workers are full-time, part-time, or casual employees. Part-time employees may be assigned to work regularly scheduled hours or flexible hours as needed. Casual employees are hired to supplement the regular workforce, full time and part time. Almost four-fifths of postal employees are full-time employees. The proportion has varied little since the Postal Service took over direction of operations. Casual employment has been reduced, however, in both absolute numbers and proportionally.

The changing composition of full-time, part-time, and casual employees affects total time worked in the Postal Service. Although total employment fell 8.4 percent in the period 1970–76, total man-years worked was reduced only 5.8 percent.

To reduce employment, the Postal Service in 1971 announced an early-retirement program featuring a six-months' salary bonus. The program encouraged 13,000 employees to retire before normal retirement, while another 17,000 left on regular or disability retirements during the last six months of 1972. Many of the retirees were experienced managers.[7] The retirement program, together with a hiring freeze imposed earlier, accomplished the goal of reducing employment. However, normal attrition became the policy for later reductions.

Approximately one-fifth of the Postal Service workforce is black, and another 4 percent are members of other minority races. The proportions have not changed significantly in the last decade. Racial minority employment reflects geographic concentration. These employees, in proportion to their share of the population, also are overrepresented as mail handlers and clerks in bulk-mail centers. About one-fifth of the workforce is female. Although women are employed in many classifications, the largest numbers are clerks and postmasters in small communities. In 1977, no women were national officers of the employee organizations that bargained collectively with the U.S. Postal Service.

Unions

Postal employees have been organized for many years. From the outset organizations were structured along "craft" lines, e.g., city carriers, clerks. Initially, the organizations were local social and benefit societies which sometimes sent a member to Washington to lobby in Congress.[8] Several national organizations were founded around 1890: National Association of Letter Carriers, National Association of Railroad Postal Clerks, and National Association of Postal Clerks. Even President Roosevelt's 1902 "gag order" to prohibit postal employees from lobbying proved a temporary restraint to the growth of employee organizations.

Congressional lobbying and administering benefit programs continued to be the primary focus of postal unions until President Kennedy issued Executive Order 10988 in 1962. By then, each occupational craft among the nonsupervisory workforce had been organized and was well established. Six of the seven craft organizations were affiliated with the AFL-CIO. The percentage of actual to potential membership varied, but was strikingly high among city letter carriers and maintenance employees. In addition to the seven craft unions were two industrial-type organizations, National Postal Union and National Alliance of Postal and Federal Employees, and three supervisory organizations.

The Postal Reorganization Act left to the National Labor Relations Board (NLRB) the determination of appropriate bargaining units, but it also provided that during the first-year transition period collective bargaining would be conducted by the labor unions which had held

[7] *Investigation of the Postal Service*, 1974, pp. 11–12.
[8] Spero, p. 57.

national exclusive recognition under Executive Order 10988. This pressure, together with the prospects of full-scale bargaining, encouraged a merger of four craft organizations (postal clerks, maintenance, motor vehicle employees, special delivery messengers) and the National Postal Union into a new quasi-industrial union, the American Postal Workers Union. Hence, four major organizations represented employees for collective bargaining, and three supervisory organizations maintained consultation rights (Table 2). A local lodge of the International Association of Machinists represented tool-and-die workers in Washington. A number of other organizations later achieved bargaining rights in local areas.

Periodically, pressures for and interest in additional mergers have arisen among the four postal employee organizations that currently hold exclusive bargaining rights for craft employees. The American Postal Workers Union and the National Letter Carriers Association in particular have considered merger. Interest in an all-communications union along European models was also explored with the Communications Workers of America. Political, economic, and philosophic differences have prevented further amalgamation.

The number of employees represented by labor organizations is dependent on total employment in the Postal Service; the number of members is dependent on total employment and the success of the organizations in gaining members among represented employees. As Postal Service employment has fallen throughout most of the period since postal reorganization, the number of employees in exclusive recognition units has declined. However, the proportion of employees represented to total employment in the Postal Service was an astonishing 88 percent.[9] Since reorganization, postal unions have convinced a larger proportion of represented employees to become union members, though a disparity remained in the percentage of eligible employees who were members between the Letter Carriers and the other three unions with bargaining rights.

A brief description of each labor organization will highlight some other differences.

AMERICAN POSTAL WORKERS UNION (APWU)

The largest of the postal unions is also the most complex. Even prior to the 1971 merger, organizing clerks was difficult because of dissimilarity in clerks' duties and because of traditional promotional paths from clerk to supervisor. Merger added numerical strength but created

---

[9] U.S. Civil Service Commission, *Federal Labor-Management Consultant*, No. 77-5, March 11, 1977, p. 4.

TABLE 2

Major Employee Organizations of Postal Service Employees, 1976

	Organization	Employees Represented	Number Represented	Reported Membership
A. With collective bargaining rights	American Postal Workers Union, AFL-CIO	Postal clerks, special delivery messengers, vehicle maintenance, mail equipment shops,[a] postal data centers, building maintenance in USPS headquarters, mailbag depositories,[a] repair and supply centers[a]	298,168	256,478
A.	National Association of Letter Carriers, AFL-CIO	City delivery carriers, vehicle service drivers	188,890	177,433 (active) 47,438 (other)
A.	National Rural Letter Carriers Association	Rural delivery carriers	52,013	44,782 (active) 11,434 (retired)
A.	National Post Office Mail Handlers Division of the Laborers' International Union, North America, AFL-CIO	Mail handlers, watchmen, messengers, mail equipment shop employees, mail-bag depositories,[a] repair and supply-center employees[a]	37,841	27,950
B. With consultation rights	National Association of Postal Supervisors		40,400	34,460
B.	National League of Postmasters; National Association of Postmasters of the United States		29,273	20,000 \ 25,000

Sources: Membership information supplied by employee organizations. All other information from the U.S. Civil Service Commission, Office of Labor-Management Relations, Union Recognition in the Federal Government as of November 1976.

[a] Denotes joint certification by American Postal Workers Union and Laborers' International Union for mail-bag depository, repair and supply-center, and mail equipment-shop employees.

new problems. The governing body of the union is a 49-member executive board representing executive positions of the five predecessor organizations. It has been characterized by the late president of the union as "unwieldly, overloaded, unnecessarily expensive and counterproductive." [10] All in all, there are 112 elected and appointed officials in the national office.

Craft separation in an industrial union was a legacy of the original unions. Yet the crafts have been uncertain of their role and, in some cases, believed the continuation of separate conventions to be an exercise in futility. Clerk domination of the organization, with approximately 85 percent of the membership, may have contributed to the feeling of lost craft identity.

Local autonomy has been a union tradition. Any postal installation with at least three employees can request a charter from the national office, and 6,500 locals have been created. Local autonomy is expressed not only in refusing to join state organizations, but also in collective bargaining behavior.

The annual budget of the union's national headquarters was $7.5 million in 1976. Slightly over $500,000 was allocated to legislative and public relations activities, and a similar amount for industrial relations. The union had also accumulated a $300,000 contingency fund, originally designed as a strike fund but now used to publicize adverse effects of mail cutbacks and position excessing.

The death in May 1977 of the president of the union since the 1971 merger removed a strong leader. His place was filled by the union's former Director of Industrial Relations.

NATIONAL ASSOCIATION OF LETTER CARRIERS (NALC)

The Letter Carriers is a proud, independent organization. Before collective bargaining, the union was widely acknowledged as probably the most powerful and effective employee group to lobby in Congress. Postmasters drawn from employee ranks were likely to have had letter carrier experience.

The union is composed of over 5,000 local branches organized into 15 regions. Many branches have few members, but local autonomy is prized. The titles of officers at headquarters have become meaningless in relation to their actual duties. More serious has been the suggestion by the former president: "There is a need for more officers in the field and less at Headquarters." [11]

---

[10] American Postal Workers Union, *The American Postal Worker* (January 1977), p. 6.

[11] National Association of Letter Carriers, *Postal Record* (August 1976), p. 46.

Although long affiliated with the AFL and later the AFL-CIO, the Letter Carriers alone among the three AFL-CIO postal unions did not join the Federation's Public Employee Department until December 1977. Unlike the American Postal Workers Union, the Letter Carriers has also not been represented on the AFL-CIO Executive Council. The Letter Carriers has been reluctant to merge with other unions.

The union's elitism and independence have not made it immune from jurisdictional disputes. A traditional rivalry has existed with the clerks, a rivalry that has been exacerbated by reclassifying tasks from the carriers to the clerks. In 1971, the impartial umpire appointed under the AFL-CIO constitution to enforce no-raiding provisions found that the Letter Carriers had attempted to organize and represent special delivery messengers.[12] The union has also had differences with the rural carriers.

The president of the Letter Carriers from 1968 to 1977 was close to the Nixon-Ford Administrations and was the principal union spokesman for postal reorganization before the postal strike of 1970. After four terms in office, he retired because of internal union opposition. His successor gained a plurality in a close election, but was defeated in 1978 by the president of the New York City branch, who was considered more militant. These political changes reflected continued divided feelings within the union.

MAIL HANDLERS

The Mail Handlers changed from a small autonomous public employee organization to part of a much larger union experienced in private-sector industrial relations when in 1968 it became the Mail Handlers, Watchmen, Messengers and Group Leaders Division of the Laborers' International Union of North America, AFL-CIO. The Mail Handlers constituted less than 10 percent of the Laborers' union, but the division became the cornerstone of the union's plan to organize in the public sector.

Mail handlers are concentrated in approximately 250 cities throughout the United States. When the merger with the Laborers took place, the existing 250 locals were reduced to 31. The division has an elected director and financial director. The remainder of the national headquarters staff and the five regional directors are appointed.

The principal spokesman of the Mail Handlers has been the head of the Laborers' Federal and Public Employees unit, who is appointed by the president of the Laborers. He has represented the Mail Handlers

[12] Bureau of National Affairs, *Government Employee Relations Report* #419, September 20, 1971, pp. A5–A6 (hereafter cited as GERR).

in national negotiations with the Postal Service and in congressional hearings. Philosophic and political differences separate him from the elected leadership of the Mail Handlers.

Mail handlers and clerks often work side by side. Task and skill differences have become blurred, complicating work assignment according to craft. The aggressiveness of the Mail Handlers has been directed at the clerk craft as well as at the Postal Service.

NATIONAL RURAL LETTER CARRIERS ASSOCIATION (NRLCA)

The rural carrier organization reflects the unusual character of its members and their jobs. The rural carrier's job is different in kind and in compensation from that of his urban counterpart. The carrier operates with little supervision, performs all duties from a private vehicle or other form of transportation, and attains considerable prestige in the community. Rural carriers cover large geographic areas and develop close ties with customers. Salary is based on distance traveled and mail volume; the carrier also receives an equipment-maintenance allowance.

The National Rural Letter Carriers Association is regarded as the most conservative and least militant of the four postal unions with exclusive recognition. It is the only one not affiliated with the AFL-CIO. Resolutions seeking the right to strike have been defeated in national convention. The organization has not shirked from jurisdictional disputes, however.

The isolation of rural letter carriers presents a problem for the union. Although 2,000 locals exist, the key unit is the state organization. The national organization consists of eight officers, four of whom are at the regional level and the other four at Washington headquarters. The weekly union magazine is a vital communications link between the union and the individual member, and the annual convention is as much a social as a business meeting.

NATIONAL ALLIANCE

From postal reorganization until 1978, the National Alliance of Postal and Federal Employees had no bargaining or consultative rights with the Postal Service, but it continued to be a gadfly to the Postal Service and the four unions with exclusive representation rights.

The Alliance started in 1913 as a response to racial discrimination practiced by the Railway Mail Association. A decade later the union expanded from a railway mail craft organization to an industrial postal union. Further enlargement of the union's jurisdiction occurred in 1965 to include the remainder of federal government employees and in 1972 to state and local government employees. The Alliance has 146 locals.

In 1972 it reported a membership of over 25,000. The organization's main support in the Postal Service continues to be from black workers in major cities.

The Alliance has attempted to challenge unions with national exclusive representation rights through National Labor Relations Board actions, court suits, and proposed federal laws. None of these attempts has succeeded to date. While the Alliance is unable to represent members in matters covered by collective bargaining, it, like other organizations, may be chosen as representative in civil rights appeals in Equal Employment Opportunity hearings.

SUPERVISORY ORGANIZATIONS

Three organizations represent supervisory employees in the Postal Service. The National League of Postmasters originally was formed to promote the interests of postmasters in smaller post offices, whereas the older National Association of Postmasters of the U.S. represented postmasters in larger municipalities. The distinction has become blurred over time. The membership of the organizations overlaps, but the interests and philosophy of the groups differ. For instance, the National League of Postmasters prefers that postal operations be returned to congressional direction and supervision; the National Association of Postmasters of the U.S., on the other hand, supports the concept of a postal corporation.

Of the three organizations, the National Association of Postal Supervisors (NAPS) has taken the strongest position in dealing with the Postal Service. The association represents all supervisors except those at headquarters and regional offices. Most postal supervisors have been promoted from the rank and file.

Whatever differences may divide them, postal management and union officials share a close identification with and loyalty to postal service. All of the unions are one-industry unions, and all union leaders have extensive experience as postal employees. Indeed, one of the sharpest barbs thrown by employees, union leaders, and postal managers during the early years of postal reorganization was that top postal officials were "outsiders" who did not understand postal service. Identification with the Postal Service is reinforced by the interchange of personnel between management and unions. Several former postal officials have been employed by the unions, and union officials have been appointed to Postal Service positions.

Collective Bargaining Prior to Postal Reorganization

Besides lobbying in Congress for improved wages and working

conditions, postal employee organizations sought national legislation to permit them to bargain collectively terms and conditions of employment. Congressional hearings on several such bills were held in the 1950s. Although never voted on, these bills served as impetus and background for the issuance of Executive Order 10988 in January 1962.[13]

Executive Order 10988 introduced collective bargaining throughout the federal government. The initial effort of the federal labor relations system was devoted to organizing bargaining units and to fostering union-management relationships. Scope of bargaining was restricted to issues within the purview of the executive branch that did not conflict with organizational missions; many issues considered basic to collective bargaining were placed beyond bargaining, e.g., wages, supplementary compensation benefits, policies governed by Civil Service regulations, and, at first, all agency rules.

The postal unions and the Post Office Department led the way among federal agencies in developing relationships and bargaining in the executive order system of labor relations. Representation elections were held in 1962 and 1964, resulting in exclusive recognition at the national level for seven craft unions. These organizations were able to bargain with the Post Office Department for national agreements. Formal recognition at the national level was achieved by four organizations: National Postal Union, National Alliance, National Association of Postal Supervisors, and National League of Postmasters. These organizations had consultation rights on national issues but could not participate in negotiations.

During the period in which Executive Order 10988 was in effect, the Post Office negotiated four national agreements, signed by all organizations with national exclusive recognition. Negotiations in this period were conducted with increasing intensity but without incident. The 1968 national negotiations appeared to mark a turning point. Management adopted a firmer stance than it had in the three previous rounds. Mediation was employed for the first time, with the Postmaster General accepting the confidential recommendations of the mediator to resolve two outstanding issues. The 1968 negotiations produced an entirely new agreement rather than additions to prior agreements. Included in the last national agreement were provisions on management and union rights, disciplinary policy, grievance and adverse-action procedures culminating with advisory arbitration, promotion, reassignments, safety and health, negotiations impasse procedures, subjects for

---

[13] *Towards Postal Excellence*, Annex, Vol. 1, "Personnel Administration and Labor Relations," p. 71.

consultation, procedures for higher level pay, scheduling of vacations, and procedures for local bargaining impasses. In addition, each of the national exclusive organizations bargained a supplemental agreement with the Post Office Department on topics relevant only to its own members, such as tools for vehicle-maintenance personnel.

Organizations could also gain recognition at regional and local levels. The former enabled organizations to participate in consultation and agreement administration. Exclusive recognition at the local level permitted organizations to bargain with local management for local agreements. Just prior to passage of the Postal Reorganization Act, the Post Office Department had 24,608 local units with exclusive bargaining agents and 7,834 units in which formal recognition had been extended.

Bargaining with local units presented problems. Many topics of interest to local employees were preempted by national-level bargaining. Other topics were beyond the scope of bargaining. Local postmasters also were concerned about bargaining away rights they believed to be within the discretion of management. At the initial deadline for local negotiations in 1968, only 40 percent of negotiating units had concluded bargaining. Prior to postal reorganization, there were 6,100 local agreements. Another 7,000 local parties merely agreed to follow the national agreement in dealing with local problems. The remaining 11,000 units had no written documents.[14] The difficulty in negotiating local agreements was exemplified by the fact that 4,541 provisions in local agreements were revised or deleted because of conflict with existing law, postal regulations, or the national agreement.[15]

The rapid organization of postal employees and bargaining at the national level meant that the Post Office and postal unions discovered the limits of the executive order system of labor-management relations more quickly than other agencies and employee organizations. Local postmasters believed that too much power had been given to the unions. They were particularly concerned about discipline because discharged employees were able to retain employment until the appeals hearing at the regional level. Negotiations over new letter carrier positions and the organization of supervisors also caused uneasiness.

For the unions, the executive order system proved even more frustrating. The recognition system authorized by Executive Order 10988 permitted different unions to represent the same employees at dif-

[14] *Towards Postal Excellence*, Annex, Vol. 1, Study 3, p. 117.

[15] Comptroller General of the United States, "Report to the Subcommittee on Departments of Treasury and Post Office and Executive Office Committee on Appropriations, House of Representatives, Review of Selected Aspects of Labor-Management Program," February 1967, p. 19.

ferent levels of the Post Office Department. The limited scope of bargaining, local management's refusal to bargain, and lack of binding arbitration of grievances curbed the unions' ability to meet management on an equal footing. In dealing with management, the unions sometimes preferred to circumvent the collective bargaining machinery and work out problems informally.

Despite the difficulties perceived by both labor and management with collective bargaining in the Post Office Department in the period 1962–70, the experience played an important role in the subsequent structure and conduct of labor relations. First, the bargaining units of the postal system were defined along occupational and geographic lines. Employee organizations had laid claim to their respective jurisdictions. The bargaining structure would continue during the transition period and beyond. Second, despite the restrictions of the executive order bargaining system, the parties had an opportunity to gain experience in bargaining with each other and in implementing an agreement. They learned valuable lessons in benefits and shortcomings of the existing system, which affected changes in the later system. Third, relationships started under the executive order system of labor relations would continue. The events of 1970 and thereafter were influenced by earlier experiences. The period under the executive order provided a transition from a system dominated by management, with the postal employee organizations seeking change through lobbying with Congress, to a system where the parties would be largely responsible for determining wages, hours, and working conditions.

Collective Bargaining Since Postal Reorganization

The Postal Reorganization Act made collective bargaining for employees subject to the provisions of the private-sector National Labor Relations Act, with two major exceptions: a ban on strikes and union-shop provisions. The scope of bargaining was thus greatly expanded to include wages, many benefits, and most working conditions. Certain statutory provisions and postal regulations continued in effect. For instance, civil service retirement and disability benefits, compensation for work injuries, and veterans' preference in appointments and employee reductions were retained and made nonbargainable issues.

The act established a timetable for bargaining. At least 90 days before expiration of an agreement, notification must be given if a party desires to terminate or modify the agreement. The Federal Mediation and Conciliation Service (FMCS) must be notified 45 days later. If an impasse exists after 90 days of bargaining, the parties may agree on binding resolution procedures. If they cannot agree, the FMCS establishes a three-member fact-finding panel. The panel consists of a selection by each party from a 15-person list submitted by the FMCS and the designation of a third person by the two already selected. The fact-finding panel has 45 days to issue its report, either with or without recommendations. The FMCS has an additional 45 days to provide mediation services. If the impasse continues after 180 days of bargaining, a tripartite arbitration board is set up along lines similar to the fact-finding-panel procedure. Fact-finders may not serve as arbitrators in the same dispute, however. The arbitration board issues a binding award within 45 days of its appointment.

Managers and supervisors were denied collective bargaining rights, but they could join supervisory organizations which were "entitled to participate directly in the planning and development of pay policies, fringe benefit programs, and other programs relating to supervisory and managerial employees."

Bargaining on a total agreement was deferred so that the effective date of the agreement and that of the postal corporation would correspond. The seven craft unions and postal management negotiated one wage issue in the interim—namely, time between steps of each grade level on the salary scale. Just before the negotiations deadline, agreement was reached to reduce the time between steps for maximum salary from 21 to 8 years.[16]

While the Postal Service was being organized and a new agreement bargained, agreements negotiated under the executive order system remained in effect. Certain provisions dealing with work schedules, overtime and holiday pay, and leave were placed in abeyance for six months following July 1971. Outstanding adverse-action and grievance appeals also continued to be processed well after the effective date of postal reorganization. The last refusal-to-bargain charge under the executive order system was decided at the end of 1973.[17]

NATIONAL LABOR RELATIONS BOARD

The Postal Reorganization Act assigned determination of appropriate bargaining units and unfair labor practices to the National Labor Relations Board. The initial challenge to the existing unit structure came from charges filed with the board by the National Alliance alleging Postal Service interference with employees selecting their own representatives.[18] These charges were dropped. Further efforts to carve out bargaining units led to an NLRB ruling in February 1974 that collective

[16] GERR #376, November 23, 1970, pp. A7–A10.
[17] GERR #535, December 31, 1973, pp. A18–A19.
[18] GERR #460, July 10, 1972, pp. A14–A15.

bargaining could not be meaningful in "any less-than-nationwide unit which does not at least encompass all employees within a district or sectional center."[19] The Board's decision left intact the existing bargaining structure, comprised of occupational units on national lines.

The nationwide criterion for Postal Service units had previously been enunciated by the Board in ordering representation elections in a unit of mail-bag depositories and area supply centers and in a unit of mail-equipment shops.[20] The only exception was an existing bargaining relationship with tool-and-die shop employees of the mail-equipment shops who were excluded from the national unit.

In other units the national concept has not been observed. For instance, there are three units of guards: one for guards in Seattle, another for guards in San Francisco and Los Angeles, and a third for all other guards in the Postal Service. Likewise, a separate unit has been created for five nurses in Miami and Jacksonville, Florida. These are minor exceptions to the general rule, especially when the relative number of employees involved is considered.

No elections have been conducted by the National Labor Relations Board in collective bargaining units covering mail-processing employees. Elections have been held elsewhere, both to determine an initial bargaining representative as well as to challenge incumbent employee organizations. Between 1972 and early 1976, the Board conducted 14 representation elections in 10 geographic locations involving 3,620 eligible employees.[21]

A second function assigned to the National Labor Relations Board is to hear and judge the validity of unfair labor practice charges. A Postal Service official has estimated that perhaps up to 800 such charges are filed annually. Charges have included refusal to bargain, union's failure to represent, Postal Service's discriminating against union members or becoming involved in union activities. The overwhelming majority of charges are withdrawn or dismissed for lack of merit. In some cases, the Board has invoked the *Collyer* doctrine and referred the charges to the collective bargaining agreement grievance procedure for disposition. A few cases are settled by the parties. Even fewer are tried before an administrative law judge of the Board. The Postal Service has been found guilty in individual installations of refusing to make overtime-pay records available, interrogating applicants for employment about their union sentiments, and participating in union-

[19] National Labor Relations Board Decision, 208 NLRB No. 144, reprinted in GERR #542, February 18, 1974, pp. E1–E7.

[20] GERR #485, January 8, 1973, pp. A1–A2.

[21] Letter to author, July 16, 1976, from Data Analysis Section, Data Systems Branch, National Labor Relations Board.

sponsored social events. Despite the volume of unfair labor practice allegations, the overall impact of these cases on collective bargaining has been minor.

POSTAL SERVICE ORGANIZATION FOR LABOR RELATIONS

When the United States Postal Service came into being in July 1971, a new position was created: Senior Assistant Postmaster General for Employee and Labor Relations (SAPMGE&LR). The new position reflected the increased importance attached to the employee and labor relations function.

Initially, labor relations received major attention in the Postal Service because of the new collective bargaining relationships required by reorganization, the need to impress upon postal management the role of the function, and the first Postmaster General, who had the SAPMGE&LR report directly to him.

The first SAPMGE&LR came from private industry and was determined to make the Postal Service like the private corporation with which he was familiar. He insisted on a labor relations staff hired from outside the Postal Service and with proven labor relations experience. This mandate was issued at a time when the Postal Service had adopted a policy of promotion from within and was in the midst of a hiring freeze. He had the reputation of being a remarkable negotiator, but lacking understanding of structural requirements and organizational dynamics.

The second SAPMGE&LR was the opposite of his predecessor in many ways. He preferred accommodation to high-handed resistance and consensus to autocratic decision-making. This approach was used within the Postal Service as well as with unions. The change did not endear the labor relations staff to line management, who felt too much was being yielded to unions.

The third head of employee and labor relations was the first person from the ranks of the Postal Service to be put in charge of the function. With 40 years of postal experience and with a wide network of professional associations, he immediately contributed credibility that had been lacking within the organization.

Changes in the SAPMGE&LR, the geographic and functional organization of the USPS, and the introduction of the labor relations function affected development of the labor relations organization. Over time, the headquarters Labor Relations Department evolved into three divisions. The Office of Programs and Policy is the liaison group of labor relations to the rest of the headquarters organization and the buffer between the unions and Postal Service operating personnel. The Office of Contract Analysis is the central force in preparing for and supporting contract negotiations. Part of its mission is to ferret out problem areas and to order economic cost analyses. The Office of Grievance and Arbitration is responsible for national meetings on grievances and arranging for arbitrations of unresolved grievances.

The labor relations staff of headquarters in 1977 numbered approximately 40, down from an all-time high of 64 persons. The reduction was sharper than the overall decline of Postal Service employment and, in part, reflected changing priorities and perceptions of the role of labor relations in the Postal Service.

Other groups at headquarters participate in labor relations. The General Counsel's staff contains an Office of Labor Law which is heavily involved in arbitration hearings as well as contract negotiations and legal interpretations of labor matters. Additional labor law staff is assigned to each of the regional offices. The Operations Policies Office coordinates labor relations activities within Operations and acts as a liaison to Employee and Labor Relations. Major sections in Operations have identified their own liaison personnel.

Organizing and staffing a field organization designed to carry out uniform labor relations policies in the face of varying conditions and sometimes hostile management have been challenging. In some regions, the labor relations field staff was initially organized on a centralized basis under control of the regional office to counteract the independence of Operations line management and to ensure consistency in labor relations decisions. Other regions adopted different strategies, either assigning labor relations specialists to districts while retaining control for policy and evaluation purposes or permitting such personnel to report directly to district managers.

In fall 1973 a major reorganization of the employee and labor relations function took place in the field as well as at headquarters. Headquarters labor relations no longer directed and controlled the regional field staff. Each region was required to have a standard organization. Reporting to the regional labor relations manager were a contract administration director and a grievance and arbitration director. In some regions, identical work is performed by the incumbents of these two offices. About 75 percent of regional labor relations staff time is now spent on grievance and arbitration cases.

In 1975 the standardized organization was extended to district representatives. A single district director for employee and labor relations assumed all employee relations functions and reported to the district manager, with functional relationships to the regional employee and labor relations staff. As a result of this reorganization, line management gained direct control over all functions within a geographic area, rather than having functional specialists reporting to their counterparts at higher levels of the organization. The increased responsibilities assigned to district directors have made them less available for arbitration and grievance hearings beyond the second step.

The present field structure for employee and labor relations is not without problems. The specialist at the district or regional level may find himself at odds with his line supervisor, especially if his opinions are based on the advice of functional counterparts at higher organizational levels. Postmasters may attempt to avoid the advice and guidance of district employee and labor relations directors and try to gain favorable support for their decisions or requests from district or regional postmasters. These problems continue to be exacerbated by the fact that district employee and labor relations directors have generally not come from the postal ranks as have other district operations officials.

THE NEGOTIATIONS PROCESS

Negotiations in the Postal Service for the field service have been conducted at three levels: (1) at the national level for all mail processing employees, the so-called "main table"; (2) at the national level for each group of craft employees; and (3) at the local level for each installation. The results of the craft negotiations are appended to the national agreement. Local agreements are supplemental to the terms of the national agreement, but are in effect concurrently. To date, there have been four rounds of negotiations: 1971, 1973, 1975, and 1978. The negotiations structure reflects past practice, a desire to maintain a unified system of employee relations throughout the Postal Service, and accommodation to emerging problems.

Individual negotiations for each of the bargaining units outside the field service, e.g., mail equipment-shop employees, result essentially in supplementary agreements that follow field-service bargaining in timing and content. Special provisions are considered, such as those negotiated in field-service craft sessions.

From the outset of national negotiations with the Postal Service until 1978, the unions organized a unified bargaining committee. The committee was initially named Council of American Postal Employees (CAPE).[22] Because consensus on one union leader to be spokesman for all four unions was politically impossible, an outside negotiator was hired to represent the unions on issues that cut across craft lines, while each union handled issues of concern only to itself. The committee continued to function in the two succeeding rounds of negotiations,

[22] GERR #386, September 28, 1970, p. A8.

although its name was then changed to Postal Coordinated Bargaining Committee. The membership of the coordinated union committee was one leader, usually the president, from each of the constituent organizations and the hired negotiator. The same chief negotiator represented the unions in the first three rounds. He played the role of coordinator, adviser, and mediator in case of union differences. Although the committee worked on the premise that decisions had to be made unanimously, the organizations with larger memberships tended to have more influence in determining the outcome. Problems arose in the committee during the 1974 negotiations over substance and strategy as well as the costs of the chief negotiator's services. Some union leaders also were concerned that the committee served little function between bargaining rounds. Coordinated bargaining on major positions appeared to have been established and accepted by the four unions with exclusive representation rights, though it did not always mask real differences in the positions of the four constituents.

The 1978 negotiations revealed a schism in the coordinated position of the four unions which affected the bargaining structure and process in that round of bargaining. Initially, the four unions agreed to continue a united front in negotiations. The coordinating committee was renamed the Postal Labor Negotiating Committee, and the unions announced that the spokesmanship would rotate among committee members. In November 1977 the Rural Letter Carriers withdrew from the committee because of disagreements with the other three organizations on substantive issues, such as filling of vacancies and light-duty assignments. The Rural Letter Carriers continued to negotiate independently thereafter in the 1978 negotiations, while the remaining three organizations negotiated on a coordinated basis.

In the first three rounds of bargaining, the Postal Service team at the main table was led by the SAPMGE&LR; the chief spokesman in 1978 was the Deputy Postmaster General who had just been promoted from SAPMGE&LR. In the 1971 and 1973 negotiations the remainder of the Postal Service team consisted of persons experienced in collective bargaining and labor law, but with little background in Postal Service operations. A representative of the Operations group became a part of the management team at the main table in the 1975 negotiations, thereby increasing the Postal Service negotiating team's credibility within management as well as with its union counterpart.

The 1971 negotiations represented the parties' first attempt to draft a comprehensive agreement. Agreements under the executive order system of labor relations provided limited utility as far as subject matter was concerned. The parties, moreover, were operating under a different impasse procedure. The participants at the table, especially on the Postal Service side, were new to the postal scene, and both sides were inexperienced with conditions under the Postal Reorganization Act. An additional pressure was the expiration of the transition period of postal reorganization on June 30, 1971; after that date unions not part of the existing bargaining structure could petition for representation elections if there were no agreement in effect.

The 1971 negotiations started slowly and quickly bogged down. The number of people involved in the negotiations, intrateam difficulties, the vastness of the task confronting the parties, and unwillingness to move from opening positions hampered progress. The unions filed an unfair labor practice accusing the Postal Service of refusal to bargain in good faith; the charge was later withdrawn. Intervention of a mediator helped little, and the impasse was referred to fact-finding. The fact-finding panel found "the parties had not been able to agree on even a single provision of the kind typically included in collective agreements in the private sector," and that on most items there had been "only the most superficial exchange" between the parties.[23] Hence, the report recommended procedures for bargaining rather than substantive settlement possibilities. The 45 days between issuance of the fact-finders' report and the deadline for bargaining resulted in intensified bargaining, brought pressure from the White House and the AFL-CIO, reintroduced a high-level mediator, and culminated in a 36-hour marathon session that resulted in an economic settlement and a skeletal agreement on July 20, 1971, three weeks after the Postal Service became effective, and only hours before impasse would have been referred to compulsory arbitration. The agreement provided for further negotiations on specified outstanding issues and referral of others to joint union-management study groups.

The following two rounds of negotiations for a national agreement went more smoothly. The same mediator continued to help the parties reach agreement on both contracts. The 1973 negotiations concluded before the expiration of the extant agreement. In 1975 the New York local of the American Postal Workers Union threatened to strike if certain provisions were not made part of the agreement. Agreement was not actually reached until shortly after the expiration of the 1973 agreement, but the parties stopped the clock to avoid a formal impasse. Union jurisdictional problems also reemerged. Nevertheless, the negotiations were concluded without major incident.

Negotiations in 1978 appeared to be following prior format; a tentative settlement was announced five hours after the expiration of the

---

[23] GERR #405, June 14, 1971, pp. A13–A15.

previous agreement. Although leadership in all four unions supported the settlement, disaffection was quickly evident in walkouts of postal workers in Jersey City and San Francisco. The protests became more prominent in the course of national conventions of the Postal Workers and Letter Carriers unions in August. The results of mail-ballot ratification votes in the Letter Carriers, Postal Workers, and Mail Handlers unions confirmed member rejection of the tentative agreement. Only the Rural Letter Carriers approved the negotiated agreement. Principal discontent centered on the wage settlement. The dilemma of handling rejected agreements was intensified by the pressure of potential strikes. The convention of the Postal Workers Union had mandated the general president to call a strike within five days of contract rejection if negotiations were not reopened with the Postal Service and within 15 days of reopened negotiations if no settlement resulted. A similar resolution had been passed in convention by the Letter Carriers. The Postal Service refused to reopen negotiations. An order restraining the unions from striking was obtained in federal court. The impasse procedure specified in the Postal Reorganization Act was too lengthy to be useful at this time. The Federal Mediation and Conciliation Service proposed a new impasse procedure, which was approved by the parties. An appointed neutral would attempt to mediate the two outstanding issues (wages and the no-layoff provision) for 15 days; if he was unsuccessful in his efforts, he would be empowered to issue a binding award. The 15-day negotiation period failed to resolve the deadlock, whereupon the mediator-arbitrator determined the outcome. The two major postal unions submitted the terms to their membership for ratification, even though the vote had no bearing on the arbitration award; the membership of each union approved the award. The threat of another postal workers' strike had passed for the time being.

In 1971 craft negotiations followed national negotiations. Since 1973, however, craft provisions have been negotiated at the same time as the articles that cover all employees under exclusive bargaining representation. Each craft negotiation has taken place separately and apart from the main table. Postal Service teams have been headed by a regional director for employee and labor relations, assisted by a headquarters representative who has labor relations responsibility for dealing with the union involved and an operations representative familiar with the work of the craft. Union teams have been led by a vice president or other ranking officer. The only variation in this structure occurred in 1978 when the Rural Letter Carriers negotiated all provisions separately with the Postal Service.

Negotiating the craft provisions simultaneously with the basic parts of the national agreement incurs potential problems. Unions have tried to obtain advantages in craft negotiations that were denied them at the main table. Both parties have had to be careful that issues negotiated at craft negotiations were not also part of the main table negotiations, lest different outcomes result. An issue raised in craft negotiations that affected more than one craft could raise havoc with the structure of negotiations and create jurisdictional problems. Impasses in craft negotiations, however, have not held up ratification of national agreements.

Local negotiations have been more troublesome for the Postal Service and for the unions. The Postal Service has found that unions could easily attempt to renegotiate national provisions at the local level and that the large number of installations made control over local negotiations difficult. Unions have learned that local negotiations provide an avenue for local unions to demonstrate autonomy and to vent hostility to the national organization.

The 1971 local negotiations that followed settlement of the national agreement resulted in a complete breakdown. The unions presented long lists of demands for local negotiations. Management felt that negotiations could be restricted to local implementation of items in the national agreement. Postmasters, faced with their first experience in collective bargaining, were reluctant to consent to anything and, in some cases, refused to meet with local union leaders.[24] Approximately 100,000 impasses were submitted to the impasse machinery; all of them were supposed to be resolved in 60 days. Just to organize the paperwork involved was a major task. The Eastern Region, for instance, was able to negotiate 19 of the 20,000 impasses it faced; the remainder were submitted to headquarters. The impasses served as the basis of bad-faith bargaining charges by postal unions and picketing by postal employees in a number of cities. The monumental impasse was resolved by adopting standard guidelines to resolve major issues which involved most of the impasses.

To prevent a repetition of the 1971 fiasco, the parties incorporated into the 1973 national agreement an article that restricted local bargaining to 22 areas, e.g., wash-up periods, formulation of local leave program, and establishment of regular five-day workweek. In addition to limiting the scope of bargaining, the new article provided an expedited timetable for bargaining and for resolving impasses directly by arbitration. Fewer than 600 impasses were forwarded in 1973. The same concepts concerning local bargaining were retained in the 1975 national

---

[24] *Investigation of the Postal Service*, pp. 45-46.

agreement, and only about 100 impasses resulted from local negotiations.

The defusing of local negotiations has not left everyone happy. Some employees believe that the national unions have conspired with management to diminish local autonomy; such feelings have contributed to efforts to restructure postal bargaining at regional or lower levels. For postal management, on the other hand, the restrictions on local bargaining did not eliminate items that had appeared in prior agreements and that were retained in local agreements on a "grandfather" basis. Efforts to eliminate such clauses by allowing only local determination on the 22 issues agreed to in national negotiations have proven fruitless.

Scope of Negotiations and Results

The scope of negotiations in the Postal Service is almost as broad as that found in private-sector negotiations. Even some aspect of the few items statutorily excluded from bargaining may be bargainable. For instance, postal employees may appeal certain disciplinary actions to the Civil Service Commission as well as to the negotiated grievance procedure; the parties have limited employees' right to switch the route of appeals to the second step of the grievance procedure.

Also affecting the scope of negotiations are the handbooks and manuals of the Postal Service. In the early days of postal reorganization, these manuals frustrated management. The unions were better acquainted with the manuals than were the new management personnel. Management also hoped to establish certain rights, only to have the unions take refuge in the past practice of existing postal regulations. Reference to the 350 manuals and handbooks continues to appear in the agreement, though few people are thoroughly familiar with their contents.

These restrictions have not prevented the parties from negotiating a wide range of issues. Of course, not all items proposed by either side have found their way into the collective bargaining agreements. Yet the 1971 national agreement is impressive for its sheer volume, and subsequent agreements have been even longer. The 1971 agreement contained 34 articles covering all employees under collective bargaining, one article for each of the four craft negotiations, and two appendixes. Only four major articles were taken almost verbatim from the 1968 agreement: reassignment, assignment of ill or injured regular employees, posting, and seniority. The 1975 agreement contained 187 printed pages: 56 pages devoted to 38 articles applying to all employees, 95 pages detailing seven articles for individual craft provisions, a 25-page appendix on reassignments, and ten pages of memorandums of understanding.

Among the most significant changes authorized by the Postal Reorganization Act was the setting of wages and other conditions of employment by collective bargaining. The act further stipulated that wages and benefits of postal employees should be comparable to those paid for similar work in the private sector. The same concept had been enunciated in the Postal Service and Federal Employees Salary Act of 1962. Instead of Congress determining compensation after studies by the Civil Service Commission and the Bureau of Labor Statistics, the decision was now to be made by the parties at the negotiating table.

To support its position on comparability, the Postal Service identified 42 jobs in private industry comparable to jobs in the Postal Service. No exact equivalent was found for the two jobs with the most employees in the Postal Service, letter carrier and window clerk. The Postal Service has therefore based much of its comparative data on surveys of nonsupervisory employees in union and nonunion companies in 15 major industries in manufacturing, transportation, finance, and service. The surveys have included information on straight-time pay, average rate for actual hours worked, and total compensation.

The results of collective bargaining on major compensation items are presented in Table 3. Not included are night-shift differentials, Sunday premiums, and similar extra payments. The results show increases of $3,850 in annual salaries in the first seven years under collective bargaining. That amount has been augmented by the cost-of-living provision incorporated into the first agreement. The original limit of $166 in cost-of-living payments was removed in the second agreement. The cost-of-living feature in the first three agreements added $2,994 into the base wage rate.

The arbitration award that ended the negotiations for a new three-year agreement in 1978 ensured postal workers a $500 increase in annual wages effective July 1978, a 3 percent increase in July 1979, and another $500 increase in July 1980. Cost-of-living allowances would continue to be computed every six months without any ceiling.

Another way of viewing the salary gains of postal workers under collective bargaining is to compare the typical postal employee at Level 5, Step 9, at different periods. At the time of the postal strike in 1970, such an employee received an annual salary of $8,292. Prior to the 1971 national agreement his salary was $8,952, but by the end of that agreement in mid-1973 it had reached $10,368. By mid-1975 the employee was earning at an annual rate of $12,778, and in May 1978, $15,796. Thus, in eight years the employee's salary increased 90 percent, exclud-

TABLE 3

Negotiated Salary and Benefit Increases, 1971–1977

	1971	1972	1973	1974	1975	1976	1977
Wage increases[a]	$750	$500	$700	$400	$650	$250	$600
Cost-of-living rate		$.01 for each .4 point increase in the BLS Consumer Price Index, computed semiannually					
Maximum		$166	no maximum				
Prior increases		—	$166 into base wages		$1310 into base wages		
Health premiums, Employer contribution	40%	40%	55%	65%	75%	75%	75%
Life insurance premiums, Employer contribution	33%	33%	33%	100%	100%	100%	100%
Retirement	As provided in Chapter 83 of Title 5, U.S. Code						
Injury compensation	As provided in subchapter I of Chapter 81 of Title 5, U.S. Code						

Source: Collective bargaining agreements between United States Postal Service and unions with exclusive representation, 1971 to 1978.

[a] Wage increases are those paid at some point during the fiscal year beginning July, not necessarily the additional amount paid by the Postal Service in any given year. Wage increases exclude extraordinary $300 bonus negotiated in the 1971 agreement that was not incorporated into base wages.

ing consideration of the compression in steps negotiated in 1970 and possible promotions.

In terms of total costs, the Postal Service has reported increases in employee compensation, including nonbargaining unit employees, from $7.4 billion in 1971 to $12.1 billion in 1976 (Table 4). The Commission on Postal Service noted: "The total increase in compensation between 1971 and 1976 was $4.694 billion, or 63 percent. During the same period, the consumer price index rose 40 percent. . . ." [25] It should be noted that the increase in salaries was 48 percent, while the increase in benefits was 241 percent; in other words, benefits as a portion of total compensation rose from 7.9 percent to 16.6 percent in this period.

The rapid increase in postal employee compensation has raised questions of equity and comparability. The real issue underlying these queries is to whom should the postal employee be compared. There is no doubt that postal employees have fared far better under collective bargaining to date than have federal Civil Service employees in the same period. A report by the Library of Congress estimated that the Postal Service had paid $5.4 billion more in wages than it would have if its employees had received increases comparable to those of federal workers paid under the General Schedule system.[26] Those employees had received 28.7 percent in raises since the Postal Service went into effect, whereas postal employees had received 54.6 percent. The inclusion of fringe benefits and more rapid step increases would widen the differential.

Another researcher has compared the salary of all federal employees with the salary of equivalent segments of the labor force employed in the private sector of the economy and concluded:

> On average, federal workers, both postal and nonpostal, of both sexes, receive wages which are superior to the wages of nonunionized private sector workers of similar socioeconomic characteristics and at least comparable to unionized private sector workers. The relative wage advantage is largest in every case for females.[27]

Further, "Male . . . nonpostal federal workers do slightly better (relative to their private sector counterparts) than do male postal workers. The opposite is true for females." It should be noted that 1973 was the last year of wage data included in the study and that significant changes in wages have occurred since then.

[25] *Report of the Commission on Postal Service*, Vol. 1 (April 1977), p. 14.
[26] Richard Kogan and James P. McGrath, "Cost Differential between U.S. Postal Workers' Salaries and General Schedule Workers' Salaries, 1971–1976," in *Congressional Record*, June 3, 1976, S.8444.
[27] Smith, pp. 175–76.

TABLE 4

Postal Service Employee Compensation Costs, Fiscal Years 1971–1976
($ Millions)

Compensation	1971	1972	1973	1974	1975	1976
Salaries	$6,808	$7,317	$7,601	$8,579	$ 9,329	$10,088
Benefits paid to employees						
Health insurance	80	112	123	173	241	337
Retirement contributions	410	446	473	517	545	617
Life insurance	28	29	30	32	111	147
Other[a]	47	47	42	50	52	50
Total	564	635	668	772	974	1,150
Contribution to CSC retirement fund deficit	0	63	111	176	207	386
Other service-wide costs						
Employees compensation fund	19	155	56	95	241	405
Unemployment compensation	0	0	0	26	25	57
Other[b]	4	62	3	2	3	3
Total	23	218	59	124	269	465
Total compensation	$7,395	$8,232	$8,439	$9,652	$10,753	$12,089

Source: Reprinted from Report of the Commission on Postal Service, Vol. 1 (Washington: U.S. Government Printing Office, April 1977), p. 14.

Note: Detail may not add to total due to rounding.

[a] Includes FICA, uniform allowance, and relocation monies.
[b] Includes awards, territorial cost-of-living, and severance pay.

For the unions, the compensation comparability provided by the Postal Reorganization Act refers to wages and benefits received by employees of United Parcel Service.[28] The comparison is invariably disadvantageous to postal employees. By July 1978 the differential in hourly wage rate has been computed at $1.25. In the area of benefits, postal employees have superior terms only with respect to vacation. The inference is that full comparability remains to be achieved.

One measure of progress in economic gains under collective bargaining is overall employee satisfaction with salary and benefits negotiated in each of the national agreements. Employees recognize that similar gains in wages and benefits would have been unlikely without collective bargaining.

While economic benefits have captured public attention, noneconomic provisions have also been of interest to the parties. The unions have been concerned with job security, improved working conditions, broadening areas subject to the grievance procedure, and enhancing union rights. Management has attempted to maximize its prerogatives. Both parties have succeeded in attaining some of their goals in negotiations.

Job security was an issue from the outset and has resulted in numerous provisions. A feature of the 1971 agreement was a no-layoff guarantee. The provision was considered necessary to convince employees that the Postal Service was not established to get rid of large numbers of employees. The concession may also have been regarded as pro forma since no employee had been laid off for lack of work in almost two centuries of postal experience. Only later did management realize that past experience was not an accurate gauge of future events. Changes in mail volume, more rapid introduction of technological innovations, and reorganization of mail processing meant that the traditional policy of attrition was an inefficient method of reducing employment. Postal Service proposals to eliminate the no-layoff provision encountered strong union resistance. The Postal Service insisted that the issue be included in the reopened 1978 negotiations. The arbitrator modified the existing terms. Employment security would continue for personnel hired before the date of the arbitration award, but similar protection would be extended to a subsequent hire only if the employee completed six years of continuous service.

Casual employees have been regarded as operationally necessary to handle peak mail volume and to replace regular staff in vacation periods and other times of absence. Unions have charged that some post-

[28] See, for instance, *The National Rural Letter Carrier*, January 15, 1977, pp. 34–35, and Statement by James J. LaPenta, Jr., Laborers' International Union of North America, to Commission on Postal Services, January 1977.

masters use casual employees in lieu of regular full-time or part-time employees. The 1975–78 agreement limited casual employees to no more than 5 percent of total bargaining-unit employment except in December; an individual casual employee could be hired for two 90-day periods, plus a 21-day Christmas period. Thus, the unions have been able to protect jobs for regular employees, while management has been able to make greater use of a cadre of casual employees.

Other negotiated items protecting jobs are prohibition of supervisors from performing bargaining unit work in post offices with 100 or more bargaining-unit employees, guarantee of 90 percent full-time employees in post offices with at least 200 man-years of work annually, and a variety of measures for employees affected by technological change, such as training and rate protection.

Working conditions in the collective bargaining agreement include scheduling requirements to minimize split shifts, pay guarantees if employees are called outside of regular hours, removal of disciplinary records after set times if no further action is taken, and restriction on national implementation of work and/or time standards until the unions have had an opportunity to grieve such standards.

A standard management-rights clause, amended from the prior agreement, was made part of the 1971 agreement. Postal Service management has obtained other language to advance its interests. Flexibility was enhanced by management's being able to assign employees to work in other classifications at the same wage level on any given day and to include work within different crafts to create full-time jobs. The 1973 agreement provided management with the right to subcontract and to make changes in handbooks, manuals, and regulations as long as such changes were reasonable and consistent with the agreement. Management also has been able to institute technological changes, although the impact of such change may be grieved.

Postal Service negotiators appear to have been quite successful in obtaining and retaining provisions they have deemed essential to operations efficiency. Other provisions adversely affecting management's control of operations have become part of the agreement, however. For instance, restrictions on supervisors' performing bargaining unit work were unknown in the Postal Service prior to their being negotiated. Such provisions may have been agreed to as a consequence of the private-sector backgrounds of management negotiators.

The attention devoted to provisions pertaining to all bargaining unit employees should not diminish the importance of craft items. An expansion of such items has occurred in each round of negotiations to

COLLECTIVE BARGAINING

date. Craft negotiations have led to agreement on special allowances, job assignments, and classifications.

The thorniest issue to arise from craft negotiations occurred after the 1975 agreement between the Postal Service and the Rural Letter Carriers. The parties agreed that, in case of a rural letter carrier vacancy where no regular rural carrier bid for the position, the vacancy would be filled by the substitute rural carrier with the highest seniority in the post office unless another substitute carrier was substantially better qualified. The provision marked a continuing change in the relative status of substitute rural letter carriers to vacant carrier positions. The 1971 craft negotiations allowed substitute carriers to be considered if no qualified career employees were available in the local office before the vacancy would be posted elsewhere. The 1973 agreement provided that substitute rural letter carriers would be considered after full-time career employees but before part-time regular employees. The Rural Letter Carriers felt the 1975 provision was merely the logical culmination of the direction in which craft negotiations on rural letter carrier vacancies had been moving. The three other unions with exclusive bargaining rights believed that the negotiated provision affected other crafts as well. A jurisdictional dispute was inevitable, and the matter was forwarded to arbitration. The arbitrator upheld the craft provision on grounds that the bidding priority for substitute rural carriers entitled them to work within the same bargaining unit.[29]

ADMINISTRATION OF AGREEMENTS

Negotiating agreements initially seemed less difficult than implementing negotiated terms. Communicating new terms and conditions of employment throughout an organization as large and dispersed as the Postal Service would be difficult enough. Obtaining uniform interpretations of and compliance with the results of negotiations was complicated by management and union organizations not used to collective bargaining and sometimes unwilling to accept the results.

Following each round of national negotiations, the parties have attempted to explain the provisions of the agreements to their constituents. Aside from written communications and directives, the Postal Service Employee and Labor Relations Group undertook training sessions for all supervisors. The 1971 sessions, entitled Operation Know-How, focused on the operation of the grievance procedure as well as the terms of the agreement. The emphasis in the 1973 sessions was on a single interpretation and application of national agreement provisions

---

[29] United States Postal Service and National Association of Letter Carriers, American Postal Workers Union and National Post Office Mail Handlers, Case No. C-NAT-15, September 28, 1976, Howard G. Gamser, arbitrator.

throughout the Postal Service; this focus resulted from the lack of uniformity that developed in the first agreement.[30] Further training sessions were held throughout the Postal Service after the 1975 agreement. The unions, meanwhile, also were instructing field staff and stewards.

Despite training and directives, variations in agreement interpretation have continued. Such variations occur among regions because of different responses by regional postmasters general, employee and labor relations staffs, and union representatives. Similar variations have been found among installations within a single region.

The 1975–78 national agreement provided for a network of 13 joint labor-management committees to carry out the agreement and to resolve differences. A few of these committees pertain to a single craft, e.g., Joint City Delivery Committee, Mail Handler Labor-Management Committee. Others are concerned with particular issues, e.g., technological or mechanization changes, human rights, safety, parking, subcontracting, jurisdiction. Still others are broad in scope, e.g., Joint Labor-Management Committee, Blue Ribbon Labor-Management Committee. Local agreements may supplement the structure provided in the national agreement with additional committees on topics assigned to local implementation.

Three of the committees may be unusual. The Blue Ribbon Labor-Management Committee is composed of the national presidents of the four unions, the Senior Assistant Postmaster General for Employee and Labor Relations, and other undesignated top Postal Service officials. The committee's quarterly meetings are "for the purpose of discussing, exploring, and considering policy matters of substantial national concern to the parties."

The Joint Labor-Management Technological or Mechanization Changes Committee allows management to notify the unions of technological changes affecting jobs and/or working conditions. In addition, the committee is given the mandate to "attempt to resolve any questions as to the impact of the proposed change upon affected employees" prior to submitting the questions to the formal grievance procedure.

The Committee on Jurisdiction appeared first in the 1975 agreement, largely at the insistence of the Mail Handlers, to identify and resolve jurisdictional disputes over work duties and assignments among the crafts. Unions involved in the dispute and Postal Service representatives were to consider the dispute in terms of stipulated criteria and arrive at a binding decision. If no such decision were forthcoming within 180

---

[30] Merna, "Labor-Management Relations in the U.S. Postal Service Today."

days after the dispute was first considered, the issue could be submitted to arbitration.

The list and functions of committees appear more impressive in the agreement than in fact. Some committees have yet to meet. In other cases, attendance has left something to be desired. While the formal meeting agenda have often been of little value, the meetings have sometimes provided opportunities for informal discussions, reactions to proposals, and presentation of complaints before they become formal grievances. Even the Committee on Jurisdiction, despite its focus and time limits, bogged down over procedural matters in handling the ongoing dispute between clerks and mail handlers as to proper assignment of jobs and job duties.

The grievance procedure has borne the brunt of the problems associated with introducing a new labor relations system. The 1973 and 1975 agreements define a grievance broadly as "a dispute, difference, disagreement or complaint between the parties related to wages, hours, and conditions of employment."

The grievance procedure in the 1975–78 agreement is outlined in Table 5. A striking feature is the disparate processing of disciplinary and other grievances. Disciplinary cases, including discharge, require a special hearing, usually at the district or regional level, at which an employer representative presides, takes evidence, and renders a decision. Appeals from such decisions are referred directly to arbitration. Employees with standing under the Veteran's Preference Act may simultaneously file appeals of discharge or suspensions of 30 days or longer to the Civil Service Commission and the grievance procedure; following the decision in Step 2B, however, they must decide whether to pursue the matter to grievance arbitration or to the conclusion of the Civil Service appeals route. The contractual grievance procedure also permits disputes of agreement interpretation to be initiated at Step 4 of the procedure. The 1978–81 agreement eliminated Step 2B and also Step 4 if the grievance did not involve interpretation of the collective bargaining agreement.

Two forums for arbitration appear in the 1975–78 national agreement. The basic system requires certification of cases for arbitration by the national president of the union within 60 days after referral, or within 15 days after referral for discharge cases. The cases are heard by one of a panel of six arbitrators selected by mutual agreement "from a geographically balanced list of arbitrators provided by the Federal Mediation and Conciliation Service." Beginning in 1973, the parties agreed to the establishment of an expedited arbitration system "for disciplinary cases which do not involve interpretation of the agree-

TABLE 5

Grievance Procedure as Provided in 1975–1978 Agreement

Employee or Union Representative	Employer Representative	Procedure and Time Limits
1. Employee (may be accompanied by union representative). Union may initiate grievance or class grievance.	Immediate supervisor	Grievance to be presented within 14 days of learning of cause. Supervisors to decide within 5 days. Union may appeal adverse decision within 10 days.
2A. Union representative	Installation head	Meeting within 7 days of receipt of appeal. Employer to decide within 10 days. Union to appeal adverse decision within 10 days.
2B. (for discipline cases only) Union area or regional representative	Employer representative at higher level than 2A	Hearing and employer decision within 7 days of receipt of appeal. Union may appeal to arbitration within 21 days.
3. (for nondisciplinary cases only) Union regional representative	Regional Director of Employee and Labor Relations	Meeting and employer decision within 15 days of appeal by union. Union may appeal decision within 15 days.
4. (for nondisciplinary cases only) Union national representative	Headquarters labor relations staff	Meeting within 15 days of appeal. Employer decision within 15 days of meeting. Union may appeal to arbitration within 45 days of employer's decision.
5. Arbitration		

ment and which are not of a technical or policy-making nature." Expedited arbitration is invoked by the national union and Postal Service headquarters. The arbitrator is selected by rotation and availability from a panel of arbitrators established on an area basis. The agreement provides that hearings are to be held within ten days of notification; hearings are to be informal and without transcripts or briefs; and arbitrators' awards are to be issued no later than 48 hours after the hearing.

In practice, the grievance system works somewhat differently than just described. The parties have made additional attempts to resolve grievances between Step 4 and arbitration. This so-called Step 4½, which usually involves top union leaders and headquarters staff personnel, may be initiated by either party. One retiring union president decided to dispose of hundreds of cases because they lacked substance, or because they would not be arbitrated for years and were standing in the way of more important cases.

Another variance has been the composition of arbitration groups and the functions assigned to them. Three groups of arbitrators have operated concurrently. One umpire was named during the 1973 agreement to decide disputes involving national contractual interpretation or general application. A second umpire was added in 1976, and a third arbitrator has been called on an ad hoc basis for major national disputes. Other disputes involving contract interpretation, discharges, or suspensions of 30 days or longer are heard by a member of a three- or four-person panel of arbitrators established by the national offices of the unions and Postal Service in each region. Expedited arbitration panels of three to ten arbitrators have been established in 31 areas; to date, those selected for the expedited panels have, for the most part, been experienced arbitrators.

The lines between the regular grievance procedure and the expedited procedure have not been firmly drawn. The parties have reviewed arbitration dockets and moved pending cases from one system to another. Experience has also taught the parties that cases tend to be expedited only at and after the hearing; the time for a grievance to be certified for arbitration and for scheduling a hearing is not much different between the regular and expedited systems.

Internal political problems on both sides have caused a high rate of grievance appeals. Unions reported that some grievance settlements became undone when labor relations staffs were informed that such settlement would make local management appear inept. Some local unions have operated on the philosophy that every member must have his day in court and, therefore, each grievance should be submitted to arbitration. Union officials have conceded privately that it is difficult for elected union officials to reject an appeal to a higher step of the grievance procedure. One official revealed that of 3,000 cases handled in the last three years at Steps 3 and 2B of the grievance procedure, 94 percent had been appealed to the next step. Local union autonomy has also contributed to the rate of appeals. The American Postal Workers Union in convention adopted a resolution that local unions could appeal grievances to arbitration without national union approval. If the grievance were won, the national union would pay the union's share of the arbitration expenses; if the grievance were lost, the local union would pay the bills. Local unions have taken advantage of the latitude. While only a miniscule portion of such cases have resulted in arbitration awards upholding the union position, favorable settlements prior to arbitration have been secured in other cases. Such results have encouraged more appeals to arbitration, with or without national approval.

A major difficulty of grievance administration has been the length of time a grievance may take before it is resolved. Bottlenecks in grievance processing may arise because of the filing of many grievances in one installation, oftentimes on the same issue. Such filing may demonstrate the militancy of local union officials, a tactic to harass local management, or the emergence of a problem area. The 1973 national agreement purposely permitted class grievances in an effort to negate the need for a mass of individual grievances, but multiple filings continue.

The major problem in grievance delays has been caused by the large number of grievances initiated and appealed to higher levels. The number has risen steadily since the negotiated grievance procedure was implemented in 1972. The average annual number of appeals to Step 4 was 4,630 under the 1971 collective bargaining agreement, 8,610 under the 1973 agreement, and 9,725 in the first two years of the 1975 agreement.[31] The proportion of Step 4 appeals filed by the Postal Workers Union to the total number increased from 51.3 percent under the 1971 agreement to 68.8 percent under the 1975 agreement; the union represented just over half of all employees under exclusive representation. In mid-1977, over 8,700 appeals at Step 4 and 2,600 appeals at Step 2B of the grievance procedure remained outstanding.

Arbitration has become another bottleneck in processing grievances. Approximately 25 percent of Step 4 decisions have been appealed to arbitration; a higher proportion of discipline cases denied at Step 2B have been forwarded to arbitration. In less than three years, 4,600

---

[31] U.S. Postal Service, Labor Relations Department, *Grievance Activity Reports*; and National Association of Letter Carriers, *Postal Record*, June 1977, p. 7.

cases were referred to expedited arbitration; 2,800 cases were settled by the parties or withdrawn, and 1,800 decisions were rendered by 165 arbitrators.[32] Approximately 2,500 grievances have been appealed to arbitration annually, with about 30 percent being referred to expedited arbitration procedures, and another 10 percent comprising discharge cases. Only 15 major arbitration cases are heard each year. As of mid-1976, 3,000 cases were pending on the arbitration dockets.

To meet the problems associated with the deluge of grievances and appeals, the parties have resorted to different strategies. Grievances accumulated during the first agreement were returned to the field for decisions that could not be cited or used as precedent. About once each year, Postal Service headquarters requisitions regional labor relations personnel to assist in a crash program to handle Step 4 cases with the unions; over a two-week period, 2,400 cases can be disposed of. Similar programs have been utilized in regional offices with large grievance caseloads.

Intensified efforts at prearbitration Step 4½ sessions have also proven helpful at reducing the backlog at times. The Postal Service and the two larger unions agreed on an experimental basis to submit to expedited arbitration certain cases involving contract interpretation and other matters normally reserved for regular arbitration. Of the first 300 cases slated for this experiment, 289 were resolved after the cases had been scheduled.[33] Another device to reduce excessive grievances and appeals in particular locations has been to schedule hearings on an around-the-clock basis. In 1977 the parties increased the number of arbitrators appointed to regional panels to speed up scheduling of disciplinary cases. A joint union-management study committee was established to review the entire grievance-arbitration procedure. Other fundamental steps have been directed at reducing the number of grievance appeals. One such move was an April 1977 memorandum of understanding by all signatories to the national agreement that appeals to Step 3 from one installation involving the same facts or issues would be consolidated; the union forwarding the appeals choose one grievance as representative for further consideration, with the remaining grievances held pending the outcome of the representative grievance. Another memorandum of understanding initially formulated in 1977 provided that counseling, a first step in the disciplinary procedure, would be removed if no further disciplinary action for the same violation occurred in six months; this memorandum of understanding

[32] Benjamin Bailar, Address to Institute of Collective Bargaining and Group Relations, March 30, 1977, New York City; reprinted in GERR #703, April 11, 1977.
[33] American Arbitration Association, *News and Views* 5 (September-October 1976).

helped to reduce the number of grievances for discipline. Counseling was removed as a disciplinary action altogether in the 1978–81 agreement. National unions have also renewed their efforts to inform members and local officers of contractual interpretations and previous grievance decisions to stem unwarranted grievances. All these efforts reflect the grievance administration problem. Some success toward overcoming the problem has been reported; whether the desired result is achieved over the long run remains to be seen.

GRIEVANCE ISSUES AND OUTCOMES

A large number of grievances have protested disciplinary measures ranging from counselings to discharges. Others have concerned problems with leave, overtime, step increases, and wash-up time. As excess personnel in postal installations increased, grievances on reassignments have mounted. When such cases have been appealed to arbitration, the Postal Service has more often than not been vindicated in its position. The Letter Carriers reported that it lost 87 percent of 3,022 discipline cases arbitrated between July 1975 and May 1977; the remaining 13 percent resulted in modification and reduction of penalties.[34] The Postal Service has estimated it has won approximately four-fifths of all cases submitted to arbitration. In large part, the imbalance reflects cases brought to arbitration by unions for political and philosophical reasons. The Postal Service record is not so impressive in some major arbitration cases, however.

The principal issues raised in arbitration in recent years have focused on work rules and work assignment. When management terminated 79 Boston mail handlers who had been working part time on fixed schedules to comply with the contractual provision that large post offices be manned 90 percent with full-time personnel, the arbitrator reinstated the grievants on the grounds that the change in work schedules altered the jobs and made them new positions and that the terminations were not proven necessary.[35] On the other hand, the Postal Service was upheld in its right to transfer and assign employees as long as work rescheduling was implemented within the judisdiction of bargaining unit personnel.[36]

Work performance has become a bone of contention, particularly when changes in existing methods are introduced on grounds of increasing productivity, saving energy, or saving money. Typical of such

---

[34] *Postal Record*, May 1977, p. 9.

[35] U.S. Postal Service and Mailhandlers Division of Laborers International Union of North America, December 28, 1972, Sylvester Garrett, arbitrator.

[36] United States Postal Service and American Postal Workers Union, Grievance No. AB-C-76, August 28, 1975, Sylvester Garrett, arbitrator.

disputes was the grievance of the Letter Carriers protesting a management order to cross lawns considered safe by the carrier if the customer does not object. The issue devolved to the amount of discretion available to letter carriers in carrying out their function. The arbitrator decided that carriers make the initial decision on lawn-crossing, but not for the purpose of extending time on the street.[37]

The Postal Service has devised a number of plans designed to improve productivity, each of which has been challenged by union grievances. The most celebrated case on standards to date has been the Letter Carrier Route Evaluation System (LCRES), a management system to revise carrier routes according to time-motion standards to equalize effort on all routes and to reduce the carrier workforce by at least 10 percent. The system was grieved on grounds of being unfair and a work speed-up. The arbitrator decided that the LCRES standards were unreasonable "to the extent that they could not be met by any significant number of presently qualified carriers, now in the work force, who put forth reasonable effort in the performance of their duties."[38] While management had the right to establish new time or work standards, the particular ones employed in LCRES could not be judged as fair, equitable, and reasonable.

Work-assignment controversies frequently have contained jurisdictional overtones. Such problems are not new, having been subjects of grievances and advisory arbitrations prior to postal reorganization.[39] The problems have become more aggravated over time. One avenue for resolution has been the grievance procedure. An early award upheld management's decision to create the position of markup clerk, thereby removing the function of readdressing mail from letter carriers.[40] Transferring 800 deliveries from letter carriers to create route openings for displaced rural carriers was found inconsistent with the contract provision permitting work reassignment only "to maximixe full-time employment opportunities and provide necessary flexibility."[41] Other disputes have involved clerks and mail handlers and the rural carriers and the other crafts.

[37] United States Postal Service and National Association of Letter Carriers, Grievance No. NC-C-178, December 23, 1976, Paul J. Fasser, Jr., arbitrator.

[38] United States Postal Service and National Association of Letter Carriers, Case No. NB-NAT-6462, August 6, 1976, Sylvester Garrett, arbitrator.

[39] See, for instance, Berger and Blomstedt.

[40] United States Postal Service and National Association of Letter Carriers and American Postal Workers Union, Case No. N-NAT-3061, October 19, 1973, Howard G. Gamser, arbitrator.

[41] United States Postal Service and National Association of Letter Carriers, Case No. RA-73-1587, August 30, 1974, Sylvester Garrett, arbitrator.

PRESSURE TACTICS

Negotiations difficulties, grievance problems, interunion rivalries, and tensions associated with emerging labor-management relationships have yielded only periodic overt militancy by employees since the 1970 postal strike. From time to time, off-duty pickets have appeared to protest working conditions in particular locations.[42] A wildcat strike occurred in the New York Bulk and Foreign Mail Center in Jersey City in 1974 when employees closed the facility for four days to protest changes in the starting times of work shifts. The walkout ended after a court-ordered restoration of the original starting times pending final disposition by arbitration. Following the tentative agreement in the 1978 negotiations, postal workers walked out from the Jersey City Bulk and Foreign Mail Center and in San Francisco. The Postal Service discharged 98 employees for striking.

The lack of major strike action, both during implementation of agreements as well as during negotiations, may be attributed to a number of factors. The leaders of the national unions have recognized the sanctity of the no-strike provision in the Postal Reorganization Act and in the collective bargaining agreement. The first three agreements were concluded before the expiration of the preceding agreement. Despite the accumulation of contingency funds by some unions, no union is in a financial position to support a national strike, even if it were to authorize one. Most workers seem to recognize that conditions have changed from pre-Postal Service days. Strike action might jeopardize the entire collective bargaining framework. Whatever else workers want, they believe they are better off with collective bargaining than with the alternative that would be available to them as regular federal employees. As indicated by convention actions of the two major unions in 1978, however, strike threats remain a realistic ingredient of postal labor relations. Union discipline may be unable to control member pressure in the future.

COURTS

Parties that do not have appeals procedures available in general or for specific issues may invoke legal proceedings to challenge decisions. The courts have been petitioned on a variety of subjects.

Questions beyond the authority of the immediate parties have included the legality of scheduled pay raises in light of a presidential

---

[42] See, for instance, GERR #565, July 29, 1974, p. A13; #608, June 2, 1975, p. A18; #619, August 18, 1975, p. A11; #652, April 12, 1976, p. A9; and #656, May 10, 1976, pp. A13–A14.

wage-price freeze,[43] the constitutionality of the strike prohibition,[44] and the constitutionality of the restrictions on partisan political activity by federal employees.[45] In the latter two cases, the Supreme Court upheld the bans.

In cases more closely connected to labor-management relations, courts have ordered arbitration to resolve a dispute over a change in shift hours,[46] and dismissed a suit attempting to block carrier-route adjustments before an arbitration decision.[47] On the other hand, courts have issued temporary restraining orders on the installation of new machinery,[48] and on the conduct of a route inspection pending arbitration of a grievance that could affect the route adjustment.[49]

The courts have also provided a forum for unions to press alleged violations of Fair Labor Standards Act provisions. A 1978 settlement of such a suit, for example, provided for a fund of up to $56 million to compensate over 80,000 postal employees who performed work without proper payment.

The National Association of Postal Supervisors (NAPS) filed three suits, each affecting many employees and with far-reaching consequences. The first in 1973 protested the Job Evaluation Program (JEP), which resulted in a revised pay schedule for postal supervisors.[50] Although supervisors were alarmed that many of their number were downgraded by JEP, NAPS attacked the program on the basis that it had not been consulted in the implementation of the study and the application of the results to salary schedules. The court upheld the right of the Postal Service to implement the new salary schedule based on JEP. When the case was appealed, the Postal Service and NAPS arrived at an out-of-court settlement on the meaning of consultation. The agreement provided for the parties to conduct regular meetings to enable the supervisory organization to consult in the development of postal programs affecting working conditions.

A 1975 NAPS suit, joined by the two postmaster groups, challenged the Postal Service's failure to grant cost-of-living adjustments to super-

---

[43] NALC, et al. v. USPS, et al., USDC D.C., Civil Action 1755-71, October 20, 1971.

[44] UFPC v. William M. Blount, et al., 404 U.S. 802 (#70-328), October 11, 1971.

[45] U.S. Civil Service Commission, et al. v. NALC, et al., U.S. Supreme Court #72-634, June 25, 1973.

[46] GERR #542, February 18, 1974, p. A2.

[47] NALC Branch 2622 v. USPS, et al., USDC MD NC, No. C-75-303-G, August 18, 1975.

[48] GERR #646, March 1, 1976, p. All.

[49] NALC v. USPS, et al., heard in the federal district court in Des Moines, Iowa; cited in National Association of Letter Carriers Annual Report (August 1976), p. 20.

[50] GERR #499, April 16, 1973, p. A9; and #549, April 8, 1974, p. A7.

visors as had been granted to workers in the bargaining units. The court found the Postal Service action to be contrary to the compensation comparability policy of the Postal Reorganization Act and ordered the parties to work out necessary amounts to arrive at appropriate differentials.[51]

The third NAPS suit, filed in 1976, protested the creation of a new wage schedule, the Postal Technical, Administrative and Clerical schedule, which removed employees from the PMS schedule and placed them in a lower wage schedule. NAPS was upset by the Postal Service decision because it effectively decreased the number of persons whom it represented. The court upheld NAPS's right to represent managerial employees and to return such employees to the PMS schedule. The question of which employees were managerial remained. The court reserved the right to make the determination if the parties were unable to reach agreement.[52]

Legal action is currently the supervisory organizations' ultimate weapon. The organizations, especially NAPS, are dissatisfied with their current role in determining employee conditions affecting their members. NAPS has introduced legislation into Congress to extend arbitration rights to postal supervisors.[53] Prospects for passage of such measures are not bright.

The Role of Congress

The advent of collective bargaining in the Postal Service removed Congress from center stage in the determination of working conditions, but it did not remove Congress altogether. The first Postmaster General of the postal corporation learned this lesson the hard way. In order to remove the political spectre from employee relations, he ordered union officials not to consult with members of Congress on issues involved in collective bargaining. The ensuing protests of a Postal Service gag on union officers led to rescission of the order. Postal unions and individual postal employees continue to seek changes in Congress.

All four unions with exclusive bargaining rights devote major resources to maintaining good relations with congressmen. The two larger unions have separate staffs whose primary duty is lobbying, and all unions employ other officials in the same capacity. The four employee unions and the three postal management organizations formed an Ad Hoc Postal Committee to work jointly on legislative activities. In addi-

---

[51] *NAPS, et al.* v. *USPS, et al.*, USDC D.C., Civil Actions #25-1909 and 75-2024, May 12, 1977.

[52] National Association of Postal Supervisors, *NAPS Letter*, 29:3 (February 4, 1977).

[53] For example, H.R. 7132 (95th Cong., 1st Sess.).

tion, the Letter Carriers, the Postal Workers, and the Mail Handlers conducted a Joint Legislative Conference for the first time in January 1978.

The focus of the unions' attention (and Postal Service management's as well) had been the members of the Senate and House Committees on Post Office and Civil Service. Both committees took a full interest in postal matters, going beyond consideration of annual bills and subsidies to inquire more broadly into postal operations. In 1973, for instance, the Senate committee held hearings and visited postal installations as the basis of an investigation of the Postal Service.[54] In 1977, the 95th Congress downgraded the Senate committee to a subcommittee of the Government Affairs Committee. The postal unions opposed the change which they felt would diminish their status in Congress. The change was not expected to lessen union lobbying efforts.

Lobbying activity has been directed to:

1. *Promoting the Welfare of the Postal Service.* Postal subsidies, postal service, and the structure of the Postal Service affect the environment for collective bargaining, but even more, the future and existence of the Postal Service itself. In these areas, the unions often find themselves working jointly with Postal Service liaison to Congress.

2. *Liberalizing Federal Employee Actions.* Postal employees continue to be covered by legislation pertaining to federal employees in many instances. Postal unions have been in the vanguard in trying to change current law limiting political activity and prohibiting strikes.

3. *Changing the Postal Service Collective Bargaining System.* In addition to the right to strike, postal unions have sought authority to negotiate union-shop agreements. The Alliance has lobbied to permit postal employees to select their own representative at grievance hearings.

4. *Ameliorating Postal Service Employees' Working Conditions.* In 1975, for instance, postal unions urged Congress to pass a safety-and-health measure that would require the Postal Service to comply with OSHA regulations.[55]

Even if postal reorganization had proceeded according to schedule in all respects, some congressional involvement in Postal Service labor relations would probably have been inevitable. The original financial goals have not been met, however, and Congress is once more being asked to make decisions it thought it had laid to rest.

---

[54] *Investigation of the Postal Service*, 1974.

[55] H.R. 2559 (94th Cong., 1st Sess.). See also, GERR #597, March 17, 1975, pp. A2–A6; #598, March 24, 1975, pp. A7–A9; #608, June 2, 1975, p. A17.

Current Status and Future Directions

The development of labor-management relations in the Postal Service has taken place against an unrealistic background. All parties immediately involved concentrated on making the concept of postal reorganization succeed. Since 1976, there has been public recognition that the Postal Service could not continue as envisioned by the Postal Reorganization Act. Many of the economic problems—business volume, competition, cost-price squeeze—have been common in other industries, but their resolution would be different because of the public function involved. Any revision in the existing model would have widespread implications for all aspects of postal services, including collective bargaining.

To place postal problems in perspective, to project future requirements, and to make recommendations, Congress established a Commission on Postal Service.[56] The commission's jurisdiction covered five areas of study: (1) identification of "public service aspects" of Postal Service, (2) determination of extent of appropriations from the federal treasury, (3) rate-making procedures, (4) levels of service, and (5) implications of new communications technologies. Although collective bargaining was excluded from specific study, each area could have significant impact on employees and labor relations. The commission reported to the President and Congress in April 1977.[57]

Attacks on postal monopoly of mail services are not new, but they intensified as postal rates and reports of public dissatisfaction have increased. Within the first three months of the 95th Congress, more than 15 bills sought repeal of the postal monopoly of first class letters. Proponents could point to the success of United Parcel Service in competing with the Postal Service in fourth-class parcel post. Between 1962 and 1975, United Parcel Service increased volume from 182 million parcels to 905 million parcels; the Postal Service volume, meanwhile, decreased from 792 million to 400 million parcels.[58] Not even the implementation of bulk mail centers stemmed the trend of losing parcel business for the Postal Service. Relaxation of the postal monopoly on first class mail would invite competition and undoubtedly lead to an additional loss of market share. The commission recommended changing the present legal monopoly only to "permit private carriage of time-value letter mail if the Postal Service is not prepared to offer generally comparable service."

---

[56] Public Law 94-421, The Postal Reorganization Act Amendments of 1976, 39 USC 101.

[57] *Report of the Commission on Postal Service*, 1977.

[58] *Report of the Commission on Postal Service*, Vol. 1, p. 101.

A serious threat to the volume of postal services comes from changing technology in communications. Such change is not new. Telephone and telecommunications have reduced the market share of postal services to less than 20 percent of all communications. More recent developments in electronic communications systems threaten maintenance of existing mail levels. About 70 percent of first class mail is composed of transactions, e.g., invoices, bills, statements, payments. Much of this mail can be processed through electronic funds transfer. Computers "talking" to other computers by telephone is another example of electronic communications transmissions. The rate of introduction and acceptance of these transmissions will affect the rate of change in mail volume; sooner or later the result is likely to be a decline in total mail volume. The commission found that "The Postal Service's planning for entry into electronic communications has low priority, little money, no organizational stature, and modest top management commitment." It recommended integrating Postal Service capabilities into existing electronic communications and determining whether the Postal Service should enter such communications.

The Postal Service has attempted to modernize operations by reorganizing and mechanizing the work flow. Optical readers, mechanized processing of flats and small parcels, and computerization of markup functions are scheduled for installation by the 1980s. Each change will require capital funds, affect mail processing flexibility, and have an impact on employees.

Ability to mechanize delivery service to individual customers has been very limited, and the number of customers will grow. One way to balance revenues in the face of rising expenditures and the absence of other means to increase productivity is to reduce service. That was the underlying rationale for the Postal Commission's controversial recommendation to reduce delivery service to five days a week. The cut-back, if implemented, would not only reduce a need for carriers, but would affect schedules, routes, and the rural letter carrier pay system.

Implicit in the question of capital investment, operating deficits, and level of service is that of federal subsidization of the Postal Service. No longer does anyone pretend that the Postal Service will become self-sufficient. Financial projections of labor and other costs indicate crushing operating deficits if currently authorized subsidies are the only federal appropriations available to the Postal Service. The commission favored a variable formula for future subsidies: the Postal Service would receive appropriations equal to 10 percent of total expenses incurred in the prior year.

Ever since passage of the Postal Reorganization Act, some congressmen have expressed interest in returning control of the Postal Service to Congress and the President. In 1975, for instance, the House of Representatives first passed and later rejected a measure that would have had Congress appropriate all expenses of the Postal Service, much as it does for other federal agencies.[59] A 1978 bill, H.R. 7700, was passed by the House of Representatives but not voted on by the Senate. This bill provided additional government subsidies to the Postal Service but imposed more control by Congress. Other provisions of the bill were abolition of the Postal Service Board of Governors, presidential appointment of the Postmaster General, reinstatement of the Department of Justice as legal counsel for the Postal Service, and congressional responsibility for defining the extent of the Postal Service's mail monopoly. If Congress were to become involved again in postal operations as it had been prior to 1970, bilateral negotiations between postal management and postal unions would be subject to congressional approval of decisions. Even if congressional involvement were on a more restricted scale, the result would inevitably be more attention to lobbying and less to direct dealings between the parties.

Congress might not want to regain control over postal affairs after it had expressed a desire not to be continuously involved. The political fate of strong postal supporters since 1970 and the downgrading of the Senate postal committee suggest lack of congressional willingness to be responsible for postal matters. The Commission on Postal Services recommended retention of the postal reorganization concept, with an independent Postal Rate Commission, a Board of Governors which appoints the Postmaster General, and regular appropriations not requiring annual congressional approval.

Whatever the congressional response to the commission's recommendations, no amount of hoped-for assistance could alter the basic problems confronting the Postal Service. The prospects of continued growth, financial stability, and quasi-private corporate climate could no longer be taken for granted. The environment for Postal Service labor relations was changing. The mood of uncertainty was bound to have an unsettling effect on management and unions.

Collective bargaining in the Postal Service has not evolved as many had expected it would. It has not followed strictly the private-sector model, despite many trappings and procedures of private-sector labor relations. Lobbying continues to be an important element, not only for major terms of the system and working conditions outside the scope of bargaining, but also for essentially minor appeals of management decisions. Lobbying has also provided a forum for altering the industrial

---

[59] GERR #634, December 1, 1975, p. A10.

environment. The 1978 negotiations revealed increasing administration involvement as wage guidelines for federal employees became a factor in determining compensation. Although the scope of bargaining has greatly exceeded previous federal-sector limits, the specific language negotiated has sometimes been at variance with similar provisions found in private-sector agreements. The intent of close cooperation evinced by committees and consultation in many areas and organizational levels has not been borne out in practice. Grievance administration has remained a major problem.

These shortcomings should not obviate the accomplishments. A new system of labor relations was introduced in a relatively short time into a large, far-flung industry. It has responded to some substantive and procedural problems. In large part because of collective bargaining, the Postal Service has absorbed without major incident many changes in staffing patterns and levels, organization, and mechanization. The unchallenged and sometimes arbitrary authority of local postmasters has been curbed to a considerable extent. Negotiations were concluded in three rounds of bargaining without resort to the final impasse procedure; the parties survived a negotiations crisis and an emergency impasse procedure in the fourth round. No recurrence of a major employee walkout has taken place since collective bargaining has been in effect. Despite resistance, the existence of unions and collective bargaining agreements has become recognized. All of this in seven years is no mean feat.

In many respects, the collective bargaining system of the Postal Service is at a crossroads. The issue is: Will the collective bargaining system begun under the Postal Reorganization Act be allowed to continue? If it is, it will need to adapt to new conditions as well as to be further integrated into operations. If collective bargaining in its present form is not allowed to continue, the experiment of a large federal workforce participating in a collective bargaining system akin to that of the private sector will have been short-lived.

List of References

Berger. Harriet, and Edward A. Blomstedt. "Clerk vs. Mail Handler: Jurisdictional Dispute in the Postal Service." *Labor Law Journal* 27 (October 1976), pp. 641–47.
Blomstedt, Edward A. "The Impact of Technology Upon Postal Labor Relations." M.B.A. thesis, Drexel University, May 1975.
Commission on Postal Service. *Report of the Commission on Postal Service.* Washington: U.S. Government Printing Office, April 1977.
Committee on Post Office and Civil Service, United States Senate. *Explanation of the Postal Reorganization Act and Selected Background Material.* Washington: U.S. Government Printing Office, 1975.
———. *Investigation of the Postal Service.* Washington: U.S. Government Printing Office, 1974.

Cullinan, Gerald. *The Post Office Department.* New York: Praeger Publishers, 1968.
Fox, Milden J., and Donald A. Heinz. "Postal Reorganization Act: Postal Service Collective Bargaining Enters a New Era." *Journal of Collective Negotiations in the Public Sector* 2 (Fall 1973), pp. 371–91.
Fuller, Wayne E. *The American Mail: Enlarger of the Common Life.* Chicago: University of Chicago Press, 1972.
Loewenberg, J. Joseph. "The Post Office Strike of 1970." In *Collective Bargaining in Government: Readings and Cases,* eds. Loewenberg and Moskow. Englewood Cliffs, N.J.: Prentice-Hall, Inc., 1972.
Merna, Gerald F. "Labor-Management Relations in the U.S. Postal Service Today." Graduate School paper, George Washington University, December 1973.
Nesbitt, Murray B. *Labor Relations in the Federal Government Service.* Washington: Bureau of National Affairs, Inc., 1976.
President's Commission on Postal Reorganization. *Toward Postal Excellence.* Washington: U.S. Government Printing Office, June 1968.
Smith, Sharon P. "Are Postal Workers Over- or Underpaid?" *Industrial Relations* 15 (May 1976), pp. 168–76.
Spero, Sterling. *The Labor Movement in a Government Industry.* New York: Macmillan Co., 1927.
Sweitzer, William P. "Bargaining Units in the U.S. Postal Service." Unpublished paper submitted by the author.
U.S. Postal Service. *Annual Report of the Postmaster General.* Washington: U.S. Postal Service, annual.
Wolk, Stuart R. "Postal Reform: Fact or Fiction?" *Labor Law Journal* 22 (June 1971), pp. 365–74.
————. "Postal Reform—A Year of Failure." *Labor Law Journal* 23 (October 1972), pp. 630–35.
Woolf, Donald A. "Labor Problems in the Post Office." *Industrial Relations* 9 (October 1969), pp. 27–35.

CHAPTER 10

Public Education

ROBERT E. DOHERTY
Cornell University

Introduction

The variety associated with collective bargaining in public education is staggering. In 1977 there were approximately 10,000 teacher-school board contracts, all of them different; 29 statutes providing some form of collective bargaining rights for teachers, each with unique features; and as many administrative agencies, each with separate rules and philosophies. In addition, hundreds of collective bargaining arrangements exist, having evolved through either executive orders or school boards' voluntary recognition of local teacher organizations.

Considerable variety can also be found in the state education laws under which the public schools must operate. The method of school finance can have important implications for bargaining, as can the degree to which state legislatures impose upon the schools certain mandates, thus preempting from the bargaining table issues that in other jurisdictions would be considered conditions of work. Some states endeavor to bring local district per pupil costs into equilibrium by providing more aid to the poor districts than to the rich; others do not.

On the other hand, certain similarities do exist among districts and the collective bargaining arrangements that have grown up within them. This chapter will stress those similarities of structure and practice, noting differences only when, in the author's judgment, doing so would lead to a better understanding of how the collective bargaining system works in public education and what it might portend.

The "Industry"

The schooling made available to youngsters during most of the nation's history was, to be sure, primitive and rudimentary. Massachusetts Colony required communities to establish schools as early as 1647, but the school year lasted only a few months and few students attended classes for more than a few years.[1] As late as 1890, only about

---

[1] Butts and Cremin, p. 353. [The complete citations for all footnote references are listed at the end of the chapter.]

487

78 percent of school-age children were attending any school, public or private,[2] and for children between the ages of 14 and 17, the percentage was only 5.56.[3] Most Americans evidently believed there was little need in an agrarian society for education beyond that of learning how to read and cipher.

SCHOOLING

For the better part of American history, teaching, although dominated by men, was a casual occupation. Salaries were low and tenure short. The scattered information that is available suggests that, during most of the nineteenth century, the average tenure of a public school teacher was two to three years.

In the colonial period annual wages were comparable to those received by sailors and fishermen; by the time of the Civil War teachers' wages equaled those of semiskilled labor.[4] It was not until the late nineteenth century that state legislatures began to require that public school teachers undergo at least a normal school education. Although many teachers in New England were college graduates who taught while awaiting appointment as pastors, most teachers in the middle and southern colonies seem to have been a sorry lot. On the eve of the American Revolution, Jonathan Boucher observed, "Not a ship arrives either with redemptioners or convicts in which schoolmasters are not as regularly advertised for sale as weavers, tailors, or any other trade, with little difference that I can hear of, excepting perhaps that the former do not usually fetch as good a price as the latter."[5] Farther west, a settler complained: "The man who was disabled to such an extent that he could not engage in manual labor, who was lame, too fat, too feeble, and had the phthisic or had fits or was too lazy to work—well, they usually made schoolmasters out of them."[6]

The status of teachers has improved considerably since that time. Public school teachers ranked twenty-ninth in an occupational prestige poll in 1963, tied with accountants and ahead of artists, novelists, and economists.[7] As teacher status has improved, so too has commitment to the occupation. This "aging" of American teachers is a rather recent phenomenon, however, and probably reflects both the decline in school enrollments, with correspondingly fewer job opportunities for younger

[2] Census, *Historical Statistics,* p. 369.
[3] DComm., *Statistical Abstract,* p. 108.
[4] Butts and Cremin, pp. 32, 285.
[5] Quoted in Beale, p. 11.
[6] Buley, Vol. 2, p. 370.
[7] Hodge, Siegal, and Rossi, pp. 290–92.

teachers, and the fact that older teachers stay with the profession longer.

Certainly one of the most significant developments of the 1970s has been the gradual decline in student enrollment. The peak year in U.S. public education was 1969, when 45,619,000 school-age children attended the public schools. By 1976, that number had dropped to 44,-393,000. (The ratio of elementary and secondary public to nonpublic school enrollment in 1977 was approximately 9 to 1, a ratio that has remained fairly constant since the early 1960s.[8])

Although state legislatures and state education departments assumed larger roles in the governance of public schools during the early twentieth century, local governance structures remain much the same as they were in the colonial era. The approximately 16,000 lay boards of education (down from over 125,000 in 1930) have, with the exception of certain state-mandated policies, control over the conduct of the public schools. Most board members are elected by popular vote. In large cities, however, many tend to be mayoral appointments. In most states school boards are fiscally independent, having a tax base and taxing authority separate from that of county and municipal governments. In a large number of these states annual school budgets are submitted to the voters for approval, a matter of no small consequence for collective bargaining, particularly if a sufficient increase in the wage bill is reflected in an increase in the tax rate. In some areas (most of the New England states, for example, and several large cities), school districts are dependent upon town and city governments for financial support. That is to say, the town or city is the sole tax collector of both school and general revenues. This lack of autonomy has important implications for collective bargaining for two reasons. First, the local board in a dependent district can reach an agreement with the union only to *request* the funding for that agreement from municipal authorities. Unless there is close liaison between the city council or the mayor's office and board negotiators during negotiations, there is always a chance that the contract will not be funded.

Second, in dependent districts bargaining tends to assume a political coloration. Board members are usually elected (or selected) on a non-partisan basis; city officials tend to be highly partisan. Thus, to the degree teacher organizations support candidates for city office, there is always the temptation, at least, for the union to strike a deal with elected officials and to go outside normal collective bargaining channels in an endeavor to gain benefits that could not be won at the bargaining table. This is the so-called end-run, a lingering presence in virtually all

---

[8] DHEW, *Digest of Education Statistics*, pp. 33, 34, 36.

public-sector bargaining arrangements but seemingly more pronounced in dependent school districts.

As to the composition of local school boards, a study conducted by Ziegler, Jennings, and Peak demonstrates that board members, 90 percent of whom are male, are better educated, older, and more affluent than the general public.[9] Whether the social, economic, and political differences between board members and the population generally are greater than exist between most elected officials and their constituents is not known. Nor is it possible to say how much these characteristics matter in respect to the formulation of educational policy. There is no evidence of consistent differences in attitudes toward collective bargaining, although it has been the observation of many who have served as neutrals in teacher-board disputes that the less affluent board members appear less willing to concede on teacher salary proposals and other economic benefits than are those who are better off.

School Finance

During the early years of the republic, about the only contribution made by state governments to public elementary and secondary education was the mandate that local communities provide free public education. Later they imposed compulsory attendance for school-age children in either public or private schools and established minimum requirements for teachers. Beginning in the late nineteenth century, most states began to lend a significant amount of financial support to the public schools. As Figure 1 indicates, the percentage of state contributions to school support was 20 percent of the total by 1890, dropped to about 15 percent in the period from 1905 to 1930, and then climbed rapidly until it reached approximately 45 percent in 1950. Since that time, there has been no dramatic increase; indeed, a number of states' contributions have been in steady decline. Federal support—usually in the form of "impact" aid or aid to districts with a disproportionate percentage of children from low-income families—has never been significant, and even that amount fell in percentage terms between 1970 and 1976.

The graphic presentation in Figure 1, of course, represents only the average among the 50 states. In 1974 local contributions averaged more than 60 percent in 13 states and more than 50 percent in 26. In only six states was the local contribution 25 percent or less, excluding Hawaii, which for all practical purposes has a single statewide school system, supported almost entirely from state and federal funds. In 1974

---

[9] Ziegler, Jennings, and Peak, p. 28.

FIGURE 1

ESTIMATED PERCENTAGE OF TOTAL EXPENDITURES FOR PUBLIC
ELEMENTARY AND SECONDARY SCHOOLS IN THE UNITED STATES
BY SOURCE OF FUNDS, 1890–1976ᵃ

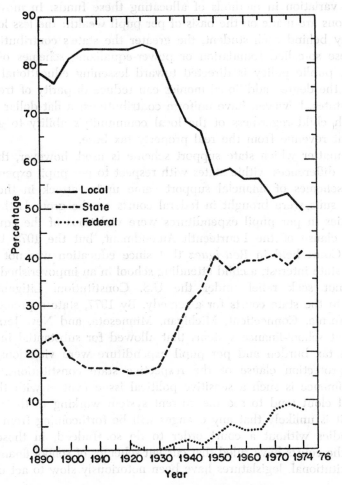

Sources: U.S. Bureau of the Census, *Historical Statistics of the United States,
Colonial Times to 1970,* Bicentennial Edition, Part 1 (Washington: U.S. Government Printing Office, 1975), p. 373; U.S. Bureau of the Census, *Statistical Abstract of the United States: 1976* (Washington: U.S. Government Printing Office,
1976), p. 129; U.S. Department of Health, Education, and Welfare, National Center for Educational Statistics, *Projections of Education Statistics,* 1970, 1974, and
1975 editions (Washington: U.S. Government Printing Office, 1970, 1974, 1975).

ᵃ 1920 is the first year for which federal statistics are available.

local contributions in the continental United States ranged from 19.9 percent in New Mexico to 85.7 percent in New Hampshire.[10]

The variation in the amount of state financial assistance is matched by the variation in methods of allocating these funds. In most states, allocations are made on the basis of per pupil wealth: the less local real property behind each student, the greater the state's contribution. Under these so-called foundation or power-equalizing schemes of school finance, public policy is directed toward lessening educational disparities to the degree additional monies can reduce disparity of treatment. Other states, however, have uniform contributions: a flat dollar amount for each child regardless of the local community's ability to generate sufficient revenue from the real property tax base.

No matter which state support scheme is used, however, there are marked differences within states with respect to per pupil expenditures. These schemes of financial support came under attack in the 1970s. Several suits were brought in federal courts on the grounds that huge disparities in per pupil expenditures were violations of the equal protection clause of the Fourteenth Amendment, but the 1973 U.S. Supreme Court held in *Rodriguez* that since education was not a compelling state interest, a child attending school in an impoverished district could not seek relief under the U.S. Constitution. Litigants then turned to the state courts for a remedy. By 1977, state supreme courts in California, Connecticut, Michigan, Minnesota, and New Jersey had held that school-finance systems that allowed for substantial inequities in both tax burden and per pupil expenditure were violations of the equal protection clause of the respective state constitutions.[11] Since school finance is such a sensitive political issue (voters with the most political clout tend to see the current system working to their advantage), it is unlikely that any changes will be forthcoming from legislative bodies without a court order to do so. Indeed, in those states where the courts have ruled that current schemes of school finance were unconstitutional, legislatures have been notoriously slow to act on these rulings.

EDUCATIONAL COST

Probably there would be considerably less concern about achieving a more equitable distribution of resources devoted to education had

---

[10] DHEW, *Statistics of State School Systems*, pp. 50–51.

[11] For an excellent summary of court opinion on the constitutionality of state school finance plans, see Chin, pp. 773–95.

not the costs themselves risen so dramatically. Per pupil costs in adjusted 1973–74 dollars rose from slightly less than $250 annually in 1930 to more than $1,200 in 1974, a 380 percent increase.[12]

With the exception of the years during the Depression and World War II, there has also been a steady increase in the percentage of the annual gross national product devoted to public secondary and elementary education, from slightly more than 1 percent in 1946 to over 4 percent in 1974.[13] The increasing burden placed on family households to support this increase has been, though uneven, equally dramatic. Revenues used to support public secondary and elementary education

FIGURE 2

PER PUPIL EXPENDITURE FOR PUBLIC ELEMENTARY AND
SECONDARY EDUCATION AS A PERCENTAGE OF PER CAPITA
PERSONAL CONSUMPTION (LEFT GRAPH) AND MEAN
SCHOLASTIC APTITUDE TEST (SAT) SCORES, 1966–1974
(RIGHT GRAPH)

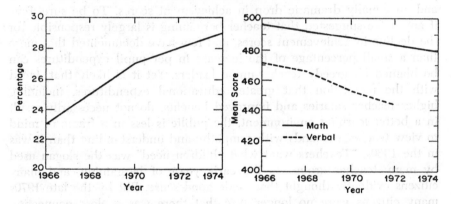

Sources: Expenditures—U.S. Department of Health, Education, and Welfare, National Center for Education Statistics, *Digest of Education Statistics: 1975 Edition* (Washington: U.S. Government Printing Office, 1976), p. 71; U.S. Bureau of the Census, *Historical Statistics of the United States, Colonial Times to 1970,* Bicentennial Edition, Part 1 (Washington: U.S. Government Printing Office, 1975), p. 225; U.S. Bureau of the Census, *Statistical Abstract of the United States: 1976* (Washington: U.S. Government Printing Office, 1976), p. 396. SAT scores—Annegret Harnischfeger and David E. Wiley, *Achievement Test Scores Decline: Do We Need to Worry?* (St. Louis, Mo.: CEMREL, Inc., 1976), p. 131.

[12] DHEW, *Digest of Education Statistics, 1975,* p. 71.

[13] U.S. Department of Commerce, Bureau of Economic Statistics, *Handbook of Basic Economic Statistics* 30:12 (Washington: U.S. Government Printing Office, 1976), pp. 224–25; U.S. Bureau of the Census, *Historical Statistics of the United States, Colonial Times to 1970,* Bicentennial Edition (Washington: U.S. Government Printing Office, 1975), p. 373; DHEW, *Statistics of State School Systems,* p. 13.

as a percentage of per capita personal consumption rose from 13 percent in 1946 to 29 percent in 1974.[14]

Between 1966 and 1974, the rapid increase in per pupil costs was accompanied by a rather substantial decline in student achievement. There is no indication, of course, that there is a cause-and-effect relationship between the two phenomena, but as Figure 2 showing increasing expenditures and declining scholastic aptitude tests demonstrates, there is at the aggregate level sufficient evidence to give pause to those who believe that all the schools need is a little more money in order to remedy educational deficiencies.

Contrary to popular belief, the decline in student achievement, at least in those areas that can be measured on standardized tests, cannot be attributed to changes in the social and economic status of the test-takers or to the increased difficulty of the tests themselves.[15] How then can one explain it? The question is important for us because, among other reasons, teacher collective bargaining is—at least in the 1970s—being carried on in the context of a dramatic increase in school costs and an equally dramatic drop in achievement scores. To be sure, few, if any, have suggested that teacher bargaining is largely responsible for the decline in achievement scores, and few have documented that more than a small percentage of the increase in per pupil expenditures can be blamed on greedy teacher-union leaders. Yet it is likely that, faced with the realization that greater educational expenditures, including higher teacher salaries and improved benefits, do not necessarily result in a better learning environment, the public is less in a frame of mind to view teacher demands with sympathy and understanding than it was in the 1960s. "Teachers want what children need" was the slogan used by many teacher groups in the early years of bargaining, and many citizens evidently thought that made good sense. But by the late 1970s many citizens were no longer sure that there was a close connection between what children needed and what teachers wanted. There seemed to have emerged an increasing public will to resist teacher demands for greater benefits, a will manifested in many quarters by overwhelming defeats of public school budgets at the polling places. In 1976 in New Jersey, for example, 60 percent of the annual school budgets were defeated by the voters.[16] At the same time, 54 percent of the more than 2,000 bond issues (authorization to borrow for capital

---

[14] DHEW, *Digest of Education Statistics, 1975*, p. 71; Census, *Historical Statistics of the United States*, p. 225; U.S. Bureau of the Census, *Statistical Abstract of the United States: 1976* (Washington: U.S. Government Printing Office, 1976), p. 396.

[15] Harnischfeger and Wiley, pp. 7–68. According to the authors, there has been a similar decline in other measurements of student achievement.

[16] *The New York Times*, June 13, 1977, p. 1.

expenditures) were defeated by voters in local school districts, although in 1965 almost 80 percent had been approved.[17]

It is at least conceivable that there would have been less public resistance to increases in budget size and the accompanying tax burden had there been some indication that there was a commensurate increase in educational benefits. Although it is not possible to provide a convincing explanation for the decline in achievement test scores beginning in the middle 1960s, several developments connected to the school environment have been noted as possible causal factors.[18] One is the decline in the percentage of students taking courses in more rigorous disciplines.

Another possible reason why student achievement has fallen off is that, in some districts at least, the actual number of hours students spend in class has declined. Dr. Charles E. Fowler, superintendent of the Fairfield, Connecticut, public schools, has reported that between 1955 and 1975 annual student hours spent in classroom instruction fell from 1,000 to 900.[19] Whether this has been a national trend and whether such a loss in instructional time has had a substantial effect on achievement scores are open questions. There is some evidence, however, that the amount of instructional time students receive is directly correlated with education achievement, particularly for so-called disadvantaged children.

If the decline in teacher-student contact hours has indeed been a partial cause of the drop in achievement scores, it would be worth knowing whether teacher absences have increased, since it is generally thought that substitute teachers are less effective than regular teachers. Collective bargaining contracts tend to provide for sick and personal leave and time off for professional and union business. But one would need to know whether there has been a significant decrease in the time teachers spend in school before a connection could be made between collective bargaining and an increase in teacher absenteeism and whether there is a causal relationship between absenteeism and student achievement. Clearly, if a teacher were absent, say, half the time, and his place were taken by a poorly trained substitute, that would make a difference. As matters stand, however, the evidence on absenteeism is scanty and no study has attempted to relate it to students' scores on standardized achievement tests. One does not know, for example, whether a collectively bargained sick-leave policy more generous than

[17] DHEW, *Bond Sales*, p. 2.

[18] Harnischfeger and Wiley, pp. 86–107 *passim*.

[19] Edward B. Fiske, "Study Finds School Children Now Getting Less Instruction," *The New York Times*, May 4, 1977, p. 50; Dr. Charles W. Fowler to the author, May 24, 1977, personal letter in the author's possession.

would otherwise have been obtained leads to abuse, or whether personal-leave days granted are automatically taken.

The dramatic rise in per pupil costs is only slightly less difficult to explain than the decline in test scores. One contributing factor is the increase in labor costs (both teachers and nonprofessional employees), which seem to have been slightly above the national average. This is due in part to salary and wage improvement but also, as Figure 3 illustrates, because the ratio of students to staff has dropped substantially in recent years. Still, the percentage of total school costs (operational *and* capital spending) attributed to teachers' salaries seems to have remained constant over the past several years—about 50 percent.[20] Probably increased fringe costs, particularly health insurance, for both teachers and nonteaching personnel have added substantially to total costs, because employers generally pay a percentage of the cost of individual and family coverage; as the cost of health care has risen dramatically since the middle 1960s, so too has the employer contribution.[21]

Two other developments that have contributed significantly to per pupil costs are the assumption by local school districts of new tasks and duties and the investment in new technology. A prime example of the first is the education of handicapped children, which may cost a district five times as much as the national average for the nonhandicapped. In the second area, schools have invested heavily in educational hardware such as television and learning machines, investments which have not modified the teacher-student ratio as many had expected. Nor, for that matter, have such investments seemed to have contributed toward improvements in achievement scores, as others had hoped.

Finally, there have been significant increases in the general cost of doing business. As new demands are made upon the schools, facilities must be established and new staff hired to meet them. There is more litigation and therefore higher legal fees, and higher insurance costs. In some large cities, schools invest heavily in "security" forces, an expenditure that may not even have existed as a budget item in the early 1960s. In the late 1970s the energy crisis caused unprecedented increases in transportation and heating costs.

---

[20] This is an estimate by W. Vance Grant, specialist in education statistics, U.S. Office of Education, June 21, 1977. There has been no systematic attempt to gather statistics on wage bill costs. Dr. Grant's estimate is based on a review of a number of local district studies.

[21] During the period 1960–75, the average cost per patient per day in community hospitals went from $32.23 to $151.20. These higher costs of health care caused the percentage of personal consumption spent on health insurance premiums to rise by 68 percent over the same period. Health Insurance Institute, pp. 49, 61.

FIGURE 3

PUPIL-TEACHER RATIOS IN ELEMENTARY AND
SECONDARY SCHOOLS,1950–1975

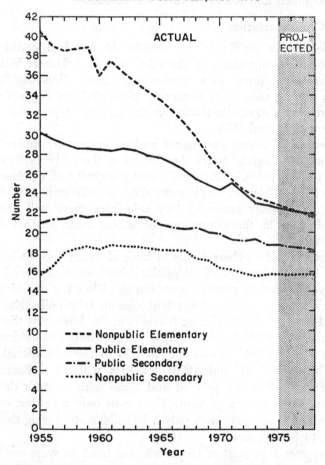

Source: U.S. Department of Health, Education, and Welfare, National Center for Education Statistics, *The Condition of Education: A Statistical Report on the Condition of Education in the United States together with a Description of the Activities of the National Center for Education Statistics* (Washington: U.S. Government Printing Office, 1976), p. 129.

The importance of these figures to the parties at the bargaining table is that the public tends not to discriminate between the cost of a school district's monthly fuel bill and the cost of a salary increase. It is rarely aware of an increase in fuel costs because they are buried deep in the school budget. It knows immediately of a teacher salary increase because it is often front-page news. Most citizens know that their tax bill has increased dramatically and consider the culprits to be avaricious union leaders and irresponsible or inept school officials who gave in too much and too often to union demands.

Teacher Characteristics

The decline in public school enrollment has had certain consequences for the composition of the educational workforce. With fewer students to teach, fewer new teachers are hired; thus the "average" teacher is getting older and is more experienced. As Figures 4 and 5 show, there was a dramatic change in the age and experience of teachers between 1970 and 1976.

The decline in school enrollment and an apparently lower turnover suggest that this "aging" trend that began in the early 1970s will continue for several years. The overwhelming majority of teachers on the job in the late 1970s were many years short of retirement, which means, of course, that under current salary schedules there will most likely be no reduction in the percentage of school costs attributed to the teacher wage bill.

The sex ratio of teachers seems to have changed very little between 1961 and 1976: 68 percent of all public school teachers were female in 1961; 15 years later 65 percent were female. Thus the argument sometimes made that one of the important reasons why collective bargaining gained hold so readily among teachers in the 1960s was the increase in the number of male teachers seems to be wanting in evidence.

Figure 6 shows two substantial changes in the educational level of teachers between 1961 and 1976: teachers without a baccalaureate declined from 12.3 to 1.1 percent and those with master's degrees increased from 25.8 to 36.2 percent. There was only a modest decline in the percentage of teachers with only a baccalaureate during that period, from 61.7 to 58.4 percent.[22]

One assumes that most of the nondegree teachers were certified and hired in a period when the states did not require that teachers hold a bachelor's degree. Many in this group began to retire in the 1960s. Since states now tend to require a baccalaureate for entry-level positions, the percentage of teachers with degrees will continue to rise; whether the trend toward an increasing percentage of teachers with a master's degree will continue is a matter of conjecture, although many teacher salary schedules provide economic incentives for holders of the M.A. and a handful of school districts require the M.A. for purposes of advancement.

---

[22] NEA, "National Opinion Poll," p. 3.

FIGURE 4

PERCENTAGE OF TEACHERS UNDER 25 YEARS OF AGE, 1960–1976

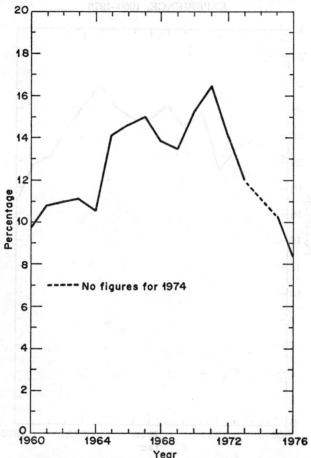

Source: National Education Association, "National Opinion Poll 1960–1976 Annual Survey" (Washington: NEA, 1977), p. 1 (mimeographed).

It is also a matter of conjecture as to whether the intellectual quality of teachers has improved over the years. Clearly, there has been advancement since the late colonial era, but as late as the middle 1960s education majors in colleges tended to score lower on standard achievement tests than all noneducation majors. The academic aptitude of teacher trainees, as measured by an examination conducted by the American Council on Education in the middle 1950s, for example, was higher only than those who had flunked out of college.[23] There is scat-

<hr>

[23] Koerner, pp. 44–45.

FIGURE 5

PERCENTAGE OF TEACHERS WITH LESS THAN THREE YEARS'
EXPERIENCE, 1960–1976

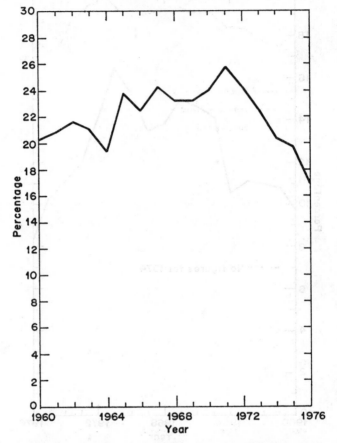

Source: National Education Association, "National Opinion Poll 1960–1976
Annual Survey" (Washington: NEA, 1977), p. 5 (mimeographed).

tered information, however, to suggest that the intellectual quality of
public school teachers began to improve in the late 1960s.[24]

Certainly the burgeoning surplus of qualified teachers in the late
1960s and 1970s made it possible for school districts to be highly selective in hiring. The surplus also provided districts with an opportunity,
though probably seldom exercised, to weed out the less competent nontenured teachers and replace them with young college graduates who
appeared to be more gifted. More will be said about the significance of

[24] See, for example, Summers and Wolfe, manuscript, p. 11, and New York State
School, "Achieving Flexible Pay Schemes," pp. 35–40 *passim.*

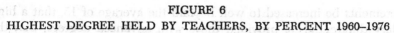

FIGURE 6
HIGHEST DEGREE HELD BY TEACHERS, BY PERCENT 1960–1976

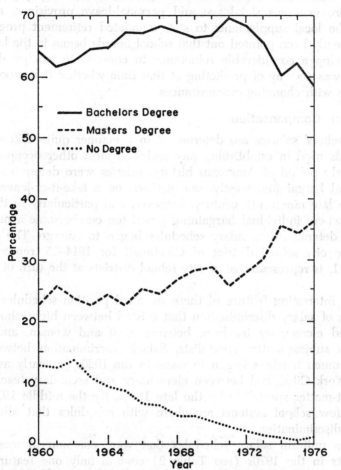

Source: National Education Association, "National Opinion Poll 1960–1976 Annual Survey" (Washington: NEA, 1977), p. 3 (mimeographed).

the intellectual climate in public education and its possible relationship to salary scheduling and student achievement in the concluding section of this chapter.

As for the possible implications the changing characteristics of the teacher population might have for collective bargaining, one would assume that union demands will begin to reflect the interests of a generally older, more experienced, more highly educated workforce. One can foresee, for example, demands that the number of automatic salary increments be increased to well beyond the average of 15, that a higher salary differential be provided those with advanced degrees, that there be more generous sick-leave and personal-leave provisions, and that there be local supplements to state-mandated retirement programs. It has already been pointed out that school boards began in the late 1970s to develop a considerable reluctance to concede to teacher demands. There was no way of predicting at that time whether that mood would change with changing circumstances.

Teacher Compensation

Teachers' salaries are determined in a manner quite different from methods used in establishing pay scales in most other occupations. In the early period of American history, salaries were determined by individual bargaining, mostly, one gathers, on a take-it-or-leave-it basis. By the late nineteenth century, however, and particularly in the larger cities where individual bargaining posed too cumbersome a method of salary determination, salary schedules began to emerge. The schedule for the city school district of Cincinnati for 1914–15, reproduced in Table 1, is representative of city school districts at the turn of the century.

An interesting feature of these so-called position schedules was the degree of salary discrimination that existed between high school teachers and elementary teachers, between men and women, and among certain subject-matter specialists. Salary discrimination between men and women teachers began to wane in the 1920s (as early as 1912 in New York City) and between elementary and secondary teachers and subject-matter specialists by the late 1930s. By the middle 1950s there were few school systems anywhere with schedules that allowed for overt discrimination.

The uniform salary schedules that were common in most school districts in the 1970s (see Table 2) contain only one feature of the position schedule: annual service increments. A new feature is the addition of a provision for salary improvement through securing graduate credits. Service increments have, in the main, been expanded from a turn-of-the-century average of 10 or 11 to 15 or 16. Most school districts seem also to grant an additional amount, on average about $200, for the master's degree.

The theory behind automatic salary progression is that teachers become more competent as they gain more experience and gather more graduate credits. It is also likely, however, that unless a school district could demonstrate that automatic salary progression was guaranteed, few prospective teachers would be secured. Unlike most occupations,

TABLE 1
Salary Schedules of City School Systems/Cincinnati, Ohio
1914–1915

Position or Grade	Minimum Yearly Salary	Yearly Increase in Salary	Years Required to Reach Maximum	Maximum Yearly Salary
High schools				
Instructors				
Male	$1,000	$100	8	$1,800
Female	900	100	9	1,800
Teachers				
Male	1,800	100	5	2,300
Female	1,300	100	5	1,800
Elementary schools				
Teachers				
If college graduates	600	50	10	1,100
If high school graduates only	450	50	13	1,100
Special teachers				
Music				
Men	1,300	100	4	1,700
Women	1,050	100	2½	1,300
Manual training				
Men	900	100	6	1,500
Women				
If college graduates	650	50	10	1,150
If high school grads only	500	50	13	1,150
German				
Men	900	100	6	1,500
Women				
If college graduates	600	50	10	1,100
If high school grads only	450	50	13	1,100
Penmanship				
Women				
If college graduates	600	50	10	1,100
If high school grads only	450	50	13	1,100
Domestic science				
Women				
If college graduates	600	50	10	1,100
If high school grads only	450	50	13	1,100
Drawing				
Men	900	100	6	1,500
Women				
If college graduates	650	50	10	1,150
If high school grads only	500	50	13	1,150
Physical training				
Men	900	100	6	1,500
Women				
If college graduates	650	50	10	1,150
If high school grads only	500	50	13	1,150

Source: Research Bureau, Public Education Association of Buffalo, *A Study of Salary Schedules in School Systems* (Buffalo, N.Y.: PEA, 1916), pp. 55–56.

there is relatively little opportunity to "move up the ranks" into a more responsible and more highly paid position. Thus, there is concern among most teachers that salary advancement be guaranteed, even though the duties of the position remain the same year after year. Even

TABLE 2

A Representative Teachers' Salary Schedule

Step	BS	BS+15	MS	MS+15	MS+30	Doctorate
0	$ 8,700	$ 8,900	$ 9,300	$ 9,500	$ 9,900	$10,450
1	9,095	9,292	9,695	9,895	10,295	10,845
2	9,490	9,690	10,090	10,290	10,690	11,240
3	9,885	10,085	10,485	10,685	11,085	11,635
4	10,280	10,480	10,880	11,080	11,480	12,030
5	10,675	10,875	11,275	11,475	11,875	12,425
6	11,070	11,270	11,670	11,870	12,270	12,820
7	11,465	11,665	12,065	12,265	12,665	13,215
8	11,860	12,060	12,460	12,660	13,060	13,610
9	12,255	12,455	12,855	13,055	13,455	14,005
10	12,650	12,850	13,250	13,450	13,850	14,400
11	13,045	13,245	13,645	13,845	14,245	14,795
12	13,440	13,640	14,040	14,240	14,640	15,190
13	13,835	14,035	14,435	14,635	15,035	15,585
14	14,230	14,430	14,830	15,030	15,430	15,980
15			15,225	15,425	15,825	16,375
16			15,620	15,820	16,220	16,770
17			16,015	16,215	16,615	17,165
18			16,410	16,610	17,010	17,560
19			16,805	17,005	17,405	17,955

under collective bargaining, where one might assume that there would be expectations of periodic salary adjustments, there seems to have been relatively little tinkering with existing schedules. The increments tend to be regarded by teachers as guaranteed ("old money"); the bargain is over how much more should be added ("new money"), usually by increasing the entry-level salary and adjusting the figures in all other stations on the schedule accordingly. The increase is either in a flat dollar amount or a percentage increase, teachers usually favoring the latter since this generally provides greater benefits to older, more experienced teachers.

A handful of school districts have experimented with so-called merit systems whereby salary adjustments were based on performance rather than mere experience and credit-gathering. Such systems have never been popular with teachers. "The use of subjective methods [merit ratings] of evaluating professional performance for the purpose of setting salaries," proclaimed a National Education Association resolution in 1960, "has a deleterious effect on the educational process." [25] Merit plans appear to be particularly difficult to establish under collective bargaining agreements since clearly all teachers cannot be meritorious and union and association leaders are reluctant to accept a settlement that many members might regard as discriminatory.[26]

---

[25] NEA, *Address and Proceedings*, p. 166.

[26] For a discussion of merit compensation schemes under collective bargaining, see New York State School, "Achieving Flexible Pay Schemes," *passim*.

Another system of compensation that gained notoriety in the late 1960s was differential staffing. Its purpose was to provide a career ladder for able and interested teachers by giving them additional responsibilities with commensurate salary differentials. A hierarchical arrangement leading from resource teachers to coordinating teachers to associate teachers, each position denoting different duties and responsibilities, would be established, thus making it possible for some teachers to earn a substantial income and still spend a good part of their time in the classroom.[27] Like merit salary plans, differential staffing schemes were infrequently implemented. Whether they proved too difficult to mesh with the egalitarianism and majoritarianism of collective bargaining or failed to pass muster for other reasons, it is not possible to say.

Teacher salaries have increased markedly since the late 1950s, both in current and adjusted dollars, as Figure 7 illustrates. There was a drop in real income between 1973 and 1976 when salary increases failed to keep up with inflation, but that was true of most workers during that period. Teachers' salaries have on average improved at a slightly better rate than those of other workers, increasing between 1960 and 1976 by 207 percent as against a 201 percent increase for all U.S. employees.[28] The highest average teachers' salaries in 1975 were in such states as New York ($15,000), California ($14,915), Michigan ($14,224), Illinois ($13,469), and Maine ($13,202), while states with the lowest average were Mississippi ($8,338), South Dakota ($8,860), and Arkansas ($9,021).[29]

Figures on average salaries must, of course, be viewed with caution, particularly those dealing with teachers' salaries. At a time when the school population was expanding rapidly, during the years 1955 to 1965, there was a comparable expansion in the workforce, and for the most part new teachers entered at the bottom of the salary schedule. Thus it is at least theoretically possible that a school district growing rapidly in pupil population could provide substantial salary increases and yet show only modest increases in average salary since the salaries of the new entrants would pull the average down. As for the 207 percent increase in average salaries from 1961–76, if one were to compare the salary of an entering teacher in 1961 (B.A., no experience) with that teacher's salary in 1976, let us say now with an M.A., the increase would be much greater. A sample of schedules of school districts in central New York suggests that the average increase over the period

[27] For a discussion of differential staffing, see NEA, *Classroom Teachers Speak Out*, and Bhaerman, *Several Educators' Cure*.
[28] NEA, "National Opinion Poll," pp. 10–11, and DComm, *The National Income*.
[29] DHEW, *The Condition of Education*, p. 133.

FIGURE 7
AVERAGE SALARIES OF INSTRUCTIONAL STAFF

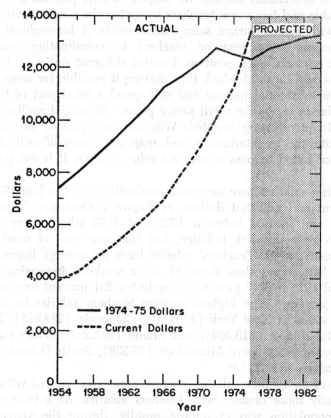

Source: U.S. Department of Health, Education, and Welfare, National Center for Education Statistics, *The Condition of Education: A Statistical Report on the Condition of Education in the United States together with a Description of the Activities of the National Center for Education Statistics* (Washington: U.S. Government Printing Office, 1976), p. 132.

would be approximately 250 percent, the range being 227 percent to 282 percent. Looked at from this perspective, teachers' salaries have improved, on average, at a significantly faster rate than those of the general workforce.

As for starting salaries, public school teachers in 1976 averaged approximately $8,700 yearly. This was on a par with the entry-level salaries of such occupations as dieticians, home economists, and community social workers, but substantially behind the beginning salaries received by accountants ($12,216) and business administration majors ($12,272).[30]

───────────

[30] NEA, "Research Information for UNISERV Units," p. 5, and College Placement Council, *CPC Salary Survey*, p. 5.

The percentage difference between entry-level teachers' salaries and those of occupations requiring similar training seems not to have changed significantly between 1966 and 1976,[31] although the salary difference between experienced teachers and their nonteacher counterparts may have become less. A comparison of salary schedules for 1976–77 with those of a decade earlier indicates that increments have become somewhat larger and the dollar amount granted for graduate credit increased, thus probably improving the salary position of the career teacher relative to career employees in occupations with similar entry-level salaries.

It is noteworthy that teachers received rather substantial improvements at a time when there was a burgeoning surplus of teachers. The National Center for Education Statistics has estimated that the number of certified teachers available for employment in 1976 was 317,000. The demand for new teachers that year was 184,000.[32] The supply, according to the National Center, will continue to grow into the 1980s, although the demand will continue to decline, also until into the 1980s when female children born in the late 1950s and early 1960s reach child-bearing age. Still, by 1983 the supply will be 359,000 to meet a demand for 164,000 new teachers.[33]

Some areas have substantially less demand than others. In New York State, for example, which has a teacher workforce of approximately 165,000, fewer than 300 new teachers would find jobs in that state's public schools during the 1977–78 school year.[34] The decline in job opportunities seems to have been uniform, at least in New York State, for almost all grade levels and all subject-matter specialties. Only teachers of such subjects as business education and distributive education seemed to hold their own in the 1970s.[35]

Although teacher salary scales seem never to have been influenced by the level of teacher supply to any marked degree, bargaining seems to have made salary even less susceptible to changes in the labor market. In some districts unions and boards have agreed to allow entry-level salaries to "float," allowing for the market to determine the salaries of new teachers; only the salaries of teachers on board would be negotiated. But this practice seems not to have caught on, and even though the teacher surplus has no doubt made it more difficult for the union to negotiate salary increases, they seem to have succeeded in doing so

[31] College Placement Council, *CPC Salary Survey*, p. 7.
[32] DHEW, *The Condition of Education*, p. 248.
[33] *Ibid.*
[34] SUNY, *The Regents*, p. 25.
[35] "Employment Prospects for New Teachers," *Postsecondary Education in New York State* 5:2 (March/April 1977), p. 1.

nonetheless. It is instructive in this regard that New York State, a state with one of the highest, if not *the* highest, percentage of teachers organized, has probably the lowest demand for teachers in relation to the size of its workforce and also has the highest average teachers' salaries.

Organizing for Collective Bargaining Purposes

TEACHER ORGANIZATIONS

Two national teacher organizations dominate collective bargaining activity in the public schools: the National Education Association (NEA) and the American Federation of Teachers (AFT). The two have held quite different views of the proper role of teacher organizations over the years (the NEA viewing themselves more as a professional group, the AFT as a trade union); but by the late 1960s it was difficult—if one examined only the rhetoric and activities of each group —to tell them apart. The NEA gravitated toward the union mold while the AFT stayed as it was. Evidently, if an organization hopes to succeed in the competition of representing teachers under a collective bargaining agreement, it must ultimately begin to act like a trade union.

There are many similarities and many differences between the two organizations. The NEA is by far the older and larger of the two. It was organized in 1857 as the National Teacher Association to "elevate the character and advance the interests of the profession of teaching, and . . . promote the cause of popular education in the United States." Although slow in starting (after more than 60 years the NEA still enrolled no more than 5 percent of American teachers),[36] by 1977 membership totaled 1.8 million. Some of this membership, however, was in higher education or held supervisory jobs.[37]

The AFT, founded and chartered by the American Federation of Labor in 1916, had as its goals: "to obtain for [teachers] all the rights to which they are entitled," and "to raise the standards of the teaching profession by securing the conditions essential to the best professional service." [38]

Like the NEA, the AFT had a rocky start. Membership was only about 13,000 in the middle 1920s, but it took a great surge forward in the 1960s, and by 1977 it had reached approximately 450,000. A portion of that membership, like the NEA's, is in higher education. Unlike the

---

[36] Wesley, *The NEA*, pp. 23–24.

[37] Except where otherwise noted, information on the NEA and the AFT was gained by the author through interviews with officials of the two organizations during the summer of 1977.

[38] Quoted from the 1916 Constitution of the Commission on Education Reconstruction, *Organizing the Teaching Profession* (Glencoe, Ill.: Free Press, 1955), p. 28.

NEA's, however, some of it is also among nonprofessional school employees (bus drivers, clerical workers, and custodial employees). The AFT actively campaigns to organize these employees, placing them in separate "special" (nonprofessional) locals.

Although neither group organizes among supervisory or administrative personnel, both represent them in isolated cases, sometimes in the same locals as teachers, sometimes separately. The NEA began to discourage supervisors from seeking membership in the middle 1970s, but many locals were reluctant to abandon members in good standing. Some locals believed that there was not sufficient conflict of interest between teachers and principals, say, to warrant exclusion. Where AFT locals do represent supervisors, usually the bargaining unit was formerly represented by the NEA and has been won over by the AFT. In any case, the percentage of supervisors or administrators who are members of either the AFT or NEA appears to be diminishing, and it is rare for one to hold elected office in either organization.

Figures on national membership do not necessarily represent bargaining strength since both organizations have large numbers of members in states that do not allow collective bargaining. Of the 1.8 million members the NEA claimed in 1977, for example, approximately 475,000 were in states that had no enabling collective bargaining statute and very little collective bargaining activity (South Carolina, Mississippi, Arkansas, and Alabama, for example).[39] The AFT, on the other hand, may represent more teachers than it has members since it has succeeded in winning bargaining rights in most of the larger cities (such as New York, Chicago, Philadelphia, Pittsburgh, Detroit, St. Louis, San Francisco, Boston), where in most instances membership is voluntary. NEA strength is concentrated in the smaller cities and in suburban and rural areas. Membership in these areas is usually voluntary, too, of course, but the number of nonmembers represented by the NEA appears to be fewer than the number of members not represented.

Both organizations provide for "unified" membership. When a teacher joins a local, he or she must also join the state and national organization. There are dues for each level. In 1977 annual national AFT dues were $31.80; NEA national dues were $30.00. State organization dues vary, but in 1977 the AFT New York statewide organization annually charged $82.00 and the NEA state affiliate charged $75.00. Local dues, which are determined by the local organization, generally ranged in 1977 for both the NEA and AFT from $25.00 to $100.00.

In both the AFT and the NEA, state and national officers are elected at the annual conventions and serve for two-year terms. The AFT

[39] NEA, *NEA Handbook: 1976–77*, p. 141.

places no restrictions on the number of terms an officer can serve, but the NEA limits its elected officers to two two-year terms. A rather significant difference exists between the formal structure of the two unions: whereas the chief administrative officers in the AFT are elected, the NEA relies on appointed executive directors to handle administrative tasks, at both the national and state levels. Before the NEA provided for consecutive two-year terms, the executive directors enjoyed considerable autonomy and authority. More recently, elected officers at the state and national level, most of whom serve full time, have begun to assert more influence in the organization.

Both AFT and NEA state organizations provide assistance to the locals in handling representation disputes in collective bargaining and in contract administration. In New York, the state AFT has a field representative for every 1,200 members approximately, and the NEA has field officers and "UNISERV" representatives to provide similar services. Both organizations also provide research and other support services for the locals and maintain lobbyists in the state capitals to promote state legislation favorable to teachers.

In regard to affiliation with other labor organizations, the AFT is affiliated with the AFL-CIO and its Public Employee Department. Some state AFT organizations are affiliated with state AFL-CIO bodies and the locals with central labor councils. Although the NEA has no direct connection with the AFL-CIO, it does, through its membership in the Coalition of American Public Employees (CAPE), work closely on legislative and other matters with such AFL-CIO unions as the American Federation of State, County, and Municipal Employees (AFSCME) and the National Treasury Employees Union. On occasion the NEA has also worked out informal cooperative arrangements with the AFSCME on state and local levels.

Membership in the AFL-CIO appears to have been one of the main stumbling blocks to a merger between the AFT and the NEA, the former insisting that affiliation with the national federation be the *sine qua non* for merger, while the latter was equally insistent that a merged teacher group would have to be outside the AFL-CIO. The 1972–76 trial merger in New York State probably engendered a sense of wariness among NEA officials about similar ventures in other states or at the national level. In 1972 the NEA state body had 100,000 members and the New York AFT 75,000, 60,000 of whom were in its New York City local. A year after the merged organization broke apart, the relationship was reversed: AFT membership was approximately 160,000 and NEA membership 25,000. Most of the locals, particularly the larger ones, opted to remain with the AFT affiliate rather than join the newly organized statewide NEA group.

Merger talks on the national level were suspended in 1976, and both NEA and AFT officials seemed resigned to several years of competition. Probably merger, or at least some form of no-raiding agreement, will some day be reached. Perhaps to most teachers it makes little sense for the two employee organizations to spend such great sums of money on organizational and representational disputes when the resources might be put to better use in collective bargaining activities. Moreover, by the mid-1970s whatever ideological differences may have divided the two groups historically had almost vanished: both organizations accepted collective bargaining and acted like trade unions. It was anybody's guess, however, how long it would take for the remaining personal and institutional differences to disappear, thus allowing a merger to take place.

SCHOOL BOARDS

Employers have also organized for collective bargaining purposes, but not nearly to the extent that teachers have. Although the National School Boards Association (NSBA) and state school-board associations frequently conduct workshops and conferences on collective bargaining, do research, provide legal advice, and distribute information on bargaining trends to local affiliates, neither lends much "at the table" bargaining assistance. Being only one of the functions of school management, collective bargaining must compete with other important matters—such as fiscal policies and racial tensions—for attention. However, bargaining does appear to be a very important concern of board members. Interestingly, those who have not experienced bargaining are somewhat more ill-disposed toward the process than are those who have.[40] With the exception of those in the South, school officials chose collective bargaining as their most important management concern, well ahead of racial tensions, declining enrollment, and problems of school finance.[41]

When bargaining began, most school districts were not equipped to handle all the chores associated with it. Few school officials had training or experience in the field, and few seemed psychologically suited to assume this new burden. Many objected strongly to the very concept of collective bargaining. In fact, as late as 1976, a national survey of school superintendents and board members found that 88 percent thought that bargaining would cause a serious reallocation of resources

---

[40] Newby, p. 2.
[41] *Ibid.*

away from services that would benefit children; 87 percent thought it would result in substantial increases in the local tax burden; 87 percent thought it would result in teachers being less responsive to the public interest; and 83 percent were persuaded that bargaining would lead to strikes and other disruptions. Employers with these views probably find it difficult to make tradeoffs, to compromise, to let go of what they regard as natural prerogatives. Like employers in the industrial sector in the late 1930s, many board members resist the process itself.[42]

It is also interesting that board members and chief school officials are so heavily represented on management bargaining teams. According to a NSBA survey, 78 percent of all management negotiating teams have at least one board member (the average is 2.5), and board members also serve as chief negotiators in 17 percent of all negotiations. School superintendents serve on management teams in 52 percent of all school negotiations, being chief negotiators in 15 percent. A professional negotiator is employed in 25 percent of teacher-board negotiations, usually as the chief spokesman, and 54 percent use central-office staff other than the superintendent for that purpose.[43]

The NSBA study does not indicate whether the same faces appear on the management teams year after year. Probably they rotate frequently. Most contracts are for a single year, and since more than one-half of all contracts take five months or more to negotiate,[44] it is unlikely that many board members volunteer for a second tour of duty. There is probably also considerable turnover among outside consultants. Thus, it is common for each new contract to be negotiated—at least on the employer's side—by novices unfamiliar with the negotiation process and its many rituals and unacquainted with the issues the parties are attempting to resolve. There is significant turnover on the union teams as well, but most local unions have state AFT or NEA representatives who provide a certain amount of continuity as chief spokesman. This frequent turnover on board teams may contribute substantially to the high number of impasses in teacher-board negotiations.

Clearly, board members need to be informed of the progress of negotiations, just as they must provide instruction to the bargaining team on the limits of their concessions and must specify what provisions of the current contract ought to be modified. But that information can usually be transmitted outside the collective bargaining arena, and there has been considerable debate over whether board members ought to be represented directly on the management team. The main difficulty

[42] *Ibid.*
[43] *Ibid.*
[44] *Ibid.*

of direct board-member participation is that whether a board member is chief spokesman or not (and most are not), the union will assume that an agreement reached on any issue, no matter how tentative, has the full sanction of the board. It is certainly difficult for the chief spokesman to say he will have to "check out" a union counterproposal with his principals when a member of the board is sitting at his side.

Whether superintendents ought to represent the board in negotiations has also been debated. Although the superintendent is expected to be the most knowledgeable person in the district on matters of finance and personnel needs, he is also the "educational leader" of the district. The *sturm und drang* associated with bargaining, some believe, tends to weaken the superintendent's ability to take a strong management stance at the bargaining table. In taking such a stance, he might alienate members of the instructional staff, thus making it difficult to win teacher cooperation later on issues of a purely educational nature that lie outside the subject matter of bargaining.

Yet in many instances there is no alternative to direct participation by superintendents and board members. Over 40 percent of all U.S. school districts have fewer than 600 students; 75 percent have fewer than 2,500.[45] Given customary ratios between students and staff and between staff and central administration, no one except board members and the chief school officer is available to serve on the bargaining team in a large number of districts. As mentioned earlier, several districts retain professional negotiators to be chief spokesmen, but this cannot be an entirely satisfactory arrangement. Although it can provide the board and the superintendent with a modicum of insulation from the heat generated at the bargaining table, these so-called "hired guns" (as teacher groups affectionately call them) cannot be expected to use the bargaining process as a mechanism for solving problems. That requires an intimate knowledge of the internal workings of the enterprise and an awareness of when a concession might hurt or benefit the educational quality. Thus, most school districts face a dilemma. Neither direct participation of school officials nor reliance on professional negotiators is a satisfactory arrangement. Yet only a minority of school districts have the resources to designate a full-time staff member to handle negotiations and the administration of the contract.

The Law

As education under the U.S. Constitution is a state rather than a federal responsibility, so, too, are the labor relations policies affecting

[45] DHEW, *Digest of Education Statistics: 1976*, p. 60.

public school teachers.[46] A review of the state laws covering collective bargaining rights for teachers and other public employees forms a patchwork quilt of many colors and designs (see Table 3 and Figure 8). Teachers can legally strike in Pennsylvania but not in New York; school boards are required to bargain over numerical limits to class size in California but not in Oregon; the agency shop is permitted in Michigan but not in Iowa; teachers are legally protected in their right to bargain collectively in Indiana but not in Illinois.

With the exception of the Wisconsin statute, which granted teachers bargaining rights in 1959, legislation providing collective bargaining rights for teachers and other public employees began to be passed in the middle 1960s. Approximately half of these laws covered teachers along with other employees, and half covered teachers only. In most instances a separate agency was established to administer the public-sector law. By 1977, beside the 29 states that had bargaining laws, there were six that had only meet-and-confer statutes; four in which employers could voluntarily extend recognition to public employee groups; and 11, mostly in the Southeast, that gave teachers and other public employees no statutory rights to bargain or even to confer on a formal and systematic basis with their employers.

It is important to remember, however, that there is a considerable amount of bargaining taking place in the schools without a statutory mandate. In 1977 thousands of teachers in Ohio and Illinois, for example, were covered by comprehensive collective bargaining agreements, even though there was no statute in these states granting collective bargaining rights.

Indeed, perhaps the greatest impetus to teacher bargaining was the negotiation of a contract between the United Federation of Teachers (UFT) and the New York City Board of Education in 1962, five years before the New York State legislature passed the Taylor Law allowing for collective bargaining for public employees. In that instance it took a representation strike to convince the city to grant the teachers the right to bargain collectively. According to board of education figures, there were only 5,949 teachers (or about 15 percent of the total workforce) absent from classes during the strike.[47] Be that as it may, the strike prompted city officials to appoint a fact-finding panel consisting of three prominent labor leaders to recommend whether there ought to be bargaining in the city's public schools. It came as a surprise to practically no one that the panel recommended bargaining. A represen-

---

[46] *National League of Cities* v. *Usery*, 96 S.Ct. 2465, 49 L.Ed 245 (1976).
[47] Leonard Buden, "City Schools Disrupted by Strike of Teachers; 4,600 Suspended by Board," *The New York Times*, November 8, 1960, p. 1.

TABLE 3

Collective Bargaining Statutes, by State

State	Coverage	Administrative Agency	Supervisors	Scope	Union Security	Impasse Resolution			Strike
						Mediation	Fact-Finding	Arbitration	
Alaska (1970)	Teachers only	Department of Labor	Administrators may form own units. Otherwise, part of teachers' unit.	Matters pertaining to employment and fulfillment of professional duties.	No provisions	5 member tripartite panel		Advisory arbitration governor appoints	Permitted
California (1975)	Teachers only	Educational Employment Relations Board	Excluded from employee unit. May form own unit.	Wages, hours, conditions plus specific issues including class size, evaluation, leave, and transfer policy.	Agency shop or maintenance of membership permitted. Dues deduction.	Appointed by Board at no cost to parties	3-member tripartite panel with recommendations		Prohibited
Connecticut (1967)	Teachers only	State Board of Education[a]	Administrators must form own units.	Salaries and all other conditions of employment.	No provisions	Secretary of Board mediates	3-member tripartite panel	Tripartite, not binding	Prohibited
Delaware (1969)	Public school employees	State Department of Public Instruction	Excluded	Salaries, employee benefits, working conditions.	Dues deduction. Union shop prohibited.	If parties cannot agree on mediator, tripartite panel chosen	Same process as mediation	Prohibited	Prohibited, lose recognition 2 yrs., dues deduction 1 yr.
Florida (1974)	All public employees	Public Employees Relations Commission	No provision	Wages, hours, and conditions of employment.	Dues deduction.	Mediator paid for by requesting party	PERC appoints special master. His decision is deemed accepted unless specifically rejected.		Prohibited. Fines, loss of dues deduction, certification
Hawaii (1970)	All public employees	PERB	No provision	Wages, hours, terms and conditions of employment. Some specific exclusions including matters inconsistent with merit principle.	Agency shop required. Dues deduction.	Mediator appointed by Board	Begins 15 days after impasse. Report issued within 10 days	Tripartite panel begins 30 days after impasse	Permitted provided impasse procedure has been complied with. May be enjoined if threat to public health or safety

TABLE 3 — Continued

TABLE 3—(*Continued*)

State	Coverage	Administrative Agency	Supervisors	Scope	Union Security	Impasse Resolution			
						Mediation	Fact-Finding	Arbitration	Strike
Idaho (1971)	Teachers only	State Superintendent of Public Instruction	Excluded by agreements	Matters and conditions by agreement of parties.	No provision	Procedure and allocation of cost set by parties	Parties or superintendent appoints single fact-finder		No provision
Indiana (1973)	Teachers only	Education Employment Relations Board	Excluded	Salaries, wages, hours and salary and wage related fringe benefits	Dues deduction	Appointed by Board at request of either	Board appoints fact-finder		Prohibited
Iowa (1974)	All public employees	PERB	Excluded	Wages, hours, several specifics.	Agency shop prohibited. Dues deduction.	Mediator appointed by Board	Fact-finder appointed by Board	Parties may use tripartite or single arbitrator. May select final offer of either party or fact-finder's report	Prohibited, fines, prison
Kansas (1970)	Teachers only	State Dept. of Education	May have own units	Wages, hours, plus specific issues	No provision	Appointed by agency	Agency appoints 3-member panel	No provision	Prohibited
Maine (1969)	Municipal employees	Labor Relations Board	Excluded	Wages, hours, and working conditions. Merit system, exams, promotions excluded.	No provision	Board appoints 1 or more mediators	Board appoints a 3-member panel of neutrals. Costs shared by parties	Tripartite panel	Prohibited
Maryland (1969)	Teachers only	State Board of Education	No provision	Salaries, wages, hours and other working conditions. Tenure excluded.	No provision	Tripartite panel	Same panel issues report if it doesn't get a settlement		Prohibited. Loss of recognition for 2 yrs., loss of dues dudection 1 year

TABLE 3—(Continued)

State	Coverage	Administrative Agency	Supervisors	Scope	Union Security	Impasse Resolution Mediation	Impasse Resolution Fact-Finding	Impasse Resolution Arbitration	Strike
Massachusetts (1973)	All public employees	Labor Relations Commission[b]	No provision	Wages, hours, and other terms and conditions of employment	Agency shop and dues deduction permitted.	Board or parties name single mediator	Board or parties name single fact-finder	Parties may voluntarily resort to arbitration	Prohibited
Michigan (1965)	All public employees	Employment Relations Commission	No provision	Wages, hours, other conditions of bargaining.	Agency shop permitted.	Board appoints single mediator	Tripartite panel. The mediator serves as chairman		Prohibited
Minnesota (1971)	All public employees	PERB[c]	May form own units	Grievance procedures and terms and conditions of employment	Fair share agreements required.	Board provides single mediator	Tripartite panel. The mediator serves as chairman	Panel of 3 neutrals, conventional arbitration	Prohibited
Montana (1971)	All public employees	Board of Personnel Appeals	Excluded	Wages, fringe benefits and other conditions of employment	Agency shop permitted. Dues deduction.	Board appoints single mediator	Board names a single fact-finder	Parties may voluntarily use arbitration	Permitted
Nevada (1969)	All public employees	Local Government Employee-Management Relations Board	Must form own units	List of specific items.	No provision	Parties may agree to use mediation	Parties may choose single fact-finder	Parties may agree in advance to be bound by fact-finder's report	Prohibited, fines, prison
New Hampshire (1975)	All public employees	PERB	Separate units	Wages, hours, and other conditions of employment. Some specific exclusions.	No provision	Parties or Board appoint a mediator	Parties or Board appoint a single fact-finder	Parties may voluntarily use arbitration on non-cost items	Prohibited
New Jersey (1968)	All public employees	Public Employment Relations Commission	Separate units	Terms and conditions of employment	Agency shop prohibited	Either party may request mediation	Commission may recommend or impose fact-finding	Tripartite panel	Prohibited

TABLE 3—(*Continued*)

State	Coverage	Administrative Agency	Supervisors	Scope	Union Security	Mediation	Fact-Finding	Arbitration	Strike
							Impasse Resolution		
New York (1967)	All public employees except New York City	PERB	No provision	Terms and conditions of employment	Agency Shop permitted. Dues deduction.	Mediator appointed by PERB	Panel of up to 3 public members	May be used voluntarily	Prohibited, loss of 2 days pay for each day on strike. Loss of dues deduction prohibited
North Dakota (1969)	Teachers only	Education Fact Finding Commission	Separate units	Salary units and other terms and conditions of employment	No provision	Parties choose single mediator	Commission acts as or names fact-finder		Prohibited
Oklahoma (1971)	Public school employees	Local Board of Education	No provision	Professionals: matters affecting professional services.	No provision	Parties can set up own impasse procedure	Tripartite panel, if parties can agree on procedure		Prohibited
Oregon (1973)	All public employees	PERB	No provision	Wages, hours, conditions of employment	Agency and union shop permitted. Dues deduction.	Board appoints single mediator	Parties or Board appoints fact-finder. Parties may request panel of 3 neutrals.	Permitted by agreement of parties	Permitted after mediation and fact-finding and 10 days notice. May be enjoined to protect public health, safety, or welfare.
Pennsylvania (1970)	All public employees	Pennsylvania Labor Relations Board[d]	Own units meet and confer	Wages, hours, terms and conditions of employment	Agency shop prohibited. Maintenance of membership permitted.	Parties call in mediator. If no settlement Bureau of Mediation called in.	Board names 1 or 3 member panel	Permitted by voluntary agreement	Permitted after impasse procedure, may be enjoined to protect public health, safety or welfare.
Rhode Island (1966)	Teachers only	State Labor Relations Board[e]	No provision	Hours, salary, working conditions, and all other terms and conditions of employment	No provision	Parties may submit to mediation	Tripartite panel		Prohibited

TABLE 3—(Continued)

State	Coverage	Administrative Agency	Supervisors	Scope	Union Security	Impasse Resolution			
						Mediation	Fact-Finding	Arbitration	Strike
South Dakota (1969)	All public employees	Department of Manpower Affairs	No provision	Wages, hours, conditions of employment	No provision	Department of Manpower Affairs intervenes in impasses			Prohibited, fines, prison
Tennessee (1978)	Teachers only	State Comm. of Education and the Court of Record	Can not be a part of a negotiating unit	List of specific items including wages and other conditions of employment	No provision	Selected by parties	Fact-finding advisory arbitration by AAA; cost borne by party requesting		Prohibited
Vermont (1969)	Teachers only	No provision	May form separate units	Salary, grievance procedure, other matters agreed upon not in conflict with state law.	No provision	Parties choose mediator	Tripartite panel		Prohibited
Washington (1975)	Teachers	Public Employment Relations Commission	May form own units or join nonsupervisory unit by agreement	Wages, hours, terms and conditions of employment.	Agency shop permitted. Dues deduction.	Commission appoints single mediator	Parties or if they can't agree, Comm. appoints single fact-finder	On agreement of parties	Prohibited
Wisconsin (1959)	Municipal employees	Wisconsin Employment Relations Commission	No provision	Wages, and conditions of employment	Agency shop permitted. Dues deduction.	May be used	Commission appoints 3-member panel		Prohibited

a In Connecticut, the State Board of Labor Relations has jurisdiction over prohibited employment practices.
b In Massachusetts, the Board of Conciliation and Arbitration has responsibility for dispute settlement.
c In Minnesota, the Director of Mediation Services provides mediation service.
d The Pennsylvania Bureau of Mediation Services provides mediation service. It reports its results to the Board.
e In Rhode Island, mediation services can be requested by the state department of education, the director of labor, or from any other source.

FIGURE 8
TEACHER COLLECTIVE BARGAINING LEGISLATION IN THE UNITED STATES

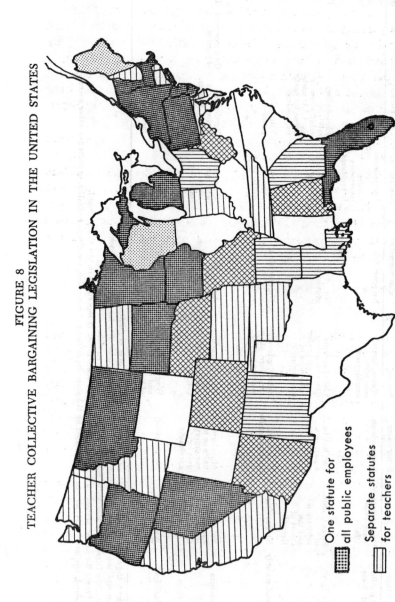

One statute for
all public employees

Separate statutes
for teachers

"Meet and confer" statutes

Separate statutes for
municipal employees

No law, or
bargaining prohibited

Voluntary bargaining

Sources: U.S. Department of Labor, Labor-Management Services Administration, *Summary of Public Sector Labor Re-*

tation election was held, which the UFT won handily, and the first contract was negotiated the following year.

It is interesting to speculate about what might have happened to the teacher bargaining movement had that strike failed. Had New York City officials held the line in the face of this rather weak showing by organized teachers and refused to permit a representation election, it is at least conceivable that enthusiasm for bargaining in other sections of the country would have been dampened. A refusal might also have caused legislatures in other states to question whether public-sector bargaining was either inevitable or appropriate.

As matters turned out, however, the New York City agreement seemed to have encouraged those favoring bargaining and broken whatever resistance to bargaining might have existed in most of the state legislatures. Between 1966 and 1976 almost 40 states granted some degree of bargaining or meet-and-confer rights to public employees. Whether New York City was the camel's nose under the tent or an inspiration of those seeking economic justice depends on the view one has of the desirability of teacher bargaining.

Bargaining Units and Union Security

UNITING ISSUES

In the main, teacher bargaining units consist of all teachers and certain satellite personnel, such as librarians, school nurses, and counselors, in a school district. Most statutes spell out uniting criteria, such as the community of interest among employees, the power of officials to make effective recommendations, and protection against Balkanization. It is rare for more than one teacher unit (elementary separate from secondary, for example) to exist in a single district because all teachers in the system tend to be on a single salary schedule, to have the same benefits, and to have similar training requirements.

The exception to this relative uniformity of treatment is the status of supervisors. Although most statutes exclude managerial and confidential employees, there is no consistency of treatment of building principals and vice-principals. In 1977, six states excluded supervisors (defined in much the same manner as defined under Section 2(11) of the National Labor Relations Act [NLRA]) from coverage; 10 states covered them under separate units; 11 states had no exclusionary provision; Pennsylvania granted them only meet-and-confer rights; and Alaska determined the status of supervisors by a *Globe*-type election— Alaskan school administrators may be in the same bargaining unit with teachers if both the teachers and the supervisors opt for that arrangement, or they can go their separate ways.

There appear to be no figures on the number of supervisors who are included in predominantly teacher units nor, for that matter, on the number represented for collective bargaining purposes. A trend seems to have developed in the early 1970s in those states where integrated units were allowed, however, for supervisors to form separate units.

Not all supervisors permitted to engage in collective bargaining have exercised their right to do so, some preferring to deal informally with school boards on salaries and other related matters. As noted earlier, both the NEA and the AFT represent supervisory units of mostly principals and vice-principals, but occasionally department chairmen and district-wide supervisors. In most instances, however, these employees are probably represented by independent organizations. Supervisors in several districts are represented by the American Federation of School Administrators (AFSA), AFL-CIO. In 1977 the federation represented approximately 12,000 supervisors in 58 locals,[48] in such school districts as New York City, Chicago, Pittsburgh, Detroit, and St. Louis.

On the question of the appropriateness of including supervisors under the coverage of state collective bargaining statutes, most state legislatures are of a mind that enough differences exist between the role and responsibilities of a building principal, say, and those of a shop foreman to cause them to ignore the precedents established under Section 2(3) and 2(11) of the NLRA and Sections 2(b) and 2(c) of the Federal Executive Order 11491. Both documents assume that management's right to manage would be weakened if the "managers" on the shop floor were possessed of a divided loyalty. A second point is that supervisors bargaining in separate units seem not to have fared nearly as well, at least in terms of salary improvements, as have teachers. The salary gap between principals and teachers with equivalent training and experience, for example, appears to have narrowed significantly between 1965 and 1975.

The application of the community-of-interest criterion has worked to exclude such nonprofessional employees as bus drivers, clericals, and custodians from professional bargaining units. In several districts where teachers bargain, these employees have organized as well, represented usually by such organizations as the Teamsters, AFSCME, Service Employees International Union, state civil service employee organizations, or independent agents. As pointed out earlier, an increasing number of these employees are represented by the AFT.

[48] Information supplied by Al Morrison, president, American Federation of School Administrators, July 28, 1977.

Like supervisors, nonprofessional employees seem to have less bargaining strength than do teachers. At least wages seem to have increased at a slower rate between 1965 and 1975 than have teachers' salaries, although benefits such as employer contributions to health and hospitalization plans appear to have kept pace.[49] This inability to win substantial gains at the bargaining table could be because much of the custodial, cafeteria, and transportation work can be readily subcontracted and since the middle 1960s a large number of school districts have decided to do just that.

Although for the most part the statutes are silent on whether multiemployer bargaining units are appropriate, such uniting arrangements have not caught on in public education. Multiemployer-multiunion or regional negotiations have been attempted in only a handful of cases, and in most instances these experiments failed. Without the discipline exercised by a competitive product market, it is difficult to persuade teachers in an affluent district to forgo whatever advantages that affluence might provide. By the same token, school boards in less affluent school systems are reluctant to provide the same benefits granted to teachers in districts that are better off. Leveling in order to merge usually means "leveling up," and districts with limited resources are either reluctant or unable to make the necessary concessions to bring salary arrangements on a par with the richer districts in the area. The meshing of salary schedules is particularly difficult when the parties (in this case several boards and several local unions) lack sufficient incentive to do so. The advantages of multiemployer bargaining— saving time at the table, securing greater bargaining expertise, and minimizing the effect of the whipsaw—appear not to be great enough to counter the fear of losing autonomy, a fear held no less by the union than by the board. Until the disparity in salary schedules and other contractual provisions in a region becomes negligible, it is unlikely that either teacher unions or school boards will voluntarily enter into multiemployer collective bargaining arrangements. Nor was there in the late 1970s any indication that state legislatures were ready to impose regional bargaining upon the parties.

UNION SECURITY

Although the union shop is rare in public education, by the late 1970s seven of the states with public-sector bargaining statutes allowed some form of union security, either an agency shop or "fair share" arrangement. Five states prohibited any form of union security, while in the remainder of the states the statutes were silent on the issue.

---

[49] Based on a sampling of school districts in central New York in the summer of 1977.

Presumably in the silent states there were few, if any, negotiated union-security provisions. In only one state, Hawaii, is the agency shop mandated. Public employees in Hawaii are granted the agency shop at the time of certification. In New York the agency shop is mandated for unions representing state employees, but bargaining agents for local employees, including teachers, must win the agency shop at the bargaining table.

Union-security provisions in the public sector differ from those in the private sector in several respects. First, it is not the usual practice for public employers to deduct the full amount of union fees and dues under an agency-shop agreement.[50] Rather, the amount deducted tends to be only a "fair share" of the cost of negotiating and administering the collective bargaining agreement. Thus, in Minnesota the Bureau of Mediation Services, the administrative agency under that state's public-employee bargaining statute, ruled in 1976 that 85 percent of the union's dues was a fair share for a nonmember to contribute; a nonmember can appeal having that amount deducted, however.[51] The reasoning applied by the bureau was similar to that used by the U.S. Supreme Court when it ruled in *Abood*[52] in 1977 that, although there was no constitutional barrier to compulsory contributions to the union by nonmembers, they cannot be obliged to lend financial support to politically or ideologically related activities in which the union might become engaged from time to time.

A second difference between the public and private sector in respect to union security is that in some states a union-security provision cannot be incorporated into the contract unless a majority of bargaining-unit members approve. There are few, if any, instances, however, where employees have voted down a union-security provision under this requirement.

A few public-sector statutes also vary from the NLRA in that the nonmember's agency fees are deducted without his or her authorization. Thus dues are subtracted from the recalcitrant employee's paycheck in the same manner as federal, state, and social security taxes. This measure saves the school board the embarrassment of firing a tenured teacher with a good record for the sole reason that the em-

---

[50] An exception to this practice is Wisconsin, where the statute defines "fair share" as an amount equivalent to full dues. However, the constitutionality of this portion of the statute is being questioned in *Browne v. Milwaukee Board of School Directors*. As of the summer of 1978 the case was still in litigation.

[51] Reported in *Government Employee Relations Report*, 696 GERR 11 (February 21, 1977).

[52] *Abood, et al. v. Detroit Board of Education, et al.*, 975 S.Ct. 1782, 52 L.Ed 2d 261 (1977).

ployee refused to authorize a contribution to the union. Under this scheme the teacher has no voice in the matter.

It could not be foreseen in the late 1970s whether the Supreme Court decision in *Abood* would encourage those states that did not provide for union-security provisions in their statutes to make such provisions. It may or may not be instructive that the New York State legislature amended that state's public employee bargaining law to allow for the agency shop only three months after the Court ruled in *Abood*. Neither was it possible to say in the late 1970s whether negotiated union-security provisions would stifle competition between the two teacher organizations. Minority organizations, both AFT and NEA, existed in hundreds of school districts, waiting for the time they might become the majority and therefore the bargaining agent. Whether the growth in the number of union-security provisions will cause these minority organizations to wither (paying dues to both the minority and majority union may be thought to be too great a burden) and make the existing bargaining agent secure against competition is problematic. Furthermore, one could only guess as to the consequences widespread adoption of union-security measures would have for the prospects of an AFT-NEA merger.

Scope of Bargaining

The scope of bargaining in public education is both narrower and broader than it is in the private sector. It is narrower in that some issues usually found on the collective bargaining table in industry have been preempted by state education or civil service law. Thus, parties do not usually negotiate retirement benefits since this is most often a matter for the state legislature to decide. Similarly, parties do not negotiate teacher job security and discipline in those districts where state education law and civil service law have jurisdiction over the order of layoffs, discharge of tenured and nontenured teachers, and due-process rights of employees subject to discipline.[53] Teacher or-

---

[53] As of this writing, all states have statewide retirement systems, and as of 1972, all but four had some sort of tenure legislation. Teacher retirement systems were first established in large city school districts around the turn of the century. Statewide plans began in the early 1900s. In 1930 there were only 22 statewide systems, but by 1950 all states made provisions for teacher retirement on a statewide basis, although some local plans still preempt statewide systems. Current plans are integrated with social security. As of 1972, all but one of the systems (New York) required employee contributions. Teacher tenure developed with civil service systems in the first 20 years of this century, though teacher tenure laws generally trailed civil service statutes in a given state by several years. The number of tenure laws grew substantially between the years 1936 and 1956, as the percentage of teachers working without the protection of tenure legislation declined from 55 to 9. Current tenure laws usually provide for a period of probationary employment—most commonly three years. Sources: Robbins, pp. 16–17; Day, pp. 8, 37, 244–45; Scott, pp. 9–12; NEA, *Trends in Teacher Tenure*, p. 3; Shapiro, p. 10.

ganizations have attempted (sometimes with success) to gain greater due-process protection than the statute provides, but the proposals tend to build on a statutory floor. Thus probationary teachers may have minimum procedural due-process rights granted under the statute, but through bargaining gain additional rights, procedural and substantive, under a "fair dismissal" clause.

The scope of bargaining in public education tends to be broader than that prevailing in the private sector because teachers view conditions of employment as transcending mere matters of salaries, hours, fringe benefits, and a grievance procedure. The contract thus becomes not only a constitution governing the working life of the teacher, but a document containing the educational philosophy of the district. It is not unusual to hear demands (and sometimes see contract language) dealing with such matters as student discipline, selection of a new superintendent, selection of teaching materials including textbooks, establishment of reference libraries, student grading, or academic freedom for both teachers and students. Teachers are the professionals, so the argument goes, and they are in a better position to know what procedures and practices constitute a sound educational program than is a lay school board. The agreement is seen by many as the vehicle for getting these professional concerns implemented.

As Table 3 shows, most statutes provide for a broad scope of bargaining, in the main obliging the employer to bargain over terms and conditions of employment. As in the private sector, it is up to the administrative agency, and behind it the courts, to determine whether a disputed issue is indeed a term and condition of employment. Also as in the private sector, the mechanism that triggers the administrative agency's attention is a refusal-to-bargain charge, usually lodged by the union against the school board.

By the late 1970s, considerable precedent had been established *within* the states as to what issues constituted appropriate bargaining subject matter. But there was clearly no consistency *among* states. In New York, for example, the administrative agency took a rather restrictive view of bargaining scope. The New York State Public Employment Relations Board (PERB) has developed the so-called "mission doctrine,"[54] under which it is argued that certain matters central to the mission of a public enterprise need not be bargained: "Underlying this determination [is] the concept that basic decisions as to public policy should not be made in the isolation of a negotiation table, but rather should be made by those having the direct and sole responsibility

[54] *Matter of New Rochelle City School District*, 4 PERB 3060 (1971); *West Irondequoit Teachers Association* v. *Helsby*, 358 N.Y.S.2d 720 (1974); *Matter of Orange County Community College Faculty Association*, 9 PERB 3068 (1976).

therefor, and whose actions in this regard are subject to review in the electoral process." [55]

Thus the level of staffing, class size, course offerings, faculty advising responsibilities, and the union's role in granting promotion and tenure to faculty were deemed central to the school system's mission and were not mandatory subjects of negotiations. Such issues could not be brought to impasse if the employer objected, although the employer was permitted to negotiate over these issues if he so chose. The PERB also ruled, however, that the "impact" of management's decision in these areas was a mandated subject of negotiations. Thus, even though a school board had complete authority to determine how many teachers it would have on its staff, if layoffs were contemplated the union could bargain over layoff procedure to the degree it was consistent with education law.

Pennsylvania, to cite another extreme example, has taken an expansive view of bargaining scope. There the supreme court ruled in 1975 that public employers cannot refuse to negotiate on certain issues merely because those issues might impinge on basic public policies: "Thus we hold that where an item of dispute is a matter of fundamental concern to the employees' interest in wages, hours, and other terms and conditions of employment, it is not removed as a matter of subject to good faith bargaining . . . simply because it may touch upon basic policy." [56]

If there is a lesson that can be drawn from the above views, it is that variety prevails among judicial and quasi-judicial bodies in the United States. The language of the New York and Pennsylvania statutes in regard to bargaining subject matter is similar; so, too, are the structures of local governments and the systems of municipal and school finance. What is different—and one could pair New Jersey and Oregon, Nevada and Michigan, or Connecticut and Wisconsin to illustrate the different approaches administrative agencies and the courts have taken in the different states—is that in Pennsylvania primacy is given to the collective bargaining statute and the rights of unions and employees under it, while in New York the PERB and the courts attempt to balance the interest of the employees with the interests of the public at large.

A broad scope of bargaining does not necessarily result in thick and unwieldy contracts. In neither the private nor the public sector are employers obliged to concede on any union proposal. Yet there are

[55] *Matter of West Irondequoit Board of Education*, 4 PERB 3727 (1971).
[56] *Pennsylvania Labor Relations Board* v. *State College Area School District, The Board of School Directors*, 9 Pa.Comm. 229 (1974).

differences between the public and private sectors that have led some observers—employers and members of administrative agencies—to favor a more restricted subject matter. First, several matters that affect teachers are also matters of consequence for citizens, students, parents, and taxpayers. If the issue is, say, the right of a teacher to suspend a student without first receiving administrative approval to do so, that could be a matter in which members of the community would take a keen interest. Although it is certainly arguable that a disruptive child has important consequences for the teacher's conditions of work, it is also arguable that a disruptive child roaming the streets during school hours is a matter of citizen concern. Except through representation by their elected and appointed officials, citizens have no input in the discussion on such an issue. The employer, so it is maintained, ought not be put in the position of negotiating on a sensitive issue like this unless he is constantly apprised of community sentiment. The nature of the collective bargaining process makes that extremely difficult, if not impossible.

Second, there is a fear shared by many that since bargaining requires compromise and tradeoffs, there is too strong a temptation for the public employer to trade off a noneconomic policy issue in order to secure an economic concession from the union. Thus the union might be granted a role in the selection of administrators in exchange for reducing its salary demand by 5 percent. In the late hours, when impasse looms near, principle gives way to expediency, and the interest in maintaining efficiency and public responsiveness surrenders to the need to settle and go home and get some sleep.

Third, many employers favor a more restrictive scope because of the nature of the impasse-resolution procedure. As we shall see, most statutes provide for fact-finding as the final step of the impasse procedure, and even though fact-finders can only make a recommendation on the resolution of a dispute, a publicly announced recommendation favoring the union's position could conceivably lend added pressure on the employer to concede. If the employer is persuaded that the issue under dispute is a policy matter that does not belong on the bargaining table in the first place, that pressure can be particularly irksome. Fact-finders have been known to be tradeoff specialists themselves on occasion, hoping that a noneconomic policy bone thrown to the union will make a disappointing salary recommendation more palatable.

Table 4 presents the results of an analysis of teacher contracts in approximately 700 school districts in New York State for the 1975–76 school year. A sampling of contracts in districts in several other states suggests strongly that in those states that allow for comprehensive

TABLE 4
Contractual Provisions in New York State Teacher Agreements, 1975–1976

Provisions	Percentage of Agreements Containing These Provisions
Leaves:	
Sick	99.5
Personal	94.6
(Average number of personal days—3)	
Length of teachers' work day	68.6
Class size[a]	54.8
Dismissal (just cause)	31.1
Grievance procedure:	
Binding arbitration arising from contract sources	82.8
Binding arbitration arising from both contract and noncontract sources	15.5
Salary schedules:	97.0
Provisions to pay longevity increments to career teachers	74.2
Payments on a merit basis	.9
Multiple-year contracts using CPI as basis for salary adjustments	13.1
Teacher aides	26.9
Time off for local union president	31.4
Maintenance of standards	12.3
Insurance:	
Health	98.9
Dental	31.3
Life	13.6
Disability	10.9
Welfare fund administered by local union	3.9
Evaluation procedure:	
Evaluation of teacher	81.2
Access to teacher's personal folder	81.0

Sources: New York State United Teachers, Division of Research and Educational Services, *1975–76 Teacher Contract Analysis Final Report Section A-R* (Albany: Division of Research and Educational Services, 1976); and New York State School Boards Association, "Negotiations Data Book: 1975–76" (Albany: 1976 [mimeographed departmental edition]).

[a] These provisions did not set exact numerical limits to class size but rather tended to obligate the employer to "strive" to maintain a certain student-teacher ratio.

collective bargaining contracts, there is very little variation from the New York experience in the kinds of provisions most commonly negotiated.

It should also be pointed out that most contracts contain provisions dealing with compensation for extracurricular activities. Other topics covered by collective bargaining range from the cost of football tickets for faculty spouses to union use of school district duplicating equipment to the methods of collecting students' "milk money," but they appear only occasionally and are not ordinarily listed as mandated subjects of bargaining.

In sum, although it would appear that there are substantial differences among the states as to what issues constitute appropriate subject matter, there is considerable similarity in the actual scope of collective bargaining contracts. It may be that in those states that allow for broad latitude of subject matter, the employers have successfully resisted demands they believe to be intrusions into policy matters. It may also be that the unions do not feel keenly enough about many of these issues to push them to impasse.

The Resolution of Bargaining Impasses

Of all public-employee groups, teachers appear to be the most inclined to take bargaining issues to impasse and to strike. Of the 2,324 impasses brought to the New York State PERB between 1974 and 1976, for example, 1,690 (73 percent) involved school districts. Most of these involved teachers, even though teacher groups accounted for less than a third of all public-employee bargaining units in the state. In 1975, approximately 75 percent of all teacher negotiations in New York reached the impasse step.[57] As for strikes, teachers accounted for almost 60 percent of all public employee work stoppages in 1975 in the U.S., although only 38 percent of all public-employee bargaining units consisted of teachers.[58]

All comprehensive public-sector statutes contain a dispute-resolution procedure. The technical impasse date is usually tied to the date on which the school budget is acted upon. With the exception of instances of multiyear agreements, the contract termination date tends to coincide with the end of the school district's fiscal year. Thus the statutes ordinarily provide that if the parties have not reached agreement a certain number of days (30, 60, 90) before the end of the current fiscal year, they are technically at impasse. It was originally thought that unless bargaining was completed before the next year's budget was prepared, it would not be possible to project costs and assess a tax rate. As time progressed, however, budget deadlines began to be ignored, with bargaining extending well into the next fiscal and contract year. The terms of the settlement, when reached, are made retroactive and the budget adjusted internally in order to fund the additional costs, if any.

Unlike the private sector, the impasse-breaking devices under public-sector statutes tend to be mandatory. If a dispute develops, the parties are obliged to avail themselves of the administrative agency's mediation services. All agencies maintain a stable of mediators for this purpose, and a few use additional ad hoc mediators during the heavy impasse season.

---

[57] PERB News, March 1977, p. 1.
[58] 698 GERR 29 (March 7, 1977). This figure is based on the assumption that 10,000 of the 13,236 school district units are teacher units.

If the parties cannot come to agreement during the mediation stage (in New York State about half are settled during this period),[59] in most instances they are obliged to request fact-finding. Depending on the state, the fact-finder is either appointed by the agency or selected by the parties from a list submitted by the agency. In most instances when the fact-finder is appointed, the agency pays for the cost of fact-finding; when selected, the parties share the cost.

The fact-finder conducts a hearing on the issues under dispute and submits a report in which he recommends settlement terms, which both parties are free to accept or reject. Fact-finders tend not to be full-time employees of the administrative agency: the seasonal nature of disputes makes it impractical for the agency to have a full-time staff of fact-finders. Some agencies appear reluctant to mesh the conciliatory role of mediation with the quasi-judicial role of fact-finding. Because a fact-finder's recommendations may alienate one or both parties, agencies prefer that the onus of an unpopular recommendation rest with an ad hoc fact-finder and not the agency.

Although not all statutes list criteria to guide the fact-finder in making his recommendation, several standards have emerged for making recommendations on the resolution of salary disputes. These are the fiscal soundness of the employer (ability to pay), comparability with salary scales in similar jurisdictions and in the region, changes in the consumer price index, the labor market, and a catch-all criterion—the public interest. Thus a fact-finder will attempt to discover how great a burden the union's salary proposal will place on the school budget and the taxpayers, what the settlements have been in comparable districts, the degree to which teachers have suffered loss of real income during an inflationary period, and the difficulty the district has in recruiting and retaining teachers. The parties, in turn, muster as many facts as possible to support their respective proposals and advise the fact-finder what inferences ought to be drawn from these facts.

In several jurisdictions the statutes provide for voluntary arbitration of interest disputes, a procedure not usually invoked until a strike appears imminent. Although by 1977 statutes in 17 states provided for mandatory arbitration as the final step in the impasse procedure for police and fire department employees,[60] only in Iowa was it mandatory that all public employee impasses go to binding arbitration if early attempts to resolve the dispute (mediation and fact-finding) failed to resolve the dispute. Under the Iowa statute an arbitration panel is

[59] *PERB News,* March 1977, p. 1.
[60] "California Rejects; New York and Massachusetts Extend Public Safety Arbitration," *LMRS Newsletter,* 8:8 (August 1977), p. 1.

obliged to select the "final offer" of either party or the fact-finder's recommendation on each of the disputed issues.[61]

The Iowa experiment seems not to have had a "chilling" effect on bargaining. As of spring 1976, about two years after the enactment of the statute, only 24 cases—8 percent of all cases reaching impasse—had gone to the arbitration step.[62] By contrast, between July 1, 1974, and December 1, 1976, 29 percent of police and firefighter impasses in New York reached the arbitration stage.[63] Pennsylvania, Michigan, and Wisconsin had similar results under their police and fire arbitration statutes.[64]

This experiment with final-offer arbitration in teacher (and other public employee) disputes is too limited to allow for generalizations. The economic and labor relations climate could be significantly different in Iowa than it is in other states. It may also be instructive that in no other state, except Wisconsin, has the legislature seen fit to adopt such a measure covering teachers. Indeed, many public employers, and probably most legislators as well, seem to prefer the granting of the right to strike over interest arbitration. That way the decision is left in their hands to either bear the cost of the strike or suffer the cost of the concessions granted to avoid the strike. An arbitrated decision takes from the employer the authority to make this calculation and to make some estimate as to what its funding priorities ought to be. As Donald H. Wollett, former director of employee relations for the State of New York, has observed:

> State and local governments have limited options for making concessions in collective bargaining because of competing claims upon the tax dollar and limited sources of public revenue. However, ability to pay or, as it is more likely to be stated, inability to pay is in reality an assertion that present programs or contemplated additions to and improvements in these programs cannot be maintained or made if the economic demands of the employee organizations are met (unless taxes are increased). Thus the problem is not one of ability or inability to pay; it is a problem of priorities and political choices. The question is how these problems are to be solved—by

---

[61] Iowa Code Ann. § 20.22 (West Supp. 1976). A 1977 Wisconsin law, effective in 1978, provides for binding arbitration of interest disputes between local governmental units and unions representing their employees. Police and firefighters have been covered by separate legislation specifying final-offer arbitration in impasse situations.

[62] "Early Impasse Settlements Characterize Iowa Bargaining," *I PERB*, 1:1 (Spring 1976), p. 3.

[63] New York State Public Employment Relations Board, unpublished data.

[64] Stern et al., pp. 5–117.

pressures brought by collective bargaining, by imposed settlements pursuant to arbitration awards, or by the usual political forces that underlie such decisions.

And what about the myriad of nonsalary issues, such as whether residency in a city should be a condition of employment, the manning scale for firefighters, whether policemen should patrol or ride alone or in pairs, and the length of the school day? These seem to be singularly inappropriate for disposition by this sterile, apolitical process of arbitration. I am inclined to think that most legislative bodies would agree.[65]

Whether state legislatures would see fit to expand the coverage of arbitration statutes to include teachers and other categories of "nonessential" public employees was an open question in the 1970s. Nor was it at all clear whether teacher organizations would choose that option over the legal right to strike. If the strike weapon proved to be less potent than expected, however, they would no doubt pressure legislative bodies to bring them under arbitration statutes. But by that time teacher organizations may have found themselves with a Hobson's choice—not powerful enough to win concessions through the strike and not strong enough to persuade legislators that, even though abused by circumstances, their services were so important that no work stoppage would be tolerable.

A handful of states allow for the strike under certain circumstances. As of 1978 a limited right to strike was expressly allowed under statute in Alaska, Hawaii, Montana, Oregon, and Pennsylvania.[66] What is meant by the limited right to strike is that before a union can legally strike, the impasse procedure, mediation, and fact-finding must have been exhausted and the strike may not jeopardize the community's health, safety, or welfare. If a court enjoins a strike on any of these grounds and the union strikes anyway, its leaders are subject to contempt proceedings. Strikes are usually enjoined on grounds that they jeopardize the welfare of the community, although as Alex Kaschock has pointed out, judges (particularly in Pennsylvania, the most strike-ridden state in recent years) are clearly not of one mind whether the welfare of the community is threatened by a teacher strike.[67]

---

[65] Donald H. Wollett, "Arbitration: Public Employees and Governmental Conflicts," manuscript of address delivered before 50th Anniversary Dinner, American Arbitration Association, Upper New York Advisory Council (Arbitration and the Law Seminar), Syracuse, N.Y., October 6, 1976, pp. 11–12.

[66] In Minnesota, the prohibition against a strike does not apply if the employer refuses to arbitrate or to abide by the arbitration award. Under Wisconsin's new law covering local government employees, only if both parties withdraw their request for arbitration does the union have the limited right to strike. Strikes are not permitted in Michigan, but the courts rarely enjoin them.

[67] Kaschock, pp. 47–90 *passim*.

Not all states prohibiting the strike provide specific penalties for violation, depending instead on the courts' injunctive action as both deterrent and penalty. New York, however, has specified the penalties: striking teachers lose two days' pay for each day out on strike and are subject to loss of tenure rights. The union, in turn, can lose checkoff rights for an indefinite period and is subject to a fine under the judicial code.[68] In Delaware, a striking union loses the right of exclusive representation for two years and dues-deduction privileges for one year.[69] In neither instance have penalties served as a complete deterrent to strikes. In 1975, Delaware teachers led the nation in percentage of working time lost due to strikes (2.6 percent); New York was fifth with 1 percent. Comparable figures for industry that year were 0.16 percent, and for teachers generally, 0.66 percent.[70]

Whether there would have been substantially more strikes and more loss of working time without these deterrents, it is not possible to say. Clearly the penalties do not deter all strikes, but then neither do penalties for other types of behavior society believes to be inappropriate always deter those bent on flouting social mores. Although there is no constitutional prohibition against a state's granting teachers and other public employees the right to strike, neither is there any constitutional protection of that right. In 1968, the New York Court of Appeals ruled in *DeLury* that the equal protection clause of the Fourteenth Amendment to the federal Constitution did not grant to any individual an absolute right to strike.[71] DeLury, the president of the New York sanitation union, had argued that New York's prohibition against public-employee strikes was unconstitutional on the grounds that it denied to public employees a right granted to similarly situated employees in the private sector. The court, however, saw substantial differences between the two sectors. "The orderly functioning of our democratic form of representative government . . . require[s] the regulation of strikes by public employees whereas there is no similar countervailing reason for a prohibition of strikes in the private sector." [72] For whatever significance it might have, the U.S. Supreme Court refused to hear an appeal from the New York court's decision for want of a properly presented federal question.[73]

---

[68] N.Y. Civil Service Law § 210, subd. 2, pars. (f) and (g) and subd. 3, par. (f).
[69] Del. Code, tit. 14, § 4011.
[70] See Table 5. These figures are based on the assumption that no days lost because of strikes were "made up" at a later time, during Christmas and spring vacations, or in the summer. There are no data on "make-up" days.
[71] *City of New York* v. *DeLury*, 295 N.Y.S.2d 901 (1968).
[72] 295 N.Y.S.2d 901, at 905.
[73] *DeLury* v. *City of New York*, 394 U.S. 455, 22 L.Ed.2d 414, 89 S.Ct. 1223 (1969).

Before the middle 1960s there were relatively few teacher strikes, or public-employee strikes of any kind, for the matter. Between 1967 and 1974, however, there was an average of approximately 100 teacher strikes each year. During the academic year 1974–75, the number increased to 235.[74] Table 5 shows the ten states in which most of the strike action has taken place. It is interesting that in most of these states the strike is illegal; in Illinois and Ohio there is no collective bargaining legislation. The strike figures do not distinguish between economic and representation work stoppages, but one can assume that the overwhelming majority are strikes over new contracts.

TABLE 5

1974–1975 School-Year Strike Activity, Ten Most Active States

Number of Work Stoppages		Number of Teachers Involved		Number of Days Idle	
Pennsylvania	55	New York	61,336	New York	387,471
Illinois	28	Illinois	34,880	Illinois	345,652
Delaware	25	Pennsylvania	13,997	Pennsylvania	168,444
New York	19	Massachusetts	7,640	Wisconsin	86,165
Ohio	18	Wisconsin	7,568	Massachusetts	61,346
New Jersey	15	Ohio	6,075	Rhode Island	46,937
Rhode Island	13	Michigan	5,783	Delaware	37,653
Michigan	13	Delaware	4,782	Michigan	32,624
California	9	Rhode Island	4,426	California	31,034
Connecticut	7	Florida	4,182	Ohio	30,382
U.S. Total	235	U.S. Total	173,491	U.S. Total	1,343,219

Sources: U.S. Bureau of the Census, Labor-Management Relations in State and Local Governments: 1975, State and Local Government Special Series No. 81 (Washington: U.S. Government Printing Office, 1977), pp. 111–38. It is difficult to compile figures on percentage of working time lost due to strikes as in many instances days on which teachers strike are made up later in the term. However, if no days were made up, American teachers would have lost .2 percent of their working time due to strikes. This compares with 1.6 percent of working time lost in the U.S. public sector. "Current Labor Statistics: Labor-Management Data, Table 37, Work Stoppages, 1946 to date," Monthly Labor Review 100 (April 1977), p. 127.

Although teacher strikes or the threat thereof have become commonplace in several jurisdictions, particularly in the large cities,[75] the public seems not to have come around to the notion that the strike is the most appropriate way of settling differences between school boards and teacher groups. A 1977 opinion poll of New York State residents, for example, found 62 percent opposed to granting the strike right to teachers, approximately the same percentage that opposed giving that right to firefighters.[76]

[74] NEA, NEA Research Memo 1970-19, NEA Research Memo 1971-28, NEA Research Memo 1972-18, NEA Research Memo 1974-3 (average figures compiled from above); Census, Labor-Management Relations in State and Local Government, p. 111.

[75] Strikes, some of them long and bitter, have occurred in such cities as New York City, Detroit, Chicago, St. Louis, Philadelphia, Pittsburgh, and Buffalo.

[76] Ithaca (N.Y.) Journal, February 14, 1977, p. 12.

Those opposed to granting the right to strike to teachers base their arguments on the following points:

1. Teachers (and other public employees) are only one of several groups who have claims on government expenditures. Other groups may want longer library hours, more and better playgrounds, better sanitation facilities, or lower taxes. But for the most part these groups cannot put the same pressure on elected officials as can a union with the power to call a strike.

2. The parallel with the private sector is not entirely appropriate. Schools and most other governmental services tend to be natural monopolies. Citizens cannot readily find alternative means of educating their children, for example, if the schools are shut down. In most instances in private-sector strikes, however, alternative commodities are usually available to consumers. Moreover, the burden of the strike tends to fall unevenly. The ultimate cost-bearers of a teachers' strike are children and, although middle-class children could probably survive several days without instruction with little loss to their intellectual growth, this is probably not the case with underprivileged children.

3. A teachers' strike presents a dilemma. If lost time is not made up, children receive fewer days of instruction. The possible relationship between days in school and student performance was discussed earlier in this chapter. If days lost due to the strike are made up, and teachers are paid for these days taught, as they usually are, then the strikers face no financial risk. Income would only be delayed, not lost. Thus, the risk of financial loss does not always serve as a deterrent to strike action by teachers.

Although the public might oppose teacher strikes by a two-to-one majority, the percentage of teachers opposing the strike as the ultimate impasse-breaker, according to an NEA survey, fell from 34 percent in 1967 to 14 percent in 1976.[77] Teacher groups argue that without the right to strike there can be no meaningful collective bargaining. If, after all the impasse procedures have been exhausted, the school board can impose a settlement anyway, it has little incentive to make concessions. There can be no real bargaining unless there is a rough balance of power, and if no meaningful strike threat can be launched, virtually all the power rests with the school board. Bargaining assumes that there will be a certain amount of compromise and the process will give to the employees somewhat more muscle than they had previously enjoyed. There can be no compromise and little exercise of muscle unless employees are able to collectively withdraw their services, thereby

[77] NEA, "National Opinion Poll," p. 6.

placing a cost on the employer for refusing to agree. Collective bargaining without the right to strike, it is alleged, is not bargaining at all.

As for the effect of time lost because of strikes on student achievement, teacher groups argue that such an effect has not been clearly demonstrated. Moreover, the effect on student learning is rarely mentioned when the schools are closed for reasons that suit the community —holidays and long vacations.

Whatever the merits of the arguments on both sides as to whether the strike should be allowed, whether disputes should be arbitrated, or whether neither is appropriate, the fact remains that teachers are most inclined of all public employee groups to take issues to impasse. Put another way, boards of education are less inclined than other public employers to settle contracts short of using the impasse procedures and are more willing to take strikes. Why this should be so is a puzzle. Perhaps it is because teachers, who as a group possess considerable professional expertise, are less inclined to accept management prerogatives on professional matters. Or perhaps it is because school management is more sensitive to community sentiment on disputed issues than are most public managers and therefore less willing to make concessions. Often the disputed issues touch upon educational policy, and it is frequently more difficult to find compromise solutions on policy matters than on questions of salary and fringe benefits, issues that seem to be of more central concern to other groups of public employees.

The Bargaining Process

The bargaining rituals employed by unions and employers in public education are similar to those used in industry. When one gets beyond the mere procedural aspects of bargaining, however, differences emerge. In most jurisdictions, for example, there is no right to strike and, although there have been a large number of teacher strikes, in most instances the strike prohibition is probably taken seriously. In general, then, the union cannot inflict the cost of a strike on the employer, and the employer is aware of that fact.

Even in those jurisdictions where the strike is permitted, or where the union can launch a meaningful strike threat without its legality, both unions and employers tend to calculate the costs and benefits of taking or calling a strike differently than do unions and employers in the private sector. As for costs to the union, working time lost because of the strike is often later recaptured through makeup days. Thus striking teachers do not always suffer loss of yearly income.

Another strike deterrent that is somewhat effective in the private sector—a fear of job loss because the struck company may lose customers to other suppliers—is almost completely absent in the public schools. For all practical purposes public schools constitute monopolies (as do some private employers, of course); thus children will come trooping back when the strike is over, taxpayers will continue to pay their taxes, and approximately the same number of teachers will be employed.

One strike deterrent that is less apparent in industry than in the public schools is that striking teachers are rarely insulated from public pressures. In most industrial settings the strike's immediate cost-bearers are company owners and officials or consumers in areas remote from the struck plant. Local merchants and others who rely on worker income will, of course, suffer from a long strike, but most private-sector strikes are short-lived, the average being 6.2 days.[78] A striking teacher, on the other hand, may live next door to an immediate cost-bearer, and since most Americans believe a teacher strike to be inappropriate in the first place, public pressure (and resentment) is sometimes intense.

A school board faced with a strike threat will also make calculations somewhat different from those of its private-sector counterpart. Like the teachers' union, it knows that it has a captured market and the demand for the product is relatively inelastic. Thus a strike does not jeopardize the long-term interests of the enterprise. Still, most school boards seem reluctant to take strikes, partly because such strikes are viewed as harmful to children, due not only to time lost but also to the antagonism the strike engenders between striking and nonstriking teachers.

The harm caused by the strike must, of course, be weighed against the harm caused by a settlement taxpayers regard as too rich, or by contractual provisions the board regards as inimical to educational quality. In an age when it appears that one-half of American communities are trying desperately to keep their industries from relocating while the other half are trying just as hard to woo them away, school tax rates become an important economic concern. For the same reason, most school boards recognize that it is also important that their districts not gain the reputation of being strike-prone.

More recently, school boards have begun to weigh the potential cost of the strike against the cost of keeping in the contract certain provisions they believe to be inappropriate incursions into management prerogatives. Beginning in about the middle 1970s many boards began to bargain hard to remove from the contract such items as maintenance

---

[78] "Current Labor Statistics: Labor Management Data, Table 37, Work Stoppages 1946 to Date," *Monthly Labor Review*, 100:4 (April 1977), p. 127.

of standards, just cause in dismissal cases, and provisions that forbade the employer from making staff cuts. This attempt to recapture rights given away in an earlier period when boards were less knowledgeable about the relationship between bargaining and effective management distressed many teacher groups, which were not accustomed to surrendering hard-won gains.

Of course, not all or even most strikes are carefully calculated risks. Strikes also occur because teachers believe legitimate aspirations have been frustrated, because of union rivalry, because board members see their political careers enhanced by taking a hard stand against the teachers, or because of ineptitude on one or both sides. Collective bargaining itself is not an entirely rational process; it should come as no surprise that the process is sometimes used in a less than rational manner.

The parties must also contend with fiscal restraints that are quite different from those prevailing in most industrial collective bargaining arrangements. Although the demands for educational services may be inelastic, the resources needed to meet that demand are frequently limited. In several states there are constitutional or statutory limits on the local tax rate or limits on the allowable tax increase over the previous year. In those districts where school budgets are voted upon, citizens can refuse to provide the necessary wherewithal to fund the contract settlement. As we have seen, there appears to be a growing reluctance on the part of the voting public to increase their tax burden. Thus, unlike most monopoly product markets, salary improvements cannot always be passed on to consumers in the form of price increases. These fiscal restraints are a lingering presence in many teacher negotiations and can bear heavily on the bargaining outcome, particularly with respect to salaries and other economic benefits.

Both teacher union and employer must also contend with the fact that theirs is a labor-intensive industry. Excessive salary demands cannot force the employer to adopt technological savings—the technological innovations adopted in education in recent years have not led to replacement of classroom teachers. About the only method of keeping unit costs relatively stable, if one can use so crass a term to describe investments in students, is to increase the student-teacher ratio. In several large city districts faced with fiscal crises, the tradeoffs were made between modest salary adjustments and rather severe reductions in staff. In New York City, for example, in order to pay previously negotiated salary increments and cost-of-living bonuses, 10,037 teachers, both regular teachers and permanent substitutes, were laid off during the 1974–75 school year,[79] causing average class size from kindergarten through junior high school to increase from 31.3 to 34.7.[80] Not all teacher organizations, of course, are willing to make that tradeoff.

There have no doubt been several instances where unions have forgone any salary adjustment in order to preserve jobs. Yet in purely economic terms there appears to be less incentive for a teacher (or any public employee) union to accept a "no increase" settlement than for a union in the industrial sector dealing with a firm in financial difficulties to do so. There the choice can be between no increase and jobs for all workers, or taking an insistence on a wage increase to impasse and facing the possibility of no jobs for anyone. If a union is concerned that the employer is indeed in financial straits and is interested in keeping the company solvent and competitive, it will probably opt for the former.[81] In the public sector, however, it is rare for that choice to be faced. There is little danger that state, city, or school district, no matter how difficult its financial problems might be, will go out of business. And although services may decline as a consequence of mass layoffs, the majority of employees, particularly those with seniority, are secure in their jobs. Under these circumstances it is not surprising that the majority of union members should pressure the union leadership to demand the increase, irrespective of the layoffs the implementation of that demand would likely cause. The surprise is that so many teacher groups in financially troubled districts have not followed that line.

Another difference between bargaining in the schools and in most industries is the amount of public interest teacher bargaining generates. The schools are the public's business, and it seems to follow that so, too, is the employment arrangement negotiated by the school board and the union. All states with collective bargaining statutes accommodate to this interest by providing that fact-finding reports be made public. Some, such as Florida, require that collective bargaining sessions be held in public.[82] The California statute mandates that all initial union and school board proposals be presented at a public meeting and

---

[79] New York State United Teachers, Division of Research and Educational Services, "New York City Educational and Physical Crisis, Table 19, New York City School District Personnel Cuts 1974–75," brief for New York State Legislature (New York: New York State United Teachers, 1975), p. 29. In addition to teachers, other categories of employees represented by the United Federation of Teachers faced cutbacks. Thus 39 percent of the guidance counselors, 16 percent of secretaries, 6 percent of school psychologists, 4 percent of laboratory specialists, and 62 percent of paraprofessionals were eliminated.

[80] New York City Board of Education, p. 25. The increase in class size was not evenly distributed: kindergarten classes increased from 43.5 to 49.1 students, a 13 percent increase; elementary classes from 28.3 to 31.4, an 11 percent increase; and junior high classes from 21.7 to 23.5, an 8 percent increase.

[81] See, for example, Henle, pp. 956–68.

[82] West's F.S.A. § 447.605.

that negotiations shall not commence on any proposal until the public has had an opportunity to inform itself on the issues and make its views known to the parties.[83] It has also been advocated by some labor relations specialists and public officials that the contract not be implemented until it has been approved in a public referendum.[84]

It is not known whether these efforts to involve the public, or at least to keep it informed, have had the desired effect. "Bargaining in the sunshine," for example, could cause both union and employer to make less extreme proposals since the public might be outraged at, say, a union demand for a 25 percent increase and an employer demand for a wage cut. Thus some of the ritualistic and time-wasting maneuvering associated with the initial stages of bargaining might be eliminated. Yet successful bargaining involves compromise, and it does not seem likely that either party can easily reduce its demands or engage in the inevitable tradeoffs when their constituents are looking over their shoulders. Thus, although few union and board negotiators would admit it publicly, it is not unusual for chief spokesmen bargaining in the sunshine to meet privately to make their deals and perhaps prepare a script that each will follow at the next public meeting.

It might not be possible to mesh completely traditional collective bargaining with the public's right to be informed about the issues. Collective bargaining has for good reason been a semiprivate affair. Statutory mandates designed to open up the process to public scrutiny have a certain appealing gloss about them, but it is doubtful if the intent of such legislation can be realized. If there is concern about the ability of elected and appointed officials to represent the public's interest at the bargaining table, the remedy—unsatisfactory as that remedy might appear to most citizens—probably lies in a more careful selection of the public's representatives.

In sum, the process of bargaining in the schools is, at a superficial level at least, similar to that used in the private sector. Whatever differences there might be can probably be attributed more to lack of knowledge and experience on the part of the negotiators than to the nature of the industry. The environment in which bargaining takes place, however, differs from perhaps most private-sector collective bargaining arrangements in several respects, probably causing school negotiators to make somewhat different calculations than do private-sector negotiators. What is common in both sectors is disappointment about outcomes and as heavy a reliance on intuition and guesswork as there is on facts and a carefully conceived strategy.

[83] 32 Cal. Code § 3547 (1977 Pocket Part).
[84] See, for example, Sam Zagoria, "Referendum Use in Labor Impasses Proposed," LMRS Newsletter, 4:9 (September 1977), p. 2.

Bargaining Outcomes

Studies that have tried to determine the effect of collective bargaining on salaries and other conditions of employment suggest that bargaining has resulted in modest gains for teachers, from approximately 1 to 5 percent in the overall, with the most significant gains being realized by those with several years' experience and large numbers of graduate credits.[85]

The finding that the greatest salary gains go to experienced teachers can be explained in at least two ways. First, many salary schedules provide for a percentage ratio between the entry-level salary and all other positions on the schedule. Thus an increase of, say, $500 at the entry level could result in as much as a $700 or $800 increase for teachers with an M.A. and a dozen years' experience. Second, teacher bargaining teams tend to consist of teachers who have both experience and significant numbers of graduate credits. Since at the time of negotiations the union does not represent potential hires, it is not surprising that salary demands should reflect the interest of "career" teachers. Moreover, school boards and school administrators seem less interested in the distribution of salary gains and the effect that distribution might have on teacher and student performance than they are in the increase in the total wage bill and the possible effect that increase might have on internal resource allocations and the tax rate.

Because total compensation rates (salaries plus fringe benefits) are more difficult to ascertain, researchers have tended not to make comparisons among them. Although it is probable that districts with high salaries also provide the most generous benefits, and vice versa, it is possible that the low salaries found in some districts reflect tradeoffs for other benefits—greater employer contributions to the health plan, longer sick-leave benefits, dental insurance, or a more liberal leave policy. Thus it is possible for salary schedules in two districts to be quite dissimilar and yet for the total wage bills (salary plus fringe benefits) to be identical. It may be that this sort of horse-trading between salary adjustments and improved fringe benefits is much easier to achieve in organized than in unorganized districts and that this is one of the most significant outcomes of bargaining.

It also seems likely that as the teacher population becomes older, a greater percentage of the compensation package will go into health and welfare plans and proportionately less into salary adjustments.

[85] The author is indebted to Professor Robert Smith, Cornell University, for explaining to him some of the more creative methodological approaches used by these researchers. The major studies consulted that deal with the impact of bargaining on teachers' salaries are as follows: Gustman and Segal; Thornton; Baird and Landon; Lipsky and Drotning; and Frey.

Indeed, that process may already have begun, thus causing an understatement of the impact of unions and collective bargaining when only the rates of salary changes are examined. There have been no recent studies of the extent and cost of fringe benefits, either in the organized or unorganized sector, but it is clear that teacher contracts contain a significant number of economic benefits. It does not seem likely that teachers would enjoy such benefits as noncontributory health and hospitalization plans, dental plans, welfare plans, and sick-leave banks[86] had there been no collective bargaining. Nor does it seem likely that teachers would have such noneconomic benefits as a grievance procedure (usually ending in binding arbitration), or fair dismissal procedures, or numerical limits on class size, or an influence over the content of the school calendar if the employee organization relied completely on the good will of school management to grant them.

It is also possible that the advent of collective bargaining has enabled teachers to improve their conditions of work indirectly. As was mentioned earlier, some working conditions are regulated by statute, particularly minimum job-security rights for tenured and probationary teachers, pensions, and minimum sick-leave benefits. Bargaining seems to have brought more teachers into the unions and dues have increased many-fold. A good portion of these dues have gone to the state NEA or AFT bodies, thus allowing for more vigorous lobbying activity and greater financial support to favored candidates for state office than was possible before bargaining. Whether substantial amounts of these additional funds have been used for political purposes is not known. Nor is it known whether efforts to elect friendly candidates to the legislature and improve working conditions through legislative changes have met with much success.

Still, to the degree bargaining outcomes mean changes in employment conditions through some form of concerted activity, one must consider attempts to influence legislation dealing with working conditions as well as what might emerge from a local collective bargaining agreement. Attempts to improve working conditions through lobbying, perhaps the most important activity of state teacher organizations in the prebargaining era, may now be somewhat less important in those jurisdictions where bargaining is allowed. That may be because teacher organizations have decided to concentrate their considerable resources at the local level where bargaining outcomes might be more directly appreciated, if not necessarily easier to attain. If that well becomes

---

[86] This is a scheme whereby a teacher who has exhausted sick-leave benefits may draw upon the unused sick days accumulated by all members of the bargaining unit. The teacher mortgages his or her sick-leave time when returning to health and to work.

dry, or if the bargaining proposals teachers most prize cannot be granted at that level, one can assume that the attention of teacher organizations will shift back to the state capitals.

Contract Administration

Nearly all teacher collective bargaining agreements contain grievance procedures. Similar in most instances to procedures found in the industrial sector, they are multistep and provide for some form of third-party adjudication as the capstone. In some of the earlier agreements it was not uncommon to find a rather broad definition of a grievance: "a grievance is a claim by any teacher or group of teachers in the negotiating unit based upon any event or conditions affecting their welfare and/or terms and conditions of employment." [87] Other early definitions included alleged violations of "regulations, administrative orders or rules of the Board of Education." [88]

More recently there has been a tightening of the grievance definition, confining its application to claimed violations or misinterpretations of the terms of the contract. This may have occurred because employers insisted at the bargaining table that the definitions be tighter, but it may also be that the unions tired of being swamped by grievances that were based on *any* event a teacher believed affected his or her welfare.

Although earlier agreements provided for advisory rather than binding arbitration, most school boards now agree to binding grievance arbitration. School boards were less reluctant to accept a binding decision if the grievance originally emerged from an alleged violation of a contract rather than from a claim that the board had violated any of its own unilaterally drawn rules and regulations. As grievance definitions became tighter, the authority of the arbitrator seemed to broaden.

A matter that time and experience have not resolved is the conflict that can occur when remedies are provided under both the grievance procedure and the statute. This conflict is most pronounced in the area of "just cause" for teacher discipline and dismissal. Many contracts contain provisions that no teacher may be disciplined or dismissed without just cause. At the same time, the education laws in several states grant a modicum of procedural-due-process protection for probationary teachers and both procedural and substantive due process for tenured teachers. It is frequently unclear in these circumstances whether the contract supersedes the statute, or vice versa. Can an aggrieved teacher

[87] *Agreement between the Downsville Central School Board of Education and the Downsville Teachers' Association,* July 1, 1973, to June 30, 1974, p. 15.

[88] *Agreement between the Bay Shore Classroom Teachers Association and Union Free School District Number One Bay Shore Public Schools,* July 1, 1970, to June 30, 1973, p. 20.

seek relief in one forum and then, if he or she is not satisfied with the result, try the other? Or can a teacher try both simultaneously? Nor has it been decided in all jurisdictions whether a union can waive an individual teacher's statutory rights by agreeing with the employer that in all cases of discipline and discharge the contractual grievance procedure will be the only source of remedy. Only gradually, and sometimes with contradictory findings, have state courts begun to separate those matters which are more appropriately handled under the collective bargaining contract from those more properly resolved in the courts.[89]

There is no detailed information available on the types of issues most commonly brought to arbitration. The NEA collects data on those arbitrations decided in its locals, but the issues may fall under two or more categories, discipline and maintenance of standards, for example, therefore making classification difficult. Be that as it may, there are a number of issues that crop up regularly at arbitration hearings. The issues cited most frequently in an informal NEA survey are discipline, salary adjustment, alleged violation of leave policy, workload and work assignment, transfer, and reduction in force.

Although the issues grieved are similar to those appearing in the industrial sector, the remedies sought frequently differ. For example, since disciplinary layoffs and fines are rare in public education, the penalty in a discipline case might be a letter of reprimand placed in the grievant's personnel folder, while the remedy sought is the removal of that letter.

For whatever reason, of all public-employee groups, teacher organizations appear to be most ready to take grievances to arbitration. Of the 1,407 public-sector grievance arbitrations handled by the American Arbitration Association (AAA) and PERB in New York State in 1976, 957 (69 percent) involved teachers,[90] although teachers accounted for less than 25 percent of all public employees in the state. Although the evidence is sketchy, it appears that similar ratios exist in other states with public-sector collective bargaining statutes.

The Continuing Issues

Probably most Americans who have dealings with the public schools

---

[89] For examples of the different ways state courts have dealt with the conflict between statutory and contractual protections, see: *Matter of Cohoes City School District,* 9 PERB 7529 (1975), and *Cohoes City School District* v. *Cohoes Teachers Association,* 40 N.Y.2d 774, 390 N.Y.S.2d 53 (1976); *Kaleva-Norman-Dickson School District No. 6, Counties of Manistee Lake and Mason, Michigan* v. *Kaleva-Norman-Dickson School Teachers' Association et al.,* 227 N.W.2d 500, 89 LRRM 2078 (Mich. Sup. Ct. 1975); *Livermore Valley Joint Unified School District of Alameda County and Costra Costa County* v. *Abraham Feinberg,* 112 Cal. Rptr. 923 (Cal Ct. App. 1974).

[90] American Arbitration Association, unpublished data; New York State Public Employment Relations Board, unpublished data.

—parents, taxpayers, students—are largely indifferent to the employment arrangements existing between teachers and school boards. Their main concerns are that there be an effective educational program, that there not be too great a school tax burden, and that school policy-makers be responsive to the interests and wishes of the public. In most instances it takes a labor dispute or the threat thereof before the public begins to suspect that there might be any connection between the goals it pursues and the objectives sought by teacher organizations. When that suspicion does arise, many citizens see the connection to be a negative one, believing that larger social goals are sacrificed when the union's goals are realized.[91]

The connection between bargaining and the quality of education is not easy to make, however. It is possible that bargaining has had very little effect on education quality, one way or the other. When Albert Shanker, president of the AFT, was asked in 1977 what evidence there was that collective bargaining had improved the quality of education, he replied that the question was not entirely relevant:

> The evidence is very mixed. It's possible in the bargaining process to negotiate things that are good for children, and it's possible to negotiate things that are bad for children. The chances are that most things that are negotiated don't have much to do with children at all. They have to do with whether teachers are going to feel happy about their jobs and whether they're going to have a better standard of living.
>
> The justification for collective bargaining in the auto industry is not that there is a better car. It is that the auto worker ought to have a decent standard of living. It's part of our democratic values. . . . That's the reason for it, not that it makes education any better.[92]

It is arguable, of course, that contract provisions that subtract from the time teachers spend with students—such as shorter school days and additional days off for personal reasons—can have a negative effect on student achievement. But it is also possible that this negative effect is countered by provisions that mandate smaller classes or require that additional educational equipment be supplied.

Clearly, bargaining has not had an unqualifiably wholesome effect on the educational enterprise. But few have suggested that it would. We have teacher bargaining in those states allowing for it because in the view of these state legislatures there seemed to be no compelling

---

[91] For a discussion of the possible negative influence bargaining may be having on the quality of public education, see Summers, *Collective Bargaining and Public Benefit Conferral.*

[92] *Chicago Tribune,* March 7, 1977, p. 4.

reason why a right enjoyed by private employees should not be shared with employees in the public sector. Put in another, perhaps more realistic, way, those who favored bargaining had more influence on legislators than did those who opposed it. The question of whether bargaining might have consequences for the quality of public education, a possibly more important legislative responsibility, may not have crossed anyone's mind.

As for the consequences bargaining may be having for efficiency, one suspects that the influence has been substantial, largely in the fringe benefit areas and to a lesser extent in salary adjustments. Probably the greatest effect bargaining has had on efficiency is that it seems to have frustrated attempts to develop more rational personnel policies. The spate of educational production-function studies that appeared in the late 1960s and early 1970s[93] suggest that scarce educational resources, particularly salary dollars, could be deployed in a much more productive manner. According to these studies, there is little relation between students' achievements and the experience level or degree status of their teachers. Indeed, there may be a negative correlation between student achievement and the age of teachers,[94] although salary schedules tend to provide substantial rewards for seniority. There is little hope that school districts will modify personnel and compensation schemes to accommodate to these findings, however, since the interests of the union, the dynamics of collective bargaining, and an insufficient will on the part of employers to change the system all tend to support the status quo.

Presumably one of the primary purposes of bargaining is to get the employer to change his mind, to do things differently than he would have done without bargaining. Since the union appears to have greater influence over how resources shall be allocated than does the public generally, and since public-sector unions sometimes have the power to elect their own "bosses," the public's influence over the conduct of the educational enterprise tends to be blunted. Thus, in some circumstances there might be a disincentive on the part of the employers to engage in vigorous and arm's-length bargaining. Commenting on the alleged "waste, inefficiency, and corruption" in the New York City schools, *The New York Times* opined: "The blame for these conditions lies in the chronic coziness between the Board of Education and the unions, often preserved with clandestine encouragement from City Hall."[95]

A similar concern brought about in 1974 the formation of a "parents'

[93] For a summary of these findings, see Heim and Perl, pp. 7–31. See also Summers and Wolfe, pp. 11–21.
[94] Firman, pp. 17–18.
[95] *The New York Times*, July 16, 1977, p. 20.

union" in Philadelphia, its main objective being to set aside certain provisions of the teacher contract on the grounds that the school board had colluded with the union to illegally transfer control over many educational policy matters from the board to the union, thus "causing immediate and direct injury" to the students. Among the provisions that the parties sought to set aside were those that limited the right of the school administration to transfer teachers, "instant tenure" for probationary teachers, and a maintenance-of-standards provision "which has frozen educational policy and practice." [96]

Parents in Rochester, New York, were similarly disturbed by contractual provisions that in their view had a deleterious effect on education quality. In 1976 they won the right to place a parent representative on the school board's bargaining team, presumably working on the theory that a parent representative, being less inclined than school administrators to make concessions that might reduce quality, would keep other team members honest.

In addition, there is the provision in the California statute that requires a public airing of union and employer proposals. Whether all these developments are illustrative of a more widespread concern about the effect bargaining may be having on educational quality is not known. It is more than likely, however, that a growing number of parents of school-age children have a less than casual interest in its possible effect.

It is also questionable whether the provisions negotiated under collective bargaining have indeed made teachers feel "happy about their jobs." As Table 6 demonstrates, there was a sharp decrease between 1966 and 1976 in the percentage of teachers, organized and unorganized, who were satisfied that they had entered a particularly rewarding occupation. Whether enthusiasm for teaching had declined at the same pace among unionized as among nonunionized teachers is unclear, but from what one can tell from the sampling techniques used in this survey, there seems to be no significant difference. Nor are there data comparing the attitudes of teachers to other professions and occupations. Possibly teachers were subject to no more and no less of the social malaise that gripped so many Americans in the 1970s.

Whether or not it is a reflection of a larger pattern of uneasiness about occupational choice, it seems to bode ill for public education when such a large number of 30- to 39-year-old teachers, most of whom

---

[96] For a summary of litigation attendant to these charges, see Brief for Appellants, *Parents' Union for Public Schools in Philadelphia, et al.* v. *Board of Education of the City of Philadelphia, et al., and Local 3, Philadelphia Federation of Teachers, et al.* (Supreme Court of Pennsylvania, Eastern District, on appeal from the Order of February 5, 1976, of the Superior Court of Pennsylvania, October Term 1975, No. 1833).

TABLE 6

Percentage of Public School Teachers Who Responded They "Would" or
"Probably Would" Become Teachers if They "Could Go Back to
(Their) College Days and Start Over Again"

	1965–66	1975–76
Total	78%	63.6%
Men	63.3	52.3
Women	84.7	69.2
Age		
Under 30	76.7	64.3
30–39	75.7	57.6
40–49	76.7	66.1
50 or more	82.6	69.5
Elementary	84.1	71.3
Secondary	71.4	56.3
District size		
Large	74.2	61.8
Medium	79.6	63.9
Small	78.9	65.5

Sources: National Education Association, Research Division, *The American Public-School Teacher, 1965–66*, Research Report 1967-R4 (Washington: National Education Association, 1967), pp. 99–100; National Education Association, Research Division, *Status of the American Public School Teacher, 1975–76* (Washington: National Education Association, 1977), pp. 273–74.

will probably have from 25 to 35 years of service remaining, are wondering whether they are in the right profession. One suspects that the negative influence on student attitudes toward learning can be substantial.

In the public's view, the first orders of business are to make the schools more effective centers of learning and more responsive to the wishes of students and parents. There are, to be sure, important public-policy issues that need to be resolved: the bargaining status of supervisors, the conflict between bargaining subject matters and subjects determined through the political process, and the resolution of bargaining impasses. But the most important issues from a public-interest perspective are that school costs have risen at a dramatic rate, the learning curve has declined almost as dramatically, public influence in the conduct of educational affairs appears to have been blunted, and there appears to be no remedy in sight. Whether these problems would have been just as acute without collective bargaining, whether bargaining has contributed to the problems, or whether there is no connection between the quality and cost of education and collective bargaining is an issue that almost defies analysis. Many school officials do see a negative connection, however, and it seems likely that any future gains teachers will receive under collective bargaining will have to be justified on the grounds that education quality will be enhanced thereby.

550 COLLECTIVE BARGAINING

At a minimum, it will have to be shown that bargaining will not do education any harm.

List of References

Baird, Robert, and John H. Landon. "The Effects of Collective Bargaining on Public School Teachers' Salaries, Comment." *Industrial and Labor Relations Review* 25 (April 1972), pp. 410–17.

Beale, Howard K. *A History of Freedom of Teaching in American Schools.* New York: Charles Scribner's Sons, 1941.

Bhaerman, Robert D. *Several Educators' Cure for the Common Cold, Among Other Things or One Unionist's View of Staff Differentiation.* AFT QUEST Occasional Paper No. 7. Washington: American Federation of Teachers, Department of Research, n.d.

Buley, R. Carlyle. *The Old Northwest.* Indianapolis: Indiana Historical Society, 1950.

Butts, R. Freeman, and Lawrence Cremin. *A History of Education in American Culture.* New York: Henry Holt, 1953.

Chin, Edward G. H. "An Analysis and Review of School Financing Reform." *Fordham Law Review* 44 (March 1976), pp. 773–95.

College Placement Council. *CPC Salary Survey.* Bethlehem, Pa.: The Council, 1977.

———. *A Salary Survey.* Bethlehem, Pa.: The Council, June 1966.

Commission on Education Reconstruction. *Organizing the Teaching Profession.* Glencoe, Ill.: Free Press, 1955.

Day, James F. *Teacher Retirement in the United States.* North Quincy, Mass.: Christopher Publishing House, 1971.

Firman, William R. "The Relationship of Cost to Quality of Education." Albany: University of the State of New York, Education Department, 1963. Mimeographed.

Frey, Donald E. "Wage Determination in Public Schools and the Effects of Unionization." In *Labor in the Public and Nonprofit Sectors,* ed. Daniel Hammermesh. Princeton, N.J.: Princeton University Press, 1975, pp. 183–219.

Gustman, Alan L., and Martin Segal. "The Impact of Teachers' Unions." Project No. 4-0316. Hanover, N.H.: U.S. Office of Education, National Institute of Education, 1976. Mimeographed.

Harnischfeger, Annegret, and David E. Wiley. *Achievement Test Score Decline: Do We Need to Worry?* St. Louis: CEMREL, Inc., 1976.

Health Insurance Institute. *Source Book of Health Insurance Data, 1976–77.* New York: The Institute, 1976.

Heim, John, and Lewis Perl. *The Educational Production Function: Implications for Educational Manpower Policy.* IPE Monograph No. 4. Ithaca: Institute of Public Employment, New York State School of Industrial and Labor Relations, Cornell University, 1974.

Henle, Peter. "Reverse Collective Bargaining? A Look at Some Union Concession Situations." *Industrial and Labor Relations Review* 26 (April 1973), pp. 956–68.

Hodge, Robert E., Paul M. Siegal, and Peter H. Rossi. "Occupational Prestige in the United States. *American Journal of Sociology* 70 (November 1964).

Kaschock, Alex A. "The Role of the Local Courts under Pennsylvania's Public Employee Relations Act: October 1970 to January 1972." M.S. thesis, New York State School of Industrial and Labor Relations, Cornell University, 1977.

Koerner, James D. *The Miseducation of American Teachers.* Boston: Houghton Mifflin Co., 1963.

Lipsky, David B., and John E. Drotning. "The Influence of Collective Bargaining on Teachers' Salaries in New York State." *Industrial and Labor Relations Review* 27 (October 1973), pp. 18–35.

National Education Association. *Address and Proceedings of the Ninety-eighth Meeting Held in Los Angeles, California, June 26–July 1, 1960.* Washington: The Association, 1960.

———. "National Opinion Poll: 1960–1976 Annual Survey." Washington: The Association, 1977. Mimeographed.

————. *NEA Handbook: 1976–77.* Washington: The Association, 1976.
National Education Association, Association of Classroom Teachers. *Classroom Teachers Speak Out on Differentiated Teaching Assignments.* Washington: The Association, 1969.
National Education Association, Research Department. "Research Information for UNISERV Units, Special Memo A-35: Salary Schedules 1975–76." Washington: The Association, 1976. Mimeographed.
————. *Trends in Teacher Tenure through Legislation and Court Decision.* Washington: The Association, 1957.
Newby, Kenneth A. *Collective Bargaining—Practices and Attitudes of School Management.* National School Board Association, Research Rep. 1977-2. Washington: National School Board Association, 1977.
New York City Board of Education. "The Impact of the 1975–77 UFT-Board of Education Contract on Class Size, Maximum Pupil/Teacher Ratios, and the 1975–76 Allocation Formula." Policy Paper No. 5. New York: The Board, September 19, 1975.
New York State School of Industrial and Labor Relations, Institute of Public Employment. "Achieving Flexible Pay Schemes in the Public Schools in the Context of Collective Bargaining: A Conversation." Ithaca: New York State School, 1973.
Robbins, Rainard B. *Pension Planning in the United States,* ed. William C. Greenough. New York: Teachers Insurance and Annuity Association of America, 1972.
Scott, Cecil Winfield. *Indefinite Teacher Tenure: A Critical Study of the Historical, Legal, Operative, and Comparative Aspects.* New York: Teachers College, Columbia University, 1934.
Shapiro, Frieda S. *Teacher Tenure and Contracts.* National Education Association Research Rep. 1972-R11. Washington: National Education Association, 1972.
Stern, James L., Charles M. Rehmus, J. Joseph Loewenberg, Hirschel Kasper, and Barbara D. Dennis. *Final-Offer Arbitration.* Lexington, Mass.: D. C. Heath and Co., 1975.
Summers, Anita S., and Barbara L. Wolfe. "Which School Resources Help Learning? Efficiency and Equity in Philadelphia Public Schools." *Federal Reserve Bank of Philadelphia Business Review* (February 1975), pp. 11–21.
Summers, Robert S. *Collective Bargaining and Public Benefit Conferral: A Jurisprudential Critique.* IPE Monograph No. 7. Ithaca: Institute of Public Employment, New York State School of Industrial and Labor Relations, Cornell University, 1974.
Thornton, Robert J. "The Effects of Collective Negotiations on Teachers' Salaries." *Quarterly Review of Economics and Business* 11 (Winter 1971), pp. 37–46.
U.S. Bureau of the Census. *Historical Statistics of Education in American Culture.* Bicentennial ed., Part 2. Washington: U.S. Government Printing Office, 1975.
————. *Labor-Management Relations in State and Local Government: 1975.* State and Local Government Special Studies No. 81. Washington: U.S. Government Printing Office, 1977.
U.S. Department of Commerce. *Statistical Abstract of the United States, 1930.* Washington: U.S. Government Printing Office, 1930.
U.S. Department of Commerce, Bureau of Economic Analysis. *The National Income and Product Accounts of the United States: 1929–1974.* Washington: U.S. Government Printing Office, 1976.
U.S. Department of Health, Education, and Welfare, National Center for Education Statistics. *Bond Sales for Public School Purposes: 1974–75.* Washington: U.S. Government Printing Office, 1976.
————. *The Condition of Education: A Statistical Report on the Condition of Education in the United States together with a Description of the Activities of the National Center for Education Statistics.* Washington: U.S. Government Printing Office, 1976.
————. *Digest of Education Statistics: 1976.* Washington: U.S. Government Printing Office, 1977.
————. *Statistics of State School Systems, 1973–74.* Washington: U.S. Government Printing Office, 1976.
University of the State of New York, State Education Department. *The Regents: 1978 Progress Report Bulletin.* Albany: The University, 1977.

Wesley, Edgar. *The NEA: The First Hundred Years.* New York: Harper & Bros., 1957.
Ziegler, L. Harmon, M. Kent Jennings, and G. Wayne Peak. *Governing American Schools: Political Interaction in Local School Districts.* North Scituate, Mass.: Duxbury Press, 1974.

Chapter 11

Collective Bargaining: Contemporary American Experience—A Commentary

Jack Barbash
University of Wisconsin

Preface

We want to do three things in this commentary: first, to set out in summary form the characteristics of American collective bargaining as it has evolved in practice and law—it is this system that sets the' background for the particular cases in this collection; second, to highlight the salient features of each of the cases reported here; third, to see the cases in the light of a bargaining framework. It needs to be stressed that although this commentary is based on the individual reports, none of the several authors should be saddled with responsibility for its contents.

The American Collective Bargaining System

Collective bargaining in the United States is a continuous process in which unions, as designated representatives of workers in specified units, and the appropriate public managements or private employers negotiate terms of employment. Collective bargaining is complemented by supporting activities like politics and public policy.

Unit describes the applicable employment territory—occupation, craft, department, multiplant, multiemployer, public jurisdiction, etc., or combinations thereof. The bargaining unit is commonly established by the National Labor Relations Board (NLRB) or a similar agency in a representation proceeding. Commonly, too, the unit established for representation is likely to change as the relationship evolves into negotiation.

The terms of employment about which the parties bargain are, fundamentally: (1) the price of labor, e.g., wages, supplements, methods of wage determination, wage structures; (2) the accompanying rules that define how the labor is to be utilized, including hours, work practices, job classifications, the effort input, etc.; (3) individual job rights, e.g., seniority, discharge for cause; (4) the rights of union and management in the bargaining relationship; and (5) the methods of enforcement, interpretation, and administration of the agreement, including the resolution of grievances. In the most fundamental sense, the stakes of collective bargaining come to price and power.

Collective bargaining is normally coordinated with two complementary strategies. In internal bargaining, the sides bargain out their eventual position *within* their respective units before presentation at the bargaining table. In public employment, the union bargains politically with public administrators and politicians. Political bargaining is also involved as the parties seek to reenforce their collective bargaining interests through public policy enactments.

The union enforces its side of the bargaining through sanctions which, by promise of benefit, threat to withhold, rational persuasion (including public relations), and direct action, induce the other side to agree and compromise. The strike is the major union sanction—even if, as in the public sector, it is largely illegal. On occasion the strike is backed up by consumer boycotts—which is the organized withholding of product demand—and direct action or violence.

Withholding of employment is the employer's major sanction, known colloquially as "taking a strike." If the employer initiates the withholding of employment, it is called a lockout. But not all sanctions are intended to disadvantage the other side. Standardization of labor costs, improving the employer's product market position (i.e., the union label), and conflict resolution on the shop floor (i.e., the grievance procedure) serve interests of both parties.

The negotiating table is figuratively and literally the forum in which the parties face each other in the making of the bargain. Negotiation, normally face-to-face or through mediation, allows the initially announced positions of the parties to be modified through continuous exchange of information and feedback. Negotiation is part of bargaining, but not all bargaining involves negotiation. That is to say, terms and sanctions can be communicated without face-to-face negotiation and without, of course, the instant feedback opportunities offered by face-to-face negotiation. Negotiation applies not only to the formal agreement, but also to subordinate bargains, including, most importantly, grievance processing.

Bargaining is of such scale and complexity that both sides require organizations to implement their representation. Organization, in turn, brings professionalization and bureaucracy. For the union this means that the traditional lay administration—that is, administration by members who are employed at other full-time jobs—tends to get displaced by full-time staff, particularly in the higher union bodies. For management, industrial relations requires expertness and is, in this respect, on a par with other management specializations.

Scale and complexity in their organizations make it necessary for the parties to bargain over the distribution of power *within* their respective organizations. Internal bargaining is most marked in public-sector management where the separation of powers inherent in constitutional government creates several, frequently competing voices, each purporting to speak in behalf of some segment of the employer-management interest. On the union side, internal bargaining is most marked in the industrial unions with their broad-based constituencies divided by skill, age, sex, and geography.

Management is normally the moving party in the direction of the enterprise. The union mostly reacts. In collective bargaining, these roles are reversed. Unions initiate and management reacts. But what the union initiates is modification of or redress from decisions first made by management. In this context, the union posture is defensive. Collective bargaining as a process thus involves a sequence of union demands and management responses. But employer initiatives are becoming more frequent, especially under cost pressures. There are atypical cases—perhaps the apparel industries come closest here—in which the union functions more positively, but these are special circumstances.

Collective bargaining is only one point, albeit a major point, along a continuum of diverse forms of joint dealing between workers and employers. At one end, the negation of joint dealing is management unilateralism where the right to make decisions is vested solely in management. At an interval along the way is human relations and its later variants. Human relations is still management-in-charge, but with greater awareness of the needs of the lower participants. Consultation, at still a further remove, is European usage and generally represents a type of formalized joint dealing in which the workers have a right to be informed, to question proposed management policies, and to get a response; but the eventual decision under consultation is made by management and is not contingent on a negotiated agreement with the workers' side. The American analogue is "meet and confer" found in several public-sector statutes.

In the collective bargaining type of joint dealing, decisions relating to the terms of employment—or more specifically, the price of labor and its attendant conditions—are contingent on negotiated agreement with an appropriate union. Codetermination—German in origin and setting—is, in its fullest development, the right of the workers' representatives to join with top management in the making of decisions in a predefined area, *whether in the employment area or not.* Industrial democracy generally means codecision-making but, in the contemporary context, on (or at least close to) the shop floor. There are instances in collective bargaining which are very close to codetermination or industrial democracy, mostly in the public sector. (Codetermination, in practice, has been mostly confined to employment terms.)

Craft unionism tends to incorporate the major terms of employment in its own internal rules rather than in the collective bargaining agreement. It is close to workers' control in that power is substantially weighted toward the union side, but without the formidable workers' control ideology. Full-dress workers' control—syndicalism in an earlier time—is the negation of joint dealing, but on the workers' side, and exists nowhere as an established arrangement.

The major variations in collective bargaining are shaped by whether the bargaining relationship is (a) in a factory or nonfactory environment—in this collection, steel and electrical products contrasted with all of the others; (b) public or private—education, postal service, and government hospitals contrasted with the others; (c) the stage of negotiations, i.e., contract vs. grievance negotiation; and (d) the stage of development of the relationship from confrontation to accommodation and possibly cooperation—perhaps agriculture contrasted to steel and airlines.

Case Profiles

In this section, the effort is made to convey the essence of the bargaining relationship, not really to summarize.

COAL

This is a bargaining relationship undergoing profound change and reeling under the impact. The new turmoil in the union began with the radically improved condition of the coal economy in the wake of the energy crisis. But the turmoil also reflects the jarring transition which the Mine Workers Union has had to make from John L. Lewis— one of the seminal and also one of the most authoritarian leaders in American trade unionism—to Tony Boyle's "corrupt kingdom" (1-29),[1] to Arnold Miller's attempt at coping with the forces unleashed by the collapse of the Lewis-Boyle tradition.

Lewis ran the Miners as a dictatorship, but its cutting edge was blunted by the Lewis charisma. Lewis innovated health insurance and pensions, not only for Miners but for the modern labor movement. At its high point, it looked as if the Miners' Welfare and Retirement Fund was on the verge of ushering in a new era for health care in Appalachia.

---

[1] The numbers in parentheses refer to page citations in individual case studies.

But actuarial weaknesses caught up with Lewis's successors to make the welfare fund a major source of dissension. Lewis approved the mechanization which made U.S. coal mining among the most efficient in the world. But mechanization in a declining market also depopulated the mines and impoverished Appalachia.

Internally, the Boyle regime of corruption and murder led to Miller's revolution which the union is still trying to digest. From without, the union is very much threatened by a growing nonunion sector and rival unionism from the Operating Engineers in the western surface mines. Concentration and conglomeration are gradually but perceptibly altering the coal industry's market structure. Destructive competitive forces are no longer the critical circumstance they were in coal's past.

The power of the state, in one form or another, has touched the coal industry and its labor relations at every main point. The federal Coal Mine Safety Act, "the strongest single code of health and safety the country has ever known" (1-8), regulates occupational health and safety. The emergency disputes provisions of Taft-Hartley have been the basis for four interventions, the latest in 1977. The Labor Management Reporting and Disclosure Act has been a major influence in the UMW internal struggles; the Employee Retirement Income Security Act (ERISA) is bringing about "a thoroughgoing change" (1-32) in retirement funds.

Power in the coal bargaining structure has moved both up and down. On the up side is the negotiation of the key bituminous contract by one employer association instead of by three associations as was the case before 1950. But within the union, power has been moving downward since the heyday of John L. Lewis. From 1974 on, union negotiations have been carried on through a bargaining council which has grown accustomed to exercising its own judgment. Decentralization has come most of all from the rekindled spirit of insurgency among the younger generation of miners.

Straight-time or hourly earnings of coal miners are among "the highest earned by industrial workers in the nation—and quite possibly in the world" (1-10). The critical bargaining issues have been health, pensions, mechanization, and the grievance-arbitration machinery. Lewis pioneered negotiated health care on an unprecedented but, as it turned out, unsustainable scale.

The union's mechanization policy permitted the operators to reduce their labor force to a level compatible with high efficiency at the same time that miners would be permitted (as Lewis said) to "maintain them[selves] and their families in comfort and with a provision for old age" (1-26). It didn't quite work out that way. A workable grievance-

arbitration mechanism which can command sufficient support from the
rank and file to put an end to wildcats has yet to be achieved.

The Lewis era evolved from turmoil to stability. The stability water-
shed was the negotiation in 1950 of a national agreement. The renewal
of struggle came in the 1970s and has dominated the industrial relations scene since then.

STEEL

In its evolution from combat to accommodation to intermittent
collaboration, steel bargaining comes close to the maturity model that
the philosophers of collective bargaining undoubtedly had in mind.

Steel, along with coal, autos, rubber, and electrical products, was
in the vanguard of the industrial union revolution of the 1930s. The
steel union was a spinoff from coal unionism, one might say. Even after
the open break with Lewis, the Steelworkers under Philip Murray carried on the Mine Workers' tradition of strong and "highly centralized"
(4-158) national union leadership—but without the repression.

Murray led the union in its militant period. Stability set in only
with the accession of David J. McDonald in 1952. Several innovations
bordering on (if not actually achieving) a modern approximation of
"union-management cooperation" originated in his administration. But
McDonald's personal leadership failed to take hold in the mills. His
critics charged (and there were many in and out of the union) that his
style was better suited to the executive's club than to the union hall
or steel mill.

McDonald faced challenges several times until I. W. Abel eventually
defeated him in 1965. Abel carried forward McDonald's "mutual trus-
teeship" in practice, if not in rhetoric or style. But Abel's roots as an
honest-to-goodness steel worker, nevertheless, did not suppress the
charge of elitism and efforts of challengers (unsuccessful) to unseat
him on that ground.

Steel management has also undergone a major metamorphosis. From
the turn of the twentieth century on, no management fought unionism
more resolutely. But from violent confrontation, steel management
found its way to accommodation. Accommodation has meant the professionalization of industrial relations, a negotiated wage structure, and
a willingness to innovate in grievance administration and strike substitutes. These are some of the most significant innovations in industrial
union bargaining. Nor have steel workers' earnings suffered under accommodation. Earnings in the industry increased more per year than
earnings of either automobile workers or all manufacturing workers
during 1947–62 (4-196).

Steel is one of the classic cases of government intervention. The strategic position of steel in the economy makes the industry particularly vulnerable to anti-inflation "jawboning" which goes back to the late 1950s. Even earlier it became clear, at least to steel management, that "Washington" was the invisible—sometimes not so invisible—participant at the bargaining table (4-179, fn. 47). Wage settlements turned on whether Washington would approve price increases. In 1962 steel provided the circumstances for President Kennedy's price crackdown.

Government intervention virtually forced the industry to recognize the union. Afterward, at one time or another, government resorted to almost every known form of intervention: mediation, fact-finding with and without recommendations, seizure, and injunction. The latest intervention resulted in an antidiscrimination consent decree.

Steel has been a strike-prone industry from the early origins of unionism to the CIO organizing period, climaxed by the longest and last national strike in 1959. It is fitting for this industry to have pioneered an Experimental Negotiating Agreement (ENA) providing for new contract arbitration in lieu of striking (4-170). "Drastic action was necessary to quell steel imports in order to maintain a domestic market for American steel and prevent postsettlement layoffs and unemployment" (4-171). The arbitration of a new contract in lieu of strike remains unused by the parties. They have been able to come to terms on their own. Nor has there been any replication of the ENA principle in other situations.

The accommodation style has not always been fully appreciated within the union ranks. Dissidents of one kind or another have denounced it at various times as elitism, bureaucracy, and proemployer. The steel experience raises the general question of whether collaboration can command general support over the long term.

Bargaining structure has also developed in the classic way from single-company bargaining "to what is in effect industrywide bargaining" (4-164, fn. 30). Structure's center of gravity is undergoing a downward pull as indicated by the more representative bargaining committees, the provision for local-issues strikes, and, as much as anything else, the heightened sensitivity of the leadership to what members will and won't take. The decentralization impulse runs through the vigorous efforts to expedite, simplify, and generally reform the grievance-arbitration process.

ELECTRICAL PRODUCTS

Up to the middle 1960s, electrical products is the situation that became noted for the successful efforts of General Electric to contain union penetration. Rival unionism, ideology, personality, and internal instability are some of the reasons why management was able to hold the unions in check.

The original union division was between the AFL's International Brotherhood of Electrical Workers (IBEW) and the CIO's United Electrical Workers (UE). The identification of UE leadership with the communist faction in the CIO led to the formation of the International Union of Electrical Workers (IUE) under the leadership of James Carey, and eventually to UE's severance from the CIO and to its displacement as the leading union in the industry. Carey's "boldness—or rashness—invective, and dramatic speechmaking" and his lack of "competence as an administrator" (5-224) cast him as a continuously abrasive influence within the union and in a confrontation posture with management. Currently, foreign competition, the "massive" southern strategy of the industry, and "the mediocre performance of IUE and UE" (5-216) are reordering union rankings; IBEW is now emerging as the leading union and "the most active organizer" (5-214) even though it continues to lag behind IUE in the very large corporations.

GE set the tone of labor relations in electrical products, with Western Electric, Westinghouse, and RCA "play[ing] ancillary roles" (5-222). Division within the union ranks made Boulwarism possible. In the NLRB's words, Boulwarism "denigrat[ed] give-and-take bargaining" (5-229) and sought to "bypass the union and attempt[ed] to disparage its importance and usefulness in the eyes of its members. . . . The aim was to deal with the union through the employees, rather than with the employees through the union" (5-232) and thereby decentralize bargaining to the local level. Later, coordinated bargaining (or "coalition bargaining," as GE preferred) tried to bring a measure of unity in the union ranks.

For a long time IUE's inability to win a strike vote undermined the credibility of its strike threats. "I owe GE a strike," Carey said in 1960 (5-236, fn. 32). The strike that came may have been "the worst setback any union . . . received in a nationwide strike since World War II" (5-237, fn. 35). The union disunity which brought about the 1960 disaster led to coordinated bargaining which, in turn, led to a strike "showdown" with GE. The "Great 1969–70 Strike," which lasted 101 days, brought about the "first fully negotiated contract in twenty years" (5-246). GE and the locals found themselves as one against the national union in preferring strikes to grievance arbitration. The end of Boulwarism brought with it also "a grudging gradual acceptance of arbitration" (5-251).

Since the Great Strike, as one union leader put it, "GE . . . entered the Twentieth Century" (5-247). The adversary relationship prevails, but there is "no real bitterness or rancor." Altogether, "union-management relations at both plant and company levels have matured" (5-261).

CONSTRUCTION

The construction industry typifies craft bargaining. Its distinguishing features are craft consciousness, multiunionism, casual employment, jurisdictional rivalry, weak employers, and employer association bargaining.

Many of the problems confronting bargaining in the industry intersect at one point or another with decentralization or "fragmentation" of bargaining and its "leap-frogging effect" (2-74). Inflation of construction wage costs, the growing nonunion sector, and jurisdictional disputes arise out of competitive craft unionism and excessive localism. Most remedies, accordingly, involve doing something about bargaining structure. All proposed reforms—whether Construction Industry Stabilization Commission or wide-area bargaining or the Dunlop bill (which almost passed only to fail because of its link with the common situs issue)—in one way or another try to deal with fragmentation by moving union power upward.

The weakness of the contractors association, the employers' bargaining vehicle, feeds decentralization. Staffing is "sparse" (2-61). Rapid turnover of personnel deprives the association of experienced negotiators. "Political turmoil" in the association is worse than in the union (2-61).

A construction strike puts "usually small and poorly capitalized" (2-75) contractors in danger of contract cancellations. The union members, on the other hand, frequently are able to find other work during a strike.

Construction is one of the major strike-prone industries in the United States, and jurisdiction is a large source of these strikes. Some branches of the industry have, however, developed sophisticated alternatives to the strike. Of the longest standing are the Council of Industrial Relations of the Electrical Construction Industry and the Impartial Board for the Settlement of Jurisdictional Disputes. During the Nixon wage-price control era, a tripartite Construction Industry Stabilization Committee (1971–74) addressed itself to reform of the bargaining structure.

Federal and some state laws are actively involved in construction industrial relations. Federal efforts to reform bargaining structure have already been noted. Federal and state law regulates wages in public construction. Federal law prohibits jurisdictional strikes and the closed shop (not altogether successfully), restricts the secondary boycott with somewhat better results, and through affirmative action forces the recruitment, training, and hiring of larger numbers of minority employees.

The open-shop drive mounted by some of the largest firms in the industry is causing construction unions to reappraise their policies in a way that state intervention has been mostly unable to do. Construction unions are now stepping up organizing, liberalizing work rules, and permitting the coexistence of union and nonunion work in the same firm, all in an effort to recapture lost territory and prevent further attrition.

TRUCKING

Collective bargaining in trucking demonstrates the same general model of weak employers confronting a powerful union; only, unlike construction, the union interest is represented by one union instead of 20.

Like construction, the multiemployer bargaining association, rent by internal divisions, is no match for the union. Nor is the individual employer whose "slim financial resources" (3-106) make him acutely vulnerable to strikes.

Bargaining consolidation received a powerful assist from Hoffa's empire-building. But Hoffa's successor, Frank Fitzsimmons, has been unable to sustain the momentum, first, because he lacks Hoffa's personal appeal to the Teamster rank and file, and second, because of fissions among employers in the unionized sector.

The Trucking Employers, Inc. (TEI), as the employer instrumentality for collective bargaining, is marked by a high degree of internal tension. The pressure on the firms to go nonunion began to accelerate with the 1970 and subsequent negotiations which increased "even further the motivation of shippers to seek out nonunion or non-Teamster modes of transportation wherever possible" (3-138).

Like construction, the Teamsters are facing an enlarging nonunion sector, the basic cause at work being "cumulative effects of . . . increases in labor costs" (3-138) since 1970. Over the long run, deregulation, as the union sees it, would likely liberalize employee entry and further threaten the unionized sector.

By all accounts, racketeering and corruption permeate some sectors of the Teamster organization, notably in the central and southern areas, in a way that is not true of construction.

Government has intervened in a variety of ways to weaken Teamster power over employers and union recalcitrants with uneven effects. The Taft-Hartley prohibitions of the secondary boycott have probably made it more difficult for the union to move against nonunion truckers. But the closed-shop prohibition has been largely ineffectual. Much of the Landrum-Griffin Act was written against a legislative history of Teamster racketeering and internal repression. ERISA provisions have provided the leverage for wholesale investigation of Teamster pension funds for "mismanagement of investment, corruption, and kickbacks, questionable loans, tie-ins with organized crime, [and] excessive disqualifications of retirees" (3-133). "Along with construction, the trucking industry is probably the most widely criticized for policies of discrimination against blacks and other minorities in hiring, assignment, transfer, and promotion" (3-130).

Notably absent from agreements is the final arbitration step in the grievance procedure. What happens, in effect, is that the union sense of fairness prevails—which employers apparently prefer to costly arbitration with an overpowering union. "Since Hoffa's departure," employers feel "that decisions [have been] fair and equitable" (3-129).

Prospects for reform from within the industry are not good. There is no strong tradition of union-management cooperation in this unbalanced power relationship to confront the industry's problems, although a new advisory committee has been established to make the attempt. So far, neither has government intervention materially altered the industrial relations condition.

AGRICULTURAL WORKERS

Bargaining in West Coast agriculture is just now emerging out of its primitive confrontation. By the signs of history, the Chicanos were not, on the face of it, the best material out of which to build a union that could survive in a hostile environment. Replacements from the "reserve army of the unemployed" across the border have always threatened the union's striking power. Denied legal protection generally available to workers, farm unions have had to face their tough employer antagonists alone.

But conditions changed. Somehow, a union and collective bargaining for farm workers has come to pass. It came to pass because their leader, César Chavez, was able to endow the dispute with a sense of mission so deeply felt as to overcome the feeling of powerlessness of this historically oppressed ethnic group. The cause—literally La Causa —attracted an auxiliary force in the churches, most significantly in the Roman Catholic Church, and university students. Indispensable to the maintenance of the organization as a going concern was the very substantial organizing and financial aid from the AFL-CIO, the United Auto Workers, and other unions.

Very early the United Farm Workers of America (UFWA) launched a consumer boycott against the products of struck employers. If the strike could not be effective, the national consumer boycott was. But the turning point in the union's fortunes came with the enactment of the California Agriculture Labor Relations Act (CALRA). The law established procedures to resolve the question of representation between the Farm Workers and the Teamsters, or alternatively no union. In the main, the Farm Workers won out. CALRA also protected the farm workers' rights of association, collective bargaining, and consumer boycott.

The termination of the bracero program helped UFWA, although the supply of farm labor continues to be augmented by the continuous flow of illegal aliens, with the union caught between ethnic loyalty and economics. Additionally, the new wave of social legislation—the Civil Rights Act, the Occupational Safety and Health Act (OSHA), and the extension of the Fair Labor Standards Act (FLSA) to larger farm operations—are bringing farm workers into the mainstream of labor legislation from which they had been traditionally excluded.

Although agreements have been signed, growing pains continue as the union evolves from movement to organization. The strains have shown up mainly in grievance handling and hiring-hall administration. For the long run, tensions in the relationship will come as technology replaces labor in the fields.

The two other agricultural organizations of importance are Local 142 of the International Longshoremen's and Warehousemen's Union (ILWU) in Hawaii and the Western Conference of Teamsters. Like the Farm Workers, Local 142's self-image is as a trade union and social movement. For many reasons, however, its organizing had easier sailing. Hawaii's sugar workers represent a more stable labor force and Hawaii represents a more favorable union environment for agricultural workers, including legal protection of the right to organize and bargain much earlier than in California. Hawaiian growers have not been resistant to agricultural unionism as have Californians. Perhaps because Local 142 is a kind of union conglomerate—actually a general workers' union with considerable economic and political power—most employers are loath to engage it in combat.

The Teamsters' importance in the fields derives from the fact that for the growers they represented a less worse alternative to the Farm Workers precisely because they were not a social movement. Although the benefits gained by Teamster groups were "roughly equivalent" (6-297) to the UFWA, they did not insist on union-controlled hiring halls and, by contrast with UFWA, seemed "business-like and efficient"

(6-298). Eventually, UFWA victories in the CALRA elections brought about a jurisdictional treaty.

AIRLINES

The collective bargaining problems of the airlines flow from two sets of circumstances that surround the industry. It is a regulated industry and, until the present period, a technologically dynamic industry.

"CAB [and/or FAA] entered into and materially influenced every major aspect of airline personnel and industrial relations" (7-346), including safety, merger displacement, employee qualifications, manning, subsidies, and dispute settlement. The airline unions have favored retention of CAB's "wide-ranging authority over air transportation" (7-318). They fear that deregulation and the likely "liquidation of the CAB" will redistribute traffic among carriers and undoubtedly disturb the existing system of employee security and vested rights based on individual carrier seniority (7-361).

Collective bargaining is governed by the craft principle built into the Railway Labor Act (RLA), which is also the basic legislation for airlines labor relations. "Single carrier bargaining remains the rule" (7-353). Multicarrier bargaining poses too many complexities to be practical, aside from the fact that the unions are not pressing for it. In lieu of multicarrier bargaining, the carriers developed the now illegal Mutual Aid Pact (MAP) (7-357). Multiunit bargaining occurs de facto when several units are represented by one union bargaining with a carrier over contracts with common expiration times. Union rivalry is common except in the pilot unit (7-349).

Following the Railway Labor Act pattern, grievances are handled through three-party boards, departing in this respect from the single-arbitrator system common elsewhere. It has its advantages, but it is "a relatively elaborate, expensive, and slow process" (7-366).

The emergency boards have been "relatively ineffective" (7-364) in curbing strikes. Mandatory mediation has been a "positive contribution" (7-370). Strikes have been "relatively infrequent" (7-365), occurring on an average of four per year in the recent period. The Mutual Aid Pact strengthened carrier defenses against strikes, "increas[ing] the number of long strikes" (7-365).

The airlines' technological evolution is epitomized in four waves of "aircraft innovation" (7-324)—the Douglas DC-3, the Douglas DC-6, the Boeing turbojets (707), and the Boeing 747—each with its threat at the time to "the survival of the various crafts" (7-332). But "the age of technological progress is over for the foreseeable future" (7-334).

The era of optimism in the airline industry gave way to uncertainty in the 1970s, accompanied by fear that even some major carriers (notably Pan Am and Eastern) might not survive their cash crises. Cost reduction became a major management bargaining goal. But the late 1970s witnessed a dramatic resurgence of traffic and profits reenforced by the CAB's adoption of policies encouraging more competition.

The Pilots have found their "increment" pay system tactically superior, for bargaining purposes, to any direct demands for higher pay. Their goal of shorter hours was more effectively pursued through piecemeal change in rules than by open reductions in hours or by mileage limitations (7-359).

On balance, "collective bargaining has worked reasonably well" (7-370). The RLA has "provided a suitable legislative framework" (7-370). Professionalism has not deterred the Pilots from becoming a militant, hard-bargaining union indistinguishable in its basic strategies from other unions. The unions seem to have been uncommonly responsive to the more pessimistic prospects for the airlines, agreeing to postponement of pay increases, variable earnings, expedited arbitration, and private fact-finding arbitration. The effects of prosperity and of deregulation on collective bargaining remain to be determined.

EDUCATION

The essential spirit of this relationship is the militancy and ardor with which teachers practice their unionism. This is all the more remarkable considering the nagging doubts that teachers voiced for a long time about the propriety of unions for professionals.

Two major unions are in the field. The strength of the American Federation of Teachers (AFT) is centered in the heavily urbanized areas and that of the National Education Association (NEA) affiliates "in the smaller cities and in suburban and rural areas" (10-509). The two are indistinguishable as to union methods except that AFT puts a high value on permanent ties to the labor movement, while NEA does not. In fact, the issue of AFL-CIO affiliation seems to be the chief sticking point in the consummation of merger between AFT and NEA.

The road to bargaining in education has been marked by much introspection on the compatibility of professionals and unions. But once the union breakthrough occurred in the early 1960s, teachers shed their inhibitions and began to function pretty much like all other unions except in one vital respect inherent in their status as public employees. Like other *public* unions, education unions deal with their employers not only as management but—to put it summarily—as politicians or, alternately, as administrators responsible to politicians.

The employer in education bargaining could hardly be more different from the private-sector employer. There is not one education employer in any given situation, but many, depending on the terms being bargained. Accordingly, the education employer can be a school administrator, a lay board of education, a city council, a state legislature, or the voters in referendum. The employer in large-scale private-sector bargaining is also bureaucratized, to be sure, but the diverse manifestations that managements take are part of an integrated hierarchical system which will act as one at showdown time. Not so in the public sector; the union strategy is not only to bargain collectively, but to bargain *politically*—to play one face of management against the other as tactical advantage seems to dictate.

Bargaining operates within what is now an intricate legal framework. The state sets professional and civil service standards and establishes the rules by which the bargaining parties conduct themselves in union-management relations. Thus, labor relations law legitimates the bargaining relationship to begin with, and then goes on to fix the bargaining unit, the terms of recognition, the scope of bargaining, and methods of dispute settlement.

The law almost invariably bars the strike, but this is just as invariably disregarded. "Of all public employee groups, teachers appear to be most inclined to take bargaining issues to impasse and to strike" (10-530). Strikes by teachers—or threats—have become "commonplace," especially in larger cities (10-535). In part, this is because strikes are likely to be less costly to teachers since lost time "is often recaptured through makeup days" (10-537). Laws also commonly provide for fact-finding and other dispute-resolution procedures.

The bargaining structure is quite involved due to the fragmentation of employer authority. In another respect, the organization is simple and decentralized since multiemployer bargaining is rare. Many of the problems in bargaining stem from the inexperience of the participants who, with few exceptions, are still in the rudimentary stages of the bargaining relationship.

Unionized teachers bring an attitude, it is not an exaggeration to say, of codetermination to the substance and enforcement of the agreement. "Teachers view conditions of employment as transcending mere matters of salaries, hours, fringe benefits, and a grievance procedure. The contract . . . becomes not only a constitution governing the working life of the teacher, but a document containing the educational philosophy of the district" (10-526). This is hardly congenial to school administrators or to boards of education who are not prepared for this sharing of power.

Education bargaining, like all public-sector bargaining, is in a period of instability as education retrenches in reaction to rising costs, demographic changes, taxpayer "revolts," and citizen doubts about the educational process. The main effect of retrenchment is to put into question the lifetime job security that teachers thought they had acquired when they entered upon their public jobs. The militant phase is likely to be an extended one as teacher unions resist retrenchment and education management seeks to capitalize on this apparently favorable shift in the terms of power.

On balance, "bargaining has resulted in modest gains for teachers. . . . The greatest salary gains go to experienced teachers" (10-542). Collective bargaining has also improved the teachers' working conditions. But teacher militancy seems to have raised a larger question: In whose interests is the public education system being run?

POSTAL SERVICE

The problems of collective bargaining in the Postal Service spring from these conditions: an immense public enterprise experimenting with more private-like management, particularly with how to meet costs without overpricing services; a network of unions stratified by craft and industrial as well as local and national interests; and a bargaining structure that attempts to give voice simultaneously to all of these diverse pressures.

Eighty-eight percent of Postal Service employees are in unions, which must be among the highest ratios anywhere in the public sector. But this high density is diffused among several craft and one semi-industrial unions. The American Postal Workers Union is the semi-industrial union. It represents a merger of previously independent craft unions, but the merger has yet to be consummated in fact as well as in form. The three remaining "craft" unions are the Letter Carriers, Mail Handlers, and Rural Letter Carriers. All of the foregoing have bargaining rights. The National Alliance is mainly a civil rights gadfly (9-447) in behalf of black postal workers, without consultative or bargaining rights. There are also three supervisory organizations, limited to consultation.

The Postal Service "is still the largest public employer and the most widespread organization" (9-437), with a large headquarters and field labor relations staff, and title to match (Senior Assistant Postmaster General for Employee and Labor Relations, or SAPMGE&LR). The Service is governed by the "jointly bargained" (9-436) Postal Reorganization Act and its law of labor relations by amendment to the National Labor Relations Act after years under Executive Order 10988. But the last and not infrequently resort is Congress, even on routine matters.

The NLRB has given its stamp of approval to "the existing bargaining structure comprised of occupational units on national lines" (9-453), with some exceptions. Negotiations are carried on at three levels: nationally for the mail-processing employees and for each group of craft employees, locally at each installation. The union side is represented through a not entirely satisfactory approximation of "coordinated" bargaining, which broke down in the 1978 negotiations.

The first negotiations "quickly bogged down" (9-458) due largely to intraorganizational problems and the sheer magnitude of the task. Until 1978 subsequent negotiations have gone more smoothly. Even so, the union tactic of using craft and local bargaining to improve on the national terms tends to entangle the negotiations. Efforts from topside to "defus[e]" (9-461) local negotiations have been rebuffed down below with the charge that the national union leaderships are conspiring with management to cut down local power. Complicated structures produce complicated results. The 1975 agreement ran to 187 printed pages.

Enforcement of agreements also runs into difficulties. There is the problem of communicating the terms of the agreements to the vast constituency on both sides. Thirteen joint committees have been established to "administer the agreement and resolve differences" (9-469). Not all committees have met. When they do meet, attendance is poor and the discussion agenda has "often been of little value" (9-470). The grievance procedure provides for five basic steps capped by arbitration. The "high rate of grievance appeals," including those going to arbitration (9-472), is a major delaying factor.

The major issue in grievances is discipline, and in arbitration, work rules and work assignment. Work-assignment grievances carry "jurisdictional overtones" (9-476) and have the effect of slowing down the Service's productivity campaigns. Management mostly wins in discipline cases. The courts are available to parties who do not have recourse to appeals mechanisms.

All things considered, there has been "little overt militancy" (9-477). The 1978 dispute seemed to be leading inexorably to a strike, but the rhetoric proved to be stronger than the acts themselves. Withal, "postal employees have fared far better under collective bargaining to date than have federal Civil Service employees in the same period" (9-464).

The expectation that collective bargaining would follow the classical private-sector model has not materialized. Political bargaining is still fundamental, and Congress is still very much a party to Postal Service bargaining. Collective bargaining is encountering all sorts of uncertainties: challenges to the postal monopoly, the changing postal technology, postal self-sufficiency, and the related question of federal subsidy.

HOSPITALS

The hospital is different. It dispenses perhaps the most public of all goods in the sense that, ideally, nobody should be denied access to quality care because of inability to pay. In fulfillment of this mission, government has become the most important "third-party" payer, thereby escalating hospital costs as to require public surveillance and containment.

In a very real sense, the hospital has become a public utility caught up in an intricate web of external regulation. Nor is management elsewhere so critically circumscribed in the exercise of authority *within* its organization.

The hospital was an almshouse and asylum—"places where the homeless and poverty stricken went to die" (8-376). It is now a "multiphase center incorporating teaching and research as well as health-care services" (8-376). Concurrently, the hospital has rapidly expanded the size of its plant, capital investment, and employment; public health care has shifted "from federal to state and local government, and nongovernment, not-for-profit hospitals have displaced investor-owned institutions" (8-376). The hospital, in short, has evolved from philanthropy and charity into a business. Increasingly its staff and employees relate to it as a business institution.

The hospital labor force consists of "large numbers of high-wage, skilled workers at the upper end of the structure, equal numbers of low-wage low-skilled at the other end, and little in between" (8-378). The upper end consists of professionals and quasi-professionals insulated from the full authority of management. The lower end is "ghettoized" with " 'overrepresentation' " (8-377) of the lowest paid ethnic minorities and women.

This is, hence, the classic segmented labor force with unionism likewise segmented. The dominating association is the guild-like physician corps. The physician, running true to guild form, is stratified into "apprentices" (interns), "journeymen" (residents), and "masters" (physicians). Whatever their legal status is finally determined to be, the residents and interns act like employees and form unions which, like all other unions, strike, bargain, and organize.

The nurses have drifted from sole reliance on a kind of nurses' "guild," the American Nurses Association, and have transformed the state branches into virtual unions which, like those of the interns and residents, also bargain and strike. The ANA by this time is not alone in the field. Contesting the territory are the Service Employees, Retail Clerks, and Local 1199.

Dramatic change has also come at the lower end of the wage structure in the unionization of the nonprofessionals who make up about two-thirds of the total hospital labor force. The forces behind unionization include increased demand and increased ability to pay, supportive federal and state legislation, militant unionism, and intensified civil rights awareness among the predominantly minority workforce. The marks of hospital unionism are rival unionism, craft and status separatism, and, unlike the other cases, the hospital situation has not produced a union national in scope with a primary mission in the field.

For all the recent activity, unionism and collective bargaining are unevenly distributed and very much a minority phenomenon. Urbanization and large-scale and federal control are good predictors of the presence of unions, as is location in a jurisdiction with supportive legislation. Thirty-four unions are active in representing hospital workers, but four "account for 75 percent of all hospital representation elections" (8-395).

Unionization has not had the radical impact that most hospital managements feared. For one thing, most managements have learned how to keep unions out. If the union does get in, management has been able to more than hold its own. Strikes occur—many are illegal—but have been proportionately fewer than in industry generally. Somehow hospitals have learned how to cope, and strikes have not brought catastrophe in their wake, although short-of-catastrophe strikes raise serious problems, too.

The Cases and the Bargaining Framework

In this part we fit the individual cases into a larger framework of collective bargaining generally, which consists of: (1) the parties to collective bargaining, (2) the rules or the law of collective bargaining, (3) the sanctions (i.e., the strike) in collective bargaining, (4) the structure or organization of bargaining, and (5) the terms or content of bargaining.

THE BARGAINERS

In this section on the changing character of the bargainers, we want to delineate the union profile in terms of growth and decline, the changing base of representation, leadership, ideology, and organization.

The union profile has remained remarkably unchanged in its general features. Union members are still mostly manual, blue-collar workers predominantly employed in manufacturing, construction, transportation, and public utilities. The union membership consists mainly of workers in the middle range of the national wage structure, thinning out among the very low and the very high paid.

Unions are predominantly white male institutions in absolute numbers. But black males are slightly more union prone than white males, and black women are considerably more union prone than white women. Unionism is strongest in the Northeast and North Central states and weakest (by less than half) in the South.[2] Unions have always represented a minority of the working population. Less than one-fourth (23.2 percent) of the labor force and just under 30 percent (28.3 percent) of nonagricultural employees are union members.[3]

The union's manufacturing base is contracting over time, with the slack being picked up by nonmanufacturing and government. Manufacturing employees as a percent of union membership has declined from 45.6 percent in 1968 to 37.8 percent in 1974, while the percentage in nonmanufacturing has increased in this period from 43.7 to 45.4 percent, and the percentage in the public sector from 10.7 to 13.5 percent.[4] The union share of the labor force has been declining slowly but continuously since the middle 1950s; the union share measured by nonagricultural employment has been in decline since the middle 1940s.[5]

U.S. unions have done better than the French, British, and West Germans in organizing manual workers, but somewhat worse than the Australians and much worse than the Swedes. It is in the private white-collar and in the public sector as a whole that American unions suffer by comparison.[6]

Union membership has not kept pace with labor force growth because employers extend union-like terms to nonunion employees. Union employers extend union terms almost automatically to their nonunion employees; others observe union conditions in order to be competitive in near-full-employment labor markets; still others hew to union terms to avoid unions.

Most of the cases are each experiencing contraction of one kind or another. Union territory in construction, trucking, and coal is diminishing because employers are trying to escape from onerous union restraints. In steel and electrical products, it is the inability of the indus-

[2] U.S. Department of Labor, Bureau of Labor Statistics, *Selected Earnings and Demographic Characteristics of Union Members, 1970* (Washington: U.S. Government Printing Office, 1970), p. 21.

[3] U.S. Department of Labor, Bureau of Labor Statistics, *Directory of National Unions and Employee Associations, 1975* (Washington: U.S. Government Printing Office, 1977), p. 63.

[4] U.S. Department of Labor, Bureau of Labor Statistics, *Handbook of Labor Statistics, 1977* (Washington: U.S. Government Printing Office, 1977), pp. 288–91.

[5] *Directory, 1975*, p. 62.

[6] Hugh A. Clegg, *Trade Unionism under Collective Bargaining* (Oxford: Basil Blackwell, 1976), p. 12.

tries to compete effectively in domestic and foreign markets that is the ultimate cause of union attrition.

Hospitals, education, and postal service are experiencing the fiscal crunch which the public sector generally is undergoing. The airlines fell from their employment peak of the 1960s because of new technology and declining markets coming at the same time. In West Coast agriculture, the potential source of employment decline is also technology, possibly accelerated to ward off the union threat. The indications are that the cases, each in its own way, are not simply caught in a cyclical phase, but are involved in long-term movements.

Significant changes are taking place within the movement of general union membership. Low-wage workers who are also likely to be blacks and other ethnics and women have historically not been strong union material. How this situation is changing dramatically is evidenced here among hospital nonprofessionals where a combination of favorable labor laws, high demand, trade union initiatives, affirmative-action hiring, and civil rights awareness has raised the union proneness of these characteristically nonunion populations.

West Coast agriculture reflects the changing union proneness of another traditional low-wage group. A charismatic leader is able to impart a sense of mission to the unionization undertaking, not only to the hitherto powerless Chicano workers, but also to hosts of activist sympathizers. But César Chavez didn't do it by charisma alone. State intervention and considerable support from outside the union, including the Roman Catholic Church, the AFL-CIO, and the UAW, among others, also had much to do with the changed situation.

Historically, union proneness on the *high* side of the occupational structure has been preeminently illustrated by the airline pilots who, despite their high salaries, continue to function like a classical craft union. More recently another group of professionals who have withstood unionization for a long time—the teachers—moved into the union fold. Other professions or near-professions, mostly in the public sector —specifically, doctors and nurses in hospitals, airline controllers, social workers, firefighters, and police—have also entered on militant bargaining relationships. The indication is that the triggering element in the emergence of these professional unions has been the legal protection accorded to public-sector bargaining.

By contrast, professionals and white-collar employees in the private sector remain largely unorganized even though similarly protected by law. The decisive influence there is probably big management's "union substitution" strategy whereby the union impulse is "bought out"—so to say—by liberal salary and personnel policies.

The mix of the collective bargaining population is being modified by the great advances in the public sector. A larger proportion of public employees are in unions than in all industries as well as a higher proportion of low and high wage earners. Public-sector bargaining represents a collective bargaining breakthrough which is, for its time, comparable in historical importance to the first collective bargaining "revolution" of the 1930s. But public-sector expansion and its union population seem to be slowing down earlier than did the private sector in an analogous stage.

High-powered leadership figures have dominated several unions examined here. John L. Lewis impressed his leadership on the labor movement at large in the early CIO period and on coal collective bargaining; he also pioneered in negotiated health and pension plans. At the end Lewis became an admired elder statesman but completely isolated from the mainline labor movement.

In the contemporary period, César Chavez is probably the most heroic figure for making agricultural organizing into a mission and movement. James R. Hoffa became the symbol of hard bargaining and empire-building until his conviction, and later his apparent assassination, forced his departure from the labor scene. Albert Shanker of the AFT has been a driving force in teacher militancy. James Carey's uncompromising anticommunism and abrasiveness of personal style undoubtedly had something to do with the turmoil in electrical products.

Some leadership styles have not been quite as dramatic, but nevertheless have imprinted their personalities on the industrial relations situations: Philip Murray with his benign but firm control of the Steelworkers; also in steel, David J. McDonald, but more authoritatively, I. W. Abel, experimenting with problem-solving relationships; and Leon Davis of District 1199 and Victor Gotbaum, both in New York City, who brought individual qualities to the unionization of hospitals.

In general, the union has become a more business-like organization, which means that a professional leadership is becoming more widespread than the traditional lay leadership. These professionals are business agents and international representatives up from the ranks, not lawyers and research technicians who, for the most part, play only limited roles.

The professionalization of union government and administration has not prevented the appearance of an increasingly assertive rank and file as counterweight to the leadership. The articulateness of local interests has been the dominant fact of life in coal, steel, and the Postal Service. In different ways, diffusion of power is very much the name of the game in most of the other cases.

In construction, localized markets produce decentralized union power based in the locals and district councils. A comparable situation exists in trucking except that it is countervailed by assertive, Hoffa-type national leadership. In airlines and hospitals, the source of power diffusion is the craft-like organization of the labor force into occupations separated not only by skill but by status. The tradition of local control preserves decentralized bargaining in education, but competitive unions give an extra fillip to diffusion. In electrical equipment, rival unionism, internal union divisions, a management strategy of *divide et impera*, and for a long time a strong-willed and unpredictable leader all joined to check monolithism.

Ideology has not recaptured its place in the unions which it had occupied in other historical eras. Nothing is left of the communist tendencies that held sway in the early CIO. The IUE was an anti-ideology spinoff from the UE. How far these unions have traveled is indicated in their joint collective bargaining undertakings. Race or ethnic consciousness, as in the Farm Workers and among black nonprofessionals in hospitals, is the nearest we come to a functioning ideology in the contemporary situation.

Corruption continues as a problem. It permeates the Teamsters, particularly in the management of central area pension finances; it erupted in the Mine Workers in the Boyle era, and it crops up intermittently in construction.

The cases typify diverse union styles. The education and nurses' associations function as unions in every way, but they steer clear of a formal relationship with the mainline labor movement. The agricultural union is a movement which is in the growing pains of becoming a union. The coal union, as this is being written, is just barely a *national* union. The construction unions and the pilots are each in their way archetypal *craft* unions, as steel is a model *industrial* union. UE tried to be an ideological union but abandoned it.

The first distinction that matters about the party which bargains with the union is whether it is employer or management. Employer connotes an owner-manager or close to it; management connotes a professional managerial corps in a large corporate enterprise. Managements are not owners, or at least not owners in any substantial way. The collective bargaining significance of the distinction is that employer-bargainers are likely to be weaker vis-à-vis the union and management-type bargainers stronger. Construction and trucking are typically employer-bargainers. So are the growers, but in a different way. Steel, electrical products, and airlines are the preeminent professionalized management-bargainers.

In the public sector, bargaining is carried on by a management corps, but the principle of separation of powers imposes a multiplicity of management entities, depending on what is being negotiated. Public-sector management in the past has been a "softer" or weaker bargainer, first because policy and fiscal authority function in separate realms of authority and the public-sector unions are not loath to put this separation to tactical use.

Public-sector bargainers are also weaker because they suffer from an identity crisis as to whether they are managers or politicians. In the latter case, the manager's vulnerability to politics impairs the will and ability to pursue the rule of the bottom line (10-546). Signs are that the power balance is shifting in management's favor as fiscal stringencies stiffen management resistance.

Public management is, paradoxically, made more difficult because the strike does not function to discipline union demands and management responses within limited bounds. This applies with special force in public education where the result of state aid formulas allows teachers to make up time lost on account of strikes.

Management strategy is affected by scale and market position. The megacorporations at first fought the unions hard because they could command the resources to do so. But once collective bargaining seemed unavoidable, they became expert bargainers. U.S. Steel and General Electric, each in their different ways, make this point. The stable relationship in these situations, emerging somewhere in the 1960s, is now being threatened by weaknesses in market position. On the other hand, increasing concentration and conglomeration in coal has yet to lay the groundwork for stable relationships in that industry.

Managements in the oligopolistic industries with their underlying staying power and professional and sophisticated staffs are fully up to bargaining with their union adversaries as equals, and more. The union challenge could be precisely what "shocked" big management into rationalizing its bargaining and personnel administration to the point where it could be as adept as the union at the bargaining game.

Professionalization of management has not always led to stability. It eventually worked out that way in steel. In GE, professionalization moved for a time in the opposite direction: It produced the ideology of Boulwarism with its strategy of union containment. In companies like IBM, not included here, professionalization has virtually foreclosed union penetration.

The competitive industries like construction, trucking, and coal have the greatest difficulty in holding their own against the powerful unions that they face at the negotiating table, the worksite, and in the industry.

But these unions are now beginning to experience the weaknesses of their strengths. The way in which they are utilizing their strength is driving substantial numbers of their employers into the nonunion domain. Not infrequently union power in competitive industries degenerates into racketeering and collusion, as in trucking and perhaps less pervasively in construction.

Competitive and weaker enterprises in construction, trucking, and coal are more likely to seek the reenforcement of multiemployer bargaining through employer associations in order to offset, in part at least, the superiority of the union position and to bring to bear professional competence in bargaining which might not otherwise be possible. Due to inadequate financing, internal divisions, and the absence of permanent staffing, employers associations have only occasionally been able to deliver on this promise.

Imbalance of power against the unions is most noticeable here in agriculture and hospitals. Only the intervention of law made bargaining at all possible.

Collective bargaining is no longer a two-party transaction. To be sure, unions and employers are still the chief players, but clearly the state is now much more than a referee; it is frequently an active participant. The state is, first of all, intervening in the bargaining relationship—as it has intermittently since the early 1960s—to dampen inflationary wage-price pressures. In the case examined here, steel and construction have been special targets of anti-inflationary pressure for nearly two decades. In hospitals, the state's interest as the major third-party payer has brought it in squarely as a bargainer to keep down costs, which get translated sooner or later into labor costs and into collective bargaining.

The civil rights movement is the other "third party" which has edged its way into collective bargaining. Construction and, in lesser measure, trucking have borne the brunt of the campaign for liberalization of entry requirements mainly for blacks and more recently for women. In the industrial union situations, steel represents the preeminent case in which seniority lines have been broadened to allow freer movement of minority workers into the higher rated jobs.

THE RULES

State intervention in union-management relations has been critical in all of the collective bargaining relationships investigated here. The Wagner Act as part of the New Deal ushered in the modern era of collective bargaining, including union recognition and freedom to organize. The NLRB's bargaining unit determinations have been crucial to industrial union bargaining, exemplified here in steel and electrical products. The bargainability of health insurance and pensions, major milestones in steel industrial relations, was first established under the forced draft of federal labor relations law.

A generation later, a new body of federal and state law made possible the breakthrough in public-sector bargaining, represented here by the teachers and postal service. Hospitals have been among the more recent objects of legal support for collective bargaining, as have farm workers via CALRA.

Just as the law of labor relations in the Wagner Act tradition favored the union side, a body of law represented by Taft-Hartley and state right-to-work laws were meant to move the pendulum of power away from the union. The restrictions on secondary boycotts, the closed shop, and picketing significantly limited the sanctions available to the construction and trucking unions. Intervention in national emergency disputes has worked mainly to restrain union power, prominently exemplified in coal and steel strikes, although there are instances when unions—steel is a case in point—have worked this title to their own tactical advantage.

Legislation has narrowed the zone within which wages are negotiated toward the high side. Davis-Bacon virtually established unionlike conditions for construction on federal account. The FLSA minimum wage has narrowed the gap between union and nonunion wages in the low-wage industries—most recently in hospitals. ERISA has legislated a detailed framework for pension bargaining and administration, particularly pertinent here to the Miners' and Teamster funds. The still-to-be-digested health and safety law (OSHA), passed in 1970, has superimposed a code on all industry and helped elevate health and safety to a major place on the collective bargaining agendas of many unions. The evolving law of equal opportunity is forcing the rewriting and reconstitution of hiring and seniority, most notably in construction, trucking, and steel. Environmental protection has undoubtedly reduced the pot available for collective bargaining.

Monetary, fiscal, and labor market policies, oscillating between full employment and inflation, have set the basic tone for collective bargaining throughout the 1960s and 1970s. Intermittent attempts to impose anti-inflationary wage restraints circumscribe collective bargaining negotiations in steel, construction, most recently in the postal service, and, in a special way, in hospitals.

We have been observing how the law of bargaining *influences* process and results. It is not fully understood, however, that law may also *compel* specific results and in so doing displace results consummated through negotiation. The law of equal opportunity is substituting its theory of broader seniority units for the negotiated narrower units, exemplified here in steel but important elsewhere as well. Another effect of equal-opportunity intervention is to establish (more or less) fixed hiring goals, most notably in construction. The law of pensions is giving greater weight to pension security in contrast to the negotiators' disposition to liberalize benefits.

The regulation of process leads almost inevitably to the regulation of substance. Nowhere is this more evident than in the NLRA's authority to set the appropriate bargaining unit; on this point compare NLRB policy favoring industry-like units to the Railway Labor Act's preservation of the craft structure on the railroads and later on the airlines. Undoubtedly, the NLRB's early support of more inclusive units accelerated the ascendancy of industrial unionism, exemplified here in steel, coal, and electrical products. Collective bargaining for health insurance and pensions in the same industries could not have happened in the way it did except for the NLRA and the NLRB. Exclusion from NLRA coverage effectively foreclosed agricultural bargaining until CALRA remedied the situation on a state level. The 1961 federal executive order and the state laws performed the same functions for public-sector bargaining.

The employer is legally obligated to bargain in good faith with the appropriate union, but not necessarily to agree to a particular outcome. However, certification of the bargaining unit combined with the duty to bargain sets in motion a course of events that leads to the *conclusion* of an agreement. (J. P. Stevens is a *cause célèbre* where this has *not* happened.) Similarly, the obligation to bargain over health insurance and pensions, subcontracting, plant relocation and closing, history indicates, creates a powerful magnetic field for the parties to come to agreement.

The NLRB decision to take jurisdiction over a firm or industry ends up with agreements for enterprises that would otherwise have been immune to bargaining. From a static viewpoint, jurisdiction is procedural; in a dynamic context, the Board's decision to take jurisdiction often paves the way for the eventual consummation of an agreement. Hospitals furnish perhaps the best example of this symbiosis between procedure and substance.

THE STRIKE

The strike is "alive and well." This is true not only for industrial relations at large, but for the microcosm represented by the cases here.

It is just as true for the public sector where strikes are in the main illegal.

Coal is consistently among the most strike-prone industries here and abroad, which applies not only to strikes for a new contract but to "strikes during the term of the contract," as the Bureau of Labor Statistics euphemistically refers to wildcats. (There are, of course, strikes during the terms of the contract which are not wildcats.) Construction and mining account for more than two-thirds of these latter strikes (1-41, fn. 108).

Until 1959, steel also represented a strike-prone relationship; its 1959 strike was the longest national steel strike—156 days—and the industry's last strike, although the 1977 negotiations led to uncommonly long "local issues" strikes in the nonferrous metals area of Minnesota. In electrical products, two long strikes, in GE and Westinghouse in the early 1960s, apparently had to happen before some sort of normalcy set in. Strikes on the airlines, all things considered, have not been common, but carriers once struck have been able to endure longer strikes because of the Mutual Aid Pact.

Strikes, although mostly illegal, continue to be almost "normal" in public-sector bargaining, teachers being the most frequent strikers. In the postal service, an unprecedented nine-day wildcat in April 1970 brought about a memorandum of agreement on wage increases and a "jointly bargained and sponsored reorganization of the Post Office Department" (9-436). Hospitals are subject to strikes, but rather less so than generally when measured by duration and number. By now it is seen as commonplace that strikes occur at all in this industry.

Agriculture is one setting in which the strike, without more, has been insufficient sanction to bring growers to the bargaining table. The strike had to be complemented by a massive consumer boycott and the passage of a labor relations act for California agricultural workers to bring about a bargaining relationship.

In the earlier postwar period, national "emergency" strikes, of the kind enjoined by Taft-Hartley in steel and coal, occupied center stage. In 1978, the government could not make the case that a national coal strike constituted a national emergency. In the period from the 1960s on, the real emergency strikes—in the sense of creating a perceived threat to law and order—appear to occur mostly in the public sector, postal service, and hospitals, as well as in cases not examined here—police, firefighters, and sanitation.

The various government jurisdictions have not been able to enforce their bans on public-sector strikes, although there is evidence that they are less loath, by now, to seek injunctions and demand penalties against violators. The no-man's-land which the strike represents in the public sector may easily be the number-one problem. This is why experiments with impasse procedures, including compulsory arbitration and the "final offer" variant, have attracted such attention. But these "moral equivalents," it is fair to say, have not yet taken full hold.

The strike in the private sector appears to have been normalized; that is, the parties seem to be able to take it in stride. It is now seen as a withholding exercise which all buyers and sellers have to rely on or threaten in order to make their bargaining positions credible. On the contrary, it is the employers in coal, steel, and electrical equipment who now insist on their right to "take a long strike" as a way of cutting the union down to size.

Violence in strikes is marginal, but it recurs, particularly when there is some question as to whether a struck plant is operating or not. Coal provides the major example. Violence flares up from time to time in construction and trucking in connection with nonunion confrontations. Wildcats, local-issues strikes, and rank-and-file rejection of contracts bring home to union leaderships that the rank and file now constitutes a permanent check and balance on their authority.

THE STRUCTURE

The problem of bargaining structure is central to many of the cases in this collection. By bargaining structure we mean the distribution and organization of power in collective bargaining. If this investigation is a fair sample, the problem of relative power is actually most acute *within* the union—rather more acute than between union and management. The most typical expression of the power struggle within the union is the rivalry between local and national elements. This is what is at stake in the Mine Workers where there is some question as to whether there is a going national union to begin with. The steel union, which has come out of the Miners' tradition of strong top leadership, has faced the problem in a more moderate way by allowing local-issues bargaining and striking, and by broadening the base of representation on the bargaining policy committees.

In the construction unions, the problem is too little rather than too much power topside. Excessive local control of bargaining is deemed to be the heart of inflation of construction costs. "The leap-frogging of settlements" spurred by localism "creates an inflationary bias" (2-74). Many attempts have been made to introduce "broader perspectives" in the bargaining relationship. The most ambitious was the Ford Administration bill of 1975—which the President subsequently vetoed

—to reform construction bargaining to bring about "a more active national involvement in local bargaining" (2-96).

In something less than half a generation, the problem of structure has shifted from concern with *too* much power on top to too much power below. Whereas the principle of democracy dominated the discussion on this point in the Landrum-Griffin era, now the principle of bargaining efficiency is ascendant—which means, among other things, the effect of power on inflation.

Inclusive vs. exclusive bargaining units is another prominent theme in the structure discussion. The craft vs. industrial unionism debate of the 1930s represented its earlier manifestation. The controversy over contracting-out construction from the factory situation between the construction crafts and the industrial unions is the more modern incarnation, as is the claim of the skilled workers within industrial unions for special treatment, noted later.

The basic craft unionism of the construction unions remains unaltered. But reforms like the multicraft, project-wide agreements negotiated by the Building and Construction Trades Department are responsive to the charge of excessive fragmentation encouraged by the craft system. Local protests that these agreements "include too many concessions to the employer . . . now threaten the continued proliferation of such agreements" (2-71).

Craft unionism, or at least craft-like unionism, is nevertheless in the saddle in a somewhat different context than the grand craft vs. industrial unionism battles of the 1930s. Craft unionism now shows up within the private-sector industrial unions like steel and electrical products, as noted above. Craft unionism's survival value is even more notable in the public-sector unions where it strongly asserted itself in the postal service, education, and hospitals, and in the quasi-public airlines.

Again, the contrast with the 1930s is interesting. In the former period, industrial unionism was the dynamic force. For much of the public sector, by contrast, militancy is sparked by such craft-like groups as teachers, nurses, doctors (most recently), as well as police, firefighters, and social workers. The craft analogy should not, however, be overdrawn. While there is a restrictive element in the public-sector crafts, it does not figure as centrally as in the construction crafts.

Inclusiveness in still another form is the issue which "coordinated" or "coalition" bargaining, preeminently in GE and Westinghouse, addresses. This is inclusiveness aimed at shoring up weaknesses in the union position caused by interunion division in bargaining with the megacorporations. "Disunity among the workers . . . powered Boulwarism. . . . Coordinated bargaining [was] the union response to Boulwarism" (5-238, 239). But coordinated bargaining is not spreading in the industry. "Managers do not like it, and the unions have run into difficulties in working together, not only because their membership rank in different companies varies greatly, but also because their organization style, leadership, and approach to bargaining differs significantly" (5-248). In the public sector, it is the public employer which mainly initiates multiunion bargaining as protection against union whipsawing.

Multiemployer bargaining is commonly initiated by relatively weak, smaller, nonfactory employers. The evidence in trucking and construction indicates that internal divisions among the employer members, inadequate financing, and short terms of office continue to plague the efforts of employers in providing an effective counterweight to strong unions.

The prevailing winds in structure are toward diffusion of power. Localization of power is the "natural" state in the nonfactory settings of trucking and construction and in the public sector generally. Hoffa's nationalization movement to reverse that state is faltering in the hands of a less inspiring leadership. Efforts to reform the locally centered construction industry are making some headway, but the center of power gravity is still in the locals and district councils. Craft distinctions are so deep-rooted in the hospitals that they amount to unbridgeable status divisions; ditto, the airlines. The public sector as a whole diffuses power as a matter of principle. The principle of separation of power has the effect of fragmenting the employer interest among the legislature, the executive, and the administrators.

Even when one union is in a leading position, as in steel and coal, the internal diffusion of power, as noted earlier, inhibits the ability of the union to function like a power monolith. Centralization in what Dunlop calls the unit of effective impact is achieved through the leading union's pacesetting role.

In a relatively few cases, the influence of an individual leader can make the difference at the showdown negotiations between settling or striking, but these cases are becoming fewer as dominant personalities like John L. Lewis, Philip Murray, James Hoffa, and (in a somewhat different style) César Chavez become fewer. At this moment only Chavez remains in this stellar category.

Decentralization is also indicative of bargaining structure at large. There are in the neighborhood of 160,000 separate agreements, not counting health, welfare, and pension supplements.[7] Small units domi-

---

[7] *Directory, 1975.*

nate in American bargaining organization; most agreements are with single employers and single plant–single employers. But they are not likely to be as influential in setting the general tone of collective bargaining as the key bargains. Collective bargaining on the union side is carried on by about 200-plus national unions including about 75,000 local unions and countless shop committees. Most unions bargain in several industries, and several unions are likely to be bargaining agents in any given industry. The typical national union, which is the linchpin of American union structure, does not have many members, although the majority of union members are found in relatively few unions.

Collective bargaining power, at the moment, seems to be moving both up and down. On the up side in the cases reported here are: (1) industry-wide negotiations in steel; (2) coordinated bargaining in electrical equipment; (3) multicarrier strike insurance in the airlines; (4) experiments in the coordination of multinational union interests, observed in steel and electrical equipment; (5) the erratic efforts at wage stabilization, which made the AFL-CIO more influential in collective bargaining; (6) mergers as in the Steelworkers' inclusion of District 50 and Mine, Mill and the Postal Workers' merger of former craft unions; (7) area-wide bargaining in construction; (8) the Hoffa nationalizing in trucking.

Indications of decentralization are: (1) the emergence of rank-and-file pressure as a permanent counterweight to leadership; (2) local-issues bargaining in steel; (3) craft self-determination as in the skilled trades and white-collar interest representation within industrial unions, i.e., USWA and IUE; (4) insurgent movements in coal, trucking, steel, and the postal service; (5) the shop-floor politics of race, as in steel; (6) the ascendancy of local-government unionism in education and hospitals; (7) political nationalization, as in Canada-steel.

THE TERMS

In this section we examine trends in the *content* of collective bargaining indicated by the specific cases studied here and the situation at large. The content or subject matter of collective bargaining is reducible to (possibly oversimplified) two headings; price and power. Price is the price of labor and means wages and all other forms of compensation including "fringe benefits," which are, as we know, not really fringe any more. Power means the contractual allocation of rights in the workplace as among employees, unions, and management, or, put another way, power means the rights that employees and their unions have in the work process as against the rights of management in directing the workforce.

Price and power are in some measure functions of the state of the economy and industry in which the bargainers find themselves. Unions are obviously in a stronger position to advance their price and power aids in an expanding economy and industry. At this writing, the condition of the American economy and in particular the condition of the industries examined here are not favorable to the enhancement of union price and power objectives. Rather, the climate is one in which cost pressures on management are more likely to lead into a hard line.

Over the long run the cases herein mostly raise a new generation of wage issues. The old question of the living wage is still pertinent only in agriculture and hospitals among the cases here. Otherwise the wages problems raised in the cases are modern ones dictated by the leading economic themes of the 1960s and 1970s: inflation and stagflation, diminishing markets, technological change, and rising aspirations.

The main new ground plowed by collective bargaining in the postwar period is the negotiation of a compensation structure rather than simply a wage or wage rate; health insurance, pensions, paid holidays and vacations, and job classification systems are the prominent examples. This era is also marked by the effort of the skilled trades in the industrial unions to recapture the ground lost through the compression of their wage structures. In a sense, public-sector unionism among such groups as teachers and nurses is part of this same tendency.

An old question in a new form is wage incentives which unions resisted historically as a speed-up device. But with production standards subject to negotiation, the field is reversed. It is the union (Steelworkers and IUE here) which now presses for extension on the ground that incentives can be made to pay off for the workers, and managements which resist on the ground that incentives no longer pay off under conditions of modern technology.

In contrast with the upward and onward spirit of the earlier period, the bargaining of the 1970s sounds a more pessimistic note, derived perhaps from pessimistic economic prospects. Unions are attaching more importance to holding their own than to innovation. Inflation, for example, makes the escalator principle relevant once again, this time whether to cap or not to cap; that is, whether to place an upper limit on the size of the cost-of-living adjustment or not.

Similarly, unemployment and layoffs have pushed job security to the fore once again. Steel's "lifetime security" is the case in point here, following along the pioneering path (with autos) of supplemental unemployment benefits. Union concessions are becoming more common. The construction unions and the Teamsters have found it necessary to relax their rules in order to keep their nonunion sectors from growing even more. In a number of instances, the teachers have softened their wage demands in exchange for stronger job-security protections. The question is whether this pessimism is a phase of the cycle or a structural downward readjustment.

The situation with respect to power is somewhat more complicated. For the private sector, again excepting agriculture and possibly hospitals, the institutional existence of the union is no longer aggressively challenged by management, although doubts on this score were expressed by union spokesmen in the course of the bitter campaign for the 1978 Labor Reform bill. In agriculture, the union still has to prove its right to survive, but it is probably farther along this road than ever before. Public-sector unions also have demonstrated conclusively that they have the strength to stay on, but the relationship has yet to be fully institutionalized, especially as to whether the union can continue to operate simultaneously on the political and management levels and resort to illegal strikes.

Most highly institutionalized in their power relationships are the industrial unions, as in steel and electrical products, who seem to have achieved some sort of power stability through the highly sophisticated grievance-arbitration system. The inability so far to institutionalize a grievance-arbitration mechanism is part of the disequilibrium in coal. Power relationships still favor the union in construction and trucking, which is also seen in the failure of a grievance-arbitration system to come to full flower. The solution that some employers in coal, construction, and trucking are seeking is not a more powerful voice, but an exit from collective bargaining altogether.

Contrary to the hopes of the earlier philosophers of collective bargaining a generation ago, the adversary relationship persists as the mode that the unions and managements find best suited to their institutional requirements. The parties depart from the adversary relationship only to the extent that collaboration is necessary to increase or preserve the common pot from which their respective shares are financed.

From time to time in the postwar period, collective bargaining in steel at the national level seemed to approach collaboration beyond "mutual survival," but shop-floor skepticism continues to deter the parties on top from playing out their collaboration too deeply. The 50-year-old Council on Industrial Relations of the Electrical Construction Industry also represents an "imaginative and effective method of disputes resolution" (2-78). Only the third-party community (government, academic, etc.) is really interested in the question as to whether there isn't a better way. In the public sector, the power relationship has not yet been sufficiently tamed or disciplined to make the question even relevant in most cases.

It is of some consequence that some questions have *not* been seriously raised in bargaining. Codetermination has not become an issue of importance. Neither has the quality of work life as commonly formulated, except as occupational health carries this meaning.

The Essence of the Problems

In this final comment, I want to get at the essences of the problems that have been raised throughout this work. It is because the themes have recurred continually that I feel justified in disposing of them in a few words at the end. The large issues raised by this investigation appear to me to be:

1. How does collective bargaining adapt to adverse market conditions after a generation of virtually uninterrupted expansion? Can the parties reverse gear without major confrontations?

2. Are there necessary limits to state intervention in collective bargaining, or are the merits of intervention determined in each case by the nature of the objective?

3. As a special case of (2) above, how should the state intervene to minimize the inflationary effects of collective bargaining in the light of the demonstrated inefficiency of previous interventions to this end?

4. How should the question of bargaining structure be resolved as between the apparently conflicting values of self-determination, which favors decentralization, and economic stability, which seems to favor centralization?

5. What should be done about public-sector strikes which (a) disrupt or threaten public order and health, and (b) defy the law in a manner amounting to mass civil disobedience?

6. How should the problem of occupational health and safety be dealt with when enterprise economy and flexibility have to be measured against the value of life?

7. What should be done when racketeering and corruption infect a union, as seems to be the Teamster case?

These are *questions* in a real sense precisely because they raise "matter(s) or point(s) of uncertainty or difficulty"[8] which do not yield ready answers. At the vital center of all these questions is power. State intervention, either as a general proposition or in the instances of inflation, racketeering, public-sector strikes, and occupational health and safety, presents the problem of state power in a free society. Finally,

---

[8] *American College Dictionary* (New York: Random House, 1966), p. 993.

power or, more exactly, forbearance in the use of power to avoid crisis confrontations is what's at stake in public-sector strikes and the shift in market positions.

It is of some interest that, if I have posed the questions validly, we are at bottom dealing here with political, and even ethical and moral, issues. The conventional wisdom in economics purports to know most of the solutions; it just doesn't know how to make the solutions work.